v.

RELIGION IN ESSENCE
AND MANIFESTATION

G. VAN DER LEEUW

RELIGION
IN ESSENCE AND
MANIFESTATION

*Translated by J. E. Turner with appendices incorporating
the additions to the second German edition
by Hans H. Penner*

*With a new foreword by
Ninian Smart*

PRINCETON UNIVERSITY PRESS
PRINCETON, NEW JERSEY

Published by Princeton University Press,
41 William Street, Princeton, New Jersey 08540
In the United Kingdom: Princeton University Press,
Guildford, Surrey

Appendices © Hans H. Penner, 1963
Foreword Copyright © 1986 by Princeton University Press
First published in Great Britain in 1938; second edition, 1964

First Princeton Paperback printing, 1986

LCC 85-43382
ISBN 0-691-07272-8
ISBN 0-691-02038-8 (pbk.)

Reprinted by arrangement with George Allen & Unwin, Ltd.

Originally published in German in Tübingen, 1933, under the title
Phänomenologie der Religion

Clothbound editions of Princeton University Press books
are printed on acid-free paper, and binding materials
are chosen for strength and durability. Paperbacks
while satisfactory for personal collections,
are not usually suitable for library rebinding
Printed in the United States of America
by Princeton University Press,
Princeton, New Jersey

"All things with God a changeless

aspect wear"

GOETHE, West-Eastern Divan
(Dowden)

CONTENTS: *Volume I*

FOREWORD

THIS book is the most famous of the works of the Dutch historian of religion and Christian theologian, Gerardus van der Leeuw. It is a model of one kind of phenomenology of religion, and its republication in English affords the chance to reappraise the achievements embodied in it. Probably few contemporary scholars in the field of religious studies would fail to feel that there are criticisms to be made of *Religion in Essence and Manifestation* but scarcely any would not recognize it as a classic in the field. It still has much to offer in the way of stimulus and systematization, and it must remain a major starting-point for further attempts at a comprehensive typology of religions and their elements. I would hope that this new edition will help widely to rekindle interest in the kind of phenomenology undertaken by van der Leeuw and will prove useful to teachers and learners alike.

The term "phenomenology of religion" (*die Phänomenologie der Religion*) goes back to P. D. Chantepie de la Saussaye, professor in Amsterdam, in 1887, and he already used a distinction which had become familiar in the Hegelian tradition, between essence and manifestation; and it is this idea of treating religion in its essential forms and manifested varieties that led to the title of van der Leeuw's book when it came out in English. In German it was entitled, more prosaically, *Phänomenologie der Religion*.

As we shall see, this conception of phenomenology fused two distinct ideas, of typology and *epochē* (the bracketing or suspension of one's own beliefs). But before we come to discuss the contemporary significance of the notion of the phenomenological method in the study of religion, let us first review Gerardus van der Leeuw's life and some of the main ideas in the book.

He lived during a stormy period in European history, from 1863 to 1950. It was also the main period for the development of the basis for the comparative study of religion or the history of religions. He bridged the time from Max Müller (1823–1900) until the first constituting of the International Association for the History of Religions, of which he was elected first President (but died shortly thereafter).

He studied in the theological faculty in Leiden from 1908 to 1913, and then had a semester each in Göttingen and Berlin. He specialized in ancient Egyptian religion, although the main thrust of his education was towards being a pastor: he was ordained a minister of the Dutch Reformed Church in 1916, which was also the year of the completion of his doctorate and his marriage. In 1918 at a remarkably early age he was called to the chair of the History of Religions at Groningen. He remained active in church affairs, and was concerned with liturgical reform (he was a fine musician, and for this and other reasons took a keen interest in the aesthetic side of religion), ethics, Christian theology and social-democratic politics. He became minister of education in the first Dutch government after the war.

His books are mainly concerned with the two areas of the phenomenology of religion and Christian theology, and include the following works, in German or Dutch: *Historical Christendom* (1919); *Roads and Boundaries—a Study Concerning the Relation of Religion and Art* (1932); *Phenomenology of Religion* (1933); *Introduction to Theology* (1935); *Primitive Man and Religion: an Anthropological Study* (1937); with K. P. Bernet Kempers *Short History of Hymnology* (1939); *Liturgics* (1940); *Man and Religion: an Attempt at an Anthropology* (1941); *Meditation Hours with Novalis* (1943); *Theology of the Sacrament* (1949). We can see that his preoccupations swung to and fro between the two main poles of his interests. Although his work on religion and art needs to be better known, there is little doubt that his chief phenomenological work is his main monument. His writings on religion and aesthetics were published after his death in 1963, with a preface by Mircea Eliade, under the title of *Sacred and Profane Beauty: the Holy in Art*.

But although it is no doubt by his phenomenology that van der Leeuw will be remembered, he was primarily a Christian theologian, and phenomenology was a propaedeutics to theology itself. It is no coincidence that the last words of his great work (leaving aside the Epilegomena) should be these: "Here there lives a faith for which God, in human form, lovingly stoops over what is deepest in the world and in man, over guilt, and for which God's almighty Power assumes life in man's fragile frame. But at this point the contemplative and comprehending servant of research reverently withdraws; his own utterance yields place to that of proclamation, his service to that in the sanctuary." Nevertheless, though this might appear to some people a much too pious ending for a scholarly work of this kind, and it might be disturbing to Jewish, Buddhist, or religiously sceptical readers, it should not lead us to think that van der Leeuw's general theory is simply subservient to his own personal faith. His theory is dependent on various influences from the tradition, and springs in part from his studies of Egyptian, Greek, and small-scale religions. Though his work in anthropology did not involve field-work and so his sources were second-hand, nevertheless he had a wide knowledge of anthropological writings, and it was from these in part that he derived the importance of the concept of *power* in his theoretical scheme.

We shall later come back to the structure of his major work. Meanwhile let us look at the methodological stance which he adopted, and which owes something to various major figures of the time, such as Brede Kristensen (1867–1953)—with whom he studied at Leiden—and Wilhelm Dilthey (1833–1911). It was delineated in the Epilegomena, originally intended as an introduction to this volume.

There he lists stages in his approach to the material. The first is the assigning of names to the types of phenomena which manifest themselves—such as "sacrifice," "priest," and so on. Second, there is the interpolation of the phenomena into our own lives. This is to avoid that woodenness in which naming merely means the transformation of observations into mere concepts. He quotes Jaspers with approval: "When the professor is told by the barbarian that once there was nothing except a great feathered serpent, unless the learned man feels a thrill and a half temptation to wish it were true, he is no judge of such things at all." Third, phenomenology is neither metaphysics nor the comprehension of empirical reality: it observes the *epochē*—standing aside and understanding what appears into view. This, as van der Leeuw remarks, is a stance given neither to god nor animal. Fourth, there is the clarification of what appears in view—by exhibiting the structural relations between types and seeing them in some wider whole (in effect within the structure of a general theory). All the foregoing stages, taken together, constitute understanding: so the chaotic real world becomes a manifestation or revelation (note here van der Leeuw's Christian-theological overtones).

The phenomenological method as thus far described needs perpetual correction by textual and archeological research. As soon as this check on results is removed, phenomenology slides into pure art or empty fantasy. The aim is objectivity and to testify to what is experienced—to the essence or essences which are manifested. Thus van der Leeuw thinks this important to theology, since while the latter can testify as can metaphysics to what lies beyond experience, so that "to see face to face is denied us, much can be observed even in a mirror; and it is possible to speak about things seen." In brief, van der Leeuw's schema involves: naming, systematic experience, *epochē*, clarification, and testimony.

There is in van der Leeuw's description of phenomenology a strange timelessness. He owes something to the philosopher Husserl in this, though Husserl's notion of phenomenology pursued quite different objectives. Actually, there is no reason why van der Leeuw's method should not be applied to a classification and clarification of the various types of religious change, as he himself recognized, for his very central category, namely Power, has a dynamic, not just a static, significance. But generally, the way in which he proceeds in this volume is to a wide classification of things, classes, persons and so on endowed with Power, in a rather motionless perspective. Perhaps there is more dynamism in his accounts of forms of religion in Part Five. But he has this model of types of phenomena which, suitably ordered, appear to us in an ahistorical way. It was thus easy for him to contrast phenomenology and the history of religions.

In a way he was conflating the method of *epochē* or "bracketing" (bracketing out that is one's own theological, philosophical, or other presuppositions) and the method of constructing ideal types. Let us pursue these lines separately.

Part of the reason why Chantepie de la Saussaye and his successors wished to draw a methodological line between phenomenology and Christian theology had to do with institutions. Although van der Leeuw himself saw a solidarity between the two kinds of enquiry, there was in the European context especially, and still is in many places, the problem of how the study of religions related to Divinity. Very often the chair or center for the study of world religions is placed in the wider context of the training of ministers or priests. The assumptions of the wider community do not apply to the narrower study—narrower that is in size but not in scope. The concept of the phenomenology of religion is thus sometimes used to demarcate the "neutral" approach of the student of religions as opposed to the "committed" approach of the Divinity School or theological seminary. In that sense it is important to distinguish the pure study of religions from the Christian (or Jewish or whatever) interpretation of other, often in principle rival, religions. But more important than this institutional reason for "bracketing" is the necessity, if we are truly to understand other people's beliefs, of not interpreting their behavior as if it implied an identical worldview to our own. The exploration of another's worldview involves empathy and imagination. It needs empathy so that we can so to speak feel our way into other people's worlds—and here the phenomenological method owes much to the thought of Dilthey and Collingwood. It needs imagination so that we can fly above and away from our own commitments and assumptions, and thus freely explore the feelings and commitments of others. Now this idea has been of major importance in the development of the historical and descriptive study of religion as it has been pursued particularly since

van der Leeuw's time. It represents one meaning of "the phenomenological method," but it is not the only strand, as we have seen in van der
Leeuw's thinking.

The other strand is to do with essences. For him the *epochē* occurs primarily in the context of his pursuit of typology and theory. His account
of the process of constructing types is subtle and complex. In some
measure he was of course influenced by Edmund Husserl (1859–1938).
His interests were philosophical rather than historical: but he was concerned with delineating clearly and accurately the structure of human
consciousness. Thus we can see on inspection that consciousness is of its
nature intentional, that is, it has an object or objects—for instance one
can be aware of the page in front of one. This intentionality does not depend on any particular object. To see something colored is seeing what
is extended, so here we have another property—extension. These features of consciousness itself are, so to say, pure essences: and Husserl by
analogy is seeking to uncover the pure essences of religious life. It happens that when Rudolf Otto published his famous book *Das Heilige*,
which later appeared in English as *The Idea of the Holy*, in 1917, Husserl
hailed it as being a masterly account of religious consciousness. And so
there was encouragement to the young van der Leeuw to see his own
project in Husserlian terms. We may see the first sense of "phenomenology" which we discussed above as constituting the Kristensen strand;
and this second sense the Husserl strand.

Yet there is something of a paradox about it. Surely the processes of
naming phenomena and checking on one's preliminary results, for instance, imply more than contemplating the states of one's own consciousness. Indeed do they imply this at all? It seems one has to range
through human history picking out instances of sacrifice, or priesthood,
or whatever. This outward–looking method seems very different from
anything which Husserl describes; and why is it that van der Leeuw
places in his account of stages in phenomenology the process of "interpolation" of the data in one's own experience?

The reason has partly to do with his debt to Lucien Lévy-Bruhl (1857–
1938). In 1940 he wrote a powerful defense of him against a variety of
misrepresentations. It was no doubt unfortunate that Lévy-Bruhl had
used the loaded terms "primitive" and "modern" mentalities to describe
the contrasting thought-forms he sought to delineate. There is nothing
especially primitive about the type of participatory thinking he high-
lighted, and it exists as much in modern circumstances as in any other.
The detached empirical attitude to human events is itself rather unnatural—and if this is what constitutes a major strand of modernity, then

perhaps modernity is a kind of aberration (so van der Leeuw was inclined to think). It is a pity, then, that Lévy-Bruhl did not use a more
neutral term (interestingly Eliade was later to try out "archaic" to refer
to a bundle of motifs in religious and symbolic thinking—again this is
maybe a misleading expression and fails properly to convey what Eliade
really has in mind). And despite van der Leeuw's worries about too ag-
gressively an empiricist stance, he was of course concerned with the objectivity of his scholarship. He used the method of *epochē* as a kind of
bridge—how to be empirical and participatory, objective and subjective,
at the same time. For the process of interpolating the phenomena as they
appeared in one's life was a means of making them live existentially. For
van der Leeuw, as we have noted, the student of religion must be prepared to sympathize with the feelings of those who operate with categories and forms other than our own. The very categories of religion
are, so to speak, soaked in values, and without an appreciation of values,
that is a kind of participation in them, you cannot understand them—
you may, as he remarks, have acquired too much of the professor and
have too little in you of the human being. And so, despite the somewhat
formal-seeming way in which he sets forth his results in the present work
at base it is for him the laying forth of a whole schema of human types
and modes of living, in which we imaginatively have to participate. The
structure which he unfolds is a timeless pattern of human response.

In this drive for the interpolation of religious phenomena into one's
own life, van der Leeuw reflects his conception of the branches of knowledge. He drew a line between the natural sciences and the cultural or human sciences. The former involved ascertaining and explaining facts.
The latter involved understanding them, and he underlined here the
concept of *verstehen*. In this he was following Dilthey. But beyond the
empathetic imagination this needed, there lay the search for meaning:
this ultimate sort of pursuit he thought of as metaphysics and theology.
There are border disciplines—psychology lies at the frontier between
the natural and the human sciences; and the phenomenology of religion
lies at the frontier between the "understanding" or human sciences and
the search for final meaning. The process of bracketing means that ultimate judgments of truth and value are cut off: what we seek is a clarification of human religiousness as it appears within, not beyond, human
experience. But nevertheless phenomenology so to speak furnishes the
material upon which Christian theology works. Theology goes beyond
human experience to the further shore of reality; but phenomenology
remains bound to the hither shore.

Because for van der Leeuw phenomenology exists at this boundary between the human sciences and Christian theology he feels less tension than we might expect between the *epochē* and faith. It is as if phenomenology in delineating the existential categories of humankind's religiosity poses questions which ultimately only some form of ultimate theology can answer: for him this was, of course, Christian theology. So although he drew a boundary between phenomenology and Christian theology he was content that the science of religion should be pursued within the ambience of a theological faculty or divinity school.

Van der Leeuw's position in all this can be clarified in a slightly different way by considering the relation between the focus of religious faith and divine existence. Let us make the simplified assumption that a believer has a primary focus of her belief, experience and practice. In many religions this focus is God. Now once we have pursued the phenomenological task of delineating the believer's faith, experience and so on, what extra is left? There is what van der Leeuw would think of as a surplus of meaning: my experience of God, thinks the believer, truly comes from God. The phenomenologist can describe this, but does not as such make the further step of asserting God's existence and activity. There seems here, though, a certain paradox, for what we as students of religion are concerned with is the power (not the truth) of religious experience, etc. So affirming the existence and activity does not add to this power: from the observer's point of view the power of religion remains exactly what it is whether God exists or not. The pieties of Vaishnavites, the hymns of Methodists, the ethical works of Quakers, the martyrdom of saints—all these testify to the power of religion whether or not the people in question are suffering from a delusion or not. It is of course true that religion would have no power, or at least much less power, were it not believed in: so the believer has to affirm God's or Vishnu's existence and so on. More generally, the power of all those categories of religious activity, experience and so on which van der Leeuw describes in this work remain as vital structures of human consciousness, etc., whatever step we take into that realm of surplus meaning which transcends this world. This perhaps helps to explain how it is that phenomenology lies at the boundary of the human sciences and theology. It also raises some interesting philosophical questions about the verification and falsification of theological claims.

We may now turn more to the content of this work, rather than to the nature of method. We have seen that van der Leeuw was deeply influenced by, and wrote in passionate defense of, Lévy-Bruhl. His studies were in ancient Greek and Egyptian religion primarily and he read widely in anthropological literature. But van der Leeuw did not, as his preface indicates, think of his work as providing any dominating theory:—as was likely at the time, such a theory would have been conceived in evolutionary terms, and van der Leeuw indeed offers no such theory. But there are some central features of his typology which do in some sense constitute a theory of religion, and they were dictated to some extent by his specialized concerns as listed above. He does not, for instance, look at religion from the main perspective of Buddhism, which would give a different slant on the primordial categories of human existence.

Rather for him the central phenomenon of religion is Power. This is that less defined energy which in its originative and more personal form is God. He thus begins the book with the claim that the main object of religion is actually a subject, namely God. This claim too might seem strange to the Buddhist or the Jain. I think that in this respect more has to be done in the phenomenology of religion than hitherto (whether by Otto, van der Leeuw or Eliade—to name perhaps the three most influential figures in this century) to reframe the field taking Buddhism more strongly into account. But for the rest his dynamistic account of religion works well. It can throw brilliant light both on the familiar and the unfamiliar. Thus in Chapter 48.2 (p. 341) he writes:

> Thus it is in no indifferent matter how the human conducts himself. His behaviour must in all respects duly respond to the goal which is power; and to that end he sets his own powerfulness as prominently as possible in the foreground. Ritual nakedness for example, the *ritus paganus*, is just such behaviour: the potency of one's own body is to ward off evil powers and awake fruitful ones. Or again, the human gives his body the appropriate pose: holding it rigid, braced up, alert, attentive and prepared, in *Standing*: allowing everything to go and abandoning himself in the abasement of *Prostration*: bowing down all that is in himself, and expressing his impotence, by *Kneeling*: raising his hands so that his "soul stream may flow freely": folding them and placing them, as though bound, within God's hands. He casts down his glance, or raises it to heaven: turns away his face, or even hides his head, as if his powerfulness were ashamed of itself, in direct contrast to the *ritus paganus*.

This indicates something of the potency of his schema.

But in addition, he sees divine Power not as something which often takes a personal form, but as lying locked away in another world, to which we cannot penetrate either in life or in phenomenology. So the divine must be mediated to human beings. The first part of this book concerns the object of religion—power and the gods; the second concerns the subject, the worshiper, the community, the soul, and so on. The third part, crucially deals with the relation between subject and object. Or rather, as he puts it, to make sure we have our priorities right, the relationship between object and subject. He expresses, especially in his schematism of outward action, a sacramental view of religion, which works well with his stress on power—for religious activities as conveying power can be regarded aptly as sacraments. Importantly too the notion of *form* in religion becomes crucial. For a mere formless Other could not stimulate activity in the human being. Thus at the outset of Chapter 73 (p. 483) he writes that "if Power possesses a form, and if it moves in some direction comprehensible by the human being, then he can follow it. This following, however, is not the non-obligatory and arbitrary attitude such as is often referred to (for example) in Protestant circles, when 'merely following Jesus' is censured, as this is advocated by the modernist group. 'To follow' always implies the union of the follower's life with that of him he follows. . . . " So the Power takes a form and it is through that form that the human being is united sacramentally, in a general sense, with the focus of her faith. This triadic concern with Object, Subject, and Relationship is natural for van der Leeuw in the light of his own Christian belief, so once again he sees no essential tension between the phenomenological approach and Christian theology.

Even if more recent work in the history of religions puts more emphasis on various aspects of the data which are less stressed by van der Leeuw (for instance, Buddhist studies, classical African religion, women's studies, new religions, mysticism), the general approach of this book is a fruitful one, and it can serve in many places as the starting point of further researches. Thus his discussion of the use of language in religion is suggestive; his categorization of the different kinds of religion remains of considerable interest; and there are treatments of phenomena which have not had much discussion, such as the notion of enmity towards God (Chapter 78). The whole book is indeed a quarry of observations each of which could form the starting-point of a research project.

Van der Leeuw's own piety no doubt made it easier for him to see close links between phenomenology and theology. This led him to see a religious significance in phenomenology itself which merits further discussion, and to this I shall return shortly. But what difference does the flavor of his Christian piety make? It would be interesting to see in the further development of the field of religious studies what would happen if we had a phenomenology written from a Jewish, a Buddhist, or a Hindu angle. There would no doubt be quite a lot of overlap, but nevertheless matters of emphasis are so important in the field, and one's own tradition can be so suggestive in the task of broader systematization, that one suspects that results would be rather different. It might be interesting from this perspective to invite students and readers to "review" van der Leeuw's *opus* with a view to outlining what parts of their own tradition, or of other people's with which they happen to be sympathetic and familiar, seem to be underplayed in the very categories which are brought to bear. We cannot treat quite at face value van der Leeuw's notion that his method is simply objective in its outcome. Our task in the plural study of religion is to evolve towards a genuinely crosscultural and global enterprise which may transcend some of the particularities of Western culture. But although this implies a limitation in van der Leeuw, it in no way implies that this book can be ignored. It is the major systematic phenomenology and has a crucial place in the ongoing study of religion.

To return to our earlier question: Does the phenomenology of religion itself have religious significance? There is a continual danger in our field of those who wish to turn the study of religion itself into a kind of religion. The guru can easily replace the teacher (and this happens in other fields where values are important). We need to stand back: we need to preserve our warm dispassion. Perhaps we should do more to underline the difference between understanding and commitment. But there are ways in which the phenomenology of religion is bound to have some religious significance. First, if you make a good film about, or write a good book about, some form of religion, for instance Theravada Buddhism, you are in effect holding up a mirror to it. If it has its own power and appeal, its own profoundity and spiritual strength, then those can be seen in the mirror. And the appeal of a faith can be mediated by a mirror as much perhaps as by a preacher. This is why some religions do not like the study of religions, for we must in the latter necessarily encounter alternatives. But of course our academic enterprise is concerned with widening knowledge and the existence of alternatives is itself a real feature of the world. Second, and more directly to the point of van der Leeuw's project, a phenomenology also holds a mirror to forms of religion which it is to be hoped reflect the structure of human religious thinking. In this self it presents to us a mode of looking at the world which is in a general sense religious. If we are to abandon sacraments, mysticism, faith, gods, what effects will this have upon our existence? The exhibition of the religious consciousness in some detail, and articulately, does represent a challenge to "secular" ways of living. Maybe we can discover many of the same patterns in the secular, for instance, in modern nationalism. If so, that becomes an important observation and extends the bounds of religion. So there is a way in which the phenomenology of religion is religious. It would perhaps be odd to labor over such a structural theory of religion without at least taking religion seriously.

A related topic that needs further reflection is the role of imaginative empathy in entering into the lives of others. What factors are there in human nature which enable us to practice *epochē*? There is much that we do not understand about the conditions of understanding.

It is over half a century since this book was launched and more than sixty years since van der Leeuw's shorter *Introduction to the Phenomenology of Religion* came out. Though there are, as have seen, places where we might wish to take issue with what he has written, the work has remarkable staying power. It has still much to offer students in our field. The criticisms which can be made of it are largely to do with scope and emphasis, but much of what remains when that is said has solid insights to give us. And even if there are those who think that it is too much in line with the sacramental religion of his own chosen tradition, they also can recognize that most of his work stands quite independently of all that. Moreover even those who are more interested in constructing their own worldviews rather than in understanding others' must recognize the importance of the categories which he gives us.

In short, this work opens important windows on religion in essence and manifestation, and it will remain a classic in the modern study of religious and other worldviews.

NINIAN SMART

SANTA BARBARA, CALIFORNIA,
December, 1985

AUTHOR'S PREFACE TO THE GERMAN EDITION

WHEN I published, in 1925, a short *Introduction to the Phenomenology of Religion*, I felt it necessary to indicate that this was actually only an *Outline* of a larger book, the construction of which lay still in the future. And now that the more substantial work has appeared I must admit that I have made little, if indeed any, advance. For in many respects, to say the least, the present Volume is of the nature of a sketch or summary; so extensive is the domain of the Phenomenology of Religion that even a detailed presentation, such as the generous consideration of the Publisher has enabled me to undertake, must often give the impression that the utmost depths of its content, and the farthest limits of its manifestations, could be adequately dealt with only in a Monograph.

In the meantime I trust that I have now given to all, whose studies include some familiarity with the History of Religion, a useful Introduction to the comprehension of the historical material; and some knowledge of this material is presupposed. As regards Phenomenology itself, Chantepie's volume should be consulted, and especially also the two compilations by Bertholet and Lehmann-Haas. In the Text of the present book, whenever it has been possible, reference has almost invariably been made to these Works in order to illuminate specific instances.

I have assigned great value throughout to the presentation of the manifestations of Religion from the most varied viewpoints possible; and for this purpose I have appealed to writers of extremely diversified opinions—and nationalities also! Whenever it seemed to me that some phenomenon had been described by anyone in a typical form I made no attempt to improve this, but utilized his own terms literally; and I hope that this method has given the book, to some extent, the character of a cooperative effort towards the accurate apprehension of the phenomena.

I need scarcely add that I am profoundly indebted to many others. But a special expression of my gratitude must be accorded to my friend and colleague, Rudolf Bultmann. He has not merely, in the most self-sacrificing and conscientious way, taken part in dealing with the Proofs, but has shown a deep interest in the Contents that has often disconcerted me by its generosity, while it has invariably and materially assisted me. To the Publisher likewise I must offer sincere thanks for the generous manner in which he has facilitated the production of this book.

In accordance with the views of Jaspers, I have tried to avoid, above all else, any imperiously dominating theory, and in this Volume there will be found neither evolutionary, nor so-called anti-evolutionary, nor indeed any other theories. More specifically, those which attempt to reveal the "primary origin" of Religion have from the outset been excluded, whether they aim at finding this in a primal Dynamism, Animism or Monotheism. What I myself consider may be opposed to theories, as the phenomenological comprehension of History, should be clear from the *Epilegomena*.

It is only too obvious to myself that this Work, in its present form, exhibits many defects, and accords too much attention to certain aspects of the History of Religion with which my own research has familiarized me, as compared with those I have studied in other authors' volumes. In spite of all this I trust that my book will contribute somewhat towards the comprehension of Religion, equally as regards its incalculable cultural wealth and the appeal to faith which it addresses to mankind.

GRONINGEN,
January 1933

AUTHOR'S NOTE TO THE ENGLISH EDITION

THE present Volume is an integral Translation of the German Edition, of which, however, I have not found it possible to undertake any revision. During the interval since its publication, research of the first order of importance and value has been pursued by many eminent investigators, of whom I may mention Herr Martin Buber, Professor Bronislaw Malinowski and Dr. R. R. Marett; and I very greatly regret that I have been unable, as yet, to give their outstanding conclusions the careful attention they call for.

My discussions of the methodological and historical aspects of the subject appear as *Epilegomena*.

1937

TRANSLATOR'S NOTE

IN translating a work which appears to me, in its wide range of comprehensiveness and its marked originality, to deserve comparison with William James's *Varieties of Religious Experience*, my obligations have been extensive and diversified: in the first place, to the author for the keen interest he has shown throughout the task, which has ensured the authoritative presentation of his own standpoint; and in this respect, it scarcely needs saying that vitally important additions to our knowledge of facts, and equally significant changes in their interpretation, have occurred since James's famous classic was first published. I am similarly indebted to Mr. W. H. Johnston, B.A., and to Mr. Norman Wells, B.A., for their very valuable assistance, and to my friends, Rev. T. Holme and Mr. H. Goodenough, for placing at my disposal the resources of the Liverpool Diocesan Library at Church House; in the same way the volumes supplied by Dr. Williams's Library, London, were most helpful, and I am glad to have this opportunity of offering my thanks to all concerned, as well as to all the authors and publishers who have kindly permitted quotations to be made, and, as on previous occasions, to Messrs. George Allen & Unwin, Ltd., for their skilled advice with regard to all the technical aspects of production, and to my wife for dealing with the proofs and various other important points. Of course I remain fully responsible for any defects that may have escaped detection.

I am equally grateful for the very generous contribution made by the Sir Halley Stewart Trust towards the expenses of translation.

A few Translator's additional Notes appear, as usual, within square brackets.

J. E. TURNER

GENERAL LITERATURE CITED

Bibliography

C. Clemen, *Religionsgeschichtliche Bibliographie*, 1914–1923.

K. D. Schmidt, *Bibliographisches Beiblatt der Theologischen Literaturzeitung*, from 1922.

O. Weinreich, *Berichte über Allg. Religionswiss. in AR.*, from 1926.

Encyclopaedias and Lexicons

ERE. (*Encyclopaedia of Religion and Ethics*), 1908 ff.

H. Th. Obbink, *Godsdienstwetenschap*, 1920.

RGG. (*Die Religion in Geschichte und Gegenwart*[2]), 1927–32.

Sources

A. Bertholet, *Religionsgeschichtliches Lesebuch*[2], 1926 ff.

C. Clemen, *Fontes historiae religionum*, from 1920.

H. Haas, *Bilderatlas zur Religionsgeschichte*, from 1924.

E. Lehmann and H. Haas, *Textbuch zur Religionsgeschichte*[2], 1922.

W. Otto, *Religiöse Stimmen der Völker*.

R. Pettazoni, *Mite e Leggende*, from 1948.

Quellen der Religionsgeschichte, published by Gesellschaft der Wiss., Göttingen.

General History of Religion

A. Bertholet and E. Lehmann, *Lehrbuch der Religionsgeschichte*, 1925 (4th Edition, P. D. Chantepie de la Saussaye, *Lehrbuch der Religionsgeschichte*, *cf. infra.*).

A. C. Bouquet, *Comparative Religion, A Short Outline* (Pelican Books), 1950.

C. Clemen, etc. *Religions of the World*, 1931.

J. G. Frazer, *The Golden Bough*[3], 1911–15 (Abridged Edition, 1923; revised ed. by Th. Gaster, 1959).

M. Gorce and R. Mortier, *Histoire Générale des Religions*, 1944 ff.

R. E. Hume, *The World's Living Religions, An Historical Sketch*, 1944.

Illustreret Religionshistorie, edited by J. Pedersen, 1948.

A. Jeremias, *Allgemeine Religionsgeschichte*[3], 1923.

G. van der Leeuw, etc., *De Godsdiensten der Wereld*, 1948.

Mana, *Introduction à L'histoire des Religions*, since 1944.

G. Mensching, *Allgemeine Religionsgeschichte*, 1949.

F. G. Moore, *History of Religions* I[2], 1920, II, 1919.

S. Reinach, *Orpheus*, 1909. Eng. Trans. 1931.

Tiele-Söderblom, *Kompendium der Religionsgeschichte*[6], 1931.

Introductions to the History and Phenomenology of Religion

Th. Achelis, *Abriss der vergleichenden Religionswissenschaft*, 1904.

Tor Andrae, *Die Letzten Dinge*, 1940.

K. L. BELLON, *Inleiding Tot De Natuurlijke Godsdienstwetenschap*, 1948.

K. BETH, *Einführung in die vergleichende Religionsgeschichte*, 1920.

C. J. BLEEKER, *Inleiding Tot Een Phaenomenologie Van Den Godsdienst*, 1934; also, *Grondlijnen Eener Phaenomenologie Van Den Godsdienst*, 1943.

P. D. CHANTEPIE DE LA SAUSSAYE, *Lehrbuch der Religionsgeschichte*[1] I, 1887.

R. DUSSAUD, *Introduction à l'Histoire des Religions*, 1914.

MIRCEA ELIADE, *Traité d'Histoire des Religions*, 1949, Engl. tr., *Patterns In Comparative Religions*, 1958.

H. FRICK, *Vergleichende Religionswissenschaft*, 1928.

J. W. HAUER, *Die Religionen*, I, 1923.

E. O. JAMES, *Comparative Religion, An Introductory and Historical Study*, 1938.

F. B. JEVONS, *An Introduction to the History of Religions*, 1896.

G. VAN DER LEEUW, *Einführung in die Phänomenologie der Religion*, 1925.

E. LEHMANN, in: CHANT. I, 1925.

G. MENSCHING, *Vergleichende Religionswissenschaft*, 1949.

H. TH. OBBINK, *De Godsdienst in zyn verschyningsvormen*, 1933.

A. SETH PRINGLE-PATTISON, *Studies in the Philosophy of Religion*, 1930.

N. SOEDERBLOM, *The Living God, Basal Forms of Personal Religion*, 1933.

C. P. TIELE, *Elements of the Science of Religion*, 1897.

G. WIDENGREN, *Religionens Värld, Religionsfenomenologiska Studier och Oversikter*, 1945.

W. WUNDT, *Völkerpsychologie* IV—VI [2-3], 1914–20.

Journals

L'Année Sociologique, from 1898.

Anthropos, Edited by W. Schmidt, from 1906.

AR. (Archiv für Religionswissenschaft), from 1898.

RHR. (Revue de l'Histoire des Religions), from 1880.

SM. (Studi e Materiali di Storia delle Religioni), from 1925.

Zalmoxis, *Revue des Études Religieuses*, edited by M. Eliade, since 1938.

Zeitschrift für Religionspsychologie, Edited by K. Beth, from 1926.

More specific Bibliographies are appended to the relevant chapters, together with special Articles, especially in *RGG*.

PART ONE

THE OBJECT OF RELIGION

CHAPTER I

POWER

1. THAT which those sciences concerned with Religion regard as the *Object* of Religion is, for Religion itself, the active and primary Agent in the situation or, in this sense of the term, the *Subject*. In other words, the religious man perceives that with which his religion deals as primal, as originative or causal; and only to reflective thought does this become the Object of the experience that is contemplated. For Religion, then, God is the active Agent in relation to man, while the sciences in question can concern themselves only with the activity of man in his relation to God; of the acts of God Himself they can give no account whatever.

2. But when we say that *God* is the Object of religious experience, we must realize that "God" is frequently an extremely indefinite concept which does not completely coincide with what we ourselves usually understand by it. Religious experience, in other terms, is concerned with a "Somewhat". But this assertion often means no more than that this "Somewhat" is merely a vague "something"; and in order that man may be able to make more significant statements about this "Somewhat", it must force itself upon him, must oppose itself to him as being Something *Other*. Thus the first affirmation we can make about the Object of Religion is that it is a *highly exceptional* and *extremely impressive "Other"*. Subjectively, again, the initial state of man's mind is amazement; and as Söderblom has remarked, this is true not only for philosophy but equally for religion. As yet, it must further be observed, we are in no way concerned with the supernatural or the transcendent: we can speak of "God" in a merely figurative sense; but there arises and persists an experience which connects or unites itself to the "Other" that thus obtrudes. Theory, and even the slightest degree of generalization, are still far remote; man remains quite content with the purely practical recognition that this Object is a departure from all that is usual and familiar; and this again is the consequence of the *Power* it generates. The most primitive belief, then, is absolutely empirical; as regards primitive religious experience, therefore, and even a large proportion of that of antiquity, we must in this respect accustom ourselves to interpret the supernatural element in the conception of God by the simple notion of an "Other", of something foreign and highly unusual, and at the same time the consciousness of absolute dependence, so well known to ourselves, by an indefinite and generalized feeling of remoteness.

3. In a letter written by the missionary R. H. Codrington, and published by Max Müller in 1878, the idea of *mana* was referred to for the first time, and naturally in the style of those days, as a "Melanesian name for the Infinite", this description of course being due to Müller;[1] while Codrington himself gave, both in his letter and his own book of 1891, a much more characteristic definition: "It is a power or influence, not physical, and in a way supernatural; but it shows itself in physical force, or in any kind of power or excellence which a man possesses. This Mana is not fixed in anything, and can be conveyed in almost anything; but spirits . . . have it and can impart it. . . . All Melanesian religion consists, in fact, in getting this Mana for one's self, or getting it used for one's benefit."[2] Taken generally, this description has completely justified itself. In the South Sea Islands *mana* always means a Power; but the islanders include in this term, together with its derivatives and compounds, such various substantival, adjectival and verbal ideas as Influence, Strength, Fame, Majesty, Intelligence, Authority, Deity, Capability, extraordinary Power: whatever is successful, strong, plenteous: to reverence, be capable, to adore and to prophesy. It is quite obvious, however, that the supernatural, in our sense of this term, cannot here be intended; Lehmann even reproached Codrington for referring to the supernatural at all, and proposed to retain the simple meaning of "successful, capable". Now *mana* actually has this significance; the warrior's *mana*, for instance, is demonstrated by his continuous success in combat, while repeated defeat shows that his *mana* has deserted him. But Lehmann, on his part, sets up a false antithesis between the ideas of "the supernormal" and "the amazing" on the one hand, and on the other the primitive ideas of "the powerful" and "the mighty" in general. It is precisely a characteristic of the earliest thinking that it does not exactly distinguish the magical, and all that borders on the supernatural, from the powerful;[3] to the primitive mind, in fact, all marked "efficiency" is *per se* magical, and "sorcery" *eo ipso* mighty; and Codrington's own phrase, "in a way

---

[1] *The Origin and Growth of Religion*, 53.   [2] *The Melanesians*, 118, Note 1.
[3] *cf.* here Rudolf Otto, *Das Gefühl des Überweltlichen (Sensus numinus)*, 1932, 55: "What is comprehended as 'Power' is also comprehended as *tremendum*. It renders its objects *tabu*"; *cf.* E. Arbmann, *Seele und Mana, AR.* 29, 1931, 332.

supernatural", appears to have expressed the accurate implication. Here we must certainly clearly distinguish such ideas from what we ourselves regard as supernatural. Power is authenticated (or verified) empirically: in all cases whenever anything unusual or great, effective or successful is manifested, people speak of *mana*. There is, at the same time, a complete absence of theoretical interest. What is "natural" in the sense of what may ordinarily be expected never arouses the recognition of *mana*; "a thing is *mana* when it is strikingly effective; it is not *mana* unless it is so", asserts a Hocart Islander. It is just as unmistakably authenticated by a dexterous plunge into the sea as by the conduct of the tribal chieftain. It indicates equally good luck (*veine*) as potency, and there is no antithesis whatever between secular acts and sacred; every extraordinary action generates the experience of Power, and the belief in Power is in the fullest sense practical; "originally therefore the conception of magical power and that of capacity in general are most probably identical".[1] Power may be employed in magic, while the magical character pertains to every unusual action; yet it would be quite erroneous to designate potency in general as magical power, and Dynamism as the theory of magic. Magic is certainly manifested by power; to employ power, however, is not in itself to act magically, although every extraordinary action of primitive man possesses a tinge of the magical.[2] The creation of the earth is the effect of the divine *mana*, but so is all capacity; the chief's power, the happiness of the country, depend on *mana*: similarly the beam of the latrine has its own mode, probably because excreta, like all parts of the body, function as receptacles of power. That any reference to magic in the technical sense is superfluous is clear from the statement that "the foreigners were after all victorious, and now the Maori are completely subjected to the *mana* of the English".[3] Yet to the primitive mind the alien authority is no such perfectly reasonable a power as it is to ourselves; again Codrington has described the situation correctly by his "in a way supernatural". Characteristic also is the manner in which the indigenes explain the power of the Christian mass:[4] "If you go to the priest and ask him to pray so that I may die, and he consents, then

---

[1] Preuss, *AR.* IX, 1906.

[2] "To seek to derive numinous power from magical is altogether to invert the situation, since long before the magician could appropriate and manipulate it, it had been 'apperceived as numinous' in plant and animal, in natural processes and objects, in the horror of the skeleton, and also independently of all these." Otto, *Gefühl des Überweltlichen*, 56.

[3] Lehmann, *Mana*, 24.   [4] *ibid.*, 58 (Wallis Island).

he celebrates mass, so that I shall die. I die suddenly, and the people say that the priest's mass is *mana*, because a youth has perished."

It is inevitable, still further, that since Power is in no degree systematically understood, it is never homogeneous nor uniform. One may possess either great or limited *mana*; two magicians may attack each other by employing two sorts of *mana*. Power enjoys no moral value whatever. *Mana* resides alike in the poisoned arrow and in European remedies, while with the Iroquois *orenda*[1] one both blesses and curses. It is simply a matter of Power, alike for good or evil.

4. Codrington's discovery was followed by others in the most diverse parts of the world. The *orenda* of the Iroquois has just been referred to; "it appears that they interpreted the activities of Nature as the ceaseless strife between one *orenda* and another".[2] The Sioux Indians, again, believe in *wakanda*, at one time a god of the type of an originator,[3] at another an impersonal Power which acquires empirical verification whenever something extraordinary is manifested. Sun and moon, a horse (a *wakanda*-dog!), cult implements, places with striking features: all alike are regarded as *wakan* or *wakanda*, and once again its significance must be expressed by widely different terms:—powerful, holy, ancient, great, *etc*. In this instance also the theoretical problem of the universality of *wakanda* is not raised; the mind still remains at the standpoint of empirically substantiating the manifestation of Power.

In contrast with *mana*, however, and together with some other ideas of Power, *wakanda* represents one specific type, since it is capable of transformation into the conception of a more or less personal god. This is also the case with the *manitu* of the Algonquins of North-West America, which is a power that confers their capacity on either harmful or beneficent objects, and gives to European missionaries their superiority over native medicine-men. Animals are *manido* whenever they possess supernatural power;[4] but *manitu* is also employed in a personal sense for spirit, and *kitshi manitu* is the Great Spirit, the Originator. The Dyaks of Borneo, similarly, recognize the power of *petara*, which is something, but also someone, while in Madagascar

---

[1] *cf.* below.
[2] Hewitt, "Orenda and a Definition of Religion", *Amer. Anthropologist*, N.S. IV, 1902.   [3] *cf.* Chap. 18.
[4] *cf.* an animal fairy tale of the Algonquins: "The elks, which were *manido*, knew in advance what the hunter would do"; and they were able, "since they were *manido*, at any time to return to life". W. Krickeberg, *Indianermärchen aus Nord-Amerika*, 1924, 69.

the *hasina*-power confers upon the king, on foreigners and whites their striking and supernormal qualities.

Among the ancient Germans, too, the idea of Power was dominant. The power of life, luck (*hamingja*), was a quantitative potency. Men fought by inciting their luck against somebody (Old Nordic: *etia hamingju*), and were defeated because they possessed too little "luck".[1] The Swedish peasant senses "power" in bread, in the horse, *etc.*, while in Nordic folklore the woman whose child has been stolen by a troll is unable to pursue her because she "has been robbed of her power".

Finally, Power may be assigned to some definite bearer or possessor from whom it emanates. Such a power is the Arabian *baraka*,[2] which is regarded as an emanation from holy men and closely connected with their graves; it is acquired by pilgrimage, and to be cured of some disease a king's wife seeks the *baraka* of a saint. This beneficent power also is confined to specific localities; thus the place in which to study is not indifferent so far as its results are concerned, and in Mecca "the attainment of knowledge is facilitated by the *baraka* of the spot".[3]

5. But even when Power is not expressly assigned a name the idea of Power often forms the basis of religion, as we shall be able to observe almost continually in the sequel. Among extensive divisions of primitive peoples, as also those of antiquity, the Power in the Universe was almost invariably an impersonal Power. Thus we may speak of Dynamism—of the interpretation of the Universe in terms of Power; I prefer this expression to both Animatism and Pre-Animism:—to the former because "Universal Animation" smacks too much of theory. The primitive mind never halts before the distinction between inorganic, and organic, Nature; what it is always concerned with is not Life, which appears to explain itself, but Power, authenticated purely empirically by one occurrence after another; thus the Winnebago (Sioux) offers tobacco to any unusual object because it is *wakan*. From the term "Pre-Animism", however, it would be inferred that, chronologically, priority is due to the idea of Power as contrasted with other conceptions such as the animistic.[4] But here there can be no question

[1] V. Grönbech, *Vor Folkeaet i Oldtiden*, I, 1909, 189 *f.*
[2] Derived from the root *brk*, to bless.
[3] O. Rescher, *Studien über den Inhalt von* 1001 *Nacht, Islam* 9, 1918, 24 *f.*
[4] Lehmann (*Mana*, 83) criticizes Marett for abandoning his conception of Pre-Animism as a stage "logically but also in some sense chronologically prior to animism" (*The Threshold of Religion*, 11), because "only the genetic method of approach can lead to the solution of our problem". But this method can in no case attain *our* goal, which is the comprehension of the phenomena in accord with their spiritual content.

whatever as to earlier or later stages in development, but quite simply of the texture or constitution of the religious spirit, as this predominated in other and earlier cultures than our own, but also as it lives and flourishes even in our own day.

- **6.** To recapitulate: I have dealt with the idea of Power which empirically, and within some form of experience, becomes authenticated in things and persons, and by virtue of which these are influential and effective. This potency is of different types: it is attributed to what we regard as sublime, such as Creation, exactly as it is to pure capacity or "luck". It remains merely dynamic, and not in the slightest degree ethical or "spiritual". Nor can we speak of any "primitive Monism", since to do so presupposes theory that does not as yet exist. Power is thought of only when it manifests itself in some very striking way; with what confers efficiency on objects and persons in ordinary circumstances, on the other hand, man does not concern himself. At the same time it is quite true that the idea of Power, as soon as it becomes incorporated within other cultural conditions, expands and deepens into the concept of a Universal Power.

To this Power, in conclusion, man's reaction is amazement (*Scheu*), and in extreme cases fear. Marett employs the fine term "awe"; and this attitude is characterized by Power being regarded, not indeed as supernatural, but as extraordinary, of some markedly unusual type, while objects and persons endowed with this potency have that essential nature of their own which we call "sacred".

K. BETH, *Religion und Magie*[2], 1927.

R. H. CODRINGTON, *The Melanesians*, 1891.

J. N. B. HEWITT, "Orenda and a Definition of Religion", *Amer. Anthropol.* N.S. IV, 1902.

R. LEHMANN, *Mana*, 1922.

R. R. MARETT, *The Threshold of Religion*.

P. SAINTYVES, *La Force Magique*, 1914.

N. SÖDERBLOM, *Das Werden des Gottesglaubens*[2], 1926.

H. WAGENVOORT, *Roman Dynamism*, 1947.

CHAPTER 2

THEORIZING ABOUT POWER

1. AN Esthonian peasant remains poor, while his neighbour grows steadily richer. One night he meets this neighbour's "luck" engaged in sowing rye in the fields. Thereupon he wakes his own "luck", who is sleeping beside a large stone; but it refuses to sow for him, because it is not a farmer's "luck" at all, but a merchant's; so he himself becomes a merchant and gains wealth.[1]

In this story Power has become a specific power; and this transition occurs very early. The power, the effects of which can be quite readily substantiated, becomes power in particular instances—royal authority, that of some craft, *etc.* In India this led to the stratification into ruling castes each of which possesses an appropriate power:—*Brahman* pertaining to brahmins, *kshatra* to *kshatriyas*.[2] In this way, too, a special magical power occasionally becomes differentiated from others, as in the case of the Egyptian *sa*, a kind of fluid transmitted by the laying on of hands and other manipulations;[3] while the advance from empirically authenticated and undefined power to theoretically specified potency is also noteworthy in the idea of Hindu *tapas*. Similarly in Australia, as elsewhere, "replete with power", "warm" and "hot" are closely related conceptions. Power develops heat, the primitive mind believes, with an almost modern scientific accuracy of observation; in Ceram a house afflicted with smallpox (in which power consequently appears) is regarded as a "warm house".[4] Similarly *tapas* is heat, that is the heat of the specific energy of chastening, its power.[5]

But there is another aspect of this systematic differentiation of potency; for the problem of the universality of Power becomes expressly postulated and affirmed. A certain Monism already constantly present, but concealed by practically oriented primitive thought, now rises

[1] A. von Löwis of Menar, *Finnische und Esthnische Volksmärchen*, 1922, No. 56. In the same way, in the *Odyssey*, Eumaeus is divine not "because he was actually Sirius and his swine the Pleiades, but because special capacities, and indeed partially magical abilities, pertained to the *major porcarius*, the swine-major, -mayor or -master, as these excellent functionaries were formerly called". Otto, *Gefühl des Überweltlichen*, 96 *f.*

[2] H. Oldenberg, *Die Lehre der Upanishaden*, 1915, 48.

[3] G. Maspero, *Études égypt.* 1, 308.

[4] F. D. E. van Ossenbruggen, *Bydr. Taal-Land-en Volkenk.*, 70, 1915; 71, 1916.

[5] Oldenberg, *Lehre*, 49; *cf.* Söderblom, *Das Werden des Gottesglaubens*, 83.

unmistakably into view; and what has hitherto been erroneously
maintained about the actual idea of Power becomes quite correct—
namely that "this interesting sketch of a unified apprehension of
Nature and of the Universe reminds us, in virtue of its principle of
unity, of Monotheism, and in the light of its realism, of dynamic
Monism"[1]:—more indubitably, it is true, of the latter than of the
former. For Power is never personal. It becomes a universal Energy,
whether in the psychological sense and in direct application to humanity,
or on the other hand as cosmological. In the first instance Power
becomes Soul, but a superpersonal Soul closely akin to Power; in the
second it assumes the form of a divine agency immanently activating
the Universe. "Pantheists and monists are the heirs of a very ancient
tradition; they sustain among ourselves a conception whose original
founders, primitive or savage peoples, deserve more respect and
sympathy than they usually receive."[2]

2. Such theoretical considerations, generally foreign to the primitive
world, attain steadily increasing influence under the conditions of so-
called intermediate or partially developed culture. The changes and
processes of the Universe are then no longer accidental and arbitrary
effects of distinct powers that emerge at each event and disappear
again; they are rather the manifestations of a unitary World-order,
appearing in conformity to rules, and indeed to laws. Many ancient
peoples were familiar with the idea of a World-course, which however is
not passively followed but rather itself moves spontaneously, and is
no mere abstract conformity to Law such as are our Laws of Nature,
but on the contrary a living Power operating within the Universe.
Tao in China, *Ṛta* in India, *Asha* in Iran, *Ma'at* among the ancient
Egyptians, *Dike* in Greece:—these are such ordered systems which
theoretically, indeed, constitute the all-inclusive calculus of the Universe, but which nevertheless, as living and impersonal powers, possess
mana-like character.

Tao, then, is the path which the Universe follows, and in a narrower
sense the regularly recurring revolutions of the seasons. The "two
shores" of warmth and heat which define this cycle together constitute
Tao; there is no place for a God "applying outward force" (to quote
Goethe).[3] Creation is the annual renewal of Nature. This regulated
cycle, still further, is completely impartial and just; and man should

[1] R. Ganschinietz, *Religion und Geisteskultur*, 8, 1914, 316 *f.*
[2] Saintyves, *La Force Magique*, 46.   [3] *cf.* p. 185.

strive to conform to *Tao*. But in so doing he need not excite himself:
Tao demands a calm, indeed an almost quietist mood. To good deeds
it is hostile: "Great *Tao* was deserted; then 'humanity' and 'justice'
came into existence, cleverness and sagacity arose, and hypocrisy
flourished." Man should do right in conformity to *Tao*, which is
"eternal without acting (*wu wei*), and yet there is nothing that it does
not effect". Thus from this belief in a primal Power there arises a type
of quietist mysticism. In itself it is self-sufficient, needing neither gods
nor men: "the Norm of men is the earth, that of the earth is heaven,
of heaven *Tao*, but the Norm of *Tao* is . . . its very self".[1] Again,
"*Tao* generates and nourishes all beings, completes and ripens them,
cares for and protects them". But just as little as *mana* is it exhaustively
manifested in the empirical: the essential nature of *Tao* is inscrutable.
"In so far as it is nameless it is the primal ground of heaven and earth;
when it has a name it is the mother of a myriad beings. For lack of a
better term, call it 'the Great'." Here the old *mana* significance returns
once more; but its content has now been "transposed", and is no
longer empirical but speculatively mystical.[2]

The Vedic *Ṛta*, again, is the Law of the Universe, identical with
moral law; it is regarded as the Law of certain gods, Varuna and Mitra,
and the World-Process is merely the apparent form behind which the
actual *Ṛta* is concealed: "The gods are thus addressed: Your *Ṛta*
(Law), which is hidden behind the *Ṛta* (the course of the Universe),
stands eternally constant, there, where the sun's chargers are un-
harnessed." Thus it becomes the ultimate court of appeal, the ground
of the Universe, its concealed and motivating Power. Just as with
Asha in the religion of Zarathustra, *Ṛta* is good disposition, correct
belief, the Law of the gods and World-Power simultaneously. The
dominating faith is that the ground of the world may be trusted, and
thus the chaotic empiricism of primitive conditions has been superseded
by a firm conviction of Order.

3. When gods exist they become either elevated above the World-
Order, or subjected thereto. Both the Israelites and the Greeks were
conscious of the flaming power of divine energy, of the *orge* which
strikes with demonic force—for there can be no question of punish-

---

[1] *cf.* p. 127.

[2] *cf.* J. J. M. de Groot, *Universismus*, 1918. [The term "transposed" indicates the variation of the significance of a phenomenon while at the same time its form remains unchanged; *cf.* more fully p. 610.]

ment here; but in contrast to the Israelites, the Greeks were unable to bring this demonic power into relation with the gods.[1] They were intensely aware of the antithesis between the arbitrary rule of potencies in this world and the idea of a just order of the Universe: *Moira* or *Aisa*, originally the lot apportioned to each man by the gods—it is διόθεν, "sent from Zeus"—becomes in the brooding mind of an Aeschylus a Power more than divine which, if so it must be, against even the gods guarantees a morally satisfactory control of the world. From the incalculable dominance of gods, whom the poets had transformed into persons, man sought escape in Destiny, as a universal ground and territory over which the gods enjoyed only limited freedom of action.

In the course of natural processes, then, man discovered a secure and, if not sympathetic, at least an impartial foundation even for human life. If for many peoples, even the most primitive, the course of the sun served as the rule of their own lives, still religious theory perceived no inexorable Fate in this necessity of Nature, but rather a guarantee of World-Order. This attitude therefore is not fatalism because the living Power, despite all theorizing, perpetually maintains its central position. Conformity to Law implies no blind Necessity, but a vital Energy realizing a purpose. It was called *Dike*, as in India *Rta*; but its path is the cycle of natural process: "the sun will not exceed his measures", said Heracleitus; "if he does, the Erinyes, the avenging handmaids of Justice, will find him out".[2] To Law, similarly, Sophocles dedicates pious resignation:

> My lot be still to lead
>   The life of innocence and fly
> Irreverence in word or deed,
>   To follow still those laws ordained on high
> Whose birthplace is the bright ethereal sky.
>   No mortal birth they own,
>   Olympus their progenitor alone:
> Ne'er shall they slumber in oblivion cold,
> The god in them is strong and grows not old.[3]

And the late-born of the tragedians, Euripides, the advocate of every doubt and the friend of all unrest, places in the mouth of his Hecuba this marvellously calm and heartfelt prayer:

[1] The Persians succeeded in this, but only by appealing to a bold Dualism and ascribing all that was demonic to the evil Spirit.

[2] Diels, *Fr.* 94 (Burnet).   [3] *Oedipus Rex*, 863 *ff.* (Storr).

Thou deep Base of the World, and thou high Throne
Above the World, whoe'er thou art, unknown
And hard of surmise, Chain of Things that be,
Or Reason of our Reason; God, to thee
I lift my praise, seeing the silent road
That bringeth justice ere the end be trod
To all that breathes and dies.[1]

Thus early Greek speculation, which set out to discover an *arche*, a primal unity and primal Power in one, ultimately discerned an impersonal, divinely living, cosmic Law; the divine, τὸ Θεῖον, more and more superseded the gods. The Stoics then drew the final conclusion: *Heimarmene*, that is what is allotted, or Destiny, is the *Logos*, the Reason of the cosmos, in accord with which all proceeds; Cleanthes prays to *Pepromene*, the predestined. But even this view of the idea of Fate was just as little an abstraction as was the Necessity of the tragedians and the pre-Socratics. Still the essence of the Universe is always Power, but now an immanent Power, a World-Soul: or better, a "Fluid" dwelling within the Universe, "the personality and the nature of the divinities pervading the substance of the several elements".[2] To the contemporary of Julian the Apostate, finally, divine Power and the creative Necessity of Nature were absolutely one: "To say that God turns away from the evil is like saying that the sun hides himself from the blind."[3]

4. The theoretic treatment of Power thus far presented bears a prominently cosmological character; but it may also possess psychological significance. The power that operates within man then becomes regarded not as his "soul", in the sense familiar to ourselves, but as a particular power subsisting in a peculiar relation to its possessor. It is his own power, though nevertheless it is superior to him.

Before *Moira* became the Power of Destiny it was already the personal lot of man, and this it still remains even to-day among modern Greeks as *Mira*. The Germanic *hamingja*, again, was not the soul, but the power ruling in and over a man. Soul is in no way a primitive concept, and even when primitive mentality began to theorize it had generally not grasped the idea of Soul. We ourselves speak of our psychical qualities, and can "verify" these whenever we wish to do so.

[1] *The Trojan Women*, 884 ff. (Murray).
[2] Cicero, *De Deorum Natura*, II, 71. (Rackham).
[3] Sallustius, in Murray, *Five Stages of Greek Religion*, 260

But to the primitive mind, on the other hand, what we regard as purely personal and pertaining to the "soul" appears as actually inherent in man but still superior to him, and in any case as distinguished from him. The Red Indian, according to his own and our ideas, may be very brave; but that avails him nought if he has no war-medicine, that is, no accumulated power for the purpose of war. Power can be bound up with all sorts of material or corporeal objects; it is this state of affairs that has led to the designation of "soul-stuff".[1] From the soul as such, however, all these ideas were distinguished by the power being impersonal, while one might have a greater or smaller quantity of it, and could either lose it or acquire it; in other terms, it was independent of man and superior to him.

In the Greek-Christian world we find the ideas of Power transformed, theoretically, into that of the single Power by means of the concept of *pneuma*. The Stoics had already placed the individual soul, the *hegemonikon*, which from the heart as centre governs the whole body, in the same category as the World-Soul, the *pneuma*, which, as Power, overflows into all things: the human *pneuma* is of the same type as the *pneuma* of the Universe. Thus the primitive idea of Power, together with the equally primitive concept of soul-breath, or rather of the breath-stuff of the soul,[2] were united in a single theory.

In Gnosticism, and also for St. Paul, the *pneuma* is the life principle of man together with the *psyche* and divine Power, which penetrates man from without and transforms him into a "pneumatized" or "spiritual" man. By St. Paul himself, however, the idea of the impersonal divine "fluid" becomes slightly changed and circumscribed through the union with Christ: "the Lord is that Spirit".[3] On the other hand, for Philo the *pneuma* emanating from the Godhead remains impersonal, though for him as for the late Stoics the *pneuma*, when contrasted with the *psyche* and the flesh, is a power superior to man.

But in spite of the identification of the spiritual and the immaterial, originating in Plato's philosophy, in the eyes of the heathen the *pneuma* was just as little purely spiritual—in our own sense—as in those of Christians. Its designation as soul-stuff was always much more than a mere name. In the New Testament, for example, the *pneuma* becomes transmitted like some sort of fluid, as are the other psychological powers *charis*, *dynamis* and *doxa*.[4] They flow from God to man, and the divine *charis* is imparted by formulas of benediction. We

---

[1] *cf.* Chap. 39.   [2] *ibid.*   [3] 2 *Cor.* iii. 17.
[4] *cf.* G. P. son Wetter, *Charis*, 1913. Joh. Schneider, *Doxa*, 1932.

translate this as the Grace of God, although it should not be understood
as friendly disposition or mercy, but as Power that is poured out and
absorbed. It enables man to perform miracles: Stephen, full of *charis*
and *dynamis*, "of faith and power, did great wonders among the
people".[1] *Charis* effects *charismata*, Gifts of Grace; these however are
no gifts of divine generosity, as we might rationalistically interpret
them, but the consequences of divine Power. Ancient Christian terminology perpetuates these ideas: in the Eucharist Christ appears with His
powers, His *pneuma*, His *doxa* or *dynamis*.[2] The "glorification" in
St. John's *Gospel* again, is a transformation of man which takes place
through the infusion of divine Power; and as Wetter affirms quite
correctly: "when classical writers refer *e.g.* to religious *gnosis*, *charis* or
doxa, who does not feel that these primitive tones (of the idea of Power)
frequently re-echo from them?"[3]

Not merely the "psychic" powers but also the deeds, thoughts and
principles of men frequently become represented as a store of power,
largely independent of the bearer. I refer here to the idea of *thesaurus*,
in consequence of which cumulative deeds constitute a potency that
is effective in favour of the doer, but eventually of another person
also; thus the treasury of grace, accumulated through the merit of
Christ and the saints, is a living power "operating" in favour of the
church. Certainly the connection between Power and the historic Christ
has long become illusory here; it has been forgotten that the Lord is
the Spirit, and the Power of Christ dispensed among believers.

In India the *thesaurus* concept is absolutely impersonal; *karma* is
Power, Law and *thesaurus* simultaneously: "not in the heavens nor
in the midst of the sea, not if he hides in the clefts of the mountains,
will man escape the power of karma". Thus action has become an
impersonal mechanism; and human worth is then appraised as a sum
of favourable or unfavourable *karma*, a sort of financial value, that can
be transferred to others.[4]

5. In India, then, there has been completed the great equalization

---

[1] *Acts* vi. 8.

[2] *cf.* G. P. son Wetter, *Altchristliche Liturgien, Das Christliche Mysterium*, 1921.

[3] G. P. son Wetter, *Die "Verherrlichung" im Johannesevangelium: Beitr. zur Rel.
wiss.* 2, 1914–1915, 72 *f.* (Published by *Rel. wiss. Ges.*, Stockholm.) Dr. Rudolf Bultmann kindly informs me that he also believes that the conception of δοξασθῆναι, as a
transformation effected by the infusion of divine power, underlies St. John's terminology, but not that the evangelist himself still retained this idea.

[4] *cf.* H. Oldenberg, *Die Lehre der Upanishaden*, 1915, 113 *f.*

that is the final word in the theory of Power, the unification of human and cosmic Power, the identification of psychology and cosmology. The substance of the self and the substance of the All are one and the same, their separation being merely provisional and, ultimately, no more than misunderstanding. The *ātman*, originally as soul-breath the most primitive soul-stuff, became in the theory of the *Upanishads* a silently operating and immanent Power conforming to Law: "If the slayer thinks he slays and the slain that he is slain, they both fail to understand; the one slays not and the other is not slain. The *ātman* reposes, subtler than the subtle and greater than the great, in the hearts of creatures. He who is free from desires and without care sees the greatness of the *ātman* by the grace of the creator. Seated, he wanders far away; reclining, he travels everywhere; apart from me, who can recognize this god who is in a state of changing ecstasy?"[1] On the other hand *Brahman*, originally the power of the word, as it reveals itself to the brahmins in the sacrificial utterances and their reciters, became the designation of cosmic Power. *Ātman* and *Brahman*, however, in the last resort are one: here is there, there is here; he who understands *tat tvam asi*, "that art thou", knows of only *one* all comprehending Power. And thus the primitive and intensely empirical idea of Power developed into religious Monism.

[1] *Kathaka Upanishad.*

CHAPTER 3

THINGS AND POWER

1. WE moderns have accustomed ourselves to regard things as mere dead objects with which we deal exactly as we please. Only a poet could vindicate things:

> Gladly do I hearken to the Things singing.
> Touch them—How stiff and mute they are!
> You kill all my Things.[1]

Here once again a philosopher is sensitive to the potency of things, which possess a life of their own despite that "loss of power that has befallen them since the days of the Greeks";[2] for the prevailing emphasis on the spiritual and internal, as contrasted with the merely institutional —*Spiritualismus*—the cult of personality, and finally modern machinery, have transformed the living, "self-activated" things into merely dead material.

To the primitive mind, on the contrary, the thing is the bearer of a power; it can effect something, it has its own life which reveals itself, and once again wholly practically. During an important expedition, for example, an African negro steps on a stone and cries out: "Ha! are you there?" and takes it with him to bring him luck. The stone, as it were, gives a hint that it is powerful. Again: an Ewe tribesman in West Africa enters the bush and finds a lump of iron there; returning home, he falls ill, and the priests explain that a *tro* (a divine being) is manifesting its potency in the iron, which in future should be worshipped.[3] Thus every thing may be a power bearer, and even if it itself provides no evidence of its influence, it suffices if someone tells it that it is powerful. What Rilke, in one of his *Stories of God*, makes the children do—they agree among themselves that the thimble shall be God: "anything may be God. You have only to tell it to be"—this is the frame of mind behind so-called Fetishism.

2. Every thing then, to repeat, can be a power bearer. Objects existing in intimate relation to soul-stuff possess indisputable potency; it is

[1] Rilke.
[2] *cf.* P. Tillich, *Die Überwindung des Persönlichkeitsideals, Logos*, XVI, 1927.
[3] J. Spieth, *Die Religion der Eweer in Süd-Togo*, 1911, 110 *ff.*

for this reason that the Maori, as has already been remarked, regard the latrine as replete with *mana*: the sick bite its beams in order to be cured.[1] This systematic reckoning with the power subsisting in things we call Fetishism, a term coined in the scientific sense by de Brosses in 1760, and originally used by the Portuguese with reference to Negro beliefs and customs.[2] But it was applied only to potent things made by man himself, and therefore not to natural objects. Gradually, however, it attained a more comprehensive meaning, sometimes so extensive that even the worship of Nature could be included, so that the concept then became formless. But if it is really desired to indicate the structure of a spiritual viewpoint by the term usually employed, then it would be advisable to apply it only to those objects that we call "things", but with no distinction between natural and artificial, because primitive man venerates what he has himself made,[3] provided this is "effective", just as much as what Nature gives him when this manifests power. In this latter respect, any peculiarity that differentiates the object from environing Nature is essentially significant: the striking shape of a crooked branch, of a round stone, *etc.*, becomes the "pointer" to the existence of power. It is necessary, further, that the object be not too large, so that one may take it away, or as it were pocket it. Although mountains and trees are regarded as sacred, like the fetish, because of their potency, still they should not be called fetishes; it is just this feeling of being able to carry the sacred power with one that is characteristic of fetishism. "Let us fetch the ark of the covenant of the Lord out of Shiloh unto us, that, when it cometh among us, it may save us out of the hand of our enemies",[4] said the Israelites when the Philistines beset them.

A good example of a fetish is the Australian *churinga*, a peculiarly shaped piece of wood on which an outline sketch of a totem emblem is scratched. The word itself means the "private secret", and the object must be kept secret from the women and children. It is the bearer of a power connected on the one hand with the individual, and on the other with his totem;[5] here again subsists the power superior to, yet nevertheless overflowing into, humanity. The *churinga* are most carefully concealed in a kind of place of refuge.[6]

[1] Lehmann, *Mana*, 50.
[2] The Portuguese *feitiço* means artificial, *factitius*, and subsequently magic.
[3] "Veneration", moreover, is to be understood here only in its most general sense. A. C. Kruyt speaks, more accurately, of "feeding" the fetish so that it may retain its power: *Het Animisme in den Indischen Archipel*, 1906, 200.
[4] 1 *Samuel* iv. 3.   [5] *cf.* Chap. 8.   [6] Chap. 57.

Earlier research assumed that the potency of a fetish is a spirit permanently residing within it, but to-day the contrasted hypothesis is in favour. At the same time it is probable that the way in which this power is represented is of secondary significance for the constitution of Fetishism as such. Thus the power of the ark of the covenant sprang from Jahveh, a god, that of the *churinga* from a totem; and the potent influence of the fetish, naturally, is very often simply presupposed quite apart from any kind of attitude to spirits or gods being implied— purely dynamically therefore. Actually, Fetishism is always dynamic; and regarded as an ideal type, it was so originally also, because its essence lies in the idea that power resides within a thing and emanates from it. Whence the power arises is, however, a question in itself.

In view of these considerations we can understand the transition from fetish to idol. In many parts of the world piles of stones were erected, each traveller adding his stone to those already thrown there; such stone heaps being found in South Africa just as in ancient Israel. In later times these cairns were looked upon as monuments or burial mounds; originally, however, it was the potency of the accumulated stones that men thus assured for themselves. In Greece these stone heaps were called *hermae* and were the origin of a divinity—"he of the stone heaps": *Hermes*. But before Hermes received his marvellous human form from the hands of Praxiteles he had to stand by the way-side, as the phallic stone or *herm*, for many years.[1] The august form of Pallas, again, was evolved from the fetish of the double thunder-shield or *palladion*. Of her, just as of Demeter, there were effigies which were half stone fetish and half woman, exactly as Aphrodite was originally a cone. The power of things, in fact, faded only very gradually before that of gods and even of animals. In ancient Egypt fetishes persisted together with animal and human forms of power, and in Greece people loved the *xoana*, the rough wooden blocks, more than Pheidias' marvellous statues; his "Attic Pallas and Rharian Ceres, which stand unsculptured in the shape of a rude and unformed log" (Tertullian), were dearer to him than the Lemnian Athene or the Cnidian Demeter. Forms contrasted with the human actually indicate a diviner remoteness, and yet at the same time a more intimate contact, than does anthropomorphic Power. And this extremely primitive association between transcendence and immanence is essentially characteristic of Fetishism. The time-honoured, time-blackened, blocks of wood, which pious faith takes to have descended from heaven, were

[1] *cf.* M. P. Nilsson, *Griechische Feste*, 1906, 388.

precious to the people's hearts; they remain so to-day in Catholic regions. For it is not before great art creations, nor forms that arouse his sympathy, that man prays most spontaneously and fervently and to which he makes pilgrimages, but the "black Madonnas".[1] It is these that work miracles; and before the fetish numinous awe unites with the intimacy and the consciousness of dominance aroused by things.[2]

The intensity of the attractive power enjoyed, even to-day, by Fetishism, is plainly evident from the use of so-called mascots in modern sport: dolls and animal figures still display themselves as potent, and this not as incarnations of gods in whom trust is no longer placed, but purely and simply as "things". At the missionary exhibition in Nice in 1925, for example, many fetishes were to be seen, and countless visitors wished to buy these at high prices. As this was naturally declined, the directors of the exhibition found themselves compelled to have these objects carefully guarded because attempts were made to steal them.[3]

3. Among potent things *tools* assume a prominent place. To primitive man, indeed, work is the very antithesis of technical occupation—it is creative. The primitive craftsman experiences the power, in virtue of which he completes his task, not as his own; capacity, moreover, is here something far more than modern efficiency. The early hand-worker therefore, particularly the smith, wields a power which he certainly understands how to employ, but of which nevertheless he is not the master; and thus we can realize why smith's work is regarded as sacred in many parts of Africa and Indonesia. In Loango, again, who-ever has cohabited the previous night may not watch the labour lest his impurity should ruin the work; for whatever comes into existence under human hands owes its being to a power superior to man. In the grips and blows of the tools, then, there dwells not only the strength of arms or legs, but also a specific power residing within the implements themselves; and this explains why tools are always made after the same model, since the slightest deviation would injure the potency. Moreover, not only are the working parts of the implements essential, but their ornamentation also.[4] The Toba-Batak of Sumatra sacrifices to his forge, hammer and anvil, to his canoe, rifle and furniture; the West African

[1] cf. Th. Trede, *Das Heidentum in der römischen Kirche*, II, 1890, 90 ff.
[2] Chap. 65.
[3] R. Allier, *Le non-civilisé et nous*, 1927, 181.
[4] Lévy-Bruhl, *How Natives Think*, 40 f.; cf. further on blacksmiths, M. Merker, *Die Masai*, 1910, 111 ff.

Ewe to his bush knife, axe, saw, *etc.*; and the gipsy, though decried as irreligious, swears his oath on the anvil.

Among implements, again, it is *weapons* that are especially potent; indeed, many weapons are nothing more than tools—the axe and hammer. The veneration of the Cretan double axe is universally familiar. The staff also was originally a weapon, which subsequently became the receptacle of royal power. In Egypt, not only was the staff worshipped, but the word denoting it, *shm*, also became an expression for "power" in general, for "to be potent", and at a later stage for a divine force which, together with other *mana*-like influences, rendered the dead king a ruler in the hereafter.[1] Thus we find here three stages: the sceptre—its power—and finally power in general. When king Tuthmosis III sent his general against Joppa he gave him his sceptre which, like the staffs of even private individuals in Egypt, bore a special name—"adorned with beauty".[2] At Chaeronea, again, the Greeks worshipped Agamemnon's sceptre with sacrifices,[3] while the Romans regarded the spear as the fetish of the god Mars. Whoever undertook a war invoked the sacred lance: *Mars vigila*:—"Mars, Awake!" And like the *hasta*, the *ancile* or shield also, which was believed to have fallen from heaven in the days of Numa, was held to be holy.

4. The last instance leads from the mere brute potency of the thing to its significance as the hoard of a communal essence. For the presence of the *ancile* guaranteed that of the supreme government. Similarly, the *palladium*, originally a stone or double shield, and subsequently the *xoanon* or wooden image of the goddess Athene, was the hoard, the power-object of Troy. Were this lost, the town would perish. In ancient Israel the same rôle was filled by the ark of the covenant. The Fox Indians too possessed a "sacred bundle", consisting of an owl, a tobacco pipe, two turtles, a firestone and a flute, which assured the tribal power.[4] The Amandebele of South Africa had their *mamchali*, a small basket without an opening containing "holy" things, a genuine palladium; if it fell into hostile hands it proved itself invulnerable.[5] On Taliabo (Sula Island) there is a sacred spot where a number of

[1] *cf.* W. Spiegelberg, *Der Stabkultus bei den Ägyptern, Rec. de Trav.* 25, 1903, 184; *cf.* 28, 1906, 163 *f.*

[2] S. G. Maspero, *Popular Stories of Ancient Egypt*, 109 *f.* G. Röder, *Altägyptische Erzählungen und Märchen*, 1927, 67.

[3] Pausanias, IX, 40, 11.

[4] K. Th. Preuss, *Glauben und Mystik im Schatten des höchsten Wesens*, 1926, 32.

[5] H. C. M. Fourie, *Amandebele van Fene Mahlangu*, 1921.

dishes, shells, *etc.*, are preserved in the soil; only one man knows where this is, and in case of plague he brings water to the *kampong* or native village in one of the shells. The Indonesians, still further, provide very many instructive examples of this belief in a tribal or communal hoard. The Macassars and Bugis ascribe special significance to the state insignia; whoever possesses these has the country also in his power, for in them the "rulership of the land is as it were concentrated";[1] during a riot in Luwu the Dutch commanding officer required only to seize the insignia of state to break down opposition immediately. Such objects are of different kinds: old spears, daggers, a Koran, stones, *etc.*—but these must usually have been handed down from the tribal ancestors. The imperial insignia of the Holy Roman Empire possessed a similarly concentrated potency even in the Middle Ages. They were regarded as sacred objects, to be approached in procession, and days when they were exhibited to the people were treated as great festival occasions. To a newly elected emperor, therefore, the possession of the insignia was extremely important;[2] like the weapons of Mars in Rome, they were *pignora imperii*:—Pledges of the realm.[3]

Not the power of the tribe or realm only, but similarly that of the family was associated with venerable objects. In Indonesia each family has its so-called *pusaka*, objects frequently of very slight value, which are, however, regarded as sacred and bequeathed from father to son. The ancient Germans too looked upon clothes, weapons and jewels as luck-bearers, the family welfare being often intimately connected with so potent an object. The power of the hero's sword, again, which rendered its wielder invincible, became the permanent *motif* of saga, myth and fairy tale.

5. From fetishes amulets are distinguished; these also are certainly containers of power, only as it were in pocket size. Representations of sacred objects, crosses, suns, *etc.*, but also knots intended to hold power together, stones and almost every imaginable thing were carried on the body as amulets to ward off danger and attract blessings. Like fetishes, these too can acquire their influence from some holy person or situation; but then they are preferably called relics.[4]

[1] C. Spat, *De Rykssieraden van Loewoe, Ned. Indie oud en nieuw*, 3, 1918.
[2] *cf.* L. von Ranke, *Weltgeschichte*, VIII⁴, 1921, 44.
[3] Escutcheons, banners and flags, which even to-day have not lost their religious significance, fall within this category.   [4] *cf.* Chap. 30.

CHAPTER 4

POTENCY. AWE. *TABU*

1. THE experience of the potency of things or persons may occur at any time; it is by no means confined to specific seasons and occasions. Powerfulness always reveals itself in some wholly unexpected manner; and life is therefore a dangerous affair, full of critical moments. If then one examines them more closely, even the most ordinary events, the customary associations with one's neighbours, or similarly one's long familiar tasks, prove to be replete with "mystic" interconnections. We may say indeed (as *e.g.* Marett maintains) that the explanation of any fact, however natural it may appear, is ultimately always "mystic". But we should probably express ourselves in more primitive fashion if we completely ignored our own scheme of explanation in terms of single causes, and in place of this interpreted life as a broad current of mighty powers whose existence we do not specifically observe, but which occasionally makes itself conspicuous by either the damming or the flooding of its waters. If, for instance, one of the Toradja tribes in Celebes is preparing for an expedition and an earthen pot is broken, then they remain at home, saying that it is *measa*.[1] This may be translated as "a sign": only not in any rationalistic sense as indicating some future misfortune, but that the current of life has been interrupted: If then one thing has been broken, why not more? Similarly, when an Ewe tribesman finds refuge from his enemies on a white ant hill he ascribes his escape to the power residing there.[2] Thus the place, the action, the person in which the power reveals itself receive a specific character. Bearers of *mana*, for example, are sharply distinguished from the rest of the world: they are self-sufficient. By the Greeks, similarly, a body struck by lightning was regarded as holy, ἱερός, because powerfulness was manifested in it.[3]

Objects, persons, times, places or actions charged with Power are called *tabu* (*tapu*), a word from the same cultural domain as *mana*. It indicates "what is expressly named", "exceptional", while the verb

---

[1] A. C. Kruyt, "Measa", *Bydr. Taal-, Land- en Volkenkunde Ned. Indie*, 74–76, 1918–1920.

[2] K. Th. Preuss, *Glauben und Mystik im Schatten des höchsten Wesens*, 1926, 25.

[3] *cf.* Euripides, *The Suppliant Women*, 934 *ff*.

tapui means "to make holy".[1] *Tabu* is thus a sort of warning: "Danger! High voltage!" Power has been stored up, and we must be on our guard. The *tabu* is the expressly authenticated condition of being replete with power, and man's reaction to it should rest on a clear recognition of this potent fullness, should maintain the proper distance and secure protection.

The *tabu* is observed in different ways and with regard to highly contrasted objects. To the Greek the *king* and the *foreigner* or *stranger* appeared as objects of *aidos*, of awe, to be duly respected by keeping one's distance.[2] Almost everywhere the king is looked upon as powerful, so that he should be approached only with the greatest caution, while the foreigner, bearer of a power unknown and therefore to be doubly feared, stands on an equal footing with an enemy; *hostis* is both stranger or foreigner, and enemy. One may either kill the alien, if one is in a position so to do, or bid him welcome; but in no case are his coming and going to be regarded with indifference. *Greeting* is therefore a religious act, intended to intercept the first onset of the power, and into which the name of God is introduced or to which an appeasing influence is attached (*e.g.* the Semitic peace greeting: *adieu*: *Grüssgott*). *Hospitality*, therefore, as well as *war*, is a religious act, intended either to repel the alien power or to neutralize it. *Sex life* is also full of potency, *woman* being distinguished from man by mysterious peculiarities; thus the *veil* served as a defence even before it became a symbol of bashfulness.[3] Everything concerned with the sexual is "exceptional": when one is sexually impure one must be careful, and not *e.g.* undertake any important matter such as war. Nor should one approach a menstruating woman, who is often excluded from a cult for this very reason:—her potent influence would antagonize the power to be acquired by means of the cult; hence the formula: *hostis vinctus mulier virgo exesto*—"Let every stranger, bound person, woman or virgin stand aside"—associated with certain Roman sacrifices. Similarly as regards Cato's warning in connection with the "vow for the cattle: a woman may not take part in this offering nor see how it is performed".[4] Some one day, again, or series of days, is regarded as being more potent than others. Sabbath, Sunday, Christmas Day and their primitive and heathen equivalents are sacred: no work is done, or at least no important affairs undertaken.

---

[1] Söderblom, *Das Werden des Gottesglaubens*, 31 *f.*
[2] *cf. Theol. Wörterbuch zum N.T.*, Αἰδώς.   [3] *cf.* 1 *Cor.* xi. 5 *ff.*
[4] *De Agri Cultura*, 83; *votum pro bubus: mulier ad eam rem divinam ne adsit neve videat quo modo fiat.*

Thus the battle of Thermopylae was lost because the "holy days" (ἱερομηνία) imposed on the Spartans a cessation of hostilities; and for the same reason they arrived at Marathon too late. On very sacred days even the slightest labour was forbidden; for critical times must never be allowed to pass unnoticed but must be met by some relevant exceptional behaviour on man's own part, such as fasting. *Tabu*, then, is the avoidance of deed and of word, springing from awe in the presence of Power. Words concerning critical affairs like hunting, war, sex intercourse, should not be uttered, but rather be replaced by a specially elaborated *tabu* language, remnants of which we still retain in our sportsmen's slang and thieves' jargon. Even a peculiar women's terminology occurs side by side with the men's.

But the mere avoidance, as such, of potency cannot suffice. Among the Kaian of Central Borneo, for example, neither man nor woman may touch slaughtered fowl during the woman's pregnancy, nor may the man pound the soil, *etc.*;[1] to our minds the connection and the purpose here are obscure. The *tabu*, however, is anything but a measure of utility: Power has revealed itself, either as cessation or as superfluity. It is therefore not only a question of avoiding it, but also of thinking of some defence against it. Sometimes the mode of protection is intelligible to us, as with the veil or some sort of ritual or discipline such as fasting; often, however, we cannot fathom it at all. Associations then appear which we moderns quite fail to understand, and feelings to which we are wholly insusceptible. But even when we do succeed, what we regard as a causative connection does not emerge, just as little as there arises an emotional reaction in the sense of our reverence or devotion, though both these may be incorporated in the primitive attitude. The *tabu*, further, may be decreed; some power bearer, a king or priest, can endow an object with his own power and proclaim a season of potency; in Polynesia the king's messenger thus announces the *tabu*:

> *Tabu*—no one may leave his house!
> *Tabu*—no dog may bark!
> *Tabu*—no cock may crow!
> *Tabu*—no pig may grunt!
> Sleep—sleep, till the *tabu* is past![2]

[1] A. W. Nieuwenhuis, *Quer durch Borneo*, II, 1907, 101.

[2] P. Hambruch, *Südseemärchen*, 1921, No. 66; *cf.* also Frazer, *The Belief in Immortality*, II, 389; no fire may be kept alight, no canoe launched, no swimming enjoyed. The dogs' and pigs' mouths are tied up so that they cannot bark nor grunt.

In Manipur, in Assam, the village priest ordains a similar communal *tabu* called *genna*; the gates of the village are closed; the friend outside must stay there, and the stranger who may chance to be within remains; the men cook their own food and eat it without the women. All the food *tabus* are carefully observed; trading and catching fish, hunting, mowing grass and felling trees are forbidden. Thus an intentionally evoked interruption of life occurs: the moment is critical, one holds one's breath! At particularly sacred times, in fact, holiday-making still retains a ritual air even in some European rural districts. In Dutch Gelderland on Christmas Eve fifty years ago, for example, everything indoors was carefully arranged; neither plough nor harrow might be left outside, all implements being brought into the barns and the gates leading to the fields closed. Everything must be locked up and under cover in its right place, "otherwise '*Derk met den beer*' (the wild huntsmen) would take it with them".[1]

Violation of the *tabu* brought in its train not punishment, but an automatic reaction of Power; it was quite unnecessary to inflict any penalties when Power assailed one spontaneously. With the best intentions, for instance, Uzzah wished to support the ark of the covenant; the touch of the sacred object, however, entailed death.[2] But it was no divine arbitrariness, and still less divine justice, that struck him down: it was the purely dynamic anger of the Lord, אַף יהוה.[3] Even a comic sidelight is instructive here:—In Thuringia every form of work was most strictly prohibited on "Golden (Trinity) Sunday"; and a lad who, in spite of this, had sewn a button on his trousers on the holy day could only with the utmost difficulty save himself from death by a lightning stroke the next day, by sacrificing the garment concerned and allowing it to slip into the water, when it was promptly carried off by Nemesis.[4] From our viewpoint, of course, only the lad was guilty and not his trousers! But Power questions not as to guilt or innocence; it reacts, exactly as the electric current shocks anyone who carelessly touches the wire. In Central Celebes death is the penalty for incest, not, however, as a punishment, but merely as a means of limiting the evil results of the outrage to the delinquents; that the latter should die was regarded as a matter of course.[5] Death by being cast from the *Saxum Tarpeium*, which the Romans inflicted upon

---

[1] H. W. Heuvel, *Oud-achterhoeksch boerenleven*, 1927, 471.   [2] 2 *Sam.* vi.
[3] Actually, not the wrath of Jahveh, but simply "wrath"; "it was not difficult for 'primitive man' to speak of wrath that was not the wrath of *anyone* whatever". Otto, *Gef. des Überwelt.* 55.
[4] O. von Reinsberg-Düringsfeld, *Das festliche Jahr*[2], 1898, 204.   [5] Kruyt, *op. cit.*

traitors, was likewise not punishment but a reaction of the Power; the *tribuni plebis*, who were sacrosanct, that is, the bearers of a most formidable potency, appear as the executioners, while whoever fell, without dying as the result, saved his life; "it is a matter less of an execution than of an intentional accident".[1]

Naturally the effectiveness of the *tabu* was believed in without any reservations whatever. A Maori would die of hunger rather than light a fire with the lighting utensils of a chief,[2] and Howitt heard of a Kurnai boy who had stolen some opossum meat and eaten this before the food *tabus* permitted. The tribal elders persuaded him that he would never be a man; he lay down, and in three weeks was dead.[3] Similar examples might be multiplied indefinitely.

2. We characterize the distance between the potent and the relatively powerless as the relationship between *sacred* and *profane*, or secular. The "sacred" is what has been placed within boundaries, the exceptional (Latin *sanctus*); its powerfulness creates for it a place of its own. "Sacred" therefore means neither completely moral nor, without further qualification, even desirable or praiseworthy. On the contrary, sacredness and even impurity may be identical: in any event the potent is dangerous. The Roman *tribunus plebis*, just referred to, was so sacred, *sacrosanctus*, that merely to meet him on the street made one impure.[4] Among the Maori also *tapu* means "polluted" just as much as "holy"; but in any case it carries a prohibition with it, and therefore prescribes keeping one's proper distance. It is, then, scarcely correct to regard the contrast between sacred and secular as developing out of the distinction between threatening danger and what is not perilous.[5] Power has its own specific quality which forcibly impresses men as dangerous. Yet the perilous is not sacred, but rather the sacred dangerous. In a quite classical way Söderblom has presented the contrast between holy and profane as the primal and governing antithesis in all religion, and has shown how the old viewpoint, that Wonder, Θαυμάζειν, is the beginning of Philosophy, can be applied with yet greater justice to Religion. For whoever is confronted with potency clearly realizes that he is in the presence of some quality with which in

---

[1] A. Piganiol, *Essai sur les Origines de Rome*, 1917, 149.   [2] Frazer, *op. cit.*, 44.
[3] Elsie C. Parsons, "Links between Morality and Religion in Early Culture," *Amer. Anthrop.*, 17, 1915, 46.
[4] Plutarch, *Quaestiones romanae*, 81. This passage seems not quite clear, but in any case impurity, involved by the sacredness of the tribune, is implied.
[5] As B. Ankermann does in Chantepie, 152; *cf.* GENERAL LITERATURE, p. 19 *ante*.

his previous experience he was never familiar, and which cannot be evoked from something else but which, *sui generis* and *sui juris*, can be designated only by religious terms such as "sacred" and "numinous". All these terms have a common relationship in that they indicate a firm conviction, but at the same time no definite conception, of the completely different, the absolutely distinct. The first impulse aroused by all this is avoidance, but also seeking: man should avoid Power, but he should also seek it. No longer can there be a "why" or "wherefore" here; and Söderblom is undeniably correct when, in this connection, he defines the essence of all religion by saying that it is mystery.[1] Of that aspect there was already a deep subjective assurance even when no god was invoked. For to religion "god" is a late comer.

3. In the human soul, then, Power awakens a profound feeling of awe which manifests itself both as fear and as being attracted. There is no religion whatever without terror, but equally none without love, or that *nuance* of being attracted which corresponds to the prevailing ethical level. For the simplest form of religious feeling Marett has suggested the fine word *Awe*, and Otto the term *Scheu*, which is somewhat less comprehensive; the Greek *aidos* too is most pertinent.[2] The expression adopted must be a very general one, since it is a question of establishing an attitude which includes the whole personality at all its levels and in countless *nuances*. Physical shuddering, ghostly horror, fear, sudden terror, reverence, humility, adoration, profound apprehension, enthusiasm—all these lie *in nuce* within the awe experienced in the presence of Power. And because these attitudes show two main tendencies, one away from Power and the other towards it, we speak of the *ambivalent* nature of awe.

Of course *tabu* means a prohibition, and Power reveals itself first of all always as something to be avoided. Everywhere, too, the prohibition announces itself earlier than the command; but Freud has very ably shown how the former always implies the latter.[3] Man is fully conscious only of the prohibition, while the command usually remains unrecognized. What we hate we love, and what we truly love we could at the same time hate. "For each man kills the thing he loves", said Oscar Wilde, and this is far more than a brilliant phrase. In the

---

[1] Very well expressed in the Essay: "Points of Contact for Missionary Work", *Int. Review of Missions*, 1919.
[2] *cf.* Murray, *The Rise of the Greek Epic*.   [3] *Totem and Taboo*, 31 *f.*, 41 *f.*

presence of the something different which we recognize as "Wholly Other", our conduct is always ambivalent. Love may be described as an attempt to force oneself into the place of the other; hate, as the fear of love.

But whether the sacred releases feelings of hate and fear, or those of love and reverence, it always confronts man with some absolute task. The *tabu* has therefore, and not without justification, been described as the oldest form of the categorical imperative.[1] Of course we must not think of Kant's argument in this connection. Nevertheless *tabu* and categorical imperative have in common the character of complete irrationality as well as absoluteness. "Thou shalt"—what one should do is a secondary issue; why one should do it is not a question at all. Confronted with Power, which he experiences as being of completely contrasted nature, man apprehends its absolute demand. An irruption occurs in his life, and he is drawn in two directions: he is seized with dread, and yet he loves his dread.

4. Having once established itself, awe develops into *observance*; and we can trace this advance in the Roman concept *religio*, which originally signified nothing more than *tabu*. In the description of an eerie place, in *Virgil*, the primal awe still glimmers: the sacred grove of the Capitol has a "dread awe" (*religio dira*).[2] But the ancient shudder lives also in custom: a sudden death is a *portentum*—a sign of potency that enters *in religionem populo*,[3] or as we should say, "renders the people impure". It was, then, preferable to put up with a ceremonial repetition of the consular election, rather than permit a *tabu* to remain in force over the people.[4] Again, an illness is thus exorcised: *hanc religionem evoco educo excanto de istis membris . . .*[5] "I call out, I draw out, I sing out, this pollution from these limbs". Thus we can comprehend the definition given by Masurius Sabinus: "*religiosum* is that which because of some sacred quality is removed and withdrawn from us".[6] This is, precisely, the sacred; and constant regard to it is the chief element in

[1] Freud, *ibid*. Preface, rather than 114 *f.*, on the equivalence with conscience. So far as I am aware, the first writer to whom the resemblance suggested itself was J. E. Harrison, *Epilegomena to the Study of Greek Religion*, 11.

[2] *Aeneid*, VIII, 347.

[3] Cicero, *De Deorum Natura*, II, 4, 10.

[4] *ibid*. 11; *quam haerere in re publica religionem*.

[5] G. Appel, *De Romanorum precationibus*, 1909, 43.

[6] Gellius, IV, ix, 8; *religiosum est, quod propter sanctitatem aliquam remotum ac sepositum a nobis est*.

the relationship between man and all that is extraordinary. The most probable derivation of the word is from *relegere*—to observe or pay attention; *homo religiosus*, therefore, is the antithesis to *homo negligens*.[1]

We can now understand, still further, how it is that awe, in the long run, must become pure observance, and intense dread mere formalism. In this respect Freud's conclusions are wholly justified: primeval prohibitions "descend, like a hereditary disease".[2] Nevertheless Freud has forgotten that no matter how much man's practical religious conduct may thus be governed by transmissible *tabus*, still profound awe and "aweful" potency must have subsisted to begin with. Observance, then, is just benumbed awe which, at any moment, can be revived. Even in our own country people's "ancient custom", in Indonesian *adat* and in court and university ceremonial, there still lives something of the awe of contact with Power. At the court of Philip IV of Spain, who died in 1665, an officer who freed the queen from the stirrup of her runaway horse had to go into exile; an incident in which it is obvious how the touch *tabu* had developed into court etiquette.

Even when vivid awe has been lost, observance continues to serve highly practical purposes. In Indonesia and Polynesia, for instance, the *tabu* is a means of asserting unquestionable right of possession to a piece of ground; some sign indicates the prohibition of stealing it or trespassing on it.[3] We should none the less be quite mistaken in concluding that the *tabu* came into being by virtue of these purely utilitarian considerations, or even that it was invented by the great ones of the earth for their own profit and benefit. Frequently it may certainly be mere routine practice, but it always has intense awe as its presupposition. The "sign", again, resembles our warning notices so closely that it may readily be confused with them; but the punishment threatened by the police is omitted, although it will doubtless appear of its own accord: on Amboina the trespasser is smitten with leprosy; and further, the prohibition itself is not rationally grounded; on the same island a rough sketch of a female sex organ—that is, something particularly "potent"—replaces the legal notification.[4] "Property" in

---

[1] *cf.* W. F. Otto, *Religio und Superstitio*, AR. 12, 1909; 14, 1911. Felix Hartmann, *Glotta*, 4, 1913, 368 *f.* Max Kobbert, *De verborum religio et religiosus usu apud Romanos quaestiones selectae*, 1910.   [2] *Faust*, Part 1.
[3] Here *Mark* vii. 11 *f.* may be referred to, where the duty of children to maintain their parents is rendered futile by an alleged *tabu* of such support as a sacrifice (*korban*).
[4] J. G. Riedel, *De Sluik- en kroesharige rassen tusschen Selebes en Papoea*, 1886, 62.

its primitive sense, then, is something quite different from what it is
with us—it is a "mystical" relation between owner and owned; the
possessor is not the *beatus possidens*, but the depositary of a power
that is superior to himself.

Once the belief in *tabu* has completely become mere observance,
an empty shell, then man breaks his fetters. In the Euripidean *Herakles*
neither Nature nor pure humanity can be defiled by the *tabu* of death;
Herakles need only take off the veil and show his head to the light:

> Eternal is the element:
> Mortal, thou canst not pollute the heavens.

Again:

> No haunting curse can pass from friend to friend.[1]

This is essentially the "modern" feeling, which opposes power in
nature and personality.

R. Caillois, *L'homme et Le Sacre*, 1939, Eng. tr., *Man and The Sacred*, 1959.
J. G. Frazer, *Taboo and the Perils of the Soul* (*The Golden Bough*, III).
S. Freud, *Totem and Taboo*.
R. Thurnwald, *Meidung*, in *Lexikon der Vorgeschichte*.

[1] *Herakles*, 1232 *ff*. (Way).

CHAPTER 5

THE SACRED ENVIRONMENT

SACRED STONES AND TREES

1. AT the close of last century, side by side with Animism, arose so-called "Naturism"—that is the hypothesis that the worship of divine beings had originated in a personification of the powers of Nature. The manifold representatives of natural potencies in Greek religion had long been familiar; the variegated and beauteous world of the Vedic deities had just been disclosed; and this also appeared, to a high degree, to have the manifestations of Nature as its basis. Thus the idea readily arose that, in reflecting on the causes of natural events, primitive man had invented gods, spirits and demons as their originators. Even to-day, indeed, every poet does the same; while in so far as language regards natural processes as activities, it likewise appears to assume an agent behind them; we too say that the storm roars, the lightning quivers, the sea rolls. Could not a sort of "disease of language", then, have seduced men into accepting these expressions quite literally? even though primarily they certainly were intended merely metaphorically, just as they are by ourselves. In this way religion could without too great difficulty be explained, since at the close of last century it occupied a comparatively superfluous and poetic position in its relations to science.

To-day, however, the need to "explain" religion has substantially lost ground; at all events we realize that reflection on the causes of natural phenomena cannot of itself constitute religion. Furthermore, it is still more difficult to regard religion as a universal error or (as Durkheim neatly puts it) a "system of hallucinatory images", an "immense metaphor with no objective value". Quite apart from such general considerations, again, the limitation to Nature is wholly untenable since, in the first place, Nature is neither the sole nor even the principal feature in religion; while in the second it is neither Nature nor natural objects that man worships, but always the Power which reveals itself in these.

It cannot therefore be the case that religion arose from "worship of Nature" simply because the concept of "Nature" is quite modern, having been first contrasted with human culture by Rousseau and the romantics. For neither the primitive nor the ancient world was there "Nature", conceived as a realm set over against man and his deeds; nor, again, were the individual objects of Nature in principle distinguished by primitive and ancient man from artificial things.[1] It is therefore not incorrect, although it is undeniably confusing, to extend the term "Fetishism", as was frequently done formerly, to so-called Nature worship; for in "Nature", exactly as in "culture", it is again and again a question of sacred Power, organic and inorganic constituting no antithesis in principle. In this respect the distinction lying nearest to that with which we are ourselves familiar is the contrast between tilled land and the surrounding uncultivated wilderness, as this actually arose first among agricultural peoples. But at that stage the potency was distributed equally between "Nature" and "culture": on the one hand, the ploughed field had its powerfulness in its fertility while, on the other, forest and heath, steppe and "barren" sea had their own powers, uncanny though these were—a distinction to be considered more fully at a later stage. It is never a contrast, however, between Power and impotence, but always between two Powers.

What we moderns call "Nature", in fact, has a prominent rôle in all religions without exception. Yet it is neither Nature, nor natural phenomena as such, that are ever worshipped, but always the Power within or behind. And as we have seen already in so many examples, this Power is substantiated empirically by exactly the same methods, and given its due reckoning in the same way. In other words, the antithesis between sacred and secular, between powerful and impotent, is always more comprehensive than that between Nature and culture, and incessantly cuts across it.

2. That Fetishism and "Naturism" are, however, separated by no unbridgeable chasm should be clear from the example of *stone worship*. With stones of any peculiar size and shape the firm subjective assurance of the presence of Power[2] has ever been associated. When for instance Jacob, his head "resting" on a stone, lay down to sleep and had his remarkable dream, he expressed himself thus—and purely empirically: "How dreadful is this place! this is none other but the house of God,

---

[1] Rudolf Bultmann draws my attention to the fact that even at the dawn of science, in the Ionian philosophy of Greece, the cosmos was apprehended as a "work of art", a product of skill, involving $\xi\rho\gamma o\nu$ and $\tau\xi\chi\nu\eta$; thus Nature's activities were interpreted on the analogy of "artificial" operations. In any case the peculiarity of Greek thought consists precisely in the Greeks being fully aware of this distinction.

[2] Here again *Ahnung*.

and this is the gate of heaven";[1] and he took the stone and set it up for a pillar, anointing it with oil. Even if this narrative is aetiological, and intended to account for the worship of a remarkable stone, still it remains typical of the way in which stones can become most intimately incorporated in man's experience.

The Hellenic peoples who immigrated to Greece from the North, again, were familiar with a stone they called *Aguieus*—"he of the ways"; and when they had permanently settled in Greece the *Aguieus* stone was set up in the market-place, decorated and garlanded: as it had protected the great migration, so it would guard the colony. The stone had the phallic form and was probably, like many other "stones set upright", originally regarded as a manifestation of fertility power. Later in Greece there arose from this stone the phallic *herm*, and eventually the god's image; in Israel, on the other hand, this development was intersected by aversion from the anthropomorphic.

While the latter examples are important with respect to the power of growth, still to be considered, thunderbolts were revelations of celestial power. The *silex* of *Jupiter Feretrius* or *Jupiter Lapis* was preserved on the Capitol and brought into use for ceremonial oaths: it was supposed to smite perjurers like a thunderbolt. The Romans also erected potent stones as boundary posts and dedicated a cult to them: the power residing within them was protective (*termini*). But other powers too could be concealed in the stone; for the ancient Romans a stone, *lapis manalis*, brought down rain—a rain charm, *aquaelicium*, whose echo still resounded in the *chanson de geste*, *Yvain*, in which, as soon as the hero pours water on a stone in the forest of Broceliande, it begins to thunder loudly and rain very heavily.

Metals too are bearers of power, and the rarer these are, the more potent. Gold, which shares its colour with the sun, also possesses something of the sun's vivifying strength; the Greeks prepared death-masks of gold while the Egyptians, for whom the metal stood in direct relationship to life, made in their later eras golden portraits of mummies. With gold, again, the kings divided life among their favourites. The golden apples of the Hesperides, from whose guardianship the fruit later passed into the power of Iduna in Iceland, were for the Greeks the symbol of life.

But *mountains* are of far greater interest. Everywhere in the world there are sacred mountains, whether Power is ascribed simply to them

---

[1] *Gen.* xxviii. 17. We should be mistaken were we to infer a necessary animating of the stone by a spirit or demon from the name *Bethel* (Greek βαιτύλιον). The *El* here is still very general; a power *post festum*.

or is imagined as a demon or god. Remote and unapproachable mountains, often volcanic and repellent, and in any case majestic, stand apart
from the normal and incorporate therefore the Power of the "wholly
other". Japan has its sacred Fujiyama, Greece its Olympus, or rather
several of them, and every region has its own holy peak. Naturally the
mountain is already there in its might before the gods make their entry
into Valhalla; but once there they can hardly reside elsewhere. The
oldest heaven is the mountain-top. Similarly in the Old Testament,
deity dwells on the mount:

> The north and south, thou madest them,
> Tabor (the mount of the gods in the north) and Hermon (the mount
> of God in the south) acclaim thee.[1]

Jahveh appears on Sinai, while in *Psalm* cxxi we find "the hills, from
whence cometh my help".

The mountain, the hard stone, was regarded as a primal and
permanent element of the world: out of the waters of Chaos rose the
primeval hill from which sprang all life. To this ancient eminence,
depicted in many temples, the Egyptians transported their creator-
god; it was looked upon as the "navel" of the earth, as its focal-point
and beginning. In Greek temples, similarly, the *omphalos* was a primitive symbol of earth and of all birth;[2] in ancient thought birth from
stone was as usual as that from the fertile earth. Mithra was regarded
as born from the rock—*ex petra natus*: and the goddess Athene was
born from Zeus' κορυφή, that is from the summit of Olympus.[3] The
story of Deucalion and Pyrrha again, who created their posterity by
throwing "their mother's bones", that is to say stones, behind them,
is universally known.

3. Like stone and mountain, the *tree* too is a power-bearer. Naturism
interpreted the tree as a symbol of celestial phenomena; it was supposed
to be a matter of the cloud-, weather-, or light-tree, whose leaves are
the clouds, its branches the sun's rays, its fruits the stars.[4] More
realistic research, however, has shown that it is not the tree that conceals
the celestial potencies, but these the tree. The incomparable Helen

---

[1] *Ps.* lxxxix. 12.
[2] *cf.* A. de Buck, *De Egyptische Voorstellingen betreffende den Oerheuvel*, 1922. W.
H. Roscher, *Der Omphalosgedanke bei verschiedenen Völkern* (*Ber. ü. d. Verh. d. Sächs.
Ges. d. Wiss. Phil.-hist. Kl.* 70, 2, 1918). A. J. Wensinck, "The Ideas of the Western
Semites concerning the Navel of the Earth" (*Verh. d. Kon. Akad. v. Wet. te Amsterdam, Afd. Lett. N. R.* 17, 1). [3] H. Diels, "Zeus", *AR.* 22, 1923–24.
[4] W. Schwarz, in Chantepie[1], I, 64 f. *cf.* GENERAL LITERATURE, p. 19 *ante*.

was once a plane in Sparta, and in Rhodos she was styled *dendritis*, "she of the tree". She shares this title with none less than Dionysus, just as Zeus was also a tree on certain occasions. In Greece trees were probably always regarded as the seat of power:—the *hamadryads*, which "are born and die with the trees"[1]; some of these were fortunate and became famous heroines, like Helen and Europa. But the ancient Egyptians were already familiar with the sycamore "which enclosed the god", as well as with the other on which sits the merciful goddess who gives water and nourishment to the dead. Elsewhere in the most ancient Egyptian *Texts* it is recorded that the gods sit on this sycamore. It is remarkable, still further, that in Egypt and Greece it was usually the barren, dead tree that was believed to be the bearer of potency or of the god: the secret of the tree, which so deeply impressed man, was that of the vicissitudes of life and death.

The primitive mind, then, lacked that unquestioning acceptance of the regularity of natural processes which our own intellectual outlook regards as axiomatic. To primitive man life is Power, not Law. Even when it is dominated by a will it reveals itself spontaneously; in this respect, therefore, the comparison of Power with the electric current loses its applicability. To early thought the dying down and reanimation of Nature are indeed no miracle—for where no law is valid, miracle has no place—but nevertheless it is a spontaneous and astounding event which might well never have occurred. And here the power of life in the tree enters into a very peculiar relation to human life. It cannot, as Mannhardt suggests, have been the observation of growth alone that induced man to infer a similarity between his own nature and that of the tree. For though man certainly grows like the tree, still he does not continue to grow through a series of apparent deaths. It was rather the experience of the tree-power, in its constantly repeated defeat of death, which forced itself upon man and caused him to rely on the firmly assured existence of the tree as being the more powerful. The "conjoined-growth" of tree and man, recognized by Mannhardt with his brilliant insight, and which will be subsequently discussed more fully in connection with the religious aspects of agriculture, is consequently not at all a rational parallel, but a mystical union that is the effect of man's desires operating in a magical way. In Mecklenburg it is—or rather was—the custom to bury the afterbirth of a new-born infant at the foot of a young tree; in Indonesia, again, a tree is planted on the spot where the placenta has been interred; in both cases alike

---

[1] Servius, in *Ecl.* 10, 62.

the child grows up with the little tree; and R. Andree has compiled examples in which the child's life is bound up with that of the tree.[1] We too retain vestiges of this in fairy tales in which the withering or blooming of a small tree indicates the hero's danger or well-being, and also—in the modern way of showing respect—in the limes and the like planted at the birth of a royal child. But all that is merely an echo. In the Bismarck Archipelago "a coconut tree is planted on the birth of a boy. When it bears its first fruit the boy is included in the ranks of the adults . . . when the life-tree of the great Ngau chieftain Tamate-wka-Nene grew, his *mana* became very great also".[2] That is genuine "conjoined-growth".

But the presupposition of such conjunct growth is relationship in essential nature, in fact the presumption of the equivalence of man and plant, which really implies that the concept of "Nature" does not as yet exist.[3] In Indonesia, in fact, there is only one word both for the human soul and for that of the rice plant. Even where the plant world serves man as cultural material it apparently never becomes a thing: man utilizes no material whatever, but invokes the power in his environment, as well as that in himself. This means, still further, that there is actually no "environment" in the strict sense of the word. Woman is a tilled field, the tilled field a woman: and where the vegetative world has not yet been domesticated this holds good in even greater degree.

Not only does the tree grow up with the individual, but it also sustains the power of the life of the whole community. All over the world we find May-poles and Easter branches, adorned with ribbons and fruits like the *eiresione* of the Greeks and the *lulab* of the Jews, which bring new life to the social group; but to this theme I shall return. The Egyptians set up a barren tree with great ceremony, thereby restoring life; and in the days before the Greeks a similar rite occurred in Crete with a holy tree. The tree was a saviour, a life-bearer. The community gathered around it; and the French revolution showed how firmly the symbol of the tree is anchored in human consciousness—and, at the same time, how few symbols even revolutionary humanity commands!—when it set up the tree of liberty, thereby simply continuing the primeval dances around the May-pole.[4]

---

[1] *Mitt. Anthr. Gesellsch. in Wien*, 14, (62).   [2] Lehmann, *Mana*, 42.
[3] Bultmann kindly informs me that, in his opinion, the idea of the transference of the tree of life to the vine was at the basis of the well-known passage in *St. John* xv.
[4] "This traditional stake, the May-pole, the gathering-point of the peasants on festival days, became the revolutionary symbol in Périgord from May, 1790." A. Mathiez, *Les Origines des cultes révolutionnaires*, 1904, 32.

Ultimately the tree grows together with the whole world as soon as man becomes conscious of its existence, that is as soon as theoretical reflection begins, even when this retains its mythical form. Herakles found a tree of life in the garden of the gods at the end of the world, Adam in Paradise at its beginning; the Egyptians and Babylonians also were familiar with this idea, the former seeking the tall sycamore "on which the gods sit", the "wood of life on which they live", in the Eastern heavens.[1] The Persians and Indians likewise were acquainted with sacred plants which, in the form of a sacrament, brought divine life to the community: *haoma* in Persia, *soma* in India. The *tulasi* plant was regarded as the bride of the god by the Hindu, while to the Romans and the Germanic tribes the ever green leaves of the mistletoe signified the secret of life and death; and for Virgil they still opened the gates of the underworld.[2]

Eventually the world-tree, *Yggdrasil*, emerged from Germanic religious fantasy as a form of the *Vårträd*, the protective tree of the community transformed into the colossal.[3] The sacred tree of Uppsala was looked upon as its earthly image, but was more probably the original from which it had been created. Even if the Christian concept of the cross may have influenced the Germanic idea—*Yggdrasil* means "Odin's horse", that is the stake on which, according to the myth, Odin had hung—we must nevertheless regard this prodigious expansion of the conception of the holy tree as its most forcible expression. *Yggdrasil* enfolds the three worlds, stands there exalted and mighty, and yet decayed both above and below. With it the world passes away. And that it was the gallows of the dying god implies no contradiction of the heathen tree symbol (as Golther suggests),[4] but actually the most acute expression of its meaning: the secret of life and death.

E. Durkheim, *The Elementary Forms of the Religious Life.*
Mircea Eliade, *Metallurgy* (Cahiers de Zalmoxis, I) 1938.
A. de Gubernatis, *La Mythologie des Plantes*, 1878–1882.
W. Mannhardt, *Wald- und Feldkulte*, 1904–1905[2].
Max Müller, *Natural Religion*, 1889.
    Physical Religion, 1898.

[1] K. Sethe, *Die altägyptischen Pyramidentexte*, II, 1910, 1216.
[2] cf. E. Norden, *P. Vergilius Maro, Aeneis*, Buch VI[2], 1916, 163 ff.
[3] cf. the magnificent description of the relationship between the "world" of the home and the World in general, the home-tree and the World-tree, in Grönbech, *Vor Folkeaet*, II, 9.
[4] *Handbuch der germanischen Mythologie*, 1895, 527 ff.

CHAPTER 6

THE SACRED ENVIRONMENT

SACRED WATER AND FIRE

1. IN the idea of holy water, too, it is clear that so far as concerns the veneration of the potent surrounding world, it is only in a very limited sense actually a matter of *environment*. For the powerfulness becomes manifested to man in his own experience, while this experience itself implies his developing consciousness of a connection between the essential nature of the object of worship and of the individual as subject. Man feels that his own life is dependent upon, and supported by, the environmental Power. But in his eyes it is not merely the environment, since this concept presupposes an attitude of disinterested observation which is absolutely foreign to the religious man, and recognized least of all by the primitive mind; rather is it the very centre of his life. Just as man and tree grow up together, so in ancient Egypt life fluctuated with the rise and fall of the flood waters; in the old *Texts* reference is often made to the "young water" which was a libation to the dead king and procured new life for him. In scantily watered country, in fact, the most beautiful representation of the after-life that could be formed was that one might drink water there, and that a generous goddess handed down from her tree water to the fainting man.

Incidentally, however, this is by no means restricted to countries poor in water. For the well accompanies the tree, and all over the world the source of living water is accounted a joyous miracle; the "water of life" brings fruitfulness and prosperity. But its potency extends even farther: it bestows eternal life, effects miracles and great deeds, and ultimately means community with the god. It resulted in fertility and increase for primitive man, to whom the animation of the fields by floods, rains and spring water was an experience of the revelation of Power; while to the mind no longer wholly primitive the sacredness was limited to certain particular waters, to definite springs and rivers, such as the holy fountain by which Demeter rested in Greece and the sacred rivers of India; also to special "holy water" endowed with power tested and proved, or guaranteed by consecration; in such cases the potency of the water becomes miraculous. To this countless legends testify, whose heroes are saved by the precious water of life which to others, again, restores vitality; the *eau de jouvence* and the *Jungbrunnen* impart renewed youth, or even chastity. But all the world over, too, the practical rite manipulates the miraculous water. Purifications by water were effective in ancient Egypt as well as for Roman Catholic piety: the *holy water*, freed from all damaging influences by exorcism, defends the person or object sprinkled with it from all demonic sway, drives off spooks and sickness, protects entrance and egress, house and cattle.[1] And finally, in baptism, water expels the devil and pours in sanctifying grace. But to the mind straining onward from Thing to Spirit, like St. John, water becomes the expression of eternal life; and he exalts the well of water, "springing up into everlasting life", above the venerated well of Jacob.[2]

2. *Fire* occupies its proper place between the powers in which (on the one hand) man indeed participates, but which he himself does not activate, and those (on the other hand) which he certainly recognizes as superior, but nevertheless handles as he wills. "All kinds of animal have been acquainted with fire, but to them it has conveyed nothing; only for man has flame had some meaning . . . man alone possesses the genius for fire", says Rémy de Gourmont;[3] or in modern terms: Fire belongs only half to Nature, and the other moiety to culture. Of course primitive thought did not make this distinction, yet it was fully aware that fire is man's property: even if it did come down from heaven, still it was kindled and nourished by man. This is the truth in the Prometheus myth, although the celestial origin of fire is hardly the first and most essential reason for its worship. Flame, on the one hand a power spreading warmth and light, and, as such, a power *par excellence*,[4] is at the same time a human acquisition. Still we can add that the celestial fire of lightning and of the sun was doubtless very soon brought into connection with the kindled earthly flame; this persists in the Hindu belief in the dual birth of *Agni*. But in the fire cult the emphasis is everywhere laid on the terrestrial fire, kindled to flame by man and living together with him.

The oldest fires were kindled by means of a fire-stone or borer, "begotten", as we should say in accord with the primitive sense; and Indian *Agni* speculation repeatedly uses expressions taken from sex

[1] *cf.* Fr. Heiler, *Der Katholizismus*, 1923, 168 *ff.* Water, like fire, is regarded as a protection against the dead; *cf.* I. Goldziher, *AR.* XIII, 1910, 20 *ff.* E. Samter, *Geburt, Hochzeit und Tod*, 1911, 83 *ff.*   [2] *St. John* iv. 13, 14.
[3] Quoted by R. Allier, *Le non-civilisé et nous*, 238.   [4] *cf.* Chap. 2.

life. The friction between the two pieces of the borer is regarded as generation and birth; they constitute a mated couple.[1] One ritual prescribes that the officiant should "keep the fire alight this night with shavings, and warm the fire-borer at it towards daybreak. It is exactly as if a calving cow is being mounted by the bull";[2] the two pieces of wood are regarded as pregnant, bearing within them the child *Agni*.[3] For long the old method of producing fire remained the same in popular custom: in Germanic countries the *nodfyr* ("need-fire") was ignited by rubbing wood, while on Midsummer's eve, and at other times when it was extinguished, the hearth fire was revived in that way.[4] This originated from the primeval Indo-Germanic conditions when fire was the most precious of possessions, to be renewed only with difficulty probably not merely because the process itself was arduous, but certainly and primarily because the fire's living power must never be allowed to perish, and could be restored only in a traditional, sacramental manner. On that account, and because of its extremely potent quality, the *nodfyr* in the Middle Ages was looked upon as "sacrilegious", and explicitly forbidden by church councils of the eighth century,[5] just as many other vestiges of the old mightiness had to give way before the new divine Power.

How closely human life and that of fire are interwoven is apparent in the many stories of procreation by fire.[6] Just as the flame is generated by human means, so it itself can also engender man's life; thus a Dyak woman of Borneo accidentally discovered the creation of fire by rubbing a liana against a piece of wood; the same liana presented her with a child, Simpang Impang.[7] In ancient Rome, again, the marital couch, *lectus genialis*, stood beside the fire on the hearth, while old foundation legends, as for example that of Praeneste, relate how a girl sitting by the hearth was impregnated by a spark sprung from the flame, and bore the founder of the city.[8]

[1] H. Oldenberg, *Die Religion des Veda*[2], 1917, 125 *f*.
[2] W. Caland, *Das Śrautasūtra des Apastamba*, 1921, 144.   [3] *ibid.*
[4] Reinsberg-Düringsfeld, *Das festliche Jahr*[2], 1898, 231 *f.*
[5] *Concilium germanicum*, 742; Council of Lestines, 743, *de igne fricato de ligno, id est nodfyr*, *cf.* H. C. A. Grolman, *Tydschr. Ned. Aardr. Gen.*, 2. R., 46, 1929, 596.
[6] Ad. Kuhn, *Die Herabkunft des Feuers und des Göttertrankes*[2], 1886, 64 *ff.*
[7] P. Hambruch, *Malaiische Märchen*, 1922, No. 30.
[8] Wissowa, in Roscher's *Lexikon*, Article "Caeculus"; *Cato, Fr.* 59, in H. Peter, *Veterum Historicorum, romanorum reliquiae*, 1, 1870; *cf.* Pliny, *Nat. Hist.* XXXVI, 204. Compare also the ancient ecclesiastical rite, in which the Easter candle is thrust into the baptismal water, to the accompaniment of a benedictory text in which sex expressions predominate (*regenerare, admixtio, foecundare, concipere, uterus, etc.*). Fr. Heiler, *Der Katholizismus*, 1923, 229 *f*.

All these ideas are based on the fire on the *hearth*. In Indo-Germanic countries above all, but elsewhere also, the hearth is the power centre of the house. Its warming glow is a guarantee of all good things and really makes the house—as we, in this era of central heating, are unfortunately learning by its deprivation. To the Hindu, similarly, *Agni* is "the never departing, great lord of the house".[1] We moderns must try to imagine the isolated primitive farm, without fire, as it is depicted in an Iceland folk tale: "Once in Winter the fire died on the island of Grimsö, so that not a single farm had it any longer. The weather was windless and very cold, the sound frozen over so that the ice was thought to be firm enough to cross. Therefore they sent three sturdy fellows to the mainland to bring fire . . .",[2] and Frazer describes the same conditions in primitive Italy. Now I have already indicated that it was not only the difficulty of generating fire anew which made its extinction seem so fateful: fire—and with it life—*dies*, and the house in which the flames expire is thereupon deprived of the life power. The same condition, still further, holds good for the community, the state: only the regulated renewal of its fire assures its prosperity, the forms of power being strikingly transferred from the family to the larger communal group. On Lemnos *e.g.* the sacred fire was extinguished every ninth year and a fresh one brought from the island of Delos: therewith, as they said, "a new life began";[3] and here there prevails that primitive systematization of life which we shall often meet with later. *We* should say that a community or state prospers and then declines. But in this change *we* do not perceive the regular rhythm, the increase and diminution of power, just as little as we can support and as it were nourish this power of the state. We distinguish to-day between life, as such, and vitality, activity, prosperity, *etc.* To primitive man, however, life is life, and he knows nothing of "flourishing civilization", just as he knows little of "living piety".[4]

We find the forms of worship of the power of fire most beautifully and systematically developed in ancient Rome; they originated in the primeval domestic cult, wherein the hearth fire was entrusted to the care of the women (the later vestals), while the father of the family appeared as the priest of the flame and his sons (*flamines*) as the kindlers. Fire is the object of the oldest family worship, wherein the power of

[1] Oldenberg, *Rel. des Veda*, 130.
[2] H. u. I. Naumann, *Isländische Volksmärchen*, 1923, No. 22. C. Andersen, *Islandske Folkesagn*, 1877, 201.   [3] Farnell, *The Cults of the Greek States*, IV, 302, 429.
[4] New fire is as it were the renewal of creation; *cf.* Grönbech in Chantepie, II, 573. O. Huth, *Janus*, 1932, 73.

the communal essence is concentrated; and on the first of March, at the commencement of the old Roman year, the fire was extinguished and immediately rekindled. Thereby prosperity was ensured for another year. In the state the hearth fire (*vesta*) became the deepest mystery, on which the community's security depended: "the temple of Vesta, the eternal fire, and the fatal pledge for the continuance of the Roman empire deposited in the shrine".[1] Human life and the life of the fire subsisted in a reciprocal relationship: they participated in each other, and Oldenberg is quite correct in alluding to the friendly connections between man and fire, which gives his life a basis and a home. The returning Indian bard announces his success first of all to the flame on the hearth, while before her death Euripides' Alcestis takes a ceremonial farewell of the hearth, and implores it to protect her children.[2] For the hearth offers safety: it is an asylum; Hecuba leads old Priam to it: "all shall be saved by this altar".[3] In modern Calabria too, in case of death, the fire on the hearth is allowed to expire,[4] while according to old Germanic custom the flame was revived on special festival days, or when "sinking fortune made it evident that a renewal was necessary";[5] and an Indian tribe had to pay, by its gradual decline, for a girl's carelessness in permitting the fire to go out.[6] These examples afford ample proof that the idea of the potency of fire extended very far, and was by no means limited to Indo-Germanic peoples.

Fire's living power protects against evil influences: "*Agni* drives away monsters, *Agni* the brightly flaming, immortal, light, purifying, worthy of reverence."[7] On the other hand, nothing impure or dangerous to life must touch the flame; as the Romans said, "Let nothing of leather be admitted; therefore let no carrion come nigh" (*ne quod scorteum adhibeatur, ideo ne morticinum quid adsit*);[8] the fire must be sustained

---

[1] Livy, XXVI, 27, 14; *cf.* Fowler, *The Religious Experience of the Roman People*, 68 *ff.*, and *The Roman Festivals of the Period of the Republic*, 147 *ff.*

[2] 168 *ff.*   [3] Virgil, *Aeneid*, 11, 523.

[4] Th. Trede, *Das Heidentum in der Römischen Kirche*, IV, 1891, 415.

[5] V. Grönbech, *Vor Folkeaet*, 11, 1912, 57.

[6] K. Knortz, *Märchen und Sagen der nordamerikanischen Indianer*, 1871, No. 60. On the Saturday before Easter the "new light" is brought into Catholic churches candles being lit at the "new fire" to the accompaniment of the thrice repeated words, *lumen Christi*. When the light of salvation threatens to expire, a fresh one must be kindled; *cf.* J. Braun, S.J., *Liturgisches Handlexikon*[2], 1924, 86.

[7] Caland, *ibid.*, 144.

[8] Varro, *de lingua latina*, VII, 84; *cf.* Ovid, *Fasti*, I, 629 *f.* "It is not lawful to bring leather into her shrine, lest her pure hearths should be defiled by skins of slaughtered beasts" (Frazer).

Scortea non illi fas est inferre sacello,
ne violent puros exanimata focos.

by pure torches.[1] Its pure nourishment, however, could be strengthened by incantations and gestures: in many German dioceses, similarly, new fire was made and blessed after all the lights had been extinguished on Maundy Thursday, and all fresh lights and candles were lit at the new flame.[2] Such holy fire has purifying power: together with water it is the great means of purification; the "fire of the purifier", indeed, was accounted as much the more potent. John the Baptist speaks of baptism with fire,[3] and in rites of consecration the old lease of life was annulled by fire and a new one rendered possible.

Finally, fire has been transformed into even the World-principle, the idea of the hearth thus being expanded to colossal proportions. This occurred chiefly in India, where *Agni* was regarded as the universally vivifying Power, even in water. It is both human love and divine immortality: "Oh friend of all men, thou art the navel of the peoples, like a pillar standing fast thou supportest man."[4] Further: "One alone is *Agni*, who is kindled at many places; one alone the sun which penetrates all things. One alone the flush of dawn which shines over the whole world. One alone there is, and it has unfolded itself into the whole Universe."[5] To revere *Agni* the sublimest lines of the *Rig-Veda* were composed, while in the speculation of the West fire became, for Heracleitus, the *arche*, the ultimate substance and power of the Universe; and as rites gradually fell into disuse the ancient mode of controlling the renewed life was transposed, by the soul seeking firm rhythms, into the inner world-process; still the ruling force of the world, of the cosmos, is "an ever living fire, with measures of it kindling and measures being extinguished".[6] But at the Christian altar the eternal light, nourished not only by the soul, remained the assurance of an ever self-renewing Love.

Kurt Erdmann, *Das Iranische Feurheiligtum*, 1941.
Ad. Kuhn, *Die Herabkunft des Feuers und des Göttertrankes*[2], 1886.
M. Ninck, *Die Bedeutung des Wassers im Kult und Leben der Alten*, 1921.

[1] Virgil, *Aeneid*, VII, 71 : *castis taedis*.
[2] Mannhardt, *Wald- und Feldkulte*, 503.
[3] *Matt.* iii. 11; *Luke* iii. 16. Here reference may also be made to the Mandean fire baptism.
[4] Bertholet, *op. cit.*, 9, 48.
[5] *ibid.*
[6] *Fr.* 30 (Diels; Cornford).

CHAPTER 7

THE SACRED WORLD ABOVE

1. WHEN man seeks the frontiers of his own being, he finds these within himself, in his environment, and in the world above. "Where heaven is, there is God", said an Ewe tribesman;[1] and it is easy to understand that heaven and its phenomena have not only always taken a prominent place in the poetry and thought of all peoples, but have also been the connecting links with the concepts of the "Wholly Other". For these the forms assumed by the celestial god, or gods, are unnecessary. Heaven, simply as such, preceded its characters or inhabitants. In Mexico, for instance, Preuss found that the concept of heaven, in its entirety, enjoyed precedence over that of the individual stars;[2] and in a different connection the relationship between heaven, or the celestial god, and the cosmic and social order, will at a later stage become more intelligible.[3] At present, however, we are investigating not the laws and ordered processes dominating human life from above, but those dramatic events in the upper world which seem to be parallel, or even akin, to those of the lower world of earth.

2. This implies that primitive man regards celestial events not as the domain of Law. He is by no means certain about the daily return of the heavenly light,[4] and the fear that the sun may some day fail in its course is to him in no way a mere phantom of the brain. The sun indeed, to our minds the pivot of the regularity of the whole solar system, appears to him neither constant nor even single; the Togo negroes, for example, formerly believed that each village had its own special sun, and it was only at a later date that they altered this opinion.[5]

The events of the higher world, therefore, form no completed process, but rather a revelation of Power. Life in the heavens deploys itself spontaneously just as it does on earth. The Cora Indians, for instance, speak of stars as "opening buds",[6] while in an ancient Babylonian hymn to Sin, the moon-god, the orb is styled "the fruit that

---

[1] J. Spieth, *Die Religion der Eweer*, 1911, 5.
[2] K. Th. Preuss, *Die geistige Kultur der Naturvölker*[2], 1923.   [3] Chap. 18.
[4] Boll, *Die Sonne*, 9.   [5] Spieth, *ibid.*, 355.
[6] K. Th. Preuss, *Die Nayarit-Expedition*, I, 1912, XXXIX.

forms itself".[1] The old Egyptian heaven- or sun-god, again, was always called "he who originates from himself"; and thus in the world above potent life manifests itself.

But since this life is not yet subjected to any ordered regularity the "naturalness" of Nature, to our own minds so axiomatic, is absent. The powerful is apprehended, therefore, not in its invariability but in its potency, which can most forcibly reveal itself, but which may also withdraw itself or even fail altogether; the way in which primitive peoples interpreted eclipses of the sun and moon is universally familiar, and the Egyptians had a tradition relating how the sun, in its wrath, once deserted men and departed to a foreign country.[2] The primitive or semi-primitive mind, then, regards the daily return of light by no means as a matter of course, but as the subject of perpetual fear and hope. What Chesterton has said of sunrise in a fine passage—that it is no repetition but a theatrical *da capo*, and "that God says every morning, 'Do it again' to the sun; and every evening, 'Do it again' to the moon",[3] is genuinely "primitive" in feeling, just as his association of this type of idea with that of the fairy tale is quite correct.[4]

The feelings of hope and of anxiety connected with sunrise produced the great light myth, as this acquired its form in the most varied cultural circles. Light, the sun, or even the moon, is a conquering hero, a warrior who annihilates the monster of darkness. The sun "rejoiceth as a strong man to run a race";[5] while the magnificent Babylonian hymn addresses this acclamation to the moon:

O Lord! Who is like unto thee? Who is equal to thee?
Great hero! Who is like unto thee? Who is equal to thee?
Lord Nannar! Who is like unto thee? Who is equal to thee?
When thou liftest up thine eyes, who can flee?
When thou drawest near, who can escape?[6]

The dawn of light is a triumph over enemies: the dragon, the snake, or some other atrocity of death and darkness is defeated; and this *light myth* dominates extensive tracts of the religious imagination in general: God as victor or as king—this entire realm of ideas is based on the dawn, while with it thoughts of creation are interwoven,[7] and the Christian Christmas symbolism of *crescit lux* is also a reinterpreta-

[1] Lehmann, *Textb.*, 302.
[2] K. Sethe, *Zur altägyptischen Sage vom Sonnenauge, das in der Fremde war*, 1912.
[3] *Orthodoxy*, Chap. IV, "The Ethics of Elfland", 107.
[4] Chap. 60.   [5] *Ps.* xix. 5.
[6] H. Zimmern, *Babylonische Hymnen und Gebete*, II, 1911, 6.   [7] Chap. 87.

tion of this natural process.[1] Victory and light, lordship and the sun:
they must all be connected together; and the relations between the
Roman imperator's dignity and conquering light have been con-
vincingly presented by Cumont, while in naming Cleopatra's twins
Helios and Selene, Antony designated them as *kosmokratores*—rulers
of the universe.[2]

The light myth, still further, may be concerned with the *sun* just
as much as with the *moon*. There are "moon peoples" as well as "sun
peoples", and in the history of a *single* nation, like the Babylonians,
there are both moon- and sun-periods. Argument over the priority of
sun or moon would be futile; both predominate in various places and
at different times,[3] and in many myths and fairy tales we find competition
between the two orbs.

3. The mighty events of the higher world arouse not merely reverence
on man's part; they are also regarded as a celestial model and source
of power. Between upper world and human world there prevails an
essential kinship, and the primeval sun riddle set by the Sphinx to
Oedipus reflects an even older idea:[4]

> When it rises in the morn
> It has four feet.
> When day turns to noon
> Two feet are granted it.
> As night comes on
> It stands on three feet.[5]

In a Slovak fairy tale the scullion asks the sun why he climbs higher
and higher in the morning, but sinks lower and lower in the afternoon.
The sun replies: "Ah, my dear fellow, ask your master why after birth
he grows bigger and bigger in body and strength, and why in old age
he stoops towards the ground and becomes weaker. With me it is just
the same. Each morning my mother gives birth anew to me as a beautiful
boy, and every evening she buries me as a feeble old man."[6]

In Egypt, where this comparison was familiar from quite early times,
the analogy between the sun's fate and that of man was transformed

[1] Boll, *Die Sonne*, 23.   [2] Boll, *ibid.*, 22.
[3] Ankermann, in Chantepie, *op. cit.*, I, 189.
[4] *cf*. P. Pierret, *Le Dogme de la Résurrection chez les Anciens Égyptiens*, 17.
[5] A fifteenth-century version in R. Köhler, *Kleine Schriften*, I, 1898, 115 *f*. The
Greek in Athanaeus, X, 456 B.
[6] H. Usener, *Kleine Schriften*, IV, 1913, 386 *ff*.

from the authentication of their parallel reviving and decease into a joyful belief in the renovation of human life. Just as each morning the sun renews its life, so it is with man, while death is no actual death but life with Ra, the sun-god. A very ancient *Text* says of a dead king: "His mother, the sky, gives birth to him, alive, each day that it pleases Ra; with him he rises in the East and with him sets in the West; so that on no day is his mother, the heavens, empty of him."[1] Man thus interweaves his own life with the greater and mightier continuity of Nature. Here again, however, this association is by no means regularly ordered, but is a quite spontaneous manifestation of the solar power. To the Romans, *mater matuta* was the goddess of the morning light and at the same time of birth.[2] He "who sees the light of the world" enters thereby into intimate relationship with the light that is his life.

Stars too were regarded as related to man; again and again we find the idea that the dead live again as stars in the heavens.[3] Similarly, the Egyptian custom of sewing a sun amulet into the grave linen is an instance of this way of bringing one's lot into close connection with celestial power.[4] It is just as if one were taking the solar potency with one into the grave.

4. The light of heaven is man's salvation. His life is bound up with the sun in its rising, as his death to its setting.[5] Many peoples sing and speak of the sun's treasure, preserved at the end of the world in the uttermost West, which the hero wins for himself. Thus Hermes steals the sun's cattle: here prosperity implies, in the good old antique way, the possession of cattle; but this can also be interpreted as gold, or a beautiful woman or some other treasure,[6] and countless fairy tales and myths relate how in this way heavenly bliss was attained. In all these narratives, however, the thought of death is always presupposed, since the sun's path of salvation traverses death. Hence the dreadful guardians of the hoard, the gloomy place whence the hero must fetch it, *etc.*

Sun-worship assumed its most magnificent raptures, as celestial

---

[1] *Pyramidentexte* (Sethe), 1835; *cf.* W. B. Kristensen, *Livet efter döden*, 1896, 69 *f.*
[2] G. Wissowa, *Religion und Kultus der Römer*[2], 1912, 97.
[3] Preuss, *Nayarit-Expedition*, XXX *ff.* As regards Egypt, Sethe, *Sage vom Sonnenauge*, 5, Note 2; *cf. Pyramidentexte*, 251.
[4] *Pyramidentexte*, 285: "Thou who in thy bonds seest Ra, who praisest him in thy fetters, as the great amulet which is in thy red linen clothing."
[5] Boll, *Die Sonne*, 17.
[6] H. Usener, *Kleine Schriften* IV, 1913, 44 *ff.*, 226 *ff.*, 464.

salvation, in ancient Egypt. There, under the influence of the priesthood of the sun-city Heliopolis, immense temples were erected to the
sun even as early as the first half of the third pre-Christian millennium;
temples that were vastly different from the usual form of sacred
Egyptian edifices. Worship was offered in the open at a great altar
in the midst of a huge court; neither *naos* nor cult image played any
part. Only a gigantic obelisk was erected on a colossal plinth: the old
and probably originally phallic symbol of prosperity and fullness of
power. Through a passage at first in semi-darkness, and then in complete obscurity, representing the sun's nocturnal course, the base of
the obelisk was reached where the worshipper, his face turned to
the East, greeted the rise of the victorious orb.[1] The Pharaohs of the
Fifth Dynasty made this sun-worship their own unique privilege, and
bringing their government into direct connection with the sun's
triumph, called themselves "sons of Ra". This form of veneration
continued to maintain its influence in Egypt until the revolution of
the heretical Akhnaton effected its culmination, and procured for it a
brief though glorious hegemony.[2] From this group of sun-concepts,
still further, originated many beautiful hymns in which the universally
nourishing, universally sustaining power, and the splendid victory of
the celestial light, are celebrated; the crown of this type of literature,
Akhnaton's hymn, interprets the triumph and guardianship of the
divine power as truth and love. Nor is the latter lacking in the earlier
hymns; for instance, in a hymn to Amon about 1420 B.C.:

> Thy love is in the Southern heaven,
> And thy grace in the Northern heaven.
> Thy beauty conquers all hearts,
> Thy love compels all arms to fall.[3]

While still finer and more impressively developed, we find in
Akhnaton's hymn the starry loveliness side by side with victory and
love:

> In beauty dost thou shine on the celestial horizon,
> Thou living Aton (sun) who art from of old.[4]

---

[1] F. W. von Bissing (and L. Borchardt), *Das Re-heiligtum des Königs Ne-Wsr-Rē*, I,
1905; cf. L. Borchardt, *Das Grabdenkmal des Königs Sa'ḥu-Reʻ*, 1910–13.

[2] G. van der Leeuw, *Achnaton. Een religieuze en aesthetische revolutie in de veertiende
eeuw voor Christus*, 1928.—H. Schäfer, *Amarna in Religion und Kunst*, 1931.—A. de
Buck, *De zegepraal van het licht*, 1930.—K. Sethe, *Urgeschichte und älteste Religion der
Ägypter*, 1930.   [3] Al. Scharff, *Ägyptische Sonnenlieder*, 1922, 50.

[4] My *Achnaton*, 47. Scharff, *ibid.*, 61.

And it was certainly not the heart subduing beauty of sunlight that was the last thing to impress man as powerful; nor was it a mere accident that so many hymns were composed in honour of sun and moon in Babylon. In later times, too, the number of sun-songs was considerable; and in the fiercest stress of battle Aias implores Zeus to save him from the mist and allow him at least to die in the light, although the dramatic "mist" of insanity finally engulfs him; here once more are associated light, life and salvation.[1] Similarly for the poet of the *Antigone* the victorious sun's rays expel the enemy:

> Sunbeam, of all that ever dawned upon
>   Our seven-gated Thebes the brightest ray,
>   O eye of golden day,
> How fair thy light o'er Dirce's fountain shone,
> Speeding upon their headlong homeward course,
> Far quicker than they came, the Argive force;
>   Putting to flight
> The argent shields, the host with scutcheons white.[2]

The *poverello* of Assisi, on the other hand, although he regards the heavenly powers as God's creation and gift to humanity, still feels himself bound to them in a sort of brotherhood of all creatures:

> *Laudato si, mi signore, cum tucte le tue creature*
> *spetialmente messor lo frate sole,*
> *lo quale jorna, et illumini per lui;*
> *Et ellu è bellu e radiante cum grande splendore;*
> *de te, altissimo, porta significatione.*
> *Laudato si, mi signore, per sora lune e le stelle,*
> *in celu l'ai formate clarite et pretiose et belle.*[3]

Of course this relationship is a kind of monastic brotherhood, and no longer the primitive mind's interweaving with Nature. It is only divine *caritas* that sustains the community with Nature; and yet the sun continues to be the expression of the highest bliss:

> *de te, altissimo, porta significatione.*

---

[1] Boll, *Die Sonne*, 15.   [2] 100 *ff.* (Storr).

[3]   Praised be Thou, O Lord, with all Thy creatures,
        In especial my brother, the sun,
        Who brings the day, and through whom Thou shinest.
        And he is beauteous and radiant in great splendour.
        Of Thee, O Highest, he bears the image.
        Praised be Thou, O Lord, for my sister the moon, and the stars;
        In heaven Thou hast formed them bright, precious and lovely.

5. With the idea of coordinating Time according to the standard of events in the world above there appears, together with the revelation of spontaneous Power, a manifestation of immutably ordered regularity. Instead therefore of being incalculable, and incessantly requiring empirical verification, Power now becomes permanent and immovable.

From this viewpoint the Calendar[1] originated as the most familiar to us of a whole series of instances in which the terrestrial course of affairs has been adjusted to that of the heavens.[2] As it is above, so below:—this school of thought, quite inaccurately monopolized for the Near East as "the ancient Oriental concept of world-order", is in fact encountered all over the world wherever man has ceased to think altogether primitively, and has rendered his life absolute in Time by relating it to the still more potent life above. In one famous *Fragment*, previously cited in another connection, Heracleitus asserts that "the sun will not exceed his measures; if he does, the Erinyes, the avenging handmaids of Justice, will find him out".[3] This is the absolute antithesis of the idea of triumphant light: to all eternity the course of the heavenly bodies is unchangeable.

The stars too follow their immutable paths. Victory is here as it were crystallized into a triumph that knows no strife. The Egyptians were profoundly impressed by the constant presence and the unceasing return of the "everlasting" and "untiring" stars (those surrounding the Pole, and the planets)[4] and identified the fate of the dead with that of these immortal celestial bodies, while in Hellenism they became *dei aeterni*, the immutable controllers of human fate.[5]

The intimate connection between man and the depositories of Power, therefore, still persists. But now the incalculable and spontaneously operating potency has, in principle, become something that can be reckoned with; only it can no longer be resisted, and it is quite futile to curse it or pray to it; it is eternally exalted, arctically above both enmity and friendship. There is indeed, as A. van Gennep says, some kind of consistency in this advance from being linked with the activities in

---

[1] Chap. 55.
[2] cf. M. P. Nilsson, *Sonnenkalender und Sonnenreligion*, AR. 30, 1933. Herm. Fränkel, *Die Zeitauffassung in der archaiischen griechischen Literatur* (*Vierter Kongress für Ästh. u. allg. Kunstwiss.* = *Beilageheft z. Zeitschr. f. Ästh. u. allg. Kunstwiss.* 25), 1931, 97 *ff*. [3] Diels, *Frag.* 94 (Burnet).
[4] cf. Kurt Sethe, *Altägyptische Vorstellungen vom Lauf der Sonne* (*Sitz. ber. d. preuss. Akad. der Wiss. phil. Kl.* 1928, XXII).
[5] F. Cumont, *Les anges du Paganisme*, RHR. 36, 1915, 159.

animal and vegetable life to being bound to the movement of the Cosmos, to the *"grands rhythmes de l'univers"*;[1] and I by no means dispute van Gennep's estimate of this idea as magnificent. In star-worship, nevertheless, community with the arbitrarily capricious or victorious Power became a subjection under the starry yoke. The upper world was locked away: its life became a process, its might a fate.

Thereby human life is astrologically predestined. In the earliest times, for the Babylonians, the stars inscribed the "writing of the heavens" from which the erudite could read his destiny. That was, however, the only thing he could do. It is not at all to be wondered at, then, that man revolted against this celestial tyranny: "The stars who know in the midst of our laughter how that laughter will end, become inevitably powers of evil rather than good, beings malignant as well as pitiless, making life a vain thing. . . . The religion of later antiquity is overpoweringly absorbed in plans of escape from the prison of the seven planets."[2] Man hoped for an ascent of the soul from the realm of the evil "elements of the world" (στοιχεῖα τοῦ κόσμου) into the empyrean, the eighth sphere of the Universe, where Power does not imply arbitrary rule.[3] He sought a *soter* to save him from the might of the stars; Christ too saves "from the conflict and battle of the powers and gives us peace from the strife of potencies and angels",[4] and the *Epistle to the Galatians* opposes the liberty through Christ to the former "thraldom of the Elemental spirits".[5] In sublime terms, too, the *Epistle to the Romans* celebrates the love of Christ, from which no *"archontes"*, no planetary guardians nor celestial powers, which by their sevenfold circle bar the way to the other refuge of the eighth heaven, can ever separate us.[6] "From the moment of birth we begin to die, and the end of life is closely allied to its beginning":[7] this wisdom of the Roman poet accords at most with the possibility of a science, but scarcely of a religion; and while astrology amalgamates with many religions, it is itself a science,[8] knowledge about Power, but neither its veneration nor utilization. This science had its origins wherever, as in China and in ancient Greece, attempts were made to delimit days and hours exactly, according to the position of the moon,

---

[1] *Les Rites de passage*, 1909, 279.
[2] Murray, *Five Stages of Greek Religion*, 180.
[3] Chap. 46.
[4] Clem. Alex. *Theod. Exc.* 71, 72.
[5] *Gal.* iv. 3; *cf. Col.* ii. 8.   [6] *Romans* viii. 37 *ff.*
[7] Manilius: *nascentes morimur, finisque ab origine pendet.*   [8] Chap. 72, 83.

stars, *etc.*,[1] and it attains its fullest bloom when every event in human life is subjected to the almighty stars. At that stage no specific revelation of Power in mankind can be thought of apart from some quite special star: Augustus, for instance, had his *sidus julium*.[2] "His star", similarly, led the wise men from the East to the manger at Bethlehem. In contrast with this, however, the Talmudist explicitly declares: "Israel is subjected to no star, but to God alone."[3]

6. In so-called "Naturism"[4] we found the worship of Power manifesting itself in the objects of Nature, and subsequently the clear recognition of regulated order in the course of the Universe. In both standpoints, still further, there subsist the presuppositions of later speculation. The earliest Greek philosophers sought the origin and the sustaining basis of all life in some single natural phenomenon, either water, air or fire, which in its unity and divinity would include the manifold diversities of the world as it presents itself to us: the ἀρχή is the essence of the world, and at the same time its divinity. Here there enters in a later Naturism, for which natural events constitute the order in life and are, as such, divine precisely in virtue of this very orderliness. Rousseau's worship of Nature, Goethe's "Nature in God, God in Nature", seek the sacredness superior to humanity once more in totality, in life in its entirety, whose austerely rational order bears man safely over the confusion of the individual life.

But from the primitive viewpoint the essential distinction is that the Greeks discovered the concept of Spirit; and any modern Naturism must relate itself in some way to this Spirit, whether "the living garment of God" surrounds the psychical core, or Nature ultimately accords with this spiritual principle (as for Rousseau), or must serve as a corrective in contrast with the malicious inventions of a degenerate culture, as for the Encyclopaedists or Wagner.[5] The most recent "Nature" speculation, however, that of the Nietzsche-Klages school, appears once again to desire to follow this latter course. But exactly as with its direct antithesis—the Christian-Greek contempt for "mere"

---

[1] cf. M. P. son Nilsson, *Die Enstehung und religiöse Bedeutung des griechischen Kalenders* (*Lunds Univ. Aarsskrift*, N. F. Avd. 1, 14, 21), 35 f.

[2] H. Wagenvoort, *Vergils Vierte Ekloge und das Sidus Julium* (*Med. Kon. Akad. v. Wet. Afd. Lett.* 67, A. 1, 1929).

[3] Troels-Lund, *Himmelsbild und Weltanschauung im Wandel der Zeiten*[1], 1929, 140 f.

[4] Chap. 5.

[5] In the first version of *The Ring of the Nibelung*; cf. P. M. Masson, *Rousseau et la restauration religieuse*[2], 1916, 9 ff.

Nature—it is dependent on the concept of Spirit, which is completely absent from primitive religious thought.

F. Boll, *Die Sonne im Glauben und in der Weltanschauung der alten Völker*, 1922.
　*Sternglaube und Sterndeutung*², 1919.
F. Cumont, *Astrology and Religion among the Greeks and Romans*, 1912.
R. Pettazoni, *Dio* I, 1922.
Troels-Lund, *Himmelsbild und Weltanschauung im Wandel der Zeiten*⁴, 1929.

CHAPTER 8

THE SACRED "CONJOINED WORLD". ANIMALS

1. WE must now discuss the sacred world of man himself, although the surrounding and the upper worlds must also be considered to be his. But the animals with which man lives pertain to his own domain, to himself, in a still more specific sense than does the rest of "Nature". Once again Chesterton is perfectly correct in saying that "we talk of wild animals; but man is the only wild animal. It is man that has broken out. All other animals are tame animals; following the rugged respectability of the tribe or type."[1] Humanity, however, does not always break loose, while "primitive" man does so far less frequently than "modern".[2] The contrast that Max Scheler and Buytendyk drew between man and animal, therefore, namely that the former objectivizes his environment and stands in an independent and superior relation to it, while the animal belongs to its surroundings, is not at all true of primitive mankind.[3] For he too appertains to his environing sphere and only rarely "objectivizes", it may be solely in magic,[4] and then only with the help of a Power that is superior to himself and to all else. For in this environment with which he feels himself intermingled he perceives again and again the revelation of Power, and as yet no "world", in our sense of the term, exists.

In this respect it is above all what is non-human that impels man to regard animals as being bearers of power. The strong non-human beast, essentially foreign to himself, is at the same moment very familiar to him first of all as hunter, and subsequently as cattle-breeder. This fusion of awe before superiority on the one hand, and on the other intimacy with the wholly familiar, enables us, if not to explain, at all events to understand, animal cults and Totemism.[5]

The animal's superiority can now be appreciated without more ado. For it controls powers wherein man himself is deficient: muscular strength, keenness of sight and smell, sense of direction and ability in tracking, flying, running with terrific speed,[6] *etc.* On the other hand

---

[1] *Orthodoxy*, 265.   [2] *cf.* van der Leeuw, *La Structure de Mentalité Primitive*.
[3] Max Scheler, *Die Stellung des Menschen im Kosmos*, 1928, 44 *ff.* F. J. J. Buyten-dyk, *Blätter für Deutsche Philosophie*, 3, 1929, 33 *ff.*
[4] Chap. 82.   [5] Ankermann in Chantepie, *op. cit.*, I, 169.
[6] *cf.* Lévy-Bruhl, *How Natives Think*, 38.

the significant distinction which, despite all evolutionary theories, we moderns presuppose between man and animal in our ordinary feelings and thoughts is not yet present. Thus of ancient Egypt Maspero writes: "The interval separating humanity from animals was almost non-existent. . . . Their (the animals') unions with the human race were fruitful, and it was no matter for surprise that the kings of Egypt should depict the sun-falcon as the head of their line and speak of the egg from which they had originated."[1] We find the same state of affairs to-day in the Indian Archipelago, where the indigenes recognize no essential differences between animal and man, and where marriage with animals, birth from and of animals, and animal descent are regarded as something quite ordinary. A Papuan relates for example: "on that island dwells one of my own relatives; long ago one of my ancestors gave birth to twins, a real child and an iguana; the mother suckled both, and when the iguana grew big she brought him to that island; there he still lives in a cave, and is allowed to survive because of the reverence felt for him. The crested dove and the black cockatoo also belong to my tribe. Towards the latter (adds the missionary who recounts this) he shows less respect, for he shoots them whenever he can and brings them to me, only someone else must carry them for him; he will never eat nor even touch them."[2] In fairy stories, in this respect also a faithful reflection of feeling about life in the past, man stands in a similarly intimate relationship to animals: they too treat animal birth and marriage as quite common events.

Thus the animal is on the one hand the non-human, the wholly different, the sinister or sublime: on the other it is intimately attached and familiar; and this union of both aspects renders the worship of the animal as a numinous object comprehensible.

The repellent and strange animal *par excellence* is the snake. It plays a part in numberless legends as a monster (dragon, *etc.*); its emerging from the ground connects it with the secrets of death, while its resemblance to the phallus, which constitutes it a sex symbol even in modern psychical experience, whenever this is released from repressions as in neurotic cases, relates it to the mystery of racial existence. Its potency is experienced chiefly as calamitous and menacing.

The familiar and most nearly related animal, again, is the domesticated beast. With different peoples domestication followed various

[1] G. Maspero, *Études de Mythologie et d'Archéologie Égyptiennes*, 1893–99, II, 213.
[2] A. C. Kruyt, *Het Animisme in den Indischen Archipel*, 1906, 120 ff.

courses. The pig and dog are regarded here as impure (that is as sacred, but sinister), there as friends of mankind. Cattle are the best loved of all domestic animals, and the religions of India and ancient Persia compete in their esteem. Even to-day, as in olden times, cattle urine is the principal Indian means of purification, while the cow's life is sacred. The modern Hindu sends one that has become useless out into the jungle, where it is torn to pieces by dogs, or sells it to the (Mohammedan) butcher; but he will not kill it himself.

The domestic animal ranks as a member of the family. It is not so long ago that in Eastern Holland the death of the farmer was ceremonially announced to his cattle, and even to his bees; similarly the country folk in the province of Gelderland speak of "bees' luck" which is granted to worthy people; the bridal pair, too, entreats the bees for their blessing on the marriage.[1] The ancient Greeks regarded the killing of the ox as the slaying of their own brother, laments for the death of the victim being uttered during the sacrifice.[2] Not so long ago animal trials were actual institutions; the beasts could appear as witnesses, accused and plaintiffs. In 1565 the inhabitants of Arles demanded the expulsion of the grasshoppers, and the contemporary *Tribunal de l'Officialité* dealt with the suit, *Maître* Marin undertaking the representation of the insects and defending their cause with great zeal. But the grasshoppers were sentenced to depart under penalty of excommunication, and even as recently as 1845 an animal trial occurred in France.[3]

Thus if on the one hand the feeling of the equality, or even of the superiority, of the powerful animal proved itself very tenacious, yet on the other attempts have long been in progress to rationalize animals out of these human relationships. It was preferable, therefore, that the wife of Faustulus, Acca Larentia, should be a whore (*lupa*) rather than a she-wolf (*lupa*).[4] As was the case also with potent things, however, the return to primitive feeling can be discovered only by the poet, it may be by the path of longing:

> I think I could turn and live with animals, they are so placid
> and self-contain'd,
> I stand and look at them long and long.[5]

[1] H. W. Heuvel, *Oud-achterhoeksch boerenleven*, 1927, 227.
[2] G. Murray, *The Rise of the Greek Epic*, 86 *ff.* Odyssey, 3, 415 *ff.*
[3] E. Westermarck, *The Origin and Development of the Moral Ideas*, I, 254 *f.*
[4] Plutarch, *Romulus*, 4, 3.
[5] Whitman, *Leaves of Grass*: "Song of Myself", 32.

2. With the idea of the powerful animal Totemism is closely connected. It may be true that a totem may also be a plant, or indeed some
natural phenomenon; yet "the animal totem predominates to such an
extent, and one receives so firm an impression that everything else is
of later origin, that the relationship of man to animal may be regarded
as the real core of Totemism".[1]

There is individual Totemism, and also social; the former, however,
is better termed *Nagualism*, in accordance with the relevant belief of
the inhabitants of Central America or, with that of the North Americans,
Manituism.[2] From the second designation it is clear that it is a matter
of the appropriation of, and connection with, the animal's power;
thus a young Red Indian goes into the wilderness, where in a dream
his totem animal appears to him and unites itself with him, while among
the Eastern Eskimo, Kagsagsuk is a sort of Soft Johnnie, mocked and
ill-treated until on a lonely spot in the mountains he finds the *amarok*,
a demonic beast which endows him with gigantic strength.[3] In Mexican
beliefs, again, the gods also have a *nagual*, a personal protective spirit.[4]

This individual guardian spirit is closely related to the "external
soul" residing in an animal, with which we shall become acquainted
at a later stage.[5] The potency of the superior animal, still further,
becomes experienced as human power; Wundt therefore refers to
"animal souls", and from this idea attempts to derive that of totem
ancestors.[6]

But with this we reach social Totemism proper. The term itself
originated with an English interpreter, John Long, who first employed
it in 1791 in the sense of a well-meaning spirit which guards men in the
form of an animal, and which because of its protection is never killed
nor eaten [7] In modern research, however, Totemism has become the
subject of interminable dispute, in which the expression is used most
variously in the loosest and vaguest senses and with the most arbitrary
limitations. Not only do different investigators arrive at and formulate
diverse conclusions, but a single *savant* like Frazer has contrived in
the course of time to evolve three distinct theories about Totemism.
In spite of all this, as generally recognized features of the phenomenon
there may legitimately be considered: (*1*) the well-being of some human

---

[1] Ankermann in Chantepie, *op. cit.*, I, 165 *f*.   [2] Chantepie, I, 171 *f*.
[3] W. Krickeberg, *Indianermärchen aus Nordamerika*, 1924, No. 6.
[4] W. Krickeberg, *Märchen der Azteken und Inkaperuaner*, 1928, No. 4 and Note.
[5] Chap. 42.   [6] Wundt, *Völkerpsychologie*, IV, 358 *f*.
[7] Reuterskiöld, *Der Totemismus*, (*AR*. 15, 1912) I; A. van Gennep, *Religions,
Mœurs et Légendes*, 1908–1914, I, 51.

community is irrevocably bound up with the totem; and from this we may, but need not necessarily, (a) infer that the group bears the name of the totem: (b) the totem is accounted its ancestor. (2) The totem involves sundry tabus: such are (a) the prohibition of killing, or eating; but in specific cases or under special conditions the command to eat may itself become imperative, because contact between the totem and the social group must be strengthened: (b) the prohibition of inter-marriage within the same totem group (so-called exogamy). By the enumeration of these characteristics, however, we have gained no genuine understanding of Totemism; and this we can achieve, so far as the modern mind can ever succeed, only if we duly consider its religious basis. Of course totems are by no means gods, and they are as a rule not "worshipped" in the sense that sacrifices and the like are offered to them. But it is a failing of modern thought that, in connection with the term religion, it must immediately think of "gods". Totemism, however, needs no gods; but it implies submergence within the power of some animal. "When man in the hunting stage . . . forced by the necessity of life and his unvarying daily occupation, thinks only of animals which are at the same moment his enemies and his food, if as it were he merges himself wholly in the animal, then it is only natural that this content of his consciousness should press for expression";[1] and this submersion in the being of a superior power, which can nevertheless be subjugated, constitutes the essence of Totemism and transforms it into a religion. Everything social is merely secondary, and is the consequence of the experience of Power. The totem animal, as a group, is a sort of reservoir for the potency of the tribe or clan.[2]

On the totem depends the life of the community. The Bantu tribe of the Ba-ronga says of the buffalo, "the magician of the plain" which executes all sorts of tasks: "our whole life depends upon him"; if he dies there is nothing left for the tribe but collective suicide. There is in this instance no question of "Totemism" in the sense of a social system with totem classes, *etc.*, such as is to be found in Australia; all the requisite presuppositions, however, are already present,[3] and we approach a further stage nearer this system when the essential relationship with the animal is indicated in the form of descent. An Amandabele youth, for example, refuses to milk a certain cow: "it is

---

[1] Ankermann in Chantepie, *op. cit.*, I, 169.
[2] Saintyves, *Force magique*, 56 and Note 2; Reuterskiöld, *op. cit.*, 20 *ff*; *cf.* B. Schweitzer, *Herakles*, 1922, 82.
[3] Carl Meinhof, *Afrikanische Märchen*, 1921, No. 20.

too powerful for him, he is afraid to milk his mother".[1] If this point of view becomes systematic, then derivation from the totem can be taken into account instead of mere connection by blood. The totem poles, therefore, bearing the animal at the top and beneath this a series of ancestors, are (as Wundt remarks) a sort of impersonal family tree;[2] with other instances, they occur in North America.[3] It is mainly in Australia that we find any very intricate totem system in which the totem provides the standard for the entire social organization of the community.

If, however, we start not from this system, but from the idea of the accumulation of power in some animal species, then we can understand the many residues of this standpoint persisting in less primitive cultural complexes. To say, for example, that the ancient Egyptians were totemists is undeniably nonsensical, if we mean by this that they accepted a totemistic system. But it is not absurd if we mean merely the idea of essential relationship with the animal and the possibility of subsisting upon this animal's power. In this latter sense the Egyptians, as we have already seen, were certainly totemists, and a similar state of affairs holds good for the bear and wolf tribes in the old Germanic world.[4]

3. For in the intimate relationship between animal and man the former can be man, and man animal. Thus in fairy tales the animal, which was originally merely such, has become an enchanted prince, while whoever allows himself to be duly impressed by the stories of the Indians of North and South America, must feel that to their minds there was no distinction whatever between the animal and the human being. Marriage and birth, war and treaty bind them together; and hardly any metamorphosis is necessary to make an animal out of man, or conversely. This transposition becomes more imperative as the contrast between the two is more clearly grasped, and then so-called *Lycanthropy* comes into existence. Although this is best known under the form of man moving about in the guise of a wolf, the fusion of animal and man is by no means pure lycanthropy in the proper sense. In Indonesia the crocodile and dog, the cat, but above all the tiger, are "werewolves",[5] while in ancient Germanic times we find the *berserkr*, the "bear-skinned man" who can transform himself into the bear's

---

[1] Fourie, *Amandebele*, 106.   [2] Wundt, *op. cit.*, IV, 331.
[3] Besson, *Le Totémisme*, 1929, Plates XXIII *ff.*
[4] Grönbech, *Vor folkeaet*, II, 1912, 98 *ff.*   [5] Kruyt, *Animisme*, 190 *ff.*

shape. But here too the genuine werewolf occurs; Sigmundr and Sin-fjötli lurk in the forest in wolf form; this belief, indeed, was influential until quite recently, and crimes were perpetrated with it as a cloak.[1] Behind it there lies an ecstatic experience; the animal is the completely "Other", to which man flees for refuge when he is satiated with humanity. The women of the Dionysian cult sought the divine in the animal. They lived themselves, as it were, entirely into the animal not from love of "animalism" in any modern sense, since the idea was not then in existence! but only in order to gain freedom from them-selves. As in Euripides' magnificent description:

> And one a young fawn held, and one a wild
> Wolf cub, and fed them with white milk, and smiled
> In love, young mothers with a mother's breast,
> And babes at home forgotten.[2]

In the cult of Dionysus the animal was precisely the god with whom man sought to unite himself.

The same thing occurred in regularized worship. Animal masks were everywhere used in sacred games and dances to invest the performers with the characters of the (divine) animals. One played the animal, therefore, in order to be identical with it and to utilize its power. The "bees" was the name given to the priestesses of Demeter, and "fillies" to others, while the girl dancers of Artemis Brauronia were regarded as "she-bears".[3] From animal mask-dances, in fact, Greek tragedy originated.

Worship of animals, as ascribed by us and by the ancients to the Egyptians above all other peoples, is found among almost all races even if only in its rudiments. The Power that makes itself known to man in field and forest, in mountains and water, was very frequently perceived in animal form, the spirit of the corn being a buck or hare when it is not an old woman. It is then no matter for surprise that many of the "high gods" also exhibit animal characteristics, and this not in Egypt only. Demeter, whose priestesses were fillies, was herself a mare which foaled the colt Areion by the stallion Poseidon;[4] similarly Dionysus was a bull, and was invoked in that form by the women of Elis.[5]

---

[1] Charles de Coster gives a most realistic description, *La légende d'Ulenspiegel et de Lamme Goedzak*; cf. Bruno Gutmann, *Volksbuch der Wadschagga*, 1914.
[2] *The Bacchae*, 699 ff. (Murray).
[3] cf. van der Leeuw, *Goden en Menschen in Hellas*, 1927, 37.
[4] Pausanias, VIII, 24, 4.   [5] G. van der Leeuw, *ibid.*, 112.

Thus the slaughter of the animal-god had the same sacramental character as the killing of the totem. In ancient Rome the October horse (*october equus*) was sacrificed by the *flamen martialis* after it had won the race. The blood from the tail was in part allowed to drip on the sacred hearth of the *regia* and in part preserved in the sanctuary of Vesta (*penus Vestae*), while its severed head was contended for by the men belonging to two wards, the *via sacra* and the *subura*, being nailed by the victors to the *regia* or to the Mamilian tower, *turris mamilia*, until the next festival; the animal was the bearer of the harvest plenteousness, and from its neck a garland of cakes was suspended *ob frugum eventum*—for the vigorous growth of the fruits.

Not only the potency of vegetation was thus sustained by animals: in every sphere they were the superior and the wise. Animals played a part in the foundation legends of very many cities, as did the she-wolf in Rome, the pig in Alba, *etc.*; they were permitted to go their own way, leading where no human wisdom could ever reach. Similarly two "milch kine" that had borne no yoke carried the ark of the covenant back to the land of Israel so that it became dangerous to the Philistines.[1]

Animals now remain potent only in fairy tales, and only on coats of arms do they still retain their ancient magnificence; but these escutcheons were once the symbols of a life that linked itself to a stable form of superhuman existence.

M. Besson, *Le totémisme*, 1929.
J. G. Frazer, *Totemism and Exogamy*, 1910.
A. van Gennep, *Religions, Mœurs et Légendes*, 1908–1914.
V. Hehn, *Kulturpflanzen und Haustiere*[8], 1911.
E. Reuterskiöld, *Der Totemismus* (*AR.* 15, 1912).
    Die Entstehung der Speisesakramente, 1912.

[1] 1 *Samuel* vi. 7.

CHAPTER 9

WILL AND FORM

1. THE principle that the environing and the higher worlds form the world conjoined with primitive man, and that their sacredness can be experienced only in a most intimate community of essential nature, finds yet another expression besides that implied by the term "Power". For Power acquires *Will*. The environment, that is to say, not only shares man's life and exercises an intense influence over him, but also "wills" something with regard to man, who on his own part desires something therefrom.

A hint of these conditions subsists in the *theory of Animism* as, in its classical form, it dominated speculation for a long time, chiefly owing to Tylor's outstanding research. But actually it is little more than a hint; for in its entire structure and tendency this theory suits the second half of the nineteenth century far better than it does the primitive world!

It sets out from psychological data. While Dynamism attempts to understand the experience of the environment in its potency, Animism aims at interpreting it as an encounter between two wills, or souls or spirits:—those of man and of his surroundings. This is its core and its permanent significance. But unfortunately much more than this was appended to it, starting from dream experience. For in one's own dream we make long journeys; in another person's dream we can also appear to other people, since others can see me in dream exactly as I am. Conversely, I can meet others if I dream about them. But during the dream my body and theirs demonstrably remain quietly in the same place. There must then be a certain "Something" that can release itself from the body:—the Soul. Besides the dream, again, there is another condition in which this soul appears to have left the body:—Death, when the body lies apparently lifeless. Nevertheless the "Something" must continue to live somehow or other. For dead people too meet us in our dreams, appear to us, and we speak to them. There must therefore be an existence of the soul after death.

Such is the psychology of Animism. But the animist requires a cosmology as well, since he is surrounded by a spontaneously active world. Now human motion always depends on the soul's presence, apart from which torpidity sets in. The movements of Nature, therefore, waves in the waters, the flame of fire, but also the rustling in tree-tops, and rolling stones, have now to be explained similarly to man's movements. "Their (primitive men's) own personality and feelings are . . . the sole causally connected material for observation at their disposal for forming their ideas about Nature; with these observational data they put together their picture of Nature . . .";[1] and thus man argues from himself to the world and concludes that not he alone, but also all objects which move of themselves, have souls.

The whole world, then, is full of "spirits". Seas, lakes, waters, mountains, caverns, trees, forests, villages, towns, houses, the air, the heavens, the underworld: all these things and places are regarded as possessed of souls, as for example by the inhabitants of the island of Nias, near Sumatra.[2] And thus it is with countless peoples.[3] But when we go on to ask how primitive humanity came to regard not only animals as possessed of souls, but also all kinds of objects that manifestly never even have life, then the animistic theory gives two different answers. In the first place, a sort of malady of thought is supposed to have induced man to do this, just as it leads our own children to speak of the "naughty table" which has hit them, and to look on Teddy Bear as an actually living creature. But it may also well be that this malady of thought was caused by a disease of language; for this itself presupposes personification. We say—and must say: the storm howls, the sea glitters, the sun shines; but we know that the storm, the sea and the sun are not really active agents. The primitive mind, however, did not know this, but was led into personifying by language which had become accustomed to divide the surrounding world into male and female —masculine and feminine—beings.[4]

All this is of course a regrettable error, from which man recovers as soon as he has reached the grown-up era of the nineteenth century! But if we leave the erroneous, indeed the pathological, aspect aside for a moment, then little objection need be raised against Animism as an explanatory theory of the world. Tylor, indeed, admired its logical conclusiveness; in his opinion Animism is "a thoroughly coherent and rational philosophy", supported too by the conviction, familiar also to ourselves, that effects presuppose causes; the "effects" are the phenomena of movement, the "causes" are the "spirits". These spirits

---

[1] Nieuwenhuis, *Die Wurzeln des Animismus*, *Int. Arch. Ethnogr.* 24, Supp., 1917, 61.
[2] Wilken, *Verspreide Geschriften*, 1912, III, 233 f.
[3] Alviella, *L'Idée de Dieu*, 1892, 107.   [4] Alviella, *op. cit.*, 60 ff.

are really nothing other than "personified causes". And Nieuwenhuis still regards Animism as essentially the same primitive science, refers to "syllogisms" and looks upon the necessity for causality as its basic ground.

2. But it is quite incomprehensible how this theory about the inter-connectedness of the world should be a religion, indeed the origin of all religion. For "the soul cult" and "the cult of ancestors" are evidently something more than philosophical interpretations of the causal nexus. The animistic theory, in fact, attempted to explain primitive conscious life according to the model of Anglo-French Positivism, and in so doing simultaneously to account for the origin of religion! and by this failure duly to estimate religion it was wrecked. This was realized on many sides—even on the positivistic itself. Söderblom in Scandinavia, Marett in England, Durkheim in France, Preuss in Germany, Kruyt in Holland and a series of other investigators have accumulated a whole arsenal of objections to Animism. They are mainly the following: (a) Animism does not make it comprehensible why souls suddenly become worshipped after death; and incidentally, that is not the case at all with a great many "souls". This omission arises, however, from: (b) the fact that Animism did not recognize the concept of Power; it failed to realize therefore that worship always depends on the substantiation of Power. Because of this it also overlooked the fact that the universal animation of Nature and in artificial objects, or the possibility of their being charged with potency, is by no means always bound up with the idea of "soul"; for something can live and be powerful, can indeed be worshipped, without having any "soul" whatever attributed to it.[1] But the soul theory—and this is probably the chief defect—(c) is treated in a one-sided rationalistic way; Animism failed to perceive that, in the concept of souls or spirits, something like faith must be present. It forgot too that dream theory cannot be the origin of belief in souls and in the dead, in spirits and gods, unless these ideas have already been introduced into the dream from other sources; further, it overlooked the fact that primitive man, who had to struggle with dire necessity to wring sustenance from his surroundings, was hardly inclined to "philosophize" about "causes". It also completely misunderstood the intimate fusion of every *Weltanschauung*, and of all religion, with experience. Still further: (d) the relationship between the spirits of the dead and those of Nature is by no means clear. Of

---

[1] *cf.* here Otto, *Gefühl des Überw.*, 68.

course it does happen that spirits of the departed lurk hidden in mountains, *etc.*, but this is no justification for setting up the worship of the dead as a general principle to explain the endowment of Nature with a soul. Again, (*e*) the entire construction of the idea of "universal endowment with souls" rests on a gigantic error, so that according to Animism it must be supposed that humanity began, like the child, with untruths, whilst ultimately (*f*) even the analogy with the child cannot be maintained, since the child knows quite well that Teddy Bear is not alive and only makes the animal live from time to time under the stress of emotion. It would be astounded, as Durkheim remarks, if the bear actually bit it!

3. That, roughly, is the record of the sins of Animism: and it is undeniably a long record. But if only we release the facts with which it begins from the theory itself, then it becomes evident that Animism has great and permanent significance. For we can now start afresh with the child who endows its toys with life. As has just been seen, it does this under the influence of emotion. It desires to have life around it and to find another will opposed to its own; so it personifies its toys, or even things not intended as toys at all. "Personifies" is actually too calculated, too rationalistic an expression; we had better say: it grants to the lifeless and soulless object *Will and Form*. Even the latter: perhaps the cushion represents an elephant, or the broom an aunt! But the child does not wish to explain anything thereby, and to him the assigning of will is the expression of his own "immediate childish world-experience".[1] The question as to why "primitive man and the child see the world as a picture of personal life", then, is quite futile. "On the contrary, we must ask ourselves: Why do we ever lose this natural mode of observation, so that we can restore it only by artificial means?"[2] But the motive for so-called personification, at all events, lies in experience. And by the investigators of so-called pre-animistic tendency this experience was universally discerned in the necessity, in the incessant danger and the constant crisis, which threatened primitive life. These arouse the feeling of dependence upon an arbitrary will (as with the "animist" Nieuwenhuis);[3] they awaken the consciousness that someone, spirit or god, is either inimical or well disposed towards man. In this there is undoubtedly much truth, although we should

---

[1] A. A. Grünbaum, *Zeitschr. f. pädag. Psychologie*, 28, 1927, 456.
[2] *ibid.*, 457.   [3] Nieuwenhuis, *op. cit.*, 15.

do better not to imagine too much about primitive man's life in his primeval forest!

For this need still exists in our own case in the modern world. We too are animists, though we do our best to forget it! And children and poets are not victims of any maladies, nor mentally deficient, but human beings whose emotional life casts off certain artificial constraints. And in this respect the human experience which evokes the animistic endowment with will and creation of form appears to be a very general one: *Solitude*. He who lives in subjection to Powers is solitary. Whether Power stands confronting him, or whether he knows himself to be one with it, or indeed understands how to control it in some magical way—it still leaves him lonely. In his environment, then, man seeks not merely "the world of mankind", but his own equal, a will:

> Unlocked the spirit-world doth lie,
> Thy sense is shut, thy heart is dead![1]

"It is not that the child begins to endow the moon, which was originally presented to him as inanimate Nature, with psychic characteristics, but the moon is presented to the child from the outset as a being . . . endowed with a soul."[2] In the crisis of solitude therefore, which probably bore very severely on primitive man even though it is only too well known to ourselves, he succeeded in giving the Powers a will and a form. And this induced all the possibilities of objectification, of speaking and being addressed, of malediction and entreaty, of revelation and of the self-concealing God.

For primitive man, just as for our peasants, the changeful seasons were the really important factors in life together with the great events of birth, marriage and death. That Winter, like Spring, is a power which one can control by observing the rites, was for that reason something self-evident to the primitive mind. At all events the malicious or beneficent potencies of the season now became a will, a demon of fertility or a god of the harvest, which could be invoked, encountered or expelled. This is Animism. Few examples are necessary here, as we shall discover an abundance in later chapters. For in the three terms *Power*, *Will* and *Form*, there lies practically the entire concept of the Object of Religion.[3]

---

[1] *Faust*, Part I.   [2] Grünbaum, *ibid.*, 459.

[3] The term "Form", *Gestalt*, is one of the most important in the present work. It is best understood by referring to recent "*Gestalt* Psychology", which maintains that every object of consciousness is a whole or a unit, and is not merely constituted by the

In Suabia, Sweden and the Netherlands the fruit trees are wrapped in straw at Christmas time so that they shall bear heavily;[1] this is an attempt to retain and concentrate the potency of the trees, and consequently an instance of Dynamism. But if the farmer goes into the orchard, as in Pillersee, to strike the trees and call out to them: "Wake up, tree! To-night is Christmas Eve, bear many apples and pears once more", then that rests on presupposing a will and a possibility of persuading the tree, and therefore constitutes Animism, although certainly of a rudimentary type. A more fully developed Animism emerges, again, when the power of the tree is regarded as a "tree spirit", a dryad or woodsprite or whatever else it may be styled, and acquires the potentiality of free movement.

Here, however, we must guard against stating the relationship between Animism and Dynamism in such a way that the former is looked upon as the successor of the latter in point of time, as often happened owing to the gratification arising from the early discovery of "Power" and the influence of the unfortunate term "Preanimism". In many cases, certainly, we can show how impersonal power received will and form. But at all periods there has been Dynamism as well as Animism, while both still exist to-day side by side: the saint, who hears prayer, is a form and has a will, while his wonder-working relics are a power. Animism and Dynamism therefore designate not eras, but structures, and are as such eternal. It is a cheap amusement to point out the "error" that consists in regarding holy water as being especially potent, or in ascribing the growth of crops to a will. It is just as easy to smile at the "mistaken" belief in the power of baptism, or at the pious delusion that disease is cured by some superior will interfering. Poets and children, none the less, to whom it is quite natural to be confronted by power and will, know that this "error" is no error at all, but rather a living vision of reality. And just like children, poets are

elements that analysis may discover; the English name of this system is usually "Configuration Psychology". "Endowment with Form", and again "Form Creation" in this sense, will appear in what follows as equivalents for the allied term *Gestaltung*. But it is vitally important to observe that, throughout this volume, all Forms are visible, or tangible, or otherwise perceptible; and thus Endowment with Form, or Form Creation, indicates the gradual crystallization of the originally formless feelings and emotions into some kind of perceptible and unified Forms; *cf.* further Chap. 65, Section 2.

[1] O. von Reinsberg-Düringsfeld, *Das festliche Jahr*[2], 1898, 460. H. W. Heuvel, *Oud-achterhoeksch boerenleven*, 473: in Gelderland the farmer went *met bloote gat*—in his shirt—into the orchard: an example of the nakedness rite often found in fertility customs.

accustomed to look more deeply into Reality than anthropologists and historians!

4. With penetrating insight, Söderblom has given prominence to the profound significance of Animism in its connection with Dynamism and so-called primal religion. "In the impersonal Power of the *mana*-type there dawns the realization that the divine penetrates the whole Universe and is in its essence supernatural. The belief in souls and spirits initiates the apprehension of a spiritual presence which, more closely defined, is a realm of will: at first of capricious and arbitrary individuals but subsequently, as the result of prophetic influence or some other ethico-religious achievements, of a more rational, more personal and more moral Being acting from inner laws."[1] Certainly "spiritual" should not be interpreted in our sense. For Power which acquires a Will also receives a Form: Will and Form together constitute "personality" as this dominates mythical modes of thought, exactly as the most up-to-date science of "substance and force", or "energy and atom", is unable to dispense with it.

The distinction between Dynamism and Animism may also be stated thus: the "extraordinary" in Dynamism is the "unexpected" in Animism. Now what is unanticipated emanates not from Power but from Person. Thus man can complain about the incalculability of the events of the world in accordance with animistic ideas and, if this is done in such fine terms as Alviella employs, we will listen gladly: "There was nothing but chance, caprice, at most custom (in natural processes). They (primitive men) were not certain that the light of day, once it had disappeared, would return in the morning, and just as little sure that Summer would follow Winter. If after the sun has departed it approaches again each Spring, if the moon each month reassumes its lost form, if rain ends drought, if the wind dies away— all this occurs because these beings so desire it; but who knows if they always will desire it, or will always be capable of it?"[2] But I scarcely feel inclined, with Alviella, to prefer the fixed order and the brazen law of a modern *Weltanschauung*, "based on the natural sciences", to this arbitrariness. For we must realize how there subsists in this capriciousness the possibility of the good, as well as of the evil, will— of the devil as of God, of sin as of grace, of the drama of God and man.

We have been reminded too, and with perfect justice, that without that affirmation of Will in the Universe and in man which constitutes

[1] *Gottesglaube*, 283.   [2] *L'Idée de Dieu*, 178 f.

Animism, Plato's philosophy could never have been formulated; while to this Kant's may be added, and if we consider Form, Pheidias and Raphael too. From this fertile mother, whose name is *Form-creation*, spring morality, psychology, theory of knowledge, poetry and painting; but if we wish to insult her we call her Mythology! More important than Plato and Raphael, however, are Moses and St. Paul: Jahveh is an animistic God not so much because He originates from the mount, or personates the wind, but because He is nothing other than Will, than burning passionate activity. Supreme activity, again, allied with lowliest form—but what a form!—appears to us in Jesus. And with his fine feeling for primitive values, Chesterton has here too expressed beautifully how intimately connected are arbitrary will and love, fear and adoration: "For a man walking down a lane at night can see the conspicuous fact that as long as nature keeps to her own course, she has no power with us at all. As long as a tree is a tree, it is a top-heavy monster with a hundred arms, a thousand tongues, and only one leg. But so long as a tree is a tree, it does not frighten us at all. It begins to be something alien, to be something strange, only when it looks like ourselves. When a tree really looks like a man our knees knock under us. And when the whole universe looks like a man we fall on our faces."[1]

A. Bertholet, *Von Dynamismus zu Personalismus;* in *Pro Regno Pro Sanctuario*, studies for van der Leeuw's 60th year, 1950, 35 *ff.*

Cte. Goblet d'Alviella, *L'Idée de Dieu*, 1892.

A. C. Kruyt, *Het Animisme in den Indischen Archipel*, 1906.

G. van der Leeuw, *La Structure de la mentalité primitive*, 1928.

L. Lévy-Bruhl, *How Natives Think*.

A. W. Nieuwenhuis, *Die Wurzeln des Animismus*, Int. Arch. Ethnogr. 24, Suppl., 1917.

R. Otto, *Das Gefühl des Überweltlichen*, 1932.

K. Th. Preuss, *Die geistige Kultur der Naturvölker*[2], 1923.

E. B. Tylor, *Primitive Culture*[4], 1903.

G. A. Wilken, *Verspreide Geschriften*, 1912.

[1] *Heretics*, "Science and the Savages"; Chap. XI, 152.

CHAPTER 10

THE FORM OF THE MOTHER

1. "SEARCH out the ancient mother", old Bachofen warned us years ago.[1] Science has never wholly ignored this admonition, although the peculiar and profound, yet somewhat obscure, theories of this romantic *savant* have only very recently gained due attention. "There is nothing more sacred on earth than the religion of the mother, for it leads us back to the deepest personal secret in our souls, to the relationship between the child and its mother"; in these terms Otto Kern has crystallized the essence of our theme.[2] Believing that behind Power he decries the outlines of a Form, man recognizes therein the features of his own mother; his loneliness when confronted with Power thus transforms itself into the intimate relationship to the mother. Modern psychoanalysis has opened the eyes of many of us to the weighty and all-dominating significance of the mother-form in adult life; while the poets, the sole genuine animists and realists in the midst of a theorized world, have felt the need of this somewhat forced awakening, bound up though it is with so many disagreeable new speculations. Similarly St. Francis, in the marvellous hymn already quoted, speaks of "our sister Mother-earth, who sustains and cares for us, and produces so many kinds of fruit together with grasses and beautifully coloured flowers".[3]

World events are now no longer any play of potencies: they are all reduced to the one great and mysterious happening: *Birth*. Movement and change, coming into being and passing away, are now a being born and a return to the womb. The Mother is the all-nourishing earth: life is to be born of Mother-earth, death is to enter in to her; and this too the poets have never forgotten: the old man who cannot die, in Chaucer's *Canterbury Tales*, sighs and groans:

> Thus walke I, lyk a restelees caityf,
> And on the ground, which is my modres gate,
> I knokke with my staf, bothe erly and late,
> And seye: "leve moder, leet me in!"[4]

---

[1] *Urreligion und antike Symbole; antiquam exquirite matrem.*
[2] *Die griechischen Mysterien der klassischen Zeit*, 1927, 24.
[3] *Laudato si, mi Signore, per sora nostra matre terra,*
   la quale ne sustena et governa
   et produce diversi fructi con coloriti flori et herba.
[4] *The Pardoners Tale.*

In Greece the oldest divine forms were Earth-mothers. Men, and likewise fountains, stones, plants, *etc.*, were all regarded not as created nor made, but as born, autochthonous.[1] To the Greeks the earth was a form, only not in the plastic Homeric sense: she was a woman with half her body above the ground; and she lacked the mobility of the later great celestial gods: she was half Power, half human. But she *was* human, and bore her progeny in human fashion. She was styled Pandora—when not simply *Ge*, the earth—because she poured out all from her rich treasure, her coffer, which became a dangerous miracle box only to the eyes of a moralizing age. And although her motion was restricted, one movement was always assured to her: her uprising in Spring, when to all creatures she brought new life.

Many were her names: she was called Athene, *kourotrophos*, the "great mother", the many breasted: in Asia, Ephesia: by the Greeks, Artemis, Diktynna or Britomartis; she was a wild natural power, at home in forest and mountain. Probably pre-hellenic Greece already knew her as Mistress of Animals, πότνια θηρῶν. She was the oldest and the most revered, and at the same moment the most mysterious, of divine forms; and when they spoke of her poets lighted upon the exotic and violent clang of the rarest primeval sounds:

> And the eldest of deities Earth that knows not toil nor decay
> Ever he furrows and scores.[2]

Aeschylus, again, imitates the child's babbling:

> O Mother, Mother Earth, I am sore afraid;
> Beat back my fear!
> O Father, her first birth, Great Zeus![3]

The Mother, then, is anything but a theoretical invention intended to explain the world process. She is Form, just barely outlined; and everywhere that Nature gives or takes something, there is the Mother. The "god bearing fountain" became an epithet for the Madonna, and ἡ ἐν τῇ Πηγῇ (She in the well), now the title of honour of the *theotokos*, was once a suggestion of nameless Form, still half identical with the

---

[1] Ninck, *Die Bedeutung des Wassers im Kult und Leben der Alten*, 20.
[2] Sophocles, *Antigone*, 339 (Storr).
> θεῶν τε τὰν ὑπερτάταν, Γᾶν
> ἄφθιτον, ἀκαμάταν, ἀποτρύεται . . .
[3] *The Suppliant Women*, 890 *ff.* (Murray).
> μᾶ Γᾶ μᾶ Γᾶ, βόαν
> φοβερὸν ἀπότρεπε,
> ὦ πᾶ, Γᾶς παῖ, Ζεῦ.

water from Earth.[1] There were, too, many mothers, called by the Greeks nymphs:—not maidens but young women, who were invoked at marriages for their blessing.[2]

From the Greeks the Mother passed to ourselves as the Sacred Three—and at the same time as a warning that here genuine personality has not yet been achieved; and thus the *eumenides*, *semnai*, *moirai*, *charites* and *horai* find their counterparts in the three fairies or *Holden* of Celtic or German popular belief.

2. As we have learnt to recognize her thus far, the Mother is the Form of untouched wild Nature, the "mountain mother", as the Greeks styled her; under the names of Artemis, Cybele, *etc.*, she retained this character, while on Germanic territory *Holda* or *Frau Holle* is a similar figure. But side by side with this appears the mother-form of the tilled and cultivated earth. And again we must be careful not to make any theoretical distinction, and it maybe try to interpret this new Mother-earth as some "goddess of cultivation"; gods and goddesses "of" something or other prolong their miserable existence only in works of reference and decorative paintings! To primitive humanity, then, cultivation was Nature as directly experienced, while the goddess was the form assumed by this experience.

The earth, still further, offers not only rich gifts and marvellous ornamentation, but she nourishes too. To the Greeks she was *Gaia kourotrophos*; and the *kouroi* were the young, of plants as well as of the animal and human world; to her knees she drew children, young animals and flowers.[3] She was, however, not always a form; and folk customs, from ancient Egypt to those of modern husbandmen, have faithfully retained the old idea of the receptacle of Power. In many places the "last sheaf" was, and indeed still is, the object of some special rites or other; ceremonially bound or threshed, it is the holder of the potency of the ploughed field, exactly as the May-pole sustains the strength of wild Nature. The granting of form begins whenever some animal, harvest cock or goat, takes the place of the purely vegetative power reservoir; and then this develops into dressing the last of the corn as a woman or, as in La Vendée, the farmer's wife being threshed and winnowed in fun.[4]

This indeed is no "personification" in our sense of the term. Natural

[1] Otto Kern, *Die Religion der Griechen*, I, 1926, 89.   [2] Ninck, *Wasser*, 13 *f.*
[3] G. van der Leeuw, *Goden en Menschen in Hellas*, Fig. 1.
[4] Mannhardt, *Baumkultus*, 612; Frazer, *The Golden Bough*, VII (*Spirits of the Corn*, I), 149 *f.*

occurrences are not allegorized—this again is done only by decorative painters!—but the essential community between human and terrestrial life is experienced. The earth, for instance, is regarded as woman, and woman as pertaining to the earth; this is the significance of the Polish custom of calling after the man who has cut the last of the grain: "Thou hast cut off the navel cord"; while in Scotland the corn spirit is reaped under the name of "the maiden".[1]

In Greece Demeter was the corn-mother, the grain-producing earth.[2] She has her sisters all over the world, from the German and Dutch *Roggenmuhme* (Dutch *roggemeuje*), to the rice-mother in Java and the mother of the maize in Mexico. In her mysteries the ceremonial cutting of an ear of corn was the climax; to her the plough was sacred, and she herself was once impregnated on the thrice-ploughed field.[3] She had a daughter called Kore, "the maiden", just as in Scotland; origin-ally she was probably alone, and the "maiden" was another earth-mother from elsewhere, who later became her daughter; both are actually only variant forms of Gaia.[4] The first is the mother in complete motherhood, the ripe fruit; the second, the maiden, the flower. The fate of both is the same: the grain must fall into the ground and die, so that it may bear fruit; subsequently the myth transformed this descent into the underworld into the rape of youth and the mother's sorrow. But in the countryman's festal calendar the *katagogia*, the "going down", still correctly signifies the transference of the seed to its underground receptacle.[5]

The birth and death of corn and men are intimately connected: "arising" and "going down", *anhodos* and *katagogia*, are the eternal crises, the sudden changes of fortune, in life. Kore-Persephone is not only the dying youth of the grain, but also the beauteous leader of the village youth, with whom she picks flowers on the meadow, and who must also grow old and die. And Demeter is the assistant at birth, Eileithyia, Eleutho, Eleusia;[6] on the other hand the dead were called after her: Δημητρεῖοι:—"Demeter's People."[7]

---

[1] Frazer, *ibid.*, 155, 164.   [2] Euripides, *The Bacchae*, 276.

[3] *cf.* Chantepie, *op. cit.*, II, 301.

[4] Farnell, *The Cults of the Greek States*, III, 116 *ff.*

[5] Farnell, *ibid.*, III, 114.—M. P. Nilsson, *A History of Greek Religion*, 123.

[6] Probably the name is not to be divorced from Eleusis and Eleusinia; *cf.* S. Wide, *Lakonische Kulte*, 1893, 175, and W. Roscher, *Ausführliches Lexikon der griechisch-römischen Mythologie*, Article "Kora".—Chantepie, *op. cit.*, II, 318; *cf.* also: F. Muller, *De "Komst" van den hemelgod, Meded. Kon. Akad. v. Wet. Afd. Lett.* 74, B, 7, 1932.

[7] Harrison, *Prolegomena to the Study of Greek Religion*, 267. Plutarch, *On the Face which Appears on the Orb of the Moon*, XXVIII.

To this corresponded a very close relationship of woman to the tilling of the land; the cult of Demeter was the affair of the women. And everywhere in the world it is woman who concerns herself with husbandry and its rites. In all this, too, very ancient social conditions play their part. Many tribes represent a transition from the hunting to the settled stage—the agricultural, the men being occupied in hunting and fishing while the women cultivate the fields. This state of affairs, however, which has its repercussions in agriculture for long periods, should be ascribed neither to indolence nor to the masculine desire to rule, and just as little should a hypothetical substitution of patriarchal conditions for matriarchy be assumed here. Women and the soil are in fact associated in the religious sense: woman is the ploughed field, the field a fertile woman: "In some parts of India, naked women drag a plough across a field by night";[1] and all this can be understood only if woman's greater potency is recalled. Like the tilled field, she too is the bearer of life, and like it she conceives and gives birth.[2]

That woman is a ploughed field is indeed familiar to the poetry of all ages and regions. To the mind of the old Egyptian sage, Ptahhotep, "she is a goodly field for her lord",[3] and in the Egyptian love song the beloved assures her swain:

> I am thy favourite sister.
> To thee I am as a garden
> Full of sweetly scented herbs.[4]

Similarly, the *Vendidad* asserts that the land "is unhappy that for long is left untilled: here wanders a beautifully formed woman who has long remained childless",[5] and that the earth bestows her riches like "a loved woman lying on her bed who produces a son for her dear husband".[6] The Hindus, like the Greeks, were aware that the phallus is a plough;[7] to the Greek poets, in fact, the image of the tilled field

---

[1] Frazer, *The Golden Bough*, I (*The Magic Art*, I), 282 *f*.; *cf. AR.* XI, 1908, 154 *ff*.

[2] *cf*. Farnell, *op. cit.*, III, 106 *ff*.—Lévy-Bruhl, *Primitive Mentality*, 316 *ff*.

[3] A. Erman, *The Literature of the Ancient Egyptians*, 61.

[4] M. Müller, *Die Liebespoesie der alten Ägypter*, 1899, 27.

[5] Lehmann, *Textbuch*, 164; *cf*. GENERAL LITERATURE, p. 19 *ante*.

[6] *ibid*.; *cf*. also the Vedic marriage formula: "This woman came as a cornfield endowed with life. Ye men, sow in her the seed"; in Bertholet, *op. cit.*, GENERAL LITERATURE, p. 19 *ante*.—Conversely, in the twelfth-century church hymn the Blessed Virgin is referred to thus: *terra non arabilis, quae fructium parturiit*; *cf*. F. J. E. Raby, *A History of Christian Latin Poetry*, 349.

[7] E. Abegg, *Das Pretakalpa des Garuda-Purana*, 1921, 200 *f*.—E. Fehrle, *Die kultische Keuschheit im Altertum*, 1910, 170 *ff*.—Dieterich *Mutter Erde*, 46 *f*.

was extremely vivid: Sophocles refers to a wife whom the husband has seen

> E'en as the tiller of a distant field
> Sees it at seedtime, sees it once again
> At harvest, and no more.[1]

Modern popular poetry too still clings to this image, just as the barren queen in the fairy tale complains: "I am like a field on which nothing grows",[2] while in the rough humour of comedy the cuckold consoles himself: "he that ears my land spares my team".[3] A later romantic period also, which prefers longing to power, can yet discover no other than the primal simile of the fruitful field, even when the uncouthness of earth and fruit is replaced by the more tender flower and bud.

But this leads to a yet wider perspective wherein the maternal form was perceived. I must begin by stating definitely that Mother Earth is very human. Demeter is the loving and sorrowing mother and her most beautiful image, the Cnidian Demeter, unites something of the tearful expression of the *Madre Dolorosa* to the joyfulness of the corn-goddess;[4] Isis again is the typical "housewife", devoted to her husband and son. Indeed, in the maternal divinities is found the entire scale of feminine possibilities: the lover, and not seldom the beloved of all the world (Ishtar-Aphrodite type), together with the virgin (Artemis, Mary).[5] But she is always the mother even when she is a maid, and even when, as in the Western Asiatic religions, a peculiar relationship subsists between the mother and a young god, to whom the feelings of both lover and mother seem to be devoted.

This singular relationship, certainly, has its social presuppositions. We know little of the origins of matriarchal law. We can, however, feel assured that a hunting social organization is connected with masculine predominance, just as is the agricultural stage with that of women. Still, it seems to me that in the combination of matriarchy and agriculture the social element appears not to be the original so much as does the religious: it is very unlikely that matriarchal law began in the intimacy between women in the course of their common agricultural pursuits. This intimate feminine intercourse and the subsequent social segregation of women, much more probably, were initiated by the

---

[1] Sophocles, *Trach.*, 31 *ff.*; *cf. Oedipus Rex*, 1257.
[2] *Kinder- und Hausmärchen*, No. 144.   [3] *All's Well That Ends Well*, I, 3.
[4] Farnell, *op. cit.*, III, 277; *cf.* also his *Outline History of Greek Religion*, 77.
[5] *cf.* the utterance in this spirit of Ramakrishna in Bertholet, *Lesebuch*, 14, 83 (*cf.* GENERAL LITERATURE).

"eternal feminine", the peculiar and mysterious power of woman, which appertains to the earth as does the earth to it.[1]

3. It has already become clear that virgin and mother stand in no antithetical relationship. Only for a culture no longer quite primitive, but influenced by the ideal of virginity, does the unity of maid and mother become a problem, an offence and a marvel; the ancient world, on the other hand, regarded the maiden either as the daughter, or as about to become a mother. And here too it was Hellas that generated the ideal form of the maiden as well as of the mother.[2]

For Faith, the virgin forms are the exponents of feminine youth in everyday life. Since times immemorial the young village girls have been beloved figures as they assemble, above all around the village well: the future mothers at the springing womb of the earth. It is an eternal event: "The young maidens come from the town to fetch water— innocent and necessary employment, and formerly the occupation of the daughters of kings. As I take my rest there, the idea of the old patriarchal life is awakened around me. I see them, our old ancestors, how they formed their friendships and contracted alliances at the fountain-side; and I feel how fountains and streams were guarded by beneficent spirits."[3] Young Werther perceived correctly: at the well arises new life; according to the Greeks, there dwelt the nymphs who bless birth, and the manifold dances of the virginal goddesses or demons took their form from the village roundelays.[4] In Sicily they were the youths whom a "queen" supervises, ($\pi a\hat{\imath}\delta\epsilon\varsigma$ and $\check{a}\nu a\sigma\sigma a$), exactly as at a festival one of the village girls appeared as the leading dancer and queen.[5] Artemis had her train:

> Once Hermes, the god with the golden wand,
> Stole me from the dance of Artemis,
> The virgin with golden arrows and rustling raiment;
> Many were sporting there, young maids and noble girls.[6]

Persephone too had such a chorus; and the many Madonnas of Christian times owe their plurality to their predecessors in antiquity.[7]

[1] cf. F. Gräbner, *Das Weltbild der Primitiven*, 1924, 33.
[2] Farnell, *Cults of the Greek States*, III, 278.
[3] *The Sorrows of Werther*, Goethe's *Works*, VI, 6 (Nimmo); Book I, May 12.
[4] G. van der Leeuw, *Goden en Menschen*, 26 ff.
[5] Nilsson, *History of Greek Religion*, 112.   [6] *Hymn. Homer. in Ven.*, 118.
[7] Probably also of Celtic origin occasionally; cf. U. von Wilamowitz-Möllendorf, *Griechische Tragödien*, II[8], 1919, 215 ff., on the Three Maries on the Island of la Camargue, Provence; cf. further Trede, *Heidentum*, II, 120, IV, 241, and Heiler, *Katholizismus*, 189.

The relationship between virgin and mother is intrinsically temporal: the maid becomes a wife. Hera is maiden, bride and wife; Artemis, virgin and mother. Often an annual bath was supposed to restore the girlhood of the goddess, as is also related of the old Germanic Hertha. This of course implies not that virginity is retained, but that fertility is constantly and miraculously renewed.[1]

The adoration of the Madonna first became a cult of sacred virginity in the Roman church. To antiquity, on the other hand, fertility was far more potent and holy than chastity, although the latter too possessed power. Demeter and Isis are mothers; Mary, their successor, is mother and maiden. But despite the ideal of virginity, the church was just as little able to dispense with the mother's form as was later Buddhism in the case of Kwanyin in China and Kwannon in Japan.[2] It is true that side by side with the mother, Mary, who has borrowed her form and even her attributes from the mothers of the Mediterranean basin, Christianity recognized another mother also, the church.

4. To primitive man, still further, his environment is not a summation of vastly different things, but a unity that is experienced as such. Therefore the mother too is not Earth alone and nothing else. The Cora Indians, for instance, worship Nasisa, "our mother", the goddess of the earth, the maize crop and the moon. In the Near East, again, the fertility mother is at the same time "queen of heaven", and this title was subsequently transferred to Mary; for heaven and earth are not severed from one another; and this experience receives its most forcible expression in the idea of the *holy marriage* between these two domains, this group of forms also being developed to the highest degree of perfection by the plastic genius of the Grecian people: "Beneath them the divine earth made fresh-sprung grass to grow, and dewy lotus, and crocus, and hyacinth, thick and soft, that upbare them from the ground. Therein lay the twain, and were clothed about with a cloud, fair and golden, wherefrom fell drops of glistering dew."[3]

Thus Homer, singing the nuptials of Zeus and Hera: yet even this brilliant scene has preserved the primeval feature of the bridal couch on the ploughed field ensuring fertility. Similarly, on the night before

[1] *cf.* A. G. Bather, "The Problem of the Bacchae", *Jour. Hell. Studies*, 14, 1894, 244 *ff.*, and Fehrle, *Kultische Keuschheit.*

[2] Compare the sober indictment by L. Coulange, *La Vierge Marie*, 1925, with the lyric by Th. Zielinski, *La Sybille*, 1924, which makes the Mother theme, reinterpreted as the idea of love, the principal feature in Christianity.

[3] *Iliad*, XIV, 346 *ff.* (Murray); *cf.* also the magnificent Aeschylus *Frag.* 43.

Midsummer's Day the farmers of Moon, in Esthonia, take girls from the ring-dance into the wood, where they simulate intercourse, while in the Ukraine the rudeness of this custom became harmless joking, though nevertheless it was connected with the conviction that a good harvest would result;[1] and in the Dutch province of Groningen, even to-day, a struggle called *waolen*, between youths and maids on the ground, is still a permanent incident during harvest.[2] In Java, however, intercourse actually occurs on the rice field; and with such customs we are once again transported to the very heart of Dynamism. As a Form, man still suffices for himself and feels as yet no need for projection beyond himself. But when the magical confidence in his capacity for directing the course of events by his own activities begins to wane, then he creates figures in his stead to perform the sacred actions for him. Just as the sheaf and the farmer's wife were transformed into the mother, so was the harvest custom into the sacred marriage.

But for the nuptials a bridegroom is also required. And with this we meet an extremely momentous phase in the history of religion. We can understand the attachment to the mother; but similarly, and in accord with Freud's theories, the intimate relationship to the father is probably no longer a secret to anyone. To every man his mother is a goddess, just as his father is a god. In the history of religion this has resulted in two great groups—the religions of the *Father*, who dwells in heaven and begets and acts, "outward force applying" (again to quote Goethe); and side by side with these the religions of the *Mother* living and giving birth in the Earth, in whose womb all process has both its beginning and its end. In no religion whatever is the mother or the father completely lacking.[3] Judaism and Islam have mercilessly expelled the mother, but to Christianity she returned as *mater gloriosa*. The Old Testament, however, recognizes the image of the mother only in its moral and spiritual sense: "as one whom his mother comforteth, so will I comfort you" (*Isaiah* lxvi. 13); but in the second chapter of *St. Luke* it has returned once more in its true significance. It seems irrefutable that here racial as well as religious types are con-

---

[1] Mannhardt, *Wald- und Feldkulte*, 1, 468, 480.

[2] H. C. A. Grolman, *Tydschrift K. Ned. Aardrykskundig Gen.*, 2. *Reeks*, 46, 1929.

[3] On the disputed question whether Mother Earth occurred among the Semites, *cf.* Th. Nöldeke, *AR.* 8, 1905, 161. Ef. Briem, *AR.* 24, 1926, 179 *ff.* B. Gemser, *Stemmen voor Waarheid en Vrede*, 62, 1915, 919 *f.* All in all, it appears to me just as certain that the Semitic representation is not the same as that of the Indo-Germanic peoples, as that the Semites by no means lacked the Mother Form, and indeed that it exerted no slight influence even on Greek ideas.

cerned. Religions that are intensely oriented towards Will turn away
from the mother to the father. The relation to the father, again, can be
spiritualized and moralized; that to the mother never completely so.
From the Lord's Prayer all natural relations are remote, but not from
the *Angelic Salutation*.[1] When he may no longer be the fructifier, the
father may be creator; the mother can only bear offspring. The father
acts with power: the mother is merely potent. The father leads his
people to their goal: the mother's child-bearing renews the cycle of
life. The mother creates life: the father history. She is Form and Power:
he Form and Will; and Animism and Dynamism carry on their final
struggle with the aid of the forms of both father and mother.

Thus we can understand how, in the history of mankind, one form
never completely supplants the other; and the form of the mother
lives on in religion because it is alive in our hearts:

> Thou—despite thy minor rôle—
> Goddess of possibilities,
> Of ultimate tragedies,
> Of ultimate happiness and sorrow—
> Mother and loved one—Both . . .[2]

J. J. Bachofen, *Urreligion und antike Symbole;* selection edited by C. A.
 Bernoulli, 3 vols.
R. Briffault, *The Mothers: A Study of the Origin of Sentiments and Institu-
 tions*, 3 vols.
A. Dieterich, *Mutter Erde*[3], 1925.
Eranos Jahrbuch, 1938, "Vorträge über Gestalt und Kult der grossen Mutter".
L. Franz, *Die Muttergötten in vorderen Orient u. in Europa*, 1937.
J. E. Harrison, *Prolegomena to the Study of Greek Religion.*
K. Leese, *Die Mutter als religiöses Symbol*, 1934.
G. van der Leeuw, *Goden en Menschen in Hellas*, 1927.
Ewald Roellenbleack, *Magna Mater im alten Testament*, 1949.

[1] *Luke* i. 28.   [2] Chr. Morgenstern, *Kleine Erde.*

CHAPTER II

POWER. WILL. SALVATION

1. THE Title of the present Chapter requires brief explanation, "Salvation" having been selected as the most suitable English equivalent for the German *Heil*, together with the occasional alternative "Deliverance"; unfortunately, neither word can be regarded as an exact rendering for the wealth of ideas implied by *Heil* itself, even though we possess many closely associated terms derived from the same root, such as heal, health, hail, hale, holy, and whole; while the Latin *salus* and the French *salut* may be added in order to clarify the very wide meaning, throughout this volume, of Salvation as always implying such concepts as whole, complete, perfect, healthy, strong, vigorous, welfare, well-being, as contrasted with suffering and misery, and in some connections bliss, both earthly and heavenly. It is in fact essentially characteristic of *Heil* itself that it may involve any one of these ideas, and sometimes all of them simultaneously; it is, in other words, universal in its significance, and indicates one of the principal sources of the religious life in all its manifestations. For the same reasons terms derived from *Heil* must be accorded a far wider range of meaning than is usual. "Saviour" (*Heiland*) thus denotes one who effects the spiritual conditions implied by the foregoing equivalents of *Heil*, or any one of these. Similarly "Holy" and "Sacred" (*Heilig*) mean being in some of these conditions, or being their cause or stimulus; "Sanctuary" (*Heiligtum*) any situation where they are aroused and experienced, while finally "The Story of Salvation" (*Heilsgeschichte*) will speak for itself; in short, the accepted, but definitely limited, English significance must be invariably expanded in the directions just indicated, so as to preclude any too rigid connotation confined to Christianity alone.

In this sense, therefore, possession of the powerful object, of the potent animal, means *salvation*. Water and trees, the fruit of the fields and the beasts in the forests, are all Bringers of Salvation; the force issuing from their power transforms the gloom of life into joy and happiness. But when felicity thus comes from without, from some potent situation, it is termed *Salvation*. "Salvation has come to us"— the cry of faith of the Reformation had its dawn in the primitive conception of a deliverance wholly unearned by man himself: Salvation therefore is Power, experienced as Good.

For a long time, however, salvation lacked form. The first saviour was the phallus which brings fertility, or its female equivalent; and subsequently, all sorts of powerful entities. For many peoples the last sheaf is the receptacle for the power of all the corn; in Värmland in Sweden, again, the housewife bakes a cake out of the flour from the last sheaf in the shape of a woman:—thus Power begins to assume definite human form; and the cake is distributed as the bread of strength to all the inmates of the household.[1] Even to-day, many a festival loaf in animal or human form has a similar origin.[2]

For long, too, the animal form remained inseparable from salvation. A very ancient invocation of the women of Elis, for example, mentions the bull Dionysus, who is to come with the *Charites*, the bearers of fertility. Elsewhere it is a green branch, or a stake adorned with vegetative symbols, that incorporates fertility. The Greeks celebrated the *daphnephoria*, and their *eiresione* resembled our palm catkins and *Palmpaschen*:

> Eiresione brings
> All good things,
> Figs and fat cakes to eat,
> Soft oil and honey sweet,
> And brimming wine-cup deep
> That she may drink and sleep.[3]

In ancient Egypt, similarly, water was salvation, the fertilizing water of the Nile floods; and this saving water became one of the chief components of the figure of Osiris the saviour, whose wanderings in the floods were probably an original feature, not introduced in the myth of his murder.[4] To rivers, in fact, sacrifices were offered long before man became conscious of any river gods.[5]

In the same way the grain often received animal form, the corn-

---

[1] Reuterskiöld, *Speisesakr.*, 116.   [2] cf. *Jer.* vii. 18.
[3] J. E. Harrison, *Prolegomena*, 80; cf. A. Dieterich, *Kleine Schriften*, 1911, 324 ff. and Zielinski's version, *The Religion of Ancient Greece*, 56,

> Eiresione brings figs, and eiresione brings loaves;
> Honey it brings in a jar, and oil to rub on our bodies,
> And a strong flagon of wine, for all to go mellow to bed on.

[4] cf. J. Frank-Kamenetzky, *AR.* 24, 1927, 240 f.
[5] cf. W. A. Murray, *Zeitschr. f. ägypt. Sprache u. Altert.*, 51, 1914, 130. ERE. Sethe, "Heroes".

stag, or cock or hare, springing from the imagination.[1] But the intense emotion of willing and suffering is also transferred to the potent or weakened fruit without any form at all; thus folklore relates the "pains of the flax".[2] Everywhere seed-time is a season of mourning, an echo of this surviving in the ballad of the afflictions and death of John Barley-corn, as modernized by Burns.

2. In the succeeding phase the human form emerges on all sides from the hitherto amorphous Power; thus the last sheaf becomes the mother of the corn, whether called Demeter or by some other name, while henceforth the tree's potency, as each year it returns to life, is styled Dionysus; and vase paintings portray this god with a human head projecting from the stake.[3]

But the salvation form expands most profusely in the representations depicting the annual renewal of growth in general. Thus Spring is a "return", or a new birth, of the saviour; and the laurel branch, which a boy brought to Delphi, was soon displaced by its bearer as representing the god.[4] Folk customs again, which have preserved the primitive for us, continue to celebrate the May king or queen. The Greeks called such a god, who arose from the seasonal changes, *kouros*, which means a youth; and certainly youth in itself, then its leader, and only ultimately its mythical type, has been accepted as saviour—not in Greece alone. The young seed, the young herd, the village youth:— all this compellingly invaded the idea of *kouros* or *kore*, whether it came to be styled Apollo or *Pfingstlümmel*, Persephone or May queen.

Several powers, moreover, may receive only a single form. It is impossible, for instance, to say that Apollo is merely the god of Spring, since he is also much more; Osiris, similarly, is the god of self-renewing vegetation. His figure was frequently constructed from fertile soil out of which ears of corn were sprouting—*Osiris végétant*.[5] We have already seen that he was, too, the god of "young" water;[6] he was also the primeval king, the bringer of culture, the god of the dead and the granter of good life in the hereafter. Thus he is actually a "saviour"

---

[1] Frazer, *The Golden Bough*, VII (*Spirits of the Corn*, I), 272 *ff.*
[2] *e.g.* M. Boehm and F. Specht, *Lettisch-litauische Volksmärchen*, 1924, 248 *ff.*
[3] J. E. Harrison, *Prolegomena to the Study of Greek Religion*, 42 *ff.* Farnell, *Cults of the Greek States*, V, 118 *f.*, 241.   [4] G. van der Leeuw, *Goden en Menschen*, 90 *f.*
[5] A. Wiedemann, *Muséon*, N.S. 4, 111 *ff.*
[6] *Pyramidentexte*, Sethe Edition, 589: "Thou art young in thy name 'young water' "; *cf.* 767, and H. Junker, *Die Stundenwachen in den Osirismysterien*, 1910, 5. *Nachtstunde*, 63.

in the fullest sense, best expressed by σωτήρ; the rescuer in case of need, and this not merely in occasional but equally in regularly recurring necessity. For the primitive mind, then, "rescuer" and "preserver" merge into one.[1]

3. Many potencies compose the form of the saviour—not that of Nature alone. Culture too is a "salvation", that is a deed that is willed or volitional. We moderns accept this as a matter of course and honour the discoverer, the author of peace, the sage. Primitive man also revered them; but he placed them on the same level as sun and Spring, as rain and animals; for to his mind, what was willed and achieved by man was in principle no different from natural events and processes. Nature and culture were one: both impelled by *a single* power and willed by *a single* will.

Thus everywhere we find prehistoric forms that taught man to plough or mine and gave him laws, but also fixed the sun in its course and rid the world of monsters and plagues of every kind. Herakles is a saviour of this type (ἀλεξίκακος), but he is at the same time *kouros*, who wins eternal life. No distinction whatever is made between occasional and permanent necessity: every necessity is in fact occasional, just as each sunrise and each Spring signify salvation. And the struggle for salvation against disaster takes on similar forms, whether it is a question of bringing a swamp under cultivation (Herakles' conflict with the Hydra), or the expulsion of darkness by the sun; fights with dragons therefore provide perhaps the most universal *motif* in the saviour myth. Whoever reads the expositions of Breysig and Ehrenreich can hardly escape the impression that the first of these investigators, in desiring to explain the idea of god as derived from some historic form of a bringer of salvation, is just as one-sided as the second, who regards the personification of Nature's power as its basis.[2] Only a combination of these two viewpoints is in fact adequate to the complexity of the actual situation.

4. God, as I have previously observed, is a late comer in the history of religion. And the remarkable thing is that, if appearances are not entirely deceptive, God the son subsisted before God the father;[3] the

[1] *cf. RGG.* Kurt Latte, Article *Heiland.*
[2] K. Breysig, *Die Entstehung des Gottesgedankens und der Heilbringer,* 1905. P. Ehrenreich, *Götter und Heilbringer, Zeitschr. für Ethnol.* 38, 1906, 536 ff.
[3] *cf.* J. E. Harrison, *Epilegomena to the Study of Greek Religion,* 18 ff.

saviour is thus a primeval form subsisting side by side with that of the mother. At all times (except during the rationalistic period) it has been easier for man to believe in the son than in the father, in youth and the future rather than in age and the past; and the saviour form is exquisitely adjusted to that of the most beautiful human figure, that of youth, whilst his will is the equivalent of youthful buoyant impetus. This is the grain of truth in the contentions of Xenophanes and Feuerbach, that man has created a God after his own image. In fact he did so create the mother and the saviour, but not the father.

K. Breysig, *Die Entstehung des Gottesgedankens und der Heilbringer*, 1905.

P. Ehrenreich, "Götter und Heilbringer", in *Zeitschr. für Ethnol.*, 38, 1906, 530 *ff*.

H. Lietzmann, *Der Weltheiland*, 1909.

A. Van Deursen, *Der Heilbringer*, 1931.

CHAPTER 12

THE SAVIOUR

1. THE *Son* brings salvation. He is not only the hope of the living, but also the consolation of the dead; and the potency of the family and the tribe is preserved by the son. When we wish for a son as the sustainer of the race we too desire salvation: we crave life, which surpasses ourselves and our own age, persists after us and is more powerful than we. Life is not only continued in the son: it is (to fall back on mathematical terms) raised to a higher power.

Where there exists a family or tribal cult, the son is its priest; this is most clearly perceived in ancient Egypt. There the *sa mr-f*, the "son whom he loves", was the administrator of the rite of sacrifice to the father and regularly brought gifts to his dead parent, thus prolonging his life in the grave. The god Horus became the prototype of the good son by safeguarding the life of his father Osiris; just as the young god imparted salvation to the old, so every good son bestowed it on his father, who had become an Osiris. He thus addressed him: "Lift up thy countenance, that thou mayest see what I have done for thee: I am thy son, I am thine heir; I have grown corn for thee, for thee I have mown wheat; the grain for thy *Wag*-festival, the corn for thy yearly feast";[1] and elsewhere: "How beautiful is it to see, how blissful to regard and view Horus when he gives life to his father, when he imparts strength to Osiris."[2]

The Egyptians expressed these acts of the good son by the word *nd*, usually translated by "revenge", but which means revenge on the father's enemy, Set, as well as all the good and the life that the son can bestow on his father:—salvation, therefore, in its most comprehensive sense.[3]

2.
>
> To another thou art child, friend;
> I see in thee the god
> Whom with awe I recognized,
> To whom flows my devotion.[4]

Into human life the saviour enters in very different forms, but his coming is always felt as the experience of Spring:

[1] *Pyramidentexte* (Sethe), 1879, *cf.* 1950.   [2] *ibid.*, 1980.
[3] *cf. ibid.*, 1558.   [4] Stefan George, *Der siebente Ring, Maximin, Kunfttag*, I.

> Now Spring has come once more . . .
> Thou sanctifiest the road and the air,
> And us also, on whom thou lookest—
> Therefore I stammer forth my thanks to thee.[1]

This is because the periodic *salvation of Spring* was probably the strongest root of belief in the saviour: in the young god's form life renews itself. His epiphany, his "day of coming" (*Kunfttag*), is the newly awakening life; and thus the saviour-god lacks that eternal constancy which is the attribute of the god of heaven and of other deities; his potency, rather, is perpetually changing, an ascending and declining power. Nature's cycle, in fact, is at one and the same moment the most saddening and the most joyous that we know. Not only the melancholy of Autumn but also Winter's famine, not merely the poetry of Spring but equally Summer's superfluity, all cooperate in the mighty form of the saviour who dies and rises again, who slumbers and awakens, who departs and reappears. Of Dionysus, for example, it was said that he had his lulling to sleep and his rising up (κατευνασμοί, ἀνεγέρσεις), and all the fully developed saviour forms show similar characteristics.[2]

But it is only rarely that Power remains merely Nature-power for long periods. To primitive man life was ever one and indivisible; and thus the visionary feelings of the mystic stimulus attached themselves to the old *kouros*-form of Dionysus, feelings that inundated Greece in early historical times; and from the periodic epiphany of the saviour there developed the historic event of the god of ecstasy's entry, overcoming the resistance of prosaic and suspicious people.[3] Thus the old Italian god of Spring, Mars, was at the same time the war-god because the commencement of the fruit year simultaneously signified the beginning of another harvest, brought in by the people as the army (*exercitus*).[4] But wherever the saviour appears the breath of Spring always dominates, whatever its narrower or later meaning may be.

3. The saviour-form appears, however, not only in the experience of the son or of Spring; there must also be considered the other type of event, already discerned in dealing with the development of the form of Power. Salvation, then, is connected not only with racial continuance,

---

[1] Stefan George, *Der siebente Ring, Maximin, Kunfttag*, III.
[2] Plutarch, *Of Isis and Osiris*, 69.
[3] Chantepie, *op. cit.*, II, 320; van der Leeuw, *Goden en Menschen*, 115 *ff.*
[4] Contrast here Kurt Latte, *AR.* 24, 1927, 251.

nor merely with the eternal repetition of Nature's life: it lives too in the inestimable boon, bestowed once for all, which is linked by memory to some single historic individual. While suffering from its childish maladies, it is true, the history of religion transformed almost all personalities that have been regarded as historical into moon-gods or some other projections of myth; but fortunately that stage has now been passed, and we see that not only many bringers of salvation actually have their roots in history, but also that at some time gods can have existed, no matter how much their human forms may be entwined with legends. This is the truth in *Euhemerism.*

But the main point here is that independently of the question, always so difficult to answer, whether a saviour has actually lived, to have existed constitutes an essential feature in his texture. Thus attempts have been made to secure a historical form for the Egyptian saviour-god Osiris,[1] and it is in fact not impossible that such a form has co-operated among the diverse components of his figure—the prehistoric god of death, the god of the Nile, the *kouros.* Still more important is it that in any case the structure of Osiris required the features of a historic man. This man was a king, or if not a king, he should have been one; for he taught men agriculture, gave them laws and culture in general,[2] as did Demeter and Triptolemus in Greece and so many more or less primitive figures to other peoples.

But we cannot assert that the bringer of culture and salvation, and the saviour, exhibit the same structure so far as Phenomenology is concerned. The bringer of salvation may also develop into a quite different form—that of the Originator.[3] This depends on whether he more resembles a son than a father, whether the characteristics in his figure have been derived from the power of age or that of youth. But this much is certain in any case:—that salvation may be historic just as well as cosmic, and that in this respect primitive man made hardly any distinction. Rites, "culture" and cosmic phenomena—all alike pertain to salvation: Jeshl or Yehl, the salvation-bringing raven of Tlingit, brings both fire and sunlight;[4] Osiris inaugurates culture, and also life from death; Herakles, again, casts down the powers inimical to culture, and overcomes death, while Christ institutes baptism and communion, bestows salvation in its most comprehensive sense, and even mediates creation.

---

[1] Frazer, *The Golden Bough*, VI (*Adonis, Attis, and Osiris*, II), 159 *f.*
[2] Plutarch, *Of Isis and Osiris*, 13.
[3] Chap. 18.   [4] Wundt, *Völkerpsychologie*, 5, 300 *ff.*

4. One root of the saviour idea, finally, springs from the experience of being healed; when man falls ill, whoever cures him is his saviour, and thus healing pertains to the operation of salvation in its most essential sense. Jesus heals: "The blind receive their sight, and the lame walk, the lepers are cleansed, and the deaf hear, the dead are raised up, and the poor have the gospel preached to them."[1] Salvation of body, and of soul, merge in the New Testament fulfilment of the prophecy of the Old Covenant: "The Spirit of the Lord is upon me, because he hath anointed me to preach the gospel to the poor; he hath sent me to heal the brokenhearted, to preach deliverance to the captives, and recovering of sight to the blind, to set at liberty them that are bruised, to preach the acceptable year of the Lord."[2] To-day too the soul's salvation still demands the cure of the body just as, conversely, every successful physician is regarded as one who, in a sense, bestows salvation. The Christian churches, however, have to some degree forgotten this connection, and are consequently penalized by the success of so many movements and prophets, like "Christian Science", that achieve faith cures. For man realizes that, despite all artificial isolation, conversion and healing go together, as will become still clearer with reference to holy men.[3]

5. The saviour myth, then, is constituted in the main by the following features:—

A. Birth, Epiphany. The saviour's appearance is miraculous; and this supernatural aspect may also be attributed to his conception. A fixed train of thought, especially among Mediterranean peoples, makes the holy child the offspring of the mother and of the divine father; and long before virginity was esteemed a moral quality, parthenogenesis was the accepted method of explaining the uniqueness of the newly born saviour—or rather of emphasizing this. Thus for the gift bestowed on the world in Plato Apollo, as well as Perictione the mother, was held responsible. Isis, again, conceived Horus, the son *par excellence*, by Osiris, only after the latter's death. For salvation rises even from death. Very beautiful in its grandiose *naïveté* is the description of Isis' joy: "Isis the excellent, who protected her brother (Osiris), who sought for him without wearying, who crossed over the whole land in her affliction without resting till she had found him; who created shade with her feathers (Isis originally had the form of a bird) and air with her

---

[1] *Matt.* xi. 5.   [2] *Luke* iv. 18 *f. Isaiah* lxi. 1, 2.   [3] Chap. 27.

wings; who cried out joyously when she brought her brother (who had been drowned) to the land; who raised the weary (*sc.* phallus) of the benumbed body (the dead man); who stole his seed and produced an heir; the child was suckled in the wilderness, the place where he was being unknown; she who, when his arm grew strong, brought him within the palace of Keb (the king of the gods)."[1]

Birth and epiphany, still further, are intrinsically the same. An old Christian tradition relates that the life of Christ as saviour commenced with His epiphany at Jordan, and cites the text: "Thou art my son, the Beloved, to-day I have become thy father."[2] Thus this is a duplicate of the account of the birth in *St. Luke* ii which follows the ordinary scheme of divine birth even though, in accordance with Hebrew feeling, it substitutes the Holy Spirit for God.[3]

But like birth, epiphany too is a springing forth from death, from the realm of the unattainable. Apollo comes from the country of the Hyperboreans: yet "neither by ships nor by land canst thou find the wondrous road to the trysting-place of the Hyperboreans".[4] It is the land at the end of the world, the fabulous country far beyond all others, whence the saviour comes. In Greece, therefore, the foreign origin of certain saviour-gods, like Apollo and Dionysus, was interpreted as an epiphany, and conversely. On the one hand Apollo is the intruder who appropriates for himself the cults of other divinities, *e.g.* that of Mother Earth at Delphi. He is the god of the victorious immigrant Hellenes, the "god of migration" (*Aguieus*) and thereby a historic saviour-form. The *paian* again, the song of victory celebrating the defeat of the python, the primeval Delphic earth snake, is the echo of a historical event; and the road which the god follows in the guise of the boy bearing the laurel, at his epiphany, is the "sacred way" of the immigrants from the North. But at the same time the country whence he comes is the mythical realm of the dead, and his unique arrival becomes a periodical event, a sojourn, *epidemia*, soon followed by a departure, *apodemia*; while the combat with the dragon is one instance of the eternal struggle between the old and the new salvations. Thus the two salvation myths, the historic and the mythical-natural, intercross, so that one becomes the expression of the other. The occurrence of salva-

---

[1] *Hymnus Bibl. Nat.* No. 20, 18th Dynasty.

[2] *Luke* iii. 22; *cf.* H. Usener, *Das Weihnachtsfest*, 1911, 40 *ff.*

[3] M. Dibelius, *Jungfrauensohn und Krippenkind (Sitz.-Ber. d. Heidelb. Akad. d. Wiss.* 1931-32, 4, 1932).—G. Erdmann, *Die Vorgeschichten des Lukas- und Matthäus-Evangeliums und Vergils vierte Ekloge,* 1932.

[4] Pindar, *Pyth.* X (Sandys).

tion bears the traits of Spring, while the experience of Spring remains eternally new and unprecedented.[1]

The epiphany is, of course, just as miraculous as the birth. The saviour performs miracles too—and not miraculous cures merely. In the Roman breviary the baptism of Christ in Jordan (that is, His epiphany) and the miracle of Cana are still linked together: before the newly appearing saviour water is converted into wine. The date of the feast of the Epiphany, January 5, was already that of the god Dionysus before it was connected with Jesus;[2] and wherever Dionysus appears, striking the earth with his thyrsus, flow forth milk, honey and wine:

> And one would raise
> Her wand and smite the rock, and straight a jet
> Of quick bright water came. Another set
> Her thyrsus in the bosomed earth, and there
> Was red wine that the God sent up to her,
> A darkling fountain. And if any lips
> Sought whiter draughts, with dipping finger-tips
> They pressed the sod, and gushing from the ground
> Came springs of milk. And reed-wands ivy-crowned
> Ran with sweet honey, drop by drop.[3]

In the struggle which the saviour must undertake, too, miracles are profuse.[4]

Miracles are portents of a new era, whether of Spring or of the World-Spring, as in Virgil's *Fourth Eclogue*. There the characteristics of the wondrous vegetation are combined with the great miracle of peace;[5] a new age of happiness dawns for the world. We too experience Spring as a marvel and understand how, conversely, the longed-for miracle of a new salvation must bear the hues of Spring.

B. Deed of Salvation. This consists in overcoming powers hostile to life, and usually bears therefore the stamp of the combat: Apollo, for example, slays the python. Similarly, Herakles' gigantic labour in performing the twelve tasks is now a cultural deed (the defeat of the hydra, *etc.*), and again a completely mythical event (procuring the

---

[1] *cf.* my Article, *Über einige neuere Ergebnisse der Psychologischen Forschung und ihre Anwendung auf die Geschichte, SM.* II, 1926, 36 *ff.*

[2] *cf.* H. Gressmann, *Tod und Auferstehung des Osiris* (*Der Alte Orient*, 23, 3), 1923, 22 *ff.* K. Holl, *Der Ursprung des Epiphanienfestes. Sitz.-Ber. d. preuss. Akad. d. Wiss.*, 1917. Ed. Norden, *Die Geburt des Kindes*, 1924. W. Bousset, *Kyrios Christos²*, 1921, 62.

[3] Euripides, *Bacchae*, 704 *ff.* (Murray).

[4] *ibid.*, 750 *ff.* and *cf.* 142 *ff.*   [5] Lietzmann, *Der Weltheiland*, 1909, 2 *ff.*

apples of the Hesperides, *etc.*), but always a struggle against death whose treasure he wins for himself—Geryon's herd, the golden apples, the horn of Achelous—by overthrowing and terrorizing death (Hades and Persephone in the underworld, Eurystheus).

But *Death* is very often linked with the deed of salvation: in the struggle the saviour himself succumbs. Here the Nature basis is perfectly clear: life in the heavens and in vegetation periodically perishes. Salvation, then, must die. Osiris, the good and just king, and at the same time the self-renewing life of the Nile, is slain by his enemy *Set*; and he shares this fate with a whole series of salvation-gods conforming to the pattern of dying Nature: *Tammuz*, *Adonis*, *Attis* in the cults of the Orient, *Hosain*, the saint of the Shiah sect, *Baldur* in the Germanic myth. "Except a corn of wheat fall into the ground and die, it abideth alone: but if it die, it bringeth forth much fruit."[1]

The saviour's death is the great sorrow, μέγα πένθος, which Egyptian *Texts* avoid naming, but which can be made good again by joy in the resurrection. In the Osiris myth joy and sorrow are divided between father and son: Horus' deed of salvation is his revenge for his father and also his resuscitation; Horus is the living and victorious saviour. But usually life and death are united in a single form.

Christianity alone, however, has transformed death itself into salvation. All saviour religions proclaim life from death, but the gospel of the Cross preaches salvation *in* death. Here complete impotence becomes the utmost development of Power: absolute disaster becomes salvation; and thus what the mystery religions dare not speak of, nor mourn, is changed to highest bliss. Death annihilates death.

C. Resurrection. Parousia. Great joy follows the great sorrow, the rejoicing of Easter morn the despair of the burial: Osiris is found by Horus or Isis and awakened from the dead. The lament for Attis precedes the *Hilaria*.

> Those who are sowing in tears
>   shall reap with shouts of joy;
> sadly they bear seed to the field,
>   gladly they bear home the sheaves.[2]

Seed-time is a time of sorrow: harvest brings an outburst of rejoicing.

Resurrection and *parousia* are interrelated as are birth and epiphany, birth and resurrection being conceived rather as mythical and periodic, epiphany and *parousia* more as unique and historic. At the end of time the saviour returns and rightly orders all. Saoshyant, for instance,

[1] *John* xii. 24.   [2] *Ps.* cxxvi. 5, 6 (Moffat).

the Persian "helper", even appears to be limited to eschatological activity, if he is not the prophet Zarathustra himself—ancient *Texts* seem to indicate this—as whose son he is usually regarded, that is in the *parousia*. Of miraculous birth, he performs the great act of salvation called *frasho kereti*, the restoration of all things, but first of all of men, who in a general resurrection receive back their bodies.[1] Many bearers of salvation remain thus concealed until the end of time, the time of greatest need: then they will appear and bring deliverance to their people. This is related of the last of the twelve Imams, one of the descendants of Ali, who disappeared in 879: bringing rescue, he will return as the *Mahdi*; and the sagas of the Emperor Frederick Barbarossa in the *Kyffhäuser* ("are the ravens still flying about the mountain?"), of the Emperor Charles in the *Unterberg*, of the three Tells in Switzerland, are all eschatological forms of one and the same yearning. To the consummating and perfecting saviour is given "all power in heaven and in earth".

6. The saviour, whose being is not of this world—for just as he "returns", so also he has existed from the beginning (*Pre-existence*)—is born when the time is "fulfilled". It is this fatefulness of the time of salvation that links the periodic form of the saviour with the historic. The May king and the *kouros* are bearers of salvation for their periods—but happiness, even if it repeats itself, is unique in our experience, and the poet knows that each Spring is equally unique, while *every* year "*everything* changes".[2] Salvation, which was granted only once and for

---

[1] Chantepie, *op. cit.*, II, 253 *f.*

[2] An ancient German *epiclesis* expresses a marvellous deliverance, and at the same time a glorification, of the Nature element in the saviour image, by connecting in its own superb yet naïve way the misery of sin and that of Winter—

> Open the heavens, O Saviour,
> From heaven, descend, descend!
> Break down the gates and doors of heaven,
> Cast off their bolts and bars!
>
> O Earth, blossom forth, blossom forth, O Earth!
> Let all be green in hill and dale!
> O Earth, bring forth this floweret,
> Arise, O Saviour, from the Earth!
>
> Here we suffer diremost need.
> Before our eyes stands eternal death.
> O come and lead us with thy powerful hand
> From misery to our Fatherland.

Everything is here: Old Testament prophecy, the hope of salvation in the new covenant, the child-bearing Mother Earth and the opening heavens, the scion of Spring and the Lord from above.

all, is nevertheless extended in festival and celebration, in sacrament and liturgy, endlessly in time and space. Around the figure of the "suffering servant of Jahveh" are united the periodic lament for Tammuz and the mourning for the lost people, the rejoicing over reawakened Nature and the cheerful hope in the descendant of David. For the outstanding factor in all salvation is that it is present, that the time is fulfilled. Thus the modern poet too finds all the ancient tones of the end of time and of new beginning, of salvation and fulfilment, in the wondrous song:

> You had eyes dimmed by distant dreams,
> And cared no more for the sacred inheritance.
> Through all space you felt the breath of the end . . .
> Now lift up your heads. For salvation has come unto you.
> In your burdened and arctic year
> A Springtime of new miracles has now burst forth.
> With flowering hand and gleaming hair
> A god has appeared and has entered your home.
>
> Now mourn no more—for you too have been chosen—
> That your days ebb away unfulfilled . . .
> Praise your city that has given birth to a god!
> Praise your days in which a god has lived![1]

[1] Stefan George, *Der Siebente Ring*, *Maximin*.

CHAPTER 13

POWER AND WILL IN MAN. THE KING

1. *LE premier qui fut roi, fut un soldat heureux.* Despite all its superficiality Voltaire's old maxim contains some truth, if only it is taken in its "primitive", and not in its original, sense. Chesterton is unquestionably right in saying that the idea of the strongest man forcibly making himself king is merely "current cant", if we disregard the mystical element of admiration which creates the ruler.[1] Yet for primitive man it is precisely power and luck that possess this mystic significance; power and will do not, as for ourselves, unite to constitute a "personality", a character, but rather an *office* or status that someone assumes; and our own expression, "his majesty", still indicates this impersonal dignity of the power which is imposed on the man and fuses with his own will. In ancient Egyptian it is called *ḥm-f*, which means literally "his club".[2] The club is both an implement and a weapon; and we have already seen that the power, emanating from the tool, meant to the primitive mind something far more than mere efficiency. It is indeed very likely, *a priori*, that the original kings were sturdy fellows who could smite hard with their clubs. But it is certain that their potency, whether attached to their clubs or their wisdom, was experienced as a power "from elsewhere". In the primitive world, then, the king is the power bearer, the saviour; and for quite a long time he remained so, while when kings *dei gratia* became constitutional monarchs, the mystic dignity became assigned to the "potent" successors, the Rienzis and Napoleons, down to the *duce* of our own time.

Thus in Melanesia the son inherits not his father's chieftainship but, if the father can so arrange affairs, that which gives him the chief's dignity, his *mana*.[3] The ruler's *mana* can, however, also be lost. When the Maori chief Hape was dying, he summoned his tribe and asked who might be in the position to stand in his footsteps and lead the people to victory. He really put this question for the benefit of his own sons, hoping to give them an opportunity to ensure the chieftainship for them-

---

[1] *The Everlasting Man* (People's Library Edition), 67.
[2] *cf.* L. Borchardt, *Die Hieroglyphe ḥm, Zeitschr. f. äg. Spr. u. Altert. K.* 37, 82. Erman-Grapow, *Wörterbuch der äg. Sprache.*
[3] Codrington, *The Melanesians,* 56 *f.*

selves; but they hesitated so long that finally a chief of low rank gave the answer, and thus they lost the authority, the *mana*.[1] Scandinavian sagas, too, tell us of a king's "luck" to which pertain victory in battle and invulnerability, healing power and good weather, particularly during sea voyages. To struggle against the king's "luck" is difficult, but "with God's help and the king (Olaf's) luck", on the contrary, one can achieve much. The king's "luck", as it were, overflows, so that under the rule of Jarl Haakon the corn grew everywhere it was sown, and herrings were to be found all round the coast; a Gothic definition of the king, again, calls him "he in whose luck we conquer". But if the harvest was bad the peasants blamed the king. Here again the "luck" is not heritable: a foundling seized the spear of the Lombard king Agilmund, and therewith the king's "luck" passed over to him, so that he was adopted and succeeded the king in the government.[2]

In describing the royal office, however, our modern expressions cannot be employed; "strong personality" is unsuitable, while "dignity" in our debased sense of a good position is equally inadequate. The term "office", or "official status" (*Amt*), then, still represents most explicitly the primitive combination of power and will that constitutes the king a saviour. How irrelevant are our present-day ideas is obvious from the familiar stories about royal children taken into combat; thus, by Tjostol Aalesön young Inge in Norway, and by Queen Fredegond young Clotaire in France, were conducted to decisive battles as guarantors of luck.[3]

The Roman *Imperium* too was regarded as an office borne by the person of an emperor or magistrate; and in the later worship of the emperors, the soul of the monarch received the *imperium* in the course of its descent through the planetary spheres. To the office, still further, corresponded potent objects as the *insignia* of kingship; the Egyptian Pharaoh was adorned with a snake, the bearer of his devastating might; and the mace and sceptre are still familiar to us to-day.

The kingship, as a power superior to its bearer himself, has been very characteristically depicted by Gerhart Hauptmann in a scene where rebels, pressing king Prospero hard, fall down before his face. Then Prospero asks:

> What has befallen me?
> Why is all dark around me? Why
> Is all my body bathed in death's cold sweat?

---

[1] Lehmann, *Mana*, 22.
[2] S. Grönbech, *Vor Folkeaet*, I, 146 *ff.*, 194; III, 49 *ff.*   [3] *ibid.*, I, 197.

and Oro the high priest replies:

> That Power, which from him struck, is all too strong
> E'en for the very soul that houses it.[1]

2. Since kingly potency is no personal capacity, all conceivable salvation is expected of it. The king's power ought to overflow; and the next most closely related consequence of this is that he should bestow gifts. "Forsooth, the king deserves the name of king only *if he distributes gifts*, rules justly, is merciful and leads a noble life before his subjects", as it says in *The Arabian Nights*. Among the old Icelandic and Anglo-Saxon *kenningar*, again, we find as poetic synonyms of "king": "dispenser of gold", "of swords", "of rings", "giver of treasures";[2] like the ancient rulers of the Orient, the German monarch too was expected to display his power by giving presents, and thus it was probably no advantage for the life purpose of the Egyptian prophet-king Akhnaton that, as we can still perceive from his monuments, he had as ruler to bestow many gifts. Those whom he favoured in this way knew how to appreciate his influence as long as it subsisted, but as soon as the royal authority had declined they allowed the king's religion to meet an ignominious end. Primitive kingship and prophetic capacity were very difficult to unite.

But royal power likewise manifests itself in matters which we moderns consider quite beyond human attainment. As a genuine saviour the king also *heals*; and until fairly recent times the "king's touch" was regarded in England as a cure for scrofula. Shakespeare describes his restorative influence, to which throngs of unfortunate people fly for aid and

> at his touch—
> Such sanctity hath heaven given his hand—
> They presently amend.[3]

Cosmic events too are subject to kingly power. The famous ruler of Bangkara in Sumatra, Si singa Mangarajah, who caused so much difficulty to the Dutch authorities, governed the rain and sunshine and blessed the harvest.[4] Similarly, the Masai king not only destroys the enemy but makes rain also, his power residing in his beard; and like Samson he loses this if he is robbed of his hair.[5] The chief of Etatin

---

[1] *Indipohdi*, Act III.   [2] A. J. Portengen, *Revue Anthr.* 35, 1925, 367.
[3] *Macbeth*, IV, 3.   [4] Wilken, *Verspreide Geschriften*, III, 166 *f.*
[5] Frazer, *The Magical Origin of Kings (Lectures on the Kingship)*, 112 *ff.*

in Southern Nigeria, again, was never permitted to leave his own house: power must be concentrated and carefully guarded. He was forced into office, and had been shut up for ten years when he gave the following description of his activities: "By the observance and performance of these ceremonies I bring game to the hunter, cause the yam crop to be good, bring fish to the fisherman and make rain to fall."[1] The curse, or the blessing, of the *datu* of Luwu in Celebes settles the prosperity of the rice harvest as well as human well-being; similarly with the sultan of Ternate in the Moluccas,[2] while Rajah Sir James Brooke (1803–1868), the ruler of Sarawak in North Borneo, was not only worshipped as a divine deliverer from the Malay power but also influenced the success of the rice crop, the water with which the women washed his feet being preserved and distributed among the farms so as to ensure a rich harvest.[3]

The classical land of royal power, however, was ancient Egypt, where the king was addressed as follows: "Thou art indeed he who canst veil the horizon; the sun rises at thy pleasure; we drink the water of the river when thou willest it, and breathe the air of heaven when thou permittest";[4] and the king makes Egypt's frontiers as wide as those "which the sun encircles". This is no swaggering nor exaggeration of a flattering Byzantinism: the king actually rules the world. Man strove to combine in one single individual all secular power and all conceivable prosperity, and the good king is thus described in excessive, yet at the same moment realistic, terms: "He illuminates the Two Lands (Egypt) more than the sun-disk. He makes the Two Lands green more than a great Nile (a plenteous flood); He hath filled the Two Lands with strength. (He is) life cooling the nostrils. . . . The king is food, His mouth is increase. He is the one creating that which is; He is the Khnum (the god who forms out of clay) of all limbs; The Begetter, who causes the people to be."[5] One of the most usual epithets applied to the monarch was "he who gives life", an expression with a double meaning since it might also signify "he on whom life was bestowed".[6] In relation to men, then, the king was the power bearer, while in

---

[1] Frazer, *The Magical Origin of Kings* (*Lectures on the Kingship*), 118.

[2] Kruyt, *Het Animisme in den Indischen Archipel*, 229 f.

[3] Wilken, *ibid.*, III, 167 f. Kruyt, *ibid.*, 231; cf. Lévy-Bruhl, *How Natives Think*, 252 ff.

[4] *Geschichte von Sinuhe*, 232 ff. cf. *Popular Stories of Ancient Egypt* (Maspero), 68 ff.

[5] Breasted, *Ancient Records of Egypt*, I, Sect. 747; cf. further Lietzmann's compilation, *Der Weltheiland*, 51 f.

[6] cf. A. Moret, *Le Rituel du Culte divin journalier*, 1902, 101.

relation to power itself he stood in need of it; and in occupying this dual position he became the original type of all the mediators between God and man.

The idea of the good king who ensures the well-being of the world is practically universal; for Confucius also knew that the general weal should be anticipated from a good prince, while the reproach for every failure could be laid on a bad one. Thus the inclination, still operative to-day among simple people, to place the blame for everything "on the government" has very old and religious roots: God, Power, really bears all the blame; only since He is too remote, man seeks some bearer of power who is nearer and can also be the scapegoat when necessary. In the Nyanza district, for instance, a hereditary king was banished from the country because of a lasting drought;[1] and Oedipus, again, had to listen to the complaint that although the land might once have extolled him as its deliverer, still it did not see why it should die of plague under his rule, and definitely expected a remedy from him.[2] Homer's description of the government of the good king is well known: "the black earth bears wheat and barley, and the trees are laden with fruit, and the sheep bring forth and fail not, and the sea gives store of fish, and all out of his good guidance, and the people prosper under him".[3] In precisely the same sense the regal power of Cyrus ensured that his soldiers, in crossing a river, should arrive safely on the other side: "the passage was considered a miraculous thing; the river had manifestly retired before Cyrus's face as for the king".[4]

In the Hellenistic era these ideas about kings received universal significance, and centred particularly upon Augustus; later, the whole of the Middle Ages is replete with them. The famous "canon attributed to St. Patrick enumerates among the blessings that attend the reign of a just king 'fine weather, calm seas, crops abundant, and trees laden with fruit' ".[5] Further, the German emperors, especially during the struggles with the Pope, stressed again and again the religious and indeed cosmic basis of their own rulership. Royal raiment, too, had possessed religious significance even when, in remote times in Egypt and elsewhere, it was only a simple primitive loin cloth. The cloak dedicated to St. Denis by Hugh Capet's consort was called *orbis terrarum*, while the emperor Henry II adorned his robe with sun,

---

[1] Frazer, *op. cit.*, 116 *f.*
[2] Sophocles, *Oedipus Rex*, 49 *f.*   [3] *Odyssey*, XIX, 109 *ff.*
[4] Xenophon, *Anabasis*, I, 4, 18; *cf.* H. Smilda, *Mnemosyne*, 1926.
[5] Frazer, *op. cit.*, 125.

moon and stars; Frederick II, similarly, "can give no completer expression to the fullness of his authority than by adorning his royal seal with a crescent couchant and a star since 1211".[1] The king's power, then, is no human might, but *the* power, the potency of the world; his imperialism is not covetousness, but an assertion of his world status, and his garb "the living garment of God". By the ancient Egyptians the "two lands" were regarded, as a matter of course, as constituting the world, while the princes of later antiquity and the Middle Ages regarded the world as their realm—no longer, however, so much as a matter of course.

3. The king, then, is a god: indeed he is one of the first and oldest gods: Power has been embodied in a living figure. For the king is no rigid god; he is rather a living, active, changeable power, a god who walks among men. But undoubtedly a god. Of course it was known all the time that this bearer of high rank was a quite ordinary man. Even the Egyptians joked about the drunkenness of the Pharaoh, Amasis,[2] and when someone called Antigonus a son of the sun and a god, he himself jocularly remarked: "Of that my bedchamber attendant knows nothing."[3] But after all it is not the man who is revered, but the official status, the power that has assumed form; and it is adored not as an immobile greatness, but as living salvation. The institution of kingship signifies, indeed, a forcible and thorough change in human life: everything was waste and misery, but now all is well. Once again the breath of Spring is wafted: "What a happy day! Heaven and earth rejoice, (for) thou art the great lord of Egypt. They that had fled have come again to their towns, and they that were hidden have again come forth. They that hungered are satisfied and happy, and they that thirsted are drunken. They that were naked are clad in fine linen, and they that were dirty have white garments. They that were in prison are set free, and he that was in bonds is full of joy."[4] That is the good tidings as it was announced at the accession of Rameses IV: the *Gospel* (*evangelium*), as people said later on.

In a still more literal sense than he is a god, the king is the son of god; and in this also he is a saviour-form. So Pharaoh declared of him-

---

[1] F. Kampers, *Vom Werdegang der abendländischen Kaisermystik*, 1924, 8 *ff*.
[2] G. Röder, *Altägyptische Erzählungen und Märchen*, 1927, 298 *ff*.
[3] Plutarch, *Of Isis and Osiris*, 24. Thus, when Alexander was wounded, he was astonished that his blood was not *ichor* "such as flows in the blessed gods". E. Bickermann, *AR*. 27, 1929, 25, Note 2.
[4] A. Erman, *The Literature of the Ancient Egyptians*, 279.

self: "I am the god, the beginning of being, nothing fails that goes out of my mouth";[1] and in the temple of Soleib Amenhotep III may still be observed adoring himself.[2] But above all the king of Egypt was literally the *son* of god, whether he appeared as the son of the sun-god, like the kings of the Fifth Dynasty, or Amon was assigned to him as his own father; and at Deir el Bahari and Luxor the temple walls exhibit in word and design a formal account of the king's birth; Amon approached the queen, and from the union of the god with mortal woman the young king sprang. Even *Psalm* ii cannot apprehend the king's intimate relationship to God otherwise than as sonship: "Thou art my Son; this day have I begotten thee".[3] Thus for the monarch a miraculous birth is quite natural.

As in birth, so at death. Even during his life the Egyptian Pharaoh was regarded as dead and endowed with eternal life. He was probably the first to whom the idea of immortality was applied; the funereal *Texts* were originally composed for him alone.[4] Similarly among the Indonesian tribes the personal continuance of life after death is thought of in connection with office, that is as limited to the tribal leaders.[5]

Naturally the sacred king is surrounded with every kind of *tabu*, to such a degree indeed that frequently kingship very closely approaches captivity, as in the case of the African ruler whose words were quoted previously. The Roman *rex* again, divested of his temporal power, of all his grandeur retained only the burdensome *tabus* as *rex sacrorum*; while in Hawaii the king was seen only by night, and whoever saw him by day was put to death; nor was he permitted to touch food with his own hand.[6] Power, concentrated in the king, must be protected.

4. The king becomes a god at the moment of his appearance; for it is precisely this *appearance* that changes the world and introduces a new era. To appear as a form is indeed the royal glory; and this we find expressed very beautifully in the song sung for the epiphany of Demetrius Poliorketes and preserved by Athenaeus: "For the other gods are too far removed from us, or they hear us not. Either they do not exist at all, or they do not concern themselves about us. But thee

---

[1] Breasted, *Records*, II, 293.

[2] G. Maspero, *Au Temps de Ramsès et d'Assourbanipal*, 1912, 46.   [3] *Ps.* ii. 7.

[4] Thus the king was the sole officiating person in worship. The Babylonian *Penitential Psalms* were composed for the king—of course in his capacity as the representative of the people—and only later used by the common folk. M. Jastrow, *Die Religion Babyloniens und Assyriens*, II, 1, 1912, 117.

[5] Kruyt, *op. cit.*, 4.   [6] Frazer, *The Belief in Immortality*, II, 388 f.

we can see with our own eyes. Thou art neither wood nor stone, but here in the very flesh. Therefore to thee we pray."[1]

The Roman cult of the emperors, too, was directed to the "god present on earth in the body, ἐπιφανής, *praesens*."[2] In him was salvation revealed and apparent; in his own era the king was the saviour. Thus in him also are to be met those historic and periodic-natural tendencies already described in dealing with the saviour. These trends even intersect most tragically. For the prince who saves his people, who has been manifested, becomes again and again the ruler who has lost his power and must depart. Far from being an "important", or even an unimportant, "personality", the king rises and sets as often as the orb with which he is frequently so intimately connected; and in *The Golden Bough* Frazer has brought out the tragic original meaning of *Le roi est mort, vive le roi* in an unforgettable manner.

Royal power, then, is world-power, but like that of the sun it is valid only for its own period. We date according to kings. In the imperial era their assumption of the government was regarded as the commencement of the world, ἀρχὴ τῶν παντών;[3] the Egyptians likewise treated the accession as a constant parallel to the commencement of all things. Thus the gospel of the new monarch is of cosmic range: he is σωτήρ in the most comprehensive sense. But he is the eternal son, and as saviour he is always the young prince; the old deposed ruler is presupposed, so that the king's first proud year succeeds the sad last year of his predecessor.

With these years of the kings a peculiar feature is associated. In Babylon the king celebrated every year a new accession day. "His reign was reckoned from the first new year's day after the death of his predecessor; his first accession he held on the first new year's day; the rest of the initial year was assigned to his dead forerunner and designated as *rêš šarruti* or the beginning of the kingship";[4] and in the earliest Egyptian era we find exactly the same procedure: on the Palermo Stone, inscribed with the oldest chronicle, the last uncompleted years of a reign are not called after any event.[5] On this feature Eduard Meyer remarks: "Here therefore full and proper years of rule are

---

[1] Bertholet, *Lesebuch*, 4, 85.
[2] H. Usener, *Dreiheit, Rh. Museum, N. F.*, 58, 23. On the peculiar and mediatory character of Roman emperor worship *cf.* E. Bickermann, *Die römische Kaiserapotheose, AR.* 27, 1929.   [3] Lietzmann, *Der Weltheiland*, 14 *f.*
[4] S. Mowinckel, *Psalmenstudien*, II, 1922, 7.
[5] *cf.* K. Sethe, *Beiträge zur ältesten Geschichte Ägyptens*, 1905, 70 *ff.* But he ascribes this peculiarity to the purely chronological purpose of the enumeration.

reckoned beginning with the day of the king's accession and ignoring the calendar year, just as at present, in charters, the years of the reign of the pope and of the king of England are calculated".[1] Each king thus begins anew, after he has put a score under the reign of his predecessor; each has his own era. Now we can understand this if we regard the monarch as the bearer of power; for the power is always new, and the king always a new king. He is never a mere continuation, but always an appearance, a new beginning; and this point of view concerns itself just as little with the particular events of any period as with the "important" personality of the ruler. Life is imprisoned within a dogma to which it must adapt itself; a net is extended over life in order to hold fast the power; its circulation is sustained by notches in the tally of time, just as is the circulation of light by the change of night and day. The king, then, signifies permanence in change.

The Egyptians said of him that he "renews life"; and this was intended in a very literal sense. For change, as it was actually experienced —and here the historic line intersects the periodic—occurred apart from the fixed times for change; but any such accidental and unforeseen waning of the power that revealed itself in the king could not be tolerated, since bodily or mental weakness in the monarch might be detrimental to the whole of life. Hence that assignment of a time limit to the monarchy, to which Frazer has devoted a great part of his work, and which found clear expression in the ancient Egyptian feast of *Sed*. Usually this is interpreted as the jubilee of a reign; but it has in fact a deeper meaning. Eduard Meyer, again, referred to "an imposing of limits to kingship", which began, as it were, for a second time with this feast.[2] During the festival a sort of coffer stood before the king in which, just as at burials, there lay a veiled form probably representing the embryo, thereby symbolizing in a drastic way the king's rebirth.[3] The "old" king, who actually wore funereal dress, was thus confronted by the new one; the king, as it were, succeeded himself.

Regal power, still further, is confined within its human form only for an appointed period. The name of the ancient Roman festival,

---

[1] In Sethe, *Beiträge zur ältesten Geschichte Ägyptens*, 1905, 73.

[2] *Geschichte des Altertums*, I, 2³, 1913, 153.

[3] Yet this muffled form was also otherwise interpreted—*e.g.* as a little princess. But it is not clear how the princess could serve as a permanent requisite of the regal ceremony. P. E. Newberry gives a very clever, but somewhat far-fetched, explanation in *Ägypten als Feld für anthropologische Forschung* (*Der alte Orient*, 27, 1), 1927, 21. On the feast of *Sed*, *cf.* W. B. Kristensen, *Meded. Kon. Akademie van Wetenschappen, Afd. Lett.* 56, B. 6, 1923, 16.

regifugium, was interpreted by Frazer as a vestige of a time when the ruler actually had to take flight after the expiration of his time limit or else, as can still be proved of the *reges nemorenses*, the kings of the woodlands, of Aricia, had to defend himself against a pretender to the throne. Even at the coronation of English kings, until that of Edward VII, a herald challenged all those to come forward who might question the sovereign's right to the throne.[1] The issue, then, is clear: Power must manifest and maintain itself, and this not only at the accession but perpetually. We must of course recall the fact that Power is no affair of mere theory, but always an empirically authenticated and experienced greatness. I do not wish, however, to cite all the examples of time-limited kingship, of which Frazer has compiled a large number:[2] I shall draw attention only to essentials.

After a certain interval therefore, after power had departed from him, the king must actually die. Of this the Egyptian feast of *Sed* and the Roman *regifugium* were modifications; and many primitive peoples are known who actually killed the "old" king. Here too the saviour must suffer and die. He might wait till he was killed, but also he might himself surrender to death; and of this too Frazer has compiled many instances. In all this the conception of sacrifice plays a part; the king should sacrifice himself for the good of his people. But yet another idea arose—that of the substitute, which attained the highest significance in the development of the concept of the saviour.

Thus once again two originally and basically different ideas are united in one. Actually, the king is always the substitute: he supervises his people's salvation, performs sacrifices, leads to war, *etc.*, and when he dies he dies for the people in order that its power should be preserved. Even his corpse could bring salvation: the body of the Swedish king Halfdan the Black was distributed to four districts, so that it might ensure a rich harvest for them all.[3] But side by side with this idea another emerges: the old custom is mitigated; the king does not actually die, but allows a substitute to be executed. This is the mock king who exercises the princely power for a brief time, usually for only one day, and is then killed; later, he is merely maltreated. This king-for-a-day, generally a slave or war prisoner, is to be found as early as Babylon, and still played his part at the Roman Saturnalia. In an Assyrian pantomime there occurs a dialogue between the mock king and his

---

[1] Frazer, *The Magical Origin of Kings* (*Lectures on the Kingship*), 275.
[2] *The Golden Bough* IV, (*The Dying God*), 14 *ff*, 46 *ff*.
[3] *Ibid.*, VI (*Adonis, Attis and Osiris*, II), 100 *ff*.

lord; the *pseudo*-king now gives orders to his master; he desires to eat, drink, love a woman, *etc.* Everything is granted him; but the end of the story is that his neck is broken and he is thrown into the river; thereby he assumes the place of the god Bel, who also dies to rise again.[1] Probably the king himself had to die originally as the substitute for the god, that is for the country's power; and then the two "substitutes" gradually fused into a single form.

For a long time this type of the innocent king-for-a-day, suffering in a ridiculous manner, vividly persisted in Literature. We recall Christopher Sly in Shakespeare's *Taming of the Shrew*, allowed as master to give orders and enjoy things for a day, but then thrown into the street again.[2] "Behind the disgraceful mask of the fallen or transient king, our ancestors perceived the tragic figure of the God-Man who died for the well-being and life of his neighbour."[3] The substitutive sacrifice for man's salvation gradually expanded into one of the great world-moving thoughts, and became linked to the change of kings. To preserve this salvation the figure of the saviour must be broken; and Frazer and other investigators have advanced the view that Jesus was maltreated by the Roman soldiers in the character of the mock-king already familiar to them from the Roman Saturnalia.[4] But even if this cannot be proved, still the King of the Jews on the Cross bears all the features of the king dying for the salvation of his people; and he still remains a king in the apotheosis, in St. John's Gospel: "Art thou a king then?—Thou sayest that I am a king."[5]

That the king must suffer is involved in the conception of the periodic change of life. The Old Testament was aware that when life is regarded historically, and when its periodic vicissitudes have been replaced by the rule of the sovereign Will, then whoso brings salvation must also suffer. The "suffering servant of Jahveh" too, particularly when he is the representative of the people, exhibits all the traits of the king.[6]

---

[1] E. Ebeling, *Keilschrifttexte aus Assur religiösen Inhalts*, 1917, *Nr.* 96. *cf.* F. M. Th. Böhl, *Stemmen des Tyds*, 10, 1920, 42 *ff.* H. Zimmern, *Berichte über die Verhandl. der sächs. Gesellsch. der Wiss.*, 1906, 1918.

[2] In other Literatures also: Dutch, *Krelis Louwen* (Langendyk); Danish, *Jeppe fra Bjerget* (Holberg).   [3] A. Moret, *Mystères Égyptiens*, 1913, 273.

[4] *cf.* P. Wendland, *Hermes*, 33, 1898, 175. H. Vollmer, *Jesus und das Sacaeenopfer*, 1905. J. Geffcken, *Hermes*, 41, 1906, 220 *ff.* Frazer, *The Golden Bough*, IX (*The Scapegoat*), 412 *ff.* Further in R. Bultmann, *Die Geschichte der Synoptischen Tradition*[2], 1931, 294. E. Klostermann, on *St. Mark* xv, 16 *ff.* in *Handbuch zum Neuen Testament*.

[5] *John* xviii. 37.

[6] F. M. Th. Böhl, *De "Knecht des Heeren" in Jezaja* 53, 1923. Böhl kindly writes to inform me that, in his opinion, the manner in which, in *Isaiah* xlix. 7, 23, liii. 15, the kings of the nation are compared with the "servant" who is identified with Israel,

5. In accordance with his type, still further, the bringer of salvation for his era always comes "again", whether as the son or as his own successor; and this hope of a definite return is also attached to the king-experience. This longing is constituted by the expectation of periodically renewed salvation and the yearning for happy "last days", for the harmonious fading away of history under a "good king".

Of such a king the ancient Egyptians had a vague anticipation: "A king will come from the South . . . the people of the days of this son of man will rejoice . . . they will remain far from evil. The godless too will humble their faces because of fear before him . . . the uraeus (royal snake) on his forehead will appease the rebels . . .";[1] the "good king's" reign was always a messianic era.[2] But as soon as the historic consciousness developed, and the idea of periodicity gave place to that of the end of the world, this epoch of salvation became transferred to the end of time, transposed to the far off and happy distance. What the Jews longed for from the branch of the line of David is universally known, and is most beautifully expressed in *Psalm* lxxii by the song of the good king:

> May he prove the champion of the weak,
>   may he deliver the forlorn,
>   and crush oppressors!
> Long may he live, long as the sun,
>   as the moon that shines for ever!
> May his rule be like rainfall upon meadows,
>   like showers that water the land!
> Justice and welfare flourish in his days,
>   till the moon be no more!
> From sea to sea may his domain extend,
>   from the Euphrates to the earth's far end! . . .
> all kings do homage to him,
>   all nations yield to him!
> For he saves the forlorn who cry to him,
>   the weak and helpless;
> he pities the forlorn and weak,
>   he saves the lives of the weak,

involves that the "servant" must also be conceived as king. "Servant" is the counterpart of "king". At the New Year Festival the king assumes the rôle of the servant, and the latter that of the king.

[1] W. Golénischeff, *Rec. de Travaux*, 15, 1893, 87 *ff*. (*Pap.* 1116 *Ermit. St. Petersburg*). *cf.* J. W. Breasted, *Development of Religion and Thought in Ancient Egypt*, 211 *f*. L. Dürr, *Ursprung und Ausbau der israelitisch-jüdischen Heilserwartung*, 1925, 1 *ff*.

[2] *cf. e.g.* Lietzmann's description of the reign of a Babylonian king, *op. cit.*, 20 *ff*.

he rescues them from outrage and oppression—
  they are not cheap to him . . .
May the land be rich in waving corn,
  right up to the top of the hills!
May the folk flourish like trees in Lebanon,
  may citizens flower like grass in the field!
For ever blessed be his name,
  sure as the sun itself his fame!
All races envy his high bliss,
  all nations hail him as the happy king![1]

In the Middle Ages these ideas became connected with the great emperors Charlemagne and Frederick II (Barbarossa); they were not dead, but were waiting in the mountain for the day of the nation's direst need, to deliver it. Perhaps owing to the general belief in a definite limit fixed for Frederick's life, in the thirteenth century people doubted that he was actually dead, and indeed on several occasions false Fredericks successfully appeared.[2] Reformation of the church, again, was included in the universal welfare to be realized by the emperor. Thus when Power can no longer be linked with any actually visible form, the saviour-form of the ruler is placed at the close of time, as was supposed to have been inscribed on king Arthur's grave:— *Hic jacet Arthurus Rex quondam Rexque futurus*: "Here lies Arthur, sometime king, and king to be."

The kingly figure, then, is one of the most momentous of all those that man has depicted for himself. To derive the entire belief in God from the deification of rulers, however, would be just as stupid as to ignore the prominent rôle which the saviour-king has played in evolving that concept of God which tends to assume the form of a *numen praesens*, a son. Again and again humanity has sought to base the transient form and changing will of man upon the changeless essence and the eternal Will controlling the Universe; and thus the Chinese mystic also assigns to the ruler a place in direct relationship to *Tao*:

There are four great ones in the space of the world,
And the ruler of men is one of these.
As his prototype Man has the Earth,
As its prototype Earth has Heaven,
As prototype Heaven has *Tao*—the Universal Order—
And as prototype *Tao*, this Universal Order, has itself.[3]

[1] Moffat.
[2] Fr. Pfister, *Die deutsche Kaisersage und ihre antiken Wurzeln*, 1928.
[3] *Tao-teh King*, 25; cf. Chap. 2.

CHAPTER 14

THE MIGHTY DEAD

1. EARLY Animism derived religion from the cult of ancestors; and in so far as, in fact, the dead are accounted powerful, this was quite correct. It is, however, not their "souls" which possess power but they themselves, their living-dead forms; and to Animism Form is always indispensable. The dead man, then, is no soul without body, but another corporeality which may be more potent even than the living, but can also lose some of its power; for the event of death, which will be discussed later,[1] enhances, but also enfeebles, power.

In no case, however, can the cult of the dead be regarded as the outcome of any primitive psychology. It is derived, rather, from an actual *experience*: its roots lie in the meeting with the dead.[2] Such an encounter is by no means rare in our own still superstitious days; but probably the theorists of Animism have seen no spectres!

It is not, however, a fact that *all* the dead are powerful. It depends on the influence they enjoyed during their life-time, and also on the circumstances under which they died. In virtue of their rank, for instance, tribal leaders usually possess power after death also, and there are even cases where continued life after death is limited to the bearers of power;[3] originally the ancient Pharaohs appear to have been alone in their enjoyment of immortality. The conditions attending death are also important: women dying in child-bed often have a specific power after death. But in many cases a special potency is ascribed, by gradual stages, to all the dead.

2. So far as *Form* is concerned, however, the might of the dead is thought of as dwindling away. They lead a shadow life; the fixed outlines and concrete substance of Form have given place to something quite nebulous and misty. On Ceramlaut, for example, the recently dead appear as a white mist, and those who have been dead for some time as shadows.[4] The dead, again, cannot be grasped, but can be seen

---

[1] Chap. 22.

[2] *cf.* K. Th. Preuss, *Glaube und Mystik im Lichte des höchsten Wesens*, 1926, 19.

[3] Söderblom, *op. cit.*, 28; Preuss, 30.

[4] J. G. F. Riedel, *De Sluik- en Kroesharige rassen tusschen Selebes en Papoea*, 1886, 163.

through; they have no bones.[1] Occasionally they are imagined as being smaller than the living.[2] But even though the form has disappeared to a great extent, it is still there: the dead man resembles the living; he can be recognized, seen and spoken to.

3. Opposed to the annihilation of power that thus affects Form, however, is an enhancement that applies to Will; and thus the opinion that the living are always "on the right side of the fence" is neither primitive nor religious. In pantheistic vein, a Dutch poet renews the honouring of the dead in writing of his dead son: "From my own immediate feeling I understand now the essence of the worship of the dead which was common to all civilized peoples. Even in his last days my child was sacred to me, when he had found peace. Now, after his departure, he is a being of a higher order: he has become divine, he is my mediator; through him the Being of the Universe became tangible and personal, something which I can love and to which I can speak, not a mere ceremonial sound nor a vague auto-suggestion."[3] The dead, then, are more potent than the living: their will imposes itself: it is irresistible. They are superior in strength and insight, they are the κρείττονες;[4] this concept is particularly explicit in Scandinavian culture, and in this connection suicide, in order to gain power to execute one's threats against the living, is a wholly practical idea.[5]

To the dead, still further, is ascribed cosmic power; here too Animism was correct in asserting that in their effectiveness Nature-spirits and the dead are not to be separated. Yet they themselves are not "spirits", but simply deceased. In New Zealand, for example, a dead medicine-man or chief is invoked for rain and fertility,[6] while in Indonesia the dead can protect in the perils of war, guard from misfortune at sea and make fishing and hunting highly productive.[7] The Greek *trito-patores*, too, were at the same moment dead ancestors and demons of the wind.[8]

Yet when human life is placed on the same level as vegetative life, and the dead are intimately allied with the grain dying in the earth and then springing up from it, Power is always a mere *unity*. The

[1] N. Söderblom, *Int. Review of Missions*, 1919, 533.
[2] Fr. von Duhn, *AR.* 12, 1909, 179 f., Table III, on the sarcophagus of Haghia Triadha.   [3] Frederik van Eeden, *Paul's ontwaken.*
[4] E. Rohde, *Psyche*, I [5-6], 1910, 246, and Note 2, who refers to Plutarch, *Cons. ad. Apoll.* 27. English Translation, 166, 201.
[5] H. and I. Naumann, *Isländische Volksmärchen*, 1923, Nr. 64.
[6] Alviella, *Idée de Dieu*, 113.
[7] Wilken, *op. cit.*, III, 190.   [8] B. Schweitzer, *Herakles*, 1922, 75 f.

altar of Consus in the *circus maximus* was simultaneously a granary
and the dwelling-place of the dead.[1] Burial is a sort of seed sowing.
The Roman family *lar*, again, expanded from a domestic god and
family ancestor to the god of a district: *lar compitalis*, the deity of the
cross-roads.[2]

4. The dead exercise their power over man in both a propitious
and a disastrous way. They are terrible, and at their approach men are
filled with dread. Of women dying in child-bed I have already spoken,
while in Indonesia the *pontianak* is a gruesome figure: hollow backed,
it sits in the tree-tops in the guise of a bird, causes miscarriages, and at
midnight robs men of their masculine vigour. On the Island of Borneo
again, before the founding by Abdu 'l Rahman of the town named
after them, one was compelled to shoot for two hours at the *pontianak*
lurking in the vicinity before approaching the settlement.[3] In ancient
Egypt, similarly, there were formulas to protect the pyramids from the
attacks of the dead.[4] Greece too had its dreadful dead, who worked
evil on the living and dragged them down to death; tormenting spirits
of this type were the harpies and sirens. Hecate's gloomy retinue
raged through the night, Dionysus too being regarded as the leader
of a "wild hunt". This notion was later developed during Germanic
antiquity and the Middle Ages: Wotan, "the furious", dashes about
with his wild company on stormy nights; he and the *Perchta* are the
exact counterparts of Dionysus and Hecate with their *thiasos* or *komos*,[5]
while in the Middle Ages the dead bore off the living to a gruesome
dance or the most wretched nuptials.[6]

From time to time this belief in the dead leads to a sort of fatalism,
especially among primitive peoples: the power of the dead is so much
stronger than that of the living that one surrenders completely to
them; they thus control custom and usage, so that any deviation draws
their anger in its train, as *e.g.* among the Bataks.[7] The excessively
powerful will of the dead dominates the whole of life; the "living
exist under the shadow of the dead".[8]

[1] A. Piganiol, *Recherches sur les Jeux romains*, 1923, 2; *cf.* 13.
[2] *cf.* S. Wide in Gercke and Norden, *Einleitung in die Altertumswissenschaft*, II[2],
1912, 241. Chantepie, *op. cit.*, II, 435.
[3] Wilken, *op. cit.*, III, 223 *ff.*   [4] *Pyramidentexte* (Sethe), 1656.
[5] *cf.* Beth, *Einführung in die vergleichende Religionsgeschichte*, 92.
[6] *cf.* my Monograph: *In den hemel is eenen dans*, 1930, 20 *f.* (*In dem Himmel ist ein
Tanz, Munich.*)
[7] *cf.* J. C. van Eerde, *Inleiding tot de Volkenkunde van Ned. Indie*, 1920, 190 *f.*
[8] N. Adriani, *Het animistisch heidendom als godsdienst*, 44. *ibid.*, Posso, 64.

But they can also exert a beneficent influence: I have previously observed how they rule the elements to the advantage of the living. Usually they protect their own people; thus the Greek *heros* was a sort of domestic demon; buried under the threshold, he occasionally showed himself to the inmates of the house in the guise of a snake.[1] In Vedic India, again, the young wife sacrificed to the ancestors and implored them to bless her with children.[2] For the dead are either the forbears, the heads of the family, whose power over their people has been enhanced by death (as will be observed later) or else they are that sinister troop, the throng of the dead. But the ghost of anyone, whether related by blood or not, can inspire dread and oppress; and with this we return to the experience of:

5. *The encounter with the dead*, which lies at the base of every form of their worship. Nordic and Icelandic sagas afford marvellous examples of the horror and devastating power emanating from the dead, as for example in the story of Grettir the Strong and the spectre Glam. The shepherd Glam, a sinister fellow, is slain by a ghost. Then he too begins to haunt the place and many people meet him: "that brought them great hurt, for when they saw him some fell fainting, and others lost their reason". He commenced to straddle the ridges of the roofs of the farm and walked both by day and night; people hardly ventured to come into the valley any longer. He continued, however, to kill cattle and people till at last he was slain once more by Grettir the Strong; but his victory procured him only bad luck.[3]

On certain days hosts of dead invade the settlements of the living:— on Ceramlaut, every Thursday, they visit their relatives from sunset to cockcrow. A meal is prepared for them: if this is omitted they lay a curse on the house.[4] In Cambodia, likewise, little boats filled with rice and cakes, *etc.*, are made for the dead, and floated on the river so that they may travel in them;[5] while on All Souls' Day a sacrifice of food or candles should be offered, lest the dead become hurtful to us. But when they have eaten their fill they are driven away: "Out of the door, ye souls, the anthesteria is over"; in Greece they were with these words ejected through the door, and with almost the same formula in

[1] *cf.* S. Wide, *Lakonische Kulte*, 1893, 280. J. E. Harrison, *Prolegomena to the Study of Greek Religion*, 325 *ff.*

[2] H. Oldenberg, *Die Religion des Veda*[2], 1917, 332, *cf.* 308.

[3] Naumann, *Isländische Volksmärchen*, Nr. 69.

[4] Riedel, *Sluik-en kroesharige rassen*, 163.

[5] Frazer, *The Golden Bough*, VI (*Adonis, Attis and Osiris*, II), 61 *f.*

Vedic India.[1] On days when the departed walk there is power in the air: we should take care, there are "polluted days"; thus in ancient Rome there were some days during which *mundus patet*, that is the ancient vault, into which also the first fruits were thrown, remained open. Then the dead walked, especially in February, the month of purification; the temples were closed, marriages should not be celebrated, the graves were adorned with flowers and sacrifices offered to the dead. For three days during May, again, the *lemures* were about; at midnight the farmer appeared at his door and threw black beans over his shoulder to buy off the terrible power: "when he has said nine times, 'Ghosts of my fathers, go forth'! he looks back, and thinks that he has duly performed the sacred rites".[2]

The *twelve nights* too were potent times, each of them deciding the weather for one month of the coming year; work was at a standstill, for spirits walked; and in Mecklenburg people avoided calling animals by their names from fear of the wild huntsman.[3] During All Souls the Tyrolese leave the uneaten cakes on the table together with burning candles for the poor souls, who are said to come from Purgatory to earth at the angelus on All Souls' Day, while in ancient Prussia it was the custom to hold a wake some days after the funeral: afterwards a priest swept the house and chased out the souls with the words: "Ye have eaten and drunken, ye departed, go out, go out."[4]

Thus in the first place sacrifice to the dead is a payment of ransom; but its purpose is also their sustenance, and if they are generously disposed they even appear as benefactors; at the Greek funeral feast the dead man was the host, ὑποδέκτης, and the saying *de mortuis nil nisi bene*, which we have converted into an affair of piety, was seriously observed.[5]

It is, however, when intercourse with the dead is interpreted as marriage that it assumes its most dreadful form: Antigone had to descend into the *thalamos* of Hades, while Iphigenia, Helen and Cassandra were regarded as brides of Hades.[6] In popular belief it is not death, but a dead man, who is the bridegroom: and Bürger's *Leonore*

---

[1] Rohde, *Psyche*, I[5-6], 236 *ff*. English Translation, 168, 197. Oldenberg, *Religion des Veda*, 550: "Avaunt, ye fathers, ye friends of *soma*, to your deep and ancient ways. But return a month hence to our home, rich in posterity, in male offspring, to eat the sacrifice."

[2] Ovid, *Fasti*, V, 429 *ff*.   [3] Reinsberg-Düringsfeld, *Das festliche Jahr*, 464 *f*.

[4] E. Samter, *Geburt, Hochzeit und Tod*, 1911, 32.

[5] Rohde, *Psyche*, I, 231 *f*.: ἐιώθεσαν οἱ παλαιοὶ ἐν τοῖς περιδείπνοις τὸν τετελητευκότα ἐπαινεῖν, καὶ εἰ φαῦλος ἦν. E. T. 170.

[6] L. Malten, *Der Raub der Kore*, AR. 12, 1909, 311.

has given this theme its classical form. But even in the horror of the
encounter with the departed there still lives the conviction that life
comes from them. The Greek festival of All Souls is called the "festival
of flowers", and even marriage with death has been transformed by
mysticism into a form of bliss:

> Death calls us to the nuptials—
> Brightly the lamps are burning—
> The virgins are at hand—
> There is no lack of oil.[1]

[1] Novalis, 5. *Hymne an die Nacht.*

CHAPTER 15

THE AWFUL FORM, THE EVIL WILL: DEMONS

1. "ANIMISM" was right, too, in maintaining that the boundary between the dead and every kind of spirit, even gods, is always plastic. But the spirit world is by no means confined to the realm of the departed. Admittedly, many demonic forms originated from belief in the dead and in spectres; I need say no more about this at present. But Power was experienced in other forms also; and in so far as the potent *will* is here again decisive in creating these forms, belief in demons is animistic. The powers of life are felt and perceived as terrifying, often indeed as devastating, and always as incalculable; and World-power, divided among many petty rulers, is placed in the hands of despotism and inconstancy. If this belief in demons predominates, a persistent fear haunts human life, as was the case among many primitive peoples; but if it can merely assume its position among other opinions—as *e.g.* in our own civilization—then it leads to superstition.

2. Neither fear nor superstition, however, is ever the outcome of reflection. Belief in demons does not mean that chance rules the Universe, but rather that I have experienced the horror of some power which concerns itself neither with my reason nor my morals;[1] and it is not fear of any definite concrete terribleness, but vague terror of the gruesome and the incomprehensible, which projects itself objectively in belief in demons. Horror and shuddering, sudden fright and the frantic insanity of dread, all receive their form in the demon; this represents the absolute horribleness of the world, the incalculable force which weaves its web around us and threatens to seize us. Hence all the vagueness and ambiguity of the demon's nature: "the characteristic of the *troll* is the malicious lack of plan which adheres to his whole way of acting, as opposed to that of man, who in all his deeds, for good or evil, is conscious of his own purpose . . . his eyes are so wicked that one glance from them suffices to burn away the fertility of a province, and it is this psychic chaos that results in his mere proximity invoking gloomy delusions".[2] The awe-inspiring character of demons is impres-

---

[1] *cf.* Otto, *The Idea of the Holy,* 126 *ff.*
[2] V. Grönbech, *Vor Folkeaet i Oldtiden,* II, 1912, 180.

sively described in the Babylonian *Prayer Against the Seven Evil Spirits*:

> Seven are they, seven are they,
> In the Ocean Deep seven are they,
> Battening in Heaven seven are they,
> In the Ocean Deep as their home they were reared,
> Nor male or female are they,
> They are as the roaming windblast,
> No wife have they, no son do they beget;
> Knowing neither mercy nor pity,
> They hearken not unto prayer or supplication.
> They are as horses reared among the hills;
> The Evil Ones of Ea,
> Throne-bearers to the gods are they.
> They stand in the highway to befoul the path.
>
> From land to land they roam,
> Driving the maiden from her chamber,
> Sending the man forth from his home,
> Expelling the son from the house of his father,
> Hunting the pigeons from their cotes,
> Driving the bird from its nest,
> Making the swallow fly forth from its hole,
> Smiting both oxen and sheep.
> They are the evil spirits that chase the great storms,
> Bringing a blight on the land. . . .
> Upon themselves like a snake they glide,
> Like mice they make the chamber stink,
> Like hunting dogs they give tongue.[1]

The malicious inadequacy of all that happens and the irrationality at the very basis of life receive their form in the manifold uncanny and grotesque apparitions that have inhabited the world from time immemorial. The demons' behaviour is arbitrary, purposeless, even clumsy and ridiculous, but despite this it is no less terrifying. In Lithuania, for instance, the *Laumen* can work very quickly, but they can neither commence nor finish anything.[2] The *trolls* again, as is well known, are hollow backed, and utter duffers. Even the Devil is absurd, the "stupid" devil who is outwitted and whom the hero of the fairy

[1] R. Campbell Thompson, *The Devils and Evil Spirits of Babylonia*, I, 1903, 77, 31, 33, 155; *cf.* O. Weber, *Die Literatur der Babylonier und Assyrier*, 1907, 166 *ff*. K. Frank, *Babylonische Beschwörungsreliefs*, 1908, 20 *f*.
[2] W. Böhm and F. Specht, *Lettisch-litauische Märchen*, 1924, No. 9.

tale reviles just as valiantly as the modern pietist.[1] Nevertheless this laughing at demons never rings true; there is too much horror mixed with it, as Ibsen, in spite of all his modern irony, understood and expressed so marvellously in the scene in *Peer Gynt* where the Hall of the Old Man of Dovrë, and the goings on of the *trolls*, are described. Otto and Karl Jaspers,[2] again, have indicated the demonic in Goethe, and whoever wishes to understand the experience of the demon will find his best teacher in the modern poet. None better than Goethe has experienced the contradictory, terror-inspiring and incomprehensible side of life and rendered it vivid to us—of course completely freed from the forms of primitive mentality. Towards the close of his *Autobiography*[3] he looks back on the life of the boy and youth which he has just depicted:—"whilst he wandered to and fro space which lay intermediate between the sensible and suprasensible regions, seeking and looking about him, much came in his way which did not appear to belong to either; and he seemed to see, more and more distinctly, that it is better to avoid all thought of the immense and incomprehensible. He thought he could detect in nature—both animate and inanimate, with soul or without soul—something which manifests itself only in contradictions, and which, therefore, could not be comprehended under any idea, still less under one word. It was not godlike, for it seemed unreasonable; not human, for it had no understanding; nor devilish, for it was beneficent; nor angelic, for it often betrayed a malicious pleasure. It resembled chance, for it evolved no consequences; it was like Providence, for it hinted at connection. All that limits us it seemed to penetrate; it seemed to sport at will with the necessary elements in our existence; it contracted time and expanded space. In the impossible alone did it appear to find pleasure, while it rejected the possible with contempt." We may designate this demonic aspect—again with a typical term from Goethe—the *inadequate*: it is at the same moment the criticism advanced by the logical human will upon the frenzy of events, and by the colossal higher Power on the feeble will of man. In the demon form, then, man's will shatters itself against the irrational harshness of the Universe, while in the demon's own will the hard world crushes the form of humanity. And the end is grotesque distortion, nightmare, madness.

---

[1] For an example of the latter *cf.* Fr. Zöller, *Die Möttlinger Bewegung, Religionspsychologie*, 4, 1928, 74, in which the leader of a sect refers to the devil as a "miserable sow".   [2] *Psychologie der Weltanschauungen*[2], 1922, 193 *ff.*
[3] *Works*, V, 422, 423; *Truth and Fiction*, Book 20. (Nimmo's Edition).

3. The demonic figure emerges from extremely diversified experiences: the wildness and fearfulness of uncultivated land, the solitude of mountain regions far from fruitful valleys :—these are the *experiences of Nature* that have contributed most towards the creation of this form. Within enclosed human dwelling-places security holds sway; but outside, in field and mountain, live the *trolls*, the *utukku* of Babylonian religion, the *jinns* of Islam; and in a Jewish legend spirits which have crept into a house are cast out into the desert, their true realm, by a decree of the courts; they too take refuge in forest and wilderness.[1] Between the Nature-demons and man rules enmity, with the sole exception that man, aware of his own superiority over the helpless figures, renders them occasional service, as for example when the human woman succours the demon woman in child-bed. Apart however from the contrast between cultivation and the desert, between subservient and arbitrarily ruling power, the experience of Nature with her manifold mysteries also tended to induce the creation of this form. Thus the power of time unites with that of place: awe-inspiring midnight is haunted by the horrid forms of the wild hunt, while sultry noon heat awakens dread in the heart of the lonely shepherd whom the *meridianus daemon* torments and who has seen the fearful and fantastically distorted figure of Pan.[2] In addition to these, again, there are all the greater and lesser fears of forest and field. Each Thing has its own mysterious and incalculable aspect, each experience of Nature its own demon: pixies, moss and wood fairies, elves, dwarfs, *etc.*, inhabit waters and forests, fields and the subterranean caverns of the mountains, in German popular belief, and to this analogies can be found everywhere.

Side by side with Nature, again, is the *experience of Dreams*. It is not so-called "free imagination", formerly held to be responsible for the creation of every form, that generates demons, but rather the organically articulated imagination of the dream, which appears with all the force of actuality therein. First of all there is the dream of *dread*: the Greek *empusa*, which has one leg of ass dung and the other of iron,[3] is a creature of the dream of dread. All the bogeys that terrorized our childhood dreams had for us the same reality as they possess in popular belief; all the fears of the day have crept into our sleep and there exert

---

[1] *Der Born Judas*, VI, 277.
[2] The "rye-aunt" too wanders at midday in the cornfield to terrify men; H. W. Heuvel, *Volksgeloof en Volksleven*.
[3] *cf.* L. Radermacher, *Aristophanes' "Frösche"*, 1922, 175 *f.*

their power in terrifying form. The Greek *Lamia*, for one, the child murderess: the Babylonian-Assyrian *Labartu* too, who lurks in morass and mountain, and against whose calamitous influence children wore amulets around their necks. The *nightmare* is an intensification of the experience of dread: in Greece *Ephialtes*, in German countries the *trude, etc.* Similarly, the sudden night attack of the demon that shuns the day (*Genesis* xxxii) is probably correctly interpreted by Roscher as the description of a nightmare.[1]

With the dream experience is connected the *sexual* root of the idea of the demon; for the sexual or ejaculatory dream called into existence the countless forms of *incubi* and *succubi*. Thus the Babylonian *ardat lile*, the "maid of the night", persisted in Jewish tradition as Lilith, "Adam's first wife".[2] In popular narrative, too, the *motif* of the dream marriage (the so-called *Märtenehe*) played a great part; union with a demonic being—Melusine, in Islam *jinn*-marriage, in Scandinavia marriage with *trolls*, in Celtic lands with fairies—may well be understood as a dream event, even though we must not overlook the fact that a practical proof of power is no less completed in the dream—even if this is subjectively or autistically distorted—than in waking experience; and unavowed fear, as well as suppressed shame, of sexual potency takes its revenge in sleep.

In other respects also it is difficult to divorce the experience of Nature from that of the dream; the satyr, for example, is certainly a Nature form, but it is equally a fantasy of the sexual day dream. Nor are the experiences of Nature and dreams the sole basis of the belief in demons; for sickness, lunacy and ecstasy are ascribed to demonic influence. Man has lost power over himself, and so another and mightier being must have taken possession of him.

Since belief in demons finds its sustenance in so many sources, it is not to be wondered at that most primitive and semi-primitive peoples think of the world as being inhabited by a multitude of demons; "they cover the earth like grass", says a Babylonian *shurpu-Text*.[3] If then a belief in God definitely establishes itself, if some attempt is made to regulate and concentrate the Power of the Universe, evil spirits must somehow or other be cleared out of the way, if not for

[1] W. H. Roscher, "Ephialtes", *Abh. der K. Sächs. Ges. d. Wiss. Phil.-hist. Kl.*, 20, 1903.
[2] The belief in the *Incubus* was admirably and vividly depicted in Charles de Coster's *Légende d'Ulenspieghel et de Lamme Goedzak*; *cf.* O. Weinreich, *AR.* 16, 1913, 623 *ff.*; Taufik Canaan, *Dämonenglaube im Lande der Bibel*, 1929, 48.
[3] Morris Jastrow, *Die Religion Babyloniens und Assyriens*, I, 1905, 283.

every-day affairs (here they rule even to-day!) at least so far as the conception of the Universe is concerned. In this respect a few spirits were lucky and made their way to divine rank. For taking everything into consideration, no essential difference can be admitted between demon and god; the idea of a god certainly has many other roots besides belief in demons, but one of these may become a god—if he does not become a devil. The Greek *daimon* does not of course mean the same as *theos*,[1] but neither does it by any means imply an inferior being; indeed, in its function as a characterization of the irrational, it leads to a peculiar conception of gods that I designate "momentary gods".[2] How little was often necessary to effect the ultimate separation between god and demon can be observed in the relation of the Iranian gods to Hindu demons, and conversely: for the Iranian designation of the devil, *Daeva*, became the title of the gods in Sanskrit (*deva*),[3] while the Iranian title of the supreme Being, *ahura*, serves in India as that of a specific and ancient type of god (*asura*), but for the enemies of the gods also. Many "great" gods of a developed pantheon still bear clear demonic features: Apollo causes plague, and at his approach the gods start in terror from their seats.[4]

Everywhere demons are older than gods; and they become evil only when they are brought into contrast with the latter. Originally just as "demonic", the gods subsequently become rational and ethical, while the evil spirits, at first merely purposeless and malicious, become the enemies of the gods, become devils. They form the horde of naughty boys held in check by the great lords, to whom a prank is frequently permitted but who are also often severely punished. As intermediate beings, again, they rule a kind of world midway between deities and men. Of course this occurs only in the religions of the higher cultures, wherein poets and theologians have co-ordinated and rationalized the domains of gods and men; while in so far as the demons have not been condemned outright they must be content with a sort of vassalage.[5]

But grievously do they revenge themselves. For the experience of the inadequate and terrifying in the world still goes far too deep. Contrasted with their God, therefore, the serious Persians were compelled to set up a demon of almost equal rank, and the Jews to transfer

---

[1] According to M. P. Nilsson (Chantepie, *op. cit.*, II, 347) the word Θεός expresses a definite individuality, and the term δαίμων an undefined power.

[2] Chap. 17; *cf.* M. P. Nilsson, *Götter und Psychologie*, AR. 22, 1923–24, 377 *ff.*

[3] Chantepie, *op. cit.*, II, 19, 214.   [4] *Hymn. Hom. in Ap.* 1 *ff.*

[5] *cf.* Plato, *Symposium*, 202; "and like all spirits he is intermediate between the divine and the mortal" (Jowett).

all sinister forms to the essential nature of Jahveh, who still shared much in common with the demon. In Islam and Christianity, too, evil spirits are recognized chiefly as powers inimical to God but subject to Him; even the gods of Greece were forced to see themselves reduced to the level of deceptive demons! Yet in the very concept of God the demonic continues to proclaim its presence, whether as absolute incalculability (predestination), or as inestimable mercy.

But even if the Devil is still a demon, whose form is moulded on the Grecian Pan, in popular belief he yet remains the "stupid" and inadequate, yet awful, Devil. But more and more he became the figure of the radically evil which can never be assimilated to the idea of God, the will that opposes itself to God's Will.

CHAPTER 16

THE SPECIAL FORM OF POWER: ANGELS

1. ANGELS are soul-beings: that is, not independent Power forms, but potencies which emanate from some other Power and appear as forms. Gods can thus send forth angelic beings, but men also; and the idea of the angel is intimately connected with that of the external soul.[1] Angels, then, are Powers that have widened outwards in their extension.

Even the name, ἄγγελος, מלאך, indicates that they are sent forth. We still speak of the angel who protects children, but we seldom realize that it is not an angel sent by God that guards the little one, but the power which the child itself has emitted. The beautiful saying of Jesus: "Take heed that ye despise not one of these little ones; for I say unto you, That in heaven their angels do always behold the face of my Father which is in heaven",[2] indicates the correct interpretation. These beings are not confined within themselves, in the sense of any modern Atomism. Each has not only relations to its environment, but part of itself therein; in other words, this is as yet no environment. Its life may thus subsist not only in its body, nor only in a "soul" supposedly immaterial, but also externally. We may recall certain fetishes, the tree of life, *etc.*; and then we perceive that the power exercised by man in the world is not to be regarded as a mere operation concentrated in the *ego*, but advances towards man, or stands over against him, as a form. Later I shall refer specifically to wraiths and soul-beings, but already we perceive the soul as a guardian spirit.

Babylonian hymns recognized a god and goddess of their own for each individual, playing no part in the pantheon but praying for their possessor and necessary to his good fortune.[3] In their absence a sick person suffered; here, then, the angels were almost gods. In Egypt on the other hand, where the *ka* formed the very condition of life and the assurance of security, the angel remained a soul.[4] In Iran, again, each thing had its *fravashi*, a concept bearing a closer relationship to the

---

[1] Chap. 42.   [2] *Matt.* xviii. 10.

[3] A. H. Edelkoort, *Het zondebesef in de babylonische boetepsalmen*, 1918, 138. *cf.* further A. M. Blackman, *Journal of Egypt. Arch.* III, 1916, 239 *f.*

[4] *cf.* my Article, *External Soul, Schutzgeist und der ägyptische Ka*, *Zeitschr. f. Ägypt. Sprache und Altertumsk.*, 54, 1918.

protected object than is expressed by the term guardian spirit. The *fravashi* was the power of a dead or living man, and subsequently of any being in general, but leading an independent existence. The gods also had a *fravashi*; and as a portion of its possessor, the *fravashi* had no separate existence.[1] The *fravashis* thus constitute an extremely instructive example of how ideas intersect in primitive religion: the soul, the dead, angels, guardian spirits, with these and other terms are they designated; but little is to be achieved with general theories here!

In Jewish popular belief, too, we find a similar outlook: the maid Rhoda claimed to see Peter, but the others did not believe her and asserted that "it is his angel".[2] The Talmud also speaks of guardian angels,[3] while in the legend about the emperor Jovinian, in the *Gesta Romanorum*, the guardian angel appears as the emperor's wraith. In ancient Germanic folklore, again, the *Fylgja* is the bearer of a man's power, who appears to him in a dream in the form of an animal or woman and announces his death;[4] families too have their *Fylgjur*. And although Wagner dealt very arbitrarily with the old sagas, still he had a sensitive comprehension of the essentials of the ancient faith and created, in his Brunnhilde, a magnificent angelic being in the primitive sense: she is "Wotan's Will", the soul sent forth by the god, and in relation to the hero she is the genuine *Fylgja*, the "death warning":

> Death-doomed are they
> Who look upon me;
> Who sees me
> Bids farewell to the light of life . . .
> Nay, having looked
> On the Valkyrie's face
> Thou must follow her forth.[5]

It is the profound idea that whoever sees his own power taking shape before him must die.

2. The *angels of the god*, then, are potencies emanating from him. When the vulture, in an Egyptian animal fable, has stolen the cat's

---

[1] N. Söderblom, *Les Fravashis*, 1899, 32 *ff.*, 60. H. Lommel, *Zarathustra*, 1930, has coined the fine term "*Heilküre*" for the *fravashi*.   [2] *Acts* xii. 15.

[3] A. Kohut, *Über die jüdische Angelologie und Dämonologie*, 1866, 19.

[4] *cf.* Hugo Gering, *Vollständiges Wörterbuch zu den Liedern der Edda*, 1903, 300. In Iceland, during the transitional period before the introduction of Christianity, people believed in a kind of form intermediate between the *valkyrie-fylgja* and the five angels of God who protect man; *cf.* A. Olrik, *Nordisches Geistesleben*[2], 1925, 97.

[5] *The Valkyrie*, Act II (Armour).

litter, the god Ra sends a "power" to exact vengeance for her.[1] As yet this liberated fragment of the god has no form, but in the true home of angels, Persia, it is very different. For the *Amesha Spentas* are energies sent forth by Ahura Mazda: their names designate his qualities: *Vohu Manah*, the good thought, *Khshathra Vairya*, divine dominion, *Ameretat*, immortality, *etc*. Under the influence of the religion of Zarathustra, however, with its strict ethical and spiritual character, a certain degree of abstraction became attached to this angelic being. But that the theoretical intellectualism of Christian speculation on the attributes of God did not prevail here is clear from their ancient description as "rulers who by their glance alone are effective, the sublime superior forces, the mighty ones":[2] this is no abstraction in our sense, but a powerfulness that has not attained a completed form because it is still too closely bound up with the supreme Power. For the effectiveness of Ahura Mazda is due to these energies which are severed from him: with his "good thought" (*Vohu Manah*) he rules, in virtue of his "divine dominion" (*Khshathra Vairya*) and in accord with his "radiant righteousness" (*Asha*).[3] Subsequently, however, the forms of these angels received outlines of constantly increasing clarity; *Vohu Manah* became the guardian of the gates of Paradise and the heaven of Ahura Mazda the court of an oriental prince surrounded by his *divan*. In this form angelology passed over to Judaism and Islam. But there too the angels still remained the concrete attributes of God: *Uriel*, the glory of God, *Raphael*, God's salvation, *etc*.[4] At the same time they became, like the Persian angels, more and more the messengers of God, his satraps and couriers. But it is scarcely to be doubted that all these angelic powers were originally independent revelations of the one Power, and only attached themselves to a single divine figure later as his ambassadors. In the case of Persia this is very clear: *Asha* is the world order, in the guise of a power, which we have already considered. For the angels are older than the gods.

Of this a different kind of proof is provided in the pre-Persian Jewish belief in angels, which is bound up with the מלאך יהוה, the angel of the Lord. Actually, this is not the servant of Jahveh but his external soul, identical with him, and yet in itself a form. In *Genesis* xlviii. 15 *f*., "angel" is used simply as another expression for the God who has

[1] Günther Röder, *Altägyptische Erzählungen und Märchen*, 1927, 303.
[2] Edv. Lehmann, *Zarathustra, en bog om Persernes gamle Tro*, 1899–1902, 138.
[3] *ibid.*, 67.
[4] Kohut, *op. cit.*, 25.

led Jacob.[1] In this respect, however, we need consider no reluctance to humanize Jahveh as having induced the idea of the angel. And the מלאך (angel) too is no pale copy. He is Jahveh himself, or rather a fragment of the mighty will that has assumed form. Only later does he become a messenger.

And the more the angel takes this status, the more is he severed from the idea of Power and soul. For Power and Will disappear, and there remains only the form: imposing, it is true. The Greek Iris and Hermes are messengers of this type, while Hermes (and also the *angelus bonus* in the cult of Sabazios[2]) still remains loosely connected with the soul in his character, as its conductor to Hades, of *psychopomp*. Odin's ravens are similarly attributes (*Hugin*, thought, and *Munin*, memory) and external souls at the same time. Jupiter, again, can send forth his eagle in precisely the same way as the magician or witch can send out soul-animals.[3]

3. Thus angels become intermediate beings, powers of subordinate rank. To the Jews, according to St. Paul, they were the mediators of the Law as an addition to the promise of God.[4] To Mary they announced that the Saviour was to be born of her: to the shepherds the "great joy" of the miracle that had occurred, and to the women and disciples the resurrection. In Christianity, still further, their task is to praise God to all eternity,[5] while in Islam their food is "Praised be Allah", their drink "Allah is holy".

In those religions that apprehend God as personal Will the angels remained servants whose work it was to announce or execute God's Will. There may also be rebellious, fallen and evil angels; but all are dependent on the sovereign Will which ultimately decides their fate. Their forms may be those of Nature, but it is Nature dominated and swayed by God's Will. This is most beautifully expressed in *St. John* i. 51: "Ye shall see heaven open, and the angels of God ascending and descending upon the Son of Man". The angelic power, then, must always have a bearer.

But it could also once again become "power" completely, as with the

---

[1] A. Lods, *L'ange de Jahvé et l'âme extérieure*, (*Zeitschr. für die Alttest. W. Beih.*, 27, 1914), 266 *ff.*; van der Leeuw, *Zielen en Engelen*, Theol. Tydschrift, N.R. 11, 1919; *cf. Exodus* xxiii. 21, where the name—that is, the essence of Jahveh—is in the angel who goes before the Israelites.

[2] F. Cumont, *Les Anges du Paganisme*, RHR. 36, 1915.

[3] S. H. Hubert and M. Mauss, *Esquisse d'une Théorie générale de la Magie, Année Sociologique*, 7, 78 *ff.*   [4] *Gal.* iii. 19.   [5] *Rev.* vii. 11.

belief in stars in the Hellenistic era, which has its echo, too, in the New Testament.[1] The "visible gods",[2] who tried to hinder the soul's journey to heaven, were powers that strove amongst themselves and which, in relation to man, constituted an inexorable necessity; while in magic angels and demons were invoked as *nomina barbara*.[3]

But power devoid of any bearer can be valued differently too, and in this sense, again, there are good angels and evil; the "powers celestial, rising and descending" of Faust's *Monologue*,[4] are the classical instance of this, while in Fechner's speculations belief in angels attained an apotheosis with later dynamistic colouring: the potencies—and this in the true spirit of Goethe—are not dead but living beings. The earth, just as in Hellenism, is "an angel who is so rich, fresh and radiant, and at the same moment so steadfast and serene as he moves through heaven, his vivacious countenance turned wholly towards heaven and carrying me with him on his journey".[5] Even the *psychopomp*, the conductor of the soul, is not absent. But whether good or evil, terrifying or beautiful, these angels have lost their soul-character and are powers devoid of all relation to any bearer; they are no longer actual angels, that is to say, but demons.

For the belief in angels reverts to the dual experience of Form, in the first place *in actu*, either as one's own, or as some foreign, power, yet lacking form, and in the second *idealiter*, as a power released and having some definite form. Exactly as man experiences himself dually, once as himself—and in this way he can imagine nothing and represent nothing to himself—and a second time as a wraith-soul-angel, so he experiences God in the same dual way, first as a Power and a Will that can neither be imagined nor represented, and again as a presence with definite form.[6] The belief in angels, therefore, is equally momentous for the idea of revelation and for the type of the concept of God.

And it is no mere matter of chance that fundamentally Christian ideas still retain something of the angel concept: thus Christ was called an angel, and in *The Shepherd of Hermas* the expressions "Son of God", "Holy Spirit", the Archangel Michael, and the "glorious" or "most holy angels" are so employed that they cannot be distinguished. Justin, again, calls the heavenly Christ "the angel of great counsel", "the Son of God", "angel and messenger of God", "Lord of the powers"

[1] *cf*. Chap. 7.   [2] Cumont.
[3] *cf*. E. Peterson, *Rh. Museum*, N. F. 75, *Engel- und Dämonennamen*.
[4] *Faust*, Part I.   [5] *Über die Seelenfrage*, 1861, 170.
[6] G. van der Leeuw, *Psychologie und Religionsgeschichte*, 11.

(that is of angels), and "wisdom" (another angel idea), while *The Ascension of Isaiah* mentions "the angel of the Holy Ghost".[1] The Holy Spirit also has the form of a dove, that is of a veritable external soul, and the *Logos* finds its prototype in "Rumour, the messenger of Zeus", *Ὄσσα Διὸς ἄγγελος*:[2] but after all the Word was the purpose of the Gospel mission. We should therefore feel no astonishment at all this, since the essence of all Christian preaching is ultimately the imparting of God through a Form which is with Him one Being, and in this way a "dual experience" of God. Hence it is no accident that, at the climax of Christian adoration, the great eucharistic hymn of praise is taken up by both men *and angels*; for the powers have only one task—to praise God Who has assumed Form: "Therefore with Angels and Archangels, with Thrones and Dominions, and with all the company of heaven, we laud and magnify thy glorious Name".

[1] G. van der Leeuw, *Zielen en Engelen*, 228 f.   [2] *Iliad*, II, 93.

CHAPTER 17

POWER AND WILL GIVEN FORM IN THE NAME

1. WE have already had occasion to observe that the idea of a god who is in some way or other personal is not an absolutely necessary element in the structure of religion. On the whole, the concept of "personality" is fairly modern and artificial; in the sphere of religion, therefore, it is more advisable to retain "Will" and "Form", while Form, again, is not always bound up with Will. Still further, the man who must come to some understanding with a power, and who therein experiences a will, attempts by every possible means to give an outline to this experience, in order to delimit it from other similar experiences; and this he does by assigning to it a *Name*. For the Name is no mere specification, but rather an actuality expressed in a word. Thus Jahveh creates the animals and leads them to Adam; he says something to them, and that is their name.[1] The names of things subsist before they acquire a "personality"; and the name of God is there even before "God" exists.

In the Name, then, is reflected experienced Will: but experienced Power also. For the extraordinary, the striking, when it receives a name, generally remains nevertheless often *mana*-like. Giant cedar trees, for example, are "cedars of *El*".[2] The vocabulary of execration, indeed, has retained this primitive application of the name as an indication of the super-potent; while whoever encounters something peculiar cries: "my God": *nom de Dieu*; or he describes anything striking as "*sakermentsch*", and quite fails to realize how much primeval experience he thus utters! Power is thus authenticated and assigned a name; plural forms being intended to express the indeterminateness wherein the experience is more powerful than form creation: God is *Elohim*. Similarly the Germanic peoples experienced the power of the *Waltenden* who rule in sea, forest and field:[3] Greece too was familiar with such collective powers whose impersonality was expressed by the plural, and who only rule together, as a genus: the nymphs in wells and woods, *semnai*, muses, *moirai*, *horai*, *artemides* (these also in the plural originally!), *panes*, *silenoi*, *anakes* (rulers), *etc*. The Celtic world, again, knew of the "mothers" who appear in threes, persisting in popular belief as the "three Marys". Even ancient Egypt had its seven Hathors, female

[1] *Gen.* ii. 19.   [2] *Ps.* lxxx. 10.   [3] Nilsson, *AR.* 22, 1923–24, 384.

predecessors of the *Eileithyias* and the seven fairies who stand by the cradle of the newborn child.

This, however, is neither polytheism nor polydemonism. It is a creation of form for Power and Will, the chorus of the drama as it were; only the actual *dramatis personae* are still absent. Just as man fashions his own power into a plurality of "souls",[1] so the Power of the Universe reveals to him not the sharp outlines of any single person but the dance of the *charites*, the stormy procession of the *horai*.

But whenever a second and self-moulded experience thus follows the immediacy of the experience of Power, personal features become sharpened. The actual numinous experience itself is formless and structureless: it is the collision with Power, the encounter with Will. Only the dual experience of Form produces demons and gods, and it would therefore be incorrect to ascribe any considerable rôle to "imagination"; for no unregulated play of fantasy predominates here, but the creation of Form. In this manner formless Power and purposeless Will are endowed with structural relations which fuse to constitute a unity stamped with individuality.

The name at first borne by the divinity is just as general and collective as is the divinity itself; it is not yet a proper name, but merely adjectival. Man first names his experiences according to their type, exactly as Adam named the animals: "the dark or fair, the wild or winterly and the radiant person are far older pairs than Aegeus and Lycus, or even than Lycurgus and Dionysus, Nestor and Lyaeus".[2] The name assigns to Power and Will a definite form and some settled content, and is therefore by no means any abstraction. Quite the contrary: it is not simply essential, but is also concrete and even corporeal. The ancient Egyptians, indeed, regarded the gods' names as their limbs: "It is Ra, who as the lord of the ennead created his names. Who then is this? It is Ra, who creates his own limbs: thus arose the gods who follow in his train".[3] Only by virtue of their names, then, do gods attain to story and myth; for myth is nothing other than "dual experience of the form", that is the experience of the god encountered anew, but henceforth indirectly, structuralized, and endowed with form.[4] That is why man

---

[1] Chap. 40.   [2] H. Usener, *Göttliche Synonyme, Kleine Schriften*, IV, 1913, 304.
[3] *Totenbuch* (Naville), *Kap.* XVII, 6 *f.*
[4] Lévy-Bruhl probably implies this in his excellent suggestion: "Can myths then likewise be the products of primitive mentality which appear when this mentality is endeavouring to realize a participation no longer directly felt—when it has recourse to intermediaries and vehicles designed to secure a communion which has ceased to be a living reality?" *How Natives Think*, 368.

longs to know the god's name; for only then can he begin to do something with his deity, live with him, come to some understanding and—
in magic—perhaps even dominate him. The children of Israel, said
Moses, will ask what is the name of Him that has sent him.[1]

The condition for all intercourse with deity therefore is to know
its name. Thus the Roman distinguished *di certi* from *incerti*: the
former he knew by name, he could invoke them, their power invaded
his life. But the second category should not be ignored. For there are
countless powers, and if we are not sure that we know their names
correctly, then we should at all events leave for them an empty space,
an altar dedicated to the unknown god", ἄγνωστος θεός, a formula
like *sive deus sive dea, sive quo alio nomine fas est appellare*:—"whether
god or goddess, or by whatever name it is lawful to call".[2] Then we
shall have made due provision for them, and there will be no power
whatever that can elude the prayer. Thus it became possible for an entire
hymn to consist of merely two phrases, like the ancient Egyptian:
"Awake in peace; thine awakening is peaceful", while all the rest is
constituted only of twenty-nine names; the intoner could then vary
and extend it himself.[3] In many hymns to the gods the names are like
the *basso continuo* executed by the suppliant according to his own
judgment.

2. In their *indigitamenta* the Romans had secret lists of divine
names which were introduced during the official invocation of the gods;
similarly the names of the domestic and family gods were kept secret.
It is indeed chiefly the ideas of the Romans that are the principal source
of our deepest insight into the essence of divine names and their
functions as the creation of forms of Power. But this must not be interpreted as though there was nothing else of significance in this respect:
for the structure of the gods' names, or of particular or individual gods,
is everywhere an indispensable intermediate link between formless
Power and the completed god-form. An intermediate link, of course,
not in the chronological sense, but in the structural and psychological;
or still better: a structural relation.

Everywhere, too, extremely different powers reveal themselves.
The Greek term *daimon* "is merely a mode of expressing the belief

---

[1] *Exodus* iii. 13.
[2] Gellius, *Attic Nights*, II, 28, 2 *ff.* G. Appel, *De Romanorum precationibus*, 1909,
14, 76 *ff.* E. Norden, *Agnostos Theos.*[2] 1926, 143 *ff.* *Theol. Wörterb. zum Neuen Test.*
Ἄγνωστος.
[3] A. Erman, *Hymn to the Royal Serpent, The Literature of the Ancient Egyptians*, 12.

that a certain effect is produced by a higher power".[1] Actually, then, every experience of power, and every encounter with a superior will, should have led to the formation of some divine form; and this indeed is often the case. But not always; and therefore we need not regard the individual or special gods as indispensable members of the evolution of the idea of God, but merely as a structural relation which, whether it actually occurs or not, is necessary to the structure. From the many, nay the innumerable, potencies which reveal themselves to man in forest and field, in home and work: from the "rulers" which in popular belief are frequently designated simply as "he" or "she": from the infinite diversity of the sheaves (does not each conceal a marvellous power?): from mountains (does not each separate peak awaken its own feeling of awe?): from labour (does not each individual type demand its specific strength?): there arises by means of the name a possibility of denomination and of enumeration.

All this, however, is no process of abstraction. The endowment with form by means of names is often incorrectly confused with allegory as *we* understand this;[2] but there is a vast contrast between our hope that Pluvius will not be too unreasonable, and the invocation of a rain god by primitive and ancient peoples. In our eyes the "rain god" is an abstraction from a reference book on mythology, but to men of the primitive and classical eras he was a living power, to which by a name had been given some kind of sketchy form.

An experience, then, does not belong to the god, but rather has its "god pertaining to it"; when for example the plague was devastating Attica Epimenides, the prophet and purifying priest, released black and white sheep on the Areopagus. Where they lay down sacrifice should be offered τῷ προσήκοντι θεῷ, to the god concerned; and the altars of these deities were "nameless altars".[3] When Odysseus, again, is cast on the coast of Scheria he arrives at the mouth of a stream and invokes its god: "Hear me, O King, whosoever thou art, as one to whom prayer is made."[4] No abstraction, then, but a most concrete experience: not theory, but the empirical verification of Power, created the "particular" or "special gods". There is here no question of Power in general, still less of any abstract idea of Power, but of *this* actual power with which one is at this very moment concerned and which

---

[1] Nilsson, *A History of Greek Religion*, 166.
[2] Thus Heiler, *Prayer*, 42 ff.
[3] Diog. Laert., *Epimenides*. C. Pascal, *Il Culto degli Dei gnoti a Roma, Bull. della Comm. arch.*, 1894, 191.   [4] *Odyssey*, V, 445.

"the situation demands". Thus when Horatius Cocles leaped into the Tiber he implored not the divinity, but simply the river itself: "Holy father Tiberinus, I pray that thou wouldst receive these arms, and this thy soldier, in thy propitious stream."[1] Horatius knew the name of the river: Odysseus knew it not and had to content himself with the general title ἄναξ. As the Greeks would say, the name gives consistency to "some good spirit", Θεός τις, and facilitates the possibility of invocation.[2]

In this connection, Usener has introduced the expressions "momentary gods" and "special gods"; and especially as regards the first of these, we must always realize (to repeat) that it by no means represents any definite phase in the evolution of the concept of God. For there would be only few genuine "momentary gods", since the major part of such momentary experiences pass away, it may be with the invocation of some unnamed "good spirit". But occasionally this gained a name: the god who compelled Hannibal to retreat from the *Porta Capena*, for instance, received a fane as *Rediculus*, and the voice which proclaimed the Gauls' approach an altar under the name of *Aius Locutius*.[3] Usener interprets the creation of the god of lightning as follows: "He was the god who in the lightning flash travelled to earth and there took up his abode. It is a clear example of what I have termed a momentary god, that is of a religious idea aroused by a single phenomenon and not extending beyond this." Then the single *keraunos* might have become an individual or "special" god of lightning in general, and eventually under the epithet *keraunios* absorbed by some more comprehensive divine form—*e.g. Zeus keraunios*. This holds true also of Rome, where *Fulgur* appears side by side with *Jupiter Fulgur* and *Jupiter Fulminator*.[4] Now it is true that, apart from isolated cases of actual worship, the momentary god is an "abstraction in so far as the primitive capacity of conception is, as it were, being purely bred".[5] The expression "structural relations", however, is better than the term "abstraction", which involuntarily stresses the theoretical aspect. Thus by means of the "momentary god", or god of "momentary function" (to adopt Fowler's term), we apprehend the transition from the solitary and instantaneous experience to the permanent form.

---

[1] Livy, II, 10 f. (Spillan).

[2] Θεός τις guided Agamemnon's ship in the storm: Aeschylus, *Agam.* 661.

[3] G. Wissowa, *Religion und Kultus der Römer*², 1912, 55.

[4] H. Usener, "Keraunos", *Kleine Schriften*, IV, 481 ff.

[5] M. P. Nilsson, *Primitive Religion*, 1911, 41 ff.; cf. also Wundt, *Völkerpsychologie*, IV, 560 ff.; R. M. Meyer, *AR.* 11, 1908, 333.

Nevertheless Usener is fundamentally correct: "The feeling of the Infinite can enter only into finite, limited phenomena and relationships. Not *the* Infinite, but *something* infinite and divine, manifests itself to man, is grasped by his spirit and expressed in his language."[1] In the paradox of this "something infinite" lives the whole marvel of religious comprehension; in it is depicted the limitation not only to anthropomorphic form but also in dogma and in words in general.

It is, then, the name that makes the actual "special god". It is this that compels the form to persist and guarantees that man can always rediscover it. The number of these numinous entities is unlimited: every action in life, every experience, has its god. "Thus the moment in which an object, or its striking characteristics, appears in human feeling and life in any perceptible relationship, whether agreeable or repulsive, is to the consciousness of the Ewe native the birth hour of a *tro*";[2] and thus he worships a mother of the market, *Asino*, the market itself, *Asi*, and also riches, *Ablo*.[3] To our minds the market is a very concrete thing, wealth merely an abstraction; but to the Ewe native both alike are living powers which he can approach through the medium of a name.

As has already been observed, the Romans possessed to a high degree the genius for this endowment with form by means of the name;[4] and in fact they associated the slightest event with the invocation of a "special god". Since the field was ploughed thrice, agriculture recognized three gods of the plough, *Vervactor, Reparator, Imporcitor. Insitor* watched over seed sowing, *Sarritor* the eradication of weeds, *Messor* the reaping, *Conditor* storing in the granary, *Sterculinius* the manuring, *etc.* Seed growth in the soil was under the guardianship of *Seia*; germination and sprouting were protected by *Proserpina*; *Segesta* took care of growth above the surface, *Volutina* of the development of the bud, *Flora* of the blossoms and *Matura* of the ripening. The other cares of the husbandman too all had their specific or individual gods: cattle breeding had *Bubona*, horse rearing *Epona*, bee keeping *Mellona*, while *Pomona* superintended arboriculture.[5] In human life it was exactly the same: *Domiducus* watched over the bringing home of the bride, *Liber* assisted the husband in sex intercourse and *Libera* the

[1] Usener, *Götternamen*[2], 276.
[2] J. Spieth, *Die Religion der Eweer in Süd-Togo*, 1911, 8.
[3] *ibid.*, 132 *ff.*   [4] Bertholet, *Götterspaltung*, 10.
[5] S. Wide, *Einleitung in die Altertumswissenschaft*, II, 1912, 240 *f.* (4th Edition, S. Wide and M. P. Nilsson, 1931).

wife.[1] The newborn babe, too, was as it were divided between potencies down to the minutest trivialities: *Alemona* nourished the fetus, *Vagitanus* opened the child's mouth at its first cry, *Levana* raised it from the ground, *Cunina* protected the cradle, *Statanus* taught it to stand, *Fabulinus* to speak, *etc.*[2] But concrete things too became powers in virtue of their names, powers that could be invoked: in the house *Janus* was the door, *Vesta* the hearth, while *Cardea* and *Limentinus* pertained to the threshold.[3]

The religion of the special gods is therefore far more practical than abstract, the severance from actual experience being still very slight. Of Rome Wissowa asserts that "all the divinities are, as it were, thought of in a purely practical manner as operative in all those things with which the Romans had to do in their ordinary life. . . . The great number of gods' names, and the unlimited multitude of divine beings, which we meet with in ancient Roman religion, therefore depend by no means on any special many-sidedness of the religious imagination, but only on the necessity, in the most immediate and everyday affairs, of recognizing the divine governance and bringing oneself into accord with it."[4] In this sense, then, we must also interpret those deities who to our mode of thought appear as *pure* abstractions, as so-called attribute-gods.[5] Instead of saying: these deities are nothing but attributes, that is abstractions, we should rather express ourselves as follows: The "attributes" that we still recognize in the deities, in the God of Judaism and Christianity, their strength, loving-kindness and justice, are actual experiences that have been transformed into ideas; originally they possessed some specific form, however sketchy and mediated through the name this may have been. First of all there were attributes of the god: subsequently, the god himself; just as there were at first shady trees, sunlit fields and blue skies, and only later the landscape. This is what Usener discovered, even if the experiential character of the idea of god had not become clear to him, when in a lecture following a sleepless night, he contradicted his opinion that the plurality of deities had arisen by splitting away from a single one, by the view that the multiplicity subsisted first, while from this the individual "great" gods had gradually developed.[6] Of course here too we must understand the expressions "originally" and "at first" not in the purely historical, still less in the chronological sense, but merely structurally and psycho-

---

[1] Lehmann-Haas, *Textbuch*, 221 *f.*   [2] Wide, *op. cit.*, 241.
[3] *ibid.*   [4] *Religion und Kultus*, 20 *ff.*   [5] Wissowa, *op. cit.*, 271 *ff.*
[6] *cf.* A. Dieterich, *Kleine Schriften*, 1911, 354 *ff.*

logically. Here as always we are concerned with understanding the structure of the idea of God, not with the facts of its origin.[1]

To the Greeks, similarly, *Paian* was the healing power, or rather the potency involved in the exorcism of the sick: or as we should say, the prescription personified. *Damia* and *Auxesia* similarly appear to us as "personifications" of growth, the second with her eloquent name at least being very transparent; but in Aegina and the Peloponnese they possessed an ancient cult.[2] For us, again, *Nike* is the "goddess of victory", that is a decorative figure; but to the Greeks she was the concrete power of victory.

So, too, the most real *Brahman*, the potent sacrificial formula, became the supreme deity to the Hindus, and as connected with it the power of isolated objects was indicated by compounds of *pati*: *Brahmanaspati* (*Bṛhaspati*), the lord of prayer, *Kṣetrasyapati*, lord of the field.[3] This again is no development of concepts, but an elementary endowment of form (*Gestaltung*). Medieval allegorical figures also, which we are inclined to condemn as mere bloodless metaphors, actually had something of the vivacity of the special gods; for to a great extent in the Middle Ages every thought, every experience, still assumed form. "It is only with difficulty that we could imagine anything by *Bel accueil*, *Doulce Mercy*, *Humble Requeste* (characters in *Roman de la Rose*). But for their contemporaries they had a reality clothed with living form and coloured with passion, which brings them wholly into line with the Roman special gods."[4] We should therefore not be surprised at *Quarème* being a figure in Literature and Painting,[5] since *Karneval, Kirmes, etc.*, still live as such in popular customs.

The Romans carried the reality of attributes so far that they could think of a large number of the gods only as linked to a bearer, so that we cannot decide whether we are concerned with gods or with souls. Thus there were divinities of the army: *Bonus Eventus, Fortuna, Victoria*, which could have Augustus, the army (*exercitus*), the *legio, etc.*, as bearers.[6] Every imperator, again, had his own *Victoria*:[7] every power was immediately specialized. Power in general became that of

[1] *cf.* further Wundt, *Völkerpsych.* VI, 8.   [2] Usener, *Götternamen*, 129 ff.
[3] Beth, *Einführung*, 20; (*cf.* GENERAL LITERATURE); *cf.* E. Cassirer, *Philosophie der symbolischen Formen*, II. *Das mythische Denken*, 1925, 256 f., with reference to the termination *tar* (*savitar*, etc.). Oldenberg, *Rel. d. Veda*, 63 ff.
[4] J. Huizinga, *Het Herfstty der Middeleeuwen*, 1919, 351.   [5] *ibid.*, 354.
[6] A. von Domaszewski, *Abhandlungen zur römischen Religion*, 1909, 104 ff.
[7] A. Piganiol, *Recherches sur les jeux romains*, 1923, 122 f., 139. A. von Domaszewski, *Die Religion des römischen Heeres*, 1895, 37. Wissowa, *op. cit.*, 127 ff.

victory, and this again the power of victory of a definite leader or some specific legion: thus there was a *Victoria Sullana*, *Victoria Caesaris* and *Victoria Augustana*. Similarly with the potencies *Honor*, *Virtus*, *Pietas*, *Disciplina*; and to what a slight degree our modern distinction between concrete and abstract subsisted is clear from the fact that Jupiter, Mars, *Victoria*, the *Genius*, *Virtus*, the *aquilae sanctae* and the *signa* of a *legio* were all alike worshipped as *di militares*.[1] According to our ideas, however, these comprise two "great gods", a sort of protective-spirit-soul (*genius*), two abstract concepts (*Victoria* and *Virtus*), and a kind of fetish (the eagles and the ensigns). But to this difference the Romans attached no meaning whatever.

For a moment, certainly, we might suppose that an exception must be made so far as concerns a partial creation of form in the Roman belief in gods. For in Gellius[2] divine pairs are to be found which at first sight seem to presuppose divine marriage. *Nerio Martis*, *Salacia Neptuni*, *Lua Saturni:* were not these simply the spouses of the gods so named, and was not the whole specific Roman creation of form by means of names an error? But a second glance shows that *Nerio Martis* was only the masculine strength of the god, *Salacia Neptuni* the flux of water, *Lua Saturni* the seed's potency of germination.[3] We too still find a tendency to this creation of form by the name when we speak of the king's majesty, the holiness of the pope or the excellency of a minister. But this is assuredly no affair of attempting to transform personalities so named into abstractions. The title is rather a compromise between individuality and power, an intermediary between the special form of the bearer and the superpersonal power which he carries.

But when the name is no longer regarded as a living potency, then the special god decays or declines, and becomes an epithet of some "great god", that is really of some special god who has had better fortune: it becomes one of the retinue of the great god.[4] The "mistress", who originally had her own realm of authority as the local goddess of the surrounding dells, thus became a title of Demeter, Isis, Cybele or Mary, as δέσποινα, *domina*, *Donna*.[5] Meilichios again, "*He of appeasement*", "is nothing else. He is merely the personified shadow or dream

[1] von Domaszewski, *Religion des römischen Heeres*, 44, 19.

[2] *Noctes atticae*, 13, 23.

[3] von Domaszewski, *Abhandl.*, 104 *ff*. Wissowa, *op. cit.*, 134 *ff*. W. Warde Fowler, *The Religious Experience of the Roman People*, 481 *ff*. G. van der Leeuw, *God, Macht en Ziel*, *Theol. Tydschr.* 1918, 123 *ff*. Kurt Latte, *AR.* 24, 1927, 253 *f*.

[4] Usener, *op. cit.*, 272.   [5] *ibid.*, 216 *ff*.

generated by the emotion of the ritual—very much, to take a familiar instance, as Father Christmas is a 'projection' of our Christmas customs";[1] he became an epithet of Zeus Meilichios. In the same way *Aphiktor* ("the Suppliant"), the name form of the prayer of the community and of the cry of the commonwealth, likewise passed as a title to the Olympian deity.[2]

Thus the construction of form by means of the name simplified the eternally changing experience of power, the encounter with ever new superiority. From the many hearth fires arose one *Vesta Publica*, one *Janus* on the Forum from the numberless doors, ultimately one *Terminus* on the Capitol from the many boundary stones, and one *Juno* out of the thousandfold soul-like guardian spirits of the women.[3] At first an event is just itself; and so long as it is apprehended as it originally occurred it opposes any endowment with form. In primitive languages, for instance, the man who arrives is another than the man who leaves; and in primitive religion, similarly, the god who appears is another than the god who departs: the experience in its original momentariness is still present.[4] But religion was also concerned when, "for every propitious event, the ancients endowed the god to whom this pertained with a specific epithet and erected to him a special temple; they had apprehended an activity of the Universe, and designated thus its individuality and its character".[5]

3. "God", therefore, is not the specialist of the works of reference. In these we find "gods" of trade, love and knowledge. Each has his own calling. But the god is not the director of such affairs: he is an actual experience. Thus we understand how indubitably polytheistic religions, such as the ancient Egyptian or Greek, speak simply of "god" whenever it is a case of regarding some definite event as the revelation of superior power. Thus "God" preserves the life of the shipwrecked mariner and brings him to safety on an island;[6] that is precisely the god "whom it concerns", "some good spirit", $\Theta\epsilon\acute{o}s$ $\tau\iota s$.

This practical or empirical significance of belief in a god is what von Wilamowitz implied in calling "god" the exponent of a belief or

---

[1] Murray, *Five Stages of Greek Religion*, 30.
[2] *ibid.*, 43; "the assembled prayer, the united cry"; *cf.* Wide, *op. cit.*, 176 *f.*
[3] E. Samter, *Die Entwicklung des Terminuskults*, *AR.* 16, 1913, 142 *ff.*
[4] Usener, *op. cit.*, 317 *ff.*
[5] Thus wrote Schleiermacher in 1799, in his *Discourses upon Religion*, with admirable powers of observation even if in romantic terms. (First German Edition, 56 *f.*)
[6] A. Erman, *The Literature of the Ancient Egyptians*, 30.

a feeling:[1] "god" is above all the name for some experience of Power. From the emotions of the young maidens of Troezen, for instance, who before marriage sacrificed their tresses, there arose the name and later the form of Hippolytus. This, however, implies no anthropomorphic theory nor Feuerbachean wisdom. The power in the experience leads to endowment with form. Surrender of maidenhood involves contact with some strange power, and this contact receives name and form.

A more suitable appellation, however, for the semi-formalized potency than the much too personal term "god" is the Roman *numen*. A *numen* is, first of all, only a nod of the head: that is the will element therein. But further, it is also power, and has a name. It is, however, still so vague that it exhibits no human features at all, and can also be ascribed to some power as an attribute.[2] But the "attributes" are nearer to the experience than is the fully developed god.

Indeed it almost appears that the Romans were familiar with the structure of this semi-formalized will-power, as it were, in its "pure culture". For they also had an adequate term instead of "person", which would here be too copious and modern; they spoke of *capita*, meaning by *caput* a legal person, and therefore someone with whom relations are possible and who himself can do something.[3] Bickel has rightly stressed the fact that this juridical personality was no abstraction, but always remained connected with the demon;[4] that is, probably, that the powerful will had received a name, and that this legal personality was attributed to the gods.[5] In connection with what has been previously observed,[6] we might also describe these divine personalities as offices: just as the king's power is his status, so divine power is something "official". Just as the monarch, as such, is no acquisitive nor cowardly personality, but always shows kingly courtesy, generosity, *etc.*, so the god is not some good or wise person but, simply as god, ever divine. His name is known—that is to say, men know what they require him for and what they expect from him. He was *deus certus*, and in Rome indeed was included in social relationships as *pater or mater*. It was, then, from these conditions that the possibility of a cult first of all arose; and whatever is addressed to nameless Power is *magic*.

[1] U. von Wilamowitz-Möllendorff, *Griechische Tragödien*, I[8], 1919, 100.

[2] Chantepie, *op. cit.*, II, 444. Latte, *AR.* 24, 1927, 256. G. van der Leeuw, *Theol. Tydschr.*, 1918, 123 *ff.*   [3] E. Bickel, *Der altrömische Gottesbegriff*, 1921, 35, 63.

[4] *ibid.* Whether his historical construction of the *di certi* from the ancestral spirits of the Italici, as connected with the juridical "person" of the Romans, is correct, is dubious.   [5] *ibid.*, 40 *f.*   [6] Chap. 13.

"*Les Saints successeurs des dieux*"[1]—the structure of special gods is still realized to-day: the *saints* of the church have become their successors.[2] "If someone has toothache, he fasts and extols St. Apollonia; if he fears danger from fire he makes St. Laurence his helper in his distress; if he is afraid of plague he makes his vows to St. Sebastian or Ottilia; Rochus is invoked for eye disease, Blase in case of sore throat, while St. Anthony of Padua returns lost objects."[3] Thus the successors of the *genius* and the *lares* as house and family deities are the saints, whose altars in houses and whose statues at cross-roads persist in giving form to the ancient isolated experience;[4] and as the cult of St. Thaddeus shows, even the momentary god still arises spontaneously: "In her special need some pious woman or other has turned to a new saint and been successful; she praises her helper and then others follow her example— thus is to be explained how the apostle Thaddeus, who a few years ago was practically unknown in Catholic circles, possesses to-day in countless churches devotional statues surrounded by votive tablets."[5] The church has always been very well able to reconcile itself to the indestructible structures of the idea of God, and has adopted and christianized them rather than sacrifice them to a barren Monotheism. In fact, in the sixth century Gregory the Great expressly recommended that the cults should be retained in the ancient places of worship, and merely the holy martyrs set up instead of demons, in accordance with the wise principle that "he who seeks to ascend to the highest point climbs not by leaps, but by steps or strides".[6]

H. Usener, *Götternamen*[2], 1929.
A. Bertholet, *Götterspaltung und Göttervereinigung*, 1933.

---

[1] P. Saintyves, 1907.

[2] In origin, the sheiks of Mohammedan popular piety are also divinities to some degree; *cf.* C. Clemen, *Die nichtchristliche Kulturreligionen in ihrem gegenwärtigen Zustand*, 1921, II, 87 *f.*

[3] Luther in *The Large Catechism* in N. Söderblom's *Einführung in die Religionsgeschichte*, 1920, 52; *cf.* Heiler, *Prayer*, 47. H. Usener, *Sonderbare Heilige*, I, 1907, 34. Heiler, *Katholizismus*, 190 *f.*

[4] Wide, *op. cit.*, 242.   [5] Heiler, *Katholizismus*, 191.

[6] The pope's letter to the abbot Mellitus; *in extenso* in J. Toutain, *RHR.* 40, 1919, 11 *ff.*

CHAPTER 18

THE SACRED WORLD IN THE BACKGROUND

POWER AND WILL IN THE BACKGROUND

1. THE History of the History of religion is just as meagre as the History of religion itself is profuse. It seems as though only very few ideas could arise within it; even till to-day, unfortunately, a more profound historical comprehension has but seldom been applied to it. In this respect investigators have too often been content to smile at Hegel as an arbitrary constructor and oppressor of History, while in the interval they themselves have done naïvely and badly what they reproached Hegel for doing, and what at all events he self-confidently and brilliantly executed.

Thus the dominant but shallow Evolutionism of the nineteenth century led to the concept of God, as held in the recent past, being regarded as the climax of a long development from quite crude beginnings: while in accordance with this, every ancient or primitive idea of God was estimated by the standard of this ultimate achievement. And then a reaction set in, equally superficial according to the ideals of the Philosophy of History, which while announcing itself as "anti-evolutionism" nevertheless restricted itself merely to inverting the development, so that it placed the concept of God of the "Enlightenment" and the nineteenth century, which to the reaction was also a matter of course, at the summit and derived everything else from this beginning by way of "degeneration". Both tendencies, however, are completely unanimous in holding that "God" can be applied only to what a modern Western European, descended from the Christianity of the age of "Enlightenment", is accustomed to designate by this name without further philosophical or phenomenological reflection.[1]

It is true that in the course of this controversy one important discovery was made; for it became clear that another belief prevailed among many primitive peoples besides that in spirits and fetishes, which had hitherto been almost the only one known. This belief was regarded by its first exponent, Andrew Lang, as the idea of a supreme being, a

[1] cf. my Review of Fahrenfort's *Het hoogste Wezen der Primitieven, Deutsche Lit.-Ztg.*, 1929, I *Heft*.

"high god". In the main this supreme being resembles the God whom the "proverbial plain man" imagines to himself even to-day: the Creator, the sustainer of the Universe, eternal and primal, benevolent and the Father of men, invisible, omniscient and the guardian of morality.[1] With Animism, whose orthodox doctrine Lang henceforth vehemently opposed, although he had himself previously supported it, this supreme being had of course no connection: such a God could never have originated from any spirit of the dead. By Animism, then, people had been led astray; even in the past, in barbarism, humanity had to a great extent believed what it still believes, even though it neither theologizes nor philosophizes: a God to whom there is no need to sacrifice (cults implying degeneration), who is no revengeful spirit (like the Jahveh of the Old Covenant) but a Lord of the heavens (like the Jahveh of the prophets), and a loving Father (like the God of Jesus). He has created all things: the Eskimo believes that there must be some being that has made all,—"Ah! if only I could, how I would love and honour this being"; and this is confirmation of St. Paul's doctrine that man knows God through creation.[2] Again, he has given moral commands and watches over their observance: the inhabitant of Terra del Fuego believes that killing brings rain, snow and hail; there is a "big man in the wood" who dislikes that, and whom it angers. And such a children's bogey stands higher, despite all the crudeness in the idea, than the Jewish God who permitted Agag to be slain: "The black man of shivering communistic savages is nearer the morality of our Lord than the Jehovah of Judges."[3]

To all these contentions Evolutionism naturally opposed itself, and insisted on ascribing the development of the worship of a supreme being to the influence of Christian missionaries. It seemed altogether too insane to suppose that the end should subsist at the beginning. But gradually it became clear that the supreme beings are indeed, in the great majority of cases, original and autochthonous. And the anti-evolutionists endeavoured to show that the beginning was a beginning in fact, and that what until their day had been so regarded was merely the product of mythical luxuriance and animistic degeneration. With an extensive equipment of knowledge, facts and cooperators, and with passion and scientific self-reliance, Father W. Schmidt undertook to vindicate the honour of the supreme being. He attempted to show that amongst those primitive peoples who really possess the oldest culture (the so-

---

[1] Lang, *The Making of Religion*, 173.   [2] *Romans* i.
[3] Lang, *ibid.*, 175 *f.*, 183 *ff.*, 192 *ff.*, 203 *ff.*, 218 *ff.*, 237, 271 *ff.*, 280 *f.*, 294.

called pygmy tribes), there subsists in its purest form the belief in a single sublime Creator-God, combined with an elevated moral order sustained by that God. With the assistance of the theory of so-called cultural cycles prevalent in Ethnography,[1] he believed himself able to prove that these oldest peoples, nourished by the herbs they collect, possess the belief in a supreme being, a moral code of a high status and monogamous marriage. And that section of their ideas and customs which does not agree with this is then to be explained by the influence of neighbouring cycles of culture, which have had to pay for their higher civilization (cattle breeding, hunting and agriculture) by a degeneration of their belief in God into mythical-animistic-magical concepts, and of their moral code to polygamy and licentiousness, *etc.*

Schmidt herewith transfers the controversy to historical territory, where I do not wish to follow him.[2] I need observe merely that the idea of the supreme being has amalgamated everywhere with animistic and dynamistic viewpoints, and that a genuine Monotheism has nowhere been proved, while the chronology of cultural cycles has remained matter of dispute until to-day.

But one thing is certain: there does exist a primitive worship of some Being, which can be interpreted neither as Power nor as Will, and which possesses a remarkable similarity to the God of the "proverbial plain man" so dear to Lang.

2. How then must this Being be interpreted? The constructions hitherto offered were influenced to a great extent by three errors: (*1*) That it is historically important to discover the oldest, because this is the most significant; (*2*) That in any case there pertains to religion a "God" as he is depicted in the Catechism or perhaps in the *Confession du Vicaire savoyard*; (*3*) That, as was taught in ancient church doctrine, there is a "natural" religion which contains the genuine belief in God and was originally common to all men, upon which through a special revelation Christendom erects the specific Christian religion of salvation in Christ. If however we free ourselves from these errors and from the pursuit after the historically demonstrable God— or still better—one God, then we find:

The Semang, a pygmy tribe on the Malacca Peninsula, worship a thunder-god *Keii*, who has created all things except the earth, this being made by another god *Ple*, who had formerly been a man. *Keii*

---

[1] *cf.* F. Gräbner, *Methode der Ethnologie*, 1911.
[2] But *cf.* Clemen and Fahrenfort, *op. cit.*

punishes sinners; his son—for he has a wife—is his policeman who
roves about in the form of a tiger: among other things he punishes
incest and want of respect for one's parents. He is invoked only occasionally, and has no fixed cult, the other creator, *Ple*, being the racial ancestor
of the Ple-tribe.[1] Here we must note: the connection with thunder,
with morals and creation, and with tribal origin together with occasional
invocation.

Among the Kurnai in South-East Australia again, where (as Father
Schmidt also concedes) the belief in a supreme being is still retained
in its purity, *Mungan-ngaua* is worshipped. Formerly he lived on
earth and taught men how to make nets, canoes and weapons; now he
lives in heaven, where he is a chief as he was previously on earth. He
too has a son who is the ancestor of the Kurnai; he speaks with the
voice of the bull-roarer (the imitation of thunder). The betrayal of the
secret rites he punishes by flood amongst other things, and is called
"our father". To the Kurnai, however, "father" means uncle as well
as father, and also all those who were initiated at the same time as they.
Here then we observe: the connection with the origin of the tribe,
with thunder and heaven, the moral code, rites and the arts.

In Northern Central California there are again two creators; one
created the earth and the other bestowed culture, but the former has
left the earth and now lives "above" in heaven. He is sublime, kindly
and weak, while the other, identified with the prairie dog or coyote,
is the trickster or adventurer, with traits of Owlglass as well as those
of the hero. The creator *Olelbis* has a wife and many relations, being
invoked only occasionally, principally in time of need; and because
he is in heaven, he sees everything but is not omniscient.[2] Here are
to be noticed: the connection with heaven, with creation, culture, the
sun and moon (the eternal "two brothers" in the myth all over the
world), the occasional cult only in case of need and the fact that the deity
sees all.

Similarly *Baiame*, the supreme being of the Kamilaroi of Central
Australia, once lived on earth as a benefactor and then went with his
two wives towards the East and dwells invisible in heaven, occasionally
appearing in human form. He is regarded as creator in a careless and
let-well-alone way; a Kurnai when asked, "who has made this?"

[1] Fahrenfort, *op. cit.*, 42 *ff.*
[2] R. Dangel, *Der Schöpferglaube der Nordzentralkalifornier*, in *SM.* III, 1927. For the
remainder of the citations, *cf.* the relevant works of Beth, Fahrenfort, Clemen, Söderblom and Schmidt; further, C. Strehlow, *Die Aranda- und Loritja-Stämme in Zentral-
Australien*, 1907 *ff.*

replied, "*Baiame*, I think". He rules the rain and speaks in the thunder, is eternal and punishes transgressors. *Alchera*, the god of the Arunta, is a strong giant with the feet of an emu. His wives have dogs' feet, his sons being emus and his daughters dogs, which corresponds to the division into Emu and Dog clans. His dwelling too is in heaven, which, however, he did not create, but which it would appear he protects from collapse. Side by side with him there is an entire series of forefathers, *alcheringamichena*, who are also cultural heroes and participate in eternal uncreatedness with *Alchera*.[1] Here we observe a clear connection with totemistic ideas, together with the features already enumerated.

Among the African Bantu tribes, again, where the rule of magic (*juju*) is supreme, a god *Nzambi* is recognized who has withdrawn into heaven and does not trouble himself about terrestrial affairs; he is looked upon as creator, but possesses no cult. In times of direst need he is invoked by the tribes, but they are not at all surprised if he does not hear them.

With *Kitshi Manitu* in the next place we were familiar from youth as the "great spirit" of the Algonquins. He is closely connected with the *mana*-power *Manitu*, already discussed, and also stands in intimate relationship to the totemistic ideas of Nagualism, while the significance of *Manitu* itself appears to vacillate between impersonal power, protective spirit and supreme being.

The classical land of the supreme being, however, is China. *Shang-Ti* is the lord in the heights, the supreme lord who is concerned with heaven, although not identical therewith, but merely a personal being dwelling on high. He stands on the same level as the ancestors, the emperor being called "the son of heaven". But he himself is not an ancestor, while fatherhood only indicates origin; he is, however, closely linked with the heavens and also the origins of the empire and dynasty. He represents the moral world order, and justly rules the world he has created and maintains; in contrast to *Tao*,[2] he is conceived as personal, but is scarcely any more anthropomorphic than is this Power: only once does an ancient *Text* say: "the lord spoke to king Wen".[3] As creator he was neglected, but his moral significance became the standard for Chinese religious sentiment; he has proclaimed laws and prohibitions and punishes evil-doers. In the cult, only the emperor

---

[1] Beth, *Religion und Magie*; *cf.* also J. Wanninger, *Das Heilige in der Religion der Australier*, 1927, 192 *f.*   [2] Chap. 2.

[3] What this implies with respect to the Phenomenology of belief in God may be estimated by comparing it with the endlessly repeated "Thus spake Jahveh" of the Old Testament.

approaches him when worshipping the "imperial heaven", the "supreme emperor", at the "altars of heaven". It is true that all can pray to him; but Confucius significantly asserted that he could hardly remember the last time he prayed.[1] Söderblom is right, therefore, in saying that only in China has the structure of the idea of the supreme being attained a culture of its own:

> Be in awe of Heaven's wrath,
>   No idle dallying venture!
> Be in awe of Heaven's course,
>   Risk not too long your idle ways!
> High Heaven sees everywhere,
>   With you it goes forth, and returns;
> High Heaven sees all clearly,
>   And ever goes with you.[2]

In Vedic India *Varuna* and *Mitra* are the chief figures of the *Adityas*, a type of god which, while maintaining its own place in the Hindu pantheon, is probably of different origin from *Indra* and his companions. The *Adityas* are connected with the kingdom, with heaven and the sun; further, they are intimately related to the path of life, to *Ṛta*[3]; sometimes *Varuna* is accounted its creator, at other times its chief attendant. His character, as contrasted with that of the drunken swashbuckler *Indra*, is described by Oldenberg as "the tranquilly shining sublimity of a sacred kingship that preserves the order of the cosmos and punishes sin". "The one slays the enemy in battle, the other always upholds the laws." *Varuna* sees all, has ordained all and appointed each thing its place. To him one prays: "What was then the grievous sin, O *Varuna*, which makes thee wish to destroy thy friend who praiseth thee? Reveal it to me, thou who art not to be deceived, thou who art mighty in thyself! With obeisance would I implore thy pardon, that I may be free from the guilt of my actions."[4]

3. I believe that all these examples, adduced from cultures most widely separated in time and space, fully justify the Title assigned to this Chapter:—"The Sacred World in the Background: Power and Will in the Background". The God in whom, to his astonishment, man had now discovered his own enlightened ideas, and whom he again

---

[1] Bertholet, *op. cit.*, 6, 67.
[2] Lehmann-Haas, *Textbuch*, 11.   [3] Chap. 2.
[4] Bertholet, *op. cit.*, 9, 51; *cf.* 40 *ff.*, 45. Oldenberg, *Die Religion des Veda*, 96 *ff.*, 178 *ff.*, 200 *ff.*, 299 *ff.*, 322 *ff.*

jubilantly greeted as the sole God of primal revelation, but whom, as Söderblom perceived, he could more easily have found in eighteenth century Deism—this God is a God in the background, and his sublimity and remoteness from the world are those of a passive pre-existent being who is taken into consideration only occasionally. The concept itself originates with Preuss, whose *Glaube und Mystik*, together with Söderblom's *Gottesglaube*, probably form the most important contributions to the understanding of the structure of belief in the supreme being.[1]

Man, then, exercises power, particularly in the rites which he performs and which rule his world; they subject to him, at least partially, other powers, rain and wind, animals and plants. By means of rites he can dominate the world; there might therefore be no power but his own, and his potency might have subsisted from the very beginning: to quote *Faust*, "the world was not, till I created it". But these conclusions he hesitates to draw; for he experiences the need of setting up a higher court, even if only in the background, some Power from which he can derive all others, including his own, a Power that as it were authorizes his rites but does not concern itself overmuch about him, nor disturbs him in his own fullness of power: only what has been instituted by the supreme being, rites, laws and prohibitions, should be observed. To this it gives close attention, and in order to be able better to do so it goes to heaven, where originally it did not exist: from there it can see everything and take care that the world does not run off the rails. Thus it is God as preserver rather than as creator, although at the same time the entire existence of the world may be derived from the divine predecessor, the Power in the background. But the creative process very often advances no farther than the individual objects that it is supposed to have created; it does not act continually, but initiated once for all, although all further activity is inconceivable without its own. Hence the name "originator" assigned to it by Söderblom, which indeed indicates one of the principal features in its nature.

Thus it approximates both to the bringers of culture and salvation[2] and to tribal ancestors. As originator of rites it is as it were the original medicine-man, and also the first lawgiver:[3] in this manner it ensures the order of the world and is responsible for its emergence. "Probably *Baiame* made it!": so man indicates the Power in the background.

---

[1] *cf.* my Review, *Deutsche Literaturzeitung*, 1928, 13 *Heft*.   [2] Chap. 12,
[3] *cf.* further Father Schmidt, *Settimana intern. di Etnol. relig.*, IV. *Sess.* 1925 (1926), 247 *ff.*

"Actually the primeval-father is superfluous, since it is merely the moon's phases that are magically represented in the festivals; but man requires an originator to make the world, to organize it and introduce ceremonies";[1] the "background" character of the primal father could not be better emphasized. Hence, too, the lack of cult worship; only in time of need, that is when all other means have failed, is he invoked, although even then one hardly expects a hearing. Thus far Lang is quite correct: the religion of the supreme being is certainly that of the "proverbial plain man", even though it is scarcely that of Jesus and the prophets.[2] Man blasphemes in his name, and also calls on him in pious exclamation; he emerges, too, in proverbs, that treasure of the "plain" man.[3] All this means that he is the God in the background, to whom one refers but does not bring down from heaven, and who also does not come forth from there spontaneously.

In this connection, then, two features are of the utmost importance: but *not* the relationship between the highest being and Nature: Söderblom is quite right in regarding this as of merely secondary significance. The originator is a god of neither the heavens nor the sun although, residing as he does in sublime remoteness, he is naturally closely linked with both phenomena. But for the historical consciousness his significance is very great, since here—and this is something fundamentally new—Power is placed in relationship to History: "there are narratives about them", asserts Söderblom of the originators.[4] But the Power-activity does not become a living actuality in history: it is transferred instead to the beginning; it is reserved, antecedent Power, and the Australian tribes have a special name for the "primeval age, unattainable in time" (*Alcheringa* among the Arunta).[5]

The second highly important characteristic of this belief is the intimate union between Power and morality, although the necessity of submitting one's actions to a certain order, and the further need of adapting events in general to a fixed rule, assume in the supreme being a somewhat vague form. It is, however, the court of appeal for human conduct and the guarantee of the orderly world process.

4. Thus in the concept of the supreme being the "appertaining god" becomes the background of the Universe. He is the Will in the

---

[1] K. Th. Preuss, *Religion und Mythologie der Uitoto*, I, 1921, 32.
[2] G. van der Leeuw, *Struktur der Vorstellung des höchsten Wesens*.
[3] Thus among the Bataks: "all depends on God", "we are in God's hands", *etc.* Nieuwenhuis, *Das höchste Wesen*, 33.   [4] *cf.* Preuss, *Glaube und Mystik*, 58.
[5] K. Beth, *Primitive Religion*, in *Die Religionen der Erde*, 1929, 8.

world behind us, but not an articulate and active Will; he is also the Power in the world of the background, but only meagrely personified.[1] He subsists in all cultural religions; and also in Judaism and Christianity, where, however, the fundamental activity of God prevents the full attainment of his characteristic attributes. The God in the parable of the Prodigal Son might be the supreme being, except for one feature: that of the Father hastening to meet the penitent sinner. The originator hastens not: he has done so once, but has become weary!

In eighteenth century Deism the worship of the supreme being attained its highest prime. The God Who, in the Incarnation, in sacrament, was too near, thus became a God in the background who sustained morality and gave, in immortality, a further guarantee of the reward of virtue and the punishment of evil-doing. A Voltaire's sceptical police-belief, like the warm enthusiasm for virtue of a Rousseau, turns to the Power in the background; while by Robespierre it was honoured as *l'Être Suprême*, in whose name he had his political opponents, people of evil conduct—guillotined!

When devoutness accompanies this belief, however, it assumes the form of *humility*: it is not we that rule the world, for what are we in contrast to the eternally sublime Father, the venerable background of the Universe? and this lowliness has found its most touching expression in Goethe's poem:

> When the All-Holy
> Father Eternal,
> With indifferent hand,
> From clouds rolling o'er us,
> Sows his benignant
> Lightnings around us,
> Humbly I kiss the
> Hem of his garment,
> Filled with the awe of
> A true-hearted child.
>
> What doth distinguish
> Gods from us mortals?
> That they before them
> See waves without number,
> One infinite stream;

[1] Although the expression "*mana*-gods", which I applied to the supreme beings in my *Einführung in die Phänomenologie der Religion* (1925), may seem to stress the aspect of Power too exclusively, still this factor cannot be allowed to remain unnoticed. We should remember *manitu*!

> But we, short-sighted,
> One wavelet uplifts us,
> One wavelet o'erwhelms us
> In fathomless night.[1]

In these few lines is contained the complete structure of belief in the Originator, as it lives on through the ages.

C. CLEMEN, *Der sog. Monotheismus der Primitiven, AR.* 27, 1929.

J. J. FAHRENFORT, *Het hoogste Wezen der Primitieven,* 1927.

H. FRICK, *Über den Ursprung des Gottesglaubens und die Religion der Primitiven, Theol. Rundschau,* N. F. 1–2, 1929–30.

A. LANG, *The Making of Religion*[3], 1909.

G. VAN DER LEEUW, *Die Struktur des Glaubens an höchste Wesen, AR.* 29, 1931.

A. W. NIEUWENHUIS, *Das höchste Wesen im Heidentum, Int. Arch. f. Ethnogr.* 27, 1926.

R. PETTAZONI, *Allwissende höchste Wesen bei primitivsten Völkern, AR.* 29, 1931.

K. TH. PREUSS, *Glauben und Mystik im Schatten des höchsten Wesens,* 1926.

P. W. SCHMIDT, *Der Ursprung der Gottesidee* I[2], 1926, II, 1929, III, 1931.

[1] *The Limits of Man* (Dwight).

CHAPTER 19

POWERS

1. THE indefinite and nameless multitude of Powers assumes Form in a plurality of personalities which, each endowed with a name and a sphere of activity of its own, are interconnected by organic relationships. *Polydemonism* becomes *Polytheism*. But these, of course, are not periods in the evolution of belief in God which in due sequence succeed each other. Rather are two different structures to be understood by the two terms. The one comprises the chaotic world of the many potencies with which we are already familiar: sacred beings whose realms of power are separated in either place or time, *numina* of the night and day, of Spring and Winter, of this activity or that. The other embraces precisely the same world, but as oriented according to definite viewpoints: thus the chaotic plurality becomes an ordered whole. Both structures alike are timeless, and in no case settled stages on the highway of mankind: to a great extent, indeed, Polytheism remains always Polydemonism. When for example the several corn-mothers of Greece had already been fused for some time into the single form of Demeter, the "black" Demeter of Phigalia still remained, with her ancient cult and crude myths, as a different form from that of the mother of Eleusis, just as the "black" madonna of some Italian town or other is radically different from the madonna figure of another locality.[1]

The process leading repeatedly from Polydemonism to Polytheism is termed *Syncretism*. In the development of culture man finds the Universe becoming steadily smaller; his world is no longer limited to his own village, but extends to a number of such communities linked together by manifold connections, and ultimately to a province, a state, to neighbouring states. The many potencies of the next village and the nearest state thus become familiar to him, whether in goodwill or in war. Then there arises some kind of understanding between his own and foreign powers, so that those exhibiting the closest mutual relationship unite under one name and a single form, while the remainder acquire definite reciprocal interconnections. Thus a Pantheon comes into being, although of course it is never completed: the *Adityas* in

[1] Bertholet, *Götterspaltung*, 6.

India, the *Vans* in Scandinavia, Dionysus and his circle in Greece, are never entirely merged in the world of the gods but maintain their own status and character.

One point must, however, be added: it concerns the concept, "God". Or rather *a* concept, "God". For here again we must not rest content with Christian or any other generally accepted ideas. At this stage, however, "God" is something other than simply Power or fetish, spirit or demon. The gods of Polytheism are indeed wills and forms in the animistic sense; but they are distinguished from other potencies that are likewise endowed with Will and Form. They possess something that is specific in its type, which it is not easy to include within any concept whatever, because here again we run the risk of imposing our own ideas. On that account we should not yet say that the deity is "sublime", even though what we mean thereby is not far removed from our own concept of sublimity. What should now be added to the character of complete Otherness, which the idea of God shares with all the objects of religion, is best indicated by an example: the ancient Egyptians, then, ascribed golden flesh to the gods. "Gold (is) the flesh of the gods . . . Rē said at the beginning of his words: My skin is of pure gold";[1] here the Greek idea of *ichor*, the blood of the gods, is relevant. By gold, then, very much is expressed which we too ascribe to deity: difference in nature, sublimity, beauty, immortality, since gold signifies eternal life. But the image is actually such:—it is quite concrete and no affair of concepts at all.

2. There are, again, several interconnections between powers that correspond fairly exactly to the prevailing conditions of human society; these are designated by the general expression *Theogony*. Thus the various types and ranks of the gods are brought together in relations resting on affinity, the simplest form being probably that of the *Triad*:— Father, Mother and Child: this existed in ancient Egypt:—Osiris, Isis, Horus. Horus is an older celestial god, who originally had nothing to do with Osiris: in the triad, however, he appears as the typical faithful son, just as Isis is the typical Egyptian loving sister-wife. And the family triad is so very powerful a factor in the human spirit, in so far as it thinks in patriarchal terms, that even Christianity could not dispense with it, so that the trinity of Jesus, Mary and Joseph may be regarded as the "trinity of Catholic popular piety".[2] But there are other

[1] B. Gunn and A. H. Gardiner, "The Temple of the Wady Abbad", *Jour. of Eg. Arch.* 4, 247.   [2] Heiler, *Katholizismus*, 192.

conditions also: for the matriarchal state is reflected in the duality
Mother and Son, or Lover. Here the Near East is typical:—Cybele and
Attis, Ishtar and Tammuz; and if the paternal god is combined with
them there arises another triad. The groups of gods on the bas-reliefs
of Boghazköi should probably be explained in this sense: the bearded
father-god meets the mother on the lion, who is followed by the young
god on a panther.[1]

Together with the Triad, of course, there appears *Duality*, predominantly as a pair of twin brothers whose unity and estrangement,
based on the relationship of the sun and moon, have given occasion
to many myths. The connections of the most diverse gods to some
larger group, such as we find in Egypt, are more independent of Nature.
the so-called Great *Ennead* includes, besides the already independent
composite Osiris triad, the other important gods too, and shows indeed
a tendency towards the development of the concept of totality. Here the
same mystic urge manifests itself that has rendered the Christian
dogma of the Trinity, which originally and essentially emphasizes the
unity of the Christian "Powers", again and again the starting point of
monistic and pantheistic speculation,[2] and has similarly reduced the
three gods included in the *Trimurti* of post-Vedic India, Brahma,
Rudra and Vishnu, to forms of the incorporeal Absolute.

But powers also unite to form an association exhibiting the traits of
either a Greek *polis*, a warrior tribe or an oriental despotic state, as the
case may be; in hierarchic organization, lesser powers are subjected
to the more important. One is the chief, whether as father of gods and
men, Zeus, whose lordship is patriarchially conceived, or as the great
king surrounded by his *divan*, an image still extant in later Judaism.
Demons and angels became either vassals and ministers, or rebels;
and the Persian divine state had its viziers and satraps, the Jewish
its grandees, among whom the rebellious were not lacking, and the
Germanic its court skalds.

3. Beside these connections, however, various divisions occur in the
manifoldness of powers. Thus the time distinction into periods according to two gods, one succeeding the other as in the case of Apollo and
Dionysus, is actually based on natural events; similarly the delimitation
of powers according to place and nation corresponds to natural and
cultural conditions. Cosmically, again, Power subdivides into celestial

[1] Haas, *Bilderatlas*, Part 5, Fig. 2; *cf.* Zimmern's *Text*.
[2] *cf.* H. Groos, *Der deutsche Idealismus und das Christentum*, 1927, 107.

and earthly or subterranean (chthonian), while in accord with Form, into male and female, father and mother, and sometimes child also. Then there are distinctions relevant to their spheres of operations, the "offices", or τιμαί, as Herodotus says. Aeschylus, too, was familiar with a formal classification of the gods:

> Of every god
> That guards the city, the deep, the high,
> Gods of the mart, gods of the sky,
> The altars blaze.[1]

But we must guard against reducing these divisions to the currency of works of reference which speak about gods like a *Who's Who*; for the traits of the form, the attributes and τιμαί, the cosmic or social links, are all to be understood only in the light of the numinous basis of Power. That is the truth misapprehended in *Henotheism*: man never has to deal with some community of gods as if it were a foreign superior state with which he comes into relation, but always only with Power, Will and Form as they become actual, impressive and visible at any given moment; and what has been revealed to him at that moment he afterwards co-ordinates according to his own standards.[2]

4. The Power that endows with sacredness the objects of man's environment, of the conjunct and the upper worlds, can withdraw itself into the background. But it can also come more and more prominently into the foreground. And in any case it is linked with the world; what is regarded with amazement as "Wholly Other" belongs nevertheless to the events of the world. Still further, the more thoroughly it is brought within the series of other phenomena so much the greater is the danger of its losing its original sacredness and becoming "world". In so-called Polytheism, then, there goes on an incessant struggle for the independence of the sacred Power over against the world; but in a wholly logical Polytheism world and god would fuse into one.

This, however, is no fault of Polytheism. It is rather the rendering apparent of the limits demanded by God as over against the world; although of course we can also say: the limits necessary to the world as against God. For neither the plurality of powers, nor the imaginative intensification of the outlines of the form, is in itself to blame for the fact that God threatens to become now world, and again man. For a God who is actually one, in the sense that there is no other Power

---

[1] *Agamemnon*, 88 *ff*. (Murray).   [2] *cf.* H. Schmalenbach, *Logos*, 16, 1927, 322.

whatever except him, would be wholly identical with the world; and Christianity allows the world and its overlord, the Devil, to exist in contrast to God.[1] Powers reveal themselves to us, and the ultimate unity is essentially the affair of faith, not of religion; for the religion of Power in general would be the worship of the Universe.

Anthropomorphism, too, is not wholly evil; for along with the fetish and the animal form, one possible expression of the Something Other is abandoned. But the human form of power also indicates distance; man has been unable to discover in the world any power higher than his own, and he now creeps, as it were, into this power himself.[2] He thereby renders some fragment of the world powerless, but does not necessarily make himself super-powerful; and it is precisely those attributes of the god, which raise it highest above man, that can be expressed no otherwise than in human analogies: strength of will, spirituality of outlook, certainty in fixing a goal.[3] Physical anthropomorphism, then, can be overcome, even though it is never conquered completely; but psychical anthropomorphism is given at the same time as human ideas and thoughts, and whoever desired to abandon it must remain absolutely silent about the god. For all speech is human and creates human forms; and even if animals and fetishes do seem to endow the Wholly Other with peculiarly adequate form,[4] still this is only because animals and things are themselves observed by man. The god of the animal, in fact, would first of all be a man.

"Whence the gods severally sprang, whether or no they had all existed from eternity, what forms they bore—these are questions of which the Greeks knew nothing until the other day, so to speak. For Hesiod and Homer were the first to compose *Theogonies*, and give the gods their *epithets*, to allot them their several *offices* and *occupations*, and describe their *forms*; and they lived but four hundred years before my time, as I believe."[5] In these words of Herodotus there lies the whole of classical Polytheism: the interconnection of the powers, the limitation of their operations, the development of their personality and creation of their form. This Polytheism is indeed to be found in

---

[1] Together with a whole host of "powers", φθορά, θάνατος, ἁμαρτία (corruption, death, sin), of the Pauline world; *cf*. O. Piper, *Die Grundlagen der evangelischen Ethik*, I, 1928, 127.

[2] *cf*. H. Werner, *Einführung in die Entwicklungspsychologie*, 1926, 272.

[3] *cf*. Kurt Sethe, *Amun und die acht Urgötter von Hermopolis, Abh. der preuss. Akad. der Wiss.*, 1929, *phil.-hist. Kl*. 4, §235.   [4] Chap. 3, 8.

[5] *Herodotus*, II, 53 (Rawlinson); my italics; *cf*. van der Leeuw, *Goden en Menschen*, 163 *f*.

many places, but nowhere so consistently and completely developed as in Greece.[1] Where it is an affair of names and forms it has become for ourselves a matter of course, and it is only recent decades that have perceived other possibilities, and also that the Greeks themselves were not content with the gifts of their own poets. For the criticisms of Xenophanes, of the Tragedians and the Sophists upon the Homeric idea of god, were passionately and quite seriously intended, and Plato knew full well why he excluded poets from his community.[2] In these criticisms fear of the humanizing of Power extends ultimately to its identification with the world. "Homer and Hesiod have ascribed to the gods all things that among men are a shame and a reproach—theft and adultery and deceiving one another." Thus says Xenophanes,[3] and he believes that he can draw the conclusion that man created gods in his own image: "If oxen or horses or lions had hands and could draw with them and make works of art as men do, horses would draw the shapes of gods like horses, oxen like oxen; each kind would represent their bodies just like their own forms." Again: "The Ethiopians say their gods are black and flat-nosed; the Thracians, that theirs are blue-eyed and red-haired."[4] We have already observed, however, that this anticipation of Feuerbach cannot be correct. But that a certain danger threatened here was again and again repeated by all the great Greeks in confirmation of Xenophanes. Thus Euripides is most severe with the beautiful Olympian forms; his gods are often mere machines, empty schemata with which men can screen their own deficiencies.[5] And even when they are real forms they exhibit so much human pettiness that they can merit only the poet's indignation, and not a single breath of adoration.

> Thine is unwisdom, or injustice thine,

says Amphitryon to Zeus; and Theseus substantiates this:

> Have they not linked them in unlawful bonds
> Of wedlock, and with chains, to win them thrones,
> Outraged their fathers? In Olympus still
> They dwell, by their transgressions unabashed.

Scornfully, again, Herakles asks:

> To such a goddess who shall pray now?[6]

[1] Nilsson, *A History of Greek Religion*, 144.   [2] *Republic*, 377 *ff.* and elsewhere.
[3] *Fr.* 11 (Diels; Cornford).   [4] *Fr.* 15, 16 (Diels; Cornford).
[5] *e.g. Troades*, 969 *ff.*; *cf.* U. von Wilamowitz-Möllendorff, *Griechische Tragödien*, III[5], 1919, 281 *f.*   [6] Euripides, *Herakles*, 345, 1316 *ff.*, 1308 (Way).

Here we see quite clearly where Theogony and endowment with Form have led. In the last resort neither the human gods nor their all-too-human poets were at fault, but rather the powers themselves. Who can help it if they clash with each other continually, if their will appears to be pure arbitrariness, if their rule must appear a tyranny? Poetic endowment with form by the Greeks merely gave its keenest expression to that question, addressed to the powers, which agitates many peoples, and in which the whole problem of *Theodicy* is contained: "What do ye powers desire? and why do ye desire it?" Much is presupposed here: that Power has Will: that man also has will, and indeed a will that does not operate by magic: that he has recognized some norm to which he ascribes absolute value. We shall discuss all this later; but we are now concerned with the fact that man can tolerate no plurality of forms and wills. And this indeed not merely because of the intractability of imagination—think of the Greek poets!—but because of the undeniable existence of forms and powers as such, quite apart from all fantasy. It was in fact the *Universe* that, under the form of gods, oppressed the Greeks; and it is *man* himself who causes himself this deep anxiety as to the gods' will.

Therefore the Greek attempted to free himself from gods: Euhemerus accounted for them as being men of an earlier age.[1] But the Greek mind chose a yet more resolute attitude: multiplicity and form had to give way to the Impersonal. The gods with human emotions, θεοὶ ἀνθρωποπαθεῖς, are after all too much like the world and men:

> For God hath need—if God indeed he be—
> Of nought: these be the minstrels' sorry tales.[2]

Nature itself is divine and requires no gods.[3] This indeed by no means yields any satisfaction to the poet's cry for a god "to whom one can pray", as Wilamowitz well remarks, since the divine Power in Nature, too, hears not. But from the far-reaching consequences of this flight from the Universe the Greeks were, of course, saved by their feeling for the principle, "Nothing in excess" (μηδὲν ἄγαν). But in India personal existence appeared more and more indefensible and despicable; even the existence of gods is, if not wrong, as in Greece, at least suffering: "in the unshakeable, the immovable, my heart rejoices".[4]

---

[1] Bertholet, *Lesebuch*, 4, 80 f.
[2] Euripides, *Herakles*, 1345 f. (Way); cf. U. von Wilamowitz-Möllendorf, *Herakles*², 1909, 481.
[3] *ibid.*, 1232; also *The Trojan Women*, 884 ff.; cf. my Article *Een dramatische Geloofsbelijdenis, Hermeneus*, 2, 1929.   [4] Bertholet, *Lesebuch*¹, 225.

This led ultimately to the disappearance of Form, to the eventual defeat of all will to live in Brahmanism and Buddhism—that is to religious *Atheism*.

Thus the development of Form and the humanizing of Will are not the basis of the question as to the claim of the gods. For everywhere that Power and man encounter each other, at the limits of human nature, this question appears, in ancient Babylon and *The Book of Job* just as with the Greek tragedians. Power no longer possesses its intrinsic claim; it must substantiate it; but in Polytheism, and above all in its most beautiful and profoundest revelation—the gods of Olympus—the question is shirked. Power and Nature, Nature and human life, all flow into each other: to the Homeric Greeks "the divine is neither a justifying explanation, nor an interruption and suspension, of the natural course of the world: it is the natural course of the world itself".[1]

Thus Power becomes our own life, numerability becomes intelligibility, the god's image becomes that of man. Here in fact lie the presuppositions of Greek, and at the same time of modern, science and art. But here too, ultimately, all worship ceases: Aristophanes is wholly right in his conservative criticism, in so far as he reproaches Euripides for causing the poor widow who plaited myrtle chaplets to lose half her customers by his disavowal of the gods.[2]

By relinquishing Form or Will, therefore, the solution can never be obtained, not even by simply erasing plurality. Only belief in the Creator escapes the consequences of Anthropomorphism: God created man after His own image. Only belief in Incarnation those of Polytheism: God becomes man, not world.

[1] W. F. Otto, *Die Götter Griechenlands*, 1929, 218.
[2] *Thesmophoriazousai*, 443 *ff.*

CHAPTER 20

THE FATHER

1. FORM and Will, then, can fail to such a degree that they are abandoned; and man can calm himself by the belief that his God is the world, is humanity, "growing with the world".[1] As we shall see,[2] he can even worship himself as humanity, as the human type: he can also take refuge in the Impersonal, in the Absolute, which "neither acts nor suffers, nor loves nor hates; it has no needs, desires or aspirations, no failures or successes, friends or enemies, victories or defeats".[3] After Greece, India has its say.[4]

And only that concept of God which renounces completely the specific potency of humanity can escape these consequences. For as long as man's own power attempts to destroy, to use, admire or enjoy external power, Form and Will must fail, since man is thereby compelling, using, admiring and enjoying himself over and over again. At most he can completely deny Form and Will: but that does not help him very much, since the world offers them to him every day in confusing plenteousness. And the tranquil background—as James saw quite rightly—can mean only "a moral holiday" and not a moral common round.[5] He himself took refuge in a modernized Polytheism; but recognition of manifoldness can avail just as little as its denial. Only where it is believed that Omnipotence—"all Power"—belongs to God does Form live and Will rule. Anthropomorphism need no longer be dreaded, because it is not we that impart Form to God, but He to us; anthropopathy is no longer a danger where all dominion comes from God and arises out of His Will; and plurality need no longer be destroyed by a desperate, colourless and unreal unity where His unity, to Whom all Power belongs, is comprehensible in itself, as is also the plurality of power that He has created. Thus we have expressed the essential principle: Form and Will have their real and divine life in God, *in the Creator*. But of course we do not mean that creator whom we have found reposing in the background of the Universe; rather do we think of the God Who imparts Himself in His creation, and Who even gives Himself.

[1] Typically, H. A. Overstreet, "The Democratic Conception of God", *Hibbert Journal*, XI, 1913, 394 *ff*.   [2] Chap. 37.
[3] James, *A Pluralistic Universe*, 47 *f*.   [4] Chap. 21.   [5] *ibid.*, 116 *ff*.

2. In this connection we naturally feel tempted to consider solely the Monotheism of Israel, to which indeed our description of fearless anthropomorphic belief in the Creator applies in the first instance. But it is imperatively necessary to inquire into the intelligible basis of Form and Will, and not to hesitate before anything less exalted. For man calls this God "Father", and hitherto we are familiar only with the Mother.

In this respect, too, Frazer remarks that it is chimerical to imagine that women invented the worship of goddesses, since "if women ever created gods, they would be more likely to give them masculine than feminine features".[1] But the second hypothesis would be just as false. It is true that both male and female elements, and the dominance of either at any given period, play a great part in the structure of the idea of God. But there is too much of the feminine in every man, and of the masculine in every woman, for precedence to be conceded here to either the one or the other sex. The religion of the Mother, therefore, is that of humanity exactly as is that of the Father.

In a way that produces on us moderns an almost amusing impression, we perceive the enormous interval separating the two, when in ancient Babylon we find our familiar name "father" replaced by "uncle";[2] the god is "uncle", that is the wife's brother, the most important male figure after the primarily important woman. This is a vestige of an all-embracing motherliness. But the distance in question finds its basis first of all in the contrast between father and mother, that is between active and passive: the mother gives birth, the father generates; the mother receives, the father gives. Thus next to the maternal figure there appears the paternal. And just as woman resembles the field, so does man the plough—to the Greeks Erichthonius, Erechtheus, "the earth opener".[3] Of course, the myth of the holy marriage, as has been observed,[4] has the mother as its principal person; and the father-spouse can be at the same time son. Here, where mother-earth is supreme, lie the roots of the Oedipus myth which, in our day, has been raised almost to the rank of a dogma by the Freudian school.[5] An ancient Egyptian divine title runs: "The Bull, that is, the spouse of his mother".[6] But the aspect of activity, of the giver, cannot be mistaken

---

[1] *Man, God and Immortality*, 129.

[2] B. Gemser, *De beteekenis der Persoonsnamen voor onze kennis van het leven en denken der onde Babylonieërs en Assyrieërs*, 1924, 102 ff.

[3] cf. E. Fehrle, *Die kultische Keuschheit im Altertum*, 1910, 185 f.

[4] Chap. 10.   [5] cf. C. Clemen, *Arch. für die ges. Psychologie*, 61, 1928, 26.

[6] cf. A. Wiedemann, *AR.* 21, 1922, 453.

in the figure of the father-spouse even when it subsists in the closest
proximity to the main factor of receptive passivity. For primeval—
and only to blind eyes, rude—sex symbolic language mediates theological creation of Form: most beautifully expressed in the words of
Tao-teh King:

> The spirit of the Deep never dies.
> It is the eternal feminine.
> The sallyport of the eternal feminine
> Is the root of heaven and earth.
> Eternally it urges itself forward, and yet remains steadfast.
> In its operation it remains effortless.

The "deep" is the "valley", the empty space between the walls of the
hills, matter without form, the mere possibility of being, while the
"spirit" is the active, the form-imparting.[1] The complete form would
therefore be not that of the mother, that is of "possibility"! but of
the willing and creating father.

But of course we must not interpret paternal form and will in terms
of the generative act alone; therein lies the onesidedness of Freudian
doctrine.[2] In the light of this lack of balance, also, it would be difficult
to understand how Christianity could take over belief in the Father
from the religion of Israel, wherein the Father form, as husband and
generator, is almost completely lacking. "Doubtless thou art our
father, though Abraham be ignorant of us, and Israel acknowledge us
not: thou, O Lord, art our father, our redeemer; thy name is from
everlasting. But now, O Lord, thou art our father; we are the clay,
and thou our potter; and we all are the work of thy hand."[3] This is
not the figure of the generator but of a creator, whose relations to man
are the precise opposite of those of kinship, and before whose will
man bows in deep but trustful dependence.

For many primitive and ancient peoples, that is to say, the term
"father" does not mean the same as it does for us, the "father" being
the representative of an age level, that of the older as contrasted with
the younger. For the term is older than the modern family, and presupposes a social organization in which a group of seniors was distinguished from a group of juniors. Here, then, much less importance

[1] R. Wilhelm, *Laotse, Tao Te King*, 1921, 8, 92. The creation of the form "Heaven-
earth" (male-female) is also connected with these ideas; *cf.* H. Th. Fischer, *Het heilig
huwelijk van hemel en aarde*, 1929.
[2] R. Thurnwald, *Ethnologie und Psychoanalyse*, in *Auswirkungen der Psychoanalyse
in Wissenschaft und Leben* (edited by H. Prinzhorn), 1928, 125 *ff*.
[3] *Isaiah* lxiii. 16; lxiv. 8.

attaches to the act of generation than to authority, fullness of power, the wisdom of the oldest men who, as is well known, were among many primitive societies the guardians of the secret rites. Even the Roman idea of *pater familias* regarded this power of the *pater* as independent of his actual fatherhood: "he who rules in the house is called *pater familias*, and is rightly so named even if he has no son". Power is limited to *domus*.[1] It is therefore in the light of this dual activity, firstly as generative-creative, secondly as authoritative-ruling, that the Father-form of God is to be understood: the indubitably superior, from which all Power is derived, but which communicates and imparts itself.

3. For this form the unity of God is not so important, at least not as a negation of plurality; and it is absolutely wrong therefore to conceive the history of religion as a development leading up to "Monotheism". Even for "developed religion, concepts like 'Monotheism' and 'Polytheism' are empty numerical schemes, by which the value of a religion can be measured just as little as can the worth of a marriage by the number of children sprung from it".[2]

It is a question then not of the unity, but of the uniqueness, of God: a form like that of God has nowhere been seen by our eyes: with a Will like God's we have never at any time come into contact. Who is like God? The uniqueness of God is no mere negation of His plurality, but a passionate affirmation of His potency. So deeply indeed has God's self-imparting activity bitten into human life that man must say to his God:

> Whom have I in heaven but thee?
> On earth I care for nothing else.[3]

Thus the Monotheism of Islam also was not a protest against Polytheism, but an enthusiastic belief in God's omnipotence.[4] For "omnipotence" is no bloodless "attribute" of a theoretically conceived ruler of the world or originator, but the conviction that all Power belongs to God, and none to man except what he receives from God. Here we are just as remote from the "supreme being" as from the manifold powers of Polytheism. Perhaps even farther: for here it is a case not of a "highest" being, but of *Being* itself, the sole reality, unique existent actuality, unique significance.

[1] G. May, *Eléments de Droit romain*[13], 1920, 103.
[2] Wundt, *op. cit.*, IV, 320.   [3] *Ps.* lxxiii. 25 (Moffat).
[4] A. Bertholet, *Die gegenwärtige Gestalt des Islams*, 1926, 8.

"God is One" therefore is to be regarded not as an assertion or conviction, but simply as an expression of faith in the sense of the classical acclamation εἷς θεός, "God is One".[1] God is One because from Him comes salvation, Power that has been turned to good. God is One because He is omnipresent in the inexhaustible activity of His Will: "If I ascend up into heaven, thou art there: if I make my bed in hell, behold, thou are there."[2] This burning activity of the Will of God is supremely vivid in the Old Testament, no less in quite primitive features such as in the story of Jahveh's sudden attack on Moses,[3] than in the battle-song of the Israelites, in which their joy in the active God who fights and saves, who descends from His mount to take their side, is unmistakably and resonantly heard:

> Blest be the Eternal One, my Strength,
>   who trains my hands to war,
>   my fingers how to fight!—
> my Crag, my Stronghold, my Fortalice and Deliverer
>   the Shield behind whom I shelter,
>   the subduer of nations before me!
>
> Eternal One, come down upon the bending heavens,
>   touch the mountains till they smoke,
> flash lightning out to scatter my foes,
>   shoot thine arrows to discomfit them;
> reach from on high to raise me from these floods,
>   rescue me from these alien hordes,
>
> O God, I would sing thee a new song,
>   and play to thee on a ten-stringed lute,
>
> May our sons be straight and strong like saplings,
> our daughters like cornices carved in a palace!
>
> Happy the nation that so fares!
> Happy the nation whose God is the Eternal![4]

But the all embracing activity of the Will, and the complete Father form, are declared by Christianity in the Incarnation. Unperturbed by the reproach of either Anthropomorphism or Polytheism, it beholds the figure of Him Who has come that He may perform the Will of Him who has sent Him.

[1] Chap. 63.   [2] *Ps.* cxxxix. 8.
[3] *Exodus* iv. 24 *ff.*   [4] *Ps.* cxliv (Moffat).

CHAPTER 21

THE ABSOLUTELY POWERFUL

1. OUR second Chapter dealt with Power theorized, rendered absolute, having attained dominance with no creation of form nor inclusion of will. Here, form and will having been abandoned as inadequate, we shall discuss Power unsustained by any person; Power that is not the outcome of will and that does not display itself, but absolutely *is*. Obviously the Power considered in Chapter 2 was not "previously" existent: just as little is the Power now in question only a late fruit of maturer speculation. But from the outset there is a tendency to Power simply as such, which at first concerns itself with neither will nor form; and also to the reattainment of Power after the creation of form has failed, as can be observed most clearly in the case of the Greeks. This produces a considerable structural difference, which induces me to devote a specific discussion to this flight to absolute Power.

It can be regarded, then, as an attempt to cling to the experience of Power purely in itself, while escaping from the "dual experience of form". Power overcomes us—herein all religions agree. But whoever has been undeceived in the divine will, and evaluates the second formalized experience of Power as mere appearance, tries to retain this experience in itself, as pure Power. Forthwith he hits upon the idea of *Fate*. Thus did Aeschylus: and thus did Goethe's Prometheus:

> I honour thee! For what?
> Hast thou the miseries lightened
> Of the down-trodden?
> Hast thou the tears ever banished
> From the afflicted?
> Have I not to manhood been moulded
> By omnipotent Time,
> And by Fate everlasting,
> My lords and thine?[1]

One alone is powerful: the force that here, and at this moment, binds me, the law according to which I have come into being. There may be other powers, forms and wills besides my own: but like myself

[1] The poem *Prometheus*.

these too are subject to that primeval determining Power which roots me to this very life, this very time and place. The riddle as to why I was born and why, just here and now, my life rolls on, is insoluble: it is just my lot, and the Power apportioning it my fate. Whatever holds good of me holds good also of the whole Universe: its potency too is limited and conditioned, its "Being-now", as its "Being-thus", a mystery.

Now I experience this Power of fate as pure Power only as soon as I not merely verify it, but also surrender myself to it. Then I abandon all personal adjustment to Power, I despair of any interference of Power on my own behalf, I relinquish the thought of *salvation* and deliver myself up to *Fate*.[1] I may turn out to be a failure: if so, Destiny receives demonic attributes and, as in later Greek times, I long for the "saving fate, for mercy".[2] But the old Greeks achieved this. The idea of the rightness of the Universe took the place of the idea of salvation: we have not understood God's will: his form appears dubious to us: nor can we justify his deeds. Nevertheless Fate is always right; and we address no demands to it because it is the absolutely powerful. Thus Euripides' "Natural Law" led all "to the right goal". The problem of a theodicy cannot arise, just as every personal desire from Power is excluded. So Plato thought: "God, as the old tradition declares, holding in His hand the beginning, middle, and end of all that is, moves according to His nature in a straight line towards the accomplishment of His end. Justice always follows Him, and is the punisher of those who fall short of the divine law."[3] Against *ananke* neither magic—human power—nor the art of healing, neither cult nor even Zeus—the power of the willing god—can do aught.[4]

2. We found that uniformity of the person and constancy in form were dependent on the *Name*; we need hardly be surprised, therefore, that the abandonment of will and form implies also a loss of the name of the power; Euripides, for instance, calls his god "Zeus" or "Natural Law" or even "world reason". The name has now become "empty sound", and far from being competent to guarantee essence—as was the case in the structure of primitive thought—it has sunk to the level of an unreality, or at least an inadequacy. The Greeks, who turned from the gods to the divine (θεῖον), derived from the proper

---

[1] *cf.* further Otto Piper's observations, *Die Grundlagen der evangelischen Ethik*, I, 1928, 108 *ff.*   [2] P. Tillich, *Philosophie und Schicksal, Kantstudien*, 34, 1929, 302 *ff.*
[3] *Laws*, IV, 715*e* (Jowett); *cf.* Tillich, *ibid.*, 301 *ff.*   [4] Euripides, *Alcestis* 962 *ff.*

name "Zeus" a significance which probably expressed something more general than when we say "God".[1] Thus it is primarily intended by Aeschylus in the famous apostrophe to Zeus in *Agamemnon*:

Zeus! Zeus, whate'er He be,
If this name He love to hear
This He shall be called of me.
Searching earth and sea and air
Refuge nowhere can I find
Save Him only, if my mind
Will cast off before it die
The burden of this vanity.[2]

From doubt and care, then, the poets find rest in the god who has no name—or has every name. And later reflection sees powers scattered throughout the world and invoked by different names, while only the one God is intended whose actual name no one knows.[3] Henceforth the name is regarded as a limitation; it can certainly offer a footing in the turmoil of the infinite manifold and provide firm outlines in the dissolution, but what has thus been won is not the divine. "If I called him by a hundred names, like a Turk, I should yet fall short and have said nothing in comparison to the boundlessness of his attributes."[4]

3. Thus from Form and Will man flees to the impersonal, the nameless; but also to the *Inner Life*; and then Power operates not from without, but from within. In relation to the human it is of course transcendent (otherwise it would no longer be the object of religion), but its superiority is that of the whole as over against the part. The god who is invoked in Euripides' Prayer of Hecuba, which has already been frequently quoted, is the air, the world principle advanced by Diogenes of Apollonia, the ἀρχή, which is the life-creating force in both man and beast.[5] The concepts "God" and "soul" affect each other: God becomes the world-soul; and with this the human spirit

---

[1] Therefore not "exactly the same as when we say God", even if "much less the proper name of one among countless gods other than Jahveh", and indeed "no longer a person". Wilamowitz, *Griech. Tragödien*, III[5], 1919, 283.

[2] *Agamemnon*, 160 *ff.* (Murray).

[3] Thus Maximus of Madaura, in F. Cumont, *Les religions orientales dans le paganisme romain*[2], 1909, 307.   [4] Goethe, *Conversations with Eckermann*, March 8, 1831.

[5] *cf.* Karl Joel, *Der Ursprung der Naturphilosophie aus dem Geiste der Mystik*, 1906, 112 *f.*

consciously turns back to extremely primitive paths. Power, as we saw, was "stuff" that could impart soul, the frontier between god and soul being indistinct, and the idea of *mana* comprising both. Now Power is made absolute from within as the world-soul, in conscious contrast to the powers which intrude from without:

> What were a God, who, outward force applying,
> But kept the All around his finger flying!
> He from within lives through all Nature rather,
> Nature and Spirit fostering each other;
> So that what in Him lives, and moves, and is,
> Still feels His power, and owns itself still His.[1]

Here, side by side with the humble worship of the Whole, there rings in Goethe's words a note of fear in face of the incalculability of the divine Will, which bestows its power and its spirit but which also, when it so pleases, withdraws them.

4. The Power which, nameless, moves within the Universe, is ultimately *One*; that is, there is none other beside it. Here—not in Monotheism—unity receives its full stress. The form of the Father, standing opposed to the world, is unique, while the Power which, like air, penetrates everything, is One—in the sense of One and All; and in the ancient world we find such pantheistic impulses. The name of the Egyptian god *Atum*, for example, was explained as: "Atum, that is, all the gods", while the dead were deified and each of their limbs identified with a god; thus a funeral *Text* quotes the dead man as saying that his hair is Nun, his countenance Ra, *etc.*, and "there is no member of my body which is not the member of some god".[2]

It is well known, further, how the Hindu spirit derived all individual powers from the twofold unity of *Brahman* and *Ātman*. The interval between object and subject is thereby completely annulled, and the absolute otherness, the transcendence of Power, can persist only in the feeling of submersion and plunging within the Universe. In the *Bhagavad-Gita* speaks the Sublime:

And others, sacrificing with the sacrifice of knowledge worship me as one or as several, in many ways—so they worship me, who face every way.

I am the oblation, I am the sacrifice, the offering to the fathers am I; I

---

[1] *God, Soul, and World* (Dwight); *cf.* H. Groos, *Der deutsche Idealismus und das Christentum*, 1927, 71 *f.*, on the derivation of Goethe's lines from Giordano Bruno, *De Immenso*, IV, 15.   [2] *The Book of the Dead*, Chap. 42, 10.

am the herb, the sacred formula; I am also the melted butter, I am the fire, I am the burnt offering.

I am the father of this universe, the mother, the supporter, the grand-father, that which should be known, the purifier, OM, the Rigveda, the Samaveda, the Yajurveda;[1]

The way, the supporter, the Lord, the witness, the abode, the refuge, the friend, the origin, the dissolution, the abiding-place, the storehouse, the changeless seed.

I give heat, I hold back the rain and send it forth; I am the immortal and also death; being and non-being am I, O Arjuna.[2]

Here every form, every particularity, every individuality fails. God too is superfluous, since the divine within man is all: "Who ranks the higher, he who offers sacrifices to his own self (*ātman*) or he who sacrifices to the gods? We should reply, he who offers sacrifice to himself."[3]

Unlike the Hindu, however, the Greek could never completely dispense with Form. But even Zeus does not *have* all Power—he *is* all Power; and this conception is already found in Aeschylus:

Zeus is air, Zeus is earth, Zeus is heaven;
Zeus is all things and whatsoever is higher than all things.[4]

The Stoics absorbed this idea: mythology is deceitful: "but though repudiating these myths with contempt, we shall nevertheless be able to understand the personality and the nature of the divinities pervading the substance of the several elements, Ceres permeating earth, Neptune the sea, and so on . . . under the names which custom has bestowed upon them".[5]

Thus Power becomes increasingly limitless, and constantly richer:

---

[1] *Om* is the sacred magic syllable, followed here by the three canonical Vedas.

[2] *The Song of the Lord: Bhagavad-Gita*, IX, 15. (E. J. Thomas); *cf.* also the pan-theism of romanticism:

> Argatiphontidas and Photidas,
> The citadel of Cadmus and Greece.
> Light, ether and the waters,
> What was: What is: What shall be;

(Heinrich von Kleist, *Amphitryon*, III, 11), and the objection of that typical animist, Alcmene!

> Shall I pray to this white marble block?
> If I am to think of him at all
> I need some recognizable features (II, 5).

[3] Oldenberg, *Lehre der Upanishaden*, 33.

[4] Cornford, *Greek Religious Thought*, 109; *cf.* H. Diels, *Zeus, AR.* 22, 1923–24, 11 *f.*

[5] Cicero, *De Deorum Natura*, II, 72. (Rackham).

"The heavens become a house, the stars chambers for the god who has grown rich."[1] Power becomes more and more absolute Power: each barrier, each limitation, collapses. Everything reposes on the one indivisible Potency: all longing is appeased, all struggle suppressed. All is within, nothing remains outside: except Him who came to bring not peace, but the sword.[2]

[1] G. Th. Fechner, *Über die Seelenfrage*, 1861, 197.
[2] Chesterton, *Orthodoxy*, "The Romance of Orthodoxy".

P. TILLICH, *Philosophie und Schicksal* (*Kantstudien*, 34, 1929).

PART TWO

THE SUBJECT OF RELIGION

A. THE SACRED MAN

CHAPTER 22

SACRED LIFE

1. JUST as the Object of religion, to faith, is Subject in the sense of "the active and primary Agent",[1] exactly so for Subject and Object. The sciences concerned with religion observe a person who practises religion, who sacrifices and prays, *etc.* Faith sees a person to whom something has happened; and Phenomenology describes how man conducts himself in his relation to Power. But it must never be forgotten that this person himself first decides, or alters, his attitude after he has been affected by Power. In this all believers are unanimous, from primitive man who experiences the nearness of Power and calls out "Tabu!", to the apostle who exhorts us to love God because He "first loved us".[2]

For this reason I now turn to the consideration of the life called "sacred", because human life, in directing itself towards Power, "first" of all was touched by Power: in orienting itself to the sacred, that is to say, it itself participates in sacredness. On the other hand, we must not for one moment forget that man is himself active, so that whoever speaks of faith is at the same time dealing with religious culture. The question whether animals possess faith is meaningless; the question whether they have religion can be answered merely in the negative, simply because they have no culture. How Power affects animals we know not; but we do know definitely that they do not react to Power. In this respect man, in his humanity, appears on the scene independently.

2. In its relationship to Power, then, human life is first of all not the life of the individual, but that of the *Community*; and this will be discussed later. But neither is it life in its variegated manifoldness such as we observe in the Press or the modern novel. Rather is it life in a form simplified and abbreviated to its essential factors: life, that is to say, as it is lived by all without exception, and quite apart from any differences in manner of living, talent, temperament, *etc.*: that is,

---

[1] *cf.* Chap. 1, Section 1. [2] 1 *John* iv. 19.

Birth, Marriage and Death: Life as it directs itself to Power and is seized upon by Power; therefore not the personal life of feeling, not the life of thought, but simply Life in its stark nakedness. Of this we must constantly remind ourselves, even when we are dealing with conditions only semi-primitive, or indeed not primitive at all.

Actually, even birth, marriage and death are still too ample. Birth and death suffice. For whatever else occurs in life, marriage, war, initiation and the bestowing of names, all can be included in the great polarity of life and death. As over against Power there is no history, neither collective nor individual. Whatever there is in life that is variable or contingent is forced into definite, stereotyped and diversified rites as much as is at all possible; rites which all, without exception, aim at the transition from life to death and from death to life. If, in the mood of modern mankind, we represent our life as a straight line, then at its beginning and its end we draw thick transverse strokes: what lies before birth does not belong to our life, and as to what follows death, we may cherish a belief; but "life after death" differs in every respect from the life we possess, and is at the very least a new beginning. The line between the two heavy transverse strokes we next divide into sections by finer strokes which indicate the great transitions: maturity, marriage, commencement of a career, retirement, a severe illness, *etc.* But in sacred life each stroke is equally heavy, each section equally important, each transition is one either from death to life or from life to death. This means that our secular life has the form of a line, but the sacred life the form of a circle. It is as the poet imagines Death to speak to man:

> If, with swift convulsion,
> Aught overwhelming has shown itself akin to thee,
> And thou, abandoning thyself in the great dance,
> Receivest the Universe as thine own—
> In every so truly great an hour,
> Which awed thine earthly form,
> I have touched thee in the very ground of thy soul,
> With sacred and mysterious Power.[1]

3. The important affairs in life therefore are not events as we understand them, but "transitional rites" (*Rites de passage*) as van Gennep calls them. Birth, naming, initiation, marriage, sickness and recovery, the start and the end of a long journey, the outbreak of war and con-

---

[1] Hugo von Hofmannsthal, *Der Tor und der Tod.*

clusion of peace, death and burial, are all points of contact between Power and life, and hence must not merely be experienced and then remembered, but must actually be *celebrated*. *In transitional rites, life affected by Power turns towards Power*. Instead of "events" or "experiences", therefore, the content of life is better styled "celebrations".

4. The first of these is *Birth*. This is not merely an event that occurs only once: it is rather an entry into life, the entering of a power which can be furthered, impeded and even frustrated. In China, celebrating birth is called "the passage through the gate"; a bamboo archway is erected first of all in the middle, and then in each of the four corners, of the room; then the *Tao* priest, the father and children step through these. This ceremony is repeated every year, or every third or sixth year, according to the family, until the rite of "the cessation of childhood"; but it is performed also when the child is ill, or repeated several times in the course of the year or month.[1] The celebration is intended to ensure contact between Power and life; the ordered induction of Power is necessary, and in cases of waning power the solemnizations must be more frequently repeated.

If no celebration takes place, in fact, birth does not become definitive, does not become an event. Thus the Central Australians believe that a child killed immediately after birth can afterwards be brought forth again by the same woman;[2] child murder is therefore not murder, but merely a sending back of life which has not yet been admitted to power; for one is "born" only when all the rites have been completed. Immediately after coming into the world one is still "only partially born"; what has occurred has such slight power that it can easily be reversed.[3]

The rites here in question are of various kinds. Laying the newborn infant on the ground was customary among the Romans; and elsewhere, *e.g.* in the Indonesian Seranglao Archipelago, the child is placed in contact with the earth, and as it were baptized with it.[4] Here therefore the new life is directed towards the power of Mother-earth. In Greece, again, a naked man ran around the hearth with the infant,[5] the fire's potency being thereby extracted. But since the induction of power

[1] A. van Gennep, *Les rites de passage*, 82 *f.*
[2] Spencer and Gillen, *The Native Tribes of Central Australia*, 51 *f.*
[3] Lévy-Bruhl, *How Natives Think*, 342 *f.*
[4] Riedel, *Sluik- en kroesharige rassen*, 175.
[5] *Amphidromia*; Samter, *Geburt, Hochzeit und Tod*, 113; *cf.* S. Reinach, *Cultes, Mythes et Religions*, 1, 1905, 137 *ff.*

first makes birth an actuality, it is never really perfected; new rites are continually necessary; and thus it is intelligible that certain initiatory rites, such as circumcision and baptism (naming), are equally birth rites.

Birth then is never perfected; but it also is not an actual beginning. The sacred life indeed knows neither beginning nor end, but strives after continuity by means of power. Birth is therefore rebirth: birth and death pertain to each other, and rites at birth are often exactly similar to the customs to be observed at death.[1] In case of miscarriages or still-births, for instance, the East African Wazaromo say "he has returned". But here we should not think of any theory of pre-existence. For there is nothing theoretical in this apprehension of life, which progresses not in a linear direction but in cycles, returning ever again upon itself.[2] Life is here no series of facts, but a stream in which it is always an affair of surmounting the perilous obstacles where power may fail, but where it may also become overwhelmingly strong. Birth time is a critical time, an exposed stage; and the woman who has just given birth is regarded as impure, that is as either powerless or under the influence of a foreign and dangerous potency. In Sweden, between child-bed and her first visit to church, a woman was formerly called "heathenish"; she had to be careful and to carry some steel about with her, so that the *trolls* could obtain no power over her.[3]

As the revelation of Power, however, every birth is a miracle: the extraordinary, the "Wholly Other", announces itself in the crisis of birth, in the newly appearing life. Actually, then, every birth is a "miraculous birth", this expression of course not being understood in the sense of supernaturalism; for in the transition from death to life, in the cycle of life regarded in its abbreviated form, Power reveals itself. Thus arose the myth of the origin of man, which assumes the form of "issuing from elsewhere" even where the physiological conditions of generation are known; a myth which was connected above all with great men like kings *etc.*, and which still persists in nurses' tales of Frau-Hollenteich or the stork.[4]

---

[1] A. van Gennep, *op. cit.*, 68 *f.*, 74, and Note 3.   [2] J. E. Harrison, *Themis*, 273.
[3] Klara Stroebe, *Nordische Volksmärchen*, I, 1919, No. 18.
[4] It is impossible to agree with Frazer (*Totemism and Exogamy*, IV, 57 *ff.*) in deriving the idea of marvellous birth from the ignorance of primitive man about the relationship between conception and birth. It is no matter of lack of knowledge but—positively—of the experience of arrival from elsewhere. Ignorance may certainly have furnished the condition for this, which then attained a positive import by "transposition"; (on this term *cf.* p 610.).

5. Man, however, cannot rest content with mere life: he must seek
sacred life, replete with Power. Rites guarantee him power: he himself
creates salvation; and the great majority of these rites are *purifications*.[1]
Potent water or fire must assist man to surmount some critical situation,
must neutralize the disturbing power and grant admission to the
beneficent influence. *Bathing* and *Baptism*, then, first make life "true"
life; and the *baptism of fire*, one of the most frequent initiatory rites
among primitive peoples, still survives in the fairy story about
the dwarf rejuvenated by flame,[2] and also in the Eleusinian legend
of the deification of Demophoon by fire through the agency of
Demeter.[3]

Beating also has lustrative value, especially the "stroke with the rod
of life", a freshly cut twig that bestowed fertility; the *accolade*, again,
is an initiation, a puberty rite.[4] Here the idea of purification approximates to that of mutilation, which leads anew to the profoundest
ideas about death and revivification, since mutilation is an intimation
of death. Again and again must sacred life be commenced anew, and
each *rite de passage* is a rite of birth, but of death also. Thus *circumcision*
is certainly a weakening of the man, but is nevertheless an enervation
with more potent life as its aim. In Buru in the Dutch East Indies the
boys who are to be circumcized are kept apart, and may eat only foods
which have been prepared by virgins;[5] this indicates the critical situation,
the contact with power, to which the boys expose themselves by this
rite. But circumcision, which occurs principally among Malay-Poly-
nesian and Semite-Hamitic peoples, must not be isolated; for it is only
one of various rites having as their purpose the induction or renewal
of power. Thus life is not accepted simply as it is, but is changed,
mutilated, so that it will become capable of Power; and circumcision
is a charm of the same character as filing down the teeth, tattooing, the
perforation of the maiden's hymen, the boring of the nasal bone, *etc.*,[6]
in Central Australia this last operation being performed on the men
on the occasion of the maturity ceremonies, and on the girls immediately
after marriage. For women, indeed, marriage is the entrance into life
proper.[7] Similarly among the Mandan Indians, at puberty rites, the
youths have the little finger of the left hand chopped off on the skull

[1] Chap. 49.　　　　　　　　　　　　　[2] *Kinder- und Hausmärchen*, No. 147.
[3] Lang, *The Homeric Hymns*, 197; cf. Murray, *The Rise of the Greek Epic*, 350 ff.
[4] cf. J. Huizinga, *Het herfstty der Middeleeuwen*, 1919, 129.
[5] Riedel, *Sluik- en kroesharige rassen*, 6.
[6] cf. further E. J. Dingwall, *Artificial Cranial Deformation*, 1931.
[7] Spencer and Gillen, *Native Tribes*, 214 ff.

of a buffalo by an old man with a hatchet;[1] and the Yoruba natives of
West Africa call circumcision "the cutting that saves".[2] Most of these
mutilations, moreover, occur not only at so-called puberty rites but
also at marriage, during mourning and the like; and thus the whole
of life is apprehended only as a crisis of Power.

The various *tests* and *purifications*, then, which those must undergo
who are to be initiated into manhood and unrestricted tribal membership, are also approximations to death leading to new life, moral
considerations and tests of courage and endurance actually occupying
only second place. Similarly the harassing still in vogue among ourselves,
for example among seamen and in student circles, is no affair of moral
ends, even though these are subsequently advanced; a crisis must be
gone through, as in Sparta when the *ephebi* were scourged at the altar
of Artemis Orthia till the blood ran; "from the outset this custom was
intended not as a test of endurance, but as purification and propitiation".[3] Even the instruction imparted to the novices at the ceremony
was by no means the principal concern. Occasionally, it is true, informa-
tion is imparted on religious topics such as the nature of the bull-roarer
used by Australian tribes, or the content of the rites, or on moral
affairs like conduct towards parents. But the real aim is always the
renewal of life, the induction of that power which makes possible a
new era and with which actual adult life first begins, just as with
ourselves ecclesiastical confirmation, despite all the stressing of
instruction in the practice of the Reformed churches and the pietistic
emphasis on the inner life, has remained a genuine *rite de passage*.

Even the new clothes which confirmation candidates in the country
procure for themselves (at least in Holland) find their prototype among
primitive peoples. "In Korea, on the fourteenth day of the first month
of the year, anyone who is entering on a 'critical year of his life', makes
an effigy of straw, dresses it in his own clothes, casts it on the road . . .
'Fate is believed to look upon the individual clothes as another man.' "[4]
And the connection of celebration with the idea of complete renewal
still persists to-day in the sphere of religious ritual: monks and nuns
adopt new costume, and even lay rites retain something of this attitude;
for when Marie Antoinette came to Strassburg as the *dauphin's* bride

---

[1] E. Samter, *Familienfeste der Griechen und Römer*, 1901, 78 *f.*
[2] Crawley, *The Mystic Rose*, I, 170.
[3] M. P. Nilsson, *Griechische Feste*, 1906, 192; *cf.* Webster, *Primitive Secret Societies*,
35. A very life-like description of the initiation of boys by the indigenes themselves is
to be found in Paul Hambruch, *Südseemärchen*, 1921, No. 9.
[4] Crawley, *The Mystic Rose*, I, 327 *f.*

she was completely undressed by her ladies and, according to old custom, clothed in new garments of French origin; she had to relinquish her Austrian clothing down to the minutest detail.[1]

With renewal of life conduct also is changed. A novice of the Kwakiutl tribes of Columbia, for example, acts as if he had forgotten ordinary human behaviour and must learn everything anew from the beginning.[2] In other cases the initiated man receives a new name: after circumcision the Amandebele youths in South Africa cross a river and are given fresh names,[3] the ceremony being called *wela*—"the transition", while on Nias boys change their names at marriage and girls at puberty. Similarly, at the conclusion of initiation the Tasmanians whisper a secret name to the boys,[4] just as the Hindu *Upanayana* ceremony of introduction to the teacher includes the reception of a fresh name in addition to the one normally used.[5] Here too secularized rite has preserved much: in Frisia for example, in the Netherlands, men leaving home to seek work receive an additional name, formerly an ordinary baptismal, to-day usually a historical, appellation like Alva *etc.*

This alteration of name indicates a complete change, a total renewal of life.[6] In the sources already cited this is repeatedly and unmistakably perceptible; thus the *Upanayana* ceremony is regarded as a rebirth, and the initiate as a "twice-born man", this idea being carried out with true Hindu precision: "by laying his right hand on the boy the teacher becomes pregnant; on the third day, in the invocation called *Sāvitrī*, a prayer to the inciting god *Savitar*, a genuine 'special god', the Brahman is born".[7] The Liberian *Vai* tribesmen, again, bring their young girls, at about the age of ten, into a shady grove called the *sande*, where they remain till the commencement of menstruation or till they are engaged; like the boys in the *belli* they, and the old women who attend them too, are looked upon as dead. They receive instruction in domestic and sex affairs; but this in itself is not the principal matter, the festival of their emergence being a rebirth,[8] while at Kikuyu in Kenya there is a ceremony, *ku-chiaruo ringi*, that is "to be born again", which must be observed before circumcision; the child must then lie down beside

[1] "The official ceremony took place in a wooden structure on one of the islands in the Rhine. In obedience to the requirements of etiquette the *dauphine* was almost completely unrobed and then clothed in garments brought from her new country." P. de Ségur, *Marie Antoinette*, 1921, 20.
[2] Webster, *Primitive Secret Societies*, 40.　　　[3] Fourie, *Amandebele*, 128 f., cf. 137.
[4] Crawley, *The Mystic Rose*, I, 320 ff.　　　[5] Oldenberg, *Religion des Veda*, 466.
[6] Chap. 17.　　[7] Oldenberg, *ibid.*, 466 f.　　[8] A. van Gennep, *op. cit.*, 197 f.

its mother on the bed and cry like a newborn infant.[1] In West Africa the *Belli-Paaro* is death, rebirth and incorporation in the community of spirits or souls; "the initiated receive the sign *Belli-Paaro* (several rows of incisions on the neck and the shoulder-blade) every twenty or twenty-five years, by which they are killed, roasted and completely changed, dying to their old life and nature and receiving new reason and knowledge".[2] In the Congo too this same reference to death and rebirth in connection with puberty rites is to be met with; there also the young people receive a new name and pretend to have forgotten their previous life and not to recognize their old acquaintances,[3] while in Ceram, in Indonesia, the novices take a most moving farewell of their friends, since they are going to meet death: the *nitu*, the spirits of the departed, will tear out their hearts, and give them back only on the entreaty of the grown-up men. On returning they walk with unsteady gait, look distracted, enter their houses by the rear doors and avoid the light, just as though they were coming from the other world.[4]

That initiation means death, and the renewal of life its surrender, can still be seen in many rites quite apart from specifically primitive culture. The novice who enters a Benedictine brotherhood, for instance, prostrates himself on the ground between four candles; he is covered with a shroud, and the *Miserere* is sung over him; then he rises, embraces all those standing around him and receives communion from the hands of the abbot.[5]

The rites that renew human life are therefore the very antithesis of mere ornaments. I become of age whether I celebrate the day or not: the psycho-physical process of puberty is completed in my own case whether I accompany it by ceremonies or not. But the primitive rite is by no means an ornamental ceremony; it is on the contrary a real development of power, a creative deed, executed by the community. He who has no name, then, has not been born, and whoever has not been initiated remains all his life a child;[6] no matter how aged he becomes he cannot even "grow old", since he has never grown up! Similarly, the fate of children who have died unbaptized is a sad one, because they have no names; they belong nowhere, properly speaking:

---

[1] C. W. Hobley, "Kikuyu Customs and Beliefs", *Journal As. Soc.*, 40, 441 *f.*

[2] Th. Achelis, *Die Ekstase*, 1902, 56 *f.*   [3] Crawley, *The Mystic Rose*, I, 325.

[4] Riedel, *Sluik- en kroesharige rassen*, 108 *ff.*; *cf.* Webster, *Primitive Secret Societies*, 39 *ff.*

[5] Comte Goblet d'Alviella, *L'Initiation*, RHR. 81, 1920, 17, Note 1.

[6] Thus in Fiji no distinction is made between uninitiated men and children; both groups are called: "they, the children". Webster, *Primitive Secret Societies*, 25.

they cannot really come into existence, either "here" or "there". Thus on one of the Twelve Nights a Tyrolese farmer sees the *Perchta* passing by with her train of unbaptized children; the last child in the line keeps treading on his little shirt which is too long for it, and can hardly keep up with the others. So the farmer shouts: "*Huderwachtl!* come here and I'll tie up your little dress for you"; the child replies: "Now I must thank you, for I have a name", and disappears.[1] At Whittinghame, again, the spirit of a child murdered by its mother haunted the district, and one night a drunkard greeted it with the words "How's a' wi' ye the morn, Short-Hoggers?" The child ran joyfully away, crying out:

> Oh, weel's me now, I've gotten a name;
> They ca' me Short-Hoggers of Whittinghame.

According to church doctrine, as we know, the unbaptized dead[2] go to the *limbus infantium*: certainly not to hell, but neither to heaven; while in the Middle Ages an oath sworn to anyone unbaptized was regarded as not binding, and hence the German princes held themselves released from the oath they had sworn to the child who afterwards became Frederick II.[3] Existence, then, is no fixed possession, but a possibility that becomes a reality only by the induction of power.

6. The Greeks regarded *marriage* as a dying and a resurrection, and called it a τέλος, a consecration; but the mysteries-consecration was a rebirth.[4] Only those who enjoy stupid jokes about the married state can smile at this; and in so doing they never realize that their jests are in themselves no more than a pitiful vestige of the awe that has always accompanied the complete union of two persons in a new life. Marriage is therefore a transition, a crisis; and in sacred life every crisis is one of death. The Greek marriage ritual resembled that of the mysteries to the very details; and although this may have been due in part to the mystery cults having sprung from the domestic cult, still it does not explain the use of the mystery formula, "I have fled from evil, I have found good", ἔφυγον κακόν, εὗρον ἄμεινον, in the marriage

---

[1] W. Mannhardt, *Die Götter der deutschen und nordischen Völker*, 1860, 291.

[2] W. H. F. Basevi, *The Burial of the Dead*, 117 ff.

[3] Ranke, *Weltgeschichte*, VII⁴, 1921, 182.

[4] Fustel de Coulanges, *La cité antique*²⁰, 1908, 43; *cf.* Jane E. Harrison, *Epilegomena to the Study of Greek Religion*, 16. But *cf.* here H. Bolkestien, Τέλος ὁ γάμος, *Meded. kon. Ak. v. Wet. Afd. Lett.*, 76, B, 2, who rejects, however, only the equivalence between τέλος and marriage, and not the other facts.

ritual. That is no eulogy of matrimony, but an expression of the consciousness that a new life is opening with new power. Thus we can understand why thoughts of death are frequently so much indulged in at the time of marriage; in Upper Bavaria a mass for the dead is said the day before the wedding, and in the Eifel district the day following, while in Thuringia the bridal pair decorated the graves of their relatives and godparents with their own hands. In Lower Bavaria, again, the best man says after the wedding breakfast: "Since we have eaten and drunk, we must not forget the poor souls", whereupon the guests proceed to the grave weeping and praying.[1] In all this we apprehend the family unity on the one hand, and on the other the proximity of death to life, the latter being very clearly expressed in the Frisian custom of women being wed in a widow's mourning habit; and I do not feel too inclined to accept the relater's rationalistic interpretation of the custom being intended to impress the women with the fact that death alone can part them from their husbands.[2] In Gelderland the shroud, and sometimes even the coffin boards, are made at the time of the wedding.[3]

As transition, as crisis, marriage is exposed to dangerous fullness of power. The potencies revealed in sex intercourse arouse anxiety and inspire fear: they must be restrained; and hence the custom of robbing cohabitation of its power by pre-marital defloration of the bride. For this a stranger or priest is selected, who possesses sufficient power to be able to take some risk.[4] The ceremonial *ruptura hymenis* may also be sufficient, while cohabitation with a child is a mitigation of this practice,[5] as is the observance of the so-called Tobias nights when the bridal pair abstain from marital intercourse.[6] Whether the so-called *jus primae noctis* has a religious basis (the lord or tribal chieftain being the powerful one!) or is a mere survival of the rule of the king or father, appears dubitable.[7]

The transition to marriage, still further, demands not only measures of defence, but implies also an induction of power likewise subjected

---

[1] Samter, *Geburt, Hochzeit und Tod*, 213.

[2] C. van Alkemade, *Inleidinge tot het Ceremonieel der Begraavenissen*, 1713, 152.

[3] H. W. Heuvel, *Volksgeloof en Volksleven*.

[4] Crawley, *The Mystic Rose*, II, 66 *ff*.

[5] *cf. e.g.* the marriage customs of Naxos, E. Kagarow, *AR*. 26, 1928, 362.

[6] In Vedic India, for example: Oldenberg, *Religion des Veda*, 253. A staff separates the couple, as did a sword among Germanic peoples.

[7] K. Schmidt, *Jus primae noctis*, 1881. On the landowner's consent as necessary to the marriage being a vestige of *jus primae noctis, cf.* Heuvel, *Oud-Achterhoeksch boerenleven*, 450.

to definite rules. Thus the communal meal at the wedding is wide-spread; the oldest form of Roman marriage included the custom of *confarreatio*, the bridal couple eating together from the sacrifice of spelt to the accompaniment of a fixed and solemn formula, *certa et sollemnia verba*. In Loango (West Africa), husband and wife and their parents each cut off a small piece of tobacco, place this in a pipe and then all smoke it one after the other.[1] This implies community; but it is just as much sacrament as it is *communio*.[2] A power is introduced into life and at the same time controlled: for rites are always creative, but also always regulative; they signify not only the piercing of a fountain, but further the laying of a channel for its stream. Thus in Russia the bridal night is spent in the store-room in order to ensure the fertility of the marriage,[3] while among very many primitive peoples we find phallic marriage rites, medieval *epithalamia*, and the coarse jests which even to-day the bridal pair are not spared in more primitive circles, being the vestiges of this. Both word and deed are intended to conduct power to the new life.

Hence it is no matter for surprise that like birth (as rebirth) and death (the relinquishing of the old sinful life) marriage also has very often become a symbol of the relationship with divine objects. "For this cause shall a man leave his father and mother, and shall be joined unto his wife, and they two shall be one flesh. This is a great mystery: but I speak concerning Christ and the church."[4] This means that life is regarded here also in its ultimate simplification, and reduced to its utmost and final significance: in his transition to the new community man achieves contact with power, and definitely recognizes this as ultimate.

7. *Death*, again, is not a fact, but a state of transition; no hard matter of fact, but a process that can be advanced or controlled by reflection and action. He is dead who is declared dead: opinion and estimation take the place of fact. Thus the *Talmud* prescribes a thanks-giving prayer on seeing a friend again after an absence of over twelve months: "Praised be Thou, O Lord, King of the world, that makest the dead live again."[5] According to Roman custom, similarly, he who had been proclaimed dead and then returned must avoid the door and

---

[1] A. Bastian, *Die deutsche Expedition an der Loango-Küste*, 1874 to 1875, 170 *f.*, *cf.* Riedel, *Sluik- en kroesharige rassen*, 350 *f.*
[2] Chap. 52.   [3] A. von Löwis of Menar, *Russische Volksmärchen*, *Nr.* 35.
[4] *Ephesians* v. 31, 32.   [5] K. Kohler, *AR.* III, 1900, 79 *ff.*

enter the house over the roof.[1] It is possible, then, to declare someone
dead, to regard him as non-existent; and this has the same effect as
actual death: in the Scandinavian sagas the *niding* is actually dead, for
there can be life only within the pale of the community, where the
powers are operative.[2] The subjective attitude and celebration are in
complete agreement. Only proper burial makes death valid; he who
has not been buried is not dead. In Calabar Miss Kingsley found the
dead predecessor of a tribal chief in his successor's house; the sly
chieftain did not wish to allow him burial, because after the completed
rite he would of course be properly dead, and then would be able to
return to the world; and his successor was so convinced of the persistent value of the chief's *mana* that he did not want to subject himself
to any competition. Thus the poor man was simply kept there "outside
life but not inside death".[3]

Death too is subjected to rites, and pertains to life's periodicity. It
can thus occur only "when the time has come", when the period of life
has been fulfilled and the power consumed. Therefore the death which
overtakes a man is no "natural" death; that we die is no natural affair,
and for this reason man refuses to permit it. With some difficulty he
fastens on a "cause", even where in our opinion matters are quite
clear; and when the natives of the Melbourne district lose a member
of the tribe by a "natural" death, they are dissatisfied with that explanation, and set up a sort of ordeal of God[4] in order to discover the
"murderer". Some power or other must have been employed, which
they find out; they then resort to the alleged perpetrator's hiding-place
and slay him. Therewith the power situation has once more been
cleared up: but not for the relatives of the man who has just been
killed. Although they know full well who has executed the attack, they
too set up on their own part an ordeal of God, and themselves slay a
"killer" who belongs to yet a third tribe and has had nothing whatever
to do with the affair.[5]

In this procedure, however, "killing" implies nothing ultimate. If
only the rites assure the continuity of power he who is dead goes on
living, so that what we call death, and what for us is an absolute fact
that we cannot evade, is to primitive man merely a transitional state
which can be avoided. As long as *burial* has not taken place, therefore,
the crisis has not been overcome. That is dangerous, especially for the

[1] Plutarch, *Quaestiones romanae*, V.   [2] Grönbech, *Vor Folkeaet*, II, 172 *ff.*
[3] *West African Studies*, 146 *f.*
[4] Chap. 54.   [5] Lévy-Bruhl, *How Natives Think*, 280 *f.*

dead man; but it has its good side also, since the deceased cannot return immediately, and this reappearance is often feared. Here too lies the reason for the *Mourning Period*.[1] Life, as it were, holds its breath, not only in the person of the dead but also in the whole community. For death, as a weakening of power, concerns not merely the dying man but likewise all those belonging to him. The fairy tale of the Sleeping Beauty in the thorn hedge, which is also found beyond Europe, is a reminder of this period of grieving in which life stands still. The dead has taken power with him, and now it is necessary to infuse life with new potency.[2] The *annus luctus*, the mourning period, is accordingly the actual process of death itself; if it is not observed the dead person finds no rest but remains in an intermediate state; in other words, not yet quite "dead";[3] in ancient Iran the three days of mourning were dangerous equally for the dead and the living.[4] Thus we can understand the joy at the burial also, the frequent abandoned festivities accompanying interment of which the wake, still observed among ourselves in country districts, is a vestige; it is necessary to "assist life over a critical situation in safety".[5] Hence the great expansion of power, its transformation into nourishment for the community. Similarly must the sexual licence be regarded that usually occurs during death ceremonies and, among primitive peoples, not infrequently leads to promiscuity.[6] On the Aru Islands, off New Guinea, phallic ceremonies were observed and obscene songs sung, singing and dancing being continued until the widow had discarded her mourning garb.[7] The *Funeral Games* which we find in classical antiquity also had the same purpose: the combats were intended to succour the stagnating life, and are to be found from the gates of Troy to the Tonga Islands.[8] Naturally not only the continuity of the communal life, but also the (renewed) life of the dead man himself, depend on the correct accomplishment of the grieving period and mourning customs: for him new life is effected by the rites, as will be later noted.[9]

The great extent to which life is governed by rule and fixed in

---

[1] Hertz, *Mélanges de Sociologie Religieuse et Folklore, passim*.

[2] N. Adriani, *De schoone slaapster in 't bosch, Versl. en Meded. kon. Ak. v. Wet., Afd. Lett.*, 5e Reeks, 2, 1917, 171 *ff*.

[3] *cf.* Wilken, *Verspreide Geschriften*, III, 532 *ff*.

[4] N. Söderblom, *Les Fravashis*, 1899, 10 *f.*, *cf.* Spencer and Gillen, *The Native Tribes*, 497 *ff*.

[5] Grönbech, *Vor Folkeaet*, IV, 58 *f.*

[6] As in Hawaii, J. G. Frazer, *The Belief in Immortality*, II, 422 *ff*.

[7] Riedel, *Sluik- en kroesharige rassen*, 267 *f.*

[8] Frazer, *Immortality*, II, 140. [9] Chap. 24.

periods is clearly shown by the institution of provisional burial, as this frequently occurs in Indonesia, where the corpse is interred for the time being and is finally buried only a long time, not infrequently several years, afterwards, when only the bones remain. The so-called *tiwah*, again, customary among the Borneo Dyaks, has no single meaning, but so long as it has not been completed the deceased is not regarded as really dead.[1] Death, always a precarious affair, becomes still more ticklish when it concerns persons who are bearers of a particularly dangerous power. In Indonesia, once more, the victims of certain maladies, those who have been forcibly deprived of life (including suicides and the drowned), those who have died as babies, as virgins or in child-bed, princes and priests, are frequently not properly interred —that is not with all the requisite rites. To this, however, nothing dishonourable is attached, only the people fear that the extremely powerful life might again be set in motion, and therefore prefer to leave it in the transitional condition.[2] Among the Dyaks only those who have died of illness are buried and despatched to the realm of the dead, while those who have died in child-bed or war, suicides, victims of accidents and stillborn children are merely placed underground.[3]

8. Human life, made sacred and endowed with power by rites, can also be absolutely and entirely stifled by them. It has already been observed how power seizes upon life in its critical situations and reduces it within their confines; and sacred life is life in this foreshortened form.

But this may be carried so far that nothing individual, nothing distinguishable, nothing really alive remains in life: Power has killed it. The most far reaching example of this tendency, which is, however, present everywhere, is to be found in Buddhism: there birth is merely an unessential incident in the endlessly advancing and essentially empty cycle of life. Buddhist fairy stories, at the end of which Buddha ties the knot of the so-called *Jataka* (Birth-story), speak very clearly in this respect: "At that time the foolish carpenter was Devadatta . . . but the wise carpenter was I." Here nothing further happens, nothing occurs in life, which has become a vacuum; only the sacred master still lives:

---

[1] Hertz, *op. cit.*, 1 *ff.* Wilken, *op. cit.*, III, 436.

[2] van Ossenbruggen, *Bydr. Taal-, Land- en Volkenkunde*, 70, 1915, 280 *ff.*; *cf.* G. van der Leeuw, *Primitieve religie in Indonesie, Tydschrift van het Kon. Ned. Aardrykskundig Gen.*, 2. Serie XLV, 1928, 873 *ff.*

[3] A. W. Nieuwenhuis, *Quer durch Borneo*, I, 1904, 90.

Power has suffocated life;[1] even the specific situations, wherein human dread and will to power had been concentrated, lose their hold.

E. CRAWLEY, *The Mystic Rose*[2], 1927.

A. VAN GENNEP, *Les rites de passage*, 1909.

V. GRÖNBECH, *Vor folkeaet i Oldtiden*, 1912.

R. HERTZ, *Mélanges de sociologie religieuse et folklore*, 1928.

I. und O. VON REINSBERG-DÜRINGSFELD, *Hochzeitsbuch*, 1871.

E. SAMTER, *Geburt, Hochzeit und Tod*, 1911.

J. WACH, *Typen religiöser Anthropologie*, 1932.

E. WESTERMARCK, *History of Human Marriage*, 1891.

[1] Oldenberg, *Buddha: His Life, His Doctrine, His Order*, 193 and Note 1. Else Luders, *Buddhistische Märchen*, 1921. Sylvain Lévi, *Les Jatakas, Conférences faites au Musée Guimet*, 1906, 1 ff.

CHAPTER 23

THE GIVEN AND THE POSSIBLE

1. THE sacredness of life is a matter of either *What is given*, or *Possibility*: two viewpoints which must be distinguished, even though they seldom appear in practice in their pure forms. The first of the two asserts that, together with life itself and as such, Power is given. The expansion and expression of life are the development of Power: potencies lie in the given life itself.

But this by no means implies that man has ever accepted life simply as sacred. "Reverence for life" is in fact wholly modern, and perhaps presupposes moral, though not religious, motives. For apart from some kind of criticism of life no religion whatever is conceivable. Religion means precisely that we do *not* simply accept life; it is directed always to the "Other"; and although it has sprung from human life, religion cannot orient itself to this life as such. But it can bring into prominence specific aspects of this existence as being "sacred", and give emphasis to certain phenomena in life as being potent. One part of life is thus accepted, but always at the expense of another, and in life, which is powerless, potency then reveals itself in certain situations.

Thus the *right hand* enjoys preference over the left; possibly this priority is connected with some organic asymmetry, but it is evaluated in the religious sense: the sanctuary, again, is entered with the right foot: with the right hand sacrifices are offered and blessings bestowed. Even children must learn the difference between the "nice" and the wrong little hand—in French, *bonne*, *belle* and *vilaine main*: Dutch, *mooie* and *leelyke handje*; while marriage with a person of inferior rank is contracted with the left hand. God's "right hand" is mighty and carries victory;[1] with the right hand the oath is sworn.[2] The seat on the right hand too is the place of honour: "Christ sitteth on the right hand of God".[3]

The difference between the sexes is similarly esteemed a disparity in Power, emphasis falling now on man and again on woman; life, as it were, may be sacred in either its masculine or its feminine aspect, just as from masculine, or feminine, "experience" originates the form of the Father

---

[1] *Ps.* cxviii. 15 *f*. [2] *Ps.* cxliv. 8, 11.
[3] *Col.* iii, 1; *cf.* R. Hertz, *Prééminence de la main droite, Mélanges d'Histoire des Religions*, 99 *ff*.

or the Mother.[1] Where the masculine or paternal power predominates, the entire life is ordered accordingly (Patriarchy), while where the potency of the mother or the maid prevails their life-form furnishes the standard for the whole of existence (Matriarchy). Thus when many primitive tribes allocated clearing the forest to the men and the management of cultivated land to the women, this was based on the diversity in what has been "given" to man and woman. The cultural stage of tilling with the hoe recognized this division of labour, in which hunting and warfare fell to the men; and this is not masculine laziness, but the correct allocation of feminine power to those activities connected with the secret of development and growth, and so of birth. When agriculture expands, however, the field work of sowing and reaping is transferred to man because for this the plough is employed, and this is regarded not as an indifferent piece of mechanism but as the phallus; here then it is not birth that is in the foreground, but generation.[2] But wherever it is a matter of approaching close to the power of the earth, as in rites of pulling the plough around and at harvest, then women and girls resume their ancient privileges even at the agricultural stage, and execute ritually and symbolically what has been withdrawn from them in their ordinary occupations. In this division of potency, still further, the psychology of man and of woman is quite clearly recognizable: "The man says 'Look, I am thus and so'; the woman, 'I, too, am thus and so, but don't look.'"[3] The experience of power in generation and birth, in prominence and concealment, is thereby finely characterized in its eternal antithesis, which has its origin in the physical aspect but subsequently extends far beyond this. Thus we understand the awe of man before woman and the fear of woman before man, both of which have religious foundations.[4] Each experiences in the other the fullness of power, as well as the completely antithetic type of diversity from their own being.

Much is "given". What appear to us as human characteristics are really gifts. The king's joy, the hero's conquering power, the warrior's courage, are accounted in German myths, as in Greek, practically as

---

[1] Chap. 20, 10.

[2] *cf.* Rich. Thurnwald, *Psychologie des primitiven Menschen* (*Handbuch der vergleichenden Psychologie*, edited by G. Kafka, I, 2, 194); *cf.* Rose, *Primitive Culture in Greece*, 84.

[3] K. Groos, *The Play of Man*, 268.

[4] A fear which can be intensified into terror; the Maori affirmed that "what destroys men is the *mana* of the female organ"; they called this *whare o aitna*, that is "the location or origin of death and misfortune". E. Arbmann, *AR.* 29, 1931, 341.

gifts pertaining to status, which must be accepted just as their opposites, cowardliness and ill luck, *etc.*, are to be accepted.[1] The "world" too is "given" and is scarcely to be severed from the inner life. Each individual has his own world according to what has been "given" him, woman, child, old man, hero, free man, slave, *etc.* But towards and within his own world each experiences the powerful, to which he gives preference over all the rest of his experience. And in this selection there again prevails that criticism which, in spite of everything, refuses simply to "accept", and ever seeks the "Other". Colours, for example, are "given": but some specific colour is impressive, is distinguished and experienced as powerful. Thus with red, the sole colour that occurs everywhere in painting the body;[2] some other hue, again, refers to another potency.[3]

The givenness of sacred life attains its most explicit expression, however, in the manifold myths concerning man's origin. Life is not only something that is to be filled with power: it contains power from the beginning and essentially. It comes from elsewhere, from some potency. That children grow on trees is a childish belief, but it was also a primeval human conviction. Similarly with the origin of man from mountain or stone, from water (*Frau-Hollen-Teich*), the interpretation of birth as a journey from the other side of the sea (in popular belief from "Angel-land", England), *etc.*

Finally life, already powerful in itself, can be accounted as absolutely holy or divine. Wanton joy of life is exhibited in many fairy story figures, from Hans the Strong who fears nobody and terrifies even the devil, to his Hellenic transfiguration in the form of Herakles, in whom the mortal becomes the mighty witness to the immortal:

> Having been a man,
> Now become a god,
> Having endured pain,
> Having gained heaven.[4]

Life as given, further, can become a symbol of the divine even in those religions which must reject its own divinity. I refer here to Hosea's marriage: and also to the beautiful, because unsought, fusion of human and divine life that occurs in Newman's sermon delivered in the small church at Littlemore, when he quitted the Anglican communion: "O my mother, whence is this unto thee, that thou bearest

---

[1] *cf.* Grönbech, *Vor Folkeaet*, I, 24. Otto, *Die Götter Griechenlands*, 245 *ff.*
[2] Grosse, *Die Anfänge der Kunst*, 58 *ff.*
[3] *cf.* Thurnwald, *op. cit.*, 234.
[4] B. Schweitzer, *Herakles*, 1922, 238 *f.*

children, yet darest not own them?"[1] In this lament the "mother" is the church; but Newman's mother was buried at Littlemore too.

2. As we have seen, sacred life is never accepted as given without further ado, but is always regarded as something which is also to be filled with power, as Possibility. And not infrequently this consideration has settled the precedence. Man must succour feeble life with his own magic rites, or implore the powers so to do; Pandora, the Earth-mother who bestows all life, is looked upon as a deceiver. "In human terms, our life is a deception. But that means only that we deceive ourselves if we think that life is nothing more than life."[2]

For this reason man made *Tools* for himself in order to correct life. Certainly he does not dominate these implements as his own productions, as their superior,[3] but as *homo faber* he sets to work with them and succours the weak life. As *homo formans*, indeed, he even gives life a new form from the very earliest times: *Art* perceives in life only the possibility of a new and potent creation of form; "Art is the signature of man".[4] He also enriches the treasure of these signatures of his, creating for himself a "culture". With the nakedness into which he was born, and which is "given" to him, he is satisfied no longer and makes for himself clothes,[5] the apron serving both as a protection and as an indication of genital potency. Shame is nothing more than the consciousness of the imperilling of this power, just as the king and other power bearers are surrounded by apotropaic tabus, intended to avert evil. To this there must of course be added the necessity for cover in colder regions; and in fashions, even to-day, the two tendencies of protecting and indicating still merge.[6]

Work again is first the discovery, and afterwards the utilization, of possibilities. Thus hunting leads to robbing and robbery to trading.[7] Every gift conceals some possibility. Things receive value: the wild beast is domesticated, and its sacredness rests on the gifts "of Nature" which it brings with it, as well as on the possibilities of its utility.[8]

The idea of value, in its turn, creates the further conceptions of profit

---

[1] *The Parting of Friends.*

[2] W. B. Kristensen, *De goddelyke bedrieger. Meded. der Kon. Akad. van Wetensch., afd. Lett.* 66, Serie B, 3, 1928, 23.

[3] Chap. 3.

[4] Chesterton, *The Everlasting Man*, Part I, Chap. 1.   [5] Chap. 9.

[6] So as not to charge everything against women *cf. e.g.* the diatribe on men's clothing, which shamelessly stresses the genital region, in Chaucer, *The Persones Tale.*

[7] Thurnwald, *loc. cit.*, 205.

[8] *cf.* R. Dussaud, *La Domestication de la Race Bovine, RHR.* 95, 1927.

and compensation. "Compensation" in commerce and in criminal law are one, as Nietzsche perceived,[1] although indeed he failed to add that both alike are of sacred origin. Whoever possesses something "valuable", then, ought to redeem it; and on Buin a fine drum arouses the envy of those who lack such an instrument, so that its fortunate owner must provide a "compensation gift" lest his drum be destroyed for him.[2] War too is the creator and adjuster of values; in Rome, as elsewhere, the seasons for agriculture and for war were identical. War yields power, even where God is believed in: it is help (חְּשׁוּעָה).[3] Property, finally, is the name given to the realization of possibilities; hence the sacredness and the inalienability of possessions. Culture thus provides life with a firm basis.

3. Or is everything futile? Does neither rite nor labour bear fruit? is not merely the given disillusion, but also every value that we attempt to instil therein? Cultural pessimism, in fact, is very ancient: not, however, because civilization itself, nor the life on which it is founded, produces no fruit, since this they do repeatedly. Rather it originates from the fact that neither the given life, nor the culture erected upon it, neither the country nor the tilled field, brings *salvation*. Despite all endeavour it is quite impossible to escape from oneself and lay hold on the Wholly Other. There is certainly fullness of life, but no commanding power of life.

Especially against the inventions of mankind does this pessimism direct its opposition: civilization is a sort of Tower of Babel, sheer wantonness. Man therefore turns away from it and towards "Nature". The Israelite Rechabites, for instance, cherished a nomadic ideal, building no houses but living in tents and forbidding cultivation of field and vineyard; their cry, "Back to the desert", is an anticipation of Rousseau's maxim: "*Revenons à la nature*",[4] of course with a specific religious tinge. During the festival of the Thesmophoria in Eretria the Greeks too lived the primitive life, βίος ἀρχαικός, cooking without fire by the sun's heat.[5] This refusal to accept any creation of form for life may lead further to the disparagement of rites—obedience is better than sacrifice—and even beyond this to the denial of life in general in

[1] *The Genealogy of Morals*, II, 4, 5; *cf.* B. Laum, *Heiliges Geld*, 1924.
[2] R. Thurnwald, *Reallexikon der Vorgeschichte, "Vergeltung"*.
[3] Fr. Schwally, *Der heilige Krieg im alten Israel*, 1901, 7.
[4] A. Bertholet, *Kultur und Religion, Festrede*, 1924, 15.
[5] Plutarch, *Quaestiones graecae*, 298 B.

favour of a pure subjectivity.[1] Both the givenness and the possibility of
powerful life are thus disavowed, death being greeted as a friend.

> Death is before me to-day
> As when a sick man becometh whole,
> As when one walketh abroad after sickness.
>
> Death is before me to-day
> As when a man longeth to see his house again,
> After he hath spent many years in captivity.[2]

The finest of all types of this despair of life, however, is identical
with that which the Greeks elaborated as the very symbol of life's joy—
Herakles: but now in his Euripidean transformation. Divinely born,
he has exhausted in the travail of his twelvefold labour every one of
life's possibilities, and so in his "thirteenth task" of destruction he
falls into despair.[3]

[1] *cf.* Ed. Spranger, *Lebensformen*[5], 1925, 107: "The religious *ego* means either
elevation to boundless fullness of life, or the negation of existence and a retrogression
to the primal values of formless inner life."

[2] The ancient Egyptian *Dialogue of him who is weary of life with his soul*: Erman,
The Literature of the Ancient Egyptians, 91, 92.

[3] G. van der Leeuw, *Goden en Menschen*, 81 *ff.*

CHAPTER 24

THE DEAD MAN

1. WE moderns are inclined to erase the dead man altogether from our roll: he no longer counts. But in the sacred life he is never omitted. Quite apart from any "soul" that he is supposed to have, and from any "immortality" he is believed to receive (the latter demanding conditions quite different from those hitherto considered), the dead counts just as much as the living man, since neither givenness nor possibility as yet deserts him; and precisely because it is assured by rites, his continued existence becomes a matter of course. Thus *burial in the crouching position*, frequently occurring in prehistoric and early historic ages, was probably a preparation for rebirth, the dead man being placed in the position of the embryo, so that new life commenced from the time of burial.[1] Thus many primitive peoples regard a newborn child as a dead man who has returned, and the Eskimo give the child the name of someone who has recently died; this assignment of a name is called "the resuscitation of the dead", and ends the period of mourning.[2] Similarly, when a child is born in West Africa, objects that have been used by deceased people are held out to it; if it tries to seize one they say: "Look, so-and-so recognizes his pipe", or if a child misbehaves its mother may say: "We made a bad mistake when we thought you were so-and-so".[3]

For death is not a fact nor event, but merely a condition different from life. In Melanesia, *mate* is the state which begins with illness or senile feebleness; nevertheless life after death is just as real as the existence we call life. The conditions preceding death are no more impressively distinct from those after death than is existence before

---

[1] Disputes still prevail as to the correct significance of burial in the crouching posture. But neither Virchow's hypothesis of economizing labour and space, nor Böklen's theory of the imitation of the crescent moon, and just as little Andree's idea that it was sought to prevent the dead man's return by trussing him up, are very illuminating, and least of all the suggestion that it was intended to give the dead the "natural" sleeping posture; *cf.* M. Hammarstroem, *AR.* 26, 1928, 146 *ff.* A. Scharff, *Grundzüge der ägyptischen Vorgeschichte*, 1927, 19; Haas gives a description of an Assyrian embryo-burial, *Bilderatlas*, Part 6, 1925, Fig. 43. Egyptian burial ritual provides confirmation of the embryo hypothesis, since the embryo (*tknw*) played a prominent part in it; *cf.* A. Moret, *Mystères égyptiens*, 1913, 36 *ff.*

[2] Hertz, *op. cit.*, 119.   [3] Kingsley, *West African Studies*, 145.

initiation into manhood from adult age.[1] Thus Lévy-Bruhl depicts
life as a cycle which, repeatedly set in motion anew by rites, moves on
from death through burial to the end of the mourning period, and then
into new life, rebirth, naming, initiation of the youth, manhood,
and once more to death again, *etc.*[2] This is certainly somewhat schematic,
and must be modified for each individual case. But in its essence
death is simply a transition like any other, and the dead man is not one
who has been struck off the roll, nor even one who has been reincarnated
(since reincarnation presupposes the dualism of body-soul!) but at
most one who has returned and, as a rule, who is still present.

2. The dead man, on the one hand the object of religious worship,[3]
pertains on the other to those forming the community of worshippers,
the religious Subject.[4] And with this the consideration of the dead
leads us once again to the idea of the sacred community. In Greece the
dead were originally buried in, or near, the house,[5] the provision of
power-giving nourishment being of value to the dead as well as to the
living; and although they can bestow power, the dead none the less
require its supply, since after all they are only "poor souls".

---

[1] W. H. Rivers, "The Primitive Conception of Death", *Hibbert Journal*, X, 1912,
393 *ff.*

[2] Lévy-Bruhl, *How Natives Think*, 255 *f.*　　　　　　　　[3] Chap. 14.

[4] Chap. 32.　　　　　　　[5] E. Rohde, *Psyche*, I[5-6], 1910, 228 *f.* E. T. 166.

CHAPTER 25

REPRESENTATION. THE KING

1. WE have already repeatedly encountered the idea of representation, of official action and existence, which very clearly illuminates the relationship between Objectivity and Subjectivity in religion. Man places himself over against God; but this is not his merely subjective attitude; much more is it an objective action, a being appointed. The relation to Power, then, whether as mere approach, subjection, acquisition or any other relationship, always rests only on the possession of Power. The man who seeks God is himself impelled by God.

But he is "impelled" as a *"representative"*: not, that is, as an individual and still less as a "personality", but simply as a bearer of power. In him is completed the apportioning of power to the totality, to the community. *In* him: *through* him merely in the instrumental sense. For he is no religious genius, no religious virtuoso: he is only the hand that Power utilizes, and it is his official status that sustains him.

2. The oldest representative is the king, whose office has been dealt with in detail in Chapter 13. In ancient Egyptian royal epithets the formula *di ankh* occupies an important place: usually translated by "endowed with life", it might equally well be understood in the active sense of "he who imparts life", and it must be so translated in certain cases;[1] for that the king already possessed divine life was, according to the Egyptian viewpoint, precisely the condition of his ability to impart it. He received power, and also exercised it. The Egyptian sacrificial formula, again, commenced with the stereotyped wording: "A sacrifice which the king offers", or "May the king be gracious and offer". This meant that whoever might bring it, every sacrifice was really offered by the king; private individuals could offer only a royal sacrifice, and actually only the king could sacrifice.[2]

Thus the official aspect of representation necessitates the complete severance of person from power. The Matabele king prays to the spirits

---

[1] cf. R. Weill, *Les Origines de l'Égypt pharaonique,* 1908, 76 f. W. M. Flinders Petrie, *The Royal Tombs of the First Dynasty,* 1900 f. II, 23, 199. A. Moret, *Le Rituel du culte divin journalier,* 1902, 101. G. J. Thierry, *De religieuze beteekenis van het aegyptische koningschap,* I, 1913, 79.　　[2] A. Moret, *Sphinx,* 11, 31.

of his ancestors, but to his own spirit as well,[1] while the Egyptian Pharaoh Amenhotep III is depicted as worshipping himself.[2] Sometimes he represents Power, sometimes the people, and thus he meets himself as it were. This relationship also occurs on a totally different plane: for when in the liturgy the priest says *dominus vobiscum*, the congregation responds: *et-cum spirito tuo*. In official status, then, to apportion and to receive have become identical.[3]

---

[1] Frazer, *The Magical Origin of Kings* (*Lectures on the Kingship*), 32.
[2] G. Maspero, *Au temps de Ramsès et d'Assourbanipal*, 1912, 46.
[3] The charismata of the Christian community, similarly, imply no *personal* distinction; *cf.* Piper, *Ethik*, I, 332.

CHAPTER 26

REPRESENTATION. MEDICINE-MAN AND PRIEST

1. The objectivity of religion has been exhibited in the capacity of representation resting on the possession of power, the representative being effective by virtue of his official status. Thus we can understand why masks play such a great part in the primitive world. Mask dances are very popular and imply far more than mere mummery: on the contrary, the masks in our everyday amusements are vestiges of official action alike in form and in intention; the *bal masqué* grants not only liberty in general, but also sets people free from their personality. It is, still further, hardly a matter of chance that exactly those who possess an "office" in the old sense of the term have deliberately retained their official garb—clergy and judges: and with the raiment very often the official facial expression too! The person acting officially, then, plays a part; and Preuss describes how during their festivities the Cora Indians are at one moment themselves, while they pray, and at the next they personify the gods and their followers;[1] the participants in the celebration are demons, and its performance is an activity of the powers. Here again therefore it is an interchange of *dominus vobiscum* and *et cum spirito tuo*, uniting the human rôle with the official divine. Especially in the case of phallic dances, and what appear to us to be most immoral sexual excesses, it must always be borne in mind that it is really demons who are acting, and that the superhuman power reveals itself in the human union. Thus we can understand how tribes, which normally adhere strictly to certain limitations in sex intercourse, nevertheless transcend all bounds in their feasts.

It is only in the light of these presuppositions, still further, that we can estimate the notorious deceit of which bearers of power have at all times been guilty. A shallow view might readily interpret all this pious fraud as a kind of priestly offence, and even derive a great proportion of religious ideas and institutions from such sacerdotal deception. Of course there have always been liars and men of doubtful honour, who have misused the objectivity of this official activity for their own ends. And the remark of the haruspex who smiled on meeting

---

[1] *Geistige Kultur, Kap.* 6.

his colleague has at all times found its justification.[1] But this certainly cannot be said about medicine-men and priests in general. This holds good, in the first place, of the former: "the mystery-monger is likewise a mystery to himself".[2] If they feel that their power has deserted them they frequently resign their position voluntarily. The Australian medicine-man, for example, removes from a sick person's body the darts that are believed to have caused the illness. Actually he takes some small stones from his own mouth; and this seems an obvious deception. But if the same medicine-man falls ill he sends for a colleague who performs the same process on him; he is "the actor who forgets that he plays a part".[3] Such an actor, however, is the only genuine one; absorbed in his rôle, he ceases to think of his own personal temperament and characteristics, and weeps real tears over the fate of Hecuba! The power bearer may even despair of his own potency, while nevertheless still firmly believing in that of others,[4] since if his own exercise of power produces no effect, this may be due to some more potent counter-charm being in operation, or to his own capacity declining. On Ysabel Island in Melanesia, for instance, a weather wizard had promised fine weather; but the same day his own hut was unfortunately overturned by a storm. Yet nobody doubted his meteorological skill on that account; they were merely convinced that there was a weather doctor on another island who possessed more *mana*![5]

We are confronted here, therefore, with the same relationship as we have already encountered in the case of the king: man bows before a power, residing within himself, which does not require his own self-confidence in order to be believed in.

2. In the primitive community the bearer of power, besides the king, is the *medicine-man*; here the term "medicine" is to be understood as power-stuff in general, although this can be medicine in our own sense also. Hence the medicine-man is a doctor; but he is also weather wizard, priest, bard, wise man, *etc.*

He is not, however, an institution to the same degree as is the king

---

[1] *cf.* R. R. Marett, *Faith, Hope and Charity*, 145: "It is often maintained by shallow persons that all savages are thorough humbugs, though more especially their chiefs and medicine-men. Much the same, however, is said about the leaders of modern society by those who, as Aristotle expresses it, get their view of the play from the cheap seats."

[2] Marett, "The Primitive Medicine-Man", *Hibbert Journal*, XVII, 1918, 103.

[3] H. Hubert and M. Mauss, *Esquisse d'une Théorie générale de la magie, Année sociologique*, 1902–03, 93 *ff*.

[4] Spencer and Gillen, *The Native Tribes*, 130.   [5] Söderblom, *Gottesglaube*[1], 37.

or priest. Certainly his activity also is thoroughly official, but in his person power reveals itself far more spontaneously; and there are of course schools and orders of medicine-men, though their power is of the empirical type. This is shown principally in the case of those magicians whom we are accustomed to call by their North Asiatic name, *shaman*; their potency is based on the ecstasy into which they drum and dance themselves. With these *shamans*, still further, we find ourselves on the road to prophets, but of course only in the sense in which Saul too was "among the prophets", that is as regards the ecstatic frenzy that renders possible a superhuman development of power.

But in any event their knowledge is a power that is superior to themselves. It is transferable from father to son, from teacher to pupils, or is acquired by protracted exercises, especially dancing; but it may also originate directly from a demon; the South American Arawaks relate how one medicine-man obtained his knowledge and his "bull-roarer" from the mother of the waters, exactly as the Roman king Numa was taught by the nymph Egeria.[1] In the community, medicine-men constitute a power beside that of the kings and often competing with this, somewhat as prophets partly complete the fulfilling of the priest's office and partly render it superfluous and oppose it. They are the precursors of doctors and scientists,[2] but of priests also. In Icelandic fairy lore the magician plays a prominent rôle, and now that the Icelandic world has been christianized, he is almost always a priest.

3. Having arrived at the end of this chapter, I shall discuss *priests*. As has previously been observed, originally the king is the priest too. For primitive man, whose life still remains a unity, requires no special representation for religious purposes; the social unity is always religious also. The position of the priest, side by side with that of the king, is thus the commencement of a differentiation of power, although the impossibility of the king's executing all religious functions in person will certainly have played a great part, while the activity of the medicine-man was also concerned in the development of the priestly status: the priest, therefore, is just as much the successor of the kings as of the magicians.

But he is at the same time their competitor. The struggle between priesthood and kingship, in fact, is very ancient: the Pharaohs had to combat the priests of Amon at Thebes; Samuel, Saul; the emperor,

[1] Th. Koch-Grünberg, *Indianermärchen aus Süd-Amerika*, 1920, No. 16.
[2] Chap. 27.

the pope. In Rome, again, the three dignities of the king—as judge, as priest and as commanding the army—were divided between the consuls and the *rex sacrorum*; but against the predominance of the *pontifices* the latter could maintain only the name of the ancient majesty. Thus it can be understood that the priests were not only administrators of the actual cult: the power they represented extended over the whole of life. The name of the Roman *pontifex* can mean only "builder of bridges", *qui pontes facit*, and we know how the Romans regarded the erection of bridges as sacred;[1] the priests originated in this instance, then, from primitive engineers who applied "bridge medicine". In Rome they were also interpreters of the law, and for a long time juris-prudence remained their prerogative, civil law being deposited in the priestly archives.[2]

Even the medicine-man's ecstasy is not always lacking in the priest; there are inspired priests like those of Tonga who, with trembling and perspiration and in a very altered tone of voice, utter the declaration of the god in the first person.[3] But this is restricted chiefly to the most primitive religions, while the priest usually differs from the medicine-man—and also from the prophet—precisely in the ecstasy, the being filled with the god, being in him as it were frozen or crystallized, the occasional miracle incorporated in ordered official actions and the cries of ecstatic possession in the monotonous intonation of the liturgy. In priestly functions, that is to say, power is fixed, while it breaks out, as it were, in medicine-man and prophet. The priest is thus bound to fixed times and places, actions and words, while prophet and medicine-man interfere where and when the spirit drives them or necessity manifests itself. The priest stands for the ordered, the prophet and medicine-man for the occasional, representation of power and of mankind. Prophet and medicine-man operate empirically and pneu-matically, the priest dogmatically in faith; and in this description the dangers as well as the superiority of the two positions are brought into sufficient prominence.

But the priest, no less than the king and medicine-man, is a bearer of power. On Mangaia (Cook Island) the priests are called "god-boxes",[4] the impersonal aspect of their power being thereby well expressed. The brahmins again are, in virtue of their birth alone, bearers

---

[1] Chantepie, *op. cit.*, II, 453. Plutarch, *Numa Pompilius*, 9.

[2] May, *Droit romain*, 30 *f.* The priests of our own day have also retained many "civil" functions, particularly the marriage ceremony.

[3] Frazer, *The Belief in Immortality*, II, 78.

[4] Frazer, *The Golden Bough (The Magic Art)*, I, 378.

of the divine *Brahman* power; and the deification of the priest is just as little an invention as is the cult of the emperors: as power bearer the priest is filled with the god. It is true that all sorts of perils threaten his potency: hence he is surrounded by tabus which sometimes almost obstruct him in his ordered activity, and which have certainly contributed also to the ultimate severance between kingly and priestly dignity. Thus the *flamen Dialis* must be descended from a confarreate marriage (its most ancient form), and himself contract one; he was *cotidie feriatus*:—that is to say, his whole time was festal and dedicated to the god; on festivals he must not even see anyone else working, and must always wear his priestly garb; the fire from his hearth could be used only for sacred purposes, his hair might be cut only by a freeman, while his shorn hair and nail parings were buried under an *arbor felix*; he could swear no oaths, nor wear fetters on his body, while he was forbidden not only to touch or eat all sorts of tabued things but even to speak about them.[1] The priest's life is restricted, power being as it were confined within his life. Official costume, celibacy, strict fasts, regular reading and discharge of the breviary, *etc.*, all have the same end: the representative has to undertake all the guarantees of power of which the community is incapable.

Within the priesthood, too, power is sometimes stronger and sometimes weaker. There are occasions when it is, as it were, concentrated: thus the *hierarchy* arose. Power is then disseminated downwards from the chief, from pope or Dalai Lama, through the ranks of the office-bearers. But the hierarchy, too, once again stresses impersonality, since its fullness of power is present in every priest; even in the humblest holder of sacerdotal office the full wealth of power subsists, even though it may make no brilliant display.

What the priest does, accordingly, has supermundane value: above all, in *sacrifice*. The idea of sacrifice has attained its most magnificent development in India, where the sacred activity has become the movement of the Universe itself as modified by the priest, "where the events and motions of the life of the Universe correspond to the figures of the sacrificial rites and liturgies, and are directed by the magic power residing in the Veda-word. All this is regarded with the eyes of one who feels this very power as subsisting within himself from birth, and who knows that 'the *kshatra* is formed from Brahman: but Brahman is Brahman in virtue of his own self' ".[2] In Christianity too the priest

---

[1] Wissowa, *Religion und Kultus*, 506 *f.*
[2] Oldenberg, *Die Lehren der Upanishaden*, 50.

is the custodian of the life of God, and with this the life of the Universe:
"Where in heaven is there such an authority as that of the catholic
priest? . . . Mary brought the divine child into the world once, but
the priest does this not once only but hundreds and thousands of times
as often as he celebrates. . . . To the priests He has transferred the
right over His sacred humanity, and as it were given them dominion
over His body."[1] "To serve at the altar, and to celebrate the divine
sacrifice, is the proper function of the *sacerdos dei*." The bishop represents God as over against the community and offers its sacrifice to Him,
while as God's representative he bestows divine grace on the community, or refuses this.[2] The church has in fact always been conscious
of the internal tension accompanying the priestly status, the people
just as much as the theologians; thus the Bavarian countryman says:
"Our passon be a real villun, he be, 'cept for t' holy consecration."[3]
The church had to defend the efficacy of priests' orders in severe
struggles against the Donatists, who regarded the consecrations administered by traditores, and baptisms by heretics, as invalid. The *character
indelebilis* received at his ordination permanently qualifies the priest
to administer the sacraments in a valid, even though perhaps illegal
and self-condemning, way; and that the office can damn its bearer is
an important idea which will be encountered at a later stage. The
ministry of the Word should be *obedience*; if it is not this, then certainly
the minister is condemned, but the ministry itself is not invalid. As a
priest observes in one of Sigrid Undset's books, "God's Word cannot
be defiled by the mouth of an impure priest; it can only burn and consume our lips".[4]

G. VAN DER LEEUW, *Deus et Homo*, 1953.
G. VAN DER LEEUW, *Pia fraus* (*Mensch en Maatschappij*, 8, 1932).
J. LIPPERT, *Allgemeine Geschichte des Priestertums*, 1883–84.
R. R. MARETT, "The Primitive Medicine-Man" (*Hibbert Journal XVII*, 1918).
AAKE OHLMARKS, *Studien zum Problem des Shamanismus*, 1939.

[1] Pastoral Letter of the Cardinal Archbishop Katschthaler of Salzburg, Feb. 2,
1905, in Heiler, *Katholizismus*, 226.   [2] Harnack, *History of Dogma*, II, 128 *ff*.
[3] Heiler, *Katholizismus*, 180.   [4] *Kristin Lavransdatter*, II.

CHAPTER 27

REPRESENTATION. THE SPEAKER

1. ACCORDING to the Greek derivation, a prophet is a *speaker* who relates the cult legend at festivals,[1] so that his action, as a representative, is in the first place a speech which, in Greece itself, generally had a technical and semi-priestly, semi-theological cast. We usually presuppose, however, that a prophet experiences his rôle in a much more ecstatic and more *shaman*-like way, such that representation involves a tension of personality which we call *possession*, and which excludes everything individual, at least so far as the mode of experience itself is concerned. A mentally deranged man, referred to by Karl Jaspers, may be cited in illustration of this; he asked the presiding court official, "most politely, that your honour would have my own thoughts returned to me".[2] Had this schizophrene only regarded his "own thoughts" as being slightly less valuable, he might have been a prophet; he was obviously a relative of the Melanesian demoniac who called himself not "I", but "we two!"[3]

Both types of prophet, however, the calm equally with the ecstatic, speak the word of someone other than themselves: from time to time, as it were, their own personality is totally switched off, so that they are representatives absolutely and completely. The prophet is then a mere tool of Power, "filled with the god" and emptied of himself—literally an "enthusiast". Of this the story of Balaam provides the finest example.[4] Bribed by Balak to invoke a withering curse on the people of Israel, he spoke the word "which the Lord hath put in my mouth". Balak, fearing that the malediction would be converted into a blessing on his enemies, entreated the prophet to remain quite silent instead. But for Balaam that was impossible: "Balaam the son of Beor hath said, and the man whose eyes are open hath said: he hath said, which heard the words of God, which saw the vision of the Almighty, falling into a trance, but having his eyes open." This angered Balak, and he wished to drive the seer away, but the blessing of Jahveh flowed on from Balaam's mouth: "If Balak would give me his house full of silver and gold, I cannot go

[1] O. Kern, *AR.* 26, 1928, 3 *f.* E. Fascher, *ΠΡΟΦΗΤΗΣ,* 1927.
[2] *Allgemeine Psychopathologie,* 1923, 113.
[3] Codrington, *op. cit.,* 153.   [4] *Num.* xxiii–xxiv.

beyond the commandment of the Lord, to do either good or bad of
mine own mind; but what the Lord saith, that will I speak."

We know that all the Old Testament prophets appeared with the
word of Jahveh, whether their speech had more or fewer ecstatic features.
Various excitant and intoxicating methods were employed for this; thus
Elisha sent for a minstrel: "and when the minstrel played, the hand of
the Lord came upon him".[1] Similarly, before declaring the oracle the
Pythia of Delphi had to drink water from the sacred fountain Kassotis
and eat laurel leaves as a kind of sacramental preparation for the divine
speech.

With marvellous psychological penetration, Aeschylus has described
the prophet's violent emotion and reluctant speech: a dreadful power
forces the wretched Cassandra to speak in broken utterances:

> Otototoi . . . Dreams. Dreams.
> Apollo. O Apollo!

whereupon she perceives a horrid spectacle: the bloody children of the
house of the Atreides, the axe of slaughter, the murder of Agamemnon
in the bath, her own fate: and she asks the chorus:

> Be near me as I go,
> Tracking the evil things of long ago,
> And bear me witness.

Thereupon the ecstasy seizes her anew:

> Oh, oh! Agony, agony!
> Again the awful pains of prophecy
> Are on me, maddening as they fall;

and a terrifying vision follows.[2] In our own day, the grandeur of this
description of depersonalized and objective speech is paralleled by the
figure of Kundrie in Wagner's *Parsifal*, when with terrible outcries
she is reluctantly conjured up by Klingsor.[3]

The relations between the prophetess and her lord were often interpreted sexually, as another mode of typifying the sacrament besides
eating the sacred meal.[4] Thus Cassandra was beloved of Apollo, while

---

[1] 2 *Kings* iii. 15.   [2] Aeschylus, *Agamemnon*, 1072 ff., 1184 f., 1214 ff. (Murray).
[3] cf. further the affecting lament of Jeremiah: "My bowels, my bowels! I am pained
at my very heart; my heart maketh a noise in me; I cannot hold my peace." (iv. 19).
[4] cf. the classical discussion of sacramental symbols by A. Dieterich, *Eine mithrasliturgie*², 1910, 92 ff.

the Pythia must be a virgin, and however old she might be, must be garbed like a girl; originally she prophesied only on the day of the god's epiphany.[1] The poet depicts the prophetess as a horse ridden by the god;[2] and a prayer from the world of syncretism is addressed to Hermes: "Enter into me, Lord Hermes, as babes into the bodies of women."[3] The prophetesses on the Indonesian Island of Buru, again, attribute their gift to intercourse in the forest with an earth-spirit;[4] and here we touch upon forms of communion with the god to which we shall return later.[5]

At present I shall refer merely to the utter elimination of the speaker's own personality. He has received the power of *objective speech*; and this utterance is essentially incomprehensible: objective speech cannot be understood. It must, therefore, be interpreted. At Delphi the *hosioi* translated the utterances of the enraptured prophetess into smooth hexameters; they themselves, as Farnell remarks, were "sane enough";[6] Plutarch calls these exegetes *theologians*. And it has indeed always been the theologian's task to transpose objective and unintelligible speech into subjective and comprehensible terms—and nevertheless preserve the potency of priest and prophet. We need not be surprised, therefore, that in Plutarch's opinion the theologians of Delphi seemed not to do justice to the truth![7]

2. But the speaker's objective utterance consists of no mere words. The *word*, the power-word, is equally a deed.[8] Faust's reflections on the commencement of the *Gospel of St. John*, therefore, do not hold good in view of the actual religious situation. For prophets are representatives of Power, and their pronunciations are at the same moment a celebration, and an exhibition, of Power. They can be soothsayers and doctors, exhorters, monitors, preachers and much else, their character being best observed in the Old Testament, where there are all kinds of prophets. The highest type is to be found in Isaiah and Jeremiah, Amos, Hosea, and Deutero-Isaiah, in whom the ecstatic and marvellous recedes almost completely in favour of the direct Word of God, frequently applicable to the prevailing conditions but often superior to these, or at least, as in *Isaiah* liii, soaring far above them. Less immediate and spontaneous, yet still claiming to be God's Word, is

---

[1] Plutarch, *Quaestiones graecae*, 292. E. E. Fehrle, *Die kultische Keuschheit im Altertum*, 1910, 7 *ff*., 75 *ff*. Farnell, *Cults*, IV, 186 *ff*.   [2] Virgil, *Aeneid*, VI, 98 *ff*.
[3] Dieterich, *Mithrasliturgie*, 97.   [4] Riedel, *Sluik- en kroesharige rassen*, 8 *f*.
[5] Chap. 67 *ff*.   [6] *Cults of the Greek States*, IV, 188 *f*.
[7] *On the Cessation of the Oracles*, XV, 417 *f*.   [8] Chap. 58.

the prophecy of Ezekiel and Zechariah.[1] But these names indicate the loftiest prime and the close of Israelitish prophetism, while its commencement and advance exhibit wholly different forms. Thus Samuel is the "seer" to whom Saul resorted when he sought his father's lost asses; but he is judge and priest also. The prophets wandering about the country, again, whom Saul unwillingly joined on returning from Samuel, were ecstatics raving like dervishes or members of the Dionysiac *thiasoi*, and even Elisha prophesied to the strains of the harp. The first prophet in the grand style was Elijah, while the acute psychological description of his appearance is, moreover, a fine example of the eternal struggle between objective utterance and the subjective striving and despair in the prophet's own personality; of this his "It is enough" is an absolutely classic example. Yet when the hand of Jahveh touched him he ran before Ahab's chariot to Jezreel,[2] and like Elisha he also performed miracles and cured diseases.

Plato, again, distinguished two types of mantic or "prophecy", the first the *mantike entheos*, the "inspired madness" or the ecstatic, *e.g.* that of the Pythia; the second the systematic interpretation of signs, such as augury from the flight of birds.[3] To the latter must be added the Babylonian inspection of the liver, Roman augury and the Chinese science of the water and wind sages (*fêng shui*), prophecy here very closely approaching sacred *science*,[4] with which it shares in common objective utterance. Similarly the soothsayers of primitive communities who smelt out the truth,[5] the wandering *sibyls* and *bakides* of Greek antiquity,[6] all held religious office by participating in divine wisdom, while the Scandinavian *völva*, too, was a female soothsayer and magician.

3. In the speaker's gift of healing, still further, an element of the character of the *saviour* plays a part. The "word" he speaks is a power-word; and hence a deed, a deed of salvation. The *logioi andres*, who wandered about the Grecian world from the sixth to the fourth centuries B.C., were conjurors, mountebanks, prophets, fortune-tellers, doctors, priests of purification, philosophers and *savants*, poets, divine men,

---

[1] Wundt (*Völkerpsychologie*, IV, 187 *ff.*) remarks that in genuine prophecy God and the prophet are one, while in the retrogressive and more reflective types God sends the prophet. The first is the dream, the second reflection upon the dream. But we find compulsory utterance, the almost spasmodic power of prophetic speech, in almost all the Israelitish prophets; *cf.* J. Pedersen, *Israel*, I, II, 1920, 116 *ff.*

[2] 1 *Kings* xviii. 46. [3] *Phaedrus*, 244. [4] Chap. 72.

[5] R. Thurnwald, *Lexikon der Vorgeschichte*, Art. *Orakel.*

[6] Rohde, *Psyche*, II, 63 *ff.*; English Translation, 292. Chantepie, *op. cit.*, II, 365.

gods. . . . The finest example of all this is Empedocles who, crowned as a god, permitted himself to be worshipped by the people, who came to him in thousands: "But now I walk before you no longer as mortal, but as an immortal god; everywhere I receive due honour as such a one, while garlands and fillets are twined about my head. As soon as I enter the flourishing cities, with these my followers, both men and women, I am worshipped, and thousands come after me, to discover *where the road leads to salvation.* Some desire oracles, others inquire about divers diseases, in order that they may hear some little word bringing salvation; for they have been writhing in harrowing torture for a long time."[1] Thus we perceive that the "mighty little word", εὐηκὴς βάξις, has many meanings: sin, sickness, and all sorts of life's emergencies are removed by it when they are confronted by "salvation". But Empedocles was also a great natural philosopher, and the sketch which he himself outlined in the passage quoted reminds us partly of the Gospel, and for the rest of a charlatan's consulting room. "Salvation", indeed, nearly always means healing also (as *e.g.* for Blumhardt), just as "healing", in its turn, always involves some sort of salvation; and if the doctor, even the modern practitioner, "cannot achieve magic, then the magnetopath or the quack takes his place".[2] Our artificial distinctions, then, between "spiritual", moral and bodily salvation *are* purely artificial, and cannot maintain themselves against the will to power and the human yearning for release.

To the poet too has been transmitted some part of the speaker's divine potency. For originally poet and prophet were one; Plato speaks of poets as being filled with God, and places them on the same footing as the oracular bards or soothsayers.[3]

H. ACHELIS, *Die Ekstase*, 1902.
J. VINCHON, VERGNES, P. SAINTYVES, M. GARÇON, *Les Guérisseurs* (*Revue Anthropologique*, 38, 1928).

[1] H. Diels, *Die Fragmente der Vorsokratiker*[3], 1912, I, 264 *f.*
[2] E. Kretschmer, *Medizinische Psychologie*[2], 1902, 255.
[3] *Apology*, 22; *cf.* on the Greek "man of words", Murray, *The Rise of the Greek Epic*, 118: "The ancient 'man of words' was not exactly a story-teller, not exactly a chronicler, not exactly a magician. He was all these, and something more also."

CHAPTER 28

REPRESENTATION. THE PREACHER

1. POWER, then, impels to speech, to utterance against one's will and with no intention of one's own. But it urges towards *preaching* also. Power sends someone forth with a message, either didactic or parabolic, that distinguishes him as *evangelist* from the prophet, while his ambassadorial status marks off the *apostle* from the priest. The priest *stands*, at the altar or in the pulpit: the evangelist and apostle *travel* on the highways, with neither pouch nor purse nor shoes, *per pedes apostolorum*. For something decisive has occurred, some marvel: the world has taken on quite a different aspect. Then there remains nothing else to do but set out and tell it to men, convey to them the joyful tidings, the warning, the admonition to conversion. It is no longer God Who speaks immediately by the mouth of the prophet: it is God Who *has* spoken and Who *has* acted; and His speech, His deed, have taken possession of certain men here and there, so that they can no longer endure their place of sojourn, but must set forth to relate what they have experienced. They can express this in widely different ways: in hearty admonition or ponderous theological lecture, in parable, anecdote or reprimand; but their utterance will always be preaching, *proclamation*: everything has changed, something great has happened. All else is now matter of utter indifference: let it be, then, and listen whilst ye are being told of this one thing: "Thus when I came to you, my brothers, I did not come to proclaim to you God's secret purpose with any elaborate words or wisdom. I determined among you to be ignorant of everything except Jesus Christ, and Jesus Christ the crucified."[1]

The word of Power cannot, indeed, be enclosed within the narrow limits of any single type. It grows, and often rankly increases; and thus the apostle and evangelist can become a prophet at any time. Since his word is potent, he heals as a matter of course; "he taught them as one having authority, and not as the scribes".[2] His own experience too,

[1] I *Cor.* ii. I *ff.* (Moffat); *cf.* Rud. Bultmann, *Die Bedeutung des geschichtlichen Jesus für die Theologie des Paulus, Theol. Blätter*, 8, 6, 1929 (in: *Glauben und Verstehen*, 1933, 188 *ff.*).
[2] *Matthew* vii. 29. Certainly this power can assume very various forms. It may imply the force of an outstanding moral personality, or even the revelation of some-

and also that of others with respect to himself, can expand to such a degree that he develops to the rank of saviour; and in the Gospel we possess the great example before whom we must all bow. Gerhart Hauptmann delicately describes the psychological detail of the experience. A man sets out to preach peace and love: "his ardent desire was to be able to speak with the voice of thunder"; and when he arrives at a place he must constantly repeat: "Thy king comes to thee". Ultimately the church bells do not exhort him to prayer: "He did not bow his head nor kneel down. He listened smiling as to the voice of an old friend, and yet it was God the Father Who was speaking to His son."[1]

2. The *teacher*, again, is to be distinguished from the preacher by the fading of the element of Power in the word. Of course potency is still presupposed, but the teacher's utterance is an application of this and not Power itself, nor even its proclamation. But after all no sharp distinctions can be drawn. For though teaching is not salvation itself, still it is its expression; and the teacher, like prophet and preacher, is an instrument of salvation. Nevertheless he is generally less important personally; for he neither imparts salvation nor announces it, but merely speaks *about* it, and in his teaching it must operate of itself. Thus could the Platonic Socrates tell his disciples: "I would ask you to be thinking of the truth and not of Socrates".[2] So too could Buddha speak to Ananda, even where it was a matter of first-hand religious discourse: "It may be, Ananda, that ye shall say: 'The Word has lost its master, we have a master no more'. Ye must not think thus, Ananda. The law, Ananda, and the ordinance, which I have taught and preached unto ye, these are your master when I am gone hence."[3] When however we place beside Buddha, the teacher, the Northern and Japanese Buddha, Amitabha, (Amida), who redeemed humanity by the vow that he would not accept eternal bliss for himself until all men had been saved, then the difference which makes the teacher becomes clear.[4] On the other hand the original potency, which is indeed the basis of the teacher's status also, continually compels the disciples to forget the absolute sufficiency of the doctrine in favour of their teacher. Thus the Hindu *guru* is very often revered as divine by even the most free-

thing "Wholly Other". But it may also be the direct inheritance of *shaman*-power, as F. C. Bartlett shows in the case of the negro preacher. *Psychology and Primitive Culture*, 122 f.   [1] *Der Apostel. Novellistische Studie.*
[2] *Phaedo*, 91 (Jowett).   [3] Bertholet, *Lesebuch*, II, 24.
[4] *cf. e.g.* J. Witte, *Die ostasiatischen Kulturreligionen*, 157.

thinking sects; or, as *dev-guru*, he becomes the actual object of worship.[1]

His *disciples* follow the teacher: their response is the result of a summons: "Follow me". Among them one or two special figures are particularly prominent as favourite, or principal, disciples:—Ananda, John, Peter, Elisha. *Women disciples* too are not lacking:—Mary Magdalene, St. Clare; and the imitation of the master consists not only in the adoption and propagation of his preaching, but also in the assimilation of life, to as high a degree as possible, to that of the hallowed teacher.

J. WACH, *Meister und Jünger*, 192.

[1] *cf.* H. von Glasenapp, *Religiöse Reformbewegungen im heutigen Indien*, 1928, 43.

CHAPTER 29

REPRESENTATION. THE CONSECRATED

1. LONG before Freud compelled them to admit it, wise men knew that human potency, which man directs upon his environment and its power, has its roots to no mean extent in sex life; and now many of them can give their attention to nothing else! In any case, the instincts of sex and hunger are the two great impelling factors whereby the will climbs to power and even rises to heaven; in face of these the consciousness of impotence collapses. Food and drink on the one hand, and on the other sex intercourse, are therefore not merely the two outstanding symbols of community with the god, but are also the means wherewith human potency sets to work.

That this powerfulness not only actually exists, but must also be modified by something being "celebrated", has been already sufficiently established.[1] Feminine sexual power, usually regarded as the most intense, is in many communities changed by the so-called *ruptura hymenis*, which is intended to remove the danger of initial intercourse as well as guarantee the efficiency of sex qualities. The operation is frequently performed by an old woman, but often also by a priest or stranger.[2] But the perforation may equally be a ritual defloration, for which likewise a priest or foreigner is engaged; for they are the potent ones. Here we are on the pathway to sacramental prostitution, which in the life of many peoples has played a prominent rôle.[3] Virginity then belongs to some powerful individual, not only because the husband relies on his own power too slightly to take it himself, but also because it falls essentially to the share of the greater. The offensive rite may however be replaced by a mere symbol such as intercourse with a youth, as on the isle of Naxos, or abstention during the so-called Tobias nights.[4]

But this "celebration" may also become a sacrifice to the divinity; and this again, in fact, with the purpose of enhancing power, either that

---

[1] Chap. 22. [2] Crawley, *The Mystic Rose*, I, 168 *ff*.
[3] A. van Gennep, *Rites de Passage*, 48 *f.*, 16.
[4] *cf.* M. P. Nilsson, *Griechische Feste*, 1906, 365 *ff*. F. Cumont, *Les religions orientales dans la paganisme romain*[2], 1909, 287. On obligatory prostitution among the Arabs, *ibid.*[4], 1929, 258. Fehrle, *Die kultische Keuschheit im Altertum*, 40 *ff*. (The river god takes the virginity of the Trojan women.) K. Schmidt, *Jus primae noctis*, 1881.

of the individual making the sacrifice or of the community. The stranger or priest then becomes the representative of the deity, while the woman, as a *devoted person*, represents the group. In a celebrated passage in his *History*, Herodotus tells us of the Babylonian women who, in the name of Mylitta, the goddess of birth, once in their life had to surrender to a stranger in return for money.[1] In any case there were consecrated women in Babylon who, until their marriage, spent part of their life in seclusion, dedicated to the god. Their representation consisted either in the sacrifice of sex intercourse—that is in virginity, or else in its precise opposite, surrender to the god when he visited them in human form.[2] In both cases they were women of the god, his brides, *ḫarimtu*, "the segregated", *ḳadištu*, the consecrated; in ancient Sumeria also there were women of the god, who were probably put to death in the "gloomy room" which was their grave and their bridal chamber simultaneously.[3]

Whether virgins or prostitutes, the dedicated women administered their segregated status for the benefit of the whole community whose power they preserved. In Corinth, during the Persian wars, the *hierodules* prayed for the salvation of the city, and no less a poet than Pindar praises them in eloquent terms.[4] How firmly the system of dedication to the god by the sacrifice of virginity had taken root in the Greek-Oriental mind, until the imperial era, is shown by the story of Paulina, a lady of repute who was seduced in the temple of Isis by a freed-man wearing the mask of Anubis;[5] the seducer knew full well the situation in which he could take advantage of the religious hysteria of his victim.

The Hindu *bayaderes*, similarly, are regarded as women of the god.[6] Nevertheless the most remarkable feature, from our viewpoint, is the transition from virginity to unrestrained licentiousness; and this can be understood only in the light of the concept of Power. Abstinence, that is to say, is not chastity in our sense, but is "cultural chastity",[7]

---

[1] I, 199; *cf.* 93. Lucian, *de dea Syria*, 6: "The market is open to strangers only".

[2] D. G. Lyon, "The Consecrated Women of the Hammurabi Code", *Studies Presented to Toy*, 341 *ff. cf.* A. S. Hartland, "At the Temple of Mylitta", *Anthr. Essays Presented to E. B. Tylor*, 1907, 189.

[3] F. M. Th. Böhl, *Verslag van het Zesde Congres Oostersch Genootschap*, 1929, 21 *ff.* Traces of temple prostitution in the Old Testament: 1 *Sam.* ii. 22, *Ex.* xxxviii. 7; *Hos.* iv. 14. Jephthah's daughter was similarly dedicated—though in what sense will probably always remain debatable: *Judges* xi.　　　　　　　[4] *Fr.* 122.

[5] Dill, *Roman Society from Nero to Marcus Aurelius*, 566. In Nero's day there were girls in the Capitol who believed themselves to be loved by Jupiter. (Seneca, *Fr.* 37.) H. Usener, *Das Weihnachtsfest*[2], 1911, 76 *f.*

[6] C. Clemen, *Die nicht-christlichen Kulturreligionen*, II, 1921, 15. *cf.* Crawley, *The Mystic Rose*, I, 235.　　　　　　　[7] Fehrle, *op. cit.*

or intercourse with divine power, celestial marriage. This can become realized in three ways; either by killing the bride, by virginity, or by unlimited surrender in the god's service. The mysticism centred upon death, upon the bride, and eroticism are therefore merely distinguishable but never separable; Aphrodite Pelagia, the goddess of harbour towns, was simultaneously prostitute and sacred.[1] The intoxication of love is a swooning and dying; turning towards the god, on the other hand, is the manifestation of erotic potency or of the will to power.

In bridal mysticism[2] the same schema subsists, not even always spiritualized. The brides of Christ have always devoted all their love, carnal or even hysterical as it often was, to the heavenly bridegroom. But for this they must not be despised. For I do not think that the purity of the relation to God depends on the eradication of the sex element. No one is able to remove completely the sexual from any relationship, even from that to Deity. There remains therefore only one method of differentiation:—to ascertain whether the devotion is an actual devotedness, that is to say a surrender of self, or is merely a manifestation of the will to power; in other terms, whether the dedicated woman desires to dominate the bridegroom more or less spiritually, but always erotically, or to love him genuinely.

2. Originally the Roman *vestals* were probably only the unmarried women of the household who carried water and maintained the fire.[3] They were the brides of fire[4] and wore bridal raiment all their lives. Associated with the state hearth by the state itself, they constituted a type of order, and their chastity guaranteed the power and well-being of the community.[5] A very ancient form of this idea is found in the test of chastity at Lanuvium, where a vestal had to bring food to a snake; if the animal ate it her chastity was established, and the farmers exclaimed, "the year will be fertile": (*clamantque agricolae: fertilis annus erit*).[6] Here cultural chastity is the exact parallel to intercourse on the ploughed field and other customs in which the development of

---

[1] H. Usener, *Vorträge und Aufsätze*[2], 1914, 189 ff.   [2] Chap. 75, 76.

[3] W. Warde Fowler, *The Religious Experience of the Roman People*, 135. On the duty of carrying water: Ovid, *Fasti*, III; *cf.* also R. Cagnat, *Les Vestales et leur couvent sur le forum romain* (*Conférences Faites au Musée Guimet*, 1906, 61 ff.).

[4] Chap. 6.   [5] Fehrle, *op. cit.*, 210 ff.

[6] J. Toutain, *RHR.* 89, 1924, 183 ff. Firmicus Maternus had an inkling of the polarity between cultural chastity and licence in asserting (contrary to the facts) of the vestals: "they are either forced into the sin of prostitution, or else they remain virgin, and so lose the honourable dignity of a glorious name"; *de errore profanarum religionum*, 14.

sex power promotes fertility, and in conformity with this its violation is a damaging, or rendering impure, rather than a misdeed.[1]

This type of consecration has an obvious feminine touch. But, of course, men dedicated themselves to the god also. It is, however, no accident that in so doing they approximated to the feminine; and this might happen in a horrible and perverted way, as was shown by the self-mutilation of the priests in Asia Minor in the service of the mountain mother. This was a sadistic self-laceration, as *The Book of Kings*[2] depicts it for us, and as Apuleius still more clearly describes it.[3] But it was also a direct sacrifice of virility, carried out in a state of transport, and impressively described by Lucian: "they castrate themselves in the service of Rhea"[4]; the castrated men received women's clothing.[5] The Gospel also mentions "some which have made themselves eunuchs for the kingdom of heaven's sake".[6]

In all this the sacredness of feminine life plays a prominent rôle. In ancient Rome, for example, a criminal who met a vestal saved his life;[7] similarly in the Middle Ages, when the veneration of women was at its height, their protection ensured freedom: "should a wolf (a fleeing criminal) take refuge with women, out of love to them he should be permitted to live".[8] The knight too swore his oath "by all women"; to him the whole female sex was a sacred family, while as a protection in battle Wolfram's Parzival sets woman above God; priests and women, again, enjoyed the same sacredness and might not carry arms.[9] Here, then, to dedicate oneself means to approximate to the feminine, to the mother, for the salvation of the entire community; and thus the longing to return to the mother's womb, and the will to sacrifice life, blend in a curious way, while the Christian monk vacillates between a love of Christ that exhibits feminine traits, and a reverence for the Virgin that is typically masculine. For though the church extols virginity and derives all evil from woman, still it well knows how to sublimate all that is profoundly human in a unique way; as St. Bernard affirms: "If a man fall not but through a woman, so he rises only through a woman."

3. The life of those dedicated to the god is a new life, filled with fresh power, and the rites leading to it are very similar to the rites of

[1] G. Wissowa, *AR.* 22, 1923–24, 201 *ff.*   [2] 1 *Kings* xviii. 28.
[3] Bertholet, *Lesebuch*, 5, 42 *f.*   [4] *de dea Syria*, 15.
[5] Bertholet, *Lesebuch*, 5, 43 *f.*   [6] *Matt.* xix. 12.   [7] Plutarch, *Numa*, 10, 3.
[8] San Marte, *Parzivalstudien*, III, 1862, 121.   [9] *ibid.*, 115 *f.*

transition already discussed.[1] They imply a death; in the ritual of admission to monastic orders, for instance, the liturgy of the obsequies is frequently incorporated.[2]

The vow,[3] taken by the person about to be dedicated, is of course not restricted to chastity, which is always merely the symbol of the surrender of the whole life.[4] It may however demand chastity, poverty and obedience, as with Christian orders. It operates in very different ways. In devoting his life to an uninterrupted cult, impossible in "the world", the monk represents the community. "Daily the monastic choir prays for all those who cannot pray, or who do not desire to pray; it renders to the infinite majesty of God that service and honour of which those standing without in the world, and working there, are incapable."[5] Monastic life, then, is perpetual adoration, like that of the angels ($\beta \iota o s \ \dot{\alpha} \gamma \gamma \epsilon \lambda \iota \kappa \acute{o} s$).[6] But representation is not merely that of the world as over against God; conversely, it is God's offensive against the world. Thus the Society of Jesus is a *militia Christi*, whose rules begin with the words: "Whosoever would fight under the standard of the Cross on behalf of God in our society, which we desire to seal with the name of Jesus."[7] And the calm submersion, the meditation *cum libello in angello*, the apparent unproductivity is representation: "It is not idleness to remain idle for God, but the business of all business."[8] Prayer, penance and the piety of the consecrated in fact augment the *thesaurus* on which the community can draw; the enfeebling of the individual's potency enhances the power of the whole.

4. The watchword of the consecrated, then, is the attainment of power by means of voluntary impotence. The sacrifice they offer effects greater fullness of power that may indeed be a form of magic, but which may also pertain to life after death, as well as the worship of the represented community. The *martyr* also, who surrenders his life, can generate power from complete impotence. "I must endure", the model child affirms, "more than any human being has ever had to suffer; for the crown of sorrow is the only crown to which I can attain";

---

[1] Chap. 22.   [2] A. van Gennep, *Rites*, 125, 140.   [3] Chap. 59.
[4] A peculiar form of dedication, sometimes even lifelong, prevailed among the Nazarenes of the Old Testament, who abstained from alcohol, did not cut their hair and avoided all contact with dead bodies. This type of avoidance (*cf.* Chap. 4) is to be found in the history of religion in endless variety.
[5] Heiler, *Katholizismus*, 452.
[6] *ibid.*, 438.   [7] *ibid.*, 313.   [8] *ibid.*, 474.

and the psychologist adds: "but this paragon will never realize that men can live without any sort of crown whatever".[1]

The entire situation, however, is transformed (and this holds good for *all* the consecrated) as soon as the surrendering personality accepts the power, to which he sacrifices himself, as supreme, and desires to understand his whole activity solely in its relation to this power. This constitutes the true concept of the martyr, μάρτυς, witness: even witness in blood. He who devotes himself is not, in the first place, one acting of his own accord, not one who "celebrates", but one who bears testimony[2] and has boldness, παρρησία, freedom of utterance[3] about his encounter with Power, about God's acts, and His word that has come to him. This boldness is a consecration: "It will end in your martyrdom".[4] Here, however, voluntary impotence is no longer attainment of power but simple obedience, unto death. But by his testimony God's witness wins for himself "boldness and access with confidence";[5] and thus feminine consecration has been exchanged for masculine *obedience*.

H. Delehaye, *Sanctus* (*Subsidia Hagiographica*, 17, 1927).
F. Dornseiff, *Der Märtyrer* (*AR.* 22, 1923–24).
E. Fehrle, *Die kultische Keuschheit im Altertum*, 1910.

[1] F. Künkel, *Einführung in die Characterkunde*[2], 1929, 48.
[2] Dornseiff, *Der Märtyrer*, *AR.* 22, 1923–24.
[3] E. Peterson, *R. Seeberg-Festschrift*, 293.
[4] *cf. Luke* xxi. 13.   [5] *Eph.* iii. 12.

SAINTS

1. SAINTS are no longer wholly representative; to a markedly high degree they are objects of veneration. Certainly, *orant pro nobis*—they are potent helpers of mankind as over against the great powers. But the principal feature is Power revealing itself in them. We fail however to imagine this potency sufficiently concretely; we speak, it is true, of the "odour of sanctity", and this fragrance is by no means merely metaphorical. For on approaching the human queen, the Egyptian god exhaled a scent,[1] and the dying Hippolytus sensed the nearness of Artemis by the "breath of heavenly fragrance" emitted by the goddess.[2] Thus too the medieval saints expired while glorious odours were disseminated.

In the first place, then, a saint is a person whose body possesses divinely potent attributes. Concealed in a sack, light emanates from it, while its little finger can set in motion a vehicle that is held fast.[3] These powers can be acquired, for example, by touch; in the famous El Hazar mosque at Cairo people touch a barred window with their hands: behind the lattice there is a saint's coffin. Still further, the personality of the holy one may retire completely behind his (physical) potency. Often it cannot be claimed even that it is he who performs miracles, since it is his power that effects them; thus the ashes of the mystic al-Hallaj, who was tortured to death and his body burned, caused a miraculous flood of the Tigris,[4] while kissing the saint's relics, preserved in glass cases, is still a prevailing custom in the Roman Catholic Church.[5] The saint is primarily a sacred, that is powerful, object—a relic.[6] Here also the cult of the dead exerts its influence;[7] but the desire to possess a portion of the powerful individual, a part of his body or even something that he has touched, begins even during his lifetime. On one occasion, in the fervour of his address, the American evangelist Billy Sunday

---

[1] Bertholet, *Lesebuch*, 10, 40.

[2] Euripides, *Hippolytus*, 1391 *ff.*; *cf.* E. Lohmeyer's brilliant "Study", *Vom göttlichen Wohlgeruch* (*Sitzber. der Heidelberger Ak. d. Wiss., Phil.-hist. Kl.* 1919, 9). H. Windisch (in *Meyers Kommentar*) on 2 *Cor.* ii. 15.

[3] Hertz, *Mélanges de sociologie religieuse et folklore*, 155 *f.*

[4] Louis Massignon, *Al Hallaj, martyr mystique de l'Islam*, I, 1922, 294.

[5] *cf.* Heiler, *Katholizismus*, 169.   [6] Chap. 3.   [7] Chap. 14, 24.

broke an ordinary chair; immediately the people in the front rows fought for possession of a fragment of it, one carrying its leg and another part of its back home with them.[1] From this attitude originate both the cult of relics and the Anglo-American hunt for souvenirs; it is always a matter of the power of something striking or extraordinary. But the remarkable object must spring from someone who himself remains in the background, and who may be a Catholic saint just as much as a Napoleon or a film star.

The *grave*, which contains relics in the most literal sense, is therefore the guarantee of sacred power; and in Christianity, just as much as in Islam, it was considered important to have one's last resting place *inter sanctos*, to be buried near the grave of the holy ones.[2] In ancient Egypt, similarly, the nobles had themselves interred at Abydos, near the grave of the divine and sacred Osiris. Conversely, the possession of the holy grave is of high value, as power, to the community, and the whole of Sophocles' *Oedipus at Colonus* is constructed on this idea.[3] In Greece, again, the heroes were nothing but saints whose graves occupied the best situations in or near the city.[4] Just like the medieval ecclesiastical saints, the heroes too were the objects of the struggle for power between different cities: Oedipus had four graves. Then the grave and the relics became more important than the saint himself: the thing prevailed over the person. Hence, still further, the so-called *translations*. The Spartans brought Orestes from Tegea, just as the Aeacids were lent to the Thebans by the Aegeans, and the Dioscuri to the Locrians by the Spartans.[5] Similarly the bones of Theseus were transported from Skyros to Athens,[6] and the oracle ordained that Hector's bones should be taken to Thebes, while in order to ward off plague the remains of St. Gennaros were brought to Naples.[7] People were so far misled as even to steal a saint; in 1087 merchants from Bari robbed the inhabitants of Myra of St. Nicholas, who on the first day after his translation cured thirty sick persons.[8] When the dying St. Francis was on his way to Assisi, Perugia had to be avoided lest the people there might seize the saint; and on his arrival at Assisi there were great rejoicings because it was hoped, with good reason, that he would quickly die.[9]

[1] Chapman Cohen, *Religion and Sex*, 173.   [2] Söderblom, *Gottesglaube*, 87 f.
[3] cf. H. Usener, *Der Stoff des griechischen Epos, Kl. Schriften*, IV, 1913, 214.
[4] Rohde, *Psyche*, I, 159 f. E. T. 121, 166. cf. also Nilsson, *A History of Greek Religion*, 233 f.   [5] M. P. Nilsson, *AR.* 22, 1923–24, 372.
[6] Plutarch, *Theseus*, 36.   [7] Pausanias, IX, 18. Trede, *Heidentum*, II, 327 ff.
[8] Trede, II, 324 f.   [9] P. Sabatier, *Vie de Saint François d'Assise*[10], 1894, 362 ff.

Thus, in the first place, a saint is either a corpse, or a part of one. The world has no use for living saints: they are dead persons,[1] or still better: the potency of the dead. Even apparently secularized civilization continues to aspire towards this power. Alphonso the Great of Naples, for instance, obtained one of Livy's arm-bones from the Venetians only with great difficulty;[2] for the Renaissance sought its saints among the ancients. And whoever has seen Napoleon's tomb under the *Dôme des Invalides*, and the Unknown Soldier's grave under the *Arc de Triomphe de l'Étoile* on the same day in Paris, realizes that the nineteenth and the twentieth centuries, too, still discover a source of power in the translation and worship of sacred corpses and graves.[3]

2. If therefore the upward limit of the saints, as directed towards the gods, is a fluctuating one, so that they are the objects of worship rather than representatives, on the other hand the concrete and palpable potency in their structure predominates so intensely that it becomes a matter of indifference to what person this may be attached; and thus we find, in actual fact, all sorts of figures among saints. Nameless powers, kings and noble forbears became heroes in Greece;[4] among the saints of the Catholic calendar we find martyrs, teachers, prophets, national heroes, simple pious people, "*successeurs des dieux*", particularly of heathen deities, and very many "odd saints".

3. The empirical character of the fullness of power therefore, previously substantiated at the commencement of this volume, is dominant here also; he is sacred from whom power emanates. If he is still living, then this power can be manifested mainly in two ways: by miracles and by physical signs, among which *stigmata* take a leading place. But the church demands the attestation of *miracles*, performed after death, for the process of beatification or canonization, and thus remains wholly

---

[1] Chap. 14.

[2] J. Burckhardt, *Die Kultur der Renaissance in Italien* I[12], 1919, 194.

[3] *cf.* Chap. 37.

[4] Rohde, *Psyche*, I, 165 *ff.* E. T. 116 *f.* Nilsson, *A History of Greek Religion*, 233 *f.* The list of Islamite saints, who play an equally prominent part in popular piety to that of their Christian counterparts, and with whom also everything revolves around the grave and the miracles associated with it, is almost as variegated. A Greek hero was a "dead man who by death has attained to something like deity"; Rose, *Primitive Culture in Greece*, 32. Sophocles was honoured not because of his poetry but as a *dexion*—as the host—of Asclepius, *ibid.*, 93.—Sanctity is not a moral power. "The Sicilian peasant still reckons the *decollati*—decapitated persons of notoriety—as very much on a par with the saints": Marett, *Faith, Hope and Charity*, 86.

within the realm of power conceptions; and it scarcely escapes from this idea by insisting on heroic virtue. For according to old church language, virtue and miracle are closely related (*virtus*, ἀρετή). A quite different concept of sanctity arises, again, as soon as the latter is associated no longer with personal power, but with the idea of status or office; it is in this sense that the New Testament "saints" are to be understood, who owe their sanctity to the gift of grace bestowed on them. They were not saints, but were accounted saints or made into saints; this concept of the saint, also, has passed into the realm of ideas of the Christian church.

CHAPTER 31

DEMONIC HUMAN BEINGS

1. THE terrible figure, the evil will, which revealed themselves to man as Power,[1] take possession of him and thus form a very remarkable dual unity of subject and object, of representative and represented. To a certain extent, indeed, this is to be met with in all representatives; but it receives in the present instance a thoroughly specific character that is due to the manner in which man loves the object of his fear and represents his own awe. This is possible, however, only on the basis of that fusion of subject and object which has been already frequently discussed, and which must be described both here and later as possession.[2] The demon has thus gained such complete control of the man that he speaks through him and acts within him; yet nevertheless there persists the consciousness of a dual personality, of possession, indeed of a violation of the essentially human.

2. The *werewolves* in the first place, whose acquaintance we have previously made,[3] are demonic human beings; but above all women, as the "more powerful", become victims of possession. The *witch* is naked; but by this no natural, nor even Greek, nakedness is implied, in the sense of "emancipation of the flesh", but a rite,[4] a "celebration", which accentuates the witch's powerfulness. She unites herself with her demonic paramour, the counterpart of the heavenly bridegroom, this unity being sexual; *incubi* and *succubi*, too, exercise their activities; and Charles de Coster gives a magnificent and psychologically penetrating description both of the werewolf and of the witch living in a covenant with the devil.[5] It is of course to be presupposed that the witch herself believes in her sinister *liaison*, and in this respect many victims of the witch delusion cannot be regarded as "innocent". At the same time others exposed themselves to the suspicion of being witches solely because of some striking characteristic such as beauty, rapidly increasing wealth *etc.* Here again we discover the empiricism of the powerful: the extraordinary as such merits reverence, or suspicion,

---

[1] Chap. 15.   [2] Chap. 74.   [3] Chap. 8.
[4] Chap. 48.   [5] *Eulenspiegel und Lamme Goedzak.*

and in any case is "sacred". Owing to her union with the demon, again, the witch acquires all kinds of capabilities, although in most cases, like those of the demon himself, these only cause injury; she induces disease in man and beast, and all sorts of evil in general: the evil eye, transmutation and the whole medley of witchcraft.

B. THE SACRED COMMUNITY

CHAPTER 32

COMMUNITY

1. TO every human being *solitude* is familiar. "Every woman who bears a child, every man who risks his life, every human being who dies, must pass through the utmost extremity without the help of his fellow creatures who are willing to assist him."[1] But man cannot be solitary. Whoever is thoroughly isolated weeps like an abandoned child: or like Christ in Gethsemane. From the child to the God-Man, solitude excites dread in us all: for we possess power and life only in the community. It is in fact this primeval dread, and no mere trivial fear, that created gods. Dread leads to God, or to the devil: even with the devil there still is life, still a "Thou". But in solitude there is nothing whatever.

Loneliness is the culmination of the insecurity and *care* wherein we live. Hence its terror arises whenever we approach the boundaries of life and experience most intensely its powerfulness and uncertainty: in birth, death and sex intercourse. Then all terrors fuse into the one great dread:— that of our existence in itself, of death, and of life. But unless we were beings who possessed life only within the community, we should know neither dread nor loneliness. Solitude and fellowship condition each other reciprocally: to be alone is to stand before the Ultimate, before God. But we enter into solitariness only out of the community: and conversely every man (with the exception of the God-Man, Christ) repeatedly returns from solitude to the community, even though "with eyes still unused to it".[2]

2. "Community" is not "covenant". Since the age of enlightenment there has operated the tendency to depict a community as a society: the church as a religious society based on confession or creed, the state as a secular society resting on a *contrat social*.[3] But "community"

---

[1] Künkel, *Einführung in die Charakterologie*, 58 *f.*

[2] Schmalenbach, *Kat. des Bundes*, 62. *Einsamkeit*. Lohmeyer, *Vom Begriff der religiösen Gemeinschaft*, 45.

[3] *cf.* von Schlözer, who thought of the state "as analogous to a fire insurance company" (Schmalenbach, *ibid.*, 37).

is something not manufactured, but given; it depends not upon sentiment or feeling, but on the Unconscious.[1] It need be founded upon no
conviction, since it is self-evident; we do not become members of it,
but "belong to it". To-day the finest example is still the peasant, who
has no "feelings" but simply belongs to his community, as contrasted
with the *citoyen* invented in the eighteenth century! Even peasants
who fight, or engage in law-suits, remain neighbours and brothers;[2]
a peasant in the Eastern Netherlands who has a mortal enemy in the
village nevertheless knows that on market-days he is obliged to greet
his foe and walk up and down with him once, when the peasant community of the whole district is gathered in the county town, thus
demonstrating to the eyes of "strangers" the fellowship of the village
ad oculos.

Primitive man, again, thinks and acts collectively. Without his fellows
the individual is nought; in him acts his family, his stock. To us mass
conversion is repugnant, but to primitive man it is quite normal; when
therefore the mass adopts a new religion one must act with them,
otherwise one cannot exist at all.[3] Thus to the German tribes the murder
of a relative was far more than a crime: it indicated madness, since it
was really suicide.[4] In the eyes of the Greeks, similarly, the slaying of
a relation was the deed that awakened the *Erinyes.* "The fact is that the
individual cannot act unless everyone acts in and with him, nor can he
suffer without the affliction extending over the entire community."[5]
"Alone", man cannot live. That is the great dread. To be alone is
to die.

Thus just as man is bound to the "world", being not opposed to it
but having "community" with it, so he has this community, and lives
in this "being in-common", with his fellow men.[6] And to-day we still
become "primitive" as soon as we feel ourselves among the mass of
living humanity; every revolution, every war, testifies to this. In times
of crisis, then, man flees from his actually achieved, or pretended,
independence, back to the original community that protects him from
dread. But in religion, wherein his very existence is the issue, man is
continually confronted by new crises; hence religion is, or becomes,
communal. The rite is the deed of us all, and similarly the myth is a
story, and the creed the belief, of everyone.

Thus whoever is severed from the community cannot live; home-

---

[1] Schmalenbach, *Kat. des Bundes*, 53 *ff.*   [2] *ibid.*, 57.
[3] Chantepie, *op. cit.*, II, 600.   [4] *ibid.*, 556.
[5] Grönbech, *op. cit.*, I, 28.   [6] *cf.* Chap. 8.

sickness gnaws at his soul. Even to-day we encounter the misery of recruits and the arson of which maidservants from the country are guilty; in such cases it is, however, not the "I" that has been damaged, but the "we" which has been shattered. Ban and interdict, then, are punishments synonymous with death, while prohibition of the sacrament by the church, and of intercourse with other members of the tribe in primitive communities,[1] kills the person upon whom it falls.

3. Primitive man knows only *one* community: to him the distinction between secular and spiritual communion is entirely foreign. Life is essentially a single whole, and the communality of society is precisely the powerful life. Life, however, can be communal in threefold form: (*A*) as *blood*, which implies the soul.[2] (*B*) as *totem*, signifying the conjoint world,[3] both of which are "given"; and (*C*) as *property*, which exhibits life's "possibility".[4] But these three forms by no means subsist in any exclusive relationship.

G. LE BON, *The Crowd*.

E. LOHMEYER, *Vom Begriff der religiösen Gemeinschaft*, 1925.

G. MENSCHING, *Sociologie der Religion*, 1947.

H. SCHMALENBACH, *Die soziologische Kategorie des Bundes* (*Die Dioskuren*, I, 1922).

Die Genealogie der Einsamkeit (*Logos*, 8, 1920).

J. WACH, *Einführung in die Religionssoziologie*, 1930.

J. WACH, *Sociology of Religion*, 1940.

[1] *e.g.* Sophocles, *Oedipus rex*, 259.

[2] Chap. 39.   [3] Chap. 8.   Chap. 23.

CHAPTER 33

MARRIAGE. FAMILY. TRIBE

1. *MARRIAGE* is "covenant" and "community" simultaneously: it is what is given *and* what is chosen. Its character as being something given becomes increasingly apparent to the degree that it expands into the family: choice, on the other hand, dominates it so far as it is a union of love. The common element that is sought, and at the same time discovered, is undifferentiated: it concerns the whole life. Differentiation thus relates not to the common factor but to the predominance of either the given, or the chosen, respectively. In every marriage, therefore, covenant struggles with community: in every individual, the spouse with the lover.

From the phenomenological standpoint, the old problem of primal marriage: was it monogamy or promiscuity? can be considered from this point of view—but only from this one! The older evolutionism set an absolute polygamy and polyandry at the beginning, together with polydemonism, while a more modern evolutionism enthusiastically attempts to assign a secure position to an original monogamy, side by side with an original monotheism. A circumspect ethnology, however, rejects every type of unilinear development, regards primal promiscuity as a figment of the imagination, and so-called group-marriage as a secondary formation;[1] but original monogamy is equally fantastic. Phenomenology is not concerned with any "primal conditions". It can apprehend only the element of promiscuity that is given potentially in every marriage, as well as the element of ultimate givenness involved in each relationship between man and woman. These are both expressed in the Biblical idea that the man leaves his father and mother for the sake of his wife—that is choice, but that God joins husband and wife together—that is givenness. Hence it is that the church regards marriage as a sacrament.

The communal element, in the first place, manifests itself particularly clearly in the widespread custom of so-called *couvade*, or male childbed. Rationalistic attempts at its explanation such as the man trying to secure the mother's privileges persisting from the matriarchal period, or the man submitting to the woman, are quite unsatisfactory; and

---

[1] F. Gräbner, *Das Weltbild der Primitiven*, 1924, 11.

this peculiar custom can be correctly understood only in the light of the idea of community: where one member suffers, that is to say, the other suffers also; *couvade* would then have arisen out of the same intention as the simultaneous illness of the married pair, of which Thurnwald gives a remarkable example.[1]

2. All this leads quite normally to the *family*; this is no joining together of individuals, but a form of existence in its own right, from which one cannot release oneself. Neither is it a covenant, but community in the truest sense, the common element of which embraces the entire life, even in its physical aspects. Thus a Basuto girl who ought to keep awake, but grows sleepy, can blame this on one of her relatives who may be indulging in a nap in some corner.[2] The element of covenant also, discerned in marriage, can in this way be completely expelled therefrom by the family. In the Gaboon and Ogowe territory, for example, a man has a certain right to his brother's wife; at least adultery with a sister-in-law is not, as such, punished. In one typical instance, an Ogowe man kills his brother's wife because she has rejected his love; he denies the crime, but his brother, the murdered woman's husband, says: "you are guilty; but because we are brothers, and not two men but one, your crime is mine and I will acknowledge it in your place"; the wife's family, however, is not content with this and demands the surrender of the actual murderer.[3] Thus the family perceives one thing only: one of its members has been stricken, and that must be made good. But the husband too sees only one fact: he and his brother are one, and he not merely feels no necessity for revenge, but even acknowledges the crime which he should have punished. The murderer, again, thinks of only a single point: his brother's wife naturally belongs to him also; her refusal therefore deserves death. And this leads in certain tribes even to a claim of the brother to his brother's wife, whom he calls "my wife".[4] A similar over-growing of the marriage-character by that of the family is to be found in so-called *levirate marriage*. In the Old Testament, as well as among many primitive peoples, it is the duty of the brother to marry his dead brother's wife,[5] and in the Lampongs, in Sumatra, the offspring of a levirate marriage are regarded as the children of the dead man. But if the levirate union remains

---

[1] G. van der Leeuw, *Structure*, 7.

[2] Lévy-Bruhl, *The "Soul" of the Primitive*, 88. He speaks of "physiological solidarity", which well describes the *couvade* also.   [3] *ibid.*, 90.

[4] *ibid.*, 91. The whole family has also paid the bride-price!   [5] *ibid.*, 92.

barren, the brother-in-law appoints one of his own sons to be the perpetuator of his brother's family. This son must then marry two wives: the son by the first wife becomes the successor of his own father, as though he were the son of the grandfather: the son by the second wife becomes his own successor.[1] Thus all life's power impulses are dominated by its common element: the family is all in all. In Israel the obligation to marry the widow was restricted by *Deuteronomy* to the brother, although originally it applied to the father of the dead man also. The first son who sprang from the renewed marriage counted as the son of the dead man, and perpetuated his name and inheritance.[2] Here then it is clear that the sacred that subsists in common need not be blood alone; and in this way what is given by Nature is modified, as so frequently elsewhere;[3] not however by a new union, but by an autocratic continuation of the impaired communal relations. Accordingly, marriage is in the first place the transition from one familial communality into another; the woman must become incorporated within the sacred subsisting in common with the husband. This train of ideas is presupposed by many marriage rites.[4] In ancient Rome, at the conclusion of the nuptials, the woman said "where you are Gaius I am Gaia", thereby adopting her husband's gentile name. The widow again, who by marrying has lost her old communality, would be completely solitary were not a position assigned to her in the husband's community. Thus Ruth attached herself to her mother-in-law although there was no longer the prospect of levirate marriage; Naomi dissuaded her, since she was too old to bear a new husband for her daughter-in-law (for this would have been the most desirable outcome!). But Ruth spoke the beautiful words, which should be interpreted in no merely sentimental mood: "thy people shall be my people, and thy God my God".[5] Here marriage has completely become community. Hence, too, its religious indissolubility: a covenant can be broken, but not marriage.

Blood is not the sole sacred common element; but it is probably the most important and, still further, it does not become severed from the other common factors. It is obviously the principal feature in the intense consciousness of unity ("belonging together" is far too feeble!). Of this blood vengeance is the best proof, since it is based directly on the common blood that has been shed; and in Greece "the heir could

[1] F. D. E. van Ossenbruggen, *Tydschr. Kon. Ned. Aardrykskundig Genootsch.*, 2. *Reeks*, 47, 1930, 223.   [2] *Deut.* xxv. 5 *ff.*; *Gen.* xxxviii, 26; *Ruth*.
[3] Chap. 23.   [4] Chap. 22.   [5] *Ruth* i. 12 *ff.*

evade the obligation of vengeance just as little as he could become
the son of another father".[1] Hence the murder of relatives was accounted
the most evil of all actions. Among the Greeks it awoke the *Erinyes*,
the embodiment, as it were, of the spilt blood which, because it had
turned against itself, resulted in madness. Thus in Aeschylus' *Eumenides*
Apollo, as his protector, defends Orestes by opposing the infamous
murder of Agamemnon by Clytemnestra to the matricide. But the
Erinyes reject this justification:

"'Tis no murder to take the life of your own kin."[2]

Abel's blood, again, "crieth unto (God) from the ground" for vengeance
upon Cain.[3] Among certain African tribes, likewise, community
consciousness is so intense that fratricide is regarded not as murder
but as suicide, as something abominable and insane. But it is not
punished;[4] indeed, there is no one competent to punish it. For there is
no "punishment" whatever in our sense: the power of the outraged
blood reacts upon the murderer. In the case of the murder of relations,
then, murderer and murdered are wholly and essentially one and the
same person; and therefore nothing can happen unless the blood, in
the guise ot the *Erinyes*, turns against itself as madness.

The stranger by blood is outside the community. He is an "enemy"
(*hostis*, foreigner or stranger and enemy); he participates in an alien
power and we must therefore be on our guard. Such a measure of
precaution is the greeting; when we say certain potent words and
offer food, this results in a temporary blending of the two inimical
powers.[5] The stranger or foreigner must therefore be met with either
the utmost courtesy (hospitality) or unconcealed enmity. Both are
directed against his power, before which we bow or which we assail,
since he is already severed from his own community; but in both cases
it is feared.[6] To the stranger also dangerous tasks are assigned, such
as the defloration of girls or affairs connected with harvest *etc.*

That community of blood is not the sole common element constituting the family is shown by the possibility of its modification which
we discerned in levirate marriage, while according to certain Mohammedan viewpoints, the Imam can accept someone into the family of
Mohammed by pronouncing a benedictory formula.[7] In ancient Rome,

[1] U. von Wilamowitz-Möllendorff, *Griechische Tragödien*, II[8], 1919, 127 *f.*
[2] *Eumenides*, 212; *cf.* van der Leeuw, *Goden en Menschen*, 101 *ff.*
[3] *Gen.* iv. 10.   [4] Lévy-Bruhl, *The "Soul" of the Primitive*, 93 *ff.*
[5] Chap. 4; van Gennep, *op. cit.*, 46 *f.*
[6] van Gennep, *op. cit.*, 36.   [7] Massignon, *Al-Hallaj*, 507.

again, the law originally recognized only *agnatio*, that is relationship based on paternity, while *cognatio*, the sole assured blood relationship, occupied merely second place. But *agnatio* was founded wholly on *patria potestas*:[1] the married woman *in manu* was therefore agnate to her husband.[2] Thus the family in this instance depended on a power, *patria potestas*, which (as we have seen) was not necessarily connected with blood relationship at all.

Among many peoples, still further, *property* also plays a part as the common element of the family. For property is not just the object which the owner possesses. It is a power,[3] and indeed a common power. The Australian's property dies with its owner, and can therefore be employed by no one else,[4] while the Roman idea of *familia* signified a farmhouse with its fields and cattle.[5] Later these possessions were called *familia pecuniaque*, and afterwards *patrimonium*, this "property derived from the father" being originally inalienable, as contrasted with *possessio*, which implied only the use of a field or building and not these in themselves.[6] Thus we find the common element of the family bound up with blood and with property; but it is not confined to these, for it is sacred, and therefore cannot be derived without any remainder from the given.

3. Family limits are not finally fixed. It may thus be regarded as the narrower association of man, wife and children,[7] as well as the wider group conditioned by these; in this way the family gradually expands into the *wider family*. A special and highly important form of this is the *clan*, whose bounds are calculated according to either patriarchal or matriarchial derivation, and whose centre of power is usually a totem;[8] its perpetuation, as a rule, is dominated by an intricate marriage system which, in accordance with its two principal types, is described as either exogamous or endogamous. For us the crucial point, however, is not whether this mode of mutual life was the original type, but the fact that in this form of community the individual is never the mere individual but always only one particular instance of a class: there are

---

[1] Chap. 20.
[2] May, *Droit romain*, 139. Piganiol, *Origines*, 160. [3] Chap. 3.
[4] Joseph Wanninger, *Das Heilige in der Religion der Australier*, 1927, 87. *cf.* Julius Lips, *Die Anfänge des Rechts an Grund und Boden, Festschr. für W. Schmidt*, 1928, 485 *ff.* [5] Piganiol, *ibid.*, 172. [6] May, *ibid.*, 186, 197 *f.*, 203.
[7] This is intended to exclude neither polygamy nor polyandry. A unilinear development from the monogamous family is neither fact nor phenomenon, but dogma.
[8] Chap. 8.

women whom a man may marry, but also those whom he cannot marry because they pertain to the group of "mothers" or "sisters", even in cases where close blood relationship is not involved, and also where connection by blood is totally lacking and only totem community subsists.[1] Levirate marriage, as well as the frequently very far-reaching marriage prohibitions of Christian communities, appear to be survivals of this. One marries precisely not a personality, but rather the bearer of some specific power; and many primitive tribes do not recognize *the* father nor *the* uncle, but only fathers and uncles.[2]

But the inclusive family may also possess quite different bases, the most important of these being the patriarchal. The Roman *gens*, for example, was actually only the family in its widest conceivable extent. The "father" of this great family was *dux et princeps generis*, from whom the *gens* derived its *nomen gentilicium*, while the *sacra gentilicia* constituted the power centre of the *gens*. Whoever forsook the *gens* and entered another, as for instance through adoption, had to carry out the renunciatory ceremony, *detestatio sacrorum*, since he would otherwise pertain to two powers simultaneously; and the *pontifices* decided whether the *sacra* of the person adopted were not being damaged too seriously by those of the one adopting him, the *adrogans*.[3] The *gens*, too, had its common graves and sanctuaries,[4] and the cult of its own gods was secret. As in the family, community here also was always that of the cult: the sacred is the common element, and the common element the sacred. Thus in ancient Greece only the nobility originally formed tribes, because it carried on the cult; later, however, those who were not noble were received into the *phratry* as participants in the ritual, or *orgeones*; but frequently the cult practices, as at Eleusis, remained in the hands of specific noble tribes.[5]

4. The greater family, or clan, gradually expanded into the still more comprehensive community form of the *tribe*; the Germanic *Sippe* embraced everyone in the *Ting*. But actual community has its root in the presence of Power, so that what "elders" generally are in

[1] *cf.* Cassirer, *Symb. Formen*, II, 226: "The definition of Species is not based on empirical-causal principles of generation; the concept of 'genus' does not depend on the empirical connection between *gignere* and *gigni*, but the conviction of the ideality of the genus, as this develops from its basis in the reciprocal magical relations of humanity and animals, is the primary fact, with which the idea of common 'descent' becomes indirectly associated."

[2] Spencer and Gillen, *Northern Tribes*, 74; *cf.* 95: "The native names apply not to the individual, but to the group of which he is a member."

[3] May, *Droit romain*, 140, 148.   [4] Chantepie, *op. cit.*, II, 438.   [5] *ibid.*, 386.

the clan—that is potential fathers, and what the father is in the family, and similarly in the wider family the primal ancestor and his successors, that too is the status of the nobility, or the king, in the tribe. They were bearers of the power which the German peoples called "peace"—*Sippe*, from Old High German *sippa, sibba,* meaning peace;[1] and hence, in the *Ting,* persons had to appear unarmed before the king.[2] There was therefore no community without some centre of power which might be either a *sacrum,*[3] a certain specific god or a person, while the power subsisting in the tribal community was guaranteed by the lord, the king or the nobility.[4] Thus life is valid only when it is potent life; but it possesses power, again, only within the community; "mere separation from family and country sufficed to bring life into peril",[5] and he who was expelled from the Germanic community was as good as dead.[6]

Here again, therefore, blood is the common element only in so far as it is one of the most important manifestations of powerfulness and sacredness; but it may also be replaced by other forms of the sacred. The Toradja of Celebes, who live on the seashore and adopted Mohammedanism from the Bugis, afterwards called themselves "descendants of the Bugis",[7]—a reversal of *cujus regio ejus religio.* The foreigner, then, is one who is a stranger to the sacred. Membership of the tribe, and "religion", are wholly one: God is the "God of the fathers", of Abraham, Isaac and Jacob.

M. J. Bouwman, *La Couvade* (*Revue Anthropol.* 35, 1925, 49 *ff*.).

F. de Coulanges, *La cité antique* (Eng. tr., *The Ancient City*).

M. Weber, *Gesammelte Aufsätze zur Religionssoziologie,* 1922 *ff.*

[1] J. M. N. Kapteyn, in: *Donum natalicium Schrynen,* 1929, 540.
[2] Chantepie, *op. cit.,* II, 577.   [3] *cf.* Chap. 3.   [4] Chap. 13.
[5] Grönbech, *Folkeaet,* II, 188.   [6] Chantepie, *ibid.,* 172 *ff.*
[7] N. Adriani, *Het animistisch Heidendom als godsdienst,* 54.

CHAPTER 34

THE COVENANT

1. THE *community* is essentially one unified entity, and the life that is powerful within it is one and indivisible; compared with the community, then, the *covenant* is an additional organization of an essentially different type. Thus Abraham had two sons, Isaac and Ishmael: Isaac, however, was not only the child of his body but also the son of the promise. An order of salvation separates off from that of Nature, a divine possibility from the—likewise divine—givenness: the charism,[1] the power, becomes divided.

Whether one wishes it or not, he belongs to the community. But he enters into the covenant. Together with the givenness pertaining to destiny, then, there appears the possibility of the human will which, however, is immediately apprehended as vocation. But the principal feature is that the sacredness of what is given—of blood, property or totem—is here radically (as in the previous Chapter occasionally) intersected by another form of the sacred; and this holds true of the development of the primitive secret society from the original tribe equally as of His deed, Who said with reference to His disciples: "Behold my mother and my brethren".[2]

Of course the order of salvation, which here exists along with the "natural" order, is not always, and not from the outset, the spiritual bond which the modern world understands by the term. There is at first a large number of simpler distinctions:—

2. At the frontier between what is given, and choice, stands the so-called *age-class*, the principle of differentiation being inclusion in some definite phase of life:—children, young people, adults; and thus the age-grade has a powerfulness of its own incompatible with other powers, which presses for specific differentiation. To-day this is familiar to every village clergyman who has seen newly married persons immediately withdraw from the choral union that he has formed after so much effort, not because they have lost their voices or their need of sociability, but just because they now belong to another age-group;

[1] Weber, *Gesammelte Aufsätze zur Religionssoziologie.*
[2] *Mark* iii. 34. Schmalenbach, *Soz. Kat. des Bundes*, 44.

and that youth has its own feelings about life, and its peculiar potency, is likewise quite obvious in our own day. Young country people, moreover, frequently form exclusive groups that play an important part in popular customs and which in olden days, according as it was feminine or masculine, had its *kora* or its *kouros* in Greece.[1] To-day, too, the group system in a country village has a religious tinge: the youths in the street in the evening, and the girls there also, or in earlier days in the spinning-room, and the men in the tavern *etc.*; in the German division of Transylvania the young men, from confirmation to marriage, form a "brotherhood" with seven official servants.[2]

Of course age is something that is given, and can of itself constitute no covenant. Yet it is here that the additional organization, to which I have just referred, begins, because in the first place people leave the age-grade voluntarily, usually by marriage, and in the next because this grade gradually passes over into the covenant. In Mittenwald in Upper Bavaria, for example, not every youth may belong to the "brotherhood", the "rapscallions" being excluded.[3] Among primitive peoples, again, the transition from the age-grade to the secret society is general, the entire organization of the latter being already actually given together with the age-group.[4]

3. The second division of powerfulness occurs with respect to *sex*. Man and woman have different charismata: to woman, man is sacred, and conversely. This is conditioned by the awe, or even the reverence, with which they regard each other, just as by the mutual disinclination subsisting between the sexes. Thus the youth's nervousness in the girl's presence and his ecstatic reverence for her, and similarly the coquetry with which woman both defends herself and attracts, as well as the deeply rooted disesteem the sexes entertain for each other, ultimately have a basis in religion. Power opposes power. Children go to school: with haughty self-consciousness, the boys keep apart from the girls walking about arm in arm and tittering while they look mockingly towards the lads, who have their own pride mixed with a disagreeable sense of insecurity, just as the girls too have their secrets; later on, the men have their own clubs, and the women their afternoon tea and gossip. *We* connect religious ideas with neither the profound lack of understanding between man and woman, nor with the marvel

---

[1] Chap. 11. [2] Schurtz, *Altersklassen und Männerbünde*, 112 *f.*
[3] Schurtz, *ibid. Bachbuben* is the German equivalent.
[4] On age-grades *cf.* further Merker, *Die Masai*, 71 *ff.* I leave to the reader the application to modern conditions—*e.g.* student unions, *etc.*

of their mutual discovery; to us both avoidance and community are equally mundane conceptions. But wrongly so; and we should not sigh under the burden of complicated "sex problems" if only we could recognize both the repellent and the attractive factors in the contrasted sexes as powerfulness, instead of imagining that we can solve them by any arbitrary conventions.

In the Fiji Islands every village has at least two *men's houses*, since custom does not permit the husband to spend the night in his own home; he belongs to the "strangers' house", the hotel, and early in the morning he returns to his family.[1] In Doreh in Dutch New Guinea, the *rumslam* are men's houses in which the youths remain—the age limit being identical with the sex limit! These buildings are at the same moment sanctuaries and places for dancing;[2] there the young women resort and unrestrained love-making follows; the sacred flutes are kept there too, while sex symbols decorate the entrance.[3] Here then we perceive how from the one life the most widely different forms of our modern diversity of existence have developed: house, sanctuary, club, hotel, brothel—from the one community the most highly contrasted differentiations. Here also the given still remains the chief element— the specific power of sex. But the differentiation is plastic, and in secret societies the restriction of membership to men (seldom to women too) is essential.

4. The *secret societies* to be found among primitive peoples, above all in Africa, are indeed compacts rather than communities, although of course the prevalence of the covenant principle is restricted, since inclusion in the tribe is usually requisite for membership within the covenant; and we have already seen that its organization arises directly from that of the family or clan. "The magical-religious brotherhoods are based essentially on clan organization, that is on social relationship, but nevertheless they are something quite different".[4] In fact, differentiation according to membership with respect to the totem, within the clan, was a sort of "additional organization"; and the organization of age-classes passes over directly into that of the covenant.[5] The Papuans, again, exclude illegitimate children from the compact, and the Australians half-castes.[6] Rites of initiation for the secret society are approximately the same as those for puberty in connection with the tribe.[7]

[1] Webster, *Primitive Secret Societies*, 12.   [2] Chap. 29, 57.
[3] Webster, *ibid.*, 8.   [4] A. van Gennep, *op. cit.*, 109.
[5] Alviella, *RHR.* 81, 1920, 7.   [6] Webster, *ibid.*, 27.   [7] Chap. 22.

Although secret societies arise from the community, and are bound up with this to such a degree, indeed, that the age-grades and the men's groups, which themselves presuppose separation from the women and children of the tribe, are scarcely to be distinguished from the compact,[1] there still appears in the latter an element of extraordinary importance:— the covenant, that is to say, reposes upon a more or less free selection from the tribe. Thus community is no longer given as a matter of course, since the covenant is sought for: one not merely belongs to the community, but enters into the covenant also. Its purpose is originally no other than that of the community itself: preservation and strengthening of communal power, attainment of communal salvation. But the secrecy which, as has already been observed, also appeared spontaneously in the cult of the family, has in this instance had an unfavourable result, since secret societies usually exhibit a deterioration of community. Because the common element is, in principle, abrogated, so the common law no longer holds good; and under the protection of the peculiar and secret powerfulness, now grown independent of the communal essence, all sorts of crimes are committed: those not within the covenant are terrorized, debts forcibly collected, enemies robbed, maltreated and killed. In Loango, for instance, a state official is present, but after masks have been put on he is sent back to the village—a clear indication that community is now yielding place to covenant.[2]

The sacred common element of covenants is to a great extent the same as that of communities, sacred objects playing a prominent part, like the *churinga* already referred to;[3] to the initiates is explained the function of the "bull-roarer", which imitates thunder, while from others this remains concealed; or members are taught how to prepare the hats and masks used in the performances and processions *etc.*[4] The gods and spirits too, to whom homage is paid, are the same as those worshipped by the community, but their secrets, for example their names, are supposed to be known only to the members. The rites, again, are the same as those of the tribe: tests, feigning death *etc.*, grades of initiation taking the place of age-classes; in Calabar, for instance, there are seven to nine of these.[5]

In general, we conclude that while the secret society certainly inclines

[1] Webster, *ibid.,* 21, 135 *ff.*
[2] A. Bastian, *Die deutsche Expedition an der Loango-Küste,* I, 1874, 221.
[3] Chap. 3.   [4] Codrington, *The Melanesians,* 69 *ff.*
[5] M. H. Kingsley, *West African Studies,* 562.

the idea of community in the direction of that of covenant, still this transposition has not been successful: it is either a social excrescence or it sinks to the level of a popular custom, if not indeed to that of farce. Of the latter process the *Quimba* in Loango offers an example: the initiates appear out of the forest armed with sticks, with which they chastise unfaithful or quarrelsome women.[1] Moreover, the secret society has acquired no form of life of its own which is sufficiently distinctive from the organization of tribe or family.

5. The limits of the given are also transcended by *sacrificial* and *festival communities*, such as were familiar to the Greeks: *thiasos* and *eranos*.[2] These were usually dedicated to some secret cult or other, and held communal meals for which they demanded contributions from their members, being as a rule open to women, strangers and slaves. Members wore a badge, and if they had rendered noteworthy service to the society they received a eulogy that was recorded on a tablet. These societies occupied a position intermediate between our secular societies and the religious covenant, and frequently facilitated the introduction of foreign, oriental, divinities, in this way, as well as by their neglect of tribal limits, constituting a transition to the mystery communities.

In the case of societies in antiquity we are often unable to decide what their constitutive factor was, whether some religious purpose or communal labour;[3] but the medieval *guilds* found their sacred common element in the specific character of the work;[4] the powerfulness of the craft, incorporated in the patron saint, bound the members together. But here again the given factor was stronger than the possibility of choice, since the guilds formed closed corporations in which the occupation was not open to all, but on the contrary was often hereditary: the potency was actually already there and required no searching for. The ceremonial of their meals, again, was the same as was customary at the ancient cult festivals, while transitions to the dignity of journeyman and mastership bore the character of consecration; in the parish

---

[1] J. Réville, *Les peuples non-civilisés*, I, 1883, 103.

[2] P. Foucart, *Des associations religieuses chez les Grecs*. Ziebarth, *Das griechische Vereinswesen*.

[3] A remarkable instance:—The so-called Gallipoli Inscription, which refers to a fishermen's society, but in which its detailed grades receive varied interpretations from commentators, in some cases with regard to occupation, and in others to activities in the mysteries cult. *Mém. Ac. Inscr. et B. Lettr.* 35, 1896, 36. *Bull. Corr. Hell.* I, 1877. F. Poland, *Geschichte des griechischen Vereinswesens*, 1908, 86, 119 f., 405. Ziebarth, *Das griechische Vereinswesen*, 1896, 24.   [4] Chap. 2.

church, too, the guild had its own altar and its own saint; the entire community ritual was continued there, and inclined to the covenant only because of the arbitrariness—in itself very limited—of the vocation.[1]

6. In the *mystery communities*, as these were brought into existence above all by Hellenism, power ultimately became differentiated: from life in the world, which became correspondingly reduced in value, "salvation" was distinguished.[2] The origin of these mystery societies, however, still clearly shows community forms: the cult of Isis, from which the Isis mysteries of the imperial era arose, presents in the family of Osiris the primal type that is repeated in every family;[3] originally, too, the Eleusinian cult was the festal celebration of an agricultural village community and restricted to its inhabitants;[4] and until the cessation of these mysteries, indeed, the chief dignities remained in the hands of two ancient Eleusinian families. "Thus the conclusion is at least rendered probable that the form of the mysteries service may have developed by gradual expansion from the domestic cult",[5] while we have already seen that the rites of marriage and of the mysteries were closely related.[6]

But the mystery communities increasingly developed from communities to covenants; primarily this holds good of their purpose. For in the mysteries, life in general and powerfulness were no longer universally sought for, but a "salvation" sharply distinguished from them; and this tendency was connected with the urge towards the security of life which was more and more powerfully operative in the Greek world from the sixth century B.C. to the fifth A.D., and which manifested itself above all in the yearning for immortality.[7] The real purpose of the mysteries, then, was the attainment of eternal life; but even when salvation still concerned the whole of life, as in the case of Empedocles[8] it embraced both healing the body and the needs of the soul, it nevertheless became increasingly isolated from the community of the given and made into the aim of another community, that arose anew for the communal achievement of this deliverance. Thus individuals entered a mystery community: for this they sought, and for it a personal and voluntary decision was requisite. It is true that the

[1] Chantepie, *op. cit.*, II, 549. Huizinga, *Herfstty der Middeleeuwen*, 115, 131 *ff.*
[2] Chap. 11.   [3] *cf.* A. Moret, *Mystères égyptiens*, 1913, 37.
[4] Farnell, *Outline History of Greek Religion*, 49.
[5] Anrich, *Das antike Mysterienwesen*, 7 *f.*; like the secret societies from tribal organization.   [6] Chap. 22.   [7] Chap. 46.   [8] Chap. 27.

arbitrary element in this decision was again withdrawn immediately the *invocation* of the deity took the place of the given; and Lucius, seeking the consecration of Isis, attained this only after he had patiently awaited the nod of the goddess (*deae nutus*).[1] The covenant thus arising either from free choice, or from the god's summons, sets itself more and more harshly in opposition to other communities. The relationship to the god is no longer simply present: some possess it, and others do not, the latter being commiserated, the initiated extolled as blessed.[2] Thus the concept of "world", only neither as the conjoint world nor as the world in the background,[3] but as the mere lack of potency, is already clearly exhibited here.

According therefore as the limits of the covenant were left, in increasing measure, either to human decision or to the numinous decree of the god, and also according as the community was on the one hand restricted to those entering it, or those who had the vocation, so on the other hand the limits of the original tribal membership were extended or even suspended. In this way the Eleusinian mysteries, at first closed to all strangers, altered their character owing to the hegemony of Athens, which developed the mysteries of the capital out of those of the tribe; afterwards, indeed, from the second half of the fifth century, they were open to all Hellenes, and finally even to *hetaerae*, children and slaves.[4] The essential characteristic of the mystery covenant, then, was that in apportioning salvation, it made no distinction between foreigners and native born, between nationals and barbarians, between slaves and free; admission was by either unrestrained choice or vocation, but it remained always an individual and personal approach to salvation,[5] which spread itself freely over the world without any limits being imposed upon it. The saviour whom the mysteries celebrated, the sacrament that was offered in them, was for all. Only the specific bounds, given within the mystery itself, were valid: "For as many of you as have been baptized into Christ have put on Christ. There is neither Jew nor Greek, there is neither bond nor free, there is neither male nor female: for ye are all one in Christ Jesus."[6] Tribal rites, also, no longer had any essential significance: eating with heathen was

---

[1] Apuleius, *Metam.* XI, 21.

[2] *e.g.* Sophocles, *Fr.* 753: " . . . thrice blessed are those who, after having witnessed such initiations, wander to Hades; for them alone does life bloom there, others being doomed to misery"; (Campbell); *cf.* van der Leeuw, *Goden en menschen*, 59.

[3] Chap. 8, 18.

[4] Rohde, *Psyche*, I, 286 *f.* E. T. 221. Farnell, *Cults of the Greek States*, III, 153 *ff.*

[5] *cf.* J. de Zwaan, *Antiek syncretisme en hedendaagsche zendingsvragen, Mededeelingen Ned. Zendelinggenootschap*, 1929, 3.   [6] *Gal.* iii. 27, 28.

permitted and circumcision not unconditionally necessary;[1] there were Greeks and barbarians, Jews and heathen, no more, but only the faithful on the one hand and the "world" on the other. Of course the mystery communities also recognized limitations, usually as products of the ancient restrictions valid for sacrifice and cult: thus Eleusis excluded manslayers and barbarians, the latter being a vestige of the limitation imposed by givenness. The conditions of admission too— fasting, chastity *etc.*—were no different from those holding generally for performance of the god's service.[2]

The actual cult of the mystery society will be discussed in a later chapter. Here it need only be said that some sacred event was repeated as the "story of salvation" and spread among the members; and in the centre of this story stood the saviour's figure.[3]

7. Still more sharply does the covenant sever itself from the "world" in the form of the *monastic community*; in this the power of the devotees[4] must be guarded and nourished by the compact, although we must observe at the same time that it sustains the character of polarity. A monk is first of all an individual, one who is alone; and with his solitude his powerfulness is closely connected. But then one power seeks others: the anchorites' huts (*lauren*) form together a *monasterium, coenobium, claustrum*; in certain cases, also, the monasteries combine to form a sort of monastery town such as Athos. The monastery, then, is a community in the fullest sense, having its own church, agriculture and crafts, its own administration and churchyard, while initiation exhibits the features of tribal and mysteries initiation.

In all other respects, however, the covenantal character comes clearly into prominence; here powerfulness, not to be acquired in the "world", is realized. A common sanctity is attained in and through the uninterrupted cult, a common morality by observance of the *consilia* and not merely of the *praecepta evangelica*. Thereby even the church is estimated essentially as "world", and every community except the monastic designated as powerless; *patres, fratres, sorores*, are then merely spiritual titles.[5] The order of birth, similarly, is completely suppressed by that of consecration, and so the death is announced of Sister Teresa, "in the world" Miss A. B. The priest of the church, again, is accounted a "secular priest"; for salvation, in its truest sense, is to be found only in the *ecclesiola in ecclesia* called the monastic community; thence it extends itself over church and world.[6]

[1] Weber, *op. cit.*, II, 39.   [2] Chap. 49.   [3] Chap. 12, 61, 73.   [4] Chap. 29.
[5] Also an application of *Matt.* xii. 50, "Whosoever shall do the will of my Father . . ., the same is my brother . . ."   [6] Chap. 29.

In Buddhism, still further, the monastic covenant has attained world importance. Emanating, just as Christianity did also, from a loose connection between teacher and disciples,[1] community here develops into a gigantic monastic covenant. Buddhism, however, has cast off the form of the given, but has not discovered that of the church; for it, therefore, laymen are regarded only as "worshippers" and are not united by any kind of organizing bond. Thus far, Buddhism is merely the logical consequence of the Hindu practice according to which a man, after having completed the period of marriage and generating children, quits his home to live in solitude as a forest ascetic; and originally the Buddhist monks gathered together in the rainy season when it was impossible to wander about begging; subsequently, monasteries arose in thousands. Thus the "world" is rendered impotent finally and as a matter of principle: there can be community only apart from the world.[2] The house, the family home, the tribal hearth, the dwelling-place of power:—all have here become a stumbling-block and an offence. Whoever seeks genuine community, then, must "go forth", the latter being even the name for the lower grades of ordination (*pabbajja*).[3] Thus from the brahmin's command: "thus let him go forth from his house", Buddhism formed a community,[4] accession to this[5] being a "going forth from home into homelessness".[6] "Very straitened is life in the home, a state of impurity; freedom is in leaving the home".[7] Genuine community demands the surrender of the "given", which becomes depreciated to a false community.

W. ANRICH, *Das antike Mysterienwesen*, 1894.

F. CUMONT, *Les religions orientales dans le paganisme romain*[4], 1929 (Eng. tr., *Oriental Religions in Roman Paganism*).

P. FOUCART, *Des associations religieuses chez les Grecs*, 1873.

K. H. E. DE JONG, *Das antike Mysterienwesen*[2], 1919.

O. KERN, *Die griechischen Mysterien der klassischen Zeit*, 1927.

A. LOBECK, *Aglaophamus*, 1829.

A. D. NOCK, *Conversion, The Old and The New in Religion From Alexander the Great to Augustine of Hippo*, 1933.

R. REITZENSTEIN, *Die hellenistischen Mysterienreligionen*[2], 1920.

H. SCHURTZ, *Altersklassen und Männerbünde*, 1902.

N. TURCHI, *Le religioni misteriosofiche del mondo antico*, 1923.

H. WEBSTER, *Primitive secret societies*, 1908.

E. ZIEBARTH, *Das griechische Vereinswesen*, 1896.

---

[1] Chap. 28.   [2] Christianity had a narrow escape from this development!
[3] Oldenberg, *Buddha*, 347 *ff.*   [4] *ibid.*, 348.
[5] Which, in its own turn, does not recognize the "given" caste distinctions as a matter of principle; Oldenberg, *ibid.*, 152.   [6] *ibid.*, 355.   [7] *ibid.*

CHAPTER 35

THE SECT

1. THE primitive world knew only of the sacred, and not specifically religious, communities; similarly, no specifically religious acts, but solely sacred. To it, therefore, any special cultivation of religious life, either individually or within the community, was quite foreign; and thus Scipio, who went before daybreak up to the Capitol to meditate in the *cella Jovis*, "apparently consulting Jupiter about matters of state", was a very rare exception that aroused a good deal of astonishment.[1] The first community devoted to specifically religious purposes, then, is the sect, which severs itself not only from the given community but from the "world" in general. Thus the sect does not repose on a covenant that breaks away from the church (this it does in only a secondary sense); primarily, it rests on one that releases itself from the community, and this in order to attain religious salvation in some quite distinctive way.

Thus the sect is not founded on a religious covenant that is severed from another religious community such as the church; it segregates itself, rather, from community in general, and constitutes religion a specific aim side by side with the usual purposes of life. The mysteries society also did something similar, and there were mixed forms of sects and mystery societies such as Orphism. But in general, mystery apprehends life more cosmically, more as a unity, than does the sect, which lets the world be in order tranquilly to be saved. The term "sect" is derived not from *secare* but from *sequi*; it is a religious party, a heresy, as the Greek word αἵρεσις puts it: that is, a choice or a tendency; it is the purest form of covenant that we know. As compared with the Judaic community, for instance, Nazarenes and Christians are sects;[2] but the pharisees and sadducees also, and in Islam the mutazilites. In principle these were all schismatics, belonging to the "separatist type";[3] but they severed themselves not from any particular community, but from every kind whether primitive-general, religious-national or ecclesiastical. The correlate of the sect is therefore not the church but the community; it is the most extreme outcome of the covenant.

---

[1] Gellius, *Attic Nights*, VI, 1, 6.
[2] *Acts* xxiv. 5; xxviii. 22.
[3] Wach, *Meister und Jünger*, 8.

2. The sect embraces a heterodox *doctrine*, another cultural *custom* than that of the community from which it cuts itself off: "false teachers will insinuate destructive heresies"[1] (αἱρέσεις). Phenomenologically, however, the divergent doctrinal or cultural element is not the determining feature; it is merely the manifestation of a conviction, of the sort of attitude that creates the sect. Thus Christianity as compared with Judaism and the Roman community, the Reformation as contrasted with the Roman church, Buddhism with the Hindu, and Islam with the Arabic community, were all sects which subsequently became churches, monastic societies or national unities. What constitutes the sect then, as such, is its sectionalizing and heretical disposition: adherents of the αἵρεσις are just heretics and a "factious person", αἱρετικὸς ἄνθρωπος, is a "perverted" man who should be avoided.[2] "Heresy" therefore concerns not simply opinion but life; it is sin, and schism on the heretic's part implies excommunication on that of the community; in the Middle Ages even moral aberrations, such as sadism, were accounted heresy.[3] No community, nevertheless, can be understood in its essence without some reference to the sects that have severed themselves from it,[4] since into these the community's own life has overflown. But whoever actually remains within the community cannot perceive this; to him, therefore, membership of the sect is just the proof of a different attitude and a foreign potency. In this respect, one can at best rise to the realization that "there must be also heresies among you, that they which are approved may be made manifest among you".[5]

3. The specific powerfulness of sects, then, is experienced as their special charism, and the choice as vocation; thus every trace of community can be eliminated in favour of some pure possibility, which must be realized by the *pneuma* or, again, by the pious will. Either vocation or performance attests membership: the one is *election*, the other *conversion*,[6] which may, however, accompany each other. But birth, once again, proves nothing: it was Sarah's son who triumphed; and by extreme sects sacrament and rite also are accounted impotent, or become modified as when adult baptism replaces that of children. In so far indeed—regarded phenomenologically—the sect precedes the church, which by contrast rather implies retrogression to the primitive community.

The impulse to the formation of a covenant arises from all kinds of

---

[1] 2 *Peter* ii. 1 (Moffat).   [2] *Titus* iii. 10.   [3] Huizinga, *Herfstty*, 414.
[4] Wach, *Religionswissenschaft*, 162, 53.   [5] 1 *Cor.* xi. 19.   [6] Chap. 79.

causes, among which the revival[1] assumes an important place; some intense shock to the feelings necessitates reflection on one's attitude towards the world and God, and compels the abandonment of the given and the search for new possibilities. Such were the Dionysiac outbursts in ancient Greece, the spiritual enthusiasm of the Reformation period, the Pentecostal movement *etc.*

The sect, however, can gradually lose its specific character again. But frequently it remains true to this and perfects it, this development taking the form of an increasingly thoroughgoing contraction. The demand for personal conversion, for the identification of faith and experience, for pure doctrine, becomes constantly sterner. In this connection the expansion of the views of Jean de la Badie (1610–1674) is remarkable: he attempted to form a community of those who had veritably been born again, and therefore could not be satisfied with any local congregation; so he formed a household congregation whose members were known to him as Christians who had been born anew. Thus by a wide *détour* he returned to the primitive "family": community-bond and family-bond in one. Subsequently, in the famous house congregation in Herford, spiritual jubilation and dancing became the characteristics of the communion of perfect love that, by this time, had been achieved. Marriages between members of the sect and non-members were declared invalid and new unions celebrated, the children of which would be free from original sin. After la Badie's death a further sharp distinction was made between those who had actually received God's grace and those in whom this assurance had not been manifested: the first group consisted of *frères et sœurs*, while the members of the second class were called *monsieur* or *seigneur*. Even the mode of addressing God was influenced by the degree of certainty of salvation: the brethren might call Him "Father", but not the others.[2]

Thus the world becomes ever larger: the community, the *Nova Sion*, the true Israel, the realm of the Spirit, constantly smaller, in accordance with the application of the "principle of the segregated and consecrated community which tolerates the state, but as far as possible avoids all contact with it, and austerely maintains the community apart from the world by means of clothing and customs, greetings, connubial relations and excommunication".[3] Actually, however, in this

---

[1] Chap. 94.

[2] H. Heppe, *Geschichte des Pietismus und der Mystik in der Reformierten Kirche namentlich der Niederlande*, 1879, 240 *ff.*

[3] As E. Troeltsch remarks about the baptists, but which is equally true of many other sects; *Kultur der Gegenwart*, I, IV, I², 510.

continually expanded purification, restriction and fixation of the sect's powerfulness, there is concealed a secret yearning for the dissolution of each and every community, for the return to solitude in the presence of God.[1] "He shall be the greatest who can be the most solitary";[2] and again to cite this writer, "Every community renders common". The dread of loneliness becomes a luxury, and the natural impotence arising from the sense of being abandoned by all given things is transformed into the unexpected, but all the more blissful, possibility of omnipotence.

J. LINDEBOOM, *Stiefkinderen van het Christendom*, 1929.
E. TROELTSCH, *The Social Teaching of the Christian Churches*.

[1] Lohmeyer, *Vom Begriff der religiösen Gemeinschaft*, 44 f.
[2] Nietzsche, *Beyond Good and Evil*, 155. (Foulis Edition.)

CHAPTER 36

THE CHURCH

1. THE Israelite קהל was at the same time the assembly of the people and the worshipping community,[1] the Greek word for this idea being *ecclesia*;[2] so that when Jesus chose His disciples and assigned to one of them a special status,[3] He not only called together men of like disposition, nor created a mere relationship of teacher and disciple, such as we have just observed in the case of Buddha. His founding of an *ecclesia* must rather "be understood from His total attitude to His own people, from whom, for whom, and as contrasted with whom He gathered and commissioned the Twelve as a special congregation, פְּנִישְׁתָּא, in order to represent the congregation of Jahveh, קְהַל-יְהֹוָה".[4] The Twelve were certainly disciples, but above all they were the people, the true Israel,[5] while the events of Pentecost brought to the disciples, as the assembly of the people, the gift of the Holy Spirit. In this manner, then, the "pneumatic" and the given bonds were woven together into one, without either being absent: "Now if you are Christ's, then you are Abraham's offspring; in virtue of the Promise you are heirs."[6] The church is therefore the people of God in the spiritual sense, and the Body of Christ in the actual sense, which means that covenant and community are fused together and elevated to a higher unity. Neither the accession of man, nor the givenness of his position, is decisive, although each is not unessential; they find their foundation, as well as their ratification, in the act of God, Who stoops to meet man "*in Christo*",[7] and Himself desires to be the bond of their community.

From the moment of her origin, however, the church has been repeatedly in danger either of becoming irretrievably the "people", because the church's hierarchical organization implies nothing whatever more than the perpetuation of the idea of the people as this became transposed from Israel to the Roman empire: or again of being completely "pneumatized", most of the sects being influential in this direction. But at all times its essence remains as hitherto:—that is

---

[1] *Gen.* xlix. 6. 1 *Kings* xii. 3. 1 *Kings* viii. 14. *Lev.* iv. 13. *Num.* xvi. 3. *Ps.* xxii. 23. *Joel* ii. 16.

[2] Bultmann, *Glauben und Verstehen*, 162 f.　　　　[3] *Matt.* xvi, 18.

[4] Schmidt, *Die Kirche des Urchristentums*, 291 f.　　　[5] Peterson, *Die Kirche*.

[6] *Gal.* iii. 29; Schmidt, *ibid.*, 314.　　　　[7] Bultmann, *ibid.*, 170 ff.

neither the choice of man understood as vocation, nor his givenness in accord with fate, but both together and received as the fruits of God's own action, consummated in the Lord of the church.[1]

As a people, then, the church is certainly the continuation of the community, but now as the convened community, as the chosen people; while as resting on a covenant, it is the perpetuation of the mysteries covenant formed around the figure and the life of the "Lord", but also a covenant whose mystery participates in that of the world's givenness and each individual's life. To state all this in the language of the early Christian era: the church erected on a feeble man, Peter, cannot be overcome even by hell.[2]

2. A church actually exists solely in Christianity; for neither the Buddhist monastic community, nor that of Islam resting on the principle of mere agreement and conformity,[3] nor again the Judaic assembly of the people, merits the title of church. This historic fact, still further, is intimately connected with the church's essential nature, since it arose from the concrete historical situation which the Jews' rejection of Christ, and the subsequent turning towards the heathen, brought in their train.[4] In this concrete situation, then, there subsists on the one hand the transition from community to covenant, but on the other the concentration of the heathen religious consciousness, already manifested in various types of covenant, into a community given in a new manner. Thus the church is the church of the heathen, but "salvation is of the Jews".[5]

All this implies that in its essence the church, as it lives in the consciousness of the faithful, evades Phenomenology. For it is the Body of Christ, and as such escapes all comprehension, of which indeed it is itself the primary presupposition. Certainly it is both people and covenant, but always only as subject to the presupposition of the presence of Christ, of the "Lord", Who is the bond alike in the assembling together, wherein vocation and choice are involved, and in the given as the Mediator of creation. The church is therefore visible-invisible, at once humanly organized and mystically animated, spiritual and cosmic. It is not to be verified as a fact, but to be believed in: and

---

[1] cf. G. P. Wetter, *La catholisation du Christianisme primitif* (*Revue d'Histoire et de Philosophie religieuse*, 7, 1927).

[2] cf. Maritain's fine dictum: "the great glory of the Church is to be holy with sinful members". *Religion and Culture*, 40.   [3] Wach, *Religionssoziologie*, 51.

[4] Peterson, *Die Kirche*.   [5] *John* iv. 22.

it is no accident that it is precisely here that, for the first time, we encounter *faith* in our investigations.[1]

Therefore though it is erected upon the earthly given, the church is grounded in divine possibility. Until its elevation to *ecclesia triumphans*, or its dissolution in *communio sanctorum*, it is the salt of the earth, the actual ground of the world's continued existence; the Body of Christ sustains the body of earth. Hence the dignity of the church and of its adherents: "the saints shall judge the world".[2] Here the idea of community attains almost its highest culmination, since the community, thus given in the church, possesses metaphysical significance; its limits are world wide and its essence the nature of God Himself, the love of Christ. The primitive community between the family and the dead now persists in transfigured form: community with God includes that with the departed, the bond of the church binds even beyond the grave. The church is the virgin, the bride, the throne and the bosom of God; a virgin mother who continually gives birth to the faithful:[3] "Christ is the bridegroom and the church the bride, by whom are borne each day spiritual sons to the venerable Father."[4] Thus the mother's image[5] is again presented to our eyes, but a mother whose powerfulness rests upon the generative act of the Father.

3. In the consciousness of the faithful, finally, the church has the character of *catholicity*. The primary meaning of "catholic", however, is not that the church embraces the whole world but, in accordance with the term's original significance, that it is a whole, an organism, whose head is Christ. Its catholicity concerns therefore not so much the extension of the church as its all-sufficiency: "Where Christ is", asserted Ignatius, "there is the catholic church"; and as catholic, the church, the Body of Christ, is in its Head organically united to the universal omnipotence. It is from this, then, that the all-embracing nature of the church arises, not however as a fact, but as a task, a *mission*: for where two or three are gathered together in His name, there He is and there is the catholic church.

[1] Bultmann, *op. cit.*, 172.
[2] 1 *Cor.* vi. 2. "The church is an 'eschatological' fact; the worshipping community, that is to say, regards itself not as a worldly phenomenon, but as pertaining to the Beyond." Bultmann, *ibid.*, 154.
[3] *cf.* F. C. Conybeare, *Jungfräuliche Mutter und jungfräuliche Kirche, AR.* IX, 1906. Harnack, *History of Dogma*, III, 108, 109; *cf.* Luther's hymn "The holy Christian church":—"How dear to me is the faithful handmaiden", *etc.*
[4] Firmicus Maternus, *De errore profanarum religionum*, 19.   [5] Chap. 10.

The church's catholicity, again, implies its unity and its holiness. In it is completed what in other communities and covenants was merely outlined: the essence of community, the "sacred common element", is therefore not the mere being together, the fellowship to which one flees for refuge from dread. Far more is it something wholly different, something not given in the totality of the members, which creates a new organon. And this different factor is the first and the last, the essence and the primal ground of all things.

R. BULTMANN, *Glauben und Verstehen*, 1933.

H. FRICK, *Romantik und Realismus im Kirchenbegriff*, 1929.

E. PETERSON, *Die Kirche*, 1929.

K. L. SCHMIDT, *Die Kirche des Urchristentums (Festgabe für A. Deissmann)*[2], 1927.

CHAPTER 37

NATION AND HUMANITY

1. FROM what has already been asserted about the sacred community there clearly follows the truth, as well as the one-sided exaggeration, of the so-called *sociological school*. That religion is no private affair, that in the realm of religion communality and collectivity assume an extraordinarily extensive status, in fact that the search for Power is essentially connected with the flight from solitude:—all these are facts. But all the less, therefore, have we any ground for allowing the religious to be merged in the social; for the sacred common element is not sacred because it is common but, on the contrary, common because it is sacred; and in worshipping God humanity does not worship itself, but worships God as it were in assembling itself together. Thus the sociological hypothesis is really only a new form of Feuerbach's which, as we observed,[1] ultimately originates from Xenophanes:—Man makes for himself a God after his own image: only here the image is that not of the individual but of the totality. Certainly all this is quite correct— "but the mischief is that the vital nerve of sacredness is lacking here. For it consists not in binding together in fellowship, nor in the audacious hypostatization of the spirit of common feeling, but persists obstinately in an irrationality. If that is taken away, then religion is powerless."[2]

2. Sacredness adheres to the community, however, even when it develops from tribe to *state* and *nation*, thereby gradually becoming secularized. Sacredness is thus preserved for a long time because the state is at first a city, *polis*,[3] and then the powerfulness of the locality coincides with that of the community. This city community, again, may become a world empire and yet remain essentially a city community, since the Roman empire, and in fact every empire, depended on the predominance of a town or a tribe until the development of nationality in its more modern sense; and in the course of this process power became concentrated in the figure of the ruler, who possessed an almost divine dignity.[4] The idea of the nation, then, arises very late as the coalescence of the concepts of tribe and empire. To it there

---

[1] Chap. 8. [2] Söderblom, *Gottesglaube*[1], p. 210; *cf.* Wach, *Religionssoziologie*, X.
[3] Chap. 57. [4] *ibid.*, 13.

pertain the common historical experience and the fact of having long lived together, associated with the now relatively unimportant blood relationship. The Jewish people is the first historic example of a nation, the other peoples of antiquity being either tribes or empires; and both types regarded themselves as being the actual world, while their rulers likewise had a cosmic significance. Egypt and Babylon were the world, but not nations, while Israel, oppressed among the peoples, experienced the potency of the people as something of its very own, as national. The same relationship subsists with respect to the Holy Roman empire and the European nations that have come into being since the Renaissance: Switzerland, the Netherlands, France *etc*. For long periods, however, the tribal power often combated the new idea of nation (Particularism), while it was frequently displaced by the concept of empire (Imperialism).

But in spite of all secularization the nation's potency still counts as sacred, as is perfectly obvious in times of great excitement; then a national altar is erected or, in the peril of war, the nation's God is invoked. From the standpoint of enlightened deistic belief in God, however, this is an absurdity, and considered in the light of the faith of the catholic church, even a sin. Phenomenologically, nonetheless, it possesses an intrinsic propriety, since it is precisely an attempt to bring one's own powerfulness into the closest possible relation to Power as such. *Nationalism* is always religious; and again the most grandiose example of such religious nationalism is to be discerned among the Jews. Israel is not the tribe nor empire whose limits are those of the world, or should be so: it is a people among peoples. But among all these it is the chosen: God is its God: the people is God's people. And the people's God is also the God of the history that has been experienced in common: the God of Abraham, Isaac and Jacob, who led the people out of Egypt, out of the house of bondage. But what we describe, phenomenologically, as a grand attempt to appropriate God's Power, appears to believers themselves as a glorious act of God who has chosen his people.

3. Social order also can be the expression of definite potencies, and thus *classes* and *castes* have their own religious value. Until modern enthusiasm for the working classes reminded us that these religious valuations do not belong wholly to the past, medieval knighthood offered the finest example of this principle. Frequently the caste is a tribe that has become merged within a foreign people either as rulers or as pariahs;[1] we know well,[2] for example, how profound is the separa-

[1] Weber, *op. cit.*, II, 14 *f*.   [2] *cf*. further Chap. 2.

tion between the potencies of the castes in British India. It precludes, for instance, communal eating: if an untouchable merely sees a brahmin's food it is defiled, while marriage between members of unequal castes is strictly forbidden. When the British authorities established public kitchens during a famine, the places assigned to the higher castes at the tables had to be separated from the others by chalked lines.

4. The equivalence of all potencies which the idea of *humanity* involves leads in the direction opposite from that of castes; this is however a comparatively recent development, and we can safely say that humanity, as such, was first discovered by the Stoics, and afterwards by the eighteenth century.[1] For in accordance with Schiller's dictum, from Christians Rousseau recruited men. That man as man has certain rights (*droits de l'homme!*), that humanity as such is the strongest bond that links men together, that all men are brothers so far as convention does not arbitrarily sever the connection—all this is the discovery of the age of enlightenment. Here mankind appears as itself worthy of adoration: and it is no matter of chance that the sociological theory, to which I have just referred, originated from the school of thought of the philosopher who in his later years founded a regular *culte de l'humanité*: Auguste Comte. *Humanité* is the *Grand-Être*, and the philosopher its high priest.

This "religion of humanity," however, has enjoyed scarcely any cult development in our secularized era; all the more powerfully, nonetheless, does the magic of humanity still operate: it is the sole entity worthy of worship that remained to thousands after the fierce conflagration of potencies in the nineteenth century. At one time virtuous, as for the age of enlightenment:

> He who delights not in such teachings
> Deserves not to be a man.[2]

At another time, realistically, as in Goethe's sense:

> For all human failings
> Pure humanity atones:

again, romantically: every mother a Virgin Mary: then as "reverence for life": it has persisted to our own time, especially in its woes. And

---

[1] To be human is in itself a value in the new Comedy; *cf.* the excellent history of the development of the idea in Mühl, *Die antike Menscheitsidee in ihrer geschichtlichen Entwicklung.*   [2] *The Magic Flute.*

there, at long last, it found cult forms also. Under the *Arc de triomphe de l'Étoile* burns the eternal flame from the grave of the *Unknown Soldier* who, in his anonymity, represents the whole of vast suffering humanity, and before whom the nations bow.[1]

Humanity then is the sole community that can vie with the church in catholicity. But it lacks the Head which constitutes the church a living organism;[2] nor has it any mission. And it is precisely in its mission that the paradoxical character of the church is revealed: the given people, which simultaneously is the spiritual community never existent in fact—the community that both is and is not—that is the church, and it embraces the world. On the other hand, humanity is far too existent: we all belong to it, and for us there remain no possibilities. This is the poverty of humanity as community.

E. DURKHEIM, *Les règles de la méthode sociologique*[7], 1919.
M. MÜHL, *Die antike Menschheitsidee in ihrer geschichtlichen Entwicklung*, 1928.

[1] The so-called "Mother's Day" is a less significant expression of the same consciousness of humanity.
[2] On the contrast between humanity and the church *cf.* Mühl, *op. cit.*, 115: "the idea of universality prevalent in antiquity amalgamates with the church and is absorbed in the concept of *catholicity*"; *cf.* again Maritain, *Religion and Culture*, 10, 19, 21, 37. Humanity is the "naturizing" of the kingdom of God or the church.

CHAPTER 38

COMMUNIO SANCTORUM

1. *CREDO . . . communionem sanctorum*, of the *Apostles' Creed*, was added only at a later period to *credo . . . unam sanctam catholicam ecclesiam*. Perhaps its original meaning was: "I believe that there subsists a participation in the sacred elements (of the sacrament)", while in the Middle Ages the expression acquired the significance—community of all, both living and departed. The Reformation, however, opposed the community of saints to the visible hierarchy of the Roman church, and rejoiced that "it was no longer necessary to see it with our eyes nor feel it with our hands", because the essence of this community rests on election by God and the constancy of Christ.[1] In both interpretations, nonetheless, the departure from tangibility and visibility is important, although this does not distinguish essentially between *communio sanctorum* and the church, which after all also has its actual being in God's act unrestricted by the limits of life. The idea of *communio sanctorum*, then, as regarded from the phenomenological viewpoint, is independent of all other factors, and also of course extremely momentous, only in its ancient Christian form, according to which it is the community of angels and all "the elect".[2] Thus the congregation experiences a foretaste of this highest community in the sacrament, the *praefatio* of which proclaims God's holiness "with Angels and Archangels, with Thrones and Dominions, and with all the company of heaven";[3] here, in communion with the Lord Who became flesh, the celestial community is foretasted. But though its essence is "beyond", the church has firm roots on earth, in the people and the given: *communio sanctorum* can be understood only eschatologically. It is wholly possibility, that is the hope of man and the promise of God.

2. I think that the most remarkable feature of the supreme community that is the Christian church is that it represents the deed of Him Who in His life proceeded from solitude to solitude. When all had abandoned Him, in the anguish of death God abandoned Him

---

[1] Calvin, *Institutio christianae religionis*, IV, 1, 3.
[2] Harnack, *History of Dogma*, V, 243 *ff*.   [3] Chap. 16.

too: "My God, my God, why has Thou forsaken me?" From this utmost dread, however, from this most desolate solitude as we perceive it in Gethsamene and on Golgotha, there springs the most intense communion; and this is the paradox of Christian faith, which unites solitude and community in the "Body of Christ". The struggle against dread was decided once for all by the Head of that Body: in the agony of the Mount of Olives, in the forsakenness of the Cross, all dread and loneliness are overcome. The "Body", the church, experiences this victory; but she must repeatedly attain to it anew, since she is not *communio sanctorum*. She is the mother who cherishes and protects until the ultimate victory; for "there is no other means of entering into life unless she (the church) conceive us in the womb and give us birth, unless she nourish us at her breasts and, in short, keep us under her charge and government, until (*donec*), divested of mortal flesh, we become like the angels".[1] This *donec* is the great word of eschatology:[2] with it human community ends, and divine community begins, which was, however, always at the foundation of every human community, to be believed in as its sole powerfulness.

[1] Calvin, *Institutio*, IV, 1, 4.   [2] Chap. 87.

C. THE SACRED WITHIN MAN: THE SOUL

CHAPTER 39

THE SOUL AS A WHOLE

1. "THOU canst not discover the bounds of the soul albeit thou pacest its every road: so deep is its ground";[1] and the idea of the soul has never been a means merely of systematizing the functions of human consciousness. On the contrary it was always, and in all its most widely contrasted structures, numinous in its type and a means of indicating the sacred in man. Even the unconscious object can possess a soul, while it is the numinous that endows the living entity with consciousness, and not conversely. "There is life that is not also numinous. But the numinous quickens even the non-living; the stone that affects me numinously appears to me, at the same time, as a 'Something' which conceals within itself a mysterious and secret life."[2]

To the primitive mind then the soul it not a mere part of man, but the whole man in his sacredness; and we still speak to-day of a certain number of "souls" in the sense of men, not simply portions of men. Thus the experience of the mysterious and the remarkable, which gives rise to the idea of the soul, is here constituted by concrete reality, experienced as a unity.

Many years ago, following a suggestion advanced by Chantepie de la Saussaye, Kruyt coined the fine term "soul-stuff" for this soul structure.[3] Later, however, when in accordance with Dynamism he wished to assign to the idea of Power the first place in primitive thought, he withdrew the word; but it appears to me that in this he was somewhat precipitate. For it is the very characteristic of the concept of the soul that Power displays and reveals itself in stuff of any kind whatever. All souls have bearers: never and nowhere are they independent entities; correctly understood, therefore, the term "soul-stuff" includes the idea of Power,[4] and in the realm of primitive thought Power and stuff are never two distinct ideas. Thus we can speak of "soul-power"

---

[1] Heracleitus (Diels, *Fragmente der Vorsokratiker*, I, 86).

[2] Schmalenbach, *Die Entstehung des Seelenbegriffs, Logos*, 16, 1927, 330, 333 *et passim.*   [3] *Animisme*, 2 *ff.*

[4] A. C. Kruyt, *Measa* (*Bydr. Taal-, Land- en Volkenkunde van N. I.* 74, 1918; 75, 1919; 76, 1920).

just as legitimately as of soul-stuff: in both cases it is a matter of certain powerful substances, or of a power attached to some substance.[1]

Current Greek popular belief, again, holds that widely spaced teeth make the retention of the "soul" difficult, so that whoever has these is short-lived, while at the same time they facilitate the inflow of soul-stuff: their possessor has erotic tendencies. As Hesseling remarks,[2] Homer knew long ago that "a hedge of teeth" is formed:—ἕρκος ὀδόντων: an example clearly exhibiting the connection between soul and power, "soul or *mana*", as Grönbech formulated it at the Congress at Leyden in 1912;[3] and in the interval, his thesis that soul and Power are essentially related has been brilliantly verified. Certainly this does not mean that every potency without exception is a soul entity, but that conversely the soul always implies powerfulness.[4]

This soul then, as one whole, is connected with some specific "stuff". It is not restricted to any single portion of the human body, but extends itself over all its parts according as these show themselves capable of some kind of powerfulness, just as blood is distributed throughout the whole body although certain organs are richer in blood than others. "As the sap oozes from the rubber plant whether it is notched on the trunk, a branch, or at the leaf edge: as the perfume of flowers arises from them and penetrates the surroundings: as blood flows through arteries and veins: and as perspiration runs from the pores and warmth emanates from the body: so the soul-stuff dwells in the body, proceeds from it and flows over everything that comes into contact with it."[5]

It is this powerfulness, thus conceived as "stuff", that the magician seeks to steal from his enemy or restore to his friend.[6] It is most carefully guarded, even in bodily excreta; strenuous effort is exerted to increase it and by every method prevent its disappearance. It is "stuff", matter, although in primitive modes of thought, which is aware of no dualism of body-spirit, this certainly implies no materialism. Stuff

---

[1] *cf.* also M. P. Nilsson, *Primitive Religion*, 1911, 16 f. Kruyt, *Animisme*, 1 ff.

[2] C. D. Hesseling, *Versl. & Meded. Kon. Akad. v. Wet. Afd. Lett.* 5. *Reeks*, 2, 1917.

[3] *Actes du IVe Congrès d'Hist. des Religions*, 1913, 70. *cf.* Schmalenbach, *op. cit.* Söderblom, *Gottesglaube*, 66 f.

[4] But obviously not a specific potency such as *mana*. "Power" is something more than *mana*. In the sciences concerned with religion we should accustom ourselves to say in advance when a concept like *mana*, or *tabu*, is to be understood in the original and ethnologically specified sense, and when as a general or generic idea. This would obviate much misunderstanding; *e.g.* not every Melanesian soul has *mana*. But every soul, whether Melanesian or not, has *mana* in its sense of power.

[5] Ch. Kaysser, in Beth, *Religion und Magie*, 152; *cf.* N. Adriani, *Posso*, 1919, 87 f.

[6] Beth, *ibid.*, 137 ff.

is always and simultaneously power; but both the diminution and the enhancing of soul-stuff are conceived materially. Thus a soul can be eaten: to eat the enemy's heart implies augmenting one's own soul-stuff;[1] and the Egyptian *ka* was a soul-being which could eat and which eventually was also eaten; the term is even etymologically connected with the word for food.[2] According to a very ancient concept occurring in the *Pyramid Texts*, again, the dead king ascends to heaven as victor, and with his attendants catches the gods with a lasso. A dreadful terror then seizes upon the heavens; the earth's bones tremble; the king, "who lives on his fathers and consumes his mothers", who "eats men and lives upon the gods", strangles the celestial beings and disembowels them; then they are cooked in glowing pots. The great gods he eats for breakfast, the intermediate deities at midday and the lesser gods for supper; he lives "on the essence of each of the gods, when he eats the entrails of those who come, with their stomachs filled with *ḥkaw*, (a psychic power of a magical character)". He "eats their *ḥkaw*, he devours their *iakhw* (another psychic power)". "Him whom he encounters on his way he eats quite raw." "Behold the *ba* (yet another psychic being) of the gods is within the king's stomach."[3] This is cannibalism raised to the level of the myth, but not wholly deprived of a certain grandeur despite its crass horror; and it yields profound insight into the nature of the primitive soul as a whole. One can eat power, and food has a psychic quality.

2. Soul-power was definitely regarded as being present in almost every part of the body, even in what it extrudes; and the idea of power in the *breath*, or the so-called breath-soul, has had the weightiest influence upon the psychology of almost all peoples and times down to the present day. From this concept too were derived the most important terms for the essence of the soul: *ātman, spiritus, anima, Seele, πνεῦμα,* רוּחַ.[4] Certainly the powerfulness of breath was not only established negatively, as Animism supposed, by inferring its psychic quality from its disappearance at the moment of death; rather was an independent life discerned in it, a life not relaxed even in sleep; the pulse beat,

---

[1] F. D. E. van Ossenbruggen, *Het primitieve Denken* (*Bydr. Taal-Land-en Volkenk. v. N. I.*, 1915), 34.

[2] So in the first instance, W. B. Kristensen, *Aegypternes Forestillinger om Livet efter Döden*, 1896, 14 *f.*; later, several others; *cf.* Ad. Erman and H. Grapow, *Wörterbuch der Ägyptischen Sprache*, V, 1931, 86 *ff.*

[3] *Pyramidentexte* (Sethe), 393 *ff.*, 278, 444; *cf.* van der Leeuw, *Godsvoorstellingen in de oud-aegyptische Pyramidetexten*, 41 *f.*　　　[4] Jevons, *Introduction*, 44.

the rise and fall of the chest, appeared to be specific life and to possess specific powerfulness.[1] The kiss also, which so frequently has some ritual meaning, was probably intended as a reciprocal transference of the breath-soul and as an exact parallel of blood brotherhood. But equally when it is a question of the life of the Universe, of cosmology, breath is the mighty generator. God breathes into man the breath of life through his nostrils,[2] and still more generally:

> When thou recallest their breath, they die.
> Yet a breath from thee brings them into being.[3]

Together with breath, *blood* is a highly important soul-bearer; in the course of the sacrifice for blessing a house in the Dutch East Indies, for instance, the posts and pillars of the building are sprinkled with blood,[4] while in *Exodus* xii, the blood besprinkled on the Israelites' doors was intended to avert death. I may presuppose that the part played by blood in the sacrificial ritual of the Old Testament is quite familiar: the blood was the soul of the flesh,[5] and Christian thought about the redemptive value of the blood of Christ has, in essence, conserved this concrete conception of the soul. According to this idea, blood is not only "a quite peculiar sort of juice",[6] but the power of salvation in general:

> Unclean I am, but cleanse me in Thy Blood:
> Of which a single drop, for sinners spilt,
> Can purge the entire world from all its guilt.[7]

And we know that blood, regarded concretely and physically, has held and still holds, both in theology and in popular piety, *e.g.* in the Salvation Army, a very prominent rôle that is grounded on the sacrificial

---

[1] Schmalenbach, *loc. cit.*, 332; Wundt, *op. cit.*, IV, 135.   [2] *Gen.* ii. 7.
[3] *Ps.* civ. 29 *f.* (Moffat); *cf.* the remarkable cosmological speculation concerning breath among the Annamites, Saintyves, *Force*, 72 *ff.*
[4] Kruyt, *Animisme*, 23.   [5] *Lev.* xvii. 11.   [6] *Faust*, Part I, 1386.
[7] Thomas Aquinas' hymn, *Adoro te devote:*

> *Me immundum munda*
> *Tuo sanguine,*
> *Cuius una stilla*
> *Salvum facere*
> *Totum mundum quit ab*
> *Omni scelere.*

Huizinga compares the words from Marlowe's *Faustus*: "See, where Christ's blood streams in the firmament! One drop of blood will save me": *Herfstty*, 368.

practice of the Old Testament and, like this, can be understood only in the light of the psychically powerful quality of blood.

Among bodily powers that are regarded as soul-stuff there emanate from the body, like blood and breath, *spittle, perspiration and urine.* *Corpse sweat* also pertains to this category, being used by the peoples of Madagascar, who believe that the newly incarnate soul arises from it.[1] Of a different type, again, are the souls called by Wundt *Organ-souls*, the potencies of separate parts of the body.[2] Here the *head* must be given special mention,[3] since as the receptacle of soul-stuff it became the keenly desired booty of head hunters in the Indian archipelago;[4] then the *heart*,[5] the *liver* and the *eye*.[6] The latter, painted on the bows of ships, has from ancient times protected the sailors of the Mediterranean, while in ancient Egypt the myth of the eye of Horus placed this part of the body in cosmic relations: it was brought to the dead, sometimes as the sun and again as a symbol for sacrifice as the fullness of life, "so that they may receive a soul from it".[7] Still further, the *larynx* and the *left side*,[8] the *great toes* and the *thumb*[9], must be mentioned.

In the case of all the above, further, it must be remembered that no bodily nor organ-soul embraces psychical powerfulness *entirely*, while excluding the remaining parts of the body. Soul-stuff actually exists in the whole body; but it is indicated only with reference to such place or places where it exhibits its power. Thus everything in man can be "soul", if only it is powerful; but in fact we cannot justifiably maintain this limitation to man alone. It has already been observed that in the primitive structure of the human mind, man is never opposed to his environment, but belongs to it; and in conformity with this, we discover no difference in principle between the soul of man and that of his environment, especially of the animal and the plant world. The Indonesians, for example, indicate both the human soul and that of the rice by the same word: *sumangat*,[10] while the Bahaus of Borneo call both souls *bruwa*;[11] and even so-called inorganic Nature possesses

[1] Wundt, *op. cit.*, IV, 148; Hertz, *Mort*, 77.
[2] Wundt, *ibid.*, 79; *cf.* Nilsson, *Primitive Religion*, 44. Kruyt, *Animisme*, 2 *ff.*
[3] Kruyt, *ibid.*, 17 *ff.*
[4] On the head as soul, *cf.* G. Weicker, *Der Seelenvogel*, 1902, 30 *f.*
[5] Schmalenbach, *loc. cit.*, 352.   [6] Wundt, *op. cit.*, IV, 105 *ff.*
[7] *Pyramidentexte* (Sethe), 578.   [8] By the Eskimo; Thalbitzer, *Actes*, 139.
[9] Fr. Pfister, *Blätter zur bayr. Volkskunde*, 11, 1927; *cf.* too the widespread fairy tales about Tom Thumb.
[10] Kruyt, *Animisme*, 136 *f.* W. W. Skeat, *Malay Magic*, 136 *ff.*
[11] A. W. Nieuwenhuis, *Zeitschr. f. Völkerkunde und Soziologie*, 1, 2, 1925, 1926.

soul-stuff. In all this there is certainly no "panpsychism" (a theoretical creation!), but at the same time no limits are imposed to the imparting of soul;[1] and the same absence of limitations prevails when man differentiates himself from other men. An individual therefore, in the nineteenth century sense of the term, was unknown to the primitive world: still less an "individual soul". According to our own phraseology two friends are "one heart and one soul", but to ancient German sentiment they were such without any metaphor at all. The tribe, which embraced all those who were united by "peace",[2] had a collective soul; its powerfulness, that is, was exhibited in its members, even if in varying degrees.[3]

No separation at all was possible, again, within the personality of man himself: potentially everything was soul, even if it did not manifest itself precisely as soul-power; and even what, according to our ideas, does not belong, or no longer pertains, to the person, could participate in the soul. Thus the bride in the fairy tale, who has lost the cloth with the three drops of her mother's blood, becomes "weak and powerless";[4] and the removal from the person concerned is in this instance twofold: in the first place, it is not her own soul-stuff whose loss renders her impotent but her mother's, which amounts to the same thing; and in the second, the soul-stuff has been separated from its bearer for a long time. The fairy tale *motif* of the protective, speaking, or otherwise influential drops of blood, actually belongs to another soul structure,[5] but here too it can exhibit that absence of limitations which is characteristic of soul-stuff structure. Similarly in the fairy story of *Beloved Roland*, the girl in her flight lets fall three drops of the slain man's blood, which delay the approaching witch.[6] In an Indian fairy tale, again, even moccasins play a warning part, and remind us that in the primitive structure of the human mind man was not a spirituality achieved by any artificial means but, just as he is, a totality in which everything might be "soul".[7]

For the "soul" designates not life and nothing more, and still less consciousness, but whatever is replete with power and effectiveness.

---

[1] Chap. 9.   [2] Chap. 33.   [3] Grönbech, *op. cit.*, II, 105, 111.
[4] Grimm's *Fairy Tales*, "The Goose Girl".
[5] Chap. 42; *cf.* further Arbmann, *Zur primitiven Seelenvorstellung* (*Le monde oriental*, I, XX, 1926; II, XXI, 1927); 366.
[6] Grimm, *ibid.* No. 56. In one variant, connected with Hänsel and Gretel, she spits thrice and the spittle gives the witch her answer—it is just another soul-stuff. J. Bolte und G. Polivka, *Anmerkungen zu den Kinder- und Hausmärchen der Brüder Grimm*, I, 1913, 498 f.
[7] W. Krickeberg, *Indianermärchen aus Nord-Amerika*, 1924, 164.

It implies that there is a "life" which is more than merely being alive;[1] the latter condition indeed is not observed by primitive man, who does not even appreciate the distinction between organic and inorganic; but the "numinous quickens even the non-living".[2]

Within this primary soul structure however, even that of soul-stuff, the soul is in one way a principle of separation; but it does not sever stuff from power, and still less body from soul; it only divides what is indifferent from what is full of the numinously effective.

For this type of soul, finally, *death* has but little meaning; the departed is no soul-being, but a complete, dead man.[3] In this primary form, then, the soul is not a being to be in principle differentiated from other religious forms, except in that it always requires a bearer. But even when regarded from this aspect the soul very closely resembles, for example, the power-object, the fetish. It is just one numinous formation together with others: fetishes, sacred trees, demons, spirits, gods[4]; the form of some numinous experience whose object is not even limited to man.[5]

ACTES du Ve Congrès intern. d'Hist. des Religions à Lund, 1929.

E. ARBMANN, *Zur primitiven Seelenvorstellung (Le monde oriental, I, XX*, 1926, *II, XXI*, 1927).

A. BERTHOLET, *Dynamismus und Personalismus in der Seelenauffassung*, 1930.

A. E. CRAWLEY, *The Idea of the Soul*, 1909.

G. VAN DER LEEUW, *Phénoménologie de l'âme (Revue d'histoire et de philosophie religieuses*, 1930).

L. LÉVY-BRUHL, *The Soul of the Primitive*.

H. SCHMALENBACH, *Die Entstehung des Seelenbegriffs (Logos*, 16, 1927).

---

[1] Schmalenbach, *loc. cit.*, 333.   [2] *ibid.*
[3] Chap. 14, 24; *Actes du Ve Congrès intern. d'Hist. des Religions à Lund*, 1929, 91; Nilsson.   [4] *cf.* Schmalenbach, *loc. cit.* 324.
[5] In ancient Egypt, the plural *baw* meant sometimes "souls", at other times "power", and again "divine beings" or "ancestors".

CHAPTER 40

SOULS IN THE PLURAL

1. THE second soul structure also, with which we are here concerned, includes not that differentiation between body and soul so familiar to ourselves, but merely that between soul and soul. Thus it can readily be understood how it has happened that we are able to represent the different potencies, experienced within man, as a number of more or less sharply outlined soul-beings; for the very character of soul-stuff, which is in no sense exclusive—in the heart for instance, but simultaneously in the head or elsewhere—itself leads to plurality.

Of course it is not here a matter of differentiating in accordance with our own categories—*e.g.* will, feeling, spirit *etc.* Soul-power is divided among various other powers which—and this as distinct from the previous structure—possess a certain consistency, but whose peculiar nature is determined by experiences that, to a great extent, are no longer available to us.[1] "The idea of a soul is not found among primitives. That which takes its place is the representation, usually a very emotional one, of one or more coexistent and intertwined participations, as yet not merged into the distinct consciousness of an individuality which is really one."[2] Certain influences upon definite vital activities, certain connections with specific experiences, are condensed into soul-beings—that is all that we can say. The distinction drawn by the Eskimo, for example, between body, soul and name, from which the soul then divides itself up according to its various potencies localized in different parts of the body, is quite clear to us.[3] Essentially, this is nothing more than a somewhat systematized view of soul-stuff. The division of soul-power in the *Brahmana Texts*, again, also seems fairly intelligible: spirit, breath, speech, food, the water pertaining to the body, bone, marrow, eyes and ears. These are partly body-, or organ-souls, and partly designations, like speech and spirit, which we appear to understand without difficulty, but which nevertheless we certainly do not completely apprehend in their original specific character.[4] But ancient Egypt offers us the most remarkable and most incomprehensible example. So long as bodily powers are

---

[1] Preuss, *Geistige Kultur*, 18.   [2] Lévy-Bruhl, *How Natives Think*, 89.
[3] Thalbitzer, in *Actes* . . ., 139.   [4] Oldenberg, *Lehre*, 18.

concerned we can grasp the differentiation here almost immediately, as for example: "air is in my nose, the seminal fluid in my sex organ".[1] But the precise meaning of *ka, ba, akh, šhm etc.* is no longer apparent to us at all. Again and again well-meaning scholars attempt to force the Egyptian soul-beings into our current categories, but without our understanding them even slightly more clearly; and to-day it is no longer possible to say which human potency was really meant by the idea of *ka*, although we can certainly indicate a few characteristics. It is still more impossible, however, to establish the relationship between the various soul-potencies; but this is not at all remarkable, since even modern "faculty psychology" has been able to produce little in this respect. Only two points, then, are clear: in the first place, that the soul appears here *in plurali*; secondly, that each soul occupies the entire man and that it is not a matter of "the component parts of human personality". We should dispense finally with this mode of expression, derived from faculty psychology, since it accords with neither the soul of ancient nor of modern man.[2]

The dead person is addressed thus: "thy *ba* is in thee, thy *šhm* is behind thee".[3] We know that the *ba* is a soul sometimes more of the soul-stuff type, and at other times more of the form type, appearing then in the guise of a bird. We know too that the *šhm* was originally a staff, and that probably the soul-being was really the power of this staff. But we can gain no deeper insight into the mutual relationships of these two types; we can only be certain that the Egyptian, the higher he desired to elevate the power of the person whom he was addressing, the more soul-potencies he ascribed to him: "Thou art pure, thy *ka* is pure, thy *ba* is pure, thy *šhm* is pure."[4] Further, it was possible to possess a plurality of some type of soul: already in the *Pyramid Texts*, the dead—but therefore all the more powerful—king had several *kas*;[5] subsequently, this plurality was systematized by the number fourteen, and thus each of the fourteen *kas* of the sun-god bears the name of some powerfulness such as abundance, riches, victory, splendour *etc.*[6]

---

[1] *Pyramidentexte* (Sethe), 1061.

[2] For Egypt *cf.* L. J. Cazemier, *Oud-egyptiese voorstellingen aangaande de ziel*, 1930, where a wide range of references may be found.

[3] *Pyramidentexte*, 2010, *cf.* 162, and further van der Leeuw, *Godsvoorstellingen in de oud-aegyptische Pyramidetexten, passim.*

[4] *Pyramidentexte*, 837; *cf.* 992 *ff.* K. Sethe, *Urkunden der 18. Dynastie*, I, 1906, 244.

[5] 396.

[6] A. H. Gardiner, *Proc. Soc. Bibl. Arch.* 38, 1916, 84. *cf.* F. W. von Bissing, *Versuch einer neuen Erklärung des kai*, *Ber. Münch. Akad.* 1911. J. H. Breasted, *Ancient Records of Egypt*, II, 210.

An even unlimited number could be assumed: "Ra's million *kas* were the protection of his subjects."[1] Thus on the one hand the plural expressed the quantitative character of the soul's power: one could possess more or less of it; on the other hand, the attempt was made to release this power from any mere plurality by differentiation. In this manner the specific soul-powers received a certain independence, which could further become the exact contrary of the stuff-like plurality of the soul. We can still observe the same process in the abnormal mind, in whose consciousness individual powers have become independent of each other: the sex organ is regarded as a child, hairs that have been torn out as snakes *etc.*[2]

In West Africa, for example, four souls are distinguished: that which survives the body: that dwelling within an animal in the wilderness, the so-called bush-soul: the shadow, and the dream-soul;[3] the Melanesians, again, distinguish a life-soul, *tarunga*, from the soul persisting after death, *tindalo*,[4] while the Bahaus, on the Island of Borneo, draw a distinction between a *bruwa* which can leave the body, and the *ton luwa*, the corporeal soul. At death the *bruwa* abandons the body for ever;[5] and many Malayan tribes enumerate seven souls.[6]

In this many-sided differentiation, still further, even the body itself may also be accounted a soul and included together with others; and to "modern"—that is to Greek—thought this must appear most surprising; to the Egyptians, however, the body, *d-t*, was a soul-power which is referred to together with *ka*, *ba* etc.[7] Dualism is here still remote: the body is one power among many others.

2. The plural soul thus approximates closely to the idea of undifferentiated power-stuff; quantity prevents clearly defined formation which, conversely, becomes more intelligible as differentiation is completed. To the Egyptian mind one might be "strong in *baw* (souls or soul-stuff), and manifold in being";[8] a person could have a "great *ka*"; and often we cannot tell whether the plural of *ka* and *ba* should be translated as

---

[1] P. Lacau, *Textes religieux égyptiens* I, 1910, Nr. 78.

[2] A. Storch, *Das archaisch-primitive Erleben und Denken der Schizophrenen*, 1922, 24.

[3] Mary Kingsley, *West African Studies*, 199 *ff.*; *cf.* C. G. Seligman, *Multiple Souls in Negro-Africa* (*Ancient Egypt*, 1915, 103 *ff.*).

[4] Codrington, *op. cit.*, 248 *f. cf.* Marett, *The Threshold of Religion*, 136.

[5] Nieuwenhuis, *Wurzeln des Anim.*, 36 *f.*

[6] Kruyt, *Animisme*, 6 *f.* Skeat, *Malay Magic*, 50.

[7] G. van der Leeuw, *Godsvoorstellingen*, 32 *f.*   [8] *Pyramidentexte*, 901.

plurals or as undifferentiated powerfulness.[1] The idea of the plural soul is therefore a genuinely transitional structure; and as such it constitutes the presupposition of every form of Dualism, whether body is separated from soul, or soul from spirit.

The differentiation arising here may then be compared to the formation of distinct divine forms; in both cases it is a matter of the division of power between different beings. Actual Dualism, however, is present just as little in Polypsychism as in Polytheism, although both are conditions of its coming into being.

---

[1] *Pyramidentexte*, 560. K. Hoffmann, *Die theophoren Personnamen des älteren Ägyptens*, 1915, 23: "Great are the *kas* of Ptah" (a proper name); *cf.* 24.

CHAPTER 41

THE FORM OF THE SOUL

1. SOUL-STUFF has no form other than that of the body or some part thereof, while this in itself is not thought of as soul. "Stuff" itself is formless; and a genuine form is first of all acquired by the soul when man sees his own image, when he perceives himself in a mirror. But this again we must not interpret—with Animism—as if the reflected image had become the cause or stimulus of any primitive psychology. Rather was the sight of oneself a numinous experience, and the mirror image a revelation of the power attached to the self which was yet foreign and superior to it. The awakening and slightly tremulous consciousness, which is at the same moment the dawning of a mys-terious powerfulness, has been tenderly and movingly depicted in Wagner's *Siegfried* music:

> I came to the limpid brook,
> And the beasts and the trees
> I saw reflected;
> Sun and clouds too,
> Just as they are,
> Were mirrored quite plain in the stream.
> I also could spy
> This face of mine.[1]

The Narcissus experience, then, is essentially numinous, the dis-covery of one's own powerfulness that is yet strangely foreign, uncontrollable, superior and mysterious. That man represents his soul by his own image implies, therefore, not that the soul is only one form of himself: on the contrary, it means that in the soul man seeks to fathom his own essence, which is concealed from him and yet superior to him.

Thus the image, the form of man and of things in general, is at the same time their power, their essence; and the replacing of attendants and of sacrifices by their images is very familiar, for example, in what we know of ancient Egypt. The representations of provisions, servants *etc.* in the *mastabas* or private tombs were frequently multiplied, "so

---

[1] *Siegfried*, Act I (Armour).

that if one of them was destroyed to such an extent that it seemed about
to lose its influence, then the substitutes stepped in and on their own
part brought to the dead man his revenues".[1] The image (to repeat)
is the essence; but the essence again is more than mere individuality:
it is power. Hence the danger of looking at one's own image; on the
Banks' Islands, for instance, there is a deep hole into which no one ever
ventures to look; for should the water in the cave reflect a man's face
he would die.[2]

Like the mirror image, the *name* also is the essence of the soul, and
even its form, in a stuff-like way that is very strange to ourselves; but
I have already given the name a detailed discussion.[3] Here therefore I
need add only that the rite of naming is equivalent to bestowing a soul;
and to the Germanic peoples the father's act in giving the child a
name counted as a birth just as much as did the *accouchement*.[4] In
Egypt, again, the names of gods were their limbs, created by the
sun-god;[5] one deity affirms: "I am this name, which the sole lord
created when as yet there were not two things on earth."[6]

2. A very striking human representation or image, and therefore
one of the most important forms of the soul, is the *shadow*;[7] this is
necessary to life, if indeed it is not life itself. Demonic beings belonging
to the nether world, have no shadows; thus in Java no shadows of spirit
animals, like black chickens and cats, can be seen.[8] The dead too lack
shadows, both for Dante and among Central African negroes, while
the Basutos believe that a crocodile can overcome a passer-by if it
seizes his shadow cast on the water.[9] Similarly at the erection of the main
pillar of a house, in Malacca, care must be taken not to allow the
workmen's shadows to fall on it, since that would cause all sorts of
misfortune;[10] and in Arcadia whoever entered the temple of Zeus
Lycaeus lost his shadow and died within a year.[11] But though the dead
man can have no shadow, he can be a shade, σκιά;[12] and here again the
element that is foreign, and yet is one's own, is stressed; the departed
is still *l'homme mort*, but he is at the same moment the "Other", the
stranger.

[1] G. Maspero, *Geschichte der Kunst in Ägypten*, 1913, 35.
[2] Codrington, *The Melanesians*, 186.   [3] Chap. 17.
[4] Grönbech, *op. cit.*, II, 128 f.   [5] *e.g. The Book of the Dead*, Chap. 17.
[6] Lacau, *Textes religieux*, No. 78; *cf.* A. H. Gardiner, *loc. cit.*, 37, 1915, 255.
[7] J. von Negelein, *Bild, Spiegel und Schatten im Volksglauben, AR.* 5.
[8] Kruyt, *Animisme*, 68 ff.   [9] Alviella, *op. cit.*, 33.   [10] Kruyt, *ibid.*, 70.
[11] Pausanias, VIII, 38, 6.   [12] Jevons, *Introduction*, 44.

Still more intensely do this attraction and repulsion live in the idea of the *wraith*.[1] The Egyptian *ka* was such a wraith, even if this did not exhaust its character;[2] meeting the *ka* implied life. In popular belief, however, the power to see one's wraith involves nothing good;[3] but in any case a power is revealed, and the romantics, above all E. Th. A. Hoffmann, have made us experience once more, at least at secondhand, all the horror of the foreign element that is yet one's own.

The soul has also been thought of as a little man, *homunculus*; in this the forms of certain body-souls may have played a part, as for example the pupil with its "little man inside the eye", and the phallus or (euphemistically) the thumb.[4] The Hindu *ātman* is *purusha*, the "Tom Thumb" soul,[5] and the Toradja of Celebes imagine the soul as a "mannikin", *tonoana*.[6] The same soul-figure is believed in in Malacca where, in the case of sickness or fainting, the soul is recalled with the words:

> Hither, Soul, come hither!
> Hither, Little One, come hither!
> Hither, Bird, come hither!
> Hither, Filmy One, come hither![7]

The form of the *homunculus*, still further, is the best proof that in the case of the image-soul it is a matter not only of outward resemblance, nor even of the dream figure, alone. We must therefore realize the awe of the Narcissus experience, and the grim horror of the encounter with the wraith, if we wish to understand the human form of the soul in its numinous essence.

E. Monseur, *L'âme pupilline, L'âme poucet* (*RHR*. 41, 1905, 1 ff., 361 ff.).
J. von Negelein, *Bild, Spiegel und Schatten im Volksglauben* (*AR*. 5, 1902).
O. Waser, *Über die äussere Erscheinung der Seele* (*AR*. 16, 1913, 336 ff.).

[1] J. von Negelein, *ibid.*   [2] Chap. 42.
[3] In Ireland, *e.g.*, the "fetch", H. Gaidoz, *Mélusine* II, 1912, 264.
[4] Monseur, *L'âme pupilline, L'âme poucet, RHR.* 41, 1905, 1 ff., 361 ff.
[5] Oldenberg, *Lehre*, 52 f.
[6] Ankermann, in Chantepie, *op. cit.*, I, 146.   [7] Skeat, *Malay Magic*, 47 ff.

CHAPTER 42

THE "EXTERNAL SOUL"

1. IN discussing the soul structures thus far referred to we have frequently met with the idea of a soul outside the body—an "external soul"; or as I should prefer to say: psychic powers existed apart from the bodily power of the soul: often the soul of a dead man, but not always. The "external soul", then, has its own structure: and quite a considerable time ago Frazer[1] made this the object of extensive investigations, but without succeeding in assigning to it its specific and relevant place among the many concepts of the soul. This can be done only if we bear in mind that originally the "external soul" was merely one of many souls.[2] Owing to special conditions, however, it received a distinct status; and these must now be considered.

Here also, in the first place, man discovers within himself a powerfulness that is superior to him; and the fact that this superiority is connected with his own person by no means prevents him experiencing it as such, since he reverences equally the powerful implements that he himself has made. But now power appears to man as intimately linked with the external world; and in this way a path has been opened towards modern concepts, since we too can conceive superiority outside ourselves more easily than within us. Nevertheless the essential unity of Inner and Outer, of personal and foreign elements, which meets us here as in the case of the wraith, is sufficiently non-modern. Man learns that his own being, or at least an essential part thereof, is to be found "without"; here again environment and ego are not yet separated; and our comprehension of this attitude will be somewhat less difficult if we realize that the exteriorizing of power refers not to the soul alone, but to every power alike. Thus certain human potencies can be interpreted as possession: some superior power has settled within man.[3] According to our modern standpoint this is demonology, not psychology at all; but if the human power is regarded as "external soul" we may speak of a kind of psychology, however strange this may be. For the primitive mental outlook, however, this distinction had no weight whatever.

[1] In *The Golden Bough*.
[2] *cf.* J. Böhme, *Die Seele und das Ich im homerischen Epos*, 1929, 91, 89.
[3] Chap. 31.

2. As an introduction to this situation, let us consider two typical folk-tales. The Frankish king Guntram is asleep under a tree with a single attendant; a small animal creeps out of his mouth, runs to the brook and acts as if it wants to cross. The servant, who has remained awake, lays his sword over the stream; on this the animal crosses, disappears into a hole, and some time later returns by the same route. Then the king wakens and says: "I have had a strange dream: I saw a great wide river, spanned by an iron bridge which I crossed and reached a cavern in the mountains, where there lay inestimable treasure." Then the servant tells him what he had seen while the king was sleeping, and the place being subsequently dug up much gold and silver was discovered.[1] Thus in this instance the soul leaves the body in animal form.

Of the second type of this idea there are endless variations, of which one example must here suffice.[2] The hero of the fairy tale has to release a maiden from the power of a wicked giant; and by a trick the girl learns from the stupid giant where his heart is (in variants, also "soul", "life", "death"): "far, far away in a lake, there is an island: on the island there stands a church: in the church there is a fountain: in the fountain a duck is swimming: in the duck is an egg, and in the egg— there is my heart". Thus the giant, as the fairy tale neatly puts it, did not have "his heart with him", keeping the soul at a distance in this way being of course intended to ensure the giant's invulnerability and complete security. But it turns out quite otherwise; for the hero, with the assistance of the famous "helpful animals" of the fairy story, sets out and secures possession of the heart and then has the giant completely in his power. In both cases the "external soul" is, as it were, man rising above himself, what is in man and yet is more than man; a power

---

[1] Grimm, *Deutsche Sagen*; in *Gesta Romanorum* also, and frequently elsewhere.

[2] In Asbjörnson. Further, Klara Stroebe, *Nordische Volksmärchen*, II, 1919, No. 23. To the same type belong the following: *Tausend und eine Nacht*, V, 283 *ff.* *Drei Zitronen* (E. Littmann's Edition); Stroebe, *Nordische Volksmärchen*, II, No. 4; *Meleager and the Log* (or *Natal Torch*), Ovid, *Fasti* V, 305 *ff.* *Metam.* VIII, 260 *ff.* Grimm, *Kinder- und Hausmärchen*, No. 9, 60; *Bidasari und der Goldfisch*, Wilken, *op. cit.*, III, 296 *ff.*, together with the stories about Punchkin the Magician and *Koshchei and the Egg; cf.* Frazer, *GB*, XI (*Balder the Beautiful*, II), 108 *ff. The Story of the Two Brothers* in *Popular Stories of Ancient Egypt* (Maspero). G. Röder, *Altägyptische Erzählungen und Märchen*, 1927; M. Burchardt, *Zeitschr. f. äg. Sprache*, 50, 1913, 118 *f.* W. Aichele, *Zigeunermärchen*, 1926, No. 27; Pol de Mont and A. de Cock, *Wondervertelsels uit Vlaanderen*, 1924, No. 28; *Phrixus and the Golden Fleece, cf.* Wundt, *op. cit.*, V, 426; G. Jungbauer, *Märchen aus Turkestan und Tibet*, 1923, No. 10; A. Leskien, *Balkanmärchen*, 1919, No. 26; A. Dirr, *Kaukasische Märchen*, 1920, No. 27.

essential to him can move about freely and attain a measure of security denied to man himself.

3. Those soul-powers which are only loosely connected with the body and which, in order to remain within the metaphor, we may now call "semi-detached", constitute a transitional form between soul-stuff and the "external soul", the hair being in this respect very prominent as a seat of soul-stuff among many peoples. The story of Samson, for instance, shows how the hair is regarded as the hero's strength; but at the same time how, because hair is easily removed, this might can be lost with very serious consequences.[1] In the fairy tale, similarly, some helpful animal gives the hero a hair or a feather which he must rub whenever he is in danger; then the animal will immediately appear. The most frequent form of this semi-detached soul is the shadow, which has already been discussed. But the idea of the soul's immateriality, which attains its predominance in another structure,[2] is also connected with the shadow. Fear of losing one's shadow is widespread, being very intense for example in West Africa, where going out at midday is avoided because at that time the body casts no shadow; and the negro's reply to Miss Kingsley's question, why he did not hesitate to go about in the dark, when also no shadow was to be seen, is very fine: "that was all right, because at night all shadows lay down in the shadow of the Great God, and so got stronger".[3] Here a simple trust in God is expressed in very primitive form: the great shadow of the night nourishes that of the individual from its own plenteousness. It is related about Sankara, again, that when travelling in Nepaul he quarrelled with the Grand Lama, and rose up into the air; but the Lama struck his knife into Sankara's shadow; falling to the ground, he broke his neck.[4] In ancient Egypt too the shadow counted as one of the many soul-powers, which were frequently all enumerated together whenever the king's eternal life was to be affirmed.

In the next place, the *after-birth* is a soul-being that leaves the bearer at the moment of his birth; nevertheless it remains connected with his own existence, and is for that reason carefully stored away or buried *etc.* by most primitive peoples. Thus the Baganda of Uganda regard the placenta as a twin of the newly born infant; and after the death of their

---

[1] Wilken, *op. cit.*, III, 553 *ff.*   [2] Chap. 43.

[3] *West African Studies*, 207. On similar fears in the Indian Archipelago *cf.* Riedel, *Sluik- en kroesharige rassen*, 61; also Kruyt, *Animisme*, 68 *ff*; von Negelein, *Seele als Vogel*, 1 *ff.*; Maspero, *Études égyptiennes*, I, 300.

[4] Frazer, *The Golden Bough*, III (*Taboo and the Perils of the Soul*), 78.

king, his jawbone is united with his after-birth in the grave; in this way
he returns to his soul, which was external.[1]

4. In these "semi-detached" souls the idea of power-stuff predominated. But as soon as the separation of soul from body is completed
another element appears; the environment is as it were drawn into the
ego, or rather: is not yet delimited therefrom. From childhood we
moderns are committed to the popular view that the soul somehow
resides within the body; even to-day it is only at death that popular
belief imagines a freely hovering soul escaping from the body. But
except in this last instance we refuse to assume any closer connection
between the external world and the soul; for us then, in the first place,
soul is consciousness, and tree and animal cannot possess our consciousness; and thus we become immovably fixed in the egotistic attitude of
conscious subjects dominating the objective world. The idea of the
"external soul", however, draws the conjoint and the environing realms
into our own lives and, conversely, establishes our existence within a
wider environment. For the soul is here neither consciousness nor ego,
but a power superior to the ego even though it is also connected therewith. We can understand the dead person's soul residing near, or in,
the grave; it is much more difficult, however, for us to grasp the idea
that the tombstone itself is a soul (נֶפֶשׁ), as is the case with Jewish
popular belief.[2] That the soul is born with ourselves is again a familiar
concept, but we can scarcely comprehend the soul being simultaneously
born in a tree, the life-tree, simply because we habitually oppose ego to
world.[3] It is clear that the line of demarcation between environment
and ego is absent; but how has it happened that the limit was over-
stepped at exactly this point:—this tree, this stone or animal?

To obtain as deep an insight as possible into this mode of thought,
so foreign to ourselves, we must now consider the most important form
of the "external soul", that of the bird soul. This concept is extraordinarily widespread. In the ancient Semitic world the dead were a
kind of bird; they chirped, had wings,[4] and were "attired like a bird with

---

[1] cf. the later discussion of the *ka*; also Flinders Petrie, in *Ancient Egypt*, 1914, 161.
A. M. Blackman, "The Pharaoh's Placenta and the Moon-God Khons" (*Journal of
Egyptian Archæology*, 3, 1916, 235 ff.). G. van der Leeuw, "The Moon-God Khons
and the King's Placenta" (*ibid.*, 5, 1918.

[2] Nilsson, *Actes . . .*, 95.

[3] Frazer, *Golden Bough*, XI (*Balder*, II), 165 ff. Jevons, *op. cit.*, 207; Chap. 5.

[4] *Isaiah* viii. 19. M. Jastrow, *Die Religion Babyloniens und Assyriens*, II, 1912,
957 f.

a wing-kerchief".[1] The Egyptian *ba* too was a bird, probably a stork, often depicted with a human head, while yet another soul, the *akh*, was the bird-shadow.[2] The bird soul appears also in many Greek myths, and on an amphora in the British Museum the soul, in the guise of a bird, may be seen leaving the body of the dying Procris.[3] The Hyperboreans again, who were actually the people of the dead, had wings: "there is a story of certain men in Hyperborean Pallene who gain a covering of light feathers for their bodies".[4]

The sirens, birds with human heads, were souls of the dead like the *keres, erinyes*, harpies, and *stymphalides*,[5] while the idea still persists in popular belief, wherein there are all sorts of birds which are dead people, together with persons clothed in feathers—valkyries, shield-maidens, swan-maidens *etc.*[6]—the winged angels or the departed of Christianity pertaining to the same category. I shall attempt to illustrate the structural connection between soul and bird by two examples. One is ancient: according to Dio Cassius "in 217 A.D., the people recovering from the terror inspired by Caracalla, and assembled at the races in the Roman circus to celebrate the beginning of Severus' reign, greeted a cawing jackdaw, which had perched on the obelisk, with the name of the executed murderer of the emperor, Martialis, as though by some divine inspiration".[7] Here we obtain a glimpse into the experience of the "external soul": the people, whose excited mood was most intensely engaged with the murderer, spontaneously and without any proof identified the bird, which had suddenly appeared, with the man's soul.

Still more illuminating is the second example, taken from modern popular belief. Tobler relates the tale, taken from Strackerjan: "A schoolboy learnt how to make mice—a typical magic trick; so the pastor corrected the lad, who, however, died soon afterwards. But before his death he had to promise the pastor that he would appear to him and tell him whether he had been saved; so when the minister was walking in his garden, a crow came flying and alighted on the lever used to draw water. 'That you, Johnnie?' asked the pastor; whereupon the crow replied: 'Yes. Whoever denies God and the saints once is for ever lost'; then it flew away."[8] Here the minister's attitude is very fine and characteristic, when with no hesitation he addresses the bird,

---

[1] *Ischtar's Höllenfahrt*, P. Jensen, *Assyrisch-babyl nische Mythen und Epen*, 1900, 81.
[2] Klebs, *Der ägyptische Seelenvogel*, (*Zeitschr. f. Äg. Sprache*, 61). W. Spiegelberg, *Or. Lit.-Zeit.* 29, 1926.   [3] Weicker, *Der Seelenvogel*, 167.
[4] Ovid, *Metam.* XV, 356 *f.*   [5] Weicker, *ibid., passim.*
[6] Tobler, *Epiphanie der Seele in der deutschen Sage;* von Negelein, *Seele als Vogel* (*Globus*, 79).   [7] Fr. von Duhn in *AR.* XII, 1909, 168.   [8] *op. cit.* 31.

as a matter of course, as "Johnnie". Again we encounter the experience of the "external soul"; and in general terms we can point to the speed of animals, or their sudden upward flight and strange cries, in order to understand the essential connection between man and bird. But we can advance still farther if we consider the original experience as it is depicted for us in these two examples. For emotion is far more impressive than the concept, and it is from emotion that form is born. The intensely moved people therefore, and the pastor concerned for the boy's salvation, effect the fusion of the soul with the bird suddenly appearing before their eyes.[1]

Then there naturally arises the endeavour to establish some structural connections between the soul-animal and man; and the smallness of many of these animals has certainly assisted in their being regarded as souls that can enter and leave the body. This is the case with the bee, butterfly and bat, where the power of flight must also have played its part, and with mouse and lizard, weasel and worm.[2] In the case of other soul-animals their uncanny or sinister characteristics may well have been influential; above all in the case of the snake, the mysterious creature crawling forth noiselessly out of the earth, the toad and crab.[3] The fish also, which acquired so important a place as a symbol in Christianity, pertains to this category.[4]

But all this is far from sufficient, since the unity between man and the soul-bearer is one that is directly experienced, not one that is understood. This is clear from the fact that there are also very big soul-animals that are not at all mysterious. Werewolves and bearskin folk have been dealt with already,[5] and similarly in the form of a stag, boar or ape the "external soul" kills men and eats their livers.[6] Ulf for example, a heroic figure in Icelandic sagas, became irritable and sleepy at dusk and then roamed about as a wolf, being therefore called *Kveldulf*, the evening wolf.[7] The human soul is here wolf- or bear-like, and there subsists an essential connection between man and animal.[8]

---

[1] The souls of two robber murderers, repentant of their misdeeds, fly away as white doves. St. Benedict saw the soul of his sister, St. Scolastica, fly to heaven as a dove, *op. cit.*, 29.

[2] Weicker, *ibid.*, 29 *ff*; Waser, *Über die äussere Erscheinung der Seele, AR.* 16, 1913, *passim*. Tobler, *op. cit.*, 13 *ff.*, 19 *f.*, 36 *ff.*

[3] Tobler, *op. cit.*, 20 *ff.*, 25 *ff.*; Gaidoz, *L'âme hors du corps, Mélusine*, XI, 26.

[4] I. Scheftelowitz, *AR.* 14, 1911, 1 *ff.* W. Spiegelberg, *AR.* 12, 1909, 574.

[5] Chap. 8.

[6] Adriani, *Posso*, 64; *cf.* Wilken, *op. cit.*, III, 25 *ff.* Nieuwenhuis, *Wurzeln*, 38.

[7] *Die Geschichte vom Skalden Egil* (F. Niedner), 1914, 29.

[8] Grönbech, *op. cit.*, II, 99 *f.*

But quite apart from lycanthropy, all sorts of larger soul-animals also occur—dogs, cats and horses.[1]

Here then we have once more regained, by other paths, the totemism and nagualism already discussed:[2] man's power is essentially connected with some exterior object and can therefore assume its form, and thus the "external soul" is actually merely an expression or form of this unity. Such symbols were also the favours which the gentlewomen of the Middle Ages gave, as those of the Toradja tribe still give, their lovers; on going into battle a Toradja youth requests his sweetheart to *moramè* for him; she then gives him her loincloth, head-kerchief or a coral necklet, and two pinches of *sirih*. The youth may not accept these love tokens from two girls simultaneously, for that would turn out ill for him.[3] "Soul endowed" too was the knight's blood-stained shirt which the gentlewoman of the Middle Ages wore next to her body: it was supposed to guarantee the community of their essential nature.[4]

5. The removal of the soul from the body, still further, assures man of life, if it does not result in insecurity as in the fairy tales. In any case the remoteness connected with the idea of the "external soul" is regarded as safety; and this holds good also beyond earthly life, since the external soul cannot be affected by death. On the contrary: death often counts as a union between man, or his soul, with the other, "external", soul, as it did especially in ancient Egyptian thought: "to die" was "to go with one's *ka*";[5] and of the departed it was said, "each goes with his *ka*," which was a good thing; while whoever did as the king desired would have a peaceful end, "as one who goes to his *ka*".[6] It was the destiny of the gods, again, who always accompanied their *kas*, to bear with them always their complete power of life,[7] the finest expression of this idea being afforded by the passage: "when I die my *ka* is powerful".[8] Man's essence is assured, and shows its power fully, only when that of life is

---

[1] Tobler, *op. cit.*, 44 *f.*   [2] Chap. 8.   [3] Kruyt, *Bydr.* 75, 121.

[4] As soul-bearers, besides those already considered, must be mentioned: the amulet called "houses of the soul", *Isaiah* iii. 20, A.V. Margin, lights and will-o'-the-wisps; Tobler, *op. cit.*, 82 *ff.*

[5] G. van der Leeuw, *External Soul. Pyramidentexte* (Sethe), 17, 826, 1431. "Go to his *ka*", as well as "go with", which is immaterial in this connection; occasionally "go to his *akh*", *Pyramidentexte*, 472; *cf.* Sethe, *Urkunden*, I, 34; van der Leeuw, *Godsvoorstellingen*, 13 *f.*

[6] B. Gunn and A. H. Gardiner, *Jour. Eg. Arch.* IV, 1917, 248.

[7] *Pyramidentexte*, 829, 1165.

[8] *ibid.*, 1055; van der Leeuw, *External Soul*, 62.

disappearing. Thus Persian thought about the reunion of the soul with the *fravashi* after death,[1] and the reunification of the body-soul (*liau krahang*) with the "soul-marrow" (*salumpok liau*) after the final burial among the Oloh Ngadju of Borneo, are parallels.[2] Here we perceive the distant dawn of the idea of the soul's immortality. "Distant", however: for the "immortal" component is merely safe: it is not as yet contrasted with the body or the corporeal soul as being eternal, divine, since psychological dualism has not yet arisen. The soul that continues to live, the so-called soul of the dead, is a special case of the "external soul". It is not a matter of belief in immortality, but of the experience of power in its direct relation to man;[3] and security, even in death, is only a conclusion drawn from this.

6. The dream-soul, similarly, is not a theoretical construction; dream, sickness and death are only particular instances of the soul's externality, the dream journey being one of the most frequent dream experiences, whose classical example was discerned in the story already told about Guntram. In case of sickness, fainting or sleep, again, the Indonesian peoples believe that the soul is absent, the *sumangat* being called back by name or in the same way as poultry are called,[4] while the priestess of the Bahaus of Borneo brings the soul of a sick person back along the "soul road", fastened to a cord after she has enticed it to her; then she blows the soul back into the body through the skull.[5] The Toradja of Celebes likewise believe that during sleep the soul is on a journey:

> I slept so fast and deeply
> That my soul left me.
> Sleeping and dreaming,
> I came to the realm of the dead.[6]

In Rarotonga, one of the Cook Islands, when anyone sneezes somebody calls out: "Ha! you have come back!" and the medicine-men often set a trap for a sick person's soul.[7] From all this, therefore, it is clear that it was not merely the absence and interruption of power which evoked

[1] N. Söderblom, *Les Fravashis*, 1899, 51.
[2] Hertz, *op. cit.* 57 *f*. Wilken, *op. cit.*, III, 59 *f*.
[3] *cf.* W. F. Otto, *Die Manen*, 1923.   [4] Kruyt, *op. cit.*, 82 *ff*.
[5] Nieuwenhuis, *Wurzeln*, 43; *cf.* his *Quer durch Borneo*, I, 103.
[6] Adriani, *Animistisch Heidendom*, 24.
[7] Frazer, *The Belief in Immortality*, II, 229 *f*.

the idea of the soul, as was maintained by Animism, but equally the
obvious and striking presence of power. Thus the novelty in this
structure is only the freedom of movement, the soul's capacity to leave
man or to seek him out, and powerful human beings, such as magicians
and witches, possess this liberty of movement to a special degree.[1]
In Betzingen two maids were sleeping in the same bed in the mill
when two lovers visited them; one of the girls could not be wakened,
but towards morning a beetle came crawling into her mouth while she
slept; and this is a proof of witchcraft:[2] the witch had sent out her
soul; similarly a magician sends forth his soul to deliver a letter and
bring him the answer.[3] Ecstatics also can do the same as witches and
magicians: as the apocalyptic writer says: "and immediately I was in
the spirit"; that is, he leaves his body.[4]

7. Finally, the structure of the ' external soul" is closely related to,
and indeed sometimes identical with, the idea of the angel, particularly
the *guardian angel*.[5] The "dual experience of form", which we discerned in discussing angels, has here an application to human personality
itself. Its structural basis consists in the community of essence accompanying "being a soul", and once again the finest example is the
Egyptian *ka*, "thou art the *ka* of all the gods" being asserted of one
very powerful deity,[6] which means: thou art their powerfulness, they
must obey thee. Or yet more clearly: to the god Osiris it was said:
"Thou art the *ka* of all the gods; Horus protected thee when thou
becamest his *ka*."[7] The community of soul conditions the protective
relationship, and thus it can be understood not only how the *ka* can
simultaneously be soul-stuff, an external soul and a protective spirit,[8]
but (further) the whole conception of guardian angel or spirit, as this
occurs quite early in Christianity[9] among other instances, can be
readily interpreted by means of the idea of the soul. I need not recall
the *fylgja* and similar concepts,[10] and only wish to add that the "external
soul", in accordance with its character as I have already stressed this,
can also have an obstructive and inimical effect. Of this the *erinys*, the
soul, really the blood, of a murdered relative provides a good example,

---

[1] Chap. 31.   [2] Tobler, *op. cit.*, 38 *ff.*
[3] Bin Gorion, *Der Born Judas*, VI, 103 *f.*   [4] *Rev.* iv, 2.
[5] Chap. 16.   [6] *Pyramidentexte* (Sethe), 1623, 1831.
[7] *ibid.*, 1690; *cf.* 136, 610, 647, 1653. Hoffmann, *Theophore Personsnamen*, 53, 60.
[8] G. van der Leeuw, *External Soul*.
[9] Harnack, *History of Dogma*, II, 362, Note 3; *cf.* 361, Note 3.
[10] Chap. 16.

the *erinys* being hostile to the murderer not however as an alien power, but as a personal soul related to him by blood.[1] The *keres* also are avenging soul-beings of a similar nature:

> like sleuth-hounds too
> the fates pursue.[2]

Finally, the connection existing between the idea of the "external soul" and that of personal fate must be considered.[3] The *aklama* of the Ewe natives, for example, is an "invisible thing that the god has given to man, so that it may always be around him and accompany him everywhere"; thus it is at the same time a sort of protective spirit, soul, and fate, and if something has succeeded they say: "my *aklama* was gracious to me, *aklama* was around me, or my *aklama* has given me some good advice".[4] Parallels are the Nordic *hamingja*, and the later Greek *Mira* (*moira*) which appears in fairy stories as adviser and protective spirit[5]; here the soul once again appears as a form of what man has experienced in himself as superior.

H. Gaidoz, *L'âme hors du corps* (*Mélusine*, XI, 1912).

L. Klebs, *Der ägyptische Seelenvogel* (*Zeitschr. f. Äg. Sprache*, 61, 1926).

G. van der Leeuw, *External Soul, Schutzgeist und der ägyptische ka* (*Zeitschr. f. Äg. Sprache*, 54, 1918)

J. von Negelein, *Seele als Vogel* (*Globus*, 79, 1901).

E. Rohde, *Psyche* [9-10], 1925.

O. Tobler, *Epiphanie der Seele in der deutschen Sage*, 1911.

G. Weicker, *Der Seelenvogel*, 1902.

[1] E. Samter, *Die Religion der Griechen*, 1914, 52. The *erinyes* were regarded as souls of the underworld also in the magical tablets of "defixion"; Weicker, *op. cit.*, 5.

[2] Sophocles, *Oedipus rex*, 470.   [3] Chap. 21.

[4] D. Westermann, *Über die Begriffe Seele, Geist, Schicksal bei dem Ewe- und Tschivolk* (*AR*. 8, 1905).   [5] P. Kretschmer, *Neugriechische Märchen*, 1910, Nr. 36, 48.

CHAPTER 43

THE UNIQUELY POWERFUL AND DIVINE SOUL

1. IN the structure of soul-stuff, as in that of the plural and the "external soul", we discerned superior power as being always the basic experience; and the differentiation of the second of these structures, and in the third the separation between ego and environment, alter nothing whatever in this situation. But as soon as a portion of the environment, or of the ego, is *deprived* of its power, thereby becoming incapable of being a soul bearer, everything is changed. In the three preceding structures we know of "no corporeality which was nothing more than mere stuff";[1] but now *Dualism* arises, for which the soul's power, living, potent and divine, can exist only in association with soulless, impotent and godless stuff.

The natural condition for this is the freedom of movement of the third structure just referred to; the persistence, for example, of the Egyptian *ba* depends simply on the possibility of its "going forth to the day". It left the grave in order to breathe and nourish itself; air and food were powerful and necessary, and the *ba* was merely an "external soul" that had attained a higher degree of security. But when all power-fulness is denied to the material world, and when the whole environment, including the body itself, is reduced to the level of mere "matter" or "thing", then this freedom of the soul appears entirely different;[2] and the Greek mind effected this revolution. For Heracleitus, whose dictum on the depth of the soul harmonizes with every soul structure, as for the pre-Socratics in general, the soul was one power among other powers; there was no condition whatever of complete impotence: everything was conceived in terms of stuff, and the entire life process was a sort of metabolic process, while stuff itself was divine.[3] But Plato, starting from Orphic-Dionysiac ideas, removed the soul out of the material world and changed the latter from being a divine whole to the realm of evil;[4] while in the course of the succeeding centuries this Greek concept of the soul proved itself so highly influential that even

---

[1] Otto, *Die Götter Griechenlands*, 87.   [2] Chap. 3.
[3] Rohde, *op. cit.*, II, 148 *f.*; *cf.* K. Joël, *Der Ursprung der Naturphilosophie*, 1906.
[4] The Dionysiac excitement in Greece was not, as Klages' school has recently maintained, a reversion from spirituality to the "primitive ground of life", but just the converse.

the last generation regarded the dualism of body and soul as being almost self-evident.

2. This conception of the soul, then, found the schema of the "external soul" existing ready for it; and the *transmigration of souls* is nothing more than an extreme conclusion drawn from the soul's liberty of movement. It is to be found in many regions quite apart from India and Greece, where the doctrine of soul migration attained its highest development. Originally, again, transmigration involved no disparagement whatever of matter: life was a cycle in which death marked only a stage and not a conclusion: indeed, there was no conclusion.[1] In the popular beliefs of primitive peoples reincarnation is accepted without further ado, and the newly born are identified according to definite distinguishing marks:—among others resemblance,[2] while in folk-tales the persecuted hero can adopt constantly fresh forms, like Proteus and Loki.[3] Similarly, in order to escape the dangers of the realm of the dead the Egyptian *ba* had the ability to adopt many guises; and metamorphosis yields no more than enhanced security, as so many of Ovid's stories prove. This, however, was not a static idea but continued to expand; and we can understand that, in this development, the soul becomes more and more the single stable entity in the flight of the merely apparent. Thus the world and the body were subjected to many changes, but the soul remained the same; the bearer changed, but what he bore continued unaltered. As one example: "Torsten initiates his boy into life with these words: this boy shall be called Ingemund, and I expect a *hamingja* (soul destiny) for him because of the name"; Ingemund being the mother's father.[4] Yet one step more, and the soul not only persists during change, but subsists *eternally in the transient, and powerful in the impotent.*

The expression "transmigration of souls" is, therefore, a most serious misconception: for while everything changes its place and all is transformed, the soul alone persists. It endures and will continue to endure, even when the body dies—whether we rejoice, or lament this inability to die as in Orphism and Buddhism; while in Mazda

---

[1] Chap. 22.

[2] K. Th. Preuss, *Tod und Unsterblichkeit im Glauben der Naturvölker*, 1930, 23. Wilken, *op. cit.*, III, 72.

[3] Nilsson justly observes that the gift of metamorphosis in Greece was preferably accorded to maritime creatures: *A History of Greek Religion*, 57.

[4] Grönbech, *op. cit.*, II, 124.

theology the soul was thought of as even pre-existent: as in being before the world and persisting after the world has ceased to be.[1]

The soul, thus rendered eternal, more and more receives its form from the semi-material world; the concrete soul-stuffs are allotted to a world-stuff which is reduced to impotence; and as forms, breath and wind *etc.*, are preferred. The degree of power corresponds to the grade of insubstantiality; and to the world of things the eternal and divine soul is hostile. In a universe of dead materiality, of substantiality replete with destruction, the soul is the heavenly spark, the divine shoot; and the Orphics deplored calamitous reincarnation, the "sorrowful weary wheel" which rolls on into eternity and heaps sin on sin. The soul that has escaped from this cycle returns to the world of the gods: but on its entrance into heaven its watchword is the appeal to its origin: it may approach the gods because it is akin to them. "I am indeed a 'dual being', half heavenly, half earthly", as a gold tablet discovered in a grave at Petelia represents the dead Orphic saying:

> Say: "I am a child of Earth and of Starry Heaven;
> But my race is of Heaven (alone)";[2]

and an inscription of a later period gives the soul ascending to heaven the formula:

> I am your fellow wanderer, your fellow Star.[3]

3. The simplest form of this dualism is separation at the moment of death, when the two parts, the powerful and the impotent, betake them each to its own place: "earth to earth, the *pneuma* upwards", γᾶ μὲν ἐς γᾶν, πνεῦμ' ἄνω; or, "the ether receives the souls, but the earth the bodies".[4] It is true that where this duality prevails, the spirituality of the soul is not always stressed; and the primitive breath-soul retains its validity always as to its name, *pneuma*, and very often also as to its essence. Many primitive peoples, again, are familiar with an ascent to heaven on a ladder of arrows,[5] while the ancient Egyptian *Pyramid Texts* depict the dead king as a bird, a falcon or goose, flying up to heaven, or climbing thither with ropes or on an animal's skin, or a ladder (Jacob's ladder!). In the oldest formulas, still further, a latent

---

[1] Söderblom, *Les fravashis*, 62 *ff.*

[2] A. Olivieri, *Lamellae aureae orphicae*, 1915, 12. O. Kern, *Orphicorum Fragmenta*, 1922, *Fr.* 32a, 105.   [3] A. Dieterich, *Eine Mithrasliturgie*², 1910, 8.

[4] Rohde, *op. cit.*, II, 389, 257 *ff.*, where additional instances are cited; E. T. 170, 541. *cf.* Dieterich, *Mithrasliturgie*, 200 *ff.*   [5] *e.g.* Wundt, *op. cit.*, V, 264 *ff.*, 272.

dualism is already manifest: "the soul (*akh*) to the heavens, the body to the earth", or "the soul (*ba*) to heaven, the body (*d-t*, originally the body-soul) to the earth".[1] A Chinese parallel from the *Li-ki*: "When someone died people climbed immediately on to the house roof and called out his name: 'So-and-so, come back!' "—the external soul!— "afterwards his mouth was filled with uncooked rice. . . . While he was being buried in the earth, they looked up to heaven; for while the body with the animal-soul sinks downward, the spirit soars upward."[2] Here there still subsists the idea of the plurality of souls, but the body is separated from the "spirit"; the latter goes upward, the body downward!

"To primitive thought such a contrast was foreign; and behind our concept of the soul lies a prolonged spiritual process of development. Homer and Plato, St. Paul and Christian thought have contributed towards spiritualizing, individualizing and expanding the purified idea of the soul in modern terminology, in a way that finds its counterpart only in India."[3] Here then originate all speculations leading theoretically to the manifold hypotheses of psycho-physical dualism and parallelism,[4] and mythically to the magnificent idea of the "heavenward journey of the soul".[5]

4. In these forms, too, Dualism still continues to employ the primitive mode of expression. For the soul is no pure spirit, but only a subtle stuff; its form not immaterial, but merely "similar to light winds and fleeting dream":—*par levibus ventis volucrique simillima somno*. Thus Dualism attains its truest form only when the body loses its value completely, and even becomes an object of aversion; it is the soul's prison, its grave: *soma sema* ("the body is a tomb");[6] and man's salvation is bound up indissolubly with liberation from the embrace of matter.[7] The soul is imprisoned in matter, which repeatedly pulls it down into the slime, and the many forms of this immortal myth of the soul, from Plato to the Romantics, are well known: "The soul flies away into the pure blue heaven of truth and innocence like a bird that has been set free, to hover in the clear light. And with the wretched

---

[1] *Pyramidentexte* (Sethe), 474. *Urkunden*, IV, 481 ; *cf.* 484.
[2] Lehmann, *Textbuch*[1], 11 *f.*   [3] Söderblom, *Gottesglaube*, 65.
[4] *cf.* the striking characterization of humanity as Descartes regarded this: "an angel driving a machine"; Maritain, *Religion and Culture*, 24.   [5] Chap. 44.
[6] Plato, *Gorgias*, 493*a*; *cf. Cratylus*, 400*c*. The expression was previously employed by Philolaus: Diels, *Vorsokratiker*, I, Fr. 14.
[7] *cf.* Rohde, *op. cit.*, II, 35; E. T. 342, 345.

net, with lime, the immortal is again drawn down and held fast in the mire".[1]

In this connection the so-called *Song of the Pearl*, from the Gnostic *Acts of St Thomas*, is typical. As a very little child the prince is sent from the East, his home, to Egypt to seek the one pearl (soul) which is in the sea (matter). At first he forgets the treasure which he ought to discover, and also that he is a king's son; then he finds the pearl and, returning to his home, at the frontier he receives his royal raiment so that he may make his entry garbed in splendour. Old fairy tale *motifs* again—a snake guarding the pearl: the hero forgetting his task while he eats the Egyptians' food, *etc.*—acquire the new content: the soul's salvation.[2] Similarly, and no less impressively, in Islam, as influenced by Neo-Platonism: "The soul descended upon thee from the lofty station; a dove rare and uncaptured. . . . It came to thee unwillingly. . . . It resisted at first . . . it grew accustomed to the desert place (the world). Methinks it then forgot the recollections of the protected park (heaven), and of those abodes which it left with regret . . . it was united to the infirmity of the material body. . . . It now remembers the protected park and weepeth with tears which flow and cease not till the time for setting out towards the protected park approacheth. . . . It then cooeth on the top of a lofty pinnacle . . . and it has come to the knowledge of every mystery in the universe, while yet its tattered vest hath not been mended.

"Its descent was predestined so that it might hear what it had not heard, else why did it descend from the high and lofty heaven to the depth of the low and humble earth?"[3]

From this stage man's most urgent problem is *asceticism*.[4] So far as the flesh is concerned he must die, in order to be able to live in the spirit: only thus can he be adequate to his destiny, his divine essence. We find this idea, in fact, in Plato, in connection with the σῶμα σῆμα metaphor: "And indeed I think that Euripides may have been right in saying,

'Who knows if life be not death and death life';

and that we are very likely dead; I have heard a philosopher say that at this moment we *are* dead, and that the body is a tomb."[5]

---

[1] Ludwig Tieck, XIV, 358. In Indian speculation a parallel idea is found in the relationship between *prakriti* (matter) and *purusha* (spirit).

[2] Lehmann-Haas, *Textbuch*, 218 *ff.*

[3] C. Field, *Mystics and Saints of Islam*, 101 *f.* (Avicenna's Poem).

[4] Chap. 66.   [5] *Gorgias*, 493 (Jowett).

5. In this purification however, which is equivalent to dying, man cannot remain halfway. For as soon as his corporeality has attained either moral and religious value, or disvalue, it can no longer be restricted to the body proper. The condemnation of the body does not suffice to ensure the spirituality of the soul, since this soul contains ideas and thoughts, impulses and desires, of a wholly material kind. Thus the soul must now be released not only from the body, but also from the corporeality residing within itself; within the soul itself the lower elements must sever themselves from the higher. Among the Greeks, indeed, it was the asceticism of the soul that first created *spirit*: it is only the suppression of the instincts, the rendering impotent not merely of the body but of fleshly lust, of appetite and stress, that render the spirit potent.[1] Here again we immediately encounter Plato: he depreciated not only the body but the soul also; the latter pertains to the lower "world of becoming". It certainly participates in the higher realm of the Ideas, and is immortal; but it is not absolute: it assumes an intermediate position and shares the nature of both these worlds. Thus arises the so-called *trichotomy*: above corporeality subsist soul qualities, and superior to these again pure spirituality. Spirit is elevated above soul. Psychologically, this implies a stratification of human nature in accordance with lower and higher impulses and instincts, while theologically it is the attempt to seek out the superior and the divine in man, despite all else: body and soul both manifest their inadequacy, and spirit now becomes the symbol of the soul's unfathomable depth.[2] The irony of history, however, has decided that the principal term for this spiritualizing, this ultimate elevation to a completely immaterial power, should be no other than precisely the old word from the soul-stuff-structure: *pneuma* (*Geist*, *esprit*, spirit, *etc.*). We have already observed that "soul" is not a comprehensive name for the phenomena of consciousness; and this holds good to a far greater degree of "spirit", which is in no sense a psychological concept: "for spirit may be abstract, unreal, powerless, more so than the soul. But the spirit has a clearer

---

[1] Scheler, *Die Stellung des Menschen im Kosmos* (1928), 74 *ff.* "The reciprocal penetration of the originally impotent spirit, and the originally demonic impulse blind to all spiritual ideas and values, by means of the developing idealization and spiritualizing of the misery subsisting behind the symbols of things, and the simultaneous enhancing and vitalizing of the spirit, are the aim and end of finite being and history"; *ibid.*, 83.

[2] Rohde, *op. cit.*, I, 4. E. T. 5. On the separation between spirit and soul in Plutarch *cf.* W. Bousset, *Die Himmelsreise der Seele*, *AR.* IV, 1901, 252; in Origen, *cf.* Harnack, *History of Dogma*, II, 362; for a good survey, W. Windelband, *History of Philosophy*, 301 *ff.*

recollection that it was never mere life in the purely biological, and above all never mere consciousness in the purely psychological, sense."[1] On the contrary: the concept of consciousness could arise only on the basis of some experience of superiority.[2]

6. Mysticism, in conclusion, follows the path of the enfeebling of stuff and the spiritualizing of soul to its ultimate end. "Thou canst not discover the bounds of the soul albeit thou pacest its every road: so deep is its ground. Dig as deeply as thou canst: then wilt thou come to the ground that is unfathomable; deprive thine own self of all power, then wilt thou find God"; thus the "ground of the soul", *fundus animae*, implies man's ultimate impotence, but simultaneously God's primal and true powerfulness; everything material, all desires and impulses, all thoughts and concepts, must disappear. Heavy sleep or intense rapture must deprive man of his self: "I mean by the chalice the wine of Eternity; and for me the meaning of this wine is the surrender of the self, the suppression of selfhood", asserts Hafiz.[3] Or a modern woman mystic: "The understanding sees with eyes without sight, hears with ears without hearing: the emotions, the will and its changing moods, have ceased. By this process spirit escapes from itself and from all selfhood; it also evades every activity and becomes devoid of working and of spirit."[4] Again: "Clothe thyself with this nought, this misery, and strive so that this misery and this nought may become thy daily nourishment and place of sojourn, so that thou mayest become completely merged with them; I assure thee that when thou art thus nought, God will become the All within thy soul".[5] The expressions that German mysticism in particular has coined for this ultimate deprivation of power and of value are manifold: "to deprive of being" (*entwerden*), "to renounce" (*entsagen*), "to deprive of form" (*entbilden*), "to empty oneself" (*entledigen*), "to be utterly naked", "to remove one's clothing", *etc.*[6] The spirit must become as thoroughly vanquished as the body and soul:

[1] Schmalenbach, *op. cit.*, 344.   [2] *ibid.*, 351.

[3] A. Merx, *Idee und Grundlinien einer allgemeinen Geschichte der Mystik*[1], 1893. For what follows *cf.* the entire Chap. 75.

[4] L. de Hartog-Meyes, *Mystiek* (*Nieuwe Banen*, IX, 1916, 220 *f.*).

[5] Miguel de Molinos, *Der geistliche Führer, Buch III, Kap.* 20.

[6] G. Siedel, *Die Mystik Taulers*, 1911, 99; on this, and also on what follows, *cf.* Grete Lüers, *Die Sprache der deutschen Mystik des Mittelalters im Werke der Mechtild von Magdeburg*, 1926.

> Would ye know how I came forth from Spirit?
> When in myself I perceived nought whatsover.
> Nought but sheer unplumbed Deity;
> Then no longer could I keep silent; I must proclaim it:
>   I ceased to be.[1]

There then remains only the tiny spark, the *scintilla animae*, the ground of the soul, which cannot be described because it contains nothing but the All: God:

> Since thus I have been lost in the Abyss,
> I would fain speak no more. I am dumb.
>   Thus hath Deity
> Manifestly absorbed me within Itself . . .
> I have been annihilated.[2]

"The *fundus animae* is the place where God and the soul are one and the same".[3] Thus the soul's ground is the most ultimate idea of the soul possible, which is indeed no longer even an idea, and which proves that he who seeks the soul is in the end seeking not for this, but always for something that exists beyond, *epekeina*.[4] Quite close and yet eternally sublime, God subsists in man at the place where His ineffableness coincides with that of the Ultimate in humanity:

> Why is all so well with the soul
> When it finds its long sought Good
> So near its heart?
> Now has it all, whate'er it will.
> Embraced, beloved, it lies still,
> With its God, in the ground.[5]

Never and nowhere, therefore, is the soul a rational explanation of life's activities, but always and everywhere an experience on the borderland; and the human spirit has found no rest until it has banned from the soul all that was impotent within it. Bodily asceticism, then, is quite insufficient: asceticism of the soul, and indeed of the spirit, must be added to it; and this leads to a blessed nothingness which—paradox of mysticism!—is experienced as powerfulness *par excellence*.

---

[1] Merx, *op. cit.*, 13.   [2] *ibid.*
[3] F. Delekat, *Zeitschr. f. Theol. u. Kirche*, N. F. IV, 1923, 280 *ff*.
[4] It is true that Southern Buddhism goes still farther by simply denying the soul.
[5] G. Tersteegen.

The vacuum is the richest fullness, the negative the highest degree of positivity:

> Thirty spokes meet together in a single hub.
> The waggon's usefulness depends on their nothingness; (on the empty space);
> Clay is moulded into vessels;
> The vessels' utility depends on their nothingness.
> To build a house, holes are made in the walls for doors and windows;
> On their nothingness depends the usefulness of the house.
> Hence:—Being yields possession, but Non-being utility.[1]

[1] *Tao-teh King*, 11.

CHAPTER 44

THE IMMORTAL SOUL

1. WE have already observed that ecstasy is a particular case of the "external soul";[1] and it is not difficult to understand that the evaporation of the weight of life, and the cessation of the vital functions as this occurs in ecstasy, have powerfully reinforced the idea of the ultimate duality of body and soul. The soul's destiny is to become free from the body, and to survive in another world untrammelled by all the heaviness of earth; so that what in ecstasy is a momentary liberation must after death manifest itself as eternal reality. The Tupi Guaranis of South America, for instance, attain by dancing to the "land without evil", to eternal youth and freedom from toil and hardships: "they believed that they would become light enough to cross over the sea dryshod, or straight from the dance be taken up into heaven, together with their huts, by incessant dancing combined with strict fasting";[2] while even for a less primitive culture, which no longer seeks the "land free from evil" on earth, ecstasy nevertheless means a glimpse of the other world. Thus it is related of certain rabbis that they "entered Paradise" in ecstasy;[3] and St. Paul tells us: "I knew a man in Christ caught up to the third heaven; (whether in the body, or out of the body, I cannot tell: God knoweth)", he adds significantly.[4] Greek antiquity too was familiar with a series of such ecstatic experiences in which the mysteries of the other world were perceived;[5] it was reported of Aristeas that he could leave behind his body like a corpse, but that his soul, after abandoning the body, mounted into the aether.[6] Thus the body became increasingly a garment that could be put on or off at will.

But where the element of power in humanity becomes more and more exclusively sought in soul and spirit, the idea is not far off that death, which finally separates body and soul, is genuine liberation and admission into powerful life: the soul—no longer the man!—is regarded as immortal. As regards Greece, Rohde has clearly explained in a masterly exposition this connection between immortality and the powerfulness (divinity) provisionally attained in ecstasy. In Greece

---

[1] Chap. 42. [2] Preuss, *Tod und Unsterblichkeit im Glauben der Naturvölker*, 5.
[3] Bousset, *Die Himmelsreise der Seele* (*AR.* IV, 1901, 136 *ff.*). [4] 2 *Cor.* xii. 2.
[5] Bousset, *ibid.*, 253 *f.*; *cf.* Rohde, *op. cit.*, II, 28 *ff.*, 91 *ff.* E. T. 30, 255, 293.
[6] Rohde, *ibid.*, 92. E. T. 281.

the ecstasy of Dionysiac religion led to the belief in an immortal soul;[1] but for this intoxicating liquors were also useful; and by many peoples these were sublimated into the beverage of the gods, so that the *soma* of the Hindus, the Persian *haoma* and the nectar of the Greeks, ensure eternal life.[2] They facilitate and contribute to the enfeebling of the body and of the daily activities of the soul. It is for the same reason that the Persian mystics drink:

> Knowest thou the cup-bearer who gives drink to spirits?
> Knowest thou the beverage which the cup-bearer pours forth?
> The cup-bearer is the beloved, who pours out for thee annihilation,
> The drink is fire, wherein thou drinkest illumination.
> Drink the draught of ecstasy, burn in the glow of love!
> Gladly the droplet seeks extinction in its mighty flood.
> The whole Universe is a wine lodge: every thing a goblet;
> It is our friend who holds the chalice, and we are the drinkers.
> Even wisdom is drunken and completely sunk in rapture.
> Heaven and earth are drunken: every angel is drunken.[3]

2. Rapture, deprivation of being (*das Entwerden*) and collapse assume various forms, one of the most remarkable being the flight towards heaven or the "heavenward journey of the soul". We have already observed that the soul has wings;[4] but even without these it pursues its upward way to heaven, which implies purification; and the final goal is union with the godhead. Probably of Iranian origin, this idea found its classical expression in the Gnostic, Hellenistic and Judaistic tendencies of the centuries at about the commencement of our chronological era. The universe consists of seven planetary spheres, each having a guardian, a star-god, whom the soul must pass in its ascension. Stage by stage it mounts to highest heaven, usually regarded as the eighth sphere, the empyrean. The *Hebdomad* or *Ogdoad*, again, is a purifying by degrees, the soul leaving the earthly level farther and farther behind.[5] Mithraism also recognized this seven grade ascent: a

[1] Rohde, *op. cit.*, II, *passim*. E. T. 264 f. But *cf.* Nilsson, *History of Greek Religion*, 210. [2] *cf.* G. Dumézil, *Le festin d'immortalité*, 1924.

[3] Mahmud's *Gulshan I Raz*; in Lehmann-Haas, *op. cit.*, 376.

[4] Negelein, *op. cit.*, 59. Holland, *Zur Typik der Himmelfahrt, AR.* XXIII, 1925, 215. The soul may also descend to the underworld; thus the Babylonian Ishtar seeks life below, and is compelled to leave behind portions of her clothing at each of the seven subterranean gates—an exact parallel to the ascent through the seven gates of heaven. Jensen, *Assyrisch-babylonische Mythen und Epen*, 81 *ff.* On the journey to heaven *cf.* also Dieterich, *Mithrasliturgie*, 90 *ff.*, 179 *ff.*, 200 *ff.*

[5] Bousset, *loc. cit.*, 148 f. On the Persians *cf.* Edv. Lehmann, *Zarathustra, en bog om Persernes gamle tro*, II, 1902, 250 *ff.*

ladder composed of eight gates, "of which the first seven consisted of seven different sorts of metals, served in the temples as a symbolic reminder of the path that must be traversed to attain the highest region of the fixed stars"; each gate was guarded by an angel, and "the farther the soul . . . advanced the more it discarded, like clothing, the passions and capacities it had received when it first came hovering down to earth", until naked, freed from all sensuality, it reached the eighth heaven where it found bliss.[1] There it was made part of a magnificent vision of the universe, and psychology transformed into cosmology; the angels of the stars indicated the way to the soul.[2]

In Judaistic versions of the soul myth, also, clothing symbolism is very vivid. Enoch for instance is carried off by two angels; he mounts through the seven heavens and in the seventh he sees God, who commands the archangel to remove his earthly clothes and garb him in raiment of "glory". Thus he becomes "one of the glorious".[3] The soul must become unclothed: this is the proper meaning of the myth: nakedness alone can qualify for donning the celestial garments.

And since it is not only cosmically, but at the same time psychologically apprehended, ascension can be translated wholly into the inward. Thus mysticism finds heaven within the soul itself, in the "ground"; the stations on the heavenward journey are then stages of inner purification. Mohammed's ascent to heaven, which represents an extension of the prophet's so-called "night journey" from Mecca to Jerusalem referred to in the *Koran*,[4] is by the Sufis related to the mystic union: Mohammed, conducted by Gabriel and Michael, mounts through the seven heavens; he arrives before the throne of Allah, where angels must remain behind:

> When, solitary, he communes with his God,
> Suddenly he is transformed into his God.
> Behold! Mohammed straightway disappears,
> And at the covenanting place God stands alone.[5]

In St. Paul also we find the schema of the journey to heaven interpreted ecstatically as well as cosmically.[6]

[1] F. Cumont, *Die Mysterien des Mithra*³, 1923, 129 f.; cf. Bousset, *loc. cit.*, 165 ff.
[2] Chap. 7, 16.
[3] Bousset, *ibid.*, 138 ff.; cf. further 140 (*Leviticus*), 141 (*Isaiah*), 151 ff., 268 ff.
[4] *Sura* 17 (Mecca). Lehmann-Haas, *op. cit.*, 350.
[5] Fariduddin Attar, in F. A. G. Tholuck, *Blütensammlung aus der morgenländischen Mystik*, 1825, 265; cf. Bousset, *ibid.*, 249 and Note 1.
[6] *Romans* viii. 38 ff. Bousset, *ibid.*, 136.

In all this there is expressed a yearning for the completely subtle, the unformed, the indescribable and unutterable. Riding, flying and soaring appear as the proper motions for which man is fitted; relinquishing the world and the body is the sole demand:

> Jerusalem! Thou city built on high,
> Would God I were in thee;
> My yearning heart so longs for thee,
> It *is with me no more*;
> Far over hill and dale,
> Far over open fields,
> It *soars* above them all
> And *hastens from this world*.

The soul, again:

> In a moment it will *mount*
> *Up to the firmament*,
> As it *forsakes*, so softly and marvellously,
> The *Elements' abode*;
> It *rides in* Elijah's chariot
> With the *angelic host*,
> Who bear it in their hands
> Encompassing it around.[1]

This longing is Christian, but also Platonic and even pre-Platonic, for Euripides' marvellous Chorus depicts precisely the same images and the same craving:

> Could I take me to some cavern for mine hiding,
>   In the hill-tops where the Sun scarce hath trod;
> Or a cloud make the home of mine abiding,
>   As a bird among the bird-droves of God!
>
> Where a voice of living waters never ceaseth
>   In God's quiet garden by the sea,
> And Earth, the ancient life-giver, increaseth
>   Joy among the meadows, like a tree.[2]

3. "Thus the so-called belief in immortality is not generated by the previously discovered idea of a soul, but conversely":[3] the soul concept is modified in accord with the type of experience of the beyond; here again the search for the soul reveals itself as a seeking for God. To the

---

[1] Johann Mathäus Meyfart. Italics indicate the old images.
[2] Euripides, *Hippolytus*, 732 *ff.* (Murray).
[3] Preuss, *op. cit.*, 17.

Semite the beyond was unattainable, and eternal life was reserved for the gods;[1] the soul therefore could never become the bridge to the beyond, and an "immortality of the soul" was inconceivable.

For the Greeks, however, conditions were different:[2] in his soul man finds the *arche*, the primal substance, of immortality. The Platonic soul, which in its intermediate status has the capacity of being able to remember the eternal Ideas and to raise itself up to these (*anamnesis* and *Eros*) *must* be immortal: but to attain eternal life it must pursue the path of purification. The Euripidean question, whether "life be not death, and death be not life," dominates all these ultimate thoughts concerning the soul; the experience of death leads to eternal life: the abandonment of this world conquers another. "Thither" always means in the first place "hence"; and Goethe too has expressed this in his unfinished drama, *Prometheus*, in which life is apprehended as profoundly as is death:

Prometheus. When from the innermost and profoundest depth,
           Completely shattered, thou feelest all
           Of joy and grief that ever surged within thee,
           When, in this storm, thy swelling heart
           Would find relief in tears,
           Heightening its own passion,
           And all within thee resounds and thrill and shakes,
           When all thy senses fade,
           And thou seemest to sink
           Into dissolution,
           While all around thee is swallowed up in night,
           When, in thine inmost self,
           Thou embracest a world—
           Then it is that man dies.
Pandora.   O Father, let us die.

W. Bousset, *Die Himmelsreise der Seele* (*AR.* IV, 1901, 136 *ff.*).
J. G. Frazer, *The Belief in Immortality and the Worship of the Dead*, 1913 *ff.*
R. Holland, *Zur Typik der Himmelfahrt* (*AR.* XXIII, 1925, 207 *ff.*).
W. B. Kristensen, *Livet fra döden*, 1925.
K. Th. Preuss, *Tod und Unsterblichkeit im Glauben der Naturvölker*, 1930.

[1] *Gen.* iii. 22. Kristensen, *Livet fra döden*, 10.
[2] That is as regards the Orphic-Platonic Greeks; for the Homeric Greeks, as with the monistic mysticism of the pre-Socratics, everything was different; *cf.* Rohde, *op. cit.*, II, 149, 253; E. T. 24. W. F. Otto, *Die Götter Griechenlands*, and my Article, *SM.* 7, 1931.

CHAPTER 45

THE CREATURE

1. THE Greek idea of the soul seeks the superior power within man, even if it previously releases him from all the ponderousness of earth. What remains is divine and immortal. Both these expressions have the same meaning: the Greek spirit participated first of all in the Semitic fear of *hubris* that placed man equal to the gods (but in this respect racial distinctions will not suffice!), until the religions of Dionysus and Orpheus brought immortality and identity with the god, as *one* reality, within the human sphere.[1] The seed present in man needs only to be developed, the spark only to be blown into flame; although many hindrances must undoubtedly be overcome. But however difficult this may be, it is not impossible; and for the soul, confined within the cycle of births and fallen into bondage to matter, there is the hope of liberation:—

To stop the wheel and breathe once more from ill.[2]

This classical version of the idea of the soul is harshly opposed to those others, according to which there is nothing whatever in man which might be in itself divine, nothing that could ascend, nothing which, however purified, implied any genuine powerfulness. The phrase in the Anglican church's *General Confession*, "and there is no health in us", expresses with magnificent curtness equally the most primitive conviction that there subsists no powerfulness, and the essentially Christian principle that nothing could endure before God. Man is a unity, a complete whole, consisting not of two parts, one powerful and the other impotent; rather is everything in him powerless, while all is placed in the world by the Creator's sole Power. Man therefore is a *creature*, which as such came from God's hand, and which perhaps God does not permit to leave His hand. If then an eternal life awaits him, this can never be *attained*, but merely *granted* to him: to man, that is to say, life, and eternal life, are both given. In him, then, there is nothing whatever that may approach nearer than

[1] Rohde, *op. cit.*, II, 2 *ff.* E. T. 263 *f.*
[2] Olivieri, *Lamellae aureae*, 4. Kern, *Orph. Fragm.*, Fr. 229, p. 244.

anything else to Deity; rather all that is within him is equally remote from each and every power, unless Power condescends to raise him from death. Christian belief, therefore, recognizes not immortality but *resurrection*, that is, a new creation; man at no time nor place becomes God, but remains first and last a creature, his blessedness consisting precisely in his being a creature.

The Old Testament, further, knows nothing of a soul to be saved: the soul is man himself in his essential nature, in his powerfulness, exactly as in the primitive structure of the soul;[1] God saves man, or rather the people. It is just as little a matter of a divine soul as of immortality; nor is it otherwise in the Gospel. For Jesus, too, man's soul is his essential nature.[2] For St. Paul, however, the situation is certainly altered, and a definite dualism predominates; nevertheless the soul in itself is not immortal. Undeniably the "flesh" is depreciated in value, but it is not the soul that is contrasted with it as the powerful element, but the *spirit*. And this *pneuma* is not the highest stage in a trichotomous psychology, but the gift of God, the imparting from God to man, indeed the Lord Himself.[3]

He who has received the Spirit, therefore, is a "new creation": the first man, Adam, was a "living soul', but the last Adam a "quickening spirit".[4] The "pneumatized" man is therefore not man in accord with his own highest potency, but he who has received the *pneuma* from God and thereby has become a new creature. He *is* not spirit, but *has* spirit or is "in the spirit".

But it is one of the most remarkable facts in the whole of the history of religion that this concept of man as a creature, as a unity of body and soul from the hand of God, was in later times almost lost owing to the omnipotent influence of Greek thought. Even to-day the ideas of the "immortal soul" and of the valuelessness of the body are still widely supposed to be essentially Christian. This negates, however, not only the Israelite origin, but also the New Testament foundation, of Christianity.[5] Nevertheless the church has always been able to preserve in its essentials the genuinely Christian view of man as a totality, and by the emphatic stressing of the "resurrection of the body" has erected a dam against its own Platonism and asceticism. Still further, hardly any idea remained so confused within the Christian

---

[1] For an important and fundamental discussion of the primitive basis of the Israelitish idea of the soul *cf.* J. Pedersen, *Israel*, I, II, 1920, 68 *ff.* "The body is the soul in outward form", 125.

[2] *cf.* R. Bultmann, *Jesus*, 51.

[3] "The Lord is that Spirit"; 2 *Cor.* iii. 17.

[4] 1 *Cor.* xv. 45.

[5] W. Stählin, *Vom Sinn des Leibes*, 1930.

church as did that of the soul;[1] and its members were unanimous only
in rejecting the principle of *pre-existence* maintained by Plato and
Origen. But whether soul and body originate together at conception
(*Traducianism*), or whether God implants the soul in the embryo on
each occasion by a new creation (*Creationism*), Augustine was unable
to decide, and the church remained hesitant;[2] for in Traducianism it
was probably desired not to forfeit the unity of body and soul, and in
Creationism the special creation, the immediate derivation from God.
Certainly in the second instance, however, the unchristian dualism has
had to be accepted in addition.

2. It is indisputable, then, that the Israelite-Christian conception of
the soul is much closer to the primitive structure of soul-stuff than to
the Platonic. Man is not a soul in a body, but a body-soul; he *has* no
body, but *is* a body;[3] and his soul is not an ultimate power, but is he
in himself, either powerful or impotent. This soul structure, again,
has certainly not been entirely lacking in its philosophic and psychological expansion, even though the latter occupies an unimportant
place in the scheme of popular belief. And like Plato as regards Dualism,
so Aristotle discovered the philosophical and psychological schema for
the concept of totality. The soul is an *entelechy*—that is, completeness
with the subsidiary significance of activity or energy; it is the form
that realizes itself in the functions of the organized body.[4] This presupposes an organic unity between body and soul: the soul is no longer
a foreign element within the body, but an inner form. To-day also this
Aristotelian conception, which regards Dualism as untenable and
unchristian, repeatedly asserts itself. The soul is the "concealed unity
of the body", and the body "the total expression of the psychical".[5]
To a marked degree, indeed, in this retrogression Christian theology
allowed itself to be led by its own most pronounced opponents,
Nietzsche and his present-day adherents, Ludwig Klages and his school.[6]
For the spirit, that "invention of the Greeks", is there proscribed as
being a power hostile to life, the "unsouling of the body" is controverted and life's centre transferred to the "instincts". And that

---

[1] Schmalenbach, *op. cit.* 312. The so-called Christian Materialism in England forms
an exception, since it denies immortality and believes in both the death and the resuscitation of the *whole* man; Denis Samat, *Milton et le matérialisme chrétien en Angleterre*,
1928.
[2] Harnack, *History of Dogma*, III, 259.   [3] Stählin, *ibid.*
[4] Aristotle, *De Anima*, 2, 1.   [5] E. Brunner, *Gott und Mensch*, 1930, 75.
[6] H. Prinzhorn, *Leib-Seele-Einheit*, 1927.

this reorientation is no theoretical fiction of the philosopher and the psychologist is attested by the cult of the body as this prominently appears to-day in the swimming-bath, on the sports field and in the dance.

Until quite recent times, still further, the dispute between the Platonic-Christian and the Jewish-Christian concepts of the soul has prevented any logical development of psychology. For the assertion of the soul's divinity and immortality, and the manifold difficulties of psycho-physical parallelism, have long hindered science from seeking therein for man as a totality, and have led the psychologist astray into assigning it the status of mere consciousness; only to-day is science gradually discovering the way back to the soul—and therewith to its bounds!

But in the rejection of Dualism Christianity has a still weightier interest than the scientific and psychological;[1] for it recognizes an antithesis far surpassing in depth that between flesh and spirit; with all primitive thought, with Nietzsche and Klages indeed, it replaces this in the first instance by the contrast between Power and impotence. But then, when the Christian says "there is no health in us", he knows at the same time that he has not merely told himself this, but has said it to Someone else, and that it has thus become a confession. Then Will[2] takes the place of Power, both within him and apart from him: an únholy, sinful will opposes itself to a holy Will. And at that moment when this confession becomes prayer: "O God, have mercy!", then man, who sought the utmost depth in the soul, has found it in God.

[1] cf. Wach, Typen rel. Anthropol., 23.   [2] Chap. 9.

A. GEHLEN, Der Mensch, seine Natur und seine Stellung in der Welt, 1940.
ROMANO GUARDINI, Welt und Person, 1940.
G. VAN DER LEEUW, Der Mensch und die Religion, 1940.
H. PRINGHORN, Leib-Seele-Einheit, 1927.
W. SOMBART, Vom Menschen, 1938.

CHAPTER 46

THE COUNTRY OF THE SOUL

1. THE superiority sought by man in the soul is not only of another type than the ordinary life of every day, but also, as we have already observed, is localized elsewhere. For it is precisely a life "beyond"; and the most ancient Egyptian *Texts*, in fact, speak of "that land" whither the dead go and where "to eternity they neither hunger nor thirst".[1]

To begin with, then, the country of the soul exists in the world: it is wholly an earthly Paradise. Somewhere or other there is a sinister region, an infamous heath, a dark forest, a mysterious cavern: there is a *descensus Averni*, an entrance to the underworld, a *Plutonion*. Alternatively, the entire domain is regarded as "beyond", *chthonic*, as the Greeks expressed this; in Greece and Southern Italy they could point to many of these "birdless lakes".[2] The whole area around Cumae, for example, was such a realm of the dead, a country of the soul.

Thus to the consciousness of man in primitive times and in antiquity there was nothing absurd in the idea that such a "beyond" was solitary and untrodden, and yet at the same time quite close to human dwellings, and indeed within reach in case of need. This is wholly in accordance with the "catathymia", or subjectively oriented attitude, of primitive mentality, which experiences values in its environment that can transform this either into the infernal regions or into Paradise.[3] Whatever lies outside the tilled land of the village, the enclosed home possessions, is "uncanny", the abode of demons, the sojourn of the dead. To Northern peoples moors, bogs and mountains, and to the inhabitants of the South steppes and deserts, pre-eminently appeared as such localities: the dwelling-place is *Midgard*, around this is *Utgard*, and there begins the realm of the dead. Its frontier may be removed very far away, even below the horizon; nonetheless it can be reached; the hero of the fairy tale goes into the other world as a matter of course. Further, this is regarded not merely spatially, but temporally also: as

[1] *Pyramidentexte* (Sethe), 382; *cf.* further the Antef stela, *Urkunden*, IV, 965; the "fear of the other country".

[2] ἄορνοι λίμναι; Rohde, *op. cit.*, I, 213; Ninck, *Wasser*, 76 *ff*.

[3] "Catathymia" is Kretschmer's term describing the mental state in which everything is perceived in accord with one's own subjective mood.

soon as night spreads its dark shadows, the world belongs completely to the "beyond" where everything is uncanny.[1]

The dreadful feature in "that land", however, is not always its chief characteristic; it may equally be a beautiful, marvellous country, a Paradise—that is, a lovely garden. Thus the Paradise of *Genesis* is an oasis as contrasted with the steppes which Adam had to till after the Fall.[2] The garden is far removed in space, and also by time as with the Golden Age; there the gods reside and the blessed dead.[3] It is the "garden of the gods" of Euripides, "the ancient garden of Phoibos" of Sophocles,[4] the Elysium whither the heroes are carried away, the "islands of the blessed": "the Elysian plain and the world's end, where is Rhadamanthus of the fair hair, where life is easiest for men. No snow is there, nor yet great storm, nor any rain; but always ocean sendeth forth the breeze of the shrill West to blow cool on men".[5] Greece knew several soul-realms of this type, whither one journeyed "neither by ships nor by land", and where neither disease nor destroying age ruled, where a sacred people lived released from all misery and strife.[6] Israel too recognized the realm of the future and of remoteness:

> And there instead of broad streams circling round
>   we have the glorious Eternal as our river,
>   a river never raided by a galley,
>   sailed by no ships of war;
>   the Eternal himself rules us,
>   the Eternal is our captain,
>   the Eternal is our king,
>   he, he alone, defends us.[7]

All the magnificence of the world exists in the soul's country, and the familiar "fools' Paradise" is the comically sounding echo of a much sublimer language;[8] all the dubious features of terrestrial existence are completely absent from the land of the soul. There Pindar finds the

---

[1] Grönbech, *op. cit.*, II, 7 *f.*
[2] *cf.* Edv. Lehmann, *La pensée du Jahviste, SM.* 3, 1927.
[3] Lietzmann, *Weltheiland*, 44; Preuss, *Tod und Unsterblichkeit*, 30.
[4] *cf.* Otto, *Götter Griechenlands*, 81.
[5] *Odyssey*, IV, 564 *ff.* (Butcher); *cf.* P. Capelle, *Elysium und die Inseln der Seligen*, *AR.* 26, 1928.
[6] Pindar, *Pyth.*, 10, 38, with reference to the country of the Hyperboreans; *cf.* O. Schröder, *AR.* 8, 1905, 69. G. van der Leeuw, *Goden en Menschen*, 92 *ff.*
[7] *Isaiah* xxxiii. 21 *ff.*; *cf.* H. Gunkel, *Das Märchen im Alten Testament*, 1921, 47.
[8] H. Thimme, *Das Märchen*, 1909, 91 *f.*

Muses' domain, the virgins' dance, the voice of the flutes, and the sound of the lyre.[1] Nor does food lack there; the goodness of "that country" is manifested first of all in its abundant viands. The Egyptians, for instance, believed in a "field of food", and also a "field of rushes" into which the departed, who could recite his magical formulas, entered with joy: "I know Ra's field of rushes: the surrounding wall is of bronze; the height of its Lower Egyptian barley is four ells, one ell its ear and three ells the stalk; the height of its spelt is seven ells, two ells the ear, and five ells its stalk."[2] From time immemorial, still further, the West has been regarded as the region of the world in which these splendours are to be found, whether they are localized in heaven or, as probably was originally the case, on earth. For in the West the sun sets; and there man built the great cities of the dead, there the "beauteous West", in the guise of a woman with lovely hair, makes its friendly advance to meet the dead.[3] But frequently all the emphasis falls on the decline that the sun, and also man, experience in the West. In that case the East of the world receives precedence: in the Eastern heaven stands the tree of the gods, "that high sycamore on which the gods sit, the tree of life on which they live";[4] its fruits nourish the dead. In the case of Egypt, indeed, it is often difficult to decide definitely whether the land of the soul is earthly or heavenly; it is the destiny of the blessed king to travel to and fro in heaven with the same ease as on earth.[5] But this at least is certain: the country of the dead lies always in the beyond, even when it is on earth: however near it may be, it is nevertheless always far away. The Egyptian king flies away from man: "He flies, he flies away from you men like the geese; he frees his hands from you like a falcon, he tears his body away from you like a hawk."[6] Hence the land of the dead is sought on some distant island or lofty mountain, behind the Northern mists, in heaven or the depths of the earth, and everywhere else where man feels he is not at home, and where on that account an eternal home might be supposed to be.[7] That in this way different localities often arose simultaneously troubled neither primitive mentality nor the thought of antiquity, as has already been observed in the case of Egypt; and the inhabitants of Eddystone

---

[1] *Pyth.* 10, 38.
[2] *The Book of the Dead*, Chap. 109, in Bertholet, *Lesebuch*, 10 [Kees], 52.
[3] *Pyramidentexte* (Sethe), 276 *ff.*   [4] *ibid.*, 916.
[5] *ibid.*, 186, 363, 1249.   [6] *ibid.*, 1484.
[7] Thus Pylos, on the Western sea-coast, was regarded by the most ancient inhabitants of the Peloponnesus as the sojourn of the dead: "in Pylos amid the dead", *Iliad*, 5, 397; *cf.* U. von Wilamowitz-Möllendorf, *Der Glaube der Hellenen*, I, 1931, 337 *f.*

Island (Solomon Islands) also seek the beyond in a distant country, but at the same time in a cave on their own island.[1]

2. Much the most preferable place, however, for this near-and-far, sought by the soul, is the underworld, or rather in the earth: there is the home of the mother and of all life.[2] Of course burial customs, wherever these prevailed, contributed to this subterranean idea of the beyond: the dead man is in the grave, that is beneath the earth. But so long as the grave remains a mere grave, as at a certain phase of the Egyptian viewpoint for which the dead man's whole life is spent in the grave, and his bliss consists just in being able to "go forth by day", the concept of the underworld is not yet really present. The "beyond", therefore, in the case of Egypt, was much rather the life of "day" which was bestowed on the dead than their subterranean sojourn;[3] and of a beyond in the earth we can speak only when the near-and-far is stressed in one way or another, whether *in malam* or *in bonam partem*. Such ideas of the underworld are to be found, as is well known, in Greece, the Old Testament and often elsewhere.[4]

Besides the concepts of the earth and the grave, the observation of the heavens by night has contributed to the view that was taken of the underworld, and thus in ancient Egypt the *Duat* or *Da-t* was simultaneously the heavens by night, and the underworld;[5] the latter was a kind of counter-heaven, the contrasted image of the dark earth,[6] while from the nightly heavens the sun rises like vegetation from the earth.[7] In this way there arose in Egypt the remarkable idea of the sun nightly traversing the underworld (or the night heaven), and of the dead greeting it on its entrance into the realm of the shades. The hue of the underworld, however, was generally gloomy: it was indeed the realm of shadow, as well as of shades, into which the soul descended. None the less the conviction never completely disappeared that this gloomy underworld was at the same time the mother's fruitful womb.

[1] W. H. R. Rivers, "The Primitive Conception of Death", *Hibbert Journal*, X, 1912, 393 *ff.*; *cf.* some remarkable examples in Wilken, *op. cit.*, III, 49 *ff.*
[2] Chap. 10.   [3] [*cf.* Maspero, *Popular Stories of Ancient Egypt*, lxi.]
[4] C. Clemen, *Das Leben nach dem Tode im Glauben der Menschheit* (1920), 42 *ff.*
[5] W. B. Kristensen, *Livet efter döden*, 1896, 57 *ff.* J. Lieblein, *Gammel-aegyptisk Religion*, III, 1885, 29.
[6] *Pyramidentexte* (Sethe), 820, 1275. In Egypt heaven, as the land of the soul, was more and more displaced by the West and the underworld; *cf.* H. Kees, *Totenglaube und Jenseitsvorstellungen der alten Ägypter*, 1926, 80, 220 *f.*
[7] Preuss, *Geistige Kultur*, 42 *f.* K. Th. Preuss, *Die Nayarit-Expedition*, I, 1912, XXV *ff.*

3. The Egyptian king who flies away from men "is no longer on earth, he attains heaven".[1] Indeed, as we have just seen, the heavens were not separated from the underworld, which originally was no other than the night heaven; but in course of time, in Egypt and elsewhere, heaven became increasingly the exclusive abode of the gods, as of the dead;[2] and this, in fact, precisely in the sense of that psychological dualism[3] which assigns the body to the earth, but the soul to the ether.

Thus almost from the beginning the heavens were "Heaven", that is the fullness of pleasure and well-being. Certainly, in the case of many peoples there still remained celestial dangers; but the good preponderated, and heaven was never the sombre desert such as the underworld was frequently depicted to be. For there is the home of the sun, although it is true too that the abundant fertility, enjoyed by the earth, is never to be found. However dismal its habitations may be, still the earth is always the bestower of new life, while the heavens are unfruitful, a brilliant culmination, but not a rebirth.

4. Exactly in the same way therefore as, in the dualistic structure, the soul becomes ever emptier and more contentless until finally its purity is equivalent to sheer nullity, so the soul's country can become divested of every visible and palpable concreteness. For from the beginning it was remote and pathless; and in being completely spiritualized it became the place that had no position whatever, the immeasurable and unlocalizable point. To this, indeed, the Platonic vision was an approximation—the relation to the "beyond" consists in man remembering not what he has experienced but what he has actually seen. "They might have seen beauty shining in brightness, when, with the happy band following in the train of Zeus, as we philosophers, or of other gods as others did, they saw a vision and were initiated into mysteries which may be truly called most blessed, and which we celebrated in our state of innocence; having no experience of evils as yet to come; admitted to the sight of apparitions innocent and simple and calm and happy, shining in pure light, pure ourselves and not yet enshrined in that living tomb which we carry about, now that we are imprisoned in the body, like an oyster in his shell."[4] And Buddhism goes very much farther in prohibiting for itself every type of "something". *Nirvana*, the "extinction" of every one of life's activities, the

---

[1] *Pyramidentexte*, 890.   [2] Clemen, *op. cit.*, 55 *ff*.
[3] Chap. 43.   [4] Plato, *Phaedrus*, 250 (Jowett).

cessation of detested rebirth, still shows the outlines of the blessed isles, but dissolved into complete nullity: "where there is no something, no permanence, the island, the unique, is named Nirvana, freed from age and death".[1]

This consistent spiritualizing of the country of the soul, simultaneously with an ever advancing enfeebling of "this side", as also of "this side" in the beyond, is opposed to the other tendency which seeks the soul's true home on "this side" itself. Man then finds his beyond in himself: not in a height dimension far above life, but in a depth dimension within himself.[2] Thus speaks modern Immanentism in many keys: but still more concrete and still less Platonic is Nietzsche, because he appeals not from the beyond to the innermost ground of the soul, but from the beyond directly to "this side": "I conjure you, my brethren, *remain true to the earth*, and believe not those who speak unto you of superearthly hopes! Poisoners are they, whether they know it or not."[3]

[1] Oldenberg, *Lehre der Upanishaden*, 311.
[2] Joh. Wendland, *Die neue Diesseitsreligion*, 1914, 8.
[3] *Thus Spake Zarathustra*, 7. (Foulis' Edition.)

CHAPTER 47

THE DESTINY OF THE SOUL

1. PRIMARILY life is a cycle, uninterrupted by death if only the correct rites are observed:[1] "I live after I am dead, like Ra," the sun-god,[2] if only the requisite celebrations have been executed. As has already been observed, *burial* is the most important of these celebrations; and similarly *mourning*, which in the entire primitive world had a ritual character. Man laments not merely to relieve his grief, but above all because he thereby assists the life of the departed over the critical point; as one Egyptian *Text* says: "I am one of the mourners for Osiris, who make him victorious over his enemies."[3] This victory over death is, of course, very differently described in accordance with the predominating idea of the soul. The simplest concept is that of resurrection in its literal sense, so that to the Egyptian dead it was said: "Arise: thou hast shaken off the earth from thy flesh."[4]

More complicated, however, is the idea according to which a *passport* is given to the dead man, guaranteeing his entry into the beyond; and the incantations placed in the grave with the departed, the most remarkable collection of which constitutes the so-called Egyptian *Book of the Dead*, served this purpose. They were *Guides* for the dead man, like the little golden tablets of the Orphics,[5] but not in any rationalistic sense; they were not only a kind of celestial *Baedeker* (although of course they were that as well!), but above all a key to the gate of the beyond; in Iran sacred formulas were whispered into the dying person's ear, while at the same time some of the holy beverage of the gods (*haoma*) was poured into his mouth. The passport to heaven and the *viaticum* are associated: Lehmann gives the text of a Chinese Buddhist passport to heaven which in official language prepares the way for a dead person: "Instructions for the woman Shan: as soon as thou receivest this passport, thou must prepare to set out for the place of the blessed, where thou mayest expect great bliss and peace."[6]

In still another way the *sacrificial cult* guarantees the destiny of the

---

[1] Here, and also on what follows, *cf.* Chap. 22.
[2] *Totenbuch* (Naville), *Kap.* 38, Note 8.
[3] *ibid.*, *Kap.* 1, 11 *f.*
[4] *Pyramidentexte* (Sethe), 654; *cf.* 1067 *f.*
[5] Olivieri, *Lamellae aureae.* Kern, *Orph. Fragm.*
[6] *Textbuch*[1], 23 *f.*

dead, although this term is perhaps somewhat magniloquent. For this cult it was sufficient that the life of the departed should be nourished by his relatives or their representatives, either in the grave or wherever he appeared; and in ancient Egypt it was "the son, who loves him", who sustained his father's life by sacrifices to the dead. Afterwards, however, when this sacred filial duty was left more and more to the professional priesthood, the expression became the settled name for the priest of the dead: "thine heir is on thy throne; he cultivates the grain crop for thee", they exclaimed to the dead king to pacify him.[1]

To the same category pertain masses for the dead and *oratio pro defunctis*. Here no longer the mere existence, but the salvation of the dead person (although it is difficult to separate these two ideas completely!), is assured by sacrifice and prayer; and this custom is "transposed"[2] to quite different connections when prayer for the dead expresses the persisting union of the members of the congregation before God, and the desire only to appear when together. Then the idea may even arise that the dead never release the living and that their own bliss is perturbed by the absence of those yet alive, so that they intercede for them:

> "I wish that he were come to me,
>   For he will come", she said.
> "Have I not pray'd in solemn Heaven?
>   On earth, has he not pray'd?"[3]

2. The nature of this life, thus gained, is very varied. Among primitive peoples eternity is usually not attached to it; the idea is altogether too abstract, and hence only very long life is spoken of,[4] which may be simply a continuation of earthly existence in so far as the departed experience just the same needs, pursue the same aims and are exposed to similar perils as are the living (and also, together with these, the possibility of again dying—the "second death"). But very often, when compared with terrestrial life, it represents an advance either for good or conversely; and an almost endless series of examples can be cited. Instead of this, however, I shall select a few that are characteristic: the African Yoruba, in the first place, have no high estimation of the beyond: "a place in this world is better than in that of the spirits."[5] And similarly Achilles: "Nay, speak not com-

---

[1] *Pyramidentexte*, 1388.   [2] [On "transposition" *cf.* pp. 31, Note, and 610.]
[3] Rossetti, *The Blessed Damozel*.   [4] Preuss, *Tod und Unsterblichkeit*, 24.
[5] Alviella, *Idée de Dieu*, 205.

fortably to me of death, O great Odysseus. Rather would I live on ground as the hireling of another, with a landless man who had no great livelihood, than bear sway among all the dead that be departed."[1] The life beyond is a shadow existence, not a complete life, as in the case, too, of the Israelite *Sheol*; even praising God, the highest activity of the living, was denied to the dead in the underworld.[2]

An advance to the good, however, is implied by the lot of the dead in the many ideas of the Paradise type, and as a simple example I select the Egyptian concept of the tree in the West to which the dead person attains, and under which he seats himself in the form of the *ba* bird (but frequently also as a "complete" man). A goddess, originally probably only the power of the tree, the goddess of the oasis, then Nut the goddess of heaven (for here the earthly and the celestial Paradise are already confused) bends down towards him from the tree, hands him food and pours water for him from a pitcher;[3] and thus the dead man receives divine life—"food of eternal life".

3. The soul's destiny, then, when differentiated in this way, depends on various circumstances. Since continued existence in itself, and also the enhancement of life's capacities, are both alike potencies, they are at first conditioned by the power possessed by the living person himself. Among primitive peoples, therefore, the souls of the dead often receive powerful life only when they have already had this during their lifetime;[4] whoever possesses much *mana* enjoys a better fate after death too,[5] and thus warriors, hunters and child-bearers, who were manifesting their potency at the moment of death, are more fortunate than other dead people.[6] The Tongans of Polynesia, again, assume immortality only for their nobles,[7] and the Greeks also allotted a particularly happy destiny to those who were already in possession of some extraordinary family *mana*: "But thou, Menelaus, son of Zeus, art not ordained to die and meet thy fate in Argos, the pasture-land of horses, but the deathless gods will convey thee to the Elysian plain and the world's end"—whereupon there follows the description of Elysium— "for thou hast Helen to wife, and thereby they deem thee to be son of Zeus."[8]

[1] *Odyssey*, XI, 488 *ff*. (Butcher).　　　[2] *Ps.* vi. 6; cxv. 7; *Isaiah* xxxviii. 18.
[3] *Totenbuch* (Naville), *Kap.* 59–63.　　[4] Preuss, *Glauben und Mystik*, 30.
[5] Tiele-Söderblom, *op. cit.* GENERAL LITERATURE, p. 19 *ante*.
[6] Söderblom, *Gottesglaube*, 57 *ff*.; Grönbech, *op. cit.*, II, 166.
[7] Frazer, *The Belief in Immortality*, II, 146.
[8] *Odyssey*, IV, 561 *ff*.; *cf.* Capelle, *AR.* XXV, 1927, 258 *ff*.

To a great extent, too, the type of death decides the *post mortem* power; and in Egypt it was believed that death from drowning or by snake bite made man divine, or a kind of hero.[1] To the manner of dying, however, man can make his own contribution, and Egyptian burial was a magnificent attempt to make the dead person, in his type of death, and consequently of his resurrection, equal to the god Osiris; for whoever had died like Osiris (originally, had been drowned!), been dismembered and buried, shared also in the "justification", in the blessed destiny of the god, while another "celebration" assimilated the lot of the departed to that of the sun-god. Among other peoples different ideas predominated, but the rites after death almost always mean an endowing of the dead person with power; thus burning the corpse implies hastening the severance of soul from body—recalling the dualistic structure!—bringing about the ultimate death and therewith rendering possible a new life.[2] Interment, again, signifies a renewed entrance into the mother-womb of the earth, upon which a rebirth can follow.[3]

4. The gradation of powerfulness after death then proceeds according to the standard of good or evil conduct during life: sin[4] decreases the power of the dead, while righteous behaviour strengthens it; and the earliest appearance of immortality, morally and religiously conditioned in this manner, is to be found in Egypt. In the celebrated Chapter 125 of *The Book of the Dead* the departed enters the hall of the two truths. There Osiris is enthroned, with forty-two assessors, as the judge of the dead. The departed commences with the assurance that he knows full well the names of the god and the assessors; thus he casts a spell on them. Then he continues: "Behold, I come unto thee and bring thee the truth, and have avoided sin against thee: I have not sinned against man, I have made no man miserable, I have not slaughtered the god's cattle. . . . I have committed no murder. . . . I have not shortened the ell measure. . . . I have not stolen milk from the mouth of little children. . . ." *etc.*; a "negative confession of sins", as the whole utterance has been aptly called. But now there again follows a second assurance of powerfulness in the purely magical sense: "I am pure", thrice repeated, and the renewed avowal that the person before the

---

[1] The drowned were called *hsiw*—"the exalted"; Osiris is the type. F. Ll. Griffith, *Zeitschr. f. ägypt. Sprache*, 46, 1909, 132 *ff*. W. A. Murray, *ibid.*, 51, 1914, 127 *ff*, G. van der Leeuw, *Godsvoorstellingen*, 67.

[2] Rohde, *op. cit.*, I, 27 *ff*. English Translation, 21.

[3] Chap. 10; *cf.* further Otto, *Götter Griechenlands*, 33.   [4] Chap. 66, 78.

court knows the accurate names of the assessors—and they are terrifying demons! Again a negative confession follows: "I have not stolen the god's property, I have not lied . . ." *etc.*, whereon the adjuration once more occurs with the aid of the names.[1] After this speech of the deceased comes the actual judgment of the dead. This we learn not from the *Texts*, but even better from the drawings accompanying them: a monster, a sort of Cerberus, sits before the throne of Osiris, in front a crocodile, behind, a rhinoceros and in the middle a lion: this will devour the departed if the gods' assembly condemns him. In the centre of the Hall of Truth there is a balance on which the dead man's heart is weighed against the symbol of truth; the god Anubis is "master of the scales", and Thoth the clerk of the court, while the judges are at the same time the executioners, holding knives in their hands.[2] The dead person who has been acquitted is "justified", that is, originally, his "voice has prevailed": he has recited the incantations in the correct manner; but the expression (*makhrw*) also means victorious, and ultimately blessed. The departed receives the "crown of justification" from the god's hand.[3]

It is scarcely necessary to discuss the many and extremely various ideas depicting the bliss or the damnation of the deceased. They are known universally. The dead are admitted to heaven and hell in accord with their powerfulness which on its part, again, may be either magical-religious or morally-religious, or both combined; and the very widespread *motif* of the *Two Ways* open to man after death clearly expresses this view of the soul's destiny. Heaven and hell, again, have been depicted by the most varied peoples with the utmost detail, and a very fine description of simple Christian belief in heaven and hell is given by the fifteenth-century poet François Villon, when he introduces his old mother as saying:

> *Femme je suis, pauvrette et ancienne,*
> *Qui rien ne sais; oncques lettre ne lus;*
> *Au moûtier vois, dont suis paroissienne,*
> *Paradis peint, où sont harpes et lus,*
> *Et un enfer, où damnés sont boullus:*
> *L'un me fait peur, l'aultre, joie et liesse.*[4]

---

[1] For the most important Sections of the *Text cf.* Lehmann-Haas, *Textbuch*, 272 *ff.*
[2] Haas, *Bilderatlas, Ägypt. Religion*, Fig. 138.   [3] Haas, *ibid.*, Fig. 140.
[4] *Ballade que Villon fit à la requête de sa mère pour prier Notre-Dame*: "I am a poor old woman, too ignorant to read a single letter. In the parish church I see Paradise painted, with its harps and lutes, and Hell, where the damned are being boiled. The one terrifies me, but the other gladdens and rejoices me."

If the ultimate endowment with power was thus sought in heaven, the idea of hell was also something more than merely voluptuous indulgence in the consciousness of one's own impotence. On the contrary man always retained the feeling, even when infernal punishment was regarded as eternal, that he could attain to power again through hell itself or, at all events, escape from his own impotence; and a modern mind, whose egotism has become abnormal, confirms this in strikingly profound terms: "I have learnt to know hell, and I surmise something about God. Now I also know what the medieval painters meant by their pictures of the torments of hell. These are no sadistic fancies, but genuine representations of the first stage of the way of salvation. . . ." "For this reason our earth, as the unavowed hell, is a double hell; and if we fall into the genuine, honest hell, then we are already half in heaven."[1]

It would therefore be quite wrong to attempt to derive the whole cycle of ideas about heaven and hell, and their thousand parallels, from the hope of reward or fear of punishment. For in the first place it is no affair whatever of recompense or penalty, but of power; and this power has accumulated during our earthly life: "Blessed are the dead which die in the Lord from henceforth: Yea, saith the Spirit, that they may rest from their labours; and their works do follow them."[2] Thus "works" can enhance or diminish power, deify us or deprive us of divinity.[3] But power is never taken as purely moral and never as purely eudemonistic; it is always primarily religious. And the most vivid descriptions of infernal torments are only the foil against which human longing for deliverance and trust in salvation arise:

> While the wicked are confounded,
> Doom'd to flames of woe unbounded,
> Call me with Thy Saints surrounded.

Here the oppressive power of the *tremenda majestas* and the *fascinans* of unconditioned redemption fuse into one:

> King of Majesty tremendous,
> Who dost free salvation send us,
> Fount of pity, then befriend us!

---

[1] Künkel, *Einführung in die Charakterkunde,* 180 *f.*
[2] *Rev.* xiv. 13; *cf.* E. Maass, *Orpheus,* 1895, 217 *ff.* C. Clemen, *Religionsgeschichtliche Erklärung des Neuen Testaments*[2], 1924, 152, 317.
[3] Steinmann, *Der religiöse Unsterblichkeitsglaube,* 50.

5. An Indian soothsayer possesses the "death's head formula". He drums on a skull and then communicates the dead man's place of rebirth. He also approaches Gotama Buddha, who lays the skulls of three beings before him; and the soothsayer asserts correctly that they have been reborn respectively in hell, in man's world, and in heaven. But when the Buddha shows him the skull of a man who has passed into extinction (*Nirvana*) the seer can find no answer at all; "he saw neither limit nor end", and with perspiring brow and shamed expression he had to confess that his knowledge failed.[1] For here human yearning is directed to neither the cyclic continuation of life, nor its advance to either good or evil, but against life itself. Power is striven for in complete impotence, in extinction: the life cycle must be reversed, the wheel of births stayed. Thus no curiosity as to the soul's destiny ever agitates Buddhism; it finds its bliss in release from every lot: "From the negation of Being and Non-Being . . . the presage of Nirvana meets the gaze of the pious man, who strove not to solve its riddle but to lose himself within it. The way in which thought silently turned away from this enigma may seem feeble and faint-hearted to the Faustian yearning to know 'the force that binds creation's inmost energies'. But how completely had Buddhism rejected such a longing! An intrinsic greatness, and indeed a unique poetry, subsist within, as man stands here before the veiled image of the Beyond, free from the desire to unveil the glory unseen by any eye, while in the depths of his own being, silently and blissfully, he experiences this glory itself."[2] In a Buddhist fairy tale, again, a king sees two mango trees, one standing tranquil but barren while the other, which had been richly laden with fruit, is completely plundered and its branches broken into small fragments. Then the king realizes that "life in the home"[3] is similar to that of the fruitful tree, rich but quickly poor, and he resolves henceforth to be like the sterile tree: "for me," he confesses, "the miserable hut of the maternal womb has been destroyed; torn asunder is the bond of rebirth in the three forms of being; the dunghill of the cycle of births has been cleaned; the sea of tears has been dried, the wall of bones thrown down. For me there is no longer rebirth."[4] Here life's power has turned against itself.

[1] W. Caland, *Boeddhistische Verhalen*, 1923, 33 *f.*

[2] Oldenberg, *Lehre der Upanishaden*, 332.

[3] Chap. 34.

[4] E. and H. Lüders, *Buddhistische Märchen*, 1921, No. 36; *cf.* the similar, but less passionate ideas in Orphism in Rohde, *Psyche*; van der Leeuw, *Goden en Menschen*.

6. Human thought which, in doubt or sullenness, thus withdraws from the enhancing of power as from self-destruction, often finds consolation in the return to the maternal womb of the life of the Universe. In this respect primeval and modern viewpoints encounter each other: I quote both an Egyptian *Pyramid Text* and a poem of to-day. The conflict between the two gods, Horus and Set, is adjusted by the god *Atmu* (here his name means "all the gods"), and their wounds are healed. The dead man implores the god to have pity on him also, as he has shown mercy to the two combatants, and receives the answer: "there is no divine seed that I could allow to fall into ruin; thou also shalt not be destroyed".[1] Nothing will come to destruction: everything is securely preserved by the god of the Universe. Here death and life both lose their true meaning: in their eternal change, whose perpetuation was originally also the aim of Egyptian belief in immortality, they are now only two transitional points which the all dominating divine life traverses in its measured rhythm. Similarly Heracleitus, for whom too death signified only a turning-point, so that death and life meet in the eternal flux: "it is death to souls to become water, and death to water to become earth; but from earth comes water, and from water soul";[2] "mortals are immortals, and immortals are mortals, the one living the other's death and dying the other's life".[3]

But even after two or three thousand years this attitude to life has remained precisely the same: all that lives, lives eternally in God; there is no death, just as there is no life; there is but life or death, whichever one will: the term is a matter of indifference. All this means that there is only Power, whatever form the destiny of soul and body may take; and the most impressive presentation of this belief I have always found in the poet's magnificent *Song of the Sower*:

> Make your stride rhythmic! Likewise your swing!
> Yet awhile will Earth stay young.
> There falls a grain of corn. It dies. It rests.
> Sweet is its rest, and good.

[1] *Pyramidentexte* (Sethe), 140 *ff.*; *cf.* van der Leeuw, *Godsvoorstellingen*, 53 *ff.*; *cf.* also the very fine and appropriate version of the Egyptian belief in immortality given in his own day by P. Pierret, although this has received slight notice from Egyptologists: "There is no death in the world, but merely transformations; bodies are incessantly metamorphosed owing to molecular interchanges, but without the loss of a single atom, and with no annihilation ever occurring"; *Le Dogme de la Résurrection chez les anciens Egyptiens*, 17. By replacing here the modernizing expressions "atom" and "molecule" by the "seed" of our *Text*, which was unknown to Pierret, we should obtain the genuine Egyptian standpoint.   [2] Diels, *Fr.* 36 (Cornford).
[3] Diels, *Fr.* 62 (Burnet); *cf.* Rohde, *op. cit.*, II, 149, 253. E. T. 368 *f.*

Here thrusts another upward through the soil.
Again good: for sweet is the light.
And nought is lost from the World,
While to all there comes what pleases God.[1]

In strange and yet scarcely surprising manner the firm foundation of this primal, and yet eternally young, faith in the securely fixed and enduring earth is expressed here also.

7. Continuation, enhancing, denial and also pacification of Powerfulness: all this is repudiated by that weary scepticism which, at all times and in all quarters, in the country of the soul imagines the land that knows no return and places its destiny on just the same footing as that of the leaves on the trees. Rather than cite many examples of this, a few expressions of Egyptian lassitude of power will amply suffice which, in that land of passionate faith in resurrection, speak all the more eloquently. In *The Songs of the Harpist*, then, some ancient Egyptian table songs have been transmitted to us which struck that characteristic, half melancholy and half frivolous, note in the midst of the joyousness of the funeral banquet, which we discern also in *Ecclesiastes* and *Omar Khayyám*. Everything that, according to Egyptian faith, was invigorating in the struggle against death, is here derided as powerless, while on the other hand fleeting life is praised. Correct burial, knowledge of the formulas, the "beloved son's" sacrifices for the dead: it all avails nothing:

How well have things gone for that good prince (the dead man).
It is most providential
That these disappear
And depart, while others remain.
Thus was it since the time of our forefathers,
And of the gods, that were of old:
In their pyramids they rest,
The nobles and the great together,
Buried in their pyramids;
And they have built for themselves funerary temples.
But their places no longer exist.
What has become of them?
I knew the sayings of Imhotep and Hordedef (famous sages),
Wise ones and celebrated.
Observe their places:

[1] Conrad Ferdinand Meyer, *Gedichte*, 1922, 78.

The walls are destroyed,
Their places exist no longer.
It is as though they had never been.
None returns thence,
To tell us how they fare,
Or to report their fate to us,
So as to calm our hearts . . .
Until we also go
Thither where they have gone.

Then the mood apparently changes, though like a heavy death-knell, like a *basso ostinato*, despair repeatedly rings through all the joyfulness:

Let thy heart take courage and forget!
Be of good cheer and take thy pleasure,
So long as thou livest.
Sprinkle myrrh on thy head,
Garb thyself in fine linen
Steeped in costly perfumes,
In the pure frankincense of the gods!
Increase thy pleasure!
Let not thy heart grow weary!
Follow thy wishes and thy desires;
Direct thy earthly fate
According to the dictates of thine own heart . . .
Until the day of lamentation comes to thee—
But he whose heart is stilled (the dead man) will not hear it,
And he who lies in the grave will not feel the affliction.
Celebrate the joyful day!
Sleep it not away!
For lo! none can take with him his possessions.
Lo! none returns who has gone hence.[1]

Or in one variant:

Celebrate the joyful day!
Enjoy the scent of the finest frankincense,
Wreathe lotus flowers about thy shoulders and thy neck,
And about those of the beloved who resides in thy heart,
And who sits by thy side.
Let music and song resound!
Cast the evil things behind thee.
Think only of joy,

[1] Another translation in Ad. Erman, *The Literature of the Ancient Egyptians*, 133.

Until the day of death arrives
When man goes to that land which loveth silence;
Then shall thy heart be at rest.
For life is not prolonged,
Neither for him who possessed granaries,
And bread for sacrifices and gifts,
Nor for him who had nought:
It is not prolonged, not for one single hour.

Or again:

Those who built in red granite,
Who built for themselves a burial chamber,
Who desired to be noble by erecting splendid buildings,
Who are pictured as gods:
Their sacrificial tables are empty,
As are those of the weary to death, who died by the river bank,
Without leaving behind them even one person to honour them . . .[1]

A weary mood, weary to death, prevails, which expressed itself in
ancient Egypt in the fine *Dialogue of him who is weary of life with his
soul*:[2] death he greets as a friend. In Israel, again, it was the writers of
Ecclesiastes and *Job* who experienced this weariness. The cycle of
natural life, that basic ground of all primitive hope, avails nothing here:

There is hope for a tree that is felled;
    it may flourish again,
    the shoots of it need not fail;
though its root decays in the soil,
    though its stump is dead in the ground,
it may bud at the scent of water,
    and put out boughs like a plant.
But man dies and departs,
    man breathes his last—and where is he?
Like the water of a vanished lake,
    like a dry, drained river,
man lies down, never to arise,
    never to waken, though the skies wear out,
    never to stir out of his slumber.[3]

The domain of darkness and of deepest gloom permits of no return.[4]
Compared with this despair, Greek and Roman scepticism appears

---

[1] *cf.* the parallel, *Job* iii. 11 *ff*.
[3] *Job* xiv. 7 *ff*. (Moffat).
[2] *cf.* Erman, *ibid.*, 86 *ff*.
[4] *Job* x. 20 *ff*.

colder and less tragic; "for though altogether to disown a divine nature in human virtue were impious and base, so again to mix heaven with earth is ridiculous."[1] And the sober spirit of Rome found in the course of the stars, which granted hope to the Egyptian, the most forcible refutation of any expectation of the beyond: "it is a double evil and a twofold madness to denounce destruction to the heaven and the stars, which we leave just as we find them, and to promise eternity to ourselves, who are dead and extinct—who, as we are born, so also perish."[2]

But deep and heavy as the death-knell, there rings out in religion again and again the tragic lament: could we only escape from the struggle for power! could we only have peace before the Power of God as before our own! Only peace!

> Why didst thou ever take me from the womb?
> Why could I not have died there in the dark?
> Then I would be as though I had not been,
>   borne from the womb straight to the tomb.
> My days are few! let me alone awhile,
>   that I may have life bright with a brief smile,
> before I leave it to return no more.[3]

8. Finally, there is a human destiny, though not of the soul, for body and soul are equally transient and, what is more, equally under the wrath of God, that is bestowed on man, a deed of God towards him, a new creation. His own life has no powerfulness: no celebration whatever can create nor perpetuate potency; but "Omnipotence" imparts to him the gift of eternal life, which is neither continuation nor increase of earthly life but absolutely new and original; a life that intrinsically implies powerfulness no longer, but is grace alone: a life knowing reward and punishment no more, but only God's love.[4]

Despite many contrary views within Christianity itself, this is in fact the truly Christian apprehension of man's destiny: "the gift of God is eternal life through Jesus Christ."[5] And: "this is life eternal, that they might know thee the only true God, and Jesus Christ, whom thou hast sent."[6] This means that the soul is no immortal goddess, but only a turning towards God: that neither celebrations nor moral actions have any ultimate influence on man's lot, but God alone: that while eternal

---

[1] Plutarch, *Romulus*, XXVIII, 6 (Clough).
[2] The heathen Caecilius, in Minucius Felix, XI, 3.   [3] *Job* x. 18 *ff.* (Moffat).
[4] Steimann, *Der religiöse Unsterblichkeitsglaube*, 78 *ff.*
[5] *Romans* vi. 23.   [6] *John* xvii. 3.

life is indeed bestowed on man, it comes not from himself but solely
from God; so that whatever man's destiny may be, it rests ever in the
love of God. Thus arose the magnificent idea which Dante expresses—
that this very love created even hell:

> Justice the founder of my fabric moved:
> To rear me was the task of Power divine,
> Supremest Wisdom, and primeval Love.[1]

H. Scholz, *Der Unsterblichkeitsgedanke als philosophisches Problem*, 1920.
Th. Steinmann, *Der religiöse Unsterblichkeitsglaube*[2], 1912.

[1] *Inferno*, III, 4 *ff*. (Cary); *cf*. H. Scholz, *Eros und Caritas*, 1929, 53.

PART THREE

OBJECT AND SUBJECT IN THEIR RECIPROCAL OPERATION

A. OUTWARD ACTION

CHAPTER 48

CONDUCT AND CELEBRATION

1. ONCE again I wish to recall the initial principle laid down at the outset: the Subject of religion is, in the sense of religion itself, the Object, and its Object the Subject. Even now, when it has become a question of the reciprocal relationship between Subject and Object, the expressions are to be understood only in their figurative meaning. Nor must the designation of the actions performed by the subject, as either "external" or "internal", be taken to imply any essential distinction; for Chantepie has already stressed the point that any "external" activity can always be understood as "internal". Still further, when the relationship between man and Power is to be dealt with, it is in the first instance not at all a matter of subjectivity or inwardness. It is principally and primarily a question of the way and the means which either Power, or man, must employ if they are to influence each other. In other terms, it is an affair of what we have hitherto learned to know, but only quite superficially, as "the world above" or "the conjoint world", and which I shall henceforth call simply "world".

Thus whether in seeking, or fleeing from, any relation to Power, or again in possessing it, man still exists in the world. But that means not only that he is fixed in the world like a coin in my pocket: it implies still further that he participates in the world and is seriously concerned with it; and Heidegger has clearly and acutely interpreted this being-in-the-world as "care". Man, that is to say, does not simply accept the world in which he lives: he also feels apprehensive about it; or expressed in religious terms, this means that the world *appears alien or strange* to him and alarms him. For even choice has its own power, and in fact an unfamiliar and troublous power. Man therefore, thus placed in the world, does not immediately and straightway find himself at home therein: he experiences a foreignness that can all too readily deepen into dread or even into despair. He does not resignedly assent to the world given to him, but again and again says to it: "No!" This saying "No!" is indeed the very basis of his humanity; it proves that he has spirit: "Spirit is life which itself cutteth into life."[1] In life, then, man sees far more than givenness: he perceives possibility also. But this possibility demands his activity; his sense of foreignness must therefore expand into *conduct* and his conduct, still further, into *celebration*: his behaviour, in other words, must accord with the Powerful which reveals itself to him. How he behaves, even how he sits or stands or lies down, is thus no matter of indifference, and only in sleep does he ever sink back into the choiceless affirmation of the maternal womb. But in his waking hours he must always be prepared; his "care" must never cease: he must be ever on the alert; and as has been previously observed, the word *religio* itself indicates this alertness.[2] Therefore in order to dominate life for oneself, to seize upon the possibilities concealed within it, man must force it into a fixed course of activity. This can result from the fear equally of Power and of impotence; but in any case fear resounds in care. A child from a pietist household, for instance, keenly enjoyed pushing a barrow about, but reproached itself bitterly because this was sinful pleasure. Then it pacified its conscience by thinking that the infant Jesus lay in the barrow, so that he was pushing the Lord for His pleasure.[3] Thus from the game a rite has arisen: that is, conduct out of the unconstrained game. For a game bound by rules is, as such, always a rite, conduct, dominance; and the rite gained control over life, and drew power therefrom, long before thought could do so: "man was a ritualist before he could speak".[4] The rite also discovered the way of worship far in anticipation of thought. Like the child, then, man pushes his barrow, but his sense of alienation causes him to apply some fixed standard to his activities, so that dread may be silenced and he may feel at home therein. Then he places his god in it: and now he pushes Power itself! But he can also pause, and kneel before the god in the cart of his life.

2. Thus it is no indifferent matter how man conducts himself. His behaviour must in all respects duly respond to the goal which is power; and to that end he sets his own powerfulness as prominently as possible in the foreground. Ritual nakedness for example, the *ritus paganus*, is just such behaviour: the potency of one's own body is to ward off evil

---

[1] Nietzsche, *Thus Spake Zarathustra*, 122 (Foulis Ed.); *cf.* Chap. 23, and P. Tillich, *Die religiöse Lage der Gegenwart*, 34; also Scheler, *Stellung des Menschen*, 46.
[2] *cf.* Chap. 4.
[3] H. R. G. Günther, *Jung-Stilling*, 1928, 165; *cf.* Marett, *Faith, Hope and Charity*, 12.
[4] Chesterton, *Heretics*, 97.

powers and awaken fruitful ones.[1] Or, again, man gives his body the
appropriate pose: holding it rigid, braced up, alert, attentive and prepared, in *Standing*: allowing everything to go and abandoning himself
in the abasement of *Prostration*: bowing down all that is in himself,
and expressing his impotence by *Kneeling*: raising his hands so that
his "soul stream may flow freely": folding them and placing them, as
though bound, within God's hands.[2] He casts down his glance, or raises
it to heaven: turns away his face, or even hides his head, as if his
powerfulness were ashamed of itself, in direct contrast to the *ritus
paganus*. The frontier between such conduct and celebration, however,
cannot be exactly delineated, although in celebration proper there is
more of premeditated action, of undertaking something, or of changing
or securing it. But conduct too has precisely the same purpose: Anna
Schieber's Grandfather Hollermann, the old shepherd whose cult consists in jumping thrice over his staff, is certainly already celebrating.
Some instant or other, some fragment of life, some sort of potency,
must be arrested, repeated and celebrated; for if that were not done
man would have no correct relationship to Power. I may, for example,
simply run out of the house, but I may also leave it every day at the
same time, walking deliberately. The first act is a deed; the second is
a celebration, a rite: it solidifies the flux of life and gives it support.[3]
Man therefore should not remain simply within the given and in dread:
he should make some gesture, "do something about it". But the basis of
his gesture is always the yearning for the Wholly Other:

> Now I know that you must become like a little child:
>   All dread is only a beginning;
>   But the Earth is without end,
> And fear is but the gesture
>   The meaning of which is yearning.[4]

[1] K. Weinhold, *Zur Geschichte des heidnischen Ritus* (*Abh. d. preuss. Akad. d. Wiss.,
phil.-hist. Kl.*, 1896). It is practised to increase fertility and destroy weeds (Bertholet,
Lesebuch, 4, 7), in processions and other pageants (rain-maidens, Lady Godiva at
Coventry, plough processions, *etc.*), for averting evil influences (in Brandenburg, when
the cow kicks while being milked, the milkmaid must sit on the stool with bare
posterior; then the animal will be quiet); also to confirm an oath, in prophecy (Saul,
Cassandra) *etc.*; *cf.* further, R. Thurnwald, *Reallexikon der Vorgeschichte*, Art. *Zauber*.
[2] Guardini, *Von heiligen Zeichen*, 13 *ff*.
[3] Nothing whatever can occur without rites. In Australia, when rain falls without
the rites having been observed, friendly spirits are supposed to have caused it (Lévy-
Bruhl, *How Natives Think*, 251); *cf.* Marett, *Faith, Hope and Charity*, 18: "Born in
the mud like the other beasts, man alone refuses to be a stick-in-the-mud. . . . So he
dances through his life as if he would dance until he drops, finding out, however, on
trial that he can develop as it were a second wind by dancing to a measure."
[4] Rainer Maria Rilke, *Die frühen Gedichte*.

3. Finally, whoever conducts himself in accord with the sacred, whoever celebrates the holy, acts as an officiant: he not only carries out something, but he accomplishes what must be executed, τὰ δρώμενα. He, as it were, adopts some specific posture: he wields the sacred: he repeats the acts of Power. Every cult, then, is repetition.

R. GUARDINI, *Von heiligen Zeichen*, 1929.
L. LÉVY-BRUHL, *Primitives and the Supernatural*.
H. USENER, *Heilige Handlung* (*Kleine Schriften*, IV, 1913).
R. WILL, *Le culte*, 1925–1929.

CHAPTER 49

PURIFICATION

1. NOT without profound reason does the housewife's "Spring cleaning" still retain a tinge of ritual. For the ultimate motive of purification is no more liberation from actual dirt in the sense of modern hygiene, but release from evil and the induction of good. Occasionally life's power dwindles: it grows paler and loses its freshness; and all this must be prevented by a periodical turning over a new page in the book of life, so that it begins anew. The accumulated impotence, which is really an evil power, must be removed; and thus the Roman vestal temple, a state shrine, was annually purified. The purification period, nonetheless, was calamitous; so the dirt was either carefully deposited in a *locus certus* or thrown into the Tiber. Then the *dies nefasti*, when it was unlawful to transact any secular business, ended, and in the calendar this memorandum was attached to the fifteenth of June: QStDF: "lawful when the dirt has been cleared away"—*quando stercus delatum fas.*[1]

This custom characterizes all ideas about purification: a new beginning is made, power thrust out and fresh potency drawn in. Thus the correct relationship to Power, which in the course of a long year has suffered loss, is once again established; as soon as the dirt has been removed the proper relation again predominates: it is *fas*. The ground of this, and of countless similar rites, is of course the simple carrying on of ordinary life, of washing and cleaning. Yet they have quite another purport than the morning routine in one's home; and with children, and seamen washing down the decks, something of the primeval feeling of life is still retained. Children often observe a certain washing rite, and it is frequently a matter of complete indifference to them whether they become really clean; while sailors, and Dutch housewives too, burnish and polish in quite a ritual manner even when there is no dirt at all to be found! In religious phraseology, then, "dirt" includes far more than mere filth. "Dirt" means all the hindrances and annoyances that prevent the perpetuation and renewal of life, so that

[1] Ovid, *Fasti*, VI, 713; Fowler, *Roman Festivals*, 145; L. Deubner, *AR.* 16, 1913, 134 *f.* In Greece it was customary to throw away the dirty water, with which anyone had washed, behind one with averted gaze; Aeschylus, *Choephoroe*, 98 *f.*

some celebration must set the arrested current in motion again. The means employed, however, need not "cleanse" in our modern sense, provided only it is powerful; and thus the ancient Persians used the urine of oxen as we do some sort of disinfectant.[1] This had its ground in the animal's sacredness and not in the purifying efficacy of the means.

Purification, again, has a dual purpose: to impart benevolent, and avert wicked, power. The most widespread means of purifying is *water*;[2] but water not only cleans: it has a power of its own which it communicates. It is "living water". In ancient Egypt there were innumerable purifications; and the most frequent designation of the priest was in fact *Wab*, that is, "the pure one". In the grave figures the priest or the deity himself pours water from a vessel in a curve over the dead person, and the same process occurs in the case of the king. But in certain delineations the stream of water is replaced by an arched series of little *ankh*, the hieroglyphic symbols for life; thus a purification in unison with, and for the purpose of, life is carried out.

An excellent example of the periodic purification of the community is also afforded by the ancient Roman custom of lustration, especially the *lustrum*; *lustrum condere*, it was said, which really was to bury a *lustrum*. By analogy with many popular customs elsewhere, this means that the dirt of some particular period was buried, so that a new period might be begun. *Lustrum* would then be the equivalent of **lōstrum*, **laustrum*, that is, water for washing.[3] After it has served as purifying water, however, the dangerous cleansing liquid must be removed. The positive, too, outweighs the negative: the *carmen* of the *lustrum* was intended to move the gods "to make the condition of the Roman people better and greater".[4] At the commencement of the new year also (originally on March 1) a general cleansing was undertaken in Rome; and the entire last month of the year was named after the cleaning utensils, the *februa*.[5]

I shall now place side by side two examples of what was understood by "dirt". In Central Celebes, in the first place, when a case of incest has made a village unclean, a buffalo, a pig and a cock are slaughtered by a man standing in the water of the river; and in the water, which has been mixed with the blood of the animals sacrificed, both the

---

[1] Lehmann, *Zarathustra*, 233.   [2] Chap. 6.
[3] Deubner, *Lustrum*, 127 *ff*. Usener, *Kleine Shriften*, IV, 117 *f*. Similarly the carnival, fair, year and the Greek *charila* are buried in popular customs.
[4] Valerius Max. IV, 1, 10.   [5] Fowler, *Roman Festivals*, 6.

guilty parties and the other inhabitants of the village must bathe, "in order in this way to rid themselves of the dirt of the incest".[1] The "dirt" is therefore neither moral nor purely physical, but both and something more. The second instance occurs in the Old Testament: "When he has finished the expiatory rites for the sacred place and the Trysting tent and the altar, Aaron shall bring forward the living goat; laying both hands upon its head, he shall confess over it all the iniquities of the Israelites and all their sinful transgressions, laying them on the head of the goat and sending it away to the desert in charge of a man who is held in readiness; the goat shall bear away their iniquities into solitude, and shall be set free in the desert."[2] The "iniquities" are therefore the dirt which the "scapegoat" takes with it into the wilderness after the priest has laid them on its head;[3] the "spiritual" or "moral" and the concretely dirty are conceived as wholly one.

Besides incense, which was already familiar to the ancient Egyptians, the "holy water" that purifies the faithful at the door of God's house, but with which animals are also sprinkled and in which bread is dipped so that the cattle may eat it,[4] is the means of purification most frequently employed in our own times.

2. In the religious life, then, any celebration that not only removes dirt, but also makes new life possible, must be of the greatest importance. It brings about, as it were, a new birth; and it would in fact be better to omit "as it were". For ancient Egypt the idea prevailed that purification was "an imparting of the divine life of the water, a means of resurrection";[5] and of the dead man it was said that he "purifies himself on the day of his birth", that is of his resurrection.[6] He carried out this self-cleansing in the "primeval water", which existed at the commencement of all being, and whose reproduction was to be found in a pool near the temple.[7] Thus the life of the dead person was, as it were, immersed in the act of creation: it was born anew, the water of purification being regarded as the seed of the god Atmu, who effected the rebirth. Thereby the celebration of purification became so

---

[1] Kruyt, *Measa*, II, 79.　　　　　　　　　　　　[2] *Lev.* xvi. 20 *ff.* (Moffat).
[3] *cf.* I. Benzinger, *Hebräische Archäologie*[2], 1907, 380.
[4] Heiler, *Katholizismus*, 170. A poor woman burns incense daily for her husband buried in a silver mine; a year later he is found alive and well: the incense perfume has preserved him: P. Zaunert, *Rheinlandsagen*, II, 1924, 22 *ff.*
[5] Kristensen, *Livet*, 101.　　　　　　　　　　[6] *Totenbuch* (Naville), *Kap.* 17, 20.
[7] *cf.* A. de Buck, *De egyptische voorstellingen betreffende den Oerheuvel*, 1922. A. Blackman, "Egyptian foretaste of baptismal regeneration" (*Theology*, 1, 1920). H. P. Blok, *Acta orientalia*, VIII, 3, 208 *f.*

important that it touched life in its profoundest depth: it resulted in rebirth, re-creation.

Christian baptism, again, is not merely a purifying from dirt and sin, not merely an induction of sacred power, but is the "washing of regeneration",[1] a birth "of water and of the Spirit",[2] the type of which is the waters of the flood.[3] Thus baptism washes away sins, and is closely connected with the expulsion of the devil (exorcism); it originates in man a new power. Nevertheless its real essence lies in rebirth: the baptized has become a new man. As in the case of the baptism in Jordan, it effects "adoption", $\upsilon\iota o\theta\epsilon\sigma\iota a$. Here too there is the same parallelism, between the water of creation and of baptism, as we have already found in ancient Egypt. In Roman Catholic ritual the prayer *benedictio fontis* reads: "O God, whose Spirit in the very beginning of the world moved over the waters, that even then the nature of water might receive the virtue of sanctification: O God, who by water didst wash away the crimes of the guilty world, and by the overflowing of the deluge didst give a figure of regeneration, that one and the same element might in a mystery be the end of vice and the origin of virtue."[4] This again means a warding off of evil, and induction of good, included in the one *regeneratio*; and the great baptismal passage in the *Epistle to the Romans* (Chap. VI) connects this ancient idea with justification from sin: "for once dead, a man is absolved from the claims of sin".[5] To be in the water means to be dead, to be buried. Here therefore the profoundest life-feeling and the most powerful creaturely feeling appear together. Immersion in water is regression to the primal ground, either (cosmically) of Chaos or (individually) of the maternal womb. But over the primeval waters hovers the vivifying spirit of God, which creates an entire life anew, $\kappa\alpha\iota\nu\grave{\eta}$ $\kappa\tau\iota\sigma\iota\varsigma$. Here then we are already in the heart of the realm of the sacrament.

Of course it is not only water that possesses purifying power. In the mysteries of Attis and Mithra there was a baptism of blood, *tauro-*

---

[1] *Titus* iii. 5.   [2] *John* iii. 5.

[3] 1 *Peter* iii. 20 f. cf. W. Heitmüller, *Im Namen Jesu*, 1903, 278 ff. H. Usener, *Das Weihnachtsfest*[2], 1911. Dieterich, *Mithrasliturgie*, 139 f. L. Duchesne, *Les origines du culte chrétien*[4], 1908, 299 ff.

[4] *Deus, cujus spiritus super aquas, inter ipsa mundi primordia ferebatur: ut jam tunc virtutem sanctificationis, aquarum natura conciperet. Deus, qui nocentis mundi crimna per aquas abluens, regenerationis speciem in ipsa diluvii effusione signasti: ut unius ejusdemque elementi mysterio, et finis esset vitiis, et origo virtutibus. Taufe und Firmung, nach dem römischen Missale, Rituale und Pontificale*, edited by Ildefons Herwegen (*Kleine Texte*, 144), 1920, 22; cf. further *Rom.* vi, *Gal.* iii. 26 f., *Col.* ii. 12.

[5] Moffat.

bolium; the blood of Christ too is pre-eminently the means of purification, and this in no merely figurative sense. Fire also, as was previously observed,[1] has great purifying power, while baptism by fire finds a place in primitive puberty rites;[2] in Bohemia house and stables are "smoked out" at the feast of St. Lucia,[3] while "blood and fire" is still to-day the effective summing up of the great means of purification, as coined by the Salvation Army. Sacred oil, as the *materia* of the sacrament of confirmation, originally intimately connected with Christian baptism, is also a "seal" and sign by which the faithful can be recognized, like the military brand in the Mithras mysteries.[4] It renders the Christian capable of active participation in the sacrifice of the church, makes him "worthy" in the official sense, and grants him *dignitas regalis et sacerdotalis*. Further, extreme unction purifies the entire body of the dying and endows him with new power; the old administration formula runs: *accipe sanitatem corporis et remissionem omnium peccatorum*— "receive bodily health and the remission of all thy sins".[5]

Purification, however, has not always the character of washing or cleansing. Very frequently the person to be purified is beaten; and here also we find not only apotropaic power intended to avert evil, but likewise that which imparts salvation. Women especially were beaten, usually with a green twig ("beating with the rod of life"); also cows' udders, and the *muliebria, etc.* The thongs of goat hide, again, with which the Roman bands of naked youths, the *Luperci*, struck the women, were called "Juno's mantle", *amiculum Junonis*, a reference to increased fertility.[6]

3. Belief in the potency of celebration, however, disappears not only under the influence of scepticism, but also owing to reduction to the subjective inner life of the soul. The classical expression of scepticism is provided by Ovid's familiar lines: "Fond fools alack! to fancy murder's gruesome stain by river water could be washed away";[7] while we find this reduction to the inner life wherever prophetic or moral

---

[1] Chap. 6. [2] Chap. 22.

[3] Reinsberg-Düringsfeld, *Das festliche Jahr*, 434.

[4] Heitmüller, *Im Namen Jesu*, 312 f. Thom. Michels, *Die Akklamation in der Taufliturgie (Jahrb. für Liturgiewiss.* VIII, 1928), 83 ff.

[5] Thus in imperative form; now replaced by a deprecatory formula; Jos. Braun, *Liturgisches Handlexikon*[2], 1924, 241.

[6] Fowler, *Roman Festivals*, 319 ff. Crawley, *The Mystic Rose*, I, 312 f. Reinsberg-Düringsfeld, *Festliche Jahr*, 176. Mannhardt, *op. cit.*, 251 ff.

[7] *Fasti*, II, 45 (Frazer).

intensity of feeling opposes the constraint of celebration, although the keenest and deepest antagonism must be sought in the Old Testament prophets and in the New Testament.[1] But a closely similar note resounds in other "great religions" also. *Buddha*, for example: "Man is not purified by water, however much he may bathe; he is pure, he is a brahmin, in whom truth and virtue reside."[2] The Law of *Manu* likewise: "The mouth of the girl and the hand of the worker are always clean."[3] Different again the Greek *Theano* who, in reply to the question as to how long is required for a woman to become clean after intercourse with a man, answered: "After her own at once, after another, never."[4]

Despite all rationalism and moralism, however, and all such religious subjectivity also, the necessity for purification still maintains its exceedingly important place in human life, alike in the physical and the psychical sense. For recent psychological and psychiatric studies have shown to what a high degree in life's crisis, where it is reluctantly brought to its very frontiers, this need for cleansing governs man and his conduct, in neurotic states even coercively. The "washing compulsion" was of course familiar to Shakespeare: the incredibly realistic scene in which Lady Macbeth, walking in her sleep, descends the stairs incessantly washing her hands is the tragic but splendid monument to this necessity for purification:[5]

> Yet here's a spot.
> Out, damned spot! out, I say!—
> What, will these hands ne'er be clean?
> Here's the smell of the blood still: all the perfumes of Arabia
> will not sweeten this little hand.

But in spite of this tragic element, the hopeless celebration becomes again and again the joyful consciousness of being purified. And when purification is a sacrament celebration itself is no longer the principal factor, but the Power that is operative within it, the grace of God. Then the water becomes wine, or indeed blood: the futile washing a rebirth. Nowhere is this more beautifully expressed than in Luther's *Epiphany Hymn*:

[1] Especially in the striking passage: *Mark* vii. 14 *ff.*
[2] Bertholet, *op. cit.*,[1] 263.   [3] Lehmann, *Zarathustra*, II, 205.
[4] Zielinski, *The Religion of Ancient Greece*, 126; *cf.* further the lines previously cited from Euripides, *Herakles*, 1230 *ff.* p. 51 *ante.*
[5] *Macbeth.* V, 1.

For us He would provide a bath
Wherein to cleanse from sin,
And drown the bitterness of death
In His own blood and wounds,
And so create new life.

The eye itself sees but the water
As man pours water forth.
But faith in the spirit understands
The power of Jesus Christ's blood.

Here the bathing water and human celebration are indissolubly
united with Christ's Power and the act of God.

CHAPTER 50

SACRIFICE

1. THE terms "soul" and "sacrifice" must be included among those presenting the greatest variety of meaning in the whole history of religion; and in both cases we may doubt the advisability of estimating such utterly different phenomena, as are comprised under these words, as being diverse instances of that single self-revelation which will be further discussed in the *Epilegomena*. With respect to these two ideas, nevertheless, and as indeed I hope that I have already shown with regard to the soul, the phenomena prove to constitute a fundamental unity. Usually, however, a distinction is made between the sacrificial gift or the sacrifice of homage, and the sacramental meal; in the latter case it is either the god himself who is consumed, or he is looked upon as a table companion who receives his due share. But even with this classification of the phenomena, justice has not been accorded to all the instances. For in many sacrificial ceremonies it is extremely difficult to point to the presence of the "god" at all.[1] In these circumstances, therefore, it would be quite impossible to maintain that old principle of explanation of sacrifice, the rule of *do-ut-des*[2]—"I give that thou mayest give"—which had in fact been formulated in classical times: "Bribes, believe me, buy both gods and men; Jupiter himself is appeased by the offering of gifts";[3] while the brahminic ritual expresses it equally clearly: "here is the butter; where are thy gifts?"[4] In his famous work, *The Religion of the Semites*, however, Robertson Smith has shown that besides this idea of *do-ut-des* there was at least one other that was quite different and yet was the basis of sacrifice—the idea of a communal meal at which the god is either a participant, or else is identical with the sacrifice, that is with the food consumed.[5]

---

[1] *cf.* an enumeration of the forms of sacrifice in Pfleiderer's *Philosophy of Religion*, IV, 186 *ff.*   [2] G. van der Leeuw, *Do-ut-des-Formel, passim.*

[3] Ovid, *Ars amatoria*, III, 653 (Mozley); *cf.* further Alviella, *Idée de Dieu*, 89, where the ancient Hindu formula is quoted: "Give thou to me, I shall give to thee; bring thou to me and I shall bring to thee"; also Jevons, *Introduction*, 69 *ff.* Grimm, *Schenken und Geben, Kl. Schriften*, II, 174 and Note.

[4] *RGG*². Article *Opfer* I.

[5] *cf.* further Reinach who, being the sound evolutionist he is, places the latter type, as the more enigmatical, at the beginning, and sacrificial gifts, as quite clearly comprehensible, at the close of the development.

It appears therefore that we must have interpreted the "gift", which is thus supposed to be the basis of sacrifice, in far too European and modern a sense; we have allowed ourselves to be led away by Ovid, and forgotten what "to give" actually means.[1] "To give" is believed to be "more blessed than to receive";[2] but for this maxim the *do-ut-des* theory leaves no scope whatever. It presupposes quite a different view of giving, or rather a wholly contrasted interpretation of "I give . . . ." For it is incontestable that this kind of argument is, very frequently, the actual ground of sacrifice. But *dare* does not mean merely to dispose of some arbitrary object with a quite indefinite intention; the word *dare* means, rather, to place oneself in relation to, and then to participate in, a second person by means of an object, which however is not actually an "object" at all, but a part of one's own self. "To give," then, is to convey something of oneself to the strange being, so that a firm bond may be forged. Mauss refers, together with other writers, to Emerson's fine essay, *Gifts*, with respect to this "primitive" view of giving: "The only gift is a portion of thyself. Thou must bleed for me. Therefore the poet brings his poem; the shepherd, his lamb; the farmer, corn; the miner, a gem." . . . "The gift, to be true, must be the flowing of the giver unto me, correspondent to my flowing unto him." In fact, giving demands a gift, not however in the sense of any commercial rationalism, but because the gift allows a stream to flow, which from the moment of giving runs uninterruptedly from donor to recipient and from receiver to giver: "the recipient is in the power of the giver."[3] "As a rule, certainly, the receiver of the present appears to gain and the donor to lose, but secretly the gift demands a gift in return. Whoever receives gifts unites himself to the one who bestows them: the accepted gift can bind."[4] We ourselves, in fact, continue to recognize this power whenever we give an employee his "earnest", and that presents maintain friendship we know quite as well as the East African natives who said to Livingstone: "Thou claimest to be our friend; but how are we to know that, so long as thou hast not given us any of thy food and hast not tasted ours? Give us an ox; we will give thee in return everything thou mayest demand, and then we shall be bound to each other by genuine affection."[5] With many primitive peoples, again, refusal to bestow or receive a gift amounts to a de-

---

[1] Grönbech in Chantepie, *op. cit.*, II, 581; Laum, *Heiliges Geld*, 32; Grimm, *loc. cit.*
[2] *Acts* xx. 35.   [3] Grönbech, *loc. cit.*, III, 3.
[4] Grimm, *loc. cit.*, 174.
[5] Cited by R. Kreglinger, *Grondbeginselen der godsdienstwetenschap*, 68; *cf.* further Grönbech, III, 112.

claration of war: it means that community is declined;[1] for the gift is powerful; it has binding force: it has *mana*. Gifts therefore can destroy the recipient; but they can also assist him, and in any event they forge an indissoluble bond. Thus the Maori speak of the *hau* (spirit) of the gift: I give what I have received from thee to a third person, and from him I receive a return gift. This I must now give to thee since it is actually thy gift; the *hau* of thy gift persists in it.[2] "The object received is not a dead thing. Even when it has been handed over by the giver it always retains something pertaining to him." To offer somebody something, then, is to offer someone a part of oneself; similarly, to accept a thing from another person is to receive some portion of his spiritual being, of his soul;[3] and under these circumstances the reciprocal nature of giving is quite obvious. The *Havamal* expresses all this most forcibly: "Friends should cheer each other with presents of weapons and raiment. . . . Those who repay with gifts, and those who respond in the same way, remain friends longest, provided that there is time for matters to turn out well. If you wish to know when you have a friend whom you can trust absolutely, and if you desire to be treated well by him, you must blend your own sentiments with his, interchange gifts with him, and often travel to visit him." In all this there is doubtless an element of calculation: here is the butter, where are the gifts? But there is also involved a just apprehension of friendship; and thirdly, there is something more: a mystic power attached to the gift which establishes *communio*.[4] Or to express this in Lévy-Bruhl's terms: giver and receiver participate in the gift and therefore in each other. Here, too, economic life has its roots; on the Trobriand Islands in Melanesia, for example, the dignified trade in *kula* is distinguished from the ordinary business in *gimwali*; in the first it is not so much a matter of exchange as of the distribution of gifts.[5] The Indian tribes of North-west America, again, practice the "potlatch" system, consisting in two tribes or chiefs engaging in a competition of prodigality; whoever is the richer gives the most and even destroys his own possessions if necessary. All this, however, in order that he himself may prosper,[6] since in this manner he shows that he has power; and we have already observed that the primitive king also demonstrated his power by giving presents. But here, as always, the "power" is just as secular (to use

[1] Mauss, *Essai sur le don, forme archaique de l'échange, Année Sociologique*, N.S. 1, 1925, 51.

[2] Mauss, *ibid.*, 45 f.   [3] *ibid.*, 47 ff.

[4] Chap. 32.   [5] Mauss, *ibid.*, 64 ff.   [6] *ibid.*, 93 ff.

our paltry expression) as it is "sacred", the "potlatch" system being simultaneously religious and economic, social and legal;[1] and a wealthy Maori has *mana*, which is at the same time credit, influence and power. Thus "to buy" is a magical action; and according to Mauss the three obligations of the "potlatch" system are to give, to receive and to give in return;[2] the one always has the other as a condition. For whoever buys receives something of the owner's being together with his purchase, and that would be dangerous if an exchange gift did not follow: buying must therefore always be accompanied by a return gift;[3] for objects sold are never completely detached from their possessor.[4]

Under such conditions we can hardly be astonished at *money* also having a sacramental origin; and the oldest Greek measure of value was the ox, the sacred sacrificial animal, the money being the tribute that must be paid to the deity. Thus the sacrificial meal, in the course of which the meat was equally divided, was the "germ of public financial administration". Later, coin appeared instead of the sacrifice;[5] but that the coin was money, that is valid, was also due to its originating in the sphere of sacrifice and bringing with it its powerfulness, or as we should say, its credit.[6] Here we meet with the same relationship as was discerned in the case of retaliation (punishment) and revenge:[7] a stream is released, one motion always setting the other free; therefore just as the evil deed must be balanced by revenge or punishment, so must the gift be "requited" by a gift in return or, in modern terms, be paid for.[8]

Sacrifice, then, and in the first place as the sacrificial gift, has now taken its place within a very much wider connotation. It is no longer a mere matter of bartering with gods corresponding to that carried on with men, and no longer homage to the god such as is offered to princes: it is an opening of a blessed source of gifts. We both give and receive, and it is quite impossible to say who is actually donor and who recipient. For both participate in the powerfulness of

---

[1] Mauss, *op. cit.*, 99.   [2] *ibid.*, 100.

[3] F. D. E. van Ossenbruggen, *Tydschrift van het Ned. Aardr. Genootschap.* 2. *Reeks,* 47, 1930, 221 *ff. cf.* J. C. van Eerde, *ibid.*, 230 *ff.* These considerations place such a custom as bride purchase in an entirely new light; *cf.* H. Th. Fischer, *Der magische Charakter des Brautpreises* (*Weltkreis*, 1932, 3, 3).

[4] Mauss, *ibid.*, 87.

[5] Is Laum correct in suggesting that the *obol* is really the *obelos*—that is, the roasting-spit? *op. cit.*, 106 *ff.*

[6] Laum.   [7] Chap. 23.

[8] *cf.* A. Olrik, *Ragnarök*, 1922, 460, and the typical Old Norse expression for "revenge", *uphaevelse*, that is, "setting the slain up again".

what is being presented, and hence it is neither the giver nor the receiver, even though he be a god or a divine being, who occupies the focal point of the action. The pivot of the sacrificial act, its power centre, is always the gift itself: it must be given, that is to say, be set in motion. As a rule it is given to another person who may be one's neighbour, or may be some god; but it may also be divided among the members of the community. It may, again, be "given" without any "addressee" at all. For the principal feature is not that someone or other should receive something, but that the stream of life should continue to flow. From this point of view, therefore, not only are gift and communion sacrifices not antitheses but, still further, the sacrifice is transplanted into the very midst of life. It is no *opus supererogatorium*, but the working of the power of life itself. And thus instead of the rationalistic *do-ut-des*, we must say: *do ut possis dare*—"I give in order that thou mayest be able to give": I give thee power that thou mayest have power, and that life may not stagnate because of any lack of potency.

2. "I discern a reference to such a reciprocal effect as this in the Roman sacrificial formula 'Hail to thee'; *e.g.* '*Iuppiter dapalis*, hail to thee by the offering of thy feast: hail to thee by the wine placed before thee'.[1] Probably this can have no other meaning than: 'Hail to thee! with these sacrificial gifts, which I now offer to thee; be strong through these my gifts.' Such an invocation in a fixed formula, in *verbis certis*, however, was never a merely arbitrary form of speech. For the view certainly prevailed at one time that the gods could be rendered capable of bestowing power only by the constant nourishing of their own strength. . . . The Roman, for example, sacrificed to the hearth, to Vesta, by throwing small gifts into the fire, while he was at the same time wholly dependent on this hearth fire, and worshipped it as the essence of the divine fullness of life."[2] Thus the relationship of dependence between god and man, which appears to us to be perfectly obvious, need by no means be actually present; or rather: the dependence certainly subsisted, but it was reciprocal, and may be compared to the status of the Catholic priest in popular piety: "no creature other than he has the 'power' to create God Himself in transubstantiation,

---

[1] Cato, *Agri cultura*, 132; *mactus* originally means "increased, strengthened", then "honoured"; *cf.* R. Wünsch, *Rhein. Mus.* 69, 1913, 127 *ff.*; a similar expansion of meaning to that of the concepts *augeo, auctoritas.*

[2] G. van der Leeuw, *Do-ut-des-Formel*, 244 *f.*

to call Him down from His heavenly throne to the altar by his word of consecration".[1]

If however man gives in order that he may also receive, nevertheless he externalizes part of himself in the gift. Here again I believe that I can deepen a certain rationalistic viewpoint, so as to be able to set it in its correct connection with life: that namely of so-called vicarious sacrifice. Usually it is maintained that vicarious sacrifice is a *pis aller*, just as the substitute formerly was in military service: no one ever sacrifices himself willingly, and therefore one sacrifices one's children, and later a slave or prisoner, finally an animal, and if that be too costly, a cake in animal form. In fact, we know how human sacrifice was actually replaced by that of animals, for example in the story of Isaac,[2] and also that the sacrificial cake very often retained the form of the animal whose place it had taken.[3] We recall again that the Toradja native, if he tells a lie while travelling by water, quickly pulls a hair from his head and throws it into the stream with the words: "I am guilty, I give this instead of myself."[4] But all this is not merely some acute business deal transacted with the powers. He who "gives", who sacrifices, *always* gives something of himself with it: whether it be his child which he is giving as a building sacrifice, or his hair that he is tendering as an atonement, or his grain offered as first-fruits, it is always a portion of himself.[5] He who makes a sacrifice sacrifices his property, that is, himself.[6] Just as he chooses, therefore, he can replace a part of himself, of his possessions, by something else, since all that he has has a part in him, and participates reciprocally. Certainly this substitution of something different for the gift can arise purely from a desire for comfort or from greed. But it may also be actuated by humanitarian motives; and it may even conduce to indifference so far as the value of the sacrifice is concerned: "the sacrifice of a fowl has the same value in the eyes of the god as the sacrifice of an ox", say the South African Baronga.[7] And from this attitude the path leads on to the standpoint of the prophet demanding obedience and not sacrifice.

But here yet another highly important idea is born: the sacrifice takes the place of the person offering it. With him it is essentially

---

[1] Heiler, *Katholizismus*, 181.

[2] A parallel from Samoa may be found in *Tales from old Fiji* (L. Fison), 1907, 41.

[3] Cakes shaped like stags were offered to Artemis Elaphebolos; Nilsson, *Griech. Feste*, 224; *cf.* 202; Samter, *Religion der Griechen*, 47.

[4] Kruyt, *Animisme*, 32 f.   [5] *cf.* Will, *Le culte*, I, 111.

[6] Chap. 33.   [7] Will, *ibid.*, I, 101.

connected; the sacrificer gives himself in and with his offering, and in this surrender the offering assists him. Thus a different light is cast upon the sacrifice of women, slaves *etc.*, who follow their masters to death. The Hindu burning of widows is universally familiar, while in Nubia slaves and prisoners were slain to accompany the dead man;[1] and the primary purpose of all this was not that the retainers should serve their master in the world beyond. That they must already do, since by their own death and rebirth they facilitated their lord's decease and rebirth. Here then it was a matter of suffering and dying together, whence new life arose. For the broad stream of life, the eternal flux of power, is assured by the greatest possible "expenditure"; and since sacrificer and sacrifice participate in each other, giver and gift can interchange their rôles. The idea of the vicarious sacrifice of Christ should therefore be interpreted from this viewpoint, not in the light of some juristic theory: the sacrifice demanded from man being accomplished by Him Who is simultaneously sacrificer and sacrifice, *sacerdos et hostia*.

3. Still further, sacrifice preserves the cycle of power. The stream of gifts (that is, of power), not only assures community between man and man, between man and god, but can also be conducted through all kinds of difficulties and can avert these by absorbing them within the community. Thus the *building sacrifice* removes the risks of construction: taking possession of the piece of ground, and the expulsion of the foreign demonic power residing in the soil, are rendered harmless by the *communio* of the sacrifice; only in this way can the house become a piece of property. The atoning sacrifice, again, removes the sin impeding the stream of life; life's power is set in motion in favour of the person offering the sacrifice. "In this respect it is somewhat indifferent whether this vital power resides in a god and, by means of the sacred food replete with the strength of life, is compelled to circulate by the maker of the sacrifice, or whether it subsists within the sacrifice itself and is consumed as food at first hand by the sacrificer. Originally the food, on which life depended, was probably eaten in the religious sense, that is, in accordance with later ideas, sacramentally.[2] . . . Then the primitive fare, venerated of old (milk and honey,

---

[1] *cf.* G. A. Reisner, *Zeitschrift für ägypt. Sprache und Altertumskunde*, 52, 1915, 34 *ff.*; A. Wiedemann, *AR.* 21, 1922, 467.
[2] "Every meal places man in connection with life's creative forces and with the eternal life of Deity"; Kristensen, *Livet*, 44.

the Roman *mola salsa, etc.*[1]) became the food of the gods or of their realm. But it might also be regarded as itself divine; and then the meal became a sacrifice".[2]

Pre-eminently does the sacramental meal, brought into prominence by Robertson Smith, now become comprehensible. Some sacred substance, an animal or other kind of nourishment, is divided among the members of a community and consumed by them: thus it becomes the sacred that subsists in common,[3] producing a strengthening of the community's power and binding its members more firmly to each other. The custom of dividing an animal into pieces, thereby effecting unity, is familiar in Saul's conduct during the siege of the town of Jabesh;[4] and perhaps this implied a sacrifice also. The significance of the sacrificial meal, however, becomes quite clear to us in the case of the Ainu, the primitive inhabitants of Japan.[5] The Ainu celebrate a bear feast; a very young bear is captured, suckled and carefully reared by a woman, pampered and spoilt for several years and finally killed; in the slaying the whole community participates, at least symbolically; it is then sincerely mourned, and consumed ceremonially in a communal meal. It is the animal of the community; and this follows from the fact that it can be a sacrificial animal only if it has grown up in the tribe, so that a wild bear would be useless for the purpose; it is as it were the child of the woman who brought it up, and who laments it.[6] A vestige of a similar communal meal occurred in Latin antiquity; the Latin League celebrated the *feriae latinae* on the Alban Mount: there the delegates from the Latin towns ate together a white steer: each town received its share, the ceremonial being called *carnem petere.*[7] And again, in a different way, the so-called *epulum Jovis* celebrated at the Ides of September, in which three gods took part;[8] thus in this instance the sacrifice and the god were not identical, the deity being numbered among the guests. But by both methods alike community among the participants was effected or strengthened;[9] and only from

---

[1] Heiler, *Prayer*, 66. Wide, in *Handbuch der klassischen Altertumswissenschaft*[4], II, 4, 1931, 74.

[2] G. van der Leeuw, *Do-ut-des-Formel*, 251 *f.*   [3] Chap. 32.

[4] 1 *Sam.* xi. 7; *cf. Judges* xix; Schwally, *Der heilige Krieg*, 53.

[5] Haas, *Bilderatlas*, No. 8.

[6] *cf.* further Frazer, *Golden Bough*, VIII (*Spirits of the Corn*, II), 101 *ff.*

[7] Warde Fowler, *The Religious Experience of the Roman People*, 172. Wissowa, *Religion und Kultus der Römer*, 124 *ff.* During the festival the *pax deorum* was maintained—a general tabu.

[8] Fowler, *Roman Festivals*, 218 *f.*

[9] Thomsen, *Der Trug des Prometheus, AR.* 12, 1909, 464.

the point of view of such community can we comprehend the laments over the sacrifice, and the prayers for forgiveness, met with among so many peoples. This becomes most obvious when totemistic connections with the sacrificial animal predominate. Thus the Zuni of Arizona mourn for the turtle which has been sacrificed: "Ah! my poor dear lost child or parent, my sister or brother to have been! Who knows which? Maybe my own great-grandfather or mother."[1] The sacrifice belongs to the community, indeed *is* the community, constitutes and strengthens it. The community is being sacrificed, "given up", in order to be sustained. And in this sense too only what has been lost can be gained.[2]

4. "This view of sacrifice has been developed in the most magnificent and logical manner in India. There the sacrifice (the ancient Vedic sacrifice of the horse) became a process which was executed with automatic precision: 'Events are apprehended just as they were in the most primitive type of prehistoric ideas of the Universe, as resting on the play of those forces which rule the Universe, and whose mode of operation, remotely comparable to the order of Nature which constitutes the modern concept of the world, the knower is able to calculate and to direct just as he will. But this knower is man himself.'[3] Here sacrifice has become a world process in the literal sense, and man understands how to dominate it. The centre of life's power lies in himself; he is the transitional point of the potencies that move the Universe. Here, then, gods are just as superfluous as they were in the primitive stage."[4]

Actually the sacrifice, as such, is always a sacrament. But where it is expressly called so, that is in Christianity, the concept of the stream of gifts has fused in a marvellous way with the concept of a personal God, and of a Saviour Who is not only the sacrifice, not only the

---

[1] Frazer, *Spirits of the Corn*, II, 175 *ff.* (*Golden Bough*, VIII).

[2] It may be said that the stream of powerfulness evoked by the sacrifice vivifies all the participants therein, whether men or gods. It may, however, also be expressed thus:—that this stream flows from the god, or again from some one participant, to man or to another member, through the sacrifice. The altar then becomes the point of transition—the theory of Hubert and Mauss (*Mélanges d'Histoire des Religions*). But the sacrifice is far more than such a transitional point; it is itself sacredness, power-stuff; *cf.* the Greek rule οὐκ ἐκφορά—nothing may remain over of the sacred food— a regulation very frequently encountered in sacrificial practice; *cf.* Thomsen, *Der Trug des Prometheus, AR.* 12, 1909, 466 *ff.*

[3] Oldenberg, *Lehre der Upanishaden*, 16 *f.*

[4] G. van der Leeuw, *Do-ut-des-Formel*, 252.

priest, but also a historic personage. Here the danger certainly threatens
that owing to the repetition inherent in all cult, the historic-concrete
and uniquely given element in the Saviour's sacrifice would be transformed repeatedly into that autocratic automatism which we have just
discerned in India. It is true that the bloodless reiteration of the bloody
sacrifice of Golgotha, as this is prescribed according to the decisions
of the Council of Trent,[1] need repeal neither the unique sacrificial
deed of Christ nor the making of the thank-offering on the church's
part, which is possible only in the concrete situation. Nevertheless a
soupçon of the idea of the luxuriantly flowing stream of grace—but
without God's act of volition and also without the church's gratitude
—once again makes itself constantly perceptible here: Power is striving
with Will and Form. If however the struggle just referred to is not
carried on one-sidedly, and in favour of a pure dynamism or a mere
symbolism, but persists as a living tension, then the Christian Eucharist
implies, indeed, an intensification of the mystic and primitive idea of
do-ut-des. For I cannot perceive any contradiction, such as Luther did,[2]
in the fact that the same entity is simultaneously received and offered.
On the contrary, it is precisely the essence of all sacrifice that it should
be at the same time an offering and a receiving. The centurion, whose
words occur in the mass before communion, says that he is not worthy
that the Lord should enter under his roof; nonetheless at the same
moment he does enter under the Lord's roof; "I am not worthy that
thou shouldest come under my roof", and "Then will I go unto
the altar of God",[3] are *one* celebration and *one* act of God. This
in fact found expression in the ancient Christian liturgy when, in
the anamnesis, the people appear offering thanks to the Lord with the
words "What is His own from what is His own";[4] and it has been
most beautifully interpreted in Paul Gerhardt's *Christmas Hymn*:

> Here stand I at Thy manger,
> O little Jesus, my very life.
> I come to bring and give to Thee
> What Thou hast given to me.

[1] Will, *Le culte*, I, 96 *f*.
[2] *Of the Babylonian Captivity of the Church:* the contradiction "that the mass should
be a sacrifice, because we receive the promise, but give the sacrifice. But one and the
same object can neither be simultaneously received and offered, nor simultaneously
given and received, by the same person."
[3] *Matt.* viii. 8; *Ps.* xliii. 4.
[4] τά σὰ ἐκτῶν σῶν σοὶ προσφέροντες κατὰ πάντα καὶ διὰ πάντα. H. Lietzmann,
Messe und Herrenmahl, 1926, 51.

ALFRED BERTHOLET, *Der Sinn des kultischen Opfers* (Abh. preuz. Akad. d. Wiss., 1942, Phil. Hist. Kl. 2).

J. GRIMM, *Schenken und Geben* (*Kl. Schriften*, II, 1865, 173 *ff.*).

H. HUBERT and M. MAUSS, *Mélanges d'Histoire des Religions*, 1909.

B. LAUM, *Heiliges Geld*, 1924.

G. VAN DER LEEUW, *Die Do-ut-des-Formel in der Opfertheorie* (*AR.* 20, 1920–21, 241 *ff.*).

A. LODS, *Examen de quelques hypothèses modernes sur les origines du sacrifice* (*Revue d'histoire et de littérature rel.*, 1921, 483 *ff.*).

A. LOISY, *Essai historique sur le sacrifice*, 1920.

B. MALINOWSKI, *Argonauts of The Western Pacific*, 1932.

M. MAUSS, *Essai sur le don, forme archaique de l'échange.* (*Année Sociologique, N.S.* I, 1925.)

S. REINACH, *Cultes, Mythes et Religions*, I, 1905.

W. ROBERTSON SMITH. *The Religion of the Semites*³, 1927

ADA THOMSEN, *Der Trug des Prometheus* (*AR.* 12, 1909, 460 *ff.*).

CHAPTER 51

SACRAMENTALS

1. ACCORDING to the doctrine of the Roman Catholic Church, those celebrations which endow a person or thing with a sacred character, or sacredness, are sacramentals. These are especially considered to be: consecration, blessing and exorcism;[1] and I shall discuss these celebrations more fully in dealing with sacred words. But at this stage, and before treating of sacraments, I must introduce this concept because it shows in a most impressive way that sacred action always tends towards the sacramental. For life, that is to say, a fixed number of sacraments is quite insufficient; certainly the idea of the sacrament as such is frequently restricted to some degree, both theoretically and often practically also; nevertheless its essence persists in celebration effecting superior powerfulness, activating a power. The Roman church to-day still recognizes very many sacramentals, while in the Middle Ages they accompanied almost the whole of life; and thus it becomes clearly enunciated that life cannot be "carried on", in the actual sense of the word, without powers being brought into action; existence, once again, is "care", which on its part leads to celebration; and this, finally, has no significance unless something essential to life is modified by it.

We may also express this state of affairs as follows: life consists not in man controlling things just as he himself pleases, but in his mobilizing the powerfulness of what appear as things. Actually, in other words, there are no "things": there are only conduits and containers, which under given conditions can retain power within themselves. Thus the "things", with which man comes into contact, are either receptacles which he must fill with power or wheels that he must set in motion; this then involves some magical deed, so that man appears to a certain extent as a creator, if not of the things then at least of the powers which endow them with life. Or alternatively: "things" are "creatures", *creaturae*. In yet other terms: they are connected with God directly and immediately, and God can at any moment breathe into them new life and grant them fresh potency; He makes instruments of His Power out of "things", He creates and

---

[1] Braun, *Liturgisches Handlexikon*, 304 *f*.

renews them. Thus a deed, a word, a person can at any moment become "powerful", either because of the fullness of power that is in man and that forces power into them, or because of the fullness of Power in God the Creator. In the first case man utters an incantation, in the second a prayer; but in both instances we speak of sacramentals.

2. As we have already been in the position to observe, *eating and drinking* are genuine sacramentals; and our drinking customs, or the fixed observances of the students' drinking bout, are all vestiges of a time when every occasion of communal drinking was actually a celebration—a celebration or, in other words, a consolidation, renewal and recreation of the common powerfulness. In Nordic sagas, for example, drinking is by no means a matter of mere thirst or desire; they drank in fixed succession, so that the stream of *Minne* should not be interrupted,[1] while the term *Minne* is better translated as *salus* than as *amor*. The magic drink again, also a sacramental!, is (as Grönbech remarks) actually nothing but any drink whatever which binds the drinker fast to the house or the circle that has given him the beverage; every drink "bewitches", renders the past forgotten and creates new love.[2] Exactly so as regards food: the communal meal too is binding; and when Jarl Torfin, unrecognized, breaks off a scrap of King Magnus's bread and eats it, he escapes by this celebration a death which otherwise would have been inevitable.[3] Thus every communal meal is not merely a sacrifice but a sacrament also and, while it is not officially characterized as such, a sacramental. The consecration of food on Easter morning takes account of these conditions even to-day: baskets filled with eggs, bread, salt, ham and little lambs made of sugar, are brought to church to be blessed; and in order that the blessing may actually penetrate the viands the baskets are opened, like the wine-bottles on Midsummer's Day.[4] Yet a step farther and we obtain the sacrament in its original form: people bring their gifts to church and lay them on the altar, where they then become the elements of the sacred sustenance. Of this there are examples of many kinds, quite apart from Christianity. On the island of Buru in the Moluccas, for instance, each clan holds a communal rice meal, to which each member contributes some fresh rice, and this is called "eating the soul of the rice".[5] In ancient Rome, again, at the *ludi saeculares*

[1] Grönbech, *op. cit.*, IV, 32.   [2] *ibid.*, III, 125 *ff.*
[3] *ibid.*, III, 117 *f.*   [4] Heiler, *Katholizismus*, 170 *f.*
[5] Frazer, *The Golden Bough*, VIII (*Spirits of the Corn*, II), 54.

suffimenta and *fruges* were brought to the quindecimvirs, and after they had been lustrated were again distributed to the people;[1] this is a vivid reminder of the *oblationes* of the Christian Eucharist.

3. From the inexhaustible wealth of sacramentals I shall cite two further important examples. First of all, *alms*. "Alms obliterates sin as water extinguishes fire", says Islamite tradition,[2] and the sanctification of life, the daily enhancing of the power of existence, is expressed as *zakat*: "every articulation of man's body is obliged to bestow alms daily; if the sun rises over him while he mediates between two other persons, then that is a bestowal of alms; if he assists somebody with his (own) animal by allowing him to ride on it or load it with his wares, that is one also; the kind word is another; in every step that he makes in ceremonial obeisance there lies an alms; likewise if he removes a barrier out of the road."[3] From this starting-point, indeed, are spun the threads of religious ethics, but also the fabric of the automatism of power. When a priest sends out an appeal to women, themselves in childbed, for assistance for needy mothers, in which he expresses the hope that "your gift of money may assist your complete recovery and the auspicious growth of your dear child", this is a sacramental in an almost entirely magical sense; and contrasted with this, the words: "Inasmuch as ye have done it unto one of the least of these my brethren, ye have done it unto me",[4] provide the direct connection between sacramental action and the thank-offering brought to the saviour.

A further extreme example of the sacramental is the *Ordeal*. This consists in some simplification of the conditions of life by the immediate introduction of power; in celebration one's own power is at once replaced by that of a different type. We feel as it were convinced that all our acts are futile, and then we transpose our own behaviour *in toto* into association with the activity of the powers. Actually this sacramental is a sacrament like none other, for man's effectiveness is here restricted to merely setting in motion, while everything else with no exception is performed by power. An African husband and wife, for example, lose their child by death: it is clear that one of them must be guilty of causing its death by magic. Together they drink the poisoned potion, *mwamfi*, and say: "Here is our child, dead; perhaps it is we, his parents, who have bewitched him? If it be so, *mwamfi*,

---

[1] *cf.* A. Piganiol, *Recherches sur les Jeux romains*, 1923, 92 *ff.*
[2] Bertholet, *op. cit.*, 16, 22.　　　　[3] *ibid.*, 21.　　　　[4] *Matt.* xxv. 40.

then remain in our bodies; but if it be not our fault, do not stay in us, *mwamfi*, but leave our bodies."[1] Thus all their conduct, even guilt or innocence, is brought within the province of celebration. Power not only takes the place of the judge, but replaces even the utterance of conscience; it knows better than the persons actually concerned whether they are guilty or not.

[1] Lévy-Bruhl, *Primitives and the Supernatural*, 180.

Fritz Bammel, *Das heilige Mahl im Glauben der Volker*, 1950.
G. van der Leeuw, *Sacramentstheologie*, 1949.
R. R. Marett, *Sacraments of Simple Folk*, 1933.

CHAPTER 52

THE SACRAMENT

1. THE word *sacrament* should not be interpreted merely according to its Latin meaning; the Greek expression *mysterion* has to some extent coloured the Roman significance. Thus not only *devotio*, the consecration of the Roman soldier when taking the oath to the colours, but also the entire range of the extraordinarily numinous Greek term, from fulfilled prophecy to the mysterious presence of the *numen*, came to be included in it;[1] "all the richness of the significance of *mysterion* has been transposed to *sacramentum*".[2] If therefore we disregard etymology altogether and enquire what a sacrament implies for religion, then if we do not wish to class all sacramentals with sacraments (which, incidentally, is quite easy to do), we discover a unitary and constant phenomenon by observing two main features: (*1*) the sacrament is the sublimation of some one of the simplest and most elementary of life's functions: washing, eating and drinking, sex intercourse, gestures, speaking; and it is their sublimation because in the sacrament this vital activity is disclosed from its profoundest bases upwards to where it touches the divine. Thus life itself, in its whole extent, is as it were brought into the presence of Power. But (*2*) in those celebrations which I shall henceforth exclusively term sacraments, this Power now becomes bound up with the action, under the form of the saviour.[3] Consequently the sacrament is on the one hand what is quite near, and on the other wholly different and remote: in one respect *fascinans*, in the other *tremendum*,[4] but always *mysterium*. The presupposition of all these ideas, however, is that Power resides within life, and this whether it has developed, or has been created, within it: "if Nature has been rendered impotent, then the sacrament is arbitrary and has no power".[5] On the other hand the sacrament is never the natural process itself, since either magically creating man, or the creative God, must "characterize" Nature.

A. One elementary function of life, thus "characterized", is purifi-

---

[1] *cf.* Anrich, *Mysterienwesen*, 144. H. von Soden, *Zeitschrift f. d. Neut. Wiss.*, 12, 1911, 188 *ff*. O. Casel, *Jahrb. f. Liturgiewiss.* 8, 1928, 226 *ff*. May, *Droit romain*, 228 *f*.
[2] Casel, *ibid.*, 232.   [3] Chap. 12.
[4] Heiler, *Katholizismus*, 532.   [5] Tillich, *Religiöse Verwirklichung*, 167.

cation, which has already been discussed in detail in Chapter 49; there it was explained specifically how purifying became a sacrament. In the *baptismal* act, again, man's status is rendered completely free alike from his own opinion, feeling or approval; the "water" becomes the Power of the blood of Christ. For this reason the blood bath of martyrdom also ranks as a second baptism;[1] through his testimony, the witness by blood participates in the purifying deed of Christ; and I have previously referred to *confirmation* and *extreme unction*.

B. The sacred meal, again, becomes a sacrament in virtue of its connection with the "Lord", the Saviour-God; we find therefore the first *sacramental meals* in the saviour-religions, the so-called mystery religions. "Chaeremon invites thee to dine at the table of the Lord Sarapis in the Sarapeion, to-morrow, the fifteenth, at the ninth hour", reads a very characteristic summons from the circle of Sarapis-Isis initiates.[2] In the Attis mysteries, similarly, the initiate could relate about a sacred meal which he took from the consecrated musical instruments of the cult, and by which alone he appears to have become initiated: "I have eaten out of the drum, I have drunk from the cymbal, I have become an initiate of Attis": ἐκ τυμπάνου βέβρωκα, ἐκ κυμβάλου πέπωκα, γέγονα μύστης ῎Αττεως[3]; and the convert and apologist of Christianity, Firmicus Maternus, did not omit to indicate expressly the parallels with the sacred food of his own religion. In the Eleusinian mysteries, likewise, a sacred drink, the *kykeon*, was consumed, which is referred to in a celebrated mystic formula.[4] Finally we find the ancient Persian meal of bread and water, mixed with the juice of the sacred *haoma* plant, retained in the Mithras mysteries, the *haoma* however being replaced by wine, and a pictorial representation from Konjica in Dalmatia[5] brings before our eyes the meal of Mithras. It was reserved for initiates of one particular rank; probably the designation of this grade, μετέχοντες, means nothing else than that these initiates were allowed to "participate" in the sacred meal. Tertullian, again, draws the parallel: "Mithras celebrates the sacrifice of bread".[6] In all these sacraments, then, the bond between celebration and saviour is certainly present, even though it is not transparent. Only the nocturnal Dionysian orgies, in which the god was eaten in the form of some animal, represent a genuine theophagy: the sacred food was

---

[1] Chap. 29.   [2] Haas, *Bilderatlas*, 9/11, Fig. 16.
[3] Firmicus Maternus, *De errore profanarum religionum*, 18, 1.
[4] Clement of Alexandria, *Protr.* 18.   [5] Haas, *op. cit.*, 15, Fig. 46.
[6] F. Cumont, *Die Mysterien des Mithra*[3], 1923, 145 *ff.*

expressly interpreted as the saviour-god, and so the participant became "filled with the god". From this to the Christian sacrament there is, of course, an enormous interval, since in the latter the link between celebration and Saviour becomes apprehended in a quite peculiar and historic way: the Saviour at Whose table persons meet together for the meal, Whose body they eat and Whose blood they drink, is the Lord, with Whom they have so often sat at table during His earthly life.

Thus in the Christian sacrament very different elements are connected in one living unity; and we may here follow the fine outline made by Brilioth,[1] who for his part relies to some extent on Lietzmann. (*1*) There is the actual *Eucharist*, that is the thank-offering as this originated from the Jewish meal; the blessing of the chalice, the breaking of the bread, are performed by the "Lord" Who is present in the *pneuma* and Who will come soon to feed His people; and in the liturgy *maran atha* is understood equally as in the present and the future.[2] (*2*) This meal is a *communio*, as of old; all those participating in it are united among themselves, but here through the bond in Christ: the union with the brethren is at the same time that with the Lord; and the sacramental of the *osculum pacis*, which occurs at this stage, expresses this union. (*3*) But into this celebration there now enters the remembrance of the Lord, the *anamnesis*; and with this the Eucharist leaves the group of sacramentals, that is of sacred repasts, absolutely, and becomes in the fullest sense a sacrament. Historically, this means that the brotherly meal, the *agape*, is separated from the Eucharist to which it was originally the prelude. But the *anamnesis* places in the foreground not only the glory of God in general, not only the *pneuma* of the Lord, but the historic deed of the Saviour, finally, in the mass in the words of the Institution (*Qui pridie*).[3] (*4*) The *anamnesis*, again, leads to the Eucharistic *sacrifice*. The sacrifice of Christ on Golgotha is the sole actual sacrifice: but it is continued in the dual sacrifice of the sacrament, which consists equally in the repetition of the Lord's sacrifice and of the community's thank-offering, which without His sacrifice would be impossible; from His own, that is, the church sacrifices what is His own. But the idea of sacrifice thus gives to *communio* its profoundest meaning, and conversely, the community is the deed of God *in Christo*; this act of God

---

[1] *Eucharistic Faith and Practice*, 276 *ff*.

[2] Lietzmann, *Messe und Herrenmahl*, 237.

[3] Even in Nietzsche's Parody the *anamnesis* and the eschatological reference persist: "at this (repast) there was nothing else spoken of but the higher man". *Thus Spake Zarathustra*, "The Supper", p. 350 (Foulis Edition).

is therefore no external event, but a participation of the Head in the members and, through the Head, of the members in one another. (5) All these elements of the Christian sacrament attain their highest completion, which is at the same moment their presupposition, in the *mystery* of the Eucharist. This is the sacred presence of the Lord which, in all the elements—the repast, *communio*, *anamnesis* and sacrifice—really gives the celebration the character of a new creation, of a creative deed of God, and compels man to his knees before the mystery of the Incarnation. Christ is present as priest, as sacrifice, and as the church which is His body. "I am the bread of life"; "I am the true vine": this mystical language gives expression to the Eucharistic experience equally as did the amazement of the disciples at Emmaus, who recognized the Lord on His breaking bread, and thus, it may be (according to Lietzmann's acute interpretation), took the first step from the Jewish meal to the Lord's supper—the historical recollection of the *Qui pridie* and equally the boundless praise of "Let us give thanks", εὐχαριστήσωμεν. The sacred food is simultaneously remembrance, sacrifice and the Saviour's presence:

> O thou Memorial of our Lord's own dying,
> O Bread that living art and vivifying,
> Make ever thou my soul on thee to live,
> Ever a taste of heavenly sweetness give.[1]

In this connection, therefore, transubstantiation must be considered as a theoretically grounded reversion to the most primitive aspects in the sacrament. The genuinely primitive sacramental required no transformation whatever: for it, the food in itself was already sacred. In the ancient Christian sacrament, however, this was not the case, but the *epiclesis*[2] was intended to invoke the Lord's spirit into the food. But to-day, in the mass, the consecration, the whispered formula of the Institution, effects a transformation of the elements.[3] In this way power-stuff, changed *ad hoc*, was substituted for the real presence of the Saviour in the Eucharist, equally in the elements and in the sacrificing community, equally in the past (the redemptive

---

[1]   O memoriale   Praesta meae menti
         Mortis Domini,   De te vivere
         Panis vivus, vitam   Et te illi semper
         Praestans homini: Dulce sapere.

Thomas Aquinas, *Rhythmus ad Sanctam Eucharistiam, Adoro te devote.*

[2] Chap. 62.   [3] *cf.* Heiler, *Katholizismus,* 224 *ff.*

history), in the future (*maran atha*), and at the present moment; and in this manner the bond with the historic Lord is relaxed.[1] On the other hand, as against Protestant spiritualizing it must be maintained that the sacrament, in accord with its essential nature, concerns the whole man and descends from a realm which does not differentiate at all between physical and psychical effects. The *pneuma* of the Lord, therefore, produces neither "thinghood" nor "spirituality", but gives new life to "creatures".[2] Nothing that has been created "can blend with the divine. And yet there is another union besides that of mere knowing and loving—the union of subsisting life."[3]

C. The third type of sacramental community is marriage. In the Eleusinian mysteries the "holy marriage", ἱερὸς γάμος, and the birth of the child that succeeded to this, were signs of salvation: "Is not the gloomy descent there, and the solemn meeting between the hierophant and the priestess, he alone and she alone? Are not the lamps extinguished? and does not the vast and countless assembly of the people believe that what they two accomplish in the darkness means their salvation?"[4] And when the torches were lit once more the saviour's birth was solemnly announced to the people.[5] Thus sexual union was "characterized" as the medium of union with divine Power; and since this Power had the form of a saviour we must speak here too of a "sacrament"; it is indeed well known that this celebration was actually apprehended as such, particularly in mysticism and in monastic rites:[6] Christ Himself, for instance, presented the betrothal ring to St. Catherine of Siena. In other respects, however, this sacrament has acquired no adequate form in the Christian church. Among heretics, again, matters were sometimes different: the Valentinians, for example, celebrated salvation by erecting a bridal chamber and subjecting candidates for initiation to a rite which they called spiritual—"pneumatized"—marriage, πνευματικὸς γάμος.[7] Moreover, so far as this sacrament is concerned, a remarkable transposition has

---

[1] *cf.* Heiler, *Katholischer und evangelischer Gottesdienst*[2], 1925, 18.

[2] Chap. 45. The entire famous passage, 1 *Cor.* x, xi, referring to communion with demons in the sacrificial meal and to that with Christ in the Lord's supper, is full of this idea; the physical is most clearly expressed in xi. 29 *f*. Whoever unworthily makes an *agape* out of the Eucharist in order to indulge himself, and thus "fails to distinguish the Lord's body", eats and drinks to his own condemnation, and may indeed die of it.

[3] Guardini, *Von heiligen Zeichen*, 53.

[4] Asterius, *Encom. mart.* 194, Combe; *cf.* Farnell, *Cults of the Greek States*, III, 356.   [5] Hippolytus, *Philosophoumena*, 164.

[6] Chap. 22.   [7] Anrich, *Mysterienwesen*, 77.

been effected in the Christian church; for marriage, as unique among sacraments, is not celebration of a power external to the ceremony itself, that is to say of the Saviour's Power, but became exalted to the rank of sacrament by the potency of the ceremony as such. In other words, marriage in itself is a sacrament, and the wedded pair themselves bestow it on one another; thus the profound basis of the elementary function of life has been declared as in and of itself sacred, and the union that is entered into is, in its essence, supernatural.

D. Sacramental *action*, and *E*, the sacramental *word*, will be discussed in Chapters 53 and 58.

2. It is possible, again, to confer remoteness on the sacrament by converting it into *myth*; and then neither life's own immediate sacredness, nor that bestowed by the saviour upon life in celebration, is evident forthwith, but the longed for powerfulness is perceived in the distance extending from "here" to "there". Thus, as has previously been observed, the sacred food of the sacrificial repast became the "food of the gods"—nectar and ambrosia; and the *soma* rite brought a systematized mythology to maturity. But the saviour-meal also can be removed into the far distance. In the words of the *Institution* in the Eucharist, in fact, there is an allusion to the Messianic repast which the Lord will hold hereafter with His people;[1] and this meal with the Messiah is to be discerned elsewhere too in Jewish ideas.[2] On the other hand, the repast in the Mithras mysteries was a continuation of the mythical last supper in which the god took part on earth.[3] In the legend of the Holy Grail, however, the Christian sacrament became rendered wholly mythical. The Grail, originally probably a wishing-bowl such as appears frequently in fairy tales,[4] together with the spear that had pierced the Saviour's side and which allowed —the Eucharistic—blood and water to flow, became a receptacle of *salus*, a communion vessel, and can be understood only in the light of cult experience, in accord with Burdach's acute exposition.

---

[1] *Matt.* xxvi. 29.
[2] Hölscher, *Geschichte der israelitischen und jüdischen Religion; cf.* Index, *Mahlzeit, eschatologisch.*
[3] Cumont, *Mysterien des Mithra*, 124, 146.
[4] *cf.* E. Wechssler, *Die Sage vom heiligen Gral in ihrer Entwicklung bis auf Richard Wagners Parsifal*, 1898. Hertz, *Parzival*. F. R. Schröder, *Die Parzivalfrage*, 1928. K. Burdach, *Vorspiel*, I, 1, 1925, 161 *ff.* G. Dumézil, *Le Festin d'Immortalité*, 1924, 179. W. Stärk, *Uber den Ursprung der Grallegende*, 1903.

3. From all this it follows that the sacrament may have a threefold significance.[1] It can be (*1*) a *celebration that produces activity:* the action itself brings something into being, causes the sacred power to bestir itself. (*2*) The sacrament is a *celebration which is itself activity:* in the action the Universe gets into motion, to-day as always. Everything is a sacrament, or can at least become one: the world is the living garment of God. This is the concept of the sacrament in romantic mysticism. (*3*) The sacrament may be a *celebration that is grounded in activity*, wherein a Will (of God, or of the Saviour) executes the act of creation or new creation: the sacrament is then creation and bestowal of power in one. In all three types alike, however, Nature is no inanimate object, no thing, but living Power,[2] while this powerfulness breaks forth into salvation in some miraculous way. But the bond with the historical Saviour can be forged only by the third type of significance; and therefore only this third type is a sacrament in its full sense.

But the second, mystic-romantic type requires some further consideration. In certain respects it is a regress, by way of an extensive *détour*, to the most primitive viewpoints. For as in the Dionysiac orgies milk, honey and wine issued from the earth,[3] so according to this mode of apprehending life, Nature presents sacramental power immediately and without any "characterization" at all: once again, therefore, the sacrament becomes a sacramental. No new creation whatever is necessary: without more ado Nature herself is divine food to him who knows how to perceive her in her divinity: God is always on earth, and need not first of all descend. Departing from the Christian sacrament, this idea leads to the regressive transformation of what has been "characterized" into ordinary matter of fact: the sacramental food becomes merely the daily nourishment. From the time he became an anchorite Nicholas Bulgaris, for instance, ate no food except the Eucharist; and this is related about other saints also.[4] Certainly there still persists here the limitation of what has not been characterized. But this may become an expansion of the characterized, such as occurred in Romanticism; Schleiermacher's "Christmas Thoughts" seeks Mary in every mother, while his Ferdinand passes "almost immediately from conversation" to the sacred act of

[1] G. van der Leeuw, *Strukturpsychologie und Theologie.*
[2] Tillich.   [3] Euripides, *Bacchae*, 142 *ff.*
[4] Jos. von Görres, *Mystik, Magie und Dämonie*, edited by J. Bernhart, 1927, 76 (= Görres, *Die christliche Mystik*, I², 1879, 372 *ff.*).

baptism.[1] Many romantics, too, dreamed that they would like to write a Bible themselves; and this universally sacramental piety found its finest expression in Novalis:

> Few know the secret of love;
> Few feel unsatiated, and have eternal thirst.
> To earthly sense the divine meaning of communion
> Is but an enigma;
> But whoso has, some time,
> Drawn the life breath from passionate and beloved lips,
> And whose heart has been molten
> By the sacred glow in quivering waves,
> Whose eye has been opened
> That he can plumb
> The immeasurable depths of heaven,
> He shall eat of His body
> And drink of His blood,
> To all eternity.

Here again, just as in the primitive world, the body's own specific potency is the ground of the sacrament:

> Who has fathomed the exalted meaning of the earthly body?
> Who can say that he understands the blood?

The saviour, too, is the life of the world itself:

> From plant and stone, from sea and light,
> His childlike countenance shines forth.
> In all things His childlike action,
> His warm love, will never rest;
> He nestles eternally close to every breast,
> Unconscious of Himself.
> To us God, to Himself a child,
> He loves us all most tenderly;
> He becomes our food and our drink,
> And faithfulness is the gratitude that He loves most.[2]

Y. Brilioth, *Eucharistic Faith and Practice*, 1930.
O. Casel, *Die Liturgie als Mysterienfeier* [3-5], 1923.
A. Dieterich, *Eine Mithrasliturgie*[2], 1910.
L. Duchesne, *Origines du culte chrétien*[4], 1908.
H. Lietzmann, *Messe und Herrenmahl*, 1926.
P. Tillich, *Religiöse Verwirklichung*[2], 1930.

[1] F. Schleiermacher, *Die Weihnachtsfeier*.   [2] *Geistliche Lieder*, 13, 11.

CHAPTER 53

SERVICE

1. IN the sacramental and in the sacrament sacred action is a service, a *ministerium* or an *officium*. For in the cult the actual agent is not man nor the human community, but sacred Power, whether this is merely the sacred common element or a sacred will. In worship, therefore, "to do", "to act", is always sacramental. Something different and something more is done than what is actually performed: things are manipulated to which man himself is not superior; he stands *within* a sacred activity and not above this. He does not govern, that is to say, but serves.[1] In many languages, indeed, "to do" has the subsidiary meaning of: culturally to do, to sacrifice, to perform magic.[2] A *dromenon*, then, always depends on some deed that is superior to man: it is always "re-done" or "pre-done",[3] and in *this* sense cult action is "representative" action: not however in Schleiermacher's sense, when by this expression he implied the symbolic representation of the content of faith,[4] but with the much more profound significance of representing the original sacred action. *It is done*: or, *God acts*; but in both cases man can only *repeat*, "follow", or "represent". In worship, therefore, activity is always "official", representative.

Thus the priest acts and speaks "in the name of Jesus": the actual speaker, the sole actor, is God. Similarly in countless dances, sacred games *etc.* of primitive peoples it is the gods, demons and spirits who act and speak; the priests or other "stage managers" are merely representatives of the sacred power.[5] Only thus can we understand why costume and mask are indispensable in cult activities; the Reformation itself made new priestly costumes out of Luther's scholarly robes. And whoever has ministered in customary garb, even though it may have been only the simple gown of a Protestant clergyman, knows that clothes make the man, or rather abstract the man so that only the *minister*, the *servant*, remains. This, however, holds good to a much greater extent of the *mask*: it converts the man who is acting

---

[1] *cf.* Usener, *Heilige Handlung*, 423 *f*.

[2] Ancient Egyptian *ir*, Lat. *facere*, Ital. *fattura*, Greek, *dromena*.

[3] Harrison, *Themis*, 43.

[4] *cf.* G. Mensching, *Die liturgische Bewegung in der evangelischen Kirche*, 1925, 26.

[5] Preuss, *Geistige Kultur*, 81.

in the cult into the *representative*,[1] and in the masked dances of many primitive peoples the dancers *re-present*, in the literal sense, demons or gods, and also the event that is being enacted; in other terms, they present the former afresh, and the latter they present anew; they *are* spirits or demons and the occurrence actually *takes place* once again.[2] If the derivation of the word *persona* from the Etruscan φersu be correct, this too implies the same state of affairs: the masks are then the dead, or the gods of the dead, and the name of the departed became that of the mask.[3]

An ancient Egyptian *Text* describes the deceased, that is, in fact, the priest of the dead, as thus addressing the god: "He who speaks should speak what is, and should not speak what is not; the god abhors the lying word. If I greet (?) thee, then do not say that it is I. For I am thy son, I am thine heir."[4] The dead person thus approaches the god officially, in accord with his quality; it is not he who speaks, but his "mask". Similarly in Christian worship, it is not the priest who acts but the church, and this also merely as the Body of Christ.

2. The sacred act is therefore service. But in service man is active: the body receives a rhythmic swing; whoever is celebrating, dances. "All over the world, in the magico-religious stage, primitive man dances where we should pray or praise", as Miss J. E. Harrison has pointed out.[5] Thus the *dance* is not merely an esthetic pursuit existing side by side with other more practical activities. It is the service of the god, and generates power: the rhythm of movement has a compelling force; and this still holds good for us too in the case of erotic dancing. For the dance is the aphrodisiac *par excellence*, of the coarsest as well as of the finest type. But it is not restricted to the power of love alone; and to primitive man it was simultaneously work and pleasure, sport and cult. In the dance life is ordered to some powerful rhythm and reverts to its potent primeval motion, and thus it is possible to attain to all manner of things "by dancing", from one's daily bread to heavenly bliss. There are love-, war- and hunting-dances, which

---

[1] *cf.* Chap. 25 *ff.*

[2] Lévy-Bruhl, *Primitives and the Supernatural*, 123 *f.*; *cf.* G. van der Leeuw, *Pia fraus, Mensch en Maatschappy*, 8, 1932.

[3] F. Altheim, *AR.* 27, 1929, 48 *ff.* An analogous case is *larva*, meaning both ghost and mask.

[4] *Pyramidentexte* (Sethe), 1160.   [5] *Epilegomena*, 12.

represent *in actu* the desired event, the love union, success in war and hunting. But there are also dances which, according to our standards, are of purely economic type; among the Mexican Indians, for example, dancing is equivalent to working. When the harvest is being brought in, someone remains at home and dances all day long so that it may be successful; he sets the power of life in motion. The festival season of the Cagaba Indians, again, is called the "time of work" and consists of a very strenuous dance lasting several days.[1] This economic dance however is no mere matter of business; it is rather a cult, since the sacred power of life is "celebrated" and set in motion.[2] The dance then is originally of the nature of a cult, so that whenever it is performed for pure pleasure the elements of the cult have been suppressed. "Spiritual" good can also be obtained by dancing: in the mysteries the dance was one of the principal means of expression,[3] while the miserable Indian tribes of Central Brazil have repeatedly attempted to reach the coast in their perpetual wanderings, and to become so light through the most strenuous dancing and fasting that they might reach heaven direct from the dance.[4] Indeed even in Christianity the celestial motion itself has been regarded as a dance, and earthly bliss as its imitation: "what can be more blessed than on earth to imitate the dance of the angels?"[5]

But movement in celebration has a dual character. In the first place power is concentrated, restricted, established and elevated by the rhythmic arrangement, and in the second superfluous power is released, cast away in recurrent movement. Powerfulness is either attained by dancing, or else superfluous power is danced away. The second type of motion occurs in the ecstatic dance, or rather in the dance so far as it is ecstatic (and it is almost always so to a certain extent). The dancing Dionysus, satyrs and maenads of Grecian vase paintings provide an excellent ideal picture of this ecstatic dance, which is moreover native to very many peoples. Dancing and mystical losing of self, dancing and ecstatic reeling, are so closely connected that the dance may even become the symbol of mystic unity with God; as Jalaluddin Rumi

[1] Preuss, *Geistige Kultur*, 82 *ff. Tod und Unsterblichkeit*, 33.
[2] *cf.* G. van der Leeuw, *In dem Himmel ist ein Tanz. Über die religiöse Bedeutung des Tanzes und des Festzuges, passim;* Lévy-Bruhl, *Primitives and the Supernatural*, 114 *f.*; Oesterley, *The Sacred Dance*, 2.
[3] Lucian, *De saltatione.*   [4] Preuss, *Tod und Unsterblichkeit*, 5.
[5] St. Basilius, *Epist.* ii, *ad Greg. cf.* P. Verheyden, *De Maagdendans (Handel. van den Mechelschen Kring van Oudheidkunde, Letteren en Kunst*, 27, 1922); G. van der Leeuw, *op. cit., passim.*

says: "He who knows the power of the dance dwells in God, for he knows that love slays."[1]

Movement and counter-movement, again, together constitute the *dramatic character* of service. All cult is drama: power is amassed and also repelled. Or in the language of the religion of Will: God comes to man, while man approaches God. The sacred game (*sacer ludus*) represents the process of this encounter, the approach to, and avoidance of, each other; it is found in the celebrations of all peoples, either in the form of actual performances of events as in mask-dances and sacred mystery plays, or in symbolic form as in the liturgy. The classical example of both types is provided in the Eleusinian mysteries, in which the sacred process was represented now in the purely dramatic form of the flower gathering (*anthology*), the carrying off (*harpage*) of Persephone and the wanderings (*plane*) of Demeter, and again in the symbolic dramatic form of the ear of corn mown in silence. The Christian church, however, relegated the dramatic performance type to the merely semi-ecclesiastical medieval "mysteries", while in its own worship the symbolic-sacramental form predominates exclusively.

Participation in dramatic service, still further, was obviously never a mere spectatorship nor listening, since the entire community actually or virtually took part and participated in celebration. This is most clearly demonstrated in the so-called *mock battles*, such as were customary for example in ancient Egypt in the Osiris cult, between the god's adherents and those of his antagonist Set, but which were also common in Greece and Rome and are still to be found to some extent in popular customs to-day.[2] The element of representation *in actu*, of repetition, is excellently interpreted by Piganiol in his account of the purpose of the games as "the renewal of the dead, of the gods, of the living and of the whole world";[3] and "the first introduction of games was intended as a religious expiation", as Livy says.[4] The combat in the games is always a symbol of the staking of life, the contest between life and death.[5] The two opponents (or the two parties forming the *catervae*) acted the game of the powers and its ultimate decision.[6]

---

[1] G. van der Leeuw, *op. cit.*, 50 and *passim*.

[2] For Egypt *cf.* Sethe, *Dramatische Texte;* Greece and Rome, A. Piganiol, *Recherches sur les Jeux romains*, 1923; Kristensen, *Livet*, 221; *Spelen, passim*; Usener, *Heilige Handlung*, 435.

[3] *op. cit.*, 149.   [4] VII, 3.   [5] Kristensen, *op. cit.*

[6] Usener, *Heilige Handlung*; on popular customs, *etc.*, *cf.* I. von Reinsberg-Düringsfeld, *Das festliche Jahr*, 60. E. K. Chambers, *The Mediaeval Stage*, I, 149 *ff.*

Finally, the *procession* is an elementary dance and fulfils the purpose of mobilizing the cult community, that is the sacred common element, the activating of power; and every procession is as it were a sacramental procession, so far as it sets something sacred in motion and extends its powerfulness over a certain region. Thus the blessing enclosed within the Holy of Holies is spread "over village and town, over field and plain"[1] by the blessed sacrament procession, as this is employed by the Roman Catholic Church. But the procession is not necessarily linked to the sacrament,[2] since some other powerful object can be carried around also: in many popular customs it is a naked girl (*ritus paganus*), while in Methana in Greece the husbandman led a menstruating woman round his orchard.[3] Fundamentally, then, the procession is a circuit, whether it wanders about through the village or the town, or makes an actual circle around an object, a field or a house *etc.* It restricts and concentrates power, and on the other hand can avert malicious powers. The ancient Roman farmer's procession round his field boundaries, the *ambarvalia*, aimed at ensuring fertility[4], and in Suabia reading the Gospel at the four corners of the village green at Whitsuntide was regarded as a "weather blessing".[5] But making the circuit may also have threatening significance: power is fixed within a circle in order to destroy, and at the seventh circuit Jericho fell to this charm.

3. From sacred action, the service of power, there developed on the one hand the *liturgy*, and on the other the *drama*; the latter pertains, however, to the Phenomenology of Art.[6] The liturgy is never completely verbal, but remains always dramatic action; and the most ancient Egyptian liturgies we possess already exhibited the character of dialogue and were solemnized dramatically;[7] in the Christian church, also, for a long time no sharp boundary could be drawn between dramatic and liturgical action. Christmas- and Easter-plays, again, developed from the liturgy, and the dialogue form of the Easter trope, *quem quaeritis?*, is still wholly liturgical, while the Easter sepulchre and the *praesepe* with the custom of "rocking the crib of the holy

[1] Heiler, *Katholizismus*, 177.   [2] Chap. 52.

[3] Nilsson, *History of Greek Religion*, 87 f.

[4] Macrobius, *Sat.* iii, 5, 7; *pro frugibus facere.*

[5] Reinsberg-Düringsfeld, *Das festliche Jahr*, 189.

[6] On the genealogy of the drama *cf.* H. Reich, *Der Mimus*, 1903. G. van der Leeuw, *Wegen en Grenzen, over de verhouding van religie en kunst*, 1932.

[7] Erman, *Denkmal memphitischer Theologie.* Sethe, *Dramatische Texte.*

child" are vestiges of drama in the liturgy; similarly the *elevatio crucis*, which retains the character of a dramatic mysteries celebration.[1]

In course of time, however, the liturgy has shown the tendency to restrict itself more and more to the sacramental word, the sacrament and the sacramental. In its festival calendar the church annually experiences the entire *vita Domini*, the story of salvation; but it does not really act this. It contents itself with a repetition in the potency of the word, the sacraments and the sacramental. For all liturgies, however, the idea of *repetition* remains the standard. Power is served by being actualized; it is represented by being brought into the present. All service, then, is a perpetual *da capo*. Power is either conjured up by man, or it renews itself; or else the Will, in whose guise Power became recognized, creatively makes all things new.

W. B. Kristensen, *Over de godsdienstige beteekenis van enkele oude wedstryden en spelen* (*Theologisch Tydschrift*, N. R. 2 (44), 1910).

G. van der Leeuw, *In dem Himmel ist ein Tanz. Über die religiöse Bedeutung des Tanzes und des Festzuges*, 1931.

W. O. E. Oesterley, *The Sacred Dance*, 1923.

[1] Chambers, *Mediaeval Stage*, II, 20 *ff.*, 42 *ff.* H. Brinkmann, *Xenia Bonnensia, Festschrift*, 1929, 109 *ff.*

CHAPTER 54

DIVINATION

1. "AN enquirer", observes Thurnwald, "turns to higher powers through the medium of the *oracle* with the intention of receiving instructions for his own conduct, or for the actions of others, in the form of signs";[1] and the question concerns, first of all, the *locus* of power, the *situation*. The person in doubt as to which course to pursue attempts to discover what the situation is; divination, therefore, yields prophecy with regard to the future only in a subordinate sense. For the enquirer wants to know not what will happen, but that what he himself desires will occur.[2] Thus the signs he perceives and interprets are simultaneously the causes of the event and signs that a power is somewhere operative. Bushmen, for instance, remain dissatisfied with an unfavourable answer from the dice oracle, and so they continue to question the dice till they tell them what they wish to hear;[3] very young children do exactly the same if they do not gain the desired result in a game. And this means that it is not a matter of any mere abstract foreknowledge of some indifferent future, but rather an investigation of the site of the power, pursued until the favourable place and the right time have been discovered. Power, celebrated in the cult, is in divination explored or conjectured.

This investigation into the nature of the situation, which at one time has a calm and almost scientific character and at another a more ecstatic form,[4] cannot of course interrogate the whole Universe. It must therefore select a section, or as it were a ground plan of this; and this it does in an apparently arbitrary, but actually strictly methodical, manner. The task of Chinese wind- and water-sages (*feng-shui*), for example, is to ensure "the harmony of human life with Nature"; they must discover the correct days and other conditions for all important actions (selection of days), and for this task a specific "office for obedient conformity with heaven" is responsible. Building a house, tilling the fields, choosing the site for a grave, *etc.*, must also

---

[1] *Orakel, Lexikon der Vorgeschichte.*   [2] Lévy-Bruhl, *Primitive Mentality,* 141.
[3] Lévy-Bruhl, *Quelques remarques sur la divination dans les sociétés primitives,* 85.
[4] Plato had already drawn this distinction; *Phaedrus,* 244; "Oionistic" and "Mantic".

be brought into precise accord with time, place and the "situation" in general. The whole destiny of someone, it may be the child born in some house, depends on the faithful fulfilment of the conditions,[1] and the knowledge these diviners possess has a very comprehensive basis. Less universal was the knowledge amassed by the Roman *augurs*. The *augur* was an "increaser", one who renders prosperous (*cf. augustus*); he was first of all *auspex*, one who observed the flight of birds; subsequently he interpreted other celestial signs also. State action could be executed only *auspicato*; to be able to interpret the indications a section must be made from existent reality, and this was done by a locality being set free and so declared (*locus liberatus et effatus*): "by the use of fixed and settled words it was detached from its environment and delimited from this" (*fando exempta*). This place, a quadrangle, was designated *templum*, and was thus in the most literal sense a "section" of the given reality in and with respect to which the "situation" was to be investigated.[2] The old formula for the king's augury, again, proves expressly that it was an affair of *fas*.[3]

Thus divination is far more than any mere satisfaction of curiosity or assurance of success. For it was impossible to take any step in life at all without knowing about the "situation", and also whether powers, and which specific powers, would be set in motion by the intended action. Many primitive people, indeed, do absolutely nothing without divination; thus the Dyaks: "When on a campaign, all the movements made by these same Dyaks depend upon omens. They cannot advance nor retreat, not attack nor change their position, until the auguries are known. I have known a chief who lived in a hut for six weeks, partly waiting for the twittering of birds to be in a proper direction, and partly detained by his followers. . . . The white man who commands the forces is supposed to have an express bird and lucky charm to guide him always; and to these the Dyaks trust considerably. 'You are our bird; we follow you,' as they say."[4] The correspondence between reality and the section made from reality, for example the starry heavens, the flight of birds or animals' entrails, is (to repeat) apparently purely arbitrary; yet it is derived from the universal idea that all things without exception are connected with each other, and

---

[1] J. Witte gives a good description in *Die ostasiatischen Kulturreligionen*, 62. *cf.* C. Clemen, *Die nichtchristlichen Kulturreligionen*, I, 1921, 44 *ff.* H. Hackmann, *Chineesche Wysgeeren*, I, 1930, 75.

[2] Wissowa, *Religion und Kultus der Römer*, 523 *ff.*   [3] Livy, I, 18, 7.

[4] Lévy-Bruhl, *How Natives Think*, 291, after Brooke.

that everything participates in everything else: the potency of one may therefore be found in the other. There is in fact no "other" in any actual sense, just as "there is no such thing as chance".[1] The entrails form a kind of microcosm, even where there are no cosmological ideas of the type of the so-called "ancient Oriental *Weltanschauung*". Thus on the Island of Talaut in the Dutch East Indies poultry and pigs are sacrificed before an *accouchement*, so that the signs may be read from the animals' entrails; if these are propitious the people rejoice, while if they are unfavourable a fresh sacrifice is made to induce the spirits to change their minds—that is to realize the "situation" better.[2] It is well known how the inspection of the liver became a sort of science in Babylon;[3] nor need I refer again to astrology, the nature of which has already been indicated.[4]

As regards divination by means of *words*, however, some further remarks are necessary. An old Tonga soothsayer in South Africa compared his own section of reality directly with the Bible; it was a systematic collection of bones, each of which had its special significance: a sheep's bone was a chief, that of a goat a subject *etc.* "You Christians believe in a Bible" said he; "our bible is better than yours: it is the bones of the oracle";[5] here, then, a system of things is opposed to one of words. Thus the word itself becomes powerful as soon as the thing has become merely a thing—in other terms, has had its power abstracted from it.[6] Special potency is ascribed to the written word; the arbitrary opening of the Bible, and the oracular interpretation of the text thus found, are well known, while in a similar way Virgil was opened in the Middle Ages (*sortes virgilianae*).[7]

But when the oracular word is of the ecstatic type it receives another kind of powerfulness. The Pythia, for example, belonged to the category of "enthusiasts";[8] originally she prophesied on the day of the god's epiphany (Apollo), and the fumes arising from the fissure in the ground, over which her tripod stood, threw her into ecstasy.[9] Other sections from reality, from which the situation could be dis-

---

[1] Lévy-Bruhl, *Primitives and the Supernatural*, 57.

[2] H. J. Stokking, *Mededeelingen vanwege het Ned. Zendelinggenootschap*, 63, 224.

[3] Jastrow, *Religion Babyloniens und Assyriens*, II, 213 *ff*.

[4] Chap. 7.   [5] Thurnwald, *loc. cit.*   [6] Chap. 3.

[7] J. Burckhardt, *Die Kultur der Renaissance in Italien*, II[12], 1919, 197. Two suspected persons resolve to fly because they have opened the *Aeneid* at III, 44:—"Ah! fly, fly the ruthless land"; *cf.* the detailed description in Rabelais, *Pantagruel*, III, 10, who remarks, however, that "I do not wish always to conclude that this fate is universally infallible, so that you may not be deceived on this point".

[8] Chap. 29.   [9] G. van der Leeuw, *Goden en Menschen*, 94 *ff*.

covered, were dreams (for example, in antiquity the dream-oracle of Trophonios[1]) and the lot.

2. So far as the word is employed in oracles, still further, it is an unintelligible expression; and whenever it was imparted in a state of rapture, as in ecstatic mantic, this was quite natural. But although the Virgilian or Biblical word, used oracularly, has in itself a comprehensible meaning, this too leads to no intelligible context; it merely ascertains the situation. No matter what method of enquiry has been utilized, then, the oracle furnishes actual intructions only through *interpretation*. The Pythia herself might rave, but her exegetes, the *hosioi* or "theologians", were sane enough:[2] or "the Sybil, with raving lips uttering things solemn, unadorned, and unembellished . . . because of the god in her":[3] nevertheless the Sybilline books played a quite rational rôle in the history of the religion of antiquity. The famous oracle of Amon too, which was revealed to Alexander in the Great Oasis, had a religious-political character; the god, who greeted the Macedonian as his own son, thereby acted as he had already done so frequently at dynastic changes in Egypt: he carried out a wholly reasonable, but at the same time religiously based, political system.[4] It can thus be understood that the oracle has had, in many cases, great cult significance, whether in the religious, the political or the ethical sphere; and in this respect the oracle is typical of the relationship between revelation and cult life.[5] Thus the Hebraic *torah* developed from oracles, the "interrogation of Jahveh", while the significance of the Delphic oracle for Greek culture can scarcely be over-estimated. Ancient lawgivers, too, invoked the oracle's sanction for their work;[6] the religious tendencies of the different eras, among others the cult of Dionysus and the worship of heroes, subsisted under the protection of Delphi;[7] no colonies were founded without questioning the oracle, which indeed almost fulfilled the functions of an emigration bureau;[8] and slaves might use the sanctuary of Apollo as a bank where they

---

[1] *cf.* the detailed description in Samter's *Religion der Griechen*, 40 *f.*

[2] Plutarch, *On the Cessation of the Oracles*, 15. Nilsson, *History of Greek Religion*, 191.

[3] Heracleitus, *Fr.* 92 (Diels). (Burnet.)

[4] G. Maspero, *Comment Alexandre devint Dieu en Egypte (Annuaire de l'École prat. des hautes Études*, 1897). Ed. Meyer, *Gottesstaat, Militärherrschaft und Ständewesen in Ägypten (Sitz. ber. der preuss. Akad. der Wiss., phil.-hist. Kl.*, 1928, 28).

[5] Chap. 85.   [6] Farnell, *Cults*, IV, 198 *f.*

[7] *ibid.*, 202 *ff.* According to Farnell, Delphi is a parallel to the Curia, which canonizes saints.   [8] *ibid.*, 200 *ff.*

could deposit their savings until they had amassed enough to purchase their liberty.[1]

On the other hand, rationalization of the investigation into the situation brought with it the danger that the inadequacy of the methods and practice might betray itself quite unmistakably. Thus Sophocles retains only Delphi and rejects the other oracles;[2] while "in the Second Punic War Marcellus was carried about in a litter with the blinds drawn in order to prevent the possibility of his seeing anything of ill omen":[3] a remarkable fusion of observance and brutal scepticism. But as is so often the case, together with scepticism subjectivation and moralization expanded: for as naïve belief declines, ethical convictions arise. In any case, the philosophers of the fourth century ascribed the same disposition to the Delphic oracle as is expressed in the parable of the widow's mite: it preferred the Arcadian's simple cereal gifts to the pompous piety of the Asiatic.[4] The story related by Herodotus about Glaucus is also famous: Glaucus had misappropriated some property confided to his charge, and desired to know from the oracle whether he should bring it into his indisputable possession by an oath. The Pythia allowed him to see that she knew all about the matter; so he regretted his question, but the Pythia replied "that it was as bad to have tempted the god as it would have been to have done the deed".[5]

[1] Farnell, *Cults*, IV, 178 f. [2] Nilsson, *History of Greek Religion*, 274.
[3] W. R. Halliday, *Lectures on the History of Roman Religion*, 145.
[4] Farnell, *Cults*, IV, 210; cf. R. Herzog, *Das delphische Orakel als ethischer Preisrichter*, in E. Horneffer, *Der junge Platon*, I, 1922, 149 ff.
[5] Herodotus, VI, 86 (Rawlinson); van der Leeuw, *Goden en Menschen*, 106.

CHAPTER 55

SACRED TIME

1. CELEBRATION is carried on in *time*. We moderns, of course, read time from the clock. But this is time that has already become spatialized, a "spurious concept, due to the trespassing of the idea of space upon the field of pure consciousness".[1] The spatiality of time, further, brings with it homogeneity; we count the hours and seconds —regard them, that is to say, as equivalent things. But they are neither things, nor perfectly alike: this they become only in space.[2] Homogeneous time thus measured in hours, days and years, therefore, is only a symbol of real time, of "duration":[3] but in duration itself every moment has its own unique value. On the dial the minutes all look alike; but in duration each possesses its own significance, exactly as in a melody each note has a distinct value.[4] Similarly we describe a circle as a straight line with infinitely many angles; but actually it is a curve, that is each point overflows into the adjacent point; there are no angles whatever, and no one has as yet solved the squaring of the circle.[5]

A time is therefore always some definite time, at first the given, and then the best time, the time of the due situation, *kairos*, the time of grace. For this reason we deal here with "sacred time". The year of the primitive community, for example, is by no means a year like that on an office calendar. It has value: it is a "year of salvation" that brings with it life. Similarly the ancient Greek *horai* (seasons) and *eniautos* (year) appear to ourselves as rather abstract entities; but to the Greeks "their virtue, their very being, was in the flowers and fruits they always carry in their hands".[6] Thus the year brings fruit and is indissolubly linked with the saviour.[7] But in the year, again, each season has some specific value. Spring brings salvation, while Winter withdraws it: Spring is the god's epiphany, Summer his sojourn or *epidemia*, and Winter his departure, *apodemia*; and within the seasons,

---

[1] Bergson, *Time and Free Will*, 98.
[2] Nietzsche, *Human, All Too Human*, 33, 34 (Foulis Edition).
[3] Bergson, *ibid.*, 90, 91, 115.   [4] *ibid.*, 98 *ff.*
[5] *cf.* K. Heim, *Glaubensgewissheit*[2], 81, 70.   [6] Harrison, *Themis*, 185.
[7] Chap. 11, 12.

too, days and hours have individual significance: they are either favourable or unfavourable.

This specific value of times, still further, distinguishes duration from dreamless sleep. Certainly the mythical consciousness[1] tends to allow time "to stand still"; this means however not that the clock stands still, but that every "when" has become a matter of sheer indifference. It is in this timelessness that *fairy tales* subsist: in an eternal present, or "in those days", or "once upon a time". In the sleeping beauty's castle all movement has ceased; the cook stands quite still with his hand raised to give the pantry boy a cuff on the ear, but he will strike only when the charm has been broken.[2] This cessation of duration acquires the religious designation of *eternity*:[3] Beatrice sees God

> where all time and place
> Are present.[4]

But while celebration certainly has this background of eternity, it is itself a part of the time movement; it is at the same moment, however, the deed of man, who stands stationary in the midst of time because he finds the "situation", and who therefore does not simply surrender to duration but firmly plants his feet, and for one moment concentrates both himself and time. He who is celebrating, so to say, controls time; he attempts to dominate it. For here also he cannot simply accept the given: he is first startled and then becomes alarmed; "temporality reveals itself as the significance of actual care".[5] Duration, then, is the great stream flowing relentlessly on: but man, encountering Power, must halt. He then makes a section, a *tempus*; and he celebrates a "sacred time", a festival. In this manner he shows that he declines the given as such, and seeks possibility.[6]

But in so doing, periodicity is assigned to time; duration unfolds and rolls on from section to section, and at the halting places Power manifests itself. They are the beginning and the end, and this in fact in the Greek pre-Socratic sense of the word ἀρχή, half beginning and half being.[7] All time passes in periods. A grey mannikin implores a woman in childbed to go with him, but she cannot; the mannikin

---

[1] Chap. 82.

[2] Chap. 60; *cf.* G. van der Leeuw, *Tyd en Eeuwigheid* (*Onze Eeuw*, 1922).

[3] Chap. 87.

[4] Dante, *Paradiso*, XXIX, 12 (Cary): *dove s'appunta ogni ubi ed ogni quando.*

[5] Heidegger, *op. cit.*, 326.

[6] For the cultural "distinction" of incisions in Time *cf.* Cassirer, *Philosophie der Symbolischen Formen*, II, 138.   [7] *cf.* Cassirer, *op. cit.*, 4.

departs weeping: "now I must travel on for another hundred years until I find another suitable person".[1] The *motif* of the battle that renews itself nightly is also very well known, among other sources from the saga of Hilde and Gudrun:[2] "mythical eternities are periodic";[3] even eschatology, with its millennial reigns and other periods, cannot escape this.[4] But the *tempus*, the section within the course of time, is never the figure upon the clock: it indicates the critical point which, marked out by celebration, clearly reveals the potency of duration.

2. Thus arose the calendar: not, however, the calendar hanging in an office, but the festival and holiday calendar; not the "civil", but the ecclesiastical year; not the time measurer, but the significance of salvation appearing in time; and "a calendar expresses the rhythm of the collective activities (read: of powerfulness) while at the same time its function is to assure their regularity".[5] Thus the ancient Roman calendar was proclaimed by the *pontifices* at the new moons (*kalendae*), and then by the *rex sacrorum* upon the first quarter, the *nones*; by this method it was possible to keep informed about the "days on which it was lawful, or unlawful, to transact secular business", *dies fasti* and *nefasti*.[6] The calendar, then, indicates clearly which instants of time have value and possess power[7]; each period, each instant, has specific individuality and its own potency.[8] This powerfulness, however, does not persist of its own accord; it must be assisted by celebrations; and thus we can understand what at first sight appears very strange to us in primitive modes of thought:—that time, whose continuance we regard as inexorable and self-evident, does not persist "of itself". It has power, and to this power something must happen: it is not "accepted"; and the calendar interferes, naturally at those situations where power reveals itself. Thus among the ancient Mexicans affairs were arranged according to the renewal of the fires: "the Aztecs spoke of periods of fifty-two years, on whose expiration all the fires were extinguished and kindled anew by boring—the bundles of years"; and on the occasion of a great migration the Mexicans

---

[1] Tobler, *Epiphanie der Seele*, 65.

[2] *cf.* Fr. Panzer, *Hilde-Gudrun*, 1901, 328 *f.*, with parallel cases.

[3] Hubert-Mauss, *op. cit.*, 196.   [4] Chap. 87.

[5] Durkheim, *The Elementary Forms of the Religious Life*, 11.

[6] Halliday, *History of Roman Religion*, 43. The Chinese use the paper calendar, or some of its leaves, as amulets, pills of calendar paper being rolled, for use against fever. Clemen, *Die nichtchristl. Rel.*, I, 44.   [7] *cf.* Hubert-Mauss, *op. cit.*, 226 *f.*

[8] Only thus can the personification of periods and seasons be understood: *Horai*, Year, Fair, *etc.*; *cf.* Hubert-Mauss, *op. cit.*, 200. W. Liungman, *Actes Ve Congrès*, 108 *ff.*

bored fires "in order to express figuratively in this way that their
years in Chapultepec had been linked with the past years, for they
had been unable to bore fires anew since they had been surrounded
by their enemies".[1] Elsewhere, for example in ancient Rome, the
calendar commenced with the agricultural season; in Rome, also, the
sacred fire was renewed on March 1.[2] The part played by the rising
of the stars, again, and above all by that of the moon, is sufficiently
well known, the moon's phases being paralleled by feminine periods,
so that the celestial potency accords with that of the earth; and "many
astronomical-cosmic periods entered into consciousness first of all as
the symbolic expression of the corresponding human periods".[3]

The advent of salvation, however, is pre-eminently the *tempus*. The
Christian ecclesiastical year is as it were a repetition of the divine life;
it is time filled with value, commencing with Advent. But it not merely
signifies salvation: it renews it also; liturgical time, moreover, is always
the same, filled with salvation. It is, so to say, a "succession of eternities".[4] The day is the symbol of the week, this of the year, and the
year of the world-period; the same salvation occurs in each temporal
unit, the Babylonian new year festival being the "annual repetition
of the unique, primal and universal new year celebration".[5] In the
hourly watches of the Egyptian Osiris mysteries, again, the god's life,
suffering and death were represented anew each hour; but their totality
simultaneously presented the passion of the god.[6] Similarly, at Michael-
mas, the Nordic peasant observes each hour of the day from six in the
morning till six in the evening, the weather of each hour indicating
that of each of the coming months.[7]

H. BERGSON, *Time and Free Will.*
E. CASSIRER, *Philosophie der symbolischen Formen*, II, *Das mythische Denken*,
　　1925 (Eng. tr., *The Philosophy of Symbolic Forms*, Vol. II, 1955).
JANE E. HARRISON, *Themis*, 1912.
E. PRZYBYLLOK, *Unser Kalender in Vergangenheit und Zukunft* (*Morgenland*,
　　22), 1930.
P. SAINTYVES, *Les notions de temps et d'éternité dans la magie et la religion*
　　(*RHR.* 79, 1919.)

[1] W. Krickeberg, *Märchen der Azteken und Inkaperuaner*, 1928, 351, 100.
[2] Fowler, *Roman Festivals*, 5; Ovid, *Fasti*, III, 137 *ff.*
[3] Th. W. Danzel, *Kultur und Religion des primitiven Menschen*, 1924, 40 *f.*
[4] Hubert-Mauss, *op. cit.*, 206.
[5] H. Zimmern, *Das babylonische Neujahrsfest*, 1926, 9.
[6] H. Junker, *Die Stundenwachen in den Osirismysterien* (*Denkschr. der kais. Akademie
in Wien*, LIV, 1910).　　　　[7] Reinsberg-Düringsfeld, *Das festl. Jahr*, 331 *f.*

CHAPTER 56

FESTIVALS

1. THE festival is the *tempus par excellence*, "selected" from the entirety of duration as particularly potent. In itself any time whatever may be chosen to be a festival period, since every one has its own value and specific powerfulness; and in this sense Guardini very finely observes[1] that "every hour of the day has its own note. But there are three that confront us with unusually clear features: morning, evening, and between the two the mid-day hour; and these are all sacred." Morning is a beginning: "the secret of birth renews itself every morning". The mystery of evening, again, is death, while mid-day is the moment, the pure present: "thou standest still, and all time is swallowed up. Eternity contemplates thee. In all the hours eternity speaks, but it is the intimate neighbour of mid-day. There time waits and discloses itself." Day-time and night-time, therefore, have different values; the Romans executed all public duties only between sunrise and sunset, while the Greeks sacrificed both by day and night; but the nightly sacrifice was offered to those powers that walk at night, the sinister and mystic gods, the νυκτιπόλοι.[2] Time may be selected also from the mythical past: some actual event may then be linked with a time which once proved itself potent in the most remote of bygone eras; thus the Egyptian sacred *Texts* often refer to "that day" on which some mythical happening or other occurred.[3] The powerfulness of this mythical "day" extends to the present; thus the Lord's resurrection is renewed each Easter day, then every Sunday and ultimately every morning.

The fixation of the time to be selected is therefore a most important affair, connected in many religions with divination as the choice of days.[4] The selected time is either dangerous or beneficent, *nefastus* or *fastus*; and sacred time is *tremenda*, or *fascinans*, or both. The Sabbath was a day of tabu on which work was forbidden, but it was also a day

---

[1] *Von heiligen Zeichen*, 78 *ff.*

[2] M. P. Nilsson, *Die Entstehung und religiöse Bedeutung des griechischen Kalenders* (*Lunds Universitets Aarsskrift, N. F., Avd.* 1, 14, 21), 1918, 17 *ff.*

[3] One of many examples:—the dead should protect the god "as the Father Nun protected those four goddesses *on the day*, when they defended the throne" (an obscure myth); *Pyramidentexte* (Sethe), 606.   [4] Chap. 54.

of recreation and rest; and post-exilic observance, while intensifying the severity of the ban on labour, also enhanced the sweetness of repose, as is clear from the fine tradition that on the Sabbath even the damned in hell enjoy a respite from their torments.[1] Christmas again, originally not itself a festival but a festival period, and subsequently the Twelve Nights, are symbolical of what the year will bring. It is a sinister time during which spooks rove about, but it is also the beautiful period in which the light increases: *crescit lux*![2] The Greek *anthesteria* too was a festival of blossoming, but was likewise a kind of All Souls; spirits were abroad and the days were μιαραί:— polluted, contagious, perilous.[3]

In its own proper nature the calendar, then, is a festal calendar, designating Sundays and holidays. This it was already in the most ancient days in Egypt, when a whole series of festivals was indicated on the Palermo Stone;[4] this it was, too, in Greece and Rome.[5] But our own farmers' calendar is also a festival calendar which "selects" the sacred time, for sowing and threshing, for work and holiday.[6] Among primitives choice of days extends still further into details; "it is not enough to have favourable omens; it is essential that the month, day, and hour on which an enterprise is begun shall be auspicious or 'record' days. We know that the primitive mind does not 'sense' the successive moments of time as homogeneous. Certain periods of the day or night, of the moon's phases, of the year, and so on, are able to exert a favourable or a malignant influence." Similarly for the Dyaks "every day has five 'times', which are fixed for the first day (Sunday) only, and for the others there must be recourse to divination".[7] In its own way the Christian cult also places definite times of night and day in relationship to Power, and as it were distributes the event of salvation over *horae canonicae* and over the days of the week. Thus the Lord's day is that of resurrection: Friday of pre-

[1] Bin Gorion, *Der Born Judas*, VI, 294. When the Eskimo "were told by their first missionaries that they must abstain from all work on the Lord's Day . . . they were amazed, but now they felt that they had obtained an explanation of many misfortunes, the cause of which they had never been able to discover" (Lévy-Bruhl, *Primitives and the Supernatural*, 50). They had simply not "selected" the appropriate time!
[2] A. Meyer, *Das Weihnachtsfest*, 1913. H. Usener, *Das Weihnachtsfest*, 1², 1911.
[3] Farnell, *Cults*, V, 216 *ff.*; "the tabooed days".
[4] Breasted, *Ancient Records*, 1, 90 *ff.*
[5] Fowler, *Roman Festivals*. Ovid, *Fasti*. M. P. Nilsson, *Griechische Feste*, 1906; *id. Kalender.*
[6] Nilsson, *Volkstümliche Feste*; Reinsberg-Düringsfeld, *Festl. Jahr; cf.* further examples: Reinsberg-Düringsfeld, *Calendrier belge*, 1861 *f.* Heuvel, *Oud-achterhoeksch Boerleven.* [7] Lévy-Bruhl, *Primitives and the Supernatural*, 48, 49.

paration on which we should fast *etc.* The cock announces day and new life: Christ banishes sleep and ancient guilt:

> The bird that heraldeth the day
> Foretells the sunbeam drawing nigh.
> Now Christ arouseth us that lay
> Torpid, to life beneath His eye.
>
> Come, break the spell of sluggish night.
> Sunder, O Christ, her iron chain!
> Come, showering down Thy healing light,
> And purge our nature's ancient stain.[1]

2. Holidays and festivals fall within a *festal cycle*; but this is no affair of merely secondary importance, since it is in their nature to continue, to carry onward.[2] They represent the critical points: not the point only, however, but the celebration also that carries us beyond the difficult stage. Festivals therefore are not merely recreational; on the contrary, primitive peoples regard them as affairs of duty and of useful work, since without them the powerfulness of life would be brought into stagnation. To the South American Uitoto the purpose of the festival is more important than the festal joy; "we dance only because of the sacred words", they say; "we do not dance without a reason";[3] and in the ideas of country folk with regard to the fair this opinion still predominates; "it is the pastor's duty to warn us against the fair", says a Gelderland farmer of the Netherlands, "just as much as it is our duty to attend it".[4] The Christian calendar again, which no longer produces natural "fruits", is intended to arouse grace in the hearts of the faithful and nourish spiritual life.[5]

[1] *Hymnus matutinus:* Aurelius Prudentius Clemens.
> *Ales diei nuntius*
> *Lucem proprinquam praecinit;*
> *Nos excitator mentium*
> *Iam Christus ad vitam vocat.*
> *Tu Christe, somnum discute;*
> *Tu rumpe noctis vincula,*
> *Tu solve peccatum vetus,*
> *Novumque lumen ingere.*

[2] Thus it runs in the *Oxyr. Hymn to Isis*, that she institutes Isaea everywhere, and: πασιν τὰ νόμιμα καὶ ἐνιαν τὸντέλιον παρέδωκας, cf. N. Turchi, *Fontes historiae mysteriorum*, 1930. B. van Groningen, *De papyro oxyrhinchita* 1380, 1921, 56.
[3] K. Th. Preuss, *Religion und Mythologie der Uitoto*, I, 1921, 123.
[4] Heuvel, *ibid.*, 322.   [5] Saintyves, *Notions de temps*, 94.

In the cycle, then, the festival becomes as it were a microcosm of the whole of time; for the Jews the new year was the period of judgment and the apportioning of fate, while the end of the year was the day of Jahveh. Each new year is therefore a turning-point of destiny, and each year an abbreviated world-history;[1] while in the Christian calendar every day is a *feria*,[2] and thus the idea of the festival becomes extended without any limit; as sacred, Time is as it were rendered eternal at every instant. Thus there arises the desire to superimpose longer periods on the festal cycle, and such "great years" make the notch after the lengthier eras. The ancient Egyptian feast of Sed has already been referred to in connection with the figure of the king,[3] and in Greece there were ennaeteric and trieteric periods, the festivals occurring every nine, and every three, years respectively, and in Israel a "sabbatical year" every fifty years; in Mexico, similarly, a fifty-two year period, while the Roman *lustrum* has been discussed previously, to which should now be added the *saeculum*, probably originally the time for sowing, subsequently the generation, and ultimately the age. But this "age" was "begun" at definite times; man did not simply wait for it, but brought it about and commenced a new era; originally, the old *saeculum* was buried (*saeculum condere*). Here also man selects the time and refuses simply to accept duration.[4] Particularly after a period of struggle and exhaustion is the necessity of making a fresh start experienced;[5] of this Augustus gave a magnificent example when, in the year 17, he inaugurated a new era by a secular festival: "Pheobus, and Diana mistress of the woods, ye that are the shining beauty of the sky, ye that are ever adorable and adored, grant the blessings we pray for at a hallowed season."[6]

3. Finally, festivals acquire a wholly different significance as soon as the power arrested in and by them becomes one that announces itself historically. One of the most important dates in the history of religion, therefore, was the transposition of the Israelite Nature festivals into *commemorationes* of historical dates, which were simultaneously manifestations of power and deeds of God, so that when the ancient moon and Spring festival of the *Passah*, which was connected with

---

[1] P. Volz, *Das Neujahrsfest Jahves*, 1912, 15 *ff.*

[2] H. A. Köstlin, *Geschichte des christlichen Gottesdienstes*, 1887, 43, 108.

[3] Chap. 13.

[4] Fowler, *The Religious Experience of the Roman People*, 440 *f.* E. Norden, *Aeneis, Buch* VI[2], 1916, 324. On the "great year" *cf* Chantepie, *op. cit.*, 1¹, 120 *f.*

[5] Thus in the year of peril, 249.   [6] Horace, *Carmen saeculare.*

tabus, was transformed into the festival of God's redemptive deed in the exodus from Egypt, something completely new was inaugurated. The notch in time is then no longer repeatable at will; duration is no longer entirely swallowed up in the festal cycle: God Himself makes the notch once for all: He arrests time and transforms the mere given into a promise.

O. von Reinsberg-Düringsfeld, *Das festliche Jahr*[2], 1898.
Karl Kerenyi, "Vom Wesens des Festes" (*Paideuma*, I, 1938, 59 *ff.*).
M. P. Nilsson, *Die volkstümlichen Feste des Jahres*, 1914.

CHAPTER 57

SACRED SPACE

1. WHAT is true of time is equally true of space. It is no homogeneous mass, nor a sum of innumerable spatial parts; but just as duration subsists in relation to time, so does *extensity* (*étendue*) to space.[1] Even to the animal, indeed, a locality is not some arbitrary point in space, but a resting-place in universal extensity, a "position" which it recognizes and towards which it directs itself. Parts of space, therefore, like instants of time, have their specific and independent value.[2] They are "positions"; but they become "positions" by being "selected" from the vast extensity of the world. A part of space, then, is not a "part" at all but a place, and the place becomes a "position" when man occupies it and stands on it. He has thus recognized the power of the locality, he seeks it or avoids it, attempts to strengthen or enfeeble it; but in any case he selects the place as a "position". Some *locus* becomes set free and declared so:—*liberatus et effatus*;[3] power resides within it. Thus a sanctuary in Minahassa in Celebes, consisting of sacred stones, under which planks have been buried that are supposed to represent the birds' notes heard at the foundation of the village, together with some captured human heads, is called "the salvation and strength of the village".[4]

Sacred space may also be defined as that locality that becomes a position by the effects of power repeating themselves there, or being repeated by man. It is the place of worship, independently of whether the position is only a house, or a temple, since domestic life too is a celebration constantly repeated in the regulated cycle of work, meals, washing *etc.* Thus we can understand why man clings with such obstinate tenacity to the positions he has once adopted; and a sacred position remains holy even when it has been long neglected. In the course of excavating pre-historic settlements in Drente, in the Netherlands, it was discovered that sites for cremation had been placed in the hollows of the wooden posts of still more ancient shrines. The consciousness of the sacred character of the locality that has once been chosen is, therefore, always retained.[5] And this also is the reason

---

[1] *Time and Free Will*, 97.   [2] Cassirer, *op. cit.*, II, 112 *ff.*
[3] Chap. 54.   [4] Adriani, *Animistisch Heidendom*, 33 *f.*
[5] *cf.* A. E. van Giffen, *Drentsche Volksalmanak*, 50, 1932, 61 *ff.*

why, during its expansion, Christianity has sought its sacred places preferably in localities adopted by the older cults.[1]

2. The place thus selected, because it has shown itself to be sacred, is at first merely a position: man adds nothing at all to Nature; the mysterious situation of a locality, its awe-inspiring character, suffice. It is the place of dread awe, which deeply impresses man: *religio dira loci*:

> Its dread awe made quake
> E'en then the fearful rustics; ay, e'en then
> They shuddered at the forest and the rock.[2]

In fact it is principally forests and caverns, rocks and mountains, that have been chosen as holy.[3] The Roman *lucus* was a grove in which cult activities were carried on: "Under the Aventine there lay a grove black with the shade of holm-oaks; at sight of it you could say 'There is a *numen* here'."[4] Even to-day we remain conscious that the gloomy forest has a numinous character, although to a great extent we have destroyed primitive man's dread of the seat of the powers by our romantic twilight moods. Nevertheless the sacred grove arouses its shiver of fear as well as of ecstasy: "If ever you have come upon a grove (*lucus*) that is full of ancient trees, which have grown to an unusual height, shutting out a view of the sky by a veil of pleached and intertwining branches, then the loftiness of the forest, the seclusion of the spot, and your marvel at the thick unbroken shade in the midst of the open spaces, will prove to you the presence of deity (*fidem tibi numinis faciet*). Or if a cave, made by the deep crumbling of the rocks, holds up a mountain on its arch, a place not built with hands but hollowed out into such spaciousness by natural causes, your soul will be deeply moved by an inkling, a presage, of the divine; (*animum tuum quadam religionis suspicione percutiet*). We worship the sources of mighty rivers; we erect altars at places where great streams burst suddenly from hidden sources; we adore springs of hot water as divine, and consecrate certain pools because of their dark waters or their immeasurable depth."[5] But such a direct experience of the

---

[1] Chambers, *Mediaeval Stage*, I, 95 *f.*; *cf.* Chap. 17 also.
[2] Virgil, *Aeneid*, VIII, 349 *f.* (Rhoades).
[3] Chap. 5; *cf.* among others S. Wide, *Lakonische Kulte*, 1893, 40 *f.* O. Kern, *Die Religion der Griechen*, I, 1926, 77.
[4] Ovid, *Fasti*, III, 295 *f.* (Modified from Frazer).
[5] Seneca, *Epistle* XLI, 3 (Gummere).

presence of the power, and subsequently of the deity, in a locality—an experience which has gained its finest poetic expression in Plato's *Phaedrus*—is possible only in a world which man has not yet reduced to an inanimate thing and deprived of all its power.

Thus the natural shrine is probably the oldest known to man. But side by side with this there soon appeared artificial sanctuaries; for power, man erects a dwelling. But frequently what has been built and what has simply been given, the erection and the grove, remain associated together; and until a late period a sacred grove with a holy tree and spring were found in Uppsala, together with a temple and three statues.[1] In the architecture of places of worship, too, there is much that still reminds us of the wood or the holy mountain: pillars derived from trees or plants: the tower form of the Babylonian *zikkurat*.[2] But the sacredness of the place, that is its character of "selectivity", continues unchanged. In infinite space a "sanctuary" arises; and it is no marvel that this "sanctuary" is such in the sense of a "refuge" also. This in fact applies to even the most primitive shrines; Australian *churinga*,[3] for example, are kept in a small cavern (*arknanaua*) in some lonely spot; the place may not be entered by the uninitiated and the admission of women and children is prohibited under pain of death. The environment of the sanctuary is also inviolable, all strife being forbidden there, while from such a place no wounded animal is ever taken away, and one that has sought refuge there is pursued no farther; even plants growing in the vicinity remain untouched.[4] This idea of refuge is widespread, and has obtained its poetic form in Wagner's *Parsifal*: the precinct of the castle of the Holy Grail is a sanctuary: "Thou couldest murder, here in holy forest, where quiet peace did thee enfold?" asks Gurnemanz of the simple fellow who has slain the swan.[5]

3. House and temple, still further, are essentially one: both can stand firm only in virtue of the power residing within them. The house is an organic unity, whose essence is some definite power, just

---

[1] Ax. Olrik, *Nordisches Geistesleben*², 1925, 34.
[2] Th. Dombart, *Der babylonische Turm*, 1930.   [3] Chap. 3.
[4] Söderblom, *Gottesglaube*, 34 *ff*. B. Spencer and F. Gillen, *The Native Tribes of Central Australia*, 133 *ff*. J. Wanninger, *Das Heilige in der Religion der Australier*, 1927, 42 *ff*. Strehlow-Leonhardi, *Die Aranda- und Loritjastämme*, II, 1908, 78. In South Boni (Indonesia), in earlier days, the desert limestone mountain chain Lamontjong was a place of refuge for even the gravest offences such as incest *etc. cf.* J. P. Kleiweg de Zwaan, *Het Asylrecht by overspel in den Indischen Archipel* (*Tydschr. Ned. Aardr. Gen.*, 2. *R.*, 48, 1931, 37 *ff*.).   [5] *Parsifal*, Act I.

as much as is the temple or church. But it is probably difficult for us, semi-americanized as we already are, living in flats and having what we need brought into the house, to form any idea of its unitary power as this is still experienced to some degree in isolated farmhouses, and which not very long ago was an unquestioned reality. For the house with its own fire, which must produce its own means of life, manufacture its own clothing, hew its own wood and have its own well, is a world in itself.[1] And we who purchase the objects we require when we want them, and buy furniture in this or that style, perhaps know only very little about the community of essence between all the parts of the house and its inhabitants, of that participation which fits each member of the domestic group into the same structure, whether it is a so-called "thing", an animal or a human being. In an Irish fairy tale a woman "enchants" every object in her household to prevent the entrance of evil spirits so that the key, the tongs, the axe, *etc.*, cannot move and therefore cannot open the way for the spirits; over the water in the foot-bath alone she has no power, because it does not belong to the household; and for this reason she pours it away before closing the door.[2]

But within the house, again, the power is distributed over the various parts, each of which has its own sacredness. Of this the Roman house is typical; but a similar state of affairs occurs all over the world. First of all the door is there to separate the space inside the house from the power existing outside, the door that protects and constitutes the transition from the secular to the consecrated enclosure; and in Rome the entrance became Janus, the god who was invoked first during prayer.[3] The *threshold* too was the sacred boundary possessing its own special power, and in Palestine to-day a mother may neither chastise nor suckle her child on the threshold; a child who has been punished there may become seriously ill, so that on the threshold one must neither sit nor work *etc.*[4] In Indonesia the main post of the house is regarded as most holy and is erected with sacrifice and ceremony. For the house shelters power: there are the "gods", "gods of the treasure-house within";[5] at the door,[6] or inside the house, are the domestic deities. Once again the classical example is provided by the

---

[1] For a not so distant past it is very finely described in Selma Lagerlöf's novels.
[2] Käte Müller-Lisowski, *Irische Volksmärchen*, No. 30: *Der Berg der lichten Frauen.*
[3] Ovid, *Fasti*, I. Cicero, *De Natura Deorum*, II, 67.
[4] Canaan, *Dämonenglaube im Lande der Bibel*, 37; further examples in E. Samter, *Familienfeste der Griechen und Römer*, 1901.
[5] Aeschylus, *Choëphoroe*, 800 (Murray).   [6] Sophocles, *Electra*, 1373 *ff.*

Roman *penates*, the gods of the *penus* or larder. No unclean person
might touch the *penus*; its management was one of the duties of the
—pure—children of the household.[1] In a different sense from what
he intended, therefore, the malicious Christian apologist of later days
was correct when he regarded the *penates* as the gods of those people
"who think that life is nothing but licence to feed and to drink".[2]
The possibility of eating and drinking is experienced precisely as a
divine possibility, and its position estimated as holy. This is also the
basis of the sacredness of that most important spot of all in the house,
the hearth:[3] it is its central point, the totality of its power. An old
Gelderland farmer's son thus relates an incident of his childhood:
"When the pot had been taken off the fire, we often set the hook
swinging; 'you mustn't do that', said our John, 'or our dear Lord will
get a headache'. To us this seemed profane. But we did not know that,
since ancient times, the hook has been the sacred position in the house,
around which the bride was led and which was seized to take possession
of the house."[4] The hook is a sanctuary also: a new labourer has water
poured over him, and so he slips into the house by the side door and
lays hold of the hook, and then he must no longer be teased.[5] Even
to-day the common people have preserved some of the correct feeling
that the power of the house accumulates in the kitchen, on the hearth:
the "best parlour" usually remains empty! The round Roman temple
of Vesta, again, was nothing more than the old round house or tent
which had the fire-place in the middle, and models of these prehistoric dwellings have been found in the *Forum Romanum*, as urns
for the ashes of the dead.[6]

The house, however, need not be the family dwelling-place: it may
also serve as the residence for the whole tribe, as was the case quite
recently in Scandinavia,[7] or it may be the power-position of an entire
section of the tribe, like the men's houses.[8] But whatever it may be,
and in whatever form the sacredness of the place may be "common",
its holiness gives it prominence as against the surrounding entirety of
space. Hence also the relationship between the sacred place and the
whole Universe: the shrine is a centre of power, a world in itself.
For the dedication of the Israelitish temple, as for the consecration

---

[1] Fowler, *Religious Experience*, 73 *ff*; *Roman Festivals*, 213 *f.*, 150, Note 1. Cicero,
De Natura Deorum, II, 68.
[2] Firmicus Maternus, *De errore profanarum religionum*, 14: *nihil aliud putant esse
vitam, nisi viscendi et potandi licentiam.*
[3] Chap. 6.   [4] Heuvel, *op. cit.*, 16 *f.*   [5] *ibid.*, 152.
[6] Halliday, *Roman Religion*, 25.   [7] Olrik, *op. cit.*, 17.   [8] Chap. 33, 34.

of a Christian church, the chanting of *Psalm XXIV* is prescribed; and it has a truly cosmic character. At the dedication of a Babylonian temple, similarly, creation hymns were sung, while in the Egyptian *pr duat*, the "House of the Morning", the rebirth of the sun was celebrated every day. Actually, indeed, the sanctuary exists not in this world at all, since it has been "selected";[1] and this cosmic significance of the sacred places was still haunting the mind of the bailiff in Eastern Holland when he feared that the swinging of the hook would give the dear Lord a headache.

House and temple, therefore, are one: both are the "House of God". Hearth and altar are also one, the temple-altar being the table and the fire-place of the gods.[2] As soon, however, as the locality is no longer simply provided "by Nature" as the "position", but must first be designated by man, the need of discovering the proper place becomes very evident. In other words, before building is begun it must be quite definitely ascertained whether the place selected is suitable for the "position". This really means that we *cannot* make shrines and *cannot* select their "positions", but can never do more than merely "find" them; and the art of discovering them is called *Orientation*. "The supernatural space, the sacred, is ordered. It is founded upon mystery".[3] The term "orientation" is derived from the custom of building in the direction from West to East, towards the sun; the altar end of the church should indicate the position where the sun rose when the church was founded.[4] Temple building was regulated by other heavenly bodies also: for example, in Egypt according to the rising, or so-called birth, of Sirius.[5]

But if the house becomes a mere place of residence, and the temple an oratory or meeting-place, then the "positions" gradually lose their cosmic-sacred character. They become merely places to stay in and talk, and it is no longer believed that anything really happens there; the extreme stage of this development is constituted by the buildings devoted to preaching of some Protestant communities. This change, certainly, is by no means linked to any one definite stage of the process: when Judaism and Christianity had already converted

[1] A. J. Wensinck, "The Semitic New Year"; *Acta Orientalia*, I, 181. A. M. Blackman, "The House of the Morning", *Jour. Egyptian Archeology*, 5, 1918.
[2] The altar is also a grave (even to-day every Roman Catholic altar has an altar-reliquary); originally, the dead remained in the house, or were buried by the hearth.
[3] Guardini, *Von heiligen Zeichen*, 72.
[4] H. Nissen, *Orientation*, I, 7 (1906–1907).
[5] *ibid.*, I, 36.

their synagogue and basilica into a place of prayer the Christian church arose as a sacred position and a House of God.

4. Not house and temple alone, however, but the *settlement* in general, the village, the town, is a "selected", sacred position; man forms his settlement and thus converts the discovered possibility into new powerfulness. His settlement then stands out from the surrounding extent of space: his tilled land from the uncultivated forest and desolate heath; and the enclosures he thus lays out play the part of the house door, separating the secure sphere of the human dwelling from the "uncanny" realm of demonic powers.[1] The old feeling for the sacredness of the cultivated area, the settlement, is very finely depicted in the legend of the giant's playthings: at her father's command, the giant's daughter returns the husbandman whom, with his oxen and plough, she had packed into her apron, to his own locality, since if the peasant in the valley does not work the giant in the mountains has nothing to eat! For the settlement is always a conquest, a selection.[2] Originally the *lares*, the Roman household gods associated with the *penates*, were probably the powers of the forest clearing, and subsequently the dominant powers in the house built within the cleared ground.[3] Agriculture and the foundation of cities, in fact, went on hand in hand, and in Rome the practice of marking out the line of the walls with the plough, *moenia signare aratro*, was not forgotten.[4] Thus the *pomoerium*, the town's "spiritual frontier", was a furrow, and at its founding, wherever it was intended to erect a gate, the plough was lifted and a tract left unhallowed.[5] Within this *sulcus primigenius*, then, lay the town; but its founding likewise was no chance affair: the "situation" had to be thoroughly investigated, and for this the art of *limitation* was employed which originated from the most primitive, yet at the same time most important, method of orientation man possesses—that is the distinction between right and left.[6] Then the *decumanus*, the main East to West road, was oriented by sunrise, intersected by the North-South road or *cardo*, and thus the ground plan of the town was determined. These *limites*

[1] Grönbech, *op. cit.*, II, 10; *cf.* Wilamowitz-Möllendorff, *Griech. Trag.* II, 224 *f.* Hence Ares remained on the Areopagus in Athens, and Mars *extra pomoerium* in Rome. [2] Cassirer, *op. cit.*, II, 120 *ff.*
[3] Only thus can the dual character of the *lares*, as gods of the field and of the house, be understood; *cf.* Halliday, *Roman Religion*, 28 *f.* E. Samter, *Der Ursprung des Larenkults, AR.* 10, 1907. [4] Ovid, *Fasti*, IV, 819, 825.
[5] Deubner, in Chantepie, *op. cit.*, II, 428. Halliday, *ibid.*, 65. I. B. Carter, *The Religion of Numa*, 33 *ff.* [6] Chap. 23. Cassirer, *op. cit.*, II, 119.

stood in immediate relation to the world-order, the town being in this way divided into four, as the world was too;[1] and thus each settlement constituted a world in itself, a sacred whole.[2] The sanctity of boundary stones and their immovability (in Rome *termini*, in Babylon *kudurru*) are universally known, and persisted indeed until quite recent times; in Egypt a boundary stone was set as firm "as the heavens" and based on the whole Universe.[3] Even the earth, therefore, is neither everywhere nor in itself "well founded and enduring"; first of all it is necessary to have made sure of the "situation" and to have selected the suitable place for the "position".

The various legends about the origins of cities are derived from precisely the same necessity. Animals were allowed to roam freely until they lay down in some place or other *etc.*: an origin was thus demanded in what is indubitably powerful. For it was no affair of establishing a mere place of sojourn, but of the foundation of a position where power resided. The god dwelt in the town just as he did in the temple, and whenever they wished to conquer a city the Romans attempted to "evoke" him by adjuration. The god might also forsake the city: this he does in the beautiful Jewish legend of the Jerusalem Gate of Compassion. In leaving the town, the divine majesty strode through this gate, and through it will hereafter return.[4] Jerusalem is, in fact, the city in which the idea of the sacred place appears as it were in its typical form; it was regarded as the world's central point. "In Jerusalem all the winds in the world blow. Before it executes its mission, every wind comes into the holy city to make obeisance here before the Lord".[5] And when the new world rises before the eyes of the faithful, once more it is the vision of the holy city, the new Jerusalem. On the completion of the final conditions, however, the distinction between city and temple again disappears, and in the new world the primitive sacred place is once more present: for in the new Jerusalem no temple whatever is required, because the Lord Himself is its temple.[6]

5. In the holy place, still further, power exists: there its effects become perceptible. What once occurred is repeated at the sacred

---

[1] The oldest ground-plan of the Egyptian city, also, shows this form: ⊕

[2] Nissen, *op. cit.*, I, 79 *ff.*, 90 *ff.* Usener, *Götternamen*, 190 *ff.*

[3] Grave at Beni Hassan; A. Erman, *Ägyptische Chrestomathie*, 1909, 113; *cf.* E. Samter, *Die Entwicklung des Terminuskults*, AR. 16, 1913.

[4] Bin Gorion, *Born Judas*, V, 282.

[5] *ibid.*   [6] *Rev.* xxi.

spot: at the altar, for example, Christ's death is reiterated.[1] In the Egyptian temple, similarly, the foundation of the world was renewed at a place erected for that very purpose, the "primeval hill" on which the sun for the first time appeared in the ancient days;[2] and the Babylonian temple tower was an image or model of the world.[3] It is not to be wondered at, therefore, that from time immemorial men have undertaken pilgrimages to places recognized as holy, where the Power of the Universe renewed itself daily, and where the heart of the world could be approached. In a certain sense, indeed, every entry into the temple, every appearance in church, is a *pilgrimage*. But it is places of superior sacredness that attract the faithful to themselves in the literal sense, and in primitive custom the psychology of pilgrimage becomes clear. Thus the sanctuary of Minahassa, previously referred to as "the salvation and strength of the village", is also named "the callers", because the stones forming it call back the villagers from foreign regions, or in other words arouse home-sickness in their breasts.[4] Primitive man's longing for house and home, for his native country or town, is ultimately therefore the yearning for salvation, for the consciousness of powerfulness, bestowed by one's own selected place. Of one's home it is true that

There are the vigorous roots of thy strength:

and man feels happy only in the place which he has discovered, which has stood the test for him and with whose power his own power is associated.

The place of pilgrimage, the seat of grace, is thus a sort of home of the second power. On festival days the Jew went on pilgrimage to Jerusalem, and once in his lifetime the Mohammedan must accomplish the great pilgrimage to Mecca. In Buddhism, in fact, pilgrimage is even the sole bond of this otherwise very loose religious community. For from pilgrimage man hopes for property and prosperity, fulfilment of desires, annulment of sin, admission to the divine world and eternal bliss:—indeed for almost everything powerful that man can possibly wish for himself.[5] In this way, then, whole peoples and religious communities can have their home: the Jews, Jerusalem: Mohammedans, Mecca and Christians, Rome. The world, which can

[1] *cf.* Rob. Grosche, *Catholica*, I, 1932, 91 *ff.*
[2] A. de Buck, *De Egyptische Voorstellingen betreffende den Oerheuvel*, 1927.
[3] Dombart, *Der babylonische Turm.*   [4] Adriani, *loc. cit.*
[5] J. Ph. Vogel, *De cosmopolitische beteeknis van het Buddhisme*, 1931, 15.

actually only be one's own, is then found in remote regions. Necessity compels emigration and the abandonment of the powerful subsisting in one's own place. Thus the seat of grace may become the image of the other world, and all life be regarded as a pilgrimage or a crusade. But Mysticism interprets this also in quite a different way: it can believe in no holy place whatever, and transfers all salvation inwardly to the holiest of holies in the heart. One of the reasons for the execution of the famous *sufi* al-Hallaj, in fact, was his assertion that pilgrimage might possess a purely spiritual character and be undertaken in one's own room, because the true sanctuary lay within the heart.[1] And the mystic Bayazid Bastami fulfilled his pilgrimage to Mecca by walking seven times around a sage: the real sanctuary is man.

[1] Massignon, *Al Hallaj*, 227, 348.

CHAPTER 58

THE SACRED WORD

1. "I CANNOT the mere Word so highly prize",[1] says Faust, and in its stead he places the deed. But he does not realize that in so doing he is not actually restoring or replacing it, but is merely giving a different translation of the Greek term *logos*. For the world of the primitive and of antiquity, and above all the religious world, knows nothing whatever of "empty words", of "words, words"; it never says: "more than enough words have been exchanged, now at last let me see deeds"; and the yearning no longer to have to "rummage among words" is wholly foreign to it. But this is not at all because the primitive world has a blunter sense of reality than ours; rather the contrary: it is we who have artificially emptied the word, and degraded it to a thing.[2] But as soon as we actually *live*, and do not simply make scientific abstractions, we know once more that a word has life and power, and indeed highly characteristic power. For we can go to the other powers, which we have by now converted into things, repeatedly: the communion elements, the sacred ceremonial places, always remain. But the word occurs only once for all, and it entails decision. In this living speech, then, time becomes *kairos*, the "due *season*," *hic et nunc*.[3] Whoever speaks, therefore, not only employs an expressive symbol but goes forth out of himself, and the word that he lets fall decides the matter. Even if I merely say "Good Morning" to someone I must emerge from my isolation, place myself before him and allow some proportion of my potency to pass over into his life, for good or evil.

We have already discussed Givenness and Possibility:[4] it is the word that decides the possibility. For it is an act, an attitude, a taking one's stand and an exercise of power, and in every word there is something creative. It is expressive, and exists prior to so-called actuality. Of the origin of language we know nothing, but it is probable that the most

---

[1] *Faust*, Part I, 878.

[2] "The 'nominalistic' standpoint, for which words are only conventional signs, mere *flatus vocis*, is only the outcome of later reflection, and not the expression of the 'natural' and immediate consciousness of language. This regards the 'essential nature' of the object as not merely mediately indicated by the word, but as in some way or other contained and present within it." Cassirer, *op. cit.*, II, 33 *f.*

[3] Frick, *Ideogramm, Mythologie und das Wort*, 19.   [4] Chap. 23.

primitive speech consisted of terms of wishing and feeling;[1] situations
and opportunities were summoned up or settled.[2] For a word is always
a charm: it awakens power, either dangerous or beneficent. Whoever
asserts anything "poses", and thus exerts some influence; but he also
"exposes" himself. Thus to the name of the ancient Egyptian king the
formula *ankh wza śnb* was regularly added, meaning "life, salvation,
health", since to mention his name exposed the king, and this "salvation
formula" was intended to act as a counter-charm and once more place
him in security.[3] In the light of these conditions, then, are also to be
understood the frequent prohibitions of speech and word which are
encountered among primitive peoples and in antiquity: for dangerous
things and people must not be named. This goes so far that, for example,
in Northern Rhodesia it is forbidden to say "No", because of the
consequences to be feared from it; to the question: "Is the beast in
the kraal?" the reply is: "It is in the kraal", even when it is not there;
the power of the word is feared more than that of facts.[4] Under these
conditions, of course, lying is an art, a merit, rather than a sin. And from
these lies of avoidance there sprang up a by no means negligible proportion of poetry: metaphor arose, indeed, from this fear of calling
things bluntly by their correct names, so that it was preferable to
paraphrase them and call the knife, for example, "the sharpness at the
thigh".[5] From the rule *nomina odiosa*, then, arose poetic paraphrase.
In Central Celebes, again, a man who is going hunting says that he
intends to look for rattan or pick bananas, since otherwise he would
kill nothing, and rain is called the blossom of trees, or ashes.[6] The
purpose of all this concealment and lying is attained in an even surer

---

[1] Thurnwald, *Psychologie des primitiven Menschen*, 267.

[2] So-called "Holophrasis" (or the use of "portmanteau words", as Marett calls
them), which prevails to a certain extent even to-day in primitive and child language,
and according to which it is not the isolated concept, but the situation, that is equivalent to the sentence as a unit, substantiates this view; where we for example, in our
languages, can locate a seal just as we please either on a block of ice or in the sunshine,
etc., certain Eskimo languages employ a specific expression for each situation; *cf.* van
der Leeuw, *Structure*, 11. F. Boas, *The Mind of Primitive Man*, 1922, 147 *ff.* Danzel,
Kultur und Religion des primitiven Menschen, 21 *f.*

[3] Obbink, *De magische beteekenis van den naam*, 128.

[4] R. Thurnwald, *Die Lüge in der primitiven Kultur*; in the cooperative volume *Die
Lüge*, 1927, 399.

[5] Naumann, *Isländische Volksmärchen*, No. 78. H. Werner, *Die Ursprünge der Meta-
pher*, 1919. G. van der Leeuw, *Wegen en Grenzen*, 12 *ff.* E. Nordenskiöld, *Journal des
Américanistes*, N.S. 24, 1932, 6; *cf.* further Old Norse *kenningar*, Portengen, *De
oudgermaansche dichtertaal in haar ethnologisch verband*; also Hesiod's expressions
"housebearer" (snail) *etc.* in Rose, *Primitive Culture in Greece*, 144.

[6] Kruyt, *Measa*, II, 43 *f.*

way by silence being commanded; in Roman sacrifice *favete linguis* was a demand for silence which might not be broken by a single word, and was accompanied only by the flute.[1] Similarly in Central Celebes no one may either speak or laugh during the invocation of spirits or any other religious ceremony; whoever speaks or laughs falls ill and the rite is ineffective.[2]

2. The word, then, is a decisive power: whoever utters words sets power in motion.[3] But the might of the word becomes still further enhanced in various ways. Raising the voice, emphasis, connection by rhythm or rhyme—all this endows the word with heightened energy; and from this a broad road leads to the domain of the *Phenomenology of Art*, which however we cannot here pursue.[4] But singing, rejoicing and mourning generate greater potency than mere speaking, and the power of lamentation is sufficiently well known in the mourning customs of innumerable peoples. In the Osiris myth, again, the grieving of the two goddesses Isis and Nephthys, the original models of all professional mourners, has power to awaken the dead god to new life. Certain unusual words possess intensified power: the term *eilikrineia*, for instance, gives a holy man an "excellent feeling", and to Jung-Stilling it appears "as if it had lain in splendour",[5] while James has told us of the marvellous effects on pious souls of such words as "Mesopotamia" and "Philadelphia"![6] More important still is the vast power which always emanated from such cult terms as *Hallelujah*, *Kyrie eleison*, *Amen*, *Om*; a mystical tone-colour is attached to them, while

---

[1] G. Mensching, *Das heilige Schweigen*, 1926, 101 *f.*   [2] Kruyt, *ibid.*, 39.
[3] This is very obvious in the primitive pun which, in this respect radically different from our own, places two realities in mutual relationship. The Egyptian pun, for example, invokes a god in order to *greet* "in his name" the *great*. These two ideas, *greet* and *great*, *Gruss* and *gross*, which possess for us merely accidental assonance, are essentially connected by means of the name; *cf.* Chap. 17, also Hubert-Mauss, *Mélanges*, 52; Obbink, *op. cit.*, 63; H. Werner, *Einführung in die Entwicklungs-psychologie*, 1926, 111; and Larock, *Essai, RHR.* 101, 1930, I, 42 *f.* "What we call a sentence is composed (for the non-civilized mind) of a series of aerial beings, exerting a subtle influence, which he understands, but of which he never sees anything at all, and which are therefore mysterious in the sense of being formidable, sinking into his body and manifesting their influence there; escaping from his lips, they spread wherever they circulate the principles of action." "Words are the material and active essences of things, and to speak is equivalent to causing these groups of living, personal and sonorous phantoms of things and beings to manifest themselves, thus forming verbal sequences."
[4] G. van der Leeuw, *Wegen en Grenzen.*
[5] H. R. G. Günther, *Jung-Stilling*, 1928, 56.
[6] *The Varieties of Religious Experience*, 383.

their very incomprehensibility enhances their numinous power. Frequently a special cult language thus arises, for which an older tongue no longer in use is usually employed: in Christian worship, Latin, and Sanskrit in the Buddhist Mass of China and Japan.[1] Finally, speaking softly, barely audible words have potent decisiveness: the priest of the mysteries *lento murmure susurrat*—slowly murmurs in a low voice his most sacred utterance about the waking of the god.[2]

3. Words, however, possess the greatest power when they combine into some formula, some phrase definite in the sound of its terms, their timbre and their rhythm. Even in the Middle Ages a request uttered not occasionally and in ordinary terms, but ceremonially intoned in the appointed words, had compelling power,[3] and almost universally in religion rhythm, pitch and sequence possess such a potency: they hold together, as it were, the power immanent in the words.[4] The best example of this is the Roman *carmen*,[5] which consisted of *verba certa*, "appointed words", none of which might be at all altered and which must be recited with a special cadence; a *carmen* was required for all services of dedication and prayer. From Roman religion the *certa verba* were transferred to the Christian; the entire liturgy is in fact a *carmen* and still, to some extent, enjoys compelling power. In ancient Christianity, too, the creed in St. Augustine's Rome was delivered "from an elevated place, in view of the faithful people, in a set form of words learnt by heart".[6] In ancient Egypt likewise the correctness of the recital was so important that the destiny of the departed depended on it; whoever could recite his formulas accurately and "had the right voice" could defy all the dangers of the other world and emerge from them victoriously. *Ma-a khrw*, "correct so far as the voice is concerned", ultimately acquired the meaning of "blessed", and was eventually added formally to the dead person's name, like our "late" or "deceased". To "know the utterances", that is the sacred *Texts* to be recited, was the most important matter for the dead,[7] *S-iakhw*, literally words

---

[1] Otto, *The Idea of the Holy*, 67. "The songs of the Salii are hardly understood correctly by their priests, but religion prohibits their alteration, and what has been rendered sacred must be observed", as Quintilian had remarked. Lehmann-Haas, *Textbuch*, 222.

[2] Firmicus Maternus, *De errore profanarum religionum*, c. 22; *cf.* on numinous utterances, Will, *Culte*, II, 150, and on cult language, *ibid.*, 135 *f.*

[3] Huizinga, *Herfstty der Middeleeuwen*, 404.

[4] G. van der Leeuw, *Wegen en Grenzen.*

[5] Examples in G. Appel, *De Romanorum precationibus*, 1909, 69 *f.*

[6] Augustine, *Confessions*, VIII, 2.   [7] *cf. e.g. Pyramidentexte* (Sethe), 855.

"that make the power of glory arise", being the name for the sacred ritual, which may be simply translated as *carmina*. In the ancient German world, similarly, the formula used in law, ritual drinking and sacrifice, was called *kvad*, and this again was a sort of *carmen*. So great was the potency of the formulas, indeed, that gods and divinities bore their names: thus *Paean* was originally a healing charm, and *Brahman* the power of the Universe, a chanted magical incantation.

H. Frick, *Ideogramm, Mythologie und das Wort* (*Marburger theol. Stud.* 3), 1931.

V. Larock, *Essai sur la valeur sacrée et la valeur sociale des noms de personnes dans les sociétés inférieures* (*RHR.* 101, 1930).

G. van der Leeuw, *Wegen en Grenzen. Over de verhouding van Religie en Kunst*, 1932.

H. W. Obbink, *De magische beteekenis van den naam*, 1925.

A. J. Portengen, *De oudgermaansche dichtertaal in haar ethnologisch verband*, 1915.

CHAPTER 59

THE WORD OF CONSECRATION

1. THE repetition of words, to continue, intensifies their power in the same degree as intensifying the tone and the rhythm:[1] this constitutes the Litany type.[2] "Thou must say it thrice" has always been the maxim of magic; and the accumulation of epithets in invoking the gods has the same purpose.[3] The object to which speech is directed, the power to be constrained, is thus as it were enveloped in words or, if the repetition occurs from one of several different points of vantage, for example from or towards the four points of the compass, enclosed within them.

The content of the words, also, is often expressly chosen so that power may be generated; thus among many ancient peoples lewd speaking was a sort of rite.[4] *Aischrologia*, or vituperation, as practised by the Greeks,[5] and usually indulged in by quite respectable matrons, had the same end in view. For speaking about powerful things itself generates power, and so everything referring to sex matters or to bodily secretions has always enjoyed great potency: the invective and obscenity surviving to-day sprang, in fact, from the word's powerfulness. Insult therefore is no senseless waste of words, as everyone knows who is in direct contact with life. The forcible terms of the ancient Germans also had a highly practical effect; if someone said to another person: "You lack courage for it", he was dishonoured unless he performed the action referred to, and if a woman was upbraided as a witch or whore she had to submit to the punishment for witchcraft or harlotry unless she had someone who could "avenge" her (*uphaevelse*, or setting up again).[6] Thus whether she were actually guilty or not was not at all important; the words rendered her culpable, and only some fresh manifestation of power could make her pure again.[7]

---

[1] G. van der Leeuw, *Wegen en Grenzen*, 60 f.

[2] It is remarkable that sufferers from mental disorders indulge in this type of repetition; the verbigeration of katatonics may be compared to magical formulas with which "the victims attempt to strengthen themselves and protect themselves against dangerous forces"; A. Storch, *Das archaisch-primitive Erleben und Denken der Schizophrenen*, 1922, 50.   [3] E. Maass, *Orpheus*, 1895, 199 *ff.*

[4] Lévy-Bruhl, *Primitives and the Supernatural*, 295 *f.*

[5] Also by the Romans at the Festival of Anna Perenna.

[6] *cf.* Wagner's *Lohengrin*.   [7] Grönbech, *op. cit.*, I, 101.

By means of the word, then, invective brings the person who is being abused within the power of the evil deed or detestable characteristic: it is a *word of consecration.* The reviler dedicates his opponent to those evil conditions about which he speaks;[1] and thus the curse is an effect of power that requires no gods nor spirits to execute it.[2] Once pronounced, a curse continues to operate until its potency is exhausted, and perpetually dedicates its object to the fate it has summoned into being. This was familiar not only to the primitive world, but above all to Greek tragedy, in which the persons acting are merely the instruments of the curse, of the ἀρά. The "curses", ἀραί, were conceived as personal;[3] the hereditary family curse dwelt in the house as a demon and continued to operate implacably. Certainly it lost its force as time ran on, and thus Orestes could appeal to the fact that he had already encountered so many people without this contact appearing to injure them, as a proof of the weakening of the curse.[4]

But equal in its power to the malediction is the blessing, "word-salvation" as it was called in the ancient German world.[5] It is indeed by no means a mere pious wish, but the allocation of fortune's gifts by employing words. When we were children we were astonished to find that Isaac had no benediction ready for his beloved Esau after the first had been purloined by the cunning Jacob. But Isaac was not expressing any mere wishes: he was blessing, and he could bestow the same blessing only once.[6] In blessing, also, much if not everything depends on the exactitude of the *carmen,* and in the Jewish legend an *Amen* omitted from the blessing was punished by God with a painful death.[7] All that is primitive and modern, heathen and Christian, with regard to blessing, is contained in Guardini's fine lines: "Only he who has Power can bless: only he who can create. God alone can bless. . . . For to bless is to decree what exists and is effective. . . . Only God can bless. But we are essentially suppliants."[8]

2. The word of consecration, still further, finds manifold applications. In the first place there is the *vow,* familiar in its classical form from the story of Jacob: "If God will be with me, and will keep me in

---

[1] Radermacher, *Schelten und Fluchen, AR.* XI, 1908, 11 *f.*
[2] *cf.* R. Thurnwald, *Reallexikon der Vorgeschichte, Zauber,* 497. A curse once pronounced cannot be retracted; *cf.* an Indian example in Vogel, *Meded. Kon. Akad. d. Wetensch., Afd. Lett.,* 70, B. 4, 1930, 16.
[3] Aeschylus, *Choëphoroe,* 406.   [4] Aeschylus, *Eumenides,* 285.
[5] Grönbech, *op. cit.,* I, 170.   [6] *Gen.* xxvii.
[7] Bin Gorion, *Der Born Judas,* V, 153.   [8] *Von heiligen Zeichen,* 68.

this way that I go, and will give me bread to eat, and raiment to put on, so that I come again to my father's house in peace; then shall the Lord be my God: . . . and of all that thou shalt give me I will surely give the tenth unto thee."[1] The Ewe king, again, swears to the *tro*: "If thou canst help me, so that we are not molested by any other king and always have food in our houses, then I will always serve thee."[2] But that such a contract with Power is not pure rationalism has already been observed in discussing gifts and sacrifice.[3] The vow is certainly a contract; but a contract is not governed by purely rational motives.

The Roman *votum* was a typical example of the word of consecration; and an *evocationis carmen* evoked the hostile god from his city during a siege;[4] it too bore the form of contract. A primeval formula also accompanied the *devotio* whereby the general, as simultaneously dedicator and dedicated, bound himself and the enemy's army together into a single unity and, by seeking death, consecrated both himself and the foe to ruin; if the general did not fall, then he remained impure and the prey of the under-world.[5] A similar dedication, only not of oneself, was the ancient Israelite ban חרם; if God delivered the enemy into Israel's hands, the people would lay on him the חרם (*ban*), that is destroy the enemy root and branch.[6]

The most familiar form of the word of consecration, however, is the *oath*. It actually leads us into the realm of the Phenomenology of Law, but partially, and in virtue of its essential nature, it pertains to religion. The oath, then, is an automatically effective power-word which, if his assertion cannot be confirmed, dedicates the swearer to this power. But this does not necessarily mean that the statement need even be true. Here also the word is more powerful than reality, and one may succeed in "making a matter true". In a Mohammedan story, for instance, a Christian offers a Mussulman half a banana with the words: "Sir, by the truth of thy faith, take this!" The Mohammedan is afraid

---

[1] *Gen.* xxviii, 20 *ff.*   [2] Spieth, *Ewe*, 107; *cf.* Heiler, *Katholizismus*, 65.
[3] Chap. 50.
[4] Lehmann-Haas, *Textbuch*, 226. Appel, *De Romanorum precationibus*, 15 *f.*
[5] The formula: "Janus, Jupiter, father Mars, Quirinus, Bellona, ye Lares, ye gods Novensiles, ye gods Indigetes, ye divinities, under whose power we and our enemies are, and ye dii Manes, I pray you, I adore you, I ask your favour, that you would prosperously grant strength and victory to the Roman people, the Quirites, and that ye may affect the enemies of the Roman people, of the Quirites, with terror, dismay and death. In such manner as I have expressed in words, so do I devote the legions and auxiliaries of the enemy, together with myself, to the dii Manes, and to Earth for the republic of the Quirites, for the army, legions, auxiliaries of the Roman people, of the Quirites." Livy, VIII, 9, 6 *f.* (Spillan). Appel, *op. cit.*, 14. L. Deubner, *Die Devotion der Decier*, *AR.* VIII, 1905.   [6] *Numbers* xxi. 2.

to allow the Christian's oath to become untrue, so he eats the banana, which contains a stupefying drug.[1] A modern would say: "my faith is pure independently of anyone else's assertions"; but the oath possesses the power to render true and untrue. Thus we can understand the institution of the oath of purification existing among many peoples. If someone is accused of theft, he strikes the earth with his hand and thereby has sworn an oath; but if, nevertheless, he has stolen the object, he must die.[2] Testimony on oath is thus decisive as to guilt or innocence. The oath is a "powerful word", and its potency may be intensified; for this purpose, among other things, repetition serves, frequently thrice.[3] The manner of taking the oath, again, also heightens its power; for example, in ancient German custom the oath had to be sworn naked (*ritus paganus*);[4] or the oath was reinforced by accompanying celebrations. In ancient Israel, for example, the man's genitals were touched while swearing an oath;[5] they were the seat of a powerful soul-stuff: "Pray, place your hand under my thigh, and I will make you swear an oath by the Eternal", said Abraham to his servant.[6] The most frequent method of strengthening the oath was, however, the institution of the oath-helper (compurgator), which is also the most conclusive proof that it is not an assertion in accordance with "actuality", but a power-word. In the Middle Ages the number of these "con-sacramentals" was decided according to the importance of the issue; in one case a man who had been attacked while alone took with him three straws from his thatched roof, his cat and his cock to swear to the outrage before the judge.[7] Finally, the oath, which is already in itself a form of ordeal, may be confirmed by a judgment of God,[8] for example by taking communion,[9] or by a duel. An oath, again, is false, perjury, even when broken unintentionally;[10] for the word is valid, and when it has once been spoken it produces its effect, that is it induces injury to the swearer or to the object by which the oath was sworn; thus the tree by which two persons have sworn never to part from each other withers when death separates them.[11]

[1] *The Arabian Nights.*
[2] Spieth, *Eweer*, 59. An Egyptian purificatory oath in E. Révillout, *Revue égyptienne*, V, 25 *ff*. Arabian and Israelite, Pedersen, *Der Eid bei den Semiten in seinem Verhältnis zu verwandten Erscheinungen*, 181, 186.   [3] Hirzel, *Der Eid*, 82.
[4] J. Grimm, *Deutsche Rechtsaltertümer*, I, 166. On the same custom among the Berbers: Westermarck, *The Origin and Development of the Moral Ideas*, I, 59.
[5] Pedersen, *op. cit.*, 150.   [6] *Gen.* xxiv, 2, 3 (Moffat).
[7] Grimm, *op. cit.*, 176. For Egypt, A. Wilcken, *Zeitschrift für ägyptische Sprache*, 48, 1911, 170.   [8] Chap. 54.   [9] Westermarck, *ibid.*, II, 687; I, 504 *f.*
[10] Hirzel, *op. cit.*, 49 *f.*   [11] Cretan folksong; Hirzel, *ibid.*, 35.

3. I have already observed that the similarity to a contract rationalizes neither the vow nor the oath, since the contract is not in itself a purely rational action, but a word of consecration. This it is in the form: word against word. Among the Romans a contract was a *carmen*; to all legal actions there pertained *certa verba, litterae* and gestures. May remarks, not incorrectly, that in legal affairs all three elements of religious dedication are represented: λεγόμενα, δρώμενα, δεικνύμενα, what is said, what is done, and what is exhibited. The law is spoken (*jus dicere*);[1] the word of consecration thus unites the phenomena of religion with those of law, and the legal relationship between persons is absolutely dependent on their own relation to Power.

R. Hirzel, *Der Eid*, 1902.
E. Maass, *Segnen, Weihen, Taufen* (*AR*. XXI, 1922).
J. Pedersen, *Der Eid bei den Semiten in seinem Verhältnis zu verwandten Erscheinungen*, 1914.
L. Radermacher, *Schelten und Fluchen* (*AR*. XI, 1908).

[1] May, *Droit romain* 20 and Note 16; *ibid.*, 34.

CHAPTER 60

MYTH

1. ACTUALLY, the myth is nothing other than the word itself. For it is neither speculation nor poem, neither a primitive explanation of the world nor a philosophy in embryo, although it also may be, and indeed frequently is, all of these. It is a spoken word, possessing decisive power in its repetition; just as the essential nature of sacred action consists in its being repeated, so the essence of myth lies in its being told, in being repeatedly spoken anew.[1] Generally, therefore, the attempt to understand myths and mythology has been far too abstract or esthetic; the type of mythology that has usually been relied on has been, to some degree, that luxuriance of myths springing up in periods during which they had themselves become dubious or indeed offensive, such as the culmination of Greek literature, together with its later phases, or in Christian-Germanic antiquity. But the living myth itself is the precise parallel of celebration; it is, indeed, itself a celebration, so that the discovery of the close relationship between myth and rite has, in recent years, led not only to the understanding of many myths which were previously enigmatic, but has also elucidated, for the first time, the essence of myth as such. And conversely, the myth certifies the ritual. "It refers to the past when the sacred action was first executed, and indeed often enables us even to prove that primitive man perhaps not merely *repeated* the incidents that had been elaborated, but that the initial celebration was deliberately and literally carried out as an actual occurrence, including everything that was then essential to it".[2] The myth is therefore not reflective contemplation, but actuality. *It is the reiterated presentation of some event replete with power*; verbal presentation, however, is quite as effective as the repetition; it is, then, verbal celebration.[3] The classical example is the repeating of the *Qui pridie*, the words of the Institution in the mass, which constantly recall anew the mighty event of the redemptive death of Christ.[4]

Mythical repetition in the form of narrative, however, conceals in

---

[1] Harrison, *Themis*, 328 ff.   [2] Preuss, *Gehalt der Mythen*, 7.
[3] Wundt, *op. cit.*, V, 24 f., 48; *cf.* further Chap. 17.
[4] Examples that it is really the rite which explains the myth: Pentheus, the "man of sorrows" of the Dionysiac circle; Jephthah's daughter; the Roman Anna Perenna; the Nordic myth of Baldur, *etc.*

itself an element that does not concern other sacred words—*Endowment with form*:[1] myth not only evokes or recalls some powerful event, but it also endows this with form. In this the origins of the sacred word in magically conditioned metaphor indubitably cooperate;[2] by bestowing form the mythical utterance becomes decisive. It does not kill, like the concept that abstracts from life, but calls forth life, and thus constitutes the most extreme antithesis conceivable to pure theory. The concept, for example, refers to the "Law of Gravitation" and abstracts from every actual weight, attempting in this way to include diversified concrete events within one single dead formula. But myth speaks of "that mad and quickening rush by which all earth's creatures fly back to her heart when released".[3]

Yet the life that falls within the decisiveness of the mythical word is not ordinary reality: this requires no decision at all, since it is simply "accepted". But myth accepts nothing: it 'celebrates' reality. It does with it what it will, and deals with it according to its own laws. As a single example: it arrests time, and in this it is sharply distinguished from celebration in the form of action, which utilizes the temporal instant, the *kairos*. Myth takes the event and sets it up on its own basis, in its own realm. Thus the event becomes 'eternal': it happens now and always, and operates as a type. What occurs daily in Nature, sunrise for example, becomes in the myth something unique.[4] It must be repeated so that the event may retain its vitality. The mythical occurrence, then, is typical and eternal; it subsists apart from all that is temporal. If nevertheless we attempt to fix it in time, we must place it at either the beginning or the end of all happening, either in the primeval era or at the conclusion of time,[5] that is before or after "time".

Thus myth is no "figurative mode of expression". The image it evokes has a very real significance; it proceeds inferentially not from "reality" to the picture, but rather from the picture to reality. When, for example, it calls God "Father", it does this not on the basis of any given fatherhood, but creates a paternal form to which every given fatherhood must conform (this case has been acutely elaborated

[1] On this term *cf.* Note 3, p. 87.
[2] *cf.* H. Pongs, *Das Bild in der Dichtung*, I, 1927, 14.
[3] Chesterton, *The Innocence of Father Brown*, 233 (Popular Edition).
[4] A. Réville, *Prolégomènes de l'Histoire des Religions*, 1889, 153 *f.* Further, 155 *f.* "What is permanent and frequent in Nature and in humanity is derived from some occurrence which happened once for all".
[5] Chap. 87. Hubert-Mauss, *Mélanges*, 192 *f.*

by Frick).[1] The myth proclaims, essentially and decisively; and thus it becomes possible that for a culture in which abstract tendencies prevail, either it is no longer understood at all, as with Greek myths in the days of the sophists and Christian myths in the nineteenth century, or, in quite the opposite direction, that it becomes the expression of the ultimate and the highest, withdrawing itself from all that is merely conceptual, as in Plato's myths or the conclusion of Goethe's *Faust*.

2. In the form of the *saga*[2] the myth reverts to the temporal. The saga is a myth which, during its expansion, has become attached to some specific place or other, or to some sort of historical fact. The narrative of the saga, therefore, has not the character of a decision. In the saga an attitude is assumed which, though frequently devout, is purely contemplative. The myth is eternally present,[3] while the saga refers wholly to the past. In the Old Testament the distinction is quite clear: the myths at the beginning of *Genesis* are sharply distinguishable from the succeeding patriarchal sagas.[4] The *motif* of the saga is not historical but mythical; it attaches itself repeatedly to different historic personalities, and the principal aspect is the typical as being always more important than the historical. In 1892, for instance, some cabmen were heard discussing Queen Louise in a Berlin beer dive. One of them asked whose wife she really had been, and another expressed the opinion that "she was old Fritz's wife", since "the best king had also had the best queen".[5] Thus while the typifying myth that confers eternity overrides history, its actuality has been lost; the myth of the dragon slayer, for example, persists in Worms on the Rhine and draws within its circle occurrences in world history,[6] but thereby the dragon becomes a prehistoric monster and loses its actual dreadfulness. The *fairy tale* is therefore closer to the myth than the saga.

---

[1] *Ideogramm, Mythologie und das Wort.* An antithesis, referring to the Mother form, occurs in Plato, *Menexenus*, 238: "the woman in her conception and generation is but the imitation of the earth, and not the earth of the woman" (Jowett).

[2] This term is employed in a broad literary sense, as in Galsworthy's *Forsyte Saga*.

[3] The myth knows no "Time" in the Newtonian sense. "The magical 'Now' is by no means a *mere* 'Now', no simple and detached present instant but, to use Leibniz's expression, *chargé du passé et gros de l'avenir.*" Cassirer, *Die Begriffsform im mythischen Denken*, II, 140 f.

[4] Here again in Galsworthy's literary sense. I can admit no difference in principle between myth and saga in the sense that in the myth only gods, and in the saga only human beings, appear, as *e.g.* H. Gunkel maintains (*Genesis*[3], 1910, xiv); cf. Bethe, *Märchen, Sage, Mythus*, 133.

[5] Bethe, *ibid.*, 126 f.   [6] cf. H. Schneider, *Deutsche Heldensage*, 1930, 21 ff.

3. "The historical saga usually adds something extraordinary and surprising, or even supernatural, to the ordinary, familiar and present; but the fairy tale stands quite apart from the actual world in a secluded and undisturbed sphere, beyond which it does not gaze; it mentions, therefore, neither name nor place, nor any definite home."[1] Fairy stories have deep significance not merely for the history of religion, since they contain much ancient religious material,[2] but for religion itself also. Telling fairy tales is therefore no affair of pure delight in fabulous narration, but has a magical effect, and the Pawnee Indians believe that relating them, by depicting man's subjugation of the buffalo, successfully militates against the decline of the herds.[3] Narrating fairy stories is celebration too,[4] in fact a *carmen*; their wording must never be changed; even children insist on this, and the art of telling such tales, which among ourselves is entrusted to "old grannies"— *e.g.* nursery stories going back to the old wives' tale, *fabula anilis*, of Apuleius—and by primitive peoples to professional story-tellers, rests to a large extent on their accurate recitation. The famous woman of Niederzwehrn, for instance, who recited fairy tales for the brothers Grimm, could correct each error immediately and never altered her wording at all, no matter how often she repeated them;[5] and Jacob Wassermann has given a clear and psychologically profound account of the cogent force of fairy story narrative.[6]

Like myth, the fairy tale too is "homeless, fluttering through the air like gossamer in sunlight". Its figures have neither names nor history: they are *the* prince, *the* step-mother, *the* vizier, or just simply Hans and Gretel, Yussuf and Ali.[7] Time stands still, as in the Sleeping Beauty's Castle. All at once the little girl is ready to be wed, while Penelope never grows any older; "once upon a time": in other words, it is eternal and ever-present, and Cinderella and Tom Thumb live to-day just as a thousand years ago. "Once upon a time: it will happen some day: that is the beginning of all fairy tales; there is no 'if' and no

---

[1] Wilhelm Grimm, in Wehrhan, *op. cit.*, 7.
[2] In their oldest forms fairy tales represent a very primitive level of human experience; I mention only the way in which the wish rules the event, the part played by animals, the frequently very ancient sayings that occur in even our modern fairy stories, *etc.* Huet, *Les contes populaires*, 71; Gunkel, *Genesis*, xxvii; Wundt, *op. cit.*, V, 166 f. Thimme, *Das Märchen*. On the origin of fairy tales *cf.* Bédier, *Les Fabliaux*, 42, 242 ff.   [3] Wundt, *op. cit.*, V, 110, 172 f.
[4] *cf.* P. Saintyves, *Les Contes de Perrault*, 1923.
[5] Grimm, *Kinder- und Hausmärchen, Vorrede*; Thimme, *Das Märchen*, 8; Huet, *Les Contes populaires*, 70.   [6] *Der Aufruhr um der Junker Ernst.*
[7] Bethe, *op. cit.*, 107; Thimme, *op. cit.*, 1 f., 139, 147; Huet, *ibid.*, 71.

'perhaps'."[1] Neither is there any space: "Go to the Red Sea", it says, and the girl goes there: that is perfectly simple![2] Similarly there is no constancy in the phenomena, no identity; metamorphosis is something so common that if the lion continues to be a lion, while the horse changes itself into a mouse, then we are told almost apologetically: "the lion was a lion, always".[3] There is no doubt, still further, that the sphere in which fairy tales are carried on is to a great extent the realm of dreams.[4] "The cock crowed, and it was daytime": this typical ending to French fairy stories[5] stresses the dream character of the narrative;[6] and hence the marvellous in the fairy tale is nothing in the least extraordinary, but is its own characteristic world. Originally, however, this dream aspect by no means implied that something transcending reality was intended; rather what is expressing itself here is primitive mentality, which is much more realistic than theoretical and has been conserved in the fairy tale. "The man of science says, 'cut the stalk, and the apple will fall'; but the fairy tale says, 'Blow the horn, and the ogre's castle will fall' ".[7] The latter, however, is far more realistically intended than the former, which is a mere abstract statement.

4. The *legend*, in conclusion, is really the story of some saint to be read during Christian worship. It has an edifying character: it effects something and thus pertains to sacred words; but the specifically decisive power of the word has here been enfeebled. The legend then, which in any case brings with it very much that is mythical and saga-like, approaches pious contemplation.

J. Bédier, *Les Fabliaux*, 1893.

E. Bethe, *Märchen, Sage, Mythus*.

E. Cassirer, *Die Begriffsform im mythischen Denken*, 1922.

G. Dumezil, *Naissance de Rome*, 1944.

A. van Gennep, *La formation des légendes*, 1910.

G. Huet, *Les contes populaires*.

G. Jacob, *Märchen und Traum*, 1923.

G. van der Leeuw, "Die Bedeutung der Mythen" (in *Festschr. für A. Bertholet*, 1950, pg. 287).

K. Th. Preuss, *Der religiöse Gehalt der Mythen*, 1933.

A. Thimme, *Das Märchen*, 1909.

---

[1] Tegethoff, *Französische Volksmärchen*, II, No. 33; *cf.* H. Gunkel, *Das Märchen im Alten Testament*, 1921, 161.   [2] *Kinder- und Hausmärchen*, No. 88.
[3] Stroebe, *Nordische Volksmärchen*, I, No. 12.   [4] Jacob, *Märchen und Traum*.
[5] Tegethoff, *Französische Märchen*, II, 324; *cf.* O. Weinreich, *AR.* 22, 1923–24, 333 *f.*
[6] Huet, *op. cit.*, 78 *f.*   [7] Chesterton, *Orthodoxy*, 89.

CHAPTER 61

THE STORY OF SALVATION: THE WORD OF GOD

1. IF the myth concerns the introduction of some cult, the discovery or attainment of a cult image or something similar, we then speak of a *cult legend*. Such is, for example, the dream of the Pharaoh Ptolemy which induced him to have the image of Serapis brought from Sinope, just as in a dream at Jerusalem, Bishop Gualfredus heard about an image of the Lord supposed to have been made by Nicodemus. So he contrived to procure the effigy, which arrived from Joppa at the harbour of Lucca on a ship with neither sails nor rudder. At first no one could reach this ship; then when a man of God arrived, summoned by an angel, it entered the haven of itself. This is the same story as that of the arrival of the black stone of the *magna mater* in Rome in 204 B.C., for the ship bearing it ran ashore off the harbour of Ostia and was refloated only when a chaste woman seized the cable. In such cult legends as these, however, the mythical occurrence does not become actual, but remains an affair of the venerable past.

Mythical history, again, becomes actual, but impalpable, in the Hindu form of the *Jatakas*;[1] "they are prolix comedies of a hundred scenes, with the Universe as the stage".[2] The individual event, the actual powerfulness of occurrences or persons, is in the *jataka* "linked" with the timeless history of Buddha. The event is then made eternal in the form not of uniqueness, but of never-ness: it is only an illusory manifestation of eternal salvation, and the most widely contrasted representations, for example in the reliefs of the Boro-Budur temple on the Island of Java, have only *one* meaning:[3] salvation is purchased at the cost of reality.[4]

The *hieros logos* on the other hand—the "sacred story"—follows the directly opposite path. It proclaims some definite occurrence, but it also determines the hearer's salvation, and the sacred events of the mystery religions were such "salvation stories". They were not merely recited but also acted[5] and experienced, the representation of Kore's ravishing and rediscovery, of the Mithraic bull sacrifice, of Attis'

---

[1] Chap. 22. [2] Lévi, *Les Jatakas*, 18.
[3] N. J. Krom, *De levensgeschiedenis van den Buddha op Barabudur*, 1926. Lévi, *op. cit.*, 13. Lüders, *Buddhistische Märchen, Zur Einführung*.
[4] Huet, *op. cit.*, 170 f. [5] A. van Gennep, *op. cit.*, 114 f.

dying and resurrection, Isis' "search" for her lost spouse, all being related and represented in the mysteries either symbolically or purely dramatically.[1] Thus the representation of the myth implies the salvation of the hearer and spectator. Salvation, quiescent in the event, becomes actual in the myth. A man is ritually killed, for example; he is "the man of sorrows", Pentheus, over whose death mourning resounds, and the renewal of whose life is ultimately celebrated with rejoicing.[2] Such a *hieros logos*, as in the case of Pentheus, can lose a goodly proportion of its determinative power; then it becomes simply myth or saga (again as in *The Forsyte Saga* sense), and finally literature (Euripides!). It may on the other hand retain its vitality but gradually lose its significance: this happens when it becomes a popular custom such as driving away Winter, expelling Death *etc.* But if it remains true to its real nature it is, as it were, the focus of all powerfulness, nourishing the community's life from its glow: and thus by the dramatic representation of the "sacred story", the powerfulness that has appeared in history is transferred to the life of the community and likewise of the individual.[3] In Christian worship the *hieros logos* is in fact the focal point: for not merely the sacrament of the Eucharist but the entire system of worship, in the cycle of its ever recurring celebrations,[4] is in principle a repetition of the typical story of Christ; and in this reiteration the powerfulness of the story is transferred to the church's own life.

2. But the *hieros logos* of Christianity is not merely a myth subsisting in celebration: it is also *evangelium, Proclamation;*[5] and in the Hellenistic world an *evangelium* was the proclamation of the saviour-king's accession to the throne.[6] For Christianity, still further, it is not primarily the literary form of the life of Jesus, but first of all the joyful message that Jesus is the Lord, the Saviour. Even in the biographical form of the Gospels themselves, this is the principal feature; it is no mere affair of imparting certain facts, but of preaching Him Who is recognized as Lord. In Christianity, therefore, the repetition of the story of salvation and the announcement, the proclamation, of salvation, are intimately connected.[7]

cf. O. Kern, *AR.* 26, 1928, 15.
[1] An example of symbolic representation is the ear of corn in Eleusis; *cf.* Chap. 53; also P. Wolters, *Die goldnen Ähren*, in *Festschrift Loeb*, 1930, 111 *ff.*
[3] *cf.* Wundt, *op. cit.*, V, 48 *f.* Preuss, *Gehalt der Mythen*, 31. Myth is a "necessary constituent of the cult in so far as a beginning in primeval time is held to be necessary for validity".   [4] Chap. 56.   [5] *cf.* Bultmann, *Glauben und Verst.*, 186 *f.*
[6] Chap. 12.   [7] *cf.* Bultmann, *ibid.*, 291.

3. Associated together in this way, they are called the "Word of God".[1] This is in the first place the announcement, the message of salvation;[2] but it is also this salvation itself as it is revealed in the actual event. The preaching of the message, then, is always at the same time a priestly act, and conversely.[3] The very utterance is powerful: "to a certain extent a preacher must be one of those men of whom his hearers are compelled to say: 'Whither shall I flee from this man? his speech pursues me to every hiding-place; how shall I get free from him? for he is upon me at every moment' ".[4] Such an utterance, however, is power actually present, the direct antithesis of any mere contemplation or explanation. The Word, and indeed in this its dual meaning of announcement and actually present divine Power, thus becomes the form of revelation in general.[5] In the later Greek period, indeed, the *logos* was the veritably present and effective Power of God, as it was subsequently in Christendom. But Christianity preaches the incarnate *logos* that has appeared in historical actuality; the very "Word", by which all things have been created, took flesh and dwelt among us "full of grace and truth".[6] Thus determinative announcement and determinative event both occur in the figure of the Saviour Jesus Christ. For such a form is essential to every myth.

The idea of the Word of God, however, lives in other religions besides Christianity, and above all in Islam. The world was created by God's Word; but within this there resides no specific power whatever: it is only one attribute of God. For passionate Mohammedan monotheism tolerates no independent *logos*, and still less a figure of any kind, and wages war therefore against the Christian doctrine of the *logos*.[7] But similar tendencies sprang up much earlier also; from the earliest historical times, in fact, the so-called "Monument of Memphite theology" attests a "theology of the word" in Egypt, with reference to the ancient Memphite god Ptah: "it happened that the heart and the tongue received power over all the members by teaching that he (Ptah) is in every body (as the heart), and (as the tongue) in every mouth of all the gods, all men and cattle, all reptiles (and) what

---

[1] *cf.* W. B. Kristensen, *De goddelyke heraut en het woord van God, Meded. Kon. Akad. v. Wetensch., Afd. Lett.* 70, B, Nr. 2, 1930.

[2] Chap. 28.   [3] *cf.* P. Tillich, *Die religiöse Lage der Gegenwart,* 148.

[4] S. Kierkegaard, in: Ed. Geismar, *Sören Kierkegaard,* 1929, 367.

[5] Chap. 85 *ff.*

[6] *John* i, 14. On the relation of history to the Word of God *cf.* Bultmann, *ibid.,* 287.

[7] Thus *e.g.* in popular literature like *The Arabian Nights:—Tausend und eine Nacht* (Littmann) VI, 66 *f.*

(ever else) lives, since he (as the heart) thinks and (as the tongue) commands all things as he will" . . . "it (the heart) is what permits all knowledge to emerge or arise, and the tongue it is that repeats what the heart has been thinking" . . . "but every word of the god came into being through what the heart had thought and the tongue commanded" . . . "and thus all works and arts are carried out, the arms' actions, the legs' motion and the movements of all the limbs, all in accord with this command which was conceived by the heart and expressed by the tongue, and which constitutes the meaning of all things." The organ of creation is the mouth, "which named all things", and thus heart and tongue are the two representatives of creative power.[1]

Primitive man also knows the word as primal power: the Uitoto tribe in Columbia ascribe to the sacred words, employed in their celebrations, the original beginning: "in the beginning the word gave origin to the Father". The sacred words, remarks Preuss, subsist independently of this Father to a certain extent, and existed before him;[2] thus the word has precedence here even over the god, and makes the latter really superfluous.

[1] Sethe, *Dramatische Texte zu altägyptischen Mysterienspielen*, I.
[2] *Religion und Mythologie der Uitoto*, I, 1921, 26.

THE WORD OF MAN: MAGICAL FORMULA AND PRAYER

1. WITHIN the stream of divine utterance there resounds the word of man; but we are very far from being able to distinguish, always and precisely, between God's word itself and human expression. For the word of Power is mighty in man's mouth just as it is in God's. Man's own word at first, therefore, is magical, creative, and so far as we can speak of "God" in this connection[1] man takes a divine word into his mouth.[2] Thus in their misery people came in hordes to Empedocles, to enquire the way of salvation and "to hear a little word bringing deliverance."[3] The magical formula and the prayer, again, cannot be kept apart; so that if in Roman prayer the rule held good, "in prayers there should be no ambiguity",[4] then it is clear that this prayer is a *carmen*, a magic formula.[5] The word, in and of itself, is powerful, so that if I pray for someone and make a mistake in his name, then the blessing will not reach him but the bearer of the name I have mentioned. In prayer, therefore, one must state as definitely as possible both name and place: an accurate filling in of all the details is requested![6] It has already been observed, too, that in Rome, the language of *precatio* and of *pactio*, of prayer and of contract, was the same;[7] in prayer, then, names are the chief features.[8]

To pray is therefore to exert power, and the Iroquois call praying "the laying down of one's *orenda*", perhaps because the act of praying presupposes the surrender of one's own power, but it may also be, quite conversely, because in the prayer power should manifest itself.[9] Similarly we find in Aeschylus that praying is "to show the force of the

---

[1] Chap. 1.

[2] It is true that this implies no historical development "from spell to prayer" in the evolutionary sense (Marett, *The Threshold of Religion*, Chap. II). Rather a prayer always subsisted side by side with the magical formula; "at first" refers, therefore, merely to the "structural relationship".

[3] In Diels, *Fragmente der Vorsokratiker*, I, 265.

[4] Servius, *ad Aen.*, VII, 120.   [5] Heiler, *Prayer*, 67 *f*.

[6] Plato, *Cratylus*, 400 *c*.   [7] Appel, *De Romanorum precationibus*, 76 *f.*, 145 *f.*

[8] Usener, *Götternamen*, 335 *f.*; *cf.* Chap. 17.

[9] Hewitt, *Orenda*, 40. Beth, *Reiigion und Magie*, 262.

mouth for someone's good".[1] Prayer has extremely concrete purposes; the Romans prayed "for the health of the cattle",[2] and the *epithalamium* sought to ensure the fertility of marriage; the incantation, again, wrought recovery from illness. The Greek *paean*, a power-word against diseases, became even a god, while to-day there are many people who still revere the doctor's prescription as a magical incantation. Thus prayer exercises potent influence alike over men, powers and gods.[3] "Upon speech all the gods live, on speech the *gandharvas*, animals and men . . . speech is imperishable, the first-born of the (*eternal*) law (Ṛta), the mother of the Vedas, the navel of immortality", says ancient Hindu word-philosophy which is based directly on the use of the *carmen* during sacrifice;[4] to the Germanic tribesman, likewise, prayer was a weapon which he hurled against his opponent.[5] The prayer of Christians moves the house where they are assembled:[6] that of the vestal virgins roots an escaping slave to the spot;[7] saints in prayer are levitated by the power of their supplication, and hover in the air.[8] The finest example of all is provided in the legend concerning the *sufi* al-Hallaj: "Once when he heard the *muezzin* call to prayer he cried: 'Thou hast lied', and when the people were enraged with him and sought to put him to death, al-Hallaj continued: 'No, thou hast not recited the *shahada* properly'; and when he himself said it, the minaret collapsed."[9]

2. Magical prayer owes its powerfulness to precise recitation, to rhythmical sequence, to the utterance of the name together with other factors; one very important consideration, for example, being the so-called epic introduction that occurs in many magical formulas. I call this the *magical antecedent*: thus one of the Merseburg magical incantations says: "Once some *idisi* (wise women) sat down (here and there). Some were knitting fetters, others were hindering the army, others were freeing from (the strong fetters).—Break away from the fetters! Escape from the enemy!"[10] And the second: "Phol and Wotan were

---

[1] Aeschylus, *Choēphoroe*, 721. [2] Cato, *De Agri Cultura*, 83.
[3] *cf.* Wundt, *op. cit.*, II. Heiler, *ibid.*, xiii *f.*, 53 *f.* F. B. Jevons, *The Idea of God*, 115 *ff.* Fr. Pfister in *Handwörterbuch des deutschen Aberglaubens, Gebet*.
[4] Bertholet, *op. cit.*, 9, 55. [5] Grönbech, *op. cit.*, IV, 44 *f.*
[6] *Acts* iv. 31. [7] Pliny, *Nat. Hist.* 28, 12 *f.* Appel, *op. cit.*, 74 *f.*
[8] J. von Görres, *Mystik, Magie und Dämonie*, 1927, 250. This was also said about Vintras, the prophet of "Vintrasism"; *cf.* J. Bois, *Les petites religions de Paris*, 1894, 122 *f.* [9] Massignon, *Al Hallaj*, I, 449.
[10] Bertholet, *op. cit.*, 12, 70.

RELIGION IN ESSENCE AND MANIFESTATION [62, 2

once riding in a wood. There Balder's foal sprained its foot. Then Sinthgunt charmed it, (and) Sunna her sister; then Friia charmed it, (and) Volla her sister; then Wotan charmed it, as he well knew how to do; alike the injured bone, the damaged blood, the broken limb—bone to bone, blood to blood, limb to limb, as though they were glued together!"[1] Here the actuality that has been given is corrected by means of the word, as it were by substitution; an event that occurred in prehistoric times, and which now possesses a mythical eternity and typicalness, is by the power of the formula rendered present in the literal sense and made actual and fruitful.[2] This phenomenon is also very well shown on a runic piece of wood discovered in Westeremden, one side of which bears a runic inscription recounting a mythical event, an "epic introduction", a "magical antecedent", as follows: "Amlud (Hamlet) took up his position (for battle) at Upheim. The surf bowed before his runic yew staves." This is, then, a historical occurrence of a mythical kind and of typical power. On the other side, in a different hand: "May the surf bow before this runic yew stave."[3] This practical application of the myth was probably inscribed on the wood, in some moment of dire need, by the Frisian seamen who had bought it in Denmark, and the stave was then cast into the raging sea. The wood of the yew, and the runic inscription, possessed magical power; here then it was actually the runic wood itself that was the concrete presence of the mythical event; succinctly, it may be said that the seamen threw the Hamlet-event into the sea. Man thus transforms a disagreeable reality by the creative induction of something better; and we find an extreme example of this creative, event-producing power of the word in an Indian tribe. "A telegram once came to my bungalow. 'Baloo dead, don't worry.' Baloo was a hundred miles away. . . ." He was, however, not dead at all; "a crow had momentarily perched on his head, and his uncle had sent the wire to prevent the fulfilment of this ill omen . . . to realize it in some way beforehand. The crow, by perching on the boy's head, had doomed him to an inevitable death."[4] For now Baloo *was* dead, since the word had con-

---

[1] Bertholet. Further examples: in popular custom, Usener, *Heilige Handlung*, 423 *f.* M. L. Palès, *Revue anthropologique*, 37, 1927. C. Bakker, *Ned. Tydschrift voor Geneeskunde*, 65, 1921. Christian, K. H. E. de Jong, *De magie by de Grieken en Romeinen*, 1921, 238. Ancient Egypt, *Pyramidentexte* (Sethe), 418. Ad. Erman, *Die ägyptische Religion*[2], 1909, 169 *ff.*

[2] *cf.* further Preuss, *Gehalt der Mythen.*

[3] J. M. N. Kapteyn, *Dertiende, veertiende en vyftiende Jaarverslag van de Vereeniging voor Terpenonderzoek*, 1928–1931, 72 *ff.*   [4] Chap. 54.

summated the event, and so he would not die again so soon. At all events the omen had "been exhausted".[1]

3. An intermediate form between conjuration and prayer is the *summons* which, in connection with the sacrament, has already been discussed as the *epiclesis*.[2] *Mars vigila*—"Mars, awake!"— cried the Roman general setting out for the field; that is a kind of warning cry, probably intended to remind the god of the pact that had been concluded.[3] Yet another type is the summons which invokes the saviour,[4] like the extremely ancient one of the women of Elis: "Come in springtime, O Dionysos, to thy pure temple by the sea, with the *Charites* in thy train, rushing with ox-foot (phallus). Noble bull, Noble bull."[5] Here the summons was intended to effect the epiphany of the lifebringing god: the presence of power was "bespoken". Professional magic also requires the god's presence and invokes him, often indeed in words whose sublimity far surpasses their trivial purpose: one magical papyrus in Leyden thus invokes Eros: "Come unto me . . . O thou omnipotent god, thou who hast inspired men with the breath of life. Thou, the lord of all that is beautiful on earth, hear my prayer . . . *etc.*"[6] The Christian *epiclesis* also, alike in prayer and in the sacrament, vacillates between conjuration, summons and actual prayer, while the ancient Christian *maran atha* is a cult summons. In the *Apostolic Constitutions*, again, we find the prayer: "send down thy Holy Spirit upon this sacrifice";[7] the Roman mass, however, required this *epiclesis* no longer, or placed it elsewhere because its formula of consecration (*Qui pridie*) could compel the presence of divine Power.[8]

Thus to a higher degree than the formula, the summons possesses the character of spontaneity; it is a kind of warning cry: a sort of "Hallo! Look out!" uttered to power. In its most elementary form it approaches the *exclamation*, still occurring in many prayers as a very ancient component (πομπνσμός, ὀλολυγή;[9] *hallelujah, Kyrie eleison, euoi, triumpe, etc.*), and which is similarly prominent in ecstatic forms of supplication. Similarly the Hindu syllable *om*, however much it may subsequently have been stored with speculation, was originally such a

---

[1] Lévy-Bruhl, *Primitives and the Supernatural*, 375.   [2] Chap. 52.
[3] Wissowa, *Religion der Römer*, 144. Heiler, *Prayer*, 16.   [4] Chap. 12.
[5] Plutarch, *Quaestiones graecae*, 36. Farnell, *Cults*, V, 126.
[6] De Jong, *Magie by de Grieken en Romeinen*, 157, 155 *ff.*
[7] Lietzmann, *Messe und Herrenmahl*, 68.
[8] Lietzmann, *ibid.*, 121 *f.* We find a similar vacillation in the formula of absolution (*ego te absolvo*), which was definitely changed from the deprecative to the indicative form only by the Council of Trent.   [9] Heiler, *Prayer*, 8 *f.*

"numinous primeval sound", "the long protracted nasal continuation of the deep 'o' sound".[1]

4. When man recognizes first of all Form, and later Will, within Power, then the power-word, the conjuration, changes into *prayer*; Power operates only upon power: the potency of Will requires a second will. To begin with, then, prayer is the verbal presentation of the human will before the superior, divine, Will. We cannot say, however, that prayer first arises as a practical manifestation of the will after the magical formula has served its purpose. For the latter has never completely exhausted its capacities, while prayer, as such an expression of the will, occurs even among the most primitive peoples; of this Heiler's admirable volume gives an abundance of examples. Prayer exhibits the greatest contrast in tone, from the threat to the most submissive humility, from alarmed entreaty to the most cordial trust. But wherever it appears, it is an address from man to the Will which he knows to be above him, and the reply of this Will. Essentially, therefore, prayer is a *dialogue*, usually having some very concrete aim: something definite is prayed for. Frequently, on the other hand, it is simply the expression of a pious or reverential, an anxious or some other type of mood; thus the Ana people of Atakpame in Togo daily appear before the sacred staff of the supreme god, kneel, clap their hands and say: "Good morning to-day, father".[2]

In prayer, then, the compulsion pertaining to the power-word is "transposed" to *fatigare deos*; God must be troubled; prayer should compel Him, as it were, as did the widow's request to the unjust judge in the *Gospel*.[3] The classical example of this "power of prayer", which has however completely discarded its magical character, is the story of Jacob's struggle with the angel, as conceived in the exegesis of the fervour of Christian prayer: "I will not let thee go, except thou bless me."[4]

---

[1] Otto, *The Idea of the Holy*, 197. On the modern interpretation of *om cf.* von Glasenapp, *Reformbewegung*, 44.   [2]   Heiler, *ibid.*, 29.   [3] *Luke* xviii.
[4] *Gen.* xxxii, 26. The ascent of prayer can be facilitated; among other things, *incense* may serve for this; *cf.* Lietzmann, *op. cit.*; also the fine passage in *Paradise Lost*, XI, 15 *ff.*:

> To heaven their prayers
> Flew up, nor missed the way, by envious winds
> Blown vagabond or frustrate: in they passed
> Dimensionless through heavenly doors; then, clad
> With incense, where the golden altar fumed,
> By their great Intercessor, came in sight
> Before the Father's throne.

From an early stage, however, it was doubted that any direct intercourse with deity was possible in prayer; and while the religion of absolute Power[1] diverts from magic to the rapture of the feeling of union with God, the religion for which Power and Will subsist in the background of the Universe[2] expressly turns its back on both the delirium of unity and reciprocity between two wills; Confucius' attitude is typical: "it must be a long time since I prayed".[3] Laments over the futility of prayer, too, are not lacking;[4] they are the antithesis of the expectation that the contract between God and man will be fulfilled. Certainly this contract is just as little essentially a matter of reckoning as is *do-ut-des* in sacrifice;[5] rather is it a *demande d'avoir de quoi donner*,[6] and a readiness to give what one wishes to receive. But as soon as this attitude becomes either mechanized, or based on the pure benevolence of Power, then disillusion must arise; and this can be overcome only by that courage which creates witnesses and martyrs, the boldness, παρρησία,[7] introducing the *Pater noster* in the *Text* of the mass: *praeceptis salutaribus moniti et divina institutione formati audemus dicere: Pater noster . . .*: "Taught by the precepts of salvation and following the divine commandment, we make bold to say: 'Our Father'."[8] But this prayer is never an individual act, since it is always based upon the sacred common element; and even when it is uttered by the individual, and its object is of a supremely personal character, it still reposes on the prayer of the community.[9] Prayer bearing the character of dialogue, then, is essentially intercessory, *intercessio*; in the Christian church it is the prayer of the *church*: a mode of relationship between the Body of Christ and the exalted Saviour; hence prayer is only *in Christo*.[10]

5. But to the extent that the relation between Power and man is devoid of the structure of Will, prayer loses its dialogue character and becomes a monologue saturated with religious energy; and thus, for Tauler, "prayer is nothing more than an absorption of the soul in

---

[1] Chap. 21.   [2] Chap. 18.

[3] Bertholet, *op. cit.*, 6, 67. The interpretation of the text is doubtful, but the Master's scepticism is obvious from his question, when they wished to pray for him during his serious illness:—"Will it be any use?"

[4] *e.g.* Sophocles, *Antigone*, 1336 *f.*   [5] Chap. 50.

[6] J. Segond, *La Prière*, 135 *ff.* (1911).   [7] Chap. 29.

[8] E. Peterson, *R. Seeberg-Festschrift*, 296 *f.* The formula is very old; *cf.* the beautiful Mozarabic version (at Christmas): *tibi, summe Pater, cum tremore cordis proclamemus e terris*; C. E. Hammond, *Liturgies Eastern and Western*, 343.

[9] Will, *Culte*, 221.   [10] *cf.* Fr. Heiler, *Das Geheimnis des Gebets*, 1919, 36

God".[1] Speaking and hearing then become subordinate affairs; nothing at all is rendered definite; words are indeed actually superfluous, since silent prayer[2] is the most suitable form for "effective self-surrender".[3]

Mystical prayer, still further, begins by inverting the relationship between God and the suppliant; and then the circulation of Power from man to God, and from God to man, whose essential nature we discerned in sacrifice, is indispensable alike to God and to man: God *needs* man's prayers, as with Pascal: "He was 'made sin for' me. He is more abominable even than myself; and far from detesting me, He feels it an honour that I go to Him to help Him."[4] Still more directly Angelus Silesius affirms:

> God is so blessed, and exists free from all desire,
> Because He receives from me as much as I from Him.[5]

The relationship has thus become wholly mutual, like the primitive relations between gift and return-gift, the stream of gifts[6] now being replaced by the stream of speech: God and man carry on an intimate conversation! But prayer is always at the same time an answer; God's utterance coincides with human speech, and prayer with its hearing.[7] No longer then is "something prayed for"; prayer for something definite ceases, or at least becomes regarded as imperfect and, gradually, prayer becomes pious meditation, a monologue. It requires no recipient: one prays either to one's higher self[8] or even to oneself,[9] or regards it as a matter of complete indifference to whom prayer is offered.[10] The old "godless" religion has exchanged the magical for the mystical garb; prayer remains indeed a celebration of Power, only this has now neither Form nor Will; and just as it is devoid of Will, so must the supplicant himself become. Mystical prayer is "merging in God". He who prays must be *"comme une toile d'attente devant un peintre"*,

[1] G. Siedel, *Die Mystik Taulers*, 1911, 6.
[2] Chap. 63.   [3] Segond, *La Prière*, 52.
[4] *ibid.*, 144. *"Il a été fait péché par moi. Il es: plus abominable que moi, et, loin de m'abhorrer, il se tient honoré que j'aille à lui et le secoure."*
[5] *The Cherubinic Wanderer*, I, 9.   [6] Chap. 50.
[7] *cf.* H. Groos, *Der deutsche Idealismus und das Christentum*, 1927, 121 *f.*, and Schleiermacher's definition of prayer: "The intimate connection of the desire to attain what is best with the consciousness of God"; § 146, 1; *cf.* further the whole Chapter.
[8] Segond, *ibid.*, 42.
[9] Romain Rolland, *Jean Christophe, La foire sur la place*, 42. Mystical prayer may also be a monologue by God; *cf.* B. M. Schuurman, *Mystik und Glaube, im Zusammenhang mit der Mission auf Java*, 1933, who quotes a Javanese *Text*: "It is Allah who adores Allah, but Allah is really only the name Allah"; 15.   [10] Segond, *ibid.*, 35.

like a burning candle consuming itself from love;[1] and thus this prayer attains its highest form in *submersion*,[2] while the dialogue type of supplication, on the other hand, always remains word and entreaty, practical demonstration of Will to will, even when it prays in *its* highest form: "not my will, but thine, be done".

[1] Segond, 37.   [2] *cf.* Fr. Heiler, *Die buddhistische Versenkung*[2], 1922.

CHAPTER 63

PRAISE, LALLATION, AND SILENCE

1. WHOEVER is deeply moved cries out: he "lifts up" his voice. Crying aloud and singing set power in motion.[1] But the most important type of profoundly emotional utterance is *praise*: the *song of praise*. It is distinguished from prayer by being, not an assumption of a position before the divine will on the part of man's will, but a "confirmation" of divine power. Of course this confirmation is by no means a sort of ratification, nor a sentimental assertion, but a "confirmation" in the literal sense, a consolidation of the power, of the will, with which man finds himself confronted; so the Botocudos repeat incessantly: "the chief, he knows no fear".[2] This is neither assertion nor poetry, but a *carmen*, a confirmation of the chief's power. To praise ancestors, again, is regarded by many primitive peoples as a means of influencing their "situation", and determining this to some result or other.[3] Praise is therefore no embellishment, no mere adornment, of intercourse with power: it is no beautiful or cordial superfluity. Whoever is deeply moved emotionally, praises: he cannot possibly avoid doing so; for in praise there lies self-forgetfulness, elevating itself above life in the powerfulness of the one who is praised. To praise, "to rejoice in the Lord", then, implies not that we desire nothing from God: on the contrary, we seek everything from Him: but rather that we relinquish ourselves and our own power, and rely wholly on God's Power. To praise is to turn away from self and towards God.

Thus we can understand that at all times, and by all religions, praise has been regarded as exceedingly important; "service"[4] is almost entirely the offering of praise,[5] and the *vita religiosa*, whether monastic, or in accord with the Reformation ideal vocational, has no other purpose

---

[1] G. van der Leeuw, *Wegen en Grenzen.* [2] *ibid.*, 12.

[3] Lévy-Bruhl, *Primitives and the Supernatural*, 135 *f.* Lévy-Bruhl's concept of "Disposition" and my own term "Situation" are almost exactly identical; both may be applied alike to persons, objects and circumstances. Heidegger, *op. cit.*, 161: Speech is existentially equally original as situation and understanding; "as the existential condition of what can be inferred from Being, speech is constitutive of its existence".

[4] Chap. 53.

[5] Like other *carmina* (*Brahman, etc.*) the song of praise was transformed into a person; in the Middle Ages, for the season when the Alleluia was omitted, "the Alleluia was buried"; *cf.* G. R. S. Mead, *The Quest*, IV, 1912, 110 *ff.*

than the praise of God and the never ceasing proclamation of His glory: *gloria Patri et Filio et Spiritui sancto, sicut erat in principio, nunc et semper, et in saecula saeculorum.* The sound of praise reaches eternity, and finds an outlet in the angelic song of praise; it is a cosmic movement towards God, which is the affair not only of man but of the whole Universe. "Make a joyful noise unto the Lord, all the earth: make a loud noise, and rejoice, and sing praise. Let the sea roar, and the fullness thereof; the world, and they that dwell therein. Let the floods clap their hands: let the hills be joyful together before the Lord."[1] Roman Catholicism, as I have already observed, transferred this idea to the monastery, while the reformers, and above all Calvin, expanded it into the magnificent demand that the whole of life should be devoted only to God's glory; measured by human standards, then, the purpose of life is uselessness and superfluity; this purpose is to confess to the Lord that He is the Lord and that His name is mighty. But this implies that life finds its own fulfillment only in life's surrender, and that genuine powerfulness is attained only by relinquishing all power. Thus praise takes the place of sacrifice: the Eucharist, indeed, was always[2] a thank-offering as a return gift for God's sacrifice. But the whole life of obedience also proceeds from the viewpoint of thankfulness: to fulfil the commands is no burden, but praise.

One striking form of the expression of praise is the so-called *acclamatio.* This hail, which in the Hellenic era was made by the mass of the people on the appearance of the emperor or some high official at assemblies or in the theatre *etc.*, was a genuine "confirmation". It authenticated an event, but also had legal validity and confirmed a decision or a choice. It was praise and decision simultaneously; it was, indeed, the sole possible decision where a majority of votes possessed no power.[3] A fine example, applied to a deity, is the acclamation of the Ephesians: "Great is Diana of the Ephesians", which continued for no less than two hours;[4] in *The Epistle to the Philippians,*[5] again, there is a similar acclamation: "Jesus Christ is Lord, to the glory of God the Father".[6] At the election of the bishop in Milan, too, a little child cried out: "Ambrose, Bishop!" and they all acclaimed Ambrose as their bishop;[7] this was regarded as an election, and it is still a recognized procedure in Catholic electoral law, even though it is a survival: *vox populi, vox Dei.* Confirmation is potent.

[1] *Ps.* xcviii. 4, 7 *ff.*   [2] Chap. 52.
[3] E. Peterson, $ΕΙΣ \; ΘΕΟΣ$ (1926).   [4] *Acts* xix. 28.   [5] ii, 11 (Moffat).
[6] E. Peterson, *Die Einholung des Kyrios, Zeitschrift für systematische Theologie,* 7, 1930, 699.   [7] I. H. Gosses, *Met meerderheid van stemmen,* 1929, 4.

2. Profound emotional disturbance also results in lallation. An apparent impediment is then the greatest powerfulness: ecstasy breaks forth in interrupted and spasmodic sounds. Examples of prophetic utterance have already been dealt with;[1] and the specific feature of lalling is that the speaker has no power over his own speech; it is "uncontrolled" and impulsive. We find such lallation in the glossolalia attested from early Christian times and in many religious movements, both ancient and modern—the pentecostal movement, *etc.* "The person who expresses his emotions in glossolalia speaks without desiring to do so; in many instances he appears to feel himself impelled to speak, in others perhaps even this is not the case; he speaks like a machine, or more precisely, *something speaks through him.* He knows not the content of what he says in advance, but interprets his words and understands them afterwards, as if they were those of another person."[2] Power is thus discovered in impotence; from the loss of one's own powerfulness the operation of some superior Power is inferred. St. Paul, indeed, who himself possessed the "gift" of speaking with tongues, "more than any of you", "would rather say five words with my own mind for the instruction of other people than ten thousand words" in incomprehensible glossolalia.[3]

3. Deep emotional agitation produces *silence* also; *favete linguis,* "keep silence", which was originally magically intended and supposed to overcome the power of some unpropitious word, became through "transposition"[4] the positive expression of the inexpressible, the language of the unutterable. Not man, but "it", is to speak. Glossolalia, in which "it" does indeed speak, is ultimately nothing more than verbosity; but the silence of profound emotional disturbance is the manifestation of the super-powerful itself, the wordless decision of the eternal Word.

The standard terminology of the liturgy, no detail of which can be arbitrarily changed, and which is employed with the utmost conservatism, is itself an approximation to silence;[5] and it is the experience of every celebrant and liturgist that while repeating the words of the liturgy he must himself be silent; "it", however, speaks all the more articulately through him. The strangeness of liturgical language is also

---

[1] Chap. 27.
[2] T. K. Österreich, *Einführung in die Religionspsychologie,* 1917, 60.
[3] 1 *Cor.* xiv. 18 f.   [4] [On this term *cf.* pp. 31, Note, and 610].
[5] G. Mensching, *Das heilige Schweigen* (1926), 125; Brilioth, *op. cit.,* 14.

an approach to silence: the ceremonial tones of a tongue long alien to
everyday usage as with Luther's Bible, or ecclesiastical Latin and
Greek;[1] while the subdued prayer of the priest in consecration also
belongs to this category and leads to the complete silence characterizing
the culmination of the mass.[2] This worshipful silence, however, is no
lack of audibility; it has not a negative but a positive value. Exactly as
with music, where the pauses often cause the most intense impression
and the richest expression,[3] silence during worship not merely gives
vent to the profoundest emotion, but is also the means of conveying the
profoundest revelation. "Silences in worship are not the empty moments
of devotion, but the full moments."[4] Silence filled by divine powerfulness corresponds to the darkness of sacred space, the numinous
emptiness of Islamite holy places;[5] and by mystics of all ages the most
extreme poverty is accounted as the greatest riches, emptiness as
fullness, power as impotence. Mensching distinguishes a preparatory,
a sacramentally unifying, a contemplative, a worshipful, an expectant
and a monastic-ascetic silence.[6] From the fourth century onwards,
indeed, the ancient Eastern liturgies were already familiar with silent
prayer; the Quakers also practise it,[7] and so does the Roman church,
apart from consecration, in the *Pater noster* and in the passion at the
moment of Christ's death.[8] The Greek *bacchae*, too, experienced a
sacred silence at the climax of their ecstasy.[9]

Universally, mysticism seeks silence: the strength of the Power with
which it deals is so great that only silence can create a "situation" for
it. This is the "paradox" of expression referred to by Jaspers: we
should like to say all that could possibly be said, and much more: the
greatest eloquence alternates with complete silence.[10] That mysticism
has always been very eloquent is therefore only the reverse of its essential
silence: the uniquely powerful is revealed only *per viam negationis*.
This is the reason why mysticism usually opposes *carmina*, formal
prayers, and why it cannot ultimately rest content with even free
personal prayer; Muslim mysticism warns even against the praise of
God: we "must forget even the praise that God has placed on our lips, in

---

[1] Will, *op. cit.*, I, 201 *f.*   Casel, *op. cit.*, 143 *f.*   [2] Will, *ibid.*, I, 201.
[3] G. van der Leeuw, *Wegen en Grenzen*, 148 *ff.*
[4] Amiel, *Journal*, 22 Aug. 1873 (Brooks).
[5] *cf.* Otto, *Aufsätze das Numinose betreffend*, 108 *ff.*   *The Idea of the Holy*, 70, 216.
[6] *cf.* further his *Die liturgische Bewegung in der evangelischen Kirche*, 1925, 47 *ff.*
[7] Will, *op. cit.*, I, 323.   [8] Heiler, *Katholizismus*, 411 *f.*
[9] Rohde, *Psyche*, II, 9. E. T. 259.
[10] *Psychologie der Weltanschauungen*[2], 1922; *cf.* van der Leeuw, *Mystiek*, 1925.

order to worship, on this side of His heart, Him Whom they praise".[1]
True worship, genuine *salāt*, is uninterrupted, in so far as he who
practises it is always pure because of the light in his heart.[2]

The injunction to "pray without ceasing. In every thing give thanks",
has certainly another basis: "for this is the will of God in Christ Jesus
concerning you".[3] The religion of Power in Will, of faith in the Form
that has actually appeared, also knows the inexpressibility of God, the
fullness of the void, the wealth of poverty and the eloquence of silence;
but it finds these in the *kenosis* of Him Who emptied Himself *by coming
into the world*.[4] Thus silence is primarily and principally a speaking to
God and being addressed by Him. The *sursum corda* was originally
spoken by the priest "in order that silence might be observed";[5] but
praise follows it.

Christian mysticism, however, speaks in Tersteegen's exquisite
Night Song, a song of praise which dies away in a silence that is the
utterance of God:

> Now let us sleep,
> And whoso cannot sleep.
> Shall with me pray
> To the great Name,
> To Whom by night and day
> The heavenly guardians pay
> Glory, honour, praise,
> Jesus, Amen.
>
> May Heaven's beauteous light
> Shine upon thee;
> May I be thy little star
> Shining here and there.
> I lay me down;
> Lord, do Thou alone
> In deepest silence
> Speak to me in the dark.

---

[1] Massignon, *Al-Hallaj*, 513; *cf.* N. von Arseniew: "On (the) heights of mystical
experience the song must again die away, since it is the realm of the inexpressible . . .",
with his further observations on the mystical *Jubilus* (*AR.* 22, 1923–24, 266 *ff.*). In
Javanese mysticism the song of praise (*dzikr*) is uttered in the first mystical stage with
the tongue and the heart; in the second and third with the heart; in the third the *dzikr*
is all that comes from the mystic's mouth, whether it is the usual formula of praise of
Islam or the mystic syllable *hu*, or the lallation: *la, la, la, oh, oh, oh*, or even "his weeping and trembling, his movement or his stillness"; Schuurman, *Mystik und Glaube*,
17 *f.*   [2] H. Kraemer, *Een Javaansche Primbon uit de zestiende eeuw*, 1921, 78.
[3] 1 *Thess.* v, 17 *f.*   [4] *Phil.* ii, 6 *f.*   [5] Casel, *op. cit.*, 149.

CHAPTER 64

THE WRITTEN WORD

1. "WHAT we have in black and white we can safely take home with us":—the tendency already discerned in Fetishism[1] becomes evident also in the valuation of the written word. Strictly, then, *writing* is a charm: written signs are charms. A *rune* (Gothic, *rûna*) is a secret, a secret decree or resolve, a mystery; the Old High German verb *rûnen* means *susurrare*, "to murmur or whisper". Thus the living word, filled with power and murmured in a subdued voice, persists in the written characters.[2] Runes originated with Odin, who in his turn received them from "the powers", and on the Stora Noleby Stone in Sweden may be read the inscription: "I write runes, *regenkunnar*, (derived from the powers)."[3] The greatest power was possessed by the system of twenty-four runes, the so-called *futhark*, itself in turn divided into three "families" of eight signs each.[4] The ancient Egyptian hieroglyphs, again, were magical beings: like all writing, they were originally pictures incorporating the essence of what is depicted; they were even called *ntr-w*, the term for "gods", and in the script certain hieroglyphic figures, representing something unfavourable or terrifying, were either suppressed and replaced by strokes or intentionally curtailed in their design.[5]

Writing, then, is magic:—one method of gaining power over the living word. The tradition of the sacred word is originally oral; it lives in being recited, and only later did oral tradition give place to graphic; in certain cases, indeed, as in that of the *Vedas*, only in our own times.[6] Committing sacred texts to writing therefore was not, in the first place, intended to render tradition exact (in antiquity, and for primitive peoples, oral tradition left nothing more to be desired!), but to attain

---

[1] Chap. 3.

[2] G. Ehrismann, *Geschichte der deutschen Literatur bis zum Ausgang des Mittelalters*, I, 1918, 46.

[3] Kapteyn, *Dertiende, Veertiende en Vyfriende Jaarverslag van de Vereeniging voor Terpenonderzoek*, 1928, 31, 53.

[4] *ibid.*, 54 *f. cf.* E. Mogk, *Germanische Religionsgeschichte und Mythologie*, 1921, 44 *ff.* Magnus Olsen, *Magie et Culte dans la Norvège antique* (*RHR.* 96, 1927, 1 *ff.*).

[5] W. Spiegelberg, *Zeitschrift für ägypt. Sprache und Altertumskunde*, 65, 1930, 120. P. Lacau, *ibid.*, 51, 1913, 1 *ff.*

[6] *cf.* H. von Glasenapp, *Religiöse Reformbewegungen im heutigen Indien*, 1928, V.

power, since with the written word man can do just what he will; writing is no more precise than the living word, but is more easily dealt with. Even where writing is employed the necessity for recitation still persists: unuttered, the word has no decisive power.

But with what exists in black and white we can proceed in a much more drastic way than with the merely spoken word. The crassest example of this is the *drinking* of a sentence. According to Mosaic law, for instance, a woman suspected of infidelity had to drink water with which a curse, written on a piece of paper, had been washed off; thus she literally drank the curse, of course as an ordeal.[1] In the Egyptian fairy tale, similarly, the hero drinks a whole book of magic that has been soaked in beer and dissolved in water, so that he may know everything it contains;[2] we too still swear by the Gospel to-day; not, that is, by the Word of God, but on the holy book. Scripture, again, is an *oracle*; it is opened arbitrarily to obtain instructions.[3] It had indeed the effect of a *judgment of God* when a key was placed in the Bible at *St. John* i. 1, a passage regarded as particularly sacred, in order to discover whether a woman were a witch or not; the book was tied up and suspended from the woman's finger, and if she were guilty she would let it drop.[4] At a quite early stage in the Egyptian ceremonies for the dead, also, the written magical charm played its part: persons who were ritually buried received their thousands in bread and beer; but "miserable is their flesh (nevertheless) if a written document be not there (among the sacrificial gifts)" and furnished with a great seal.[5] In China, again, the Buddhist dead receive a passport intended to open the entrance to heaven for them, and filled up with all due ceremony by the proper official; it concludes: "As soon as thou receivest this passport, thou must set out for the place of the blessed where thou mayest expect great bliss and peace. Given this eighth day of the fourth month in the sixth year of Hienfong."[6] Another remarkable example of the written sacred word is the so-called *heavenly letter*, written by God or by an angel and fallen from heaven, or obtained in some other miraculous way, and supposed to be a protection against every form of evil. The peculiar feature is that here it is a matter of a written *revelation*; the

---

[1] *Num.* v, 11 *ff. cf.* R. Kreglinger, *Grondbeginselen der Godsdienstwetenschap*, 40.
[2] G. Roeder, *Altägyptische Erzählungen und Märchen*, 1927, 145. G. Maspero, *Stories of Ancient Egypt*, 129.   [3] Chap. 54.
[4] The so-called *kaei* (key) trial. Waling Dykstra, *Friesch Volksleven*, II, 171.
[5] *Pyramidentexte* (Sethe), 474.
[6] Lehmann, *Textbuch*[1], 23 *f.*; *cf.* the small gold tablets placed in the grave with the Orphic dead, discovered in Southern Italy; chap. 47.

celestial letter is a sort of popular parallel to the Word of God.[1] Quite recently the *Book of Mormon*, the holy writ of the Mormons, as is well known, was composed by God and sent down from heaven,[2] while the sheer and pure power of letters, even though utterly meaningless, is to be found in the magical papyri of antiquity (*Abraxas, ephesia grammata*) and pre-eminently in the Jewish *kabbala*.[3]

2. From the oracular use of sacred writings, of which the finest example was perhaps the opening of the Sibylline books by the Romans in times of direst emergency,[4] is distinguished the utilization of holy writ in order to find in it the revealed word of God. This required that settled delimitation of the writings called a *canon*; from the abundance of sacred words and writings a certain portion is "selected" and elevated to the status of "holy writ", exactly as certain actions are given prominence as sacraments among the mass of sacramentals. This canonization may consist, in the first place, in placing the origin of the writings under consideration in some miraculous light, sacred writings, for example, being frequently "discovered", of course after having been deliberately concealed. In 181 B.C. a Roman secretary found a stone coffin with an inscription asserting that king Numa Pompilius was buried in it; in the coffin were books purporting to be Numa's writings, and dealing with the philosophy of Pythagoras; a *praetor* read them, however, and had them burnt as dangerous to the state. Here then an attempt had been made to create respect for a specific religion by means of books that had appeared miraculously.[5] Not only origin, but restriction also, pertains to canonization: then from the writings arises the sacred book within which the power of the sacred word is confined, the limits being most rigidly drawn in Islam, Judaism and Christianity. Other religions too have their more or less definitely fixed holy books: the *Vedas*, the *Avesta*, the Buddhist *Tipitaka*, etc. The Chinese Buddhist *Tipitaka* includes from 5000 to even 7000 volumes, arranged in rotating cases in the Japanese temples; and turning the case is regarded as the study of the holy writ and is a

---

[1] R. Stübe, *Der Himmelsbrief*, 1918.   [2] Stübe, *ibid.*, 41 *ff.*
[3] A. Dieterich, *Abraxas*, 1891. P. Vulliaud, *La Kabbale Juive, Histoire et Doctrine*, 1923.   [4] H. Diels, *Sibyllinische Blätter*, 1890.
[5] Fowler, *The Religious Experience of the Roman People*, 349. Perhaps the discovery of the "strict book of the law" by the high priest Hilkiah in B.C. 623 was also an attempt to endow the law with divine authority; *cf.* 2 *Kings* xxii. In Egypt the "process of discovery" was quite a usual affair; *cf.* R. Weill, *Les Origines de l'Égypt pharaonique*, 1908, 39 *ff.*   G. van der Leeuw, *Pia fraus, Mensch en Maatschappy*, 8, 1932.

meritorious action.[1] But only Judaism, Christianity and Islam possess one single holy book, and the last of these is pre-eminently a genuine religion of the book. The Koran comes from God: "He it is who hath sent down to thee 'the Book' . . . But they whose hearts are given to err, follow its figures, craving discord, craving an interpretation; yet none knoweth its interpretation but God. And the stable in knowledge say, 'we believe in it: it is all from our Lord'."[2] It is precisely the intensely passionate monotheism of Islam, which regards with suspicion a God possessing any attributes, that leads to the crassest belief in the letter of the writings. God speaks, and His utterance is not His attribute in the sense of the Aristotelian philosophy that has pervaded Islam, but pertains eternally to His essence; it is an "eternal attribute" which "had no beginning and is never interrupted"; the utterance of the eternally speaking God must therefore be eternal; the Koran, that is to say, did not originate in time and was not created by God, but existed uncreated from all eternity.[3] In the eyes of the Mutazilites, however, this belief was too dangerous: besides God, there could be nothing uncreated; the Koran must therefore have been created like all other creatures, and was not the immediate language of God but only a means of which He made use. On this question a vehement dispute ensued with orthodoxy, forming an exact parallel to the Christian controversies about the nature of Christ; the spoken and subsequently the written word thus assume in Islam the place of the "Word", that is of Christ and of the *logos*, in Christianity.[4] Scriptural orthodoxy triumphed, however, and even went so far as the assertion: "whatever lies between the two covers is the word of God", thereby declaring the paper and the ink to be uncreated;[5] and these contentions are typical of the difficulties of scriptural theology in Judaism and Christianity. Moses, again, was supposed to have received the tablets of the law, written by God's own hand, on Sinai; certainly the Old Testament canon was defined only in Christian times;[6] but for the Jews holy writ was always "law",[7] just as the law was its oldest and most essential constituent. Subsequently Christians too repeatedly sought the fixity of divine revelation:

[1] Clemen, *Die nichtchristlichen Religionen*, I, 107 f.
[2] *Sura* 3, 5 (Everyman's Library); cf. I. Goldziher, *Vorlesungen über den Islam*, 1910, 81 f.   [3] Goldziher, *ibid.*, 112 f.
[4] For a parallel between Mohammedan doctrine about scripture and the doctrine of the two natures in Christianity cf. Frick, *Vergl. Rel. wiss.*, 32.
[5] Goldziher, *ibid.*, 113 ff.; cf. H. Frick, *Marb. Theol. Stud.* 3, 10.
[6] Hölscher, *Geschichte der israelitischen und jüdischen Religion*, 101.
[7] cf. further below.

"It is written!"[1] The Christian church has indeed again and again found the way back to its essential nature, and continually discovered anew that her "Word" is not the written word, but the living utterance of God in the figure of Christ.[2] The church, still further, has undoubtedly made the written word fluid and vital in its liturgy, and actual and decisive in its preaching, although in its Roman and Greek forms it has admittedly diminished the ascendancy of the writings by the more supple tradition.[3] It has also, in the Greek communion, not only read the Gospel aloud, but has rendered it living in worship and in the church.[4] And finally, in the evangelical churches, it has returned repeatedly to the recollection of its actual and true nature, by asserting that it is *not* a book religion like Islam but faith in the living Word, and by substantiating this conviction either by the power of its prophetic utterances or by the sincerity of its experience. The Bible has nevertheless won a place for itself, as the written word of God, which is far more important than can ever be understood from its mere character as a document of revelation. The fact that it is *written* has exerted its own influence, while the facility with which the word of God can be manipulated and controlled has repeatedly attracted the Christian mind. So far as the Protestant church is concerned, indeed, Tillich speaks quite justifiably even of a sacrament, not of the word alone, but of the written word, which according to him has established a new hierarchy of pure doctrine.[5]

But on the other hand, there naturally occurs a periodical reaction as the outcome of the formidable problem of *interpretation*. What does the Bible say? Everything, and nothing. "When will people understand that it is useless for a man to read his Bible unless he also reads everybody else's Bible? A printer reads a Bible for misprints. A Mormon reads his Bible, and finds polygamy; a Christian Scientist reads his, and finds that we have no arms and legs."[6] The Bible, then, must be *interpreted*: but how, and by what authority? In these difficulties a by no means negligible proportion of the most important questions that have agitated

---

[1] In India, where sacred tradition is transmitted orally, it is usual to say "It has been heard" instead of "It is written"; the *Veda* is called "What has been heard".

[2] Will, *Culte*, II, 335: the Bible as sacred action, and its being read aloud as the event itself.   [3] Heiler, *Katholizismus*, 587.

[4] S. Hans Ehrenberg and Sergej Bulgakov, *Östliches Christentum und Protestantismus* (*Religiöse Besinnung*, I, 1928). On tradition in the Eastern church *cf.* S. Boulgakoff, *L'Orthodoxie*, 1932, 12 *ff.*, and on the actual procedure in reading the scriptures, ibid., 32.   [5] *Religiöse Verwirklichung*, 141.

[6] Chesterton, *The Innocence of Father Brown*, 277 (Popular Edition). J. Wach, *Zur Hermeneutik heiliger Schriften* (*Theol. Stud. und Krit.* 1930).

Christianity, in the course of its history, found its origin. In Islam, still further, the situation was exactly the same. Without a living faith, therefore, dictating the understanding of scripture, there can be no vitally operative holy writ. For Christianity, this implies that no living holy writ can subsist without the church; while in the case of Christianity and Islam, and to a certain extent of other religions also, as for example Hinduism, it involves the necessity of a *theology* which at all times shall render possible a new and living understanding of scripture.[1]

Holy writ, then, requires first of all a *tradition* subsisting concurrently with itself:—in Judaism the rabbinic, in Islam the *hadith*,[2] and in Christianity the παράδοσις. Its true significance, nevertheless, by no means lies in settling the meaning of the original author of the sacred text. Exegesis *e mente auctoris* is certainly frequently identified with the elucidation of the fundamental religious import; but this is always a subordinate matter, since the critical issue is that a living word of God should resound from the writ. Of course many theologians, in both ancient and recent times, assert that the *sensus strictus* of the writ is identical with the divine meaning. Moses implied what Christ taught. But this is correct only if we concede that one and the same divine meaning repeatedly manifests itself in distinctive forms and with reference to different affairs. Allegorical and typological interpretation in Christianity, like the rationalization of the ancient myths and prophetic and ecstatic utterances, find their analogy in Mohammedan theology. In the most recent developments of Protestant theology, however, there has arisen an endeavour to return to purely theological exegesis, and thus to turn from the written, settled and dead word of God to the living. It is true that the attempt simply to identify the divine meaning with the original import of the author can no longer be repeated; and so Christianity may be reverting, by a long and arduous road, to the understanding of the decisive power of the word; then it will no longer ask: "what says Moses?" or "what does St. Paul mean?" but "What is God saying to us?"[3] For the final and ultimate significance of holy writ is neither the meaning of its author, since indeed its real "author" is always God alone, nor that of its occasional interpreters; its deepest import always transcends us: it is "revealed" to us, that is to say, proclaimed at that moment when God speaks to us, without

---

[1] Chap. 84.   [2] Goldziher, *op. cit.*, 40 *f.*, 80 *ff.*
[3] Compare the history of the modern exposition of the Koran, which parallels the history of the interpretation of the Bible to an almost incredible degree. R. Hartmann, *Die Krisis des Islam*, 1928.

our therefore being able to maintain that we "have understood the mind of God".[1]

The mystics, of course, think otherwise. They compose their own holy writ. One day al-Makki was walking with the *sufi*-martyr al-Hallaj through one of the narrow streets of Mecca and reciting from the Koran: "he listened to me reciting and then said: 'I also could say such things'"; but, the orthodox Mohammedan adds, "I ceased to associate with him".[2] To cite another example from a totally different sphere of civilization: the Romantics cherished the ideal of writing not merely a cultural novel on the great model of *Wilhelm Meister*, but also a Bible.[3]

3. *Creeds*, still further, are a special type of holy writ. Like all that is written, they too are derived from the living, spoken word; and with this they fuse once again, in so far as they actually subsist only when they are recited. To be written down implies far less for them than for genuine holy writ; for in the case of creeds the principal feature is that they express the "sacred common element", and become recognized as such. They come to life, therefore, first of all in community worship, and may represent acts of trust, praise, adoration *etc.*, as for example the creed in Christian worship. Creeds, therefore, are fixed forms of a communal declaration before God: they are confessions. As such, again, they are scarcely to be separated from confessions of sin: the confession of faith and the confession of sin are indeed closely interconnected. They lead, too, to decision and systematize conduct, thus yielding the possibility of a new mode of life. This holds true especially of the confession of sin. "As long as the doer of the deed keeps it a secret, it is like a being that has issued from himself, living a life of its own, and in its turn engendering fatal consequences; if he openly confesses that he is the doer of the deed, he withdraws from it the life with which he had endowed it, and takes away its power to harm. As the Eskimo shaman put it, he 'takes the sting out' of the evil."[4] Among certain primitive peoples, similarly, before a campaign each warrior is asked to make an open and general confession; this however has nothing at all to do with repentance, only there may have been some dangerous element in the soldier's conduct that should be made good and therewith harmless; and thus once more the decisive power of the word

---

[1] Chap. 85 *ff.*   [2] Massignon, *Al-Hallaj*, I, 56 *f.*
[3] *cf.* R. Haym, *Die romantische Schule*[3], 1914.
[4] Lévy-Bruhl, *Primitives and the Supernatural*, 356.

is shown.[1] With this the confession of sin approximates to purification[2] and the apotropaic in general.[3] But such a confession of guilt requires no idea of God whatever, no moral obligation, and indeed hardly any conception of sin; it is just felt that something is not right as regards the holy, and the alleviating power of the word is realized; while with this apprehension of guilt there may also be connected the so-called "negative admission of sin" in ancient Egypt, in which adjurations alternate with the assurance of innocence: "I have *not* oppressed, *not* stolen", *etc.*[4] Certainly there can be no reference to any personal admission of guilt in all this; it is not at all an affair of the moral consciousness, but only of warding off evil consequences by means of the word.[5]

The confession of faith, also, is first of all a power-word; and a Bantu negro, who had been converted by the mission, was compelled by his relatives to abandon the Christian "faith" again by means of an emetic.[6] Somewhat similarly, during preparations for ancient Christian baptism in Rome, the "faith" was "handed over" to the *competetentes—traditio symboli*—originally together with the Gospel and the Lord's Prayer; then the catechumen "returned it" again (*redditio*)[7]. With the "faith", again, there was often associated a renunciation of evil powers, naturally in the form of a *carmen*:—in the early Christian world *abrenuntiatio diaboli*; in Mazdaism, too, both were connected together.[8] The Buddhist is a typical confession of faith: "I take my refuge in the Buddha. I take my refuge in the doctrine. I take my refuge in the monastic community",[9] which is thrice repeated and clearly exhibits the decisive character of the confession. Whoever confesses his faith, therefore, is not expounding any *Weltanschauung*, but is deciding, while a decision is made about himself also; this holds good too of those confessions that assume a quite different form, for example the assertory creed of Islam: "There is no God but Allah, and Mohammed is His prophet"; in confessing the oneness of God the confessor confesses *himself*. Similarly, the Christian creed is absolutely an act of confession, not merely an explicitly expressed conviction.

[1] Lévy-Bruhl, *Primitives and the Supernatural*, 348. R. Pettazoni, *La confessione dei peccati*, I, *passim* (1929).
[2] Chap. 49.   [3] Pettazoni.   [4] *Totenbuch* (Naville), *Kap.* 125.
[5] Of course this does not prevent us estimating the level of Egyptian morality from the enumeration of offences that have not been committed.
[6] Lévy-Bruhl, *Primitives and the Supernatural*, 88.
[7] Braun, *Liturgisches Handlexikon*, 350. L. Duchesne, *Origines du culte chrétien*[4], 1908, 308 *ff.*   [8] Bertholet, *Lesebuch*, 1, 16.   [9] *ibid.*, 11, 129 *f.*

The apotheosis of the confession of faith in Mazdaism is very important. The soul of the departed meets its own *daena* (a spiritual primeval being, and subsequently a confession of faith) in the form "of a girl, glorious and radiant, with shining arms, strong and well built, beautifully formed, with high breasts, and a splendid figure, of noble birth and high lineage, fifteen years old and as lovely as the most beautiful of creatures". To the spirit of the righteous man she says: "I am thy good religion, thine own personal confession";[1] conversely, an ugly old woman is the form of the *daena* of the wicked. Here the forms of the "external soul",[2] of the guardian spirit and of the faith (including good works) have been fused in one super-terrestrial beauteous figure.[3]

4. Religious *doctrine*, to continue, is the intellectual treatment of a given sacred word. It differs from myth because form here assumes less importance and conceptual thought predominates, while it is distinguished from the philosophy of religion by being the doctrine of some community and in originating from the "sacred common element". The occult knowledge in primitive secret societies, on the other hand, withheld from women and children but confided to neophytes, is not doctrine because what is known possesses no conceptual interconnection. Primitive religion in general, in fact, recognizes no doctrine:[4] celebration and myth constitute it in its entirety; it is related, not taught. So it was in the case of Egyptian and Babylonian, Greek and Roman religions; and similarly in the Old Testament. The first essential in the formation of doctrine, then, is a creed. This is the centre and the basis of every *development of dogma*; from which it follows, on the one hand, that dogma is never a collective philosophy, but always and essentially an act of worship, a celebration, and an act of praise. On the other hand, dogma is never purely existential, never merely concerned with reality, because it always represents some theoretical elaboration of the confession. It is the reflective contemplation of celebration, the expression of myth in logical form. But as soon as it ceases to be transparent and to exhibit its inherent confessional nature, it loses its specific character

---

[1] Lehmann-Haas, *Textbuch*, 162 f.

[2] Chap. 42. Persian, *Fravashi*.

[3] The "transposition" that has occurred here is very remarkable; it formed a creed, ligion and a thesaurus of good works out of the soul-being; *cf.* H. Lommel, *Die Religion Zarathustras*, 1930, 187 ff.

[4] It approaches most closely to the essential nature of doctrine when initiates in primitive communities are instructed about the existence of the gods who founded the ceremonies, the so-called originators (Chap. 18).

and sinks to the level either of some mere philosophic thesis, or religious technique; and from time to time this may well happen.

We find doctrine then, and for the first time in the history of religion, in the theological compositions of the Egyptian heretic king Akhnaton; for in the name he assigned to his god he set out the different conclusions at which he had arrived in the course of his reforming labours, and thus axiomatically fixed their relationship to the prevailing ideas of God. It is true that these dogmas were scarcely the utterance of a living community, although they were certainly so intended.[1] The doctrine of a genuine community is however to be discerned in Orphism and similar Greek spiritual movements. Here, in the form of a cosmogony and theogony, arose the doctrine of sin and salvation, based on the "story of salvation" in the death of Zagreus, in which the type of sin as original, and of salvation as release from the cycle of births, are systematically represented.

Here the form certainly remains predominantly mythical; and we must realize that doctrine can never completely discard the mythical if it wishes to avoid falling to the level of a mere philosophical thesis. The material of doctrine in general, again, is of the most various types. Precepts pertaining to worship and morality, myths, narratives about ancestors, etc., are all incorporated within doctrine, receiving a significance that is modified in accordance with the requirements of its religious theories; and this absorption of an entire religious tradition in doctrine shows, on the one hand, that this can never deliquesce into pure theory: the heterogeneity of its material constitutes the copiousness of doctrine. On the other hand, this of itself involves immense difficulties. For the entire tradition, at first preserved for centuries in verbal form, and subsequently consolidated in writing, must now be expressed as dogma and forced into one doctrinal system which, even if it is not purely conceptual, is still as self-consistent as is possible. But this never proceeds at all easily, since the fantasies of mythology, the ecstasies of enthusiasts and the pathos of prophets, chronicle and fairy story, hymn and proverb, must all be given doctrinal form which must possess power, and still at the same moment be intelligible. We should however guard against discarding, without further ado, the accompanying violation of the material as sheer falsity, since the

---

[1] cf. H. Schäfer, *Amarna in Religion und Kunst*, 1931. G. van der Leeuw, *Achnaton*, 1927. In ancient Egypt the urge towards doctrinal development of religious tradition was very powerful; cf. K. Sethe, *Amun und die acht Urgötter von Hermopolis, Abh. der preuss. Akad. der Wiss.*, 1929, *phil.-hist. kl.* 4.

completed theology which begins its activity[1] at this stage would then be radically untrue.

Certainly we can "understand Schleiermacher's conclusion that all expression involves the stagnation of religious experience, so that the definition of doctrine as 'experience that has become torpid' would not be incorrect; still, to be articulately expressed pertains to experience, as does its utterance also, while utterance in its own turn leads logically to reflection and doctrine. Again, we must not forget that all doctrine sustained by the consciousness of the religious community is essentially living and remains so, while even in the most abstruse dogma the original experience of God may repeatedly renew itself".[2]

5. Finally the *law*, as the rule of conduct, is given with religion itself: it is the guarantee of celebration. But it also receives a fixed mould and becomes a formula that is spoken, and subsequently written, which as such pertains to the category of sacred words. Traditional usage and custom, derived from ancestors, were codified only at a certain stage in the development of the cult and, in the course of this process, relatively new laws are recorded together with ancient observances. Of this the Jewish *Torah*, the Iranian *Vendidad*, the Indian *Brahmanas* and the Mohammedan *Sunna* are classical examples. The ancient Greek laws of religious communities, also, like those of the Orphics and the Pythagoreans,[3] were to a great extent changed forms of old tabu regulations.[4] In these, law and custom, moral and religious bonds all subsist together, without being distinguished from each other. The links are precisely those of religious celebration, and it is quite immaterial whether its content, according to our own criteria, pertains to law or custom, to ethics or piety. The relations between religion and law, again, are in the main of four types: (*1*) It forms an object of veneration. Here again the Old Testament is the classical example: the law demands not only obedience, but love; some of the *Psalms* (especially *Psalm* 119) express this conviction. (*2*) This veneration of the law as the revelation of God may then degenerate into formal observance, such as arose in Judaism and Parsiism. Here primitive worship of the written word (ceremonial burial of ancient *Torah* rolls *etc.*) is associated with scholarly endeavour, for which the study of the *Torah* is the highest duty. On the other hand this observance may: (*3*) lead to a revolt

---

[1] Chap. 84.   [2] *RGG*. Article *Lehre*.
[3] An example of *symbola pythagoraea* in Bertholet, *Lesebuch*, 4, 43.
[4] Chap. 4.

against the letter of the law, as in the case of the prophets and of Jesus, or against the law as such, as with St. Paul. The law, confined within its proper limits, is then: (4) frequently categorically disavowed by mysticism, as being at most of merely relative value when contrasted with that of religion.

Thus a rabbi in Warsaw, whom Jeremias questioned about his attitude towards Zionism, said as he raised the *Torah* roll: "Professor, we still have our country—a portable country".[1] That is legal piety at its highest power; the written word of the law replaces everything: celebration and sacred space, the "how" and the "where". The "what" of the divine word, fixed for all time, suffices in the actuality of obedience and love.

[1] A. Jeremias, *Jüdische Frömmigkeit*, 1927, 11. The Law may also be a power-bearer in the most primitive sense; there are miraculous laws, just as there are miraculous images; in Judaism there are accounts of miraculously saved *Torah* rolls; *cf.* Will, *Culte*, II, 311; also the *Torah* words, "Mezuza" and "Tephillin", used as amulets; W. Bousset, *Die Religion des Judentums*[3], 1926, 179.

R. Pettazoni, *La Confessione dei Peccati*, 1920–1936.
J. Wach, "Zur Hermeneutik heiliger Schriften" (*Theol. Stud. und Krit.* 1930).

CHAPTER 65

ENDOWMENT WITH FORM IN WORSHIP

1. "WORSHIP assembles together the scattered and sporadic feelings, and transforms an indefinite religious sentiment into an individual, and at the same time collective, religious consciousness."[1] Thus everything that we have so far discovered in conduct and celebration, in time and space, in action and word, is part of this thoroughgoing self-comprehension, this confronting of the self with Power, which we call *worship*. In worship, therefore, man seeks to give form not only to individual and to collective experience, not only to the conduct of himself and his community, but also to the activities of Power, indeed to its very existence. In worship the being of man and the Being of his God are comprehended within one actual "being-thus": man's being and God's Being are interpreted, and are given form, essentially as becoming profoundly moved, and as what causes this, as what is created, and as creation, respectively. In worship, the form of humanity becomes defined, while that of God becomes the content of faith, and the form of their reciprocal relation experienced in action. This holds true of *all* worship, from richest to poorest: even the most unpretentious Calvinistic type of divine service cannot satisfy itself simply by "ceremonially proclaiming the King's advent": He must also make His entry.[2]

2. The sacred, then, must possess a form: it must be "localizable", spatially, temporally, visibly or audibly. Or still more simply: the sacred must "take place". This "taking place", however, is never and on no occasion simply the event that is given: rather, in the given, possibilities must first of all reveal themselves.[3] Eating, therefore, is not a "taking place" of the sacred, but the sacrament is. But every event may be a "taking place" of the sacred, and in such cases we speak of a "*symbol*". A symbol, that is to say, is by no means something quite inessential, as our loose modern mode of expression seems to imply,

---

[1] Will, *op. cit.*, I, 23.

[2] R. Will, *Les principes essentiels de la vie cultuelle, Revue de théologie et de philosophie*, Lausanne, N.S. 14 (60), 1926. In a more highly developed cult the entrance becomes a permanent place of residence, and the cult itself a "heaven on earth"; Boulgakoff, *Orthodoxie*, 179.　　　　　　　　　　　　[3] Chap. 23.

but rather the encounter, συμ-βάλλειν, between possibility and givenness, between the event and "taking place", between secular and
sacred.[1] The symbol, then, is *a participation of the sacred in its veritable,
actual, form*: between the sacred, and its form, there exists community
of essence; and the distinction between the genuine, and the modernized,
symbol is most clearly expressed in the conception of the Eucharist:
do the bread and wine "signify" the body and blood of Christ, or *are*
they these too? Community of essence, alone, constitutes the symbol;
what signifies and manifests on the one hand, and what on the other
hand is thus signified and manifested, fuse together into one single
image.[2] In Australia, for instance, flowers made from wood and worn
in the hair symbolically represent the kangaroo flesh which the totem
ancestor carried on his head during his wanderings.[3] And this is no
mere esthetic metaphor, nor is it a technical symbol in any chemical
or mathematical sense but, in its essential nature, community.[4] The
image *is* what it represents, and that which signifies *is* what is signified.

The whole of human life, indeed, should be regarded from this point
of view. "All that is transitory is a parable": in this universally familiar
dictum of Goethe's the little word "only" may quite justifiably be
omitted in this connection, since the equivalence implies community.
The situation in which we find ourselves is essentially connected with
sacredness: of this it is an image, from this it derives its own value.
Thus earthly love symbolizes God's love, and this makes it valuable
and in itself sacred: earthly fatherhood, again, is an image of the divine:
that renders it great and potent.[5] Further, it is not that our so-called
reality is there first, and only subsequently the sacred which this
symbolizes: it is rather the sacred that first and solely exists, and our
secular entities possess value and permanence only because they are
capable, in any given instance, of symbolizing the sacred and cooperating
with it. This expresses the profoundest significance of the principle
that we are created in God's image: God is the archetype, but our
"images" can witness to Him and indicate Him. We may also assert,
with Mensching, that the symbol always has a meaning determined by
the story of salvation, and is not arbitrary but necessary.[6] The sacred
becomes "fixed", or "placed", in the concrete human situation; and

---

[1] cf. Wundt, *op. cit.*, IV, 35; Déonna, *Quelques réflexions sur le symbolisme, RHR.* 88,
18 ff.

[2] cf. Kretschmer, *Medizinische Psychologie*, 22. Reuterskiöld, *Totemismus*, 14.

[3] R. Thurnwald, *Zeitschr. f. Ästhetik und Allg. Kunstwiss.*, 21.

[4] "Participation", Lévy-Bruhl.   [5] cf. Huizinga, *Herfstty*, 345.

[6] *Buddhistische Symbolik*, 6 f., 9.

this includes persons and objects—the "things" of Chapter 3—words, actions *etc.*, all of which receive their ministerial status from the sacred and thus become symbols; while among these, "symbols" in the narrower sense such as the cross, incense, the *sacra* of the mysteries *etc.*, play a subordinate though momentous part. For it is in these that the sacred becomes actualized: in Egypt, for example, incense was regarded as "the stair to heaven";[1] and with the cross we bless. The most real symbol of all, however, is the altar, the throne or table of God, because there the sacred does in fact become "placed", and as it were establishes itself.[2] Symbols, still further, assist man in bringing the world into his own power, and with them he works magic; but in those types of religion where this impetus to exercise power over the world has yielded to being seized upon by Power, the sacred always becomes definitely "localized"; and then it is not the transient that is a "parable", but rather the creature[3] which, as such, can be a bearer of divine Power. The earthly situation implies the divine: "All creatures are shadows, echoes and pictures, mere vestiges and imitations and images."[4]

3. Upon the divine seat the god is enthroned; and now man may place his image on it. But this by no means always happens. The ark of Jahveh, for instance, was an empty throne of God;[5] and the vacant throne occurs also among primitive peoples.[6] This of course does not involve any "purely spiritual" worship of God, but merely that the deity should assume his place on the empty throne at his epiphany. The *image of the god* is a means of holding him fast, of guaranteeing his presence: thus it has the same purpose as the fetish,[7] from which it often cannot in fact be distinguished. The fetish or semi-fetish indeed, or the formless image, is usually preferred to the wholly human image;[8] and so to faith the black Madonnas have greater value than the most beautiful work of art.[9] For the dreadful and almost inhuman expresses

---

[1] *Pyramidentexte* (Sethe), 365. On the inexhaustible wealth of symbols *cf.*, together with Déonna, *op. cit.*, Danzel, *AR.* 21, 1922. A. Goblet d'Alviella, *Croyances, Rites, Institutions,* 1911.

[2] It is extremely probable that the ark of the covenant of Jahveh was also a throne of this type. The form of the sacred building, too, is symbolic: *e.g.* the cruciform church, the Hindu *stupa*, the Babylonian *ziggurat, etc.*

[3] Chap. 45.   [4] Bonaventura, *Itinerarium mentis in Deum,* 2.

[5] *cf.* H. Gressmann, *Die Lade Jahves und das Allerheiligste des salomonischen Tempels,* 1920.

[6] As on Bali Island, as Prof. J. C. van Eerde kindly informs me.

[7] Chap. 3.   [8] G. van der Leeuw, *Wegen en Grenzen,* 116.

[9] *cf.* Trede, *Heidentum in der römischen Kirche,* II, 91, with Note.

the sacred far better than does the human and is therefore preferred, since it stands closer to the "wholly other"; and Otto compares the terrible Hindu caricatures of the gods to the harsh and fearful Byzantine images of the Madonna and of Christ.[1] But still the human element breaks a way through for itself and forces itself forward, from the composite forms of Egypt and the many-limbed monsters of India to the pure humanity of the Homeric gods and the maternal form of the Madonna; so among the symbols of Power the human gains preference. The worship of images of the gods, therefore, is not founded on any error in piety towards the dead, or towards the gods of having confused them with their own images, as Euhemerism maintains:[2] "With respect to the gods too, our ancestors believed carelessly, credulously, with untrained simplicity; while worshipping their kings religiously, desiring to look upon them when dead in outward forms, anxious to preserve their memories in statues, those things became sacred which had been taken up merely as consolations."[3] By the image of the god it is essentially the *sacrum* that is indicated, the presence of the divine; and "the oldest image of the Gods", says Nietzsche, "is meant to shelter and at the same time to hide the God—to indicate him but not to expose him to view".[4] But similarly, even where fetish or semi-fetish has long yielded place to the human image, it is never a matter of mere external resemblance; for the essence of the god's image consists not in its resemblance to man but in its being filled with power, exactly as in the case of the fetish; and primitive people willingly give their fetishes to European collectors, but not their magic medicine, which is power.[5] The essential factor in the image, then, is power; hence the importance of the dedication of images, since this first endows them with potency. Arnobius represents a heathen as saying: "We too do not decide that the bronze or gold, or silver or any other materials from which images are made, are gods or divinities in themselves; but we venerate the gods in these images and worship them, whom the sacred act of dedication introduces and causes to dwell within wrought images."[6] Further, the power in the image may be either pure potency

---

[1] *cf.* the profound passage in *Human, All Too Human* (Nietzsche), II, 115 (Foulis Edition).

[2] As *e.g.* in old Arabian narrative: J. Wellhausen, *Reste arabischen Heidentums*, 1887, 14; *cf.* Negelein, *Spiegel und Schatten*. Geffcken, *Der Bilderstreit des heidnischen Altertums*, *AR*. 19, 293 *f.*

[3] Minucius Felix, XX, 6; similarly *Sap*. XIV, 15.

[4] *Human, All Too Human*, II, 116.

[5] A. Bertholet, *Journal of Biblical Literature*, 49, 3, 1930, 229.

[6] Geffcken, *loc. cit.*, 308.

(dynamistically) or some powerful person (Animism). In the latter case the god or spirit inhabits the image: if he is not present the image is a mere block of wood or stone;[1] thus the Egyptian *ka*[2] animated the statue of which he took possession. In New Guines, again, the spirit inhabits the *korwar*, from which he pronounces oracles and where he receives sacrifices *etc.*[3] The image is, as it were, the medium of the spirit.[4] The dedication of the image, further, may be replaced by its miraculous origin and characteristics. Thus it is the bearer of the sacred because it has shown itself to be filled with power and allocated thereto; and there are many cult legends relating to the marvellous origin of certain celebrated images of the gods. The image of Sarapis, for example, was transported from Sinope to Alexandria by divine command, given in a dream to the ruler Ptolemy, while the black stone of the mother of the gods was brought to Rome from Pessinus and worked miracles at the moment of its landing.[5] The same stories are told of many sacred images; and that these manifest their allocation to power by cures, oracles *etc.* is universally familiar; in ancient Egypt they were made to speak by means of some special contrivance, and in this way Alexander received his oracle from Amon.[6] Sacred images also bleed, descend from their pedestals, speak and cure if they are touched *etc.*[7]

Veneration of images is almost universal. It subsisted most vigorously in orthodox Christianity, which separated the altar space from the church by a wall of images—merely painted, it is true (*iconostasis*); the holy images constituted the space an *adyton* and the sacred acts a *mysterium*.[8] In the Greek church, again, the *festum orthodoxiae* designates the victory of those who revered images over those who, in the Byzantine empire, desired to abolish them.[9] This strife concerning images, however, was only a particularly violent outbreak of a conflict that is latent in all religions, and which had already aroused disturbances in Old Testament times and in the classical period.[10] In the course of this conflict the

---

[1] *cf. e.g.* R. Wilhelm, *Chinesische Volksmärchen*, 1919, No. 18, with Note.
[2] Chap. 42.   [3] Wilken, *op. cit.*, III, 190 *f.*
[4] *cf.* J. C. Lamster, *Tydschrift Ned. Aardr. Genootschap*, 2. Reeks, 47, 1930, 452 *ff.*
[5] Plutarch, *Of Isis and Osiris*, 28; *cf.* E. Petersen, *Die Serapislegende, AR.* 13, 1910, 47 *ff.*
[6] Maspero, *Études égyptiennes*, I, 77 *ff.* M. Weynants-Ronday, *Les statues vivantes*, 1926. O. Weinreich, *Antike Heilungswunder*, 1909.
[7] Negelein, *op. cit.*
[8] K. Holl, *Die Entstehung der Bilderwand in der griechischen Kirche, AR.* 9, 1906; *cf.* on icons, Boulgakoff, *Orthodoxie*, 461 *ff.*   [9] 842.
[10] Geffcken, *op. cit. passim.* G. van der Leeuw, *Wegen en Grenzen, passim.*

primitive awe of the image[1] was transformed, by "transposition", into the consciousness that the sacred can neither be firmly fixed nor portrayed. In this respect *Deuteronomy* provides the outstanding criterion. The ancient prohibition of images in Jewish law presupposed the concept of the real essence subsisting within the image; later, this was "transposed" into the realization of the insufficiency of every image. Jahveh speaks "out of the midst of the fire" on Sinai: "ye heard the voice of the words, but saw no similitude";[2] here the decisiveness of the word is placed above assumption of form. In the latter there is a suspicion of command over Power, whereby it may be deprived of its sacredness; awe of the numinous element in the image has been transformed into awe of the numinous in general.[3] In Greek and Roman antiquity, too, men were influenced by fear of dominating the deity by means of its image, and appealed to the absence of images (which probably had other reasons!) in the earliest religion; Varro thought that by the introduction of images religion had suffered the loss of purity.[4] And fear of the human form, of man's own work, of the no longer *"wholly* other"*, subsists equally in the Stoics and in Judaism: both were united by the early Christian apologists, for the first time in St. Paul's speech on the Aeropagus recorded in *The Acts of the Apostles*.[5] Subsequently, during the Byzantine agitations of the iconoclasts, political reasons combined with a fear of form that was to some degree influenced by Islam; similarly in the Reformation period, social motives united with rationalistic, and with the fear of form itself, in iconoclasm.[6] For in the image man dreads the idolizing of his own power.

But images have always found their defenders too, even as early as the classical era. Not merely as a makeshift, and pedagogically as a *Biblia pauperum*, but also as a matter of principle, images of God have their legitimate status. For as Posidonius maintained, the human body contains the *logos* and is therefore worthy of representing God. In the Byzantine dispute about images, further, this idea was rendered yet more profound by an appeal to the Incarnation:—if in Christ God has assumed human form, this form is thereby essentially endowed with

[1] Chap. 41.   [2] *Deut.* iv, 12.

[3] Otto. Whether there ever were images of Jahveh in Israel is a debatable question; *cf.* Obbink, *Zeitschr. f. d. altt. Wiss.*, 1929. S. Mowinckel, *Acta orientalia*, 8, 1930.

[4] Geffcken, *op. cit.*, 299. Plutarch, *Numa*, 8, 8. Fowler, *Religious Experience*, 146. Wissowa, *Religion und Kultus*, 28.

[5] *cf.* Norden, *Agnostos Theos*.

[6] G. van der Leeuw, *Wegen en Grenzen*; obedience to scripture also probably played a significant rôle; *cf. e.g. Biblioth. Reform. neerl.*, II, 1904, 601.

Power.[1] Man portrays God in human guise, then, not as a mere make-shift and because he knows not the form of God, but precisely because he does know it, in Christ. Man has not dressed God up in his own image: God has created man after His image.[2] Thus opponents of images have, often unwittingly, suppressed self-centredness and self-righteousness, while their advocates, again frequently without being aware of it, have defended the *locus standi* of God in the Universe, the "place" of God in human life.[3]

4. To the experience of the sacred, finally, *music* has also given a specific form that has in general not been regarded so mistrustfully by religion as has the visible image; musical expression of the holy occupies an extensive domain in worship. There is hardly any worship without music; and this is capable of actualizing even the most inadequate aspects of the experience. Nevertheless here too the fear of form, now in the guise of music, has not been absent, and stricter Buddhism, like Islam, has proscribed it just as Calvinism has forbidden images. But with this we encounter the formidable problem of the expression of the sacred in Art: not merely in music, but also in the word and the image, in architecture, in dance and drama; this expression always shows itself to be at once necessary and impossible. Its discussion pertains, however, to the Phenomenology of Art.[4]

W. Déonna, *Quelques réflexions sur le symbolisme (RHR.* 88, 1924).
J. Geffcken, *Der Bilderstreit des heidnischen Altertums (AR.* 19, 1919).
G. Mensching, *Buddhistische Symbolik,* 1929.

[1] Geffcken, *op. cit.* Will, *op. cit.,* II, 192.
[2] *Gen.* i. 27 probably refers to the bodily form of God.
[3] This may be carried to its extreme in the idea of images of Christ not made with hands: ἀχειροποιητοί. Will, *op. cit.,* II, 304.
[4] G. van der Leeuw, *Wegen en Grenzen.*

CHAPTER 66

ENDOWMENT WITH FORM IN CUSTOM

1. CONDUCT assumes form as *custom*. Observance of the potency of life, tabus, and purifications,[1] the obligations of worship and the other demands of Power upon life, together constitute usage, tradition and custom, whose sphere of operation is more extensive than that of law.[2] Custom then is essentially religious, because it is the endowing with form of fear and of awe before superior Power. It occupies the intermediate position between mere etiquette, good form and morality; and every now and then it changes into one of these. Good form is its empty shell; but morality may derive its own claim either from some quite independent principle, as it has been sought to do again and again in the modern world, or else it rests, exactly like custom, on the demand of Power—only not in this case, as with custom, by way of any possible endowment of life with form, but in the catastrophic type of complete failure—of sin—and of being raised up anew—of grace.[3]

Of course there already exists, in the simple fact of usage, a tendency towards this rupture which, in ethics, intersects the whole of life. For the sacredness of Power awakens the sense of distance; but conduct and custom aim at bridging this interval and rendering possible some definite and satisfactory relationship towards Power. And this usually succeeds, although failures of course occur, which must be atoned for: "no such thing ought to be done in Israel",[4] was said of such a failure. But in custom there is no question of any complete breakdown; on the contrary: life is so ordered that it accords with divine rule, whether this is simply tradition, or cosmic law (*ṛta, asha, ma-at, etc.*).[5] The state of impurity, then, has nothing whatever to do with observance of custom; it is always a condition of fullness of power, even though this may be a repletion with dangerous and undesired power. Whoever transgresses custom goes astray, and instead of celebrating as he should he sends the course of the powers off the rails; and this must be made good again. For this reason value is laid on the confession of sin[6] which sets

---

[1] Chap. 4, 49.   [2] Chap. 64.
[3] Chap. 78.   [4] 2 *Sam.* xiii. 12—a proverbial saying in the Old Testament.
[5] Chap. 4.   [6] Chap. 64. Lévy-Bruhl, *Primitives and the Supernatural*, 352.

the stagnant stream of events in motion once more, or upon the assurance of innocence, the so-called negative confession of sin[1] which we encountered in Egypt, in a rudimentary form, as early as in the *Pyramid Texts*: "He has not reviled the king", *etc.*[2] Here, of course, it is not a matter of personal "moral responsibility" in the sense of ethical autonomy, just as little as it is a "consciousness of sin" such as we find, for example, in St. Paul or in the Babylonian penitential psalms; and the offence against custom, the transgression, revenges itself on lifeless objects, or again on animals and plants, just as on man. There are, indeed, no "lifeless" objects; for every being has power, and this power can interfere with the current of potency in some undesirable way. By the Kukis of British India, for instance, the tree that has killed a human being is destroyed; Xerxes, again, commanded the Hellespont to be scourged, while the Draconian laws punished objects just as, in the Gospel, Christ cursed the barren fig tree. Until 1846, too, the law remained in force in England that a thing that had caused death to any one should, as a *deodand*, become the property of the king as the representative of God.[3] The ground of custom, therefore, is not the moral consciousness, and still less intention, but only the quality of powerfulness which is produced by some act or other.[4]

2. Custom, still further, need not remain a mere guarantee of life's potency. It may itself also become one means of the attainment of yet greater power, and in such cases we are concerned with *asceticism*. I have previously observed that the possession of power is a quality which might be called physical, since it is placed on just the same level as warmth, heat, glow;[5] thus great power is great heat, which may become dangerous to "custom", but may also promote it. The story of the creation of Masu, for example, related that the earth (that is the Island of Sumba) in its newly created condition was still very wet; then someone brought fire from heaven, and the earth became dry and had to be cooled again with raw flesh and water; and this is still always done as soon as the earth threatens to become too warm, for example as a result of illicit sex intercourse or adultery.[6] *Transgression*, therefore,

[1] Chap. 64.
[2] *Totenbuch* (Naville), *Kap.* 125. *Pyramidentexte* (Sethe), 892. Ad. Erman, *Zeitschr. für ägypt. Spr.*, 31, 75 *ff.*
[3] Westermarck, *The Origin and Development of the Moral Ideas*, I, 262.
[4] *cf.* Kurt Latte, *Schuld und Sünde in der griechischen Religion* (*AR.* 20, 1920–21, 256).   [5] Chap. 1 *f.*
[6] J. P. Kleiweg de Zwaan, *Tydschr. Ned. Aardr. Genootschap.* 2. *Reeks*, 47, 1930, 195.

causes heat. But on the other hand, heat is also produced by *celebration*. Everywhere that the operation of power proceeds, whether in the beneficial or the forbidden sense, there "heat" arises: the Hindu *tapas* has previously, in the discussion of power,[1] been found to be warmth and heat. Ascetic celebrations, again, develop a powerfulness that inspires even the gods with fear.[2] Asceticism may therefore be described as a celebration which develops power exactly as does transgression, but in the opposite sense, so that it confirms custom instead of violating it; and to this the detail of ascetic practice corresponds: chastity, fasting, self-castigation, silence, holding the breath, *etc*. Thus while custom regulates the operation of powers within life, asceticism controls them *à outrance*, so that almost nothing remains of them. Custom prescribes speech *and* silence, but asceticism silence alone; custom forbids the enjoyment of certain viands, while asceticism forbids eating in general, in so far as it is not absolutely necessary for life;[3] custom ordains speaking in defined periods and according to an accepted accentuation, but asceticism regulates even breathing and limits this to what is indispensable; custom dictates definite relations in sex intercourse, forbidding this with regard to certain persons and times; asceticism, however, proscribes such intercourse altogether.

But the deprivation of power involved in this strengthening of custom is merely apparent: rather, it intensifies the ascetic's own power. The seeming weakness becomes experienced as strength,[4] since the enfeebling of certain vital functions invigorates others. So far, then, Nietzsche is quite right in his assertion that "in every ascetic morality man worships one part of himself as a God, and is obliged, therefore, to diabolize the other parts".[5] Asceticism thus presupposes a fracture within life, quite unknown to custom; and as long as life is regarded as a totality there is no question of any "diabolizing". But for the ascetic many more tabus are in force than for the ordinary person;[6] and in this way he can avoid many transgressions of which others become guilty, while by restraint he intensifies his own power. A medicine-man therefore, or a king or priest, must submit to all sorts of tabus and observe a certain degree of asceticism. But when life is dualistically interpreted and a distinction drawn between body and soul,[7] then asceticism serves

---

[1] Chap. 2.   [2] Oldenberg, *Lehre der Upanishaden*, 49; *id.*, *Mahabharata*, 119.

[3] Thus ordinary fasting, that is to say the prohibition of specific foods at definite times, belongs to custom; abstinence from eating in general, to the verge of exhaustion, pertains to asceticism.   [4] Lévy-Bruhl, *Primitives and the Supernatural*, 241 *f*.

[5] *Human, All Too Human*, I, 140 (Foulis Edition).   [6] Chap. 4, 29.

[7] Chap. 43.

to eliminate the now completely diabolized body as much as is possible, to render it harmless, to oppose its operations, chastise it and even torture it, so that the "soul" may free itself and rule absolutely: the "best" in man, his eternal element or whatever else we may call it, is to be released. Psychologically, however, this type of celebration implies a satisfaction of natural instincts in some indirect way, since the ascetic knows how to procure various pleasures even through agony and pain; and in this connection psycho-pathology provides valuable comment, and can say much about the attainment of power by means of its loss. All ascetics, nevertheless, are not deranged, nor lustful perverts; and in the contrast with the flesh the antithesis to the unholy may at all times be patent.[1] It makes a very great difference, therefore, whether the flesh be diabolized, or the *diabolus* sought in the flesh; certainly the propriety of this latter attitude may be doubtful, but its religious value need not be disputed.

Asceticism, however, is concerned neither with autonomous morality nor with religious ethics. For it is an extreme type of celebration—essentially an acquisition of power: to it life can never be a catastrophe. And the entire interval separating asceticism from the demand that arises from the consciousness of sin and grace is shown by placing its practice of the depreciation of life, in order to heighten life's power, side by side with the Gospel teaching that he who loses his life keeps it, but that he who desires to retain it loses it.

But all this does not mean that asceticism treats life any less seriously than does autonomous, or religious, ethics: it may indeed become intensified into the very destruction of life; we have in fact already encountered such enmity towards life.[2] But this brings no deliverance; and this has been occasionally realized even in ascetic India, where the task of effecting deliverance has so often been assigned to asceticism: "asses and other animals roam about shameless and naked near houses and forests; are they therefore free from passion? If men could be released by smearing themselves with clay and ashes, would not the dog also be released, who is continually lying on clay and ashes? Are not the jackals and mice, the gazelles and other animals ascetics, who feed on grass, leaves and water alone and live in the forest? Are not frogs, fish and other aquatic animals *yogins*, since they remain from birth to death on the banks of the Ganges and other sacred streams?"[3]

[1] K. Schjelderup, *Die Askese*, 1928. [2] Chap. 47.
[3] E. Abegg, *Der Pretakalpa des Garuda-Purana*, 1921; here asceticism is contrasted with knowledge of truth.

3. Conduct, in conclusion, may also assume the form of worship, not merely in the general sense as representative action and ritual observance, but also as *taking sides.* In ancient Egyptian religious plays, for instance, two parties were formed, one led by the god and the other by his enemies. A mock battle broke out, which in the case of the Osiris mysteries was fought on water, the people choosing the side of the god against his adversaries: "I beat back those who were attacking the sacred barque of the god, and overthrew the enemies of Osiris."[1] Similar combats occurred in many popular customs of ancient times, as in modern days.[2] In that case religious custom develops into a "following" of the god, which we shall encounter at a later stage when discussing the idea of Imitation.[3]

Mircea Eliade, *Yoga Essai sur les Origines de la Mystique Indienne,* 1936.
G. Mensching, *Gut und Böse im Glauben der Völker,* 1950.
K. Schjelderup, *Die Askese,* 1928.
E. Westermarck, *The Origin and Development of the Moral Ideas,* I, II.

[1] H. Schäfer, *Die Mysterien des Osiris in Abydos,* 1904, 22.
[2] Usener, *Heilige Handlung,* 435 *ff.*
[3] Chap. 73; *cf.* further Chap. 90. Schäfer, *ibid.,* 24. "I prepared the 'great departure', and followed in the god's footsteps."

B. INWARD ACTION

CHAPTER 67

RELIGIOUS EXPERIENCE

1. THE division of our subject into Outward and Inward Action by no means implies a belief in the possibility of separating the inner from the outer:

> Wouldst thou truly study Nature?
> Seek the Whole in every feature.
> Nought's within and nought's without,
> For whatever's in will out.[1]

Everything external is closely connected with something internal; and conversely, without the outer there is no inner, or if there were it would not appear. A sacred stone, a god, a sacrament, therefore, are experiences precisely as fear, love and piety are, since in both cases it is for us a question of what appears, of what makes itself known by signs. Feeling, again, does not exist without speech and gesture; thought is not present without form and action; even mysticism requires words. It is therefore never permissible to place "institutional" religion in antithesis to the inward experience of religion. For every dogma, every act of worship, can only become understood primarily as the reflection of some experience; every act, every idea, is the expression of a need or a release, of pain or bliss.[2]

2. Nor again should we contrast experience as purely "personal" with the collective or communal element in external action. We shall find, indeed, that in a certain sense everything in religion is "personal", in so far as it can never be manifested outside the actual given situation, the existential determinateness, of humanity; but also that nothing is ever "purely" personal, since nothing whatever could be manifested were it not at some time understood by others besides any one individual. Very possibly, too, the last of all to understand is the present author!

---

[1] Goethe, *Epirrhema* (Dwight).
[2] On the relation between "Inner" and "Outer" *cf.* further Scheler, *Vom Ewigen im Menschen*, 366 *f.*

Still, he has innumerable predecessors. Everything, then, must be taken into consideration in order to constitute the experience that arises.[1]

My intention in discussing "inward action", therefore, is to maintain that every experience without exception may be regarded from two quite different sides:— from the point of view of its expression, or as it were in its external aspect, and also from the angle of its impression, or in other words in its internal aspect. I say advisedly "as it were". For the outer is always and simultaneously the inner, and conversely; only our survey may be directed either more specifically to the expression, to whatever makes itself manifest, or more towards the impression, that is to those inward emotions that have occasioned the expression. Thus it may be concerned with prayer, but equally with inner questioning: with space, but also with a yearning for some definite "situation": with what deeply moves us as well as with our being profoundly affected. Of course the contemplation of the inward can never be separated from that of the outward; here the position is analogous to our field of vision: I see the garden, for instance; that is, I see the flowers in the front of the garden, and in the background the trees near the fence; alternatively, I direct my glance towards the trees and at the same time see the flowers, although I intend to look at the trees. Investigation, in other words, can never restrict itself entirely to the external nor to the internal; only on each given occasion its direction is different. In this respect an analogy, or rather a relationship, subsists with the psychological distinction between introvert and extravert, or schizoid and cyclothyme. So long, that is to say, as it is manifested within the limits of the normal mind, neither of these two types ever exists entirely without the other; but (once again) the orientation is different in each of the two cases.

Thus our regard is now directed inwardly: the outward, nevertheless, is not forgotten but always remains within the visual field. The direction of our gaze, however, constitutes an attempt to advance from the "world" which "astonishes" us, and subsequently excites our "anxiety" and our "celebrating",[2] to that ultimate solitude where man stands, absolutely alone and with no "world", in dread before God.[3] An attempt merely— for to this goal we shall never actually attain: but on the road to the inward we hope that much will be disclosed.

3. In the spiritual life of to-day, then, religious experience is to a great degree in bad repute; and this is because it is quite wrongly restricted to "feeling", its value being then estimated according to the intensity

---

[1] Chap. 107.　　　[2] Chap. 48.　　　[3] Schmalenbach, *op. cit.*

of such feeling. Religious experience would in that case naturally mean the utmost subjectivity; but as such it should have no place, at least in religion, wherein the Object, as has repeatedly been maintained in Chapter I and in other passages, is simultaneously the Subject. Experience, however, is in no sense either mere feeling nor, specifically, religious feeling: under no conditions whatever, indeed, can any "feeling" be separated from life in its totality, except in antiquated faculty psychology! For together with feeling, other constituents are always present: will, reason, *etc.*[1]

It would therefore be better to avoid all such terminology, and speak (as Binswanger does) of a *social* ego directed from the subject to the environment: a *solitary* ego, which tends not to disclose the subject: a *conscious* self also, including the two selves previously referred to: an *accessible* self, which is not oriented by the subject to the world and of which, too, the individual himself is not aware, but which we are able to comprehend: and, finally, an ego which we can *understand* and which implies all these selves.[2] Our path then proceeds from the social and accessible ego, by way of the isolated self, to the ideal of the last ego—the ego we can understand. But whether we call the excitations within these various selves feelings, impulses or anything else, in any case the entire ego is involved in every such activity, and the whole life is present therein which becomes experience[3] owing to the disturbance (which may eventually be intensified into being profoundly moved), and consequently exists only in so far as it is referred to the object.[4]

What the nature of an experience is will be most clearly understood if it is compared with the "event". Event and experience, then, are the same "content", in the first place as a fact, and then as meaning also. A phenomenon therefore is always related to experience, since unless this is so it would not appear to us meaningfully. But outer phenomena also possess an element constituted by fact and event, a natural aspect, which cannot be understood as such. I understand the altar, for example, as a "locality" or "position"; but I cannot understand the stone of which it is made. Thus the experience is, *idealiter*, devoid of fact and of event: it is meaning in its purity.[5]

---

[1] [The brief passage that follows, in small type, is of a somewhat technical character.]

[2] Binswanger, *Psychologie*, 272.   [3] *ibid.*, 244.

[4] This is in fact implied by the term *Er-lebnis* itself; *cf.* pp. 462, 671.

[5] Thus the experience which I have previously called "dual experience of form" would here be lacking *idealiter*; on the other hand, the fact that it is never wholly absent first renders possible the descent to the worldless depths of significance; objectively, this means that experience, apart from the world of events, does not exist; and subjectively, that there is no meaning which cannot be understood. Understanding is not a supplementary activity on the part of the investigator, but pertains essentially to life itself; *cf.* Heidegger, *op. cit.*, 164; similarly, "what the disciple of Saïs unveils is not life, but form"; Dilthey, *op. cit.*, 7, 195.

But it is therefore never completely attainable, since it must always express itself in and through something that has the character of an event: it can appear only when it conceals itself within the opaqueness of the event. *For only what is concealed can become revealed.* But the solitude we seek here is a sort of treed hedge beyond which, indeed, we do not pass, but which attracts us, as a norm, to where dread of the "world" of events has yielded to the dread devoid of any object, where pure meaning would be found if it could ever be found at all, but which would then necessarily disclose itself as madness!

4. Religious experience, further, is that experience whose significance refers to the Whole; it can therefore never be understood from the standpoint merely of the moment, but only and always from that of eternity. Its meaning is an ultimate meaning, and is concerned with "the last things";[1] its nature is eschatological, and transcends itself; while for man it implies an ultimate, a boundary. But it could not attain this significance were it not primary and initial; thus its meaning becomes experienced as "wholly other", and its essence as revelation.[2] There is always a remainder therefore, something that fundamentally cannot become understood, but which religion regards as the condition of all understanding; and thus, at the frontier of the world of appearance, understanding is exchanged for being understood.

Like all experience, nonetheless, religious experience is related to the object, and this indeed in a pre-eminent sense: "in the very expression *Er-leben* there already resounds some degree of objective orientation".[3] In religious experience, however, this orientation is a presence, subsequently an encounter, and finally a union. And in this presence not he who experiences is primary, but He who is present; for He is the holy, the transcendently Powerful.

W. JAMES, *The Varieties of Religious Experience*, 1902.
R. R. MARETT, *Faith, Hope and Charity*, 1932.
F. SCHLEIERMACHER, *Über die Religion*, 1799 (*Ausg.* RUD. OTTO, 1913; Eng. tr., *On Religion*, 1958).
H. WERNER, *Einführung in die Entwicklungspsychologie*, 1926.

[1] Chap. 87.   [2] Chap. 85 *ff.*
[3] Spranger, *Einheit der Psychologie*, 175.

CHAPTER 68

THE AVOIDANCE OF GOD

1. WE have already[1] observed how isolated objects, actions *etc.*, that are "excepted" from the entire world of experience, become declared tabu; and this "excepting" then becomes a "selection" manifested in times and spaces, in persons, objects and words *etc.* In their totality, again, these "selected" factors constitute the realm of the *sacred*, as this detaches itself from the unselected and secular world, while the contrast between sacred and secular showed itself increasingly to be fundamental. With this, too, from the inner aspect or from the side of experience, awe is correlated (to use Marett's fine term) which has been compared by Murray to the Greek *aidos*;[2] and on its own part this awe appeared as ambivalent, as involving the *fascinans* just as it does the *tremendum*.[3] Thus man fears the sacred, but loves it also: he attempts to elude it, yet seeks for it too. In *fear* therefore, which we are now about to examine, we shall discover not avoidance alone, but within and about this always a simultaneous attraction: "Half drew she him, half sank he in."[4]

2. By "fear", however, we understand not reasonable alarm nor dejection due to some concrete danger.[5] Essentially, this has nothing whatever to do with religion. By fear I wish rather to indicate exclusively that experience which Kierkegaard calls "dread", and which I shall myself distinguish as *primary fear* from the first mentioned, *secondary fear*.[6] This primary fear, still further, is not based on any rational set of conditions, for it exists prior to every experience: such fear is a mode of the very state in which one subsists. "Prudence perceives what is to be feared because it is itself within the existential mode of fear; and fear as a slumbering possibility of the existential 'being in the world', faintheartedness, has already understood and appreciated the world in so far that from it something akin to the terrifying may approach." But "what arouses dread is 'being in the world' itself".[7] Thus the child's

---

[1] Chap. 4.   [2] Murray, *The Rise of the Greek Epic*, 104, 109 *f.*
[3] Otto.   [4] Goethe, *The Fisher.*
[5] On what follows *cf.* Heidegger, *op. cit.*, 140 *ff.*, 184 *ff.*
[6] Ribot, *The Psychology of the Emotions.*   [7] Heidegger, *op. cit.*, 141, 187.

dread of the dog, about which it knows nothing, the boy's dread regarding the domain of sex, just because of his ignorance, the undefined
dread that may seize us when we are alone, on a moor or in the forest,
and whose echoes vibrate in many legends and fairy tales, horror in the
dark:—all this is fear in the specifically religious sense. Or to state this
bluntly once and for all: in the secondary sense, already indicated, I
fear the car which threatens to run me down, but in the primary sense
I fear the motorless world of the steppes; secondarily, again, I dread
the idea of being attacked in the forest; primarily, I dread the very
feeling of the forest's uncanniness and would on that account greet the
appearance even of robbers with joy! The fear here referred to, therefore, is not some annoying disturbance, like the secondary type of fear,
that should be subdued. On the contrary, it has a positive value and is
intimately related to religion, as is shown by the Greek expression
deisidaimonia, and above all by the Jewish "fear of God". There always
persists in it something of that instinctive and irrational fear which is
occasionally manifested without any concealment in the Old Testament
itself, to whatever degree the Old Testament idea, in the course of time,
may have accumulated ethical content; thus it was in the case of the
"panic" of Jahveh which he sent before Israel.[1] The vision of the
prophet Isaiah is the most vivid expression of this fear; and here it is
precisely ambivalence that is very clearly exhibited, since the awe
becomes the consciousness of sin, the terror becomes worship.[2] Similarly
in the New Testament, when it is concerned with the appearance of
Jesus, not only astonishment but fear also is present; thus in the
marvellous description in *St. Mark* x, 32, where the Lord is on the
way to Jerusalem and His disciples are following Him in terror and fear;
and again in the profoundly penetrating passage in which Peter falls
at Jesus' feet: " 'Lord, leave me; I am a sinful man'. For amazement
had seized him and all his companions at the take of fish they had
caught."[3] Thus the primitive amazement, and later fear, produced by
the extraordinary and miraculous, here appear at the very centre of
religious experience, where its ambivalent aspect is presented as worship.

It seems then that the ancient dictum: "Fear was the first creator of
gods in the world",[4] is absolutely true; and desiring to express the
practical character of his religion, an Eskimo shaman said: "we do not
believe: we fear."[5] But this dread, which we have already learnt to

[1] *Exodus* xxxiii. 27; *cf. Isaiah* viii. 13; "let Jahveh be your fear and your dread".
[2] *Isaiah* vi.   [3] *Luke*, v, 8, 9 (Moffat).
[4] Statius, *Theb.* iii, 661.   [5] Lévy-Bruhl, *Primitives and the Supernatural*, 22.

recognize as the primeval experience in religion, is not mere slavish
fear, and still less feeble despondency;[1] it is essentially ambivalent, a
condition intermediate between being repelled and being attracted.
And long before Freud and the psychology of the "Unconscious",
Kierkegaard dealt most profoundly with this primal experience: the
dread to which he refers is that of Nothingness. The unrestricted
possibility of the unformed feeling of life causes the "vertigo of liberty".
Thus dread is not consciousness of guilt; it is rather the essential condition therefor. In itself, indeed, it is innocence: "that is the profound
mystery of innocence, that it is at the same time dread", a hesitation
between hastening towards the object and escaping from it, attachment
and anxiety, fear and love. The development of youth during puberty
shows this dread of Nothingness in its clearest form, while many
neuroses also provide examples. But these are merely the extreme types
of a universally human experience, which awaits all men in the hour of
death, when Nothingness confronts us: "The father and mother of all
fears being the fear of death."[2]

This dread, however, is not correlated with unpleasant feelings, as
an earlier psychology maintained. On the contrary, it is connected with
feelings of pleasure just as frequently as with the unpleasant. Thus man
loves his dread and becomes fascinated by it, like one who after staring
into the water for a long time is captivated by the horror of destruction
by the stream, or like Goethe's fisherman's fascination by the water-
sprite. This dread, still further, may be almost completely resolved
into terror, in which a considerable proportion of the fear of demons
and spirits persists; but it may also traverse the entire range of human
feeling, from terror through horror, awe, reverence and the sense of
distance, to trust and love; and in love there is always something of
horror, in horror always some degree of love. Dread itself, however, is
no haphazard feeling, but the primeval experience aroused by the unlimited possibility lying at the base of all religions without exception, and
also of life beyond the merely given in general; this dread indicates the
tension of the relationship between Power and man. It is a "sympathetic antipathy and an antipathetic sympathy",[3] so that in fear there
is always an element of love, however feeble this may be, and in love
an element of terror, however refined it may have become; and there

[1] In his own day Varro drew the distinction, "saying that the gods are feared by
the superstitious man, but are reverenced by the religious man as parents, not as
enemies"; in Augustine, *The City of God*, 6, 9.
[2] Marett, *Faith, Hope and Charity*, 41.
[3] Kierkegaard, *Begrebet Angest* (*The Concept of Dread*).

are no religious ideas from which awe, as corresponding to the primeval experience of dread, is wholly absent.[1] Only thus, in fact, can we understand that to fear God, to love and to serve Him, appear as related concepts;[2] and we all realize, in truth, that we not only hate our dreads, but also, in secret, love them. The religious element in awe, then, is given with its inexplicability and irreducibility on the one hand, and on the other with its limitlessness extending over the totality of life: "everything is possible: I stand before the Nought".[3]

3. Dread, again, is the condition of the experience of *guilt*, which will be discussed later;[4] but it is already clear that the tension of ambivalent dread has caused a rupture in the recesses of human nature. For it confronts man with himself, divides him, as it were, into two egos, one of which desires to comply with the terribly-sweet demand of the sacred, while the other strives to escape from it. One self longs to conform to the sacred, whether this self-accord be a hastening away from, or towards, the sacred; the other self attempts to place life above the infinite possibility, to survive the gnawing dread, to ignore the demand; and we may call the first ego *conscience*, provided we apply this term in its original sense and not in connection with so-called autonomous morality. For the word *conscience, conscientia,* συνείδησις, presupposes a schism within the self; it is derived not from a theoretic-ethical, but from a mythical-religious idea, as a result of which our inner psychic life stands confronted with itself as with something foreign. It is my conscience that says something to me; but it could say nothing at all to me if it were myself; and thus it is a *foreign* being, a sort of demon within me.[5] A Bechuana tribesman was once asked if he had a conscience: " 'Yes, all have one', he said in reply. 'And what does it say to them?' 'It is quiet when they do well and torments them when they sin '."[6] From this it follows that the inner voice, the inward judge, usually denies and seldom or never affirms, as we also know indeed

---

[1] *cf.* Söderblom, *Gottesglaube*; similarly for Ribot, *The Psychology of the Emotions,* who will accept *primus in orbe* only if a moment of attraction is recognized in repulsion; for Marett (*Faith, Hope and Charity*), who includes in *timor* the feelings of wonder, admiration, interest, reverence and love; for Grönbech (*op. cit.*, II, 77), who concedes fear as a primeval feeling in religion only if this implies "wanton gaiety as well as despair". (Marett observes that fear is founded in hope: "hope is of superior importance, since ultimately we fear because we hope, and not *vice versa*". *loc. cit.*, 22, 40. In the end this is nothing but a different way of emphasizing ambivalence.)

[2] *Deut.* x, 12.   [3] Chap. 67.
[4] Chap. 78.   [5] *cf.* A. Vierkandt, *Naturvölker und Kulturvölker,* 1896, 179 *f.*
[6] Westermarck, *The Origin and Development of the Moral Ideas,* I, 125.

from experience, despite much ethical theory, while even children are already aware of it. The conjoined knowledge cries out to knowledge, the associated self to the self, that man must undertake something with respect to the sacred, and that he may not live in disregard of it. The most celebrated example of this is Socrates' Demon, which ethics, but for its too positive and too moral conception of conscience, would not so frequently have refused to identify therewith; the Demon, this "revenge of the irrational" on the rationalist Socrates, as Joël says,[1] also expressed itself negatively, as is well known. "This voice, which emerges from unknown depths, appears as something foreign that does not pertain to the self, and this precisely at the moment when it arises to prevent something. For where it operates positively, *currentum instigans*, the voice of conscience is unheard in the din excited by consciousness and therefore not observed as something particular."[2] But in so far as it represents the alien and the sacred, it appears to be a god; the ancient Egyptians, indeed, called conscience, which they regarded as the heart, the god within us: Intef performs all his good works under the leadership of his heart: "I was excellent by virtue of what it told me to do: I was distinguished under its guidance; people say: it is a decree of the gods residing within everybody."[3] Paheri again: "I knew the god who dwells within man: I recognized him; I distinguished this way from that, *etc.*";[4] and there follows an assurance of honesty. Now it is possible, certainly, with Nietzsche and Freud, to ascribe the "strangeness" of the voice, which warns us to avoid, to infantilism; "not the voice of God in the heart of man, but the voice of some men in man".[5] We may however prefer the Egyptian description; on this point phenomenology has no decision to make. But this much is certain: a rupture (to repeat) manifests itself here which cleaves human personality. The self, which desires simply to live, is compelled to "avoid" by the other self which interrupts it. "Avoidance", then, means observance, *religio*; it may become flight, but it may also become a passionate seeking; in both cases alike "avoidance" reveals itself in the fact that distance is recognized together with dread. And if man simply continues to live in spite of his conscience, then it will torment him even when he is unconscious of any fault; in

---

[1] *Geschichte der antiken Philosophie*, I, 1921, 816 *f.*

[2] M. P. Nilsson, *Götter und Psychologie bei Homer*, AR. 22, 1923/24. 380; *cf.* Windelband, *History of Philosophy*, 98; *Präludien*, I⁶, 1919, 77 *f.*

[3] Sethe, *Urkunden*, IV, 974.

[4] *ibid.*, 119; *cf.* 117. Ad. Erman, *Die ägyptische Religion*², 1909, 123.

[5] *Human, All Too Human*, II, 224.

this respect "psychoanalysis confirms what the pious were wont to say, that we are all miserable sinners";[1] this confirmation, though coming somewhat late in the day, should nevertheless be welcome. On the other hand the recognition of the inner voice, either as foreign or as divinely experienced, gives to human conduct a firmness and a calm, outstanding examples of which we can perceive at the end of Socrates' *Apology* and in Luther's declaration at Worms, that "to act against conscience is neither safe nor advisable".

4. To him therefore who is seized by dread, subsequently by awe, and compelled to "avoid", different paths stand open other than the easiest way of continuing to live while ignoring all this, which has just been referred to. The first is that of presumption, of autocratic seizure of power, and with this attitude of mind we have already become familiar in countless magical customs; at a later stage I shall discuss its background[2] in turning away from the world, which is overcome only in appearance, but which in reality is abandoned. The experience accompanying this frame of mind is often an almost wanton arrogance; we find it in pure magic—for example in the Hindu idea that the *tapas* (warmth) of ascetic fulfilment of duty makes the throne of the great god in heaven hot;[3] and thus dread is overcome in a mighty trial of strength, which makes matters hot for the gods on their thrones. A titanic mood may also colour this experience; in myth the type is Herakles, who threatens Helios, appears terrible before the throne of Hades, instils fear into its mighty ruler and himself attains divinity. In the fairy tale, again, it is Strong Jack who thrashes the devil and sets out, but all in vain, to learn what fear is. The Greeks called such an arrogant disregard of awe *hubris* and looked upon it as the great sin, although they themselves could never renounce it: to render oneself like the god, not to esteem the god rightly, is *hubris*, the human element being altogether discarded; and so Aias calls down divine anger on himself, "thinking things not fit for man".[4] The ecstatic likeness of the *bacchae* to the god was likewise described as "bacchic frenzy".[5] This Titanism, however, is by no means the same as that living in disregard of Power, that failure duly to observe the sacred, which we have already encountered. On the contrary: Power is here frankly recognized, and

---

[1] Freud, *Totem and Taboo*, 121; *cf.* O. Pfister, *Die psychanalytische Methode*, 1913, 87 *ff.*   [2] Chap. 82.
[3] Lüders, *Buddhistische Märchen*, No. 53.   [4] Sophocles, *Ajax*, 776 *f.*
[5] Euripides, *The Bacchae*, 779; ὕβρισμα βακχῶν.

then a hostile attitude is adopted amounting to contempt; and thus
man turns away from the Power that arouses dread towards himself,
towards his own powerfulness, under the impression that his own likeness to the god will excite no alarm. In its other aspects too Goethe has
expressed the religion of *hubris* in its finest form (and has at the same
moment provided its keenest criticism!) in his *Prometheus*:—

> Here sit I, fashion men
> In mine own image,—
> A race to be like me,
> To weep and to suffer,
> To be happy and enjoy themselves,
> All careless of *thee* too,
> As I![1]

Similarly, *Postilion Kronos*:—

> So that Orcus may know we are coming,
> And the mighty ones below
> Are rising from their seats.[2]

This is *Herakles redivivus*! and the same heroic victory over dread
is very finely portrayed, especially with reference to conscience, in
Ibsen's *Master Builder*; Hilda's demand, that the Master Builder
should equip himself with a "robust conscience", is pure *hubris*. The
Master Builder attempts to do so and—here too criticism closely
accompanies the challenge—falls from the tower he has himself constructed. In fact, a tower became the classical type, and also the warning
example, of this heroism: the tower of Babel!

In the second place, against dread man may come to rely on *habit*.
Alarm, or care, may lead to man gaining dominance, but also to habit,
either with respect to what has been acquired, or to the impossibility of
such acquisition. A child, for instance, wonders at some object in its
environment and tries to seize it; then he becomes quite accustomed
either to the thing he possesses or to the fact that he cannot have the
object. So out of his relation to Power man forms a habit which becomes
firmly established in the various rites and customs we have encountered,
but which also represents an inner attitude. It is "justice towards the
gods", *justitia adversus deos*,[3] in which Cicero found the essence of
piety: the correct behaviour that never surpasses the limits imposed on
man and involves an equally unmoved outlook with regard to both

---

[1] Dwight's translation.   [2] In the original version.
[3] Cicero, *De Deorum Natura*, I, 41.

possibilities and impossibilities; the *justus*, in other words, is he whose demeanour is correct.[1] The Romans, indeed, placed great emphasis on practical conduct; so did the Greeks but, in accordance with their characteristic temperament, they expressed themselves more freely about the experience connected with this. It is then this spiritual condition which, as the antithesis to *hubris*, runs through so many Greek concepts about God and the Universe—*sophrosyne*. The magicians were "crafty", ὀλοόφρονες; they had pernicious ideas, while whoever was *sao-phron* had saving and healing thoughts. The mood of *sophrosyne* was related to the Apollonian calm of the soul of the Delphic god, to "Nothing in excess": μηδὲν ἄγαν.[2] It was a highly prized possession, a sort of sea-calm of the soul, which did not however prevent it being regarded by profounder minds as inferior when compared with Dionysiac ecstasy, nor hinder a poet like Euripides from putting its glorification into the mouth of the petty *bourgeois* and the philistine.[3] And no less a thinker than Plato extols the "madman", μαίνεσθαι, at the expense of the "sane man", σωφρονεῖν, in his celebrated eulogy of "mania".[4] But as regards the "Wholly Other", habit is always very foolish: in three days, just when the horse became used to eating nothing at all, it died; and when man has completely lost his capacity for surprise, he too is as good as dead! For in dread we may be blessed, or we may realize that we are damned; but in the easy-going calm of the man who has altogether forgotten astonishment and amazement there is neither blessedness nor damnation.

The third way of escape from dread is faith.[5] Dread, says Kierkegaard again, enfolds the point at which the spirit breaks through, alike in the fall and in deliverance. Then every attempt to elude astonishment or care is abandoned, and the dreadfulness of Power is not merely unreservedly acknowledged, but experienced as part of one's very own existence. This experience is vividly expressed in the passage from Luther's sermon on *Exodus* xx. 1, which Otto quotes: "For therefrom can no man refrain: if he thinketh on God aright, his heart in his body is struck with terror: yea, he would escape out of the world."[6] It lives too in the sixth chapter of *Isaiah*, in *Job*, in the Babylonian peni-

---

[1] *cf. ibid.*, II, 4, 10, and the formula of the fetial on the *hostis* who was, as such, *injustus: illum injustum esse neque jus persolvere*.

[2] G. van der Leeuw, *Goden en Menschen*, 87 ff.; *cf.* Murray, *The Rise of the Greek Epic*, 48. Samter, *Religion der Griechen*, 74.

[3] Euripides, *Medea, e.g.* 1078 ff. *The Bacchae*, 1150 ff.

[4] *Phaedrus*, 245.   [5] Chap. 80.

[6] *cf. The Idea of the Holy*, 103, and Calvin, *Institutio*, I, 1, 3.

tential Psalms and in all the horror of the Hindu experience of God in the *Bhagavad-Gita*.[1] Dread, however, finds its end in God, from Whom it emanated: "the mothers do not tell us where we are: they leave us quite alone; where dread ends and God begins we too may be allowed to be".[2] Again: "There is no fear in love; but perfect love casteth out fear: because fear hath torment."[3] Or: "That is perfect fear which is born of love and expels ordinary fear."[4]

S. F. H. J. BERKELBACH VAN DER SPRENKEL, *Vrees en Religie*, 1920.
S. KIERKEGAARD, *Begrebet Angest* (*Samlede Vaerker*, IV), 1923 (Eng. tr., *The Concept of Dread*).
A. MOSSO, *Die Furcht*, 1889.
TH. RIBOT, *The Psychology of the Emotions*.

[1] Especially 11, 15 *ff.*
[2] Rainer Maria Rilke, in P. Zech, *Rainer Maria Rilke*, 1930, 64.
[3] 1 *John* iv. 18.
[4] Abbas Dorotheus, in Nik. von Arseniew, *Religiöse Besinnung*, I, 1928, 109.

CHAPTER 69

SERVITUDE TO GOD

1. THE opposite Pole to titanic insubordination, and different also from habit as discussed in the previous Chapter, is servitude to God, wholly resigned and unreserved submission to the rule of Power. Man, realizing his own dependence on Power and compelled to assign to this dependence a form in his religious consciousness, has here chosen the form of a servant to express his unrestricted recognition of this subjection. The bodily posture associated with this recognition is προσκύνησις (הִשְׁתַּחֲוָה), prostrating oneself: before Power man humbles himself. God is *Lord*, not only of the earth like the Semitic *baalim*, but also of those who live on it and who are His slaves: He is the king who owns the land and whom all men must serve. And in his own divinity the earthly king is by no means the prototype of this "Lord" God, but is His shadow or His son;[1] thus the Hebrew expressed himself:—"I am thy slave, the son of thy female slave"[2]; in the New Testament too the designation recurs in relation to Christ: "the slave (δοῦλος) of Christ Jesus".[3] Slavish servitude may certainly be implied here, but it may equally well be the expression of awe before the sacred; this it is already in very many passages in the Old Testament. In such a spirit of serving God, for example, Abraham says to Him: "Here am I venturing to speak to the Lord, I who am mere dust and dross".[4] On the other hand, even such slavish humiliation may facilitate an excessive intensification of self-respect in being the servant of such a master,[5] just as to serve, with the *arrière pensée* of being able to rule all the more effectively, repeatedly appears in human experience.

2. The designation "servant of God" involves, however, not only complete submission but also readiness for service, obedience; here[6] servitude borders on the imitation of God, with which I shall later on deal in fuller detail.[7] Obedience is hearkening to God's decisive word. Life becomes viewed as fulfilment of this word: its whole significance

---

[1] Chap. 13, 25.
[2] *Ps.* cxvi. 16.
[3] *Phil.* i. 1; *cf. Tit.* i. 1.
[4] *Gen.* xviii. 27 (Moffat).
[5] There is a good example in Günther, *Jung-Stilling*, 93.
[6] Chap. 53.
[7] Chap. 73.

lies in decision. This is shown very beautifully in Parsiism; obedience (*sraosha*) is there one of the sacred beings which surround Ahura Mazda; and at a later period *sraosha* was assigned to the soul, as a psychopomp, on the road to the judgment of the dead—that is of decision.

All volition, in fact, has obedience as its presupposition: "A man who *wills* commands something within himself which renders obedience, or which he believes renders obedience."[1] Thus the will to power presupposes obedience, which indeed may also be one attitude of the man who listens to himself; and in such a case we have the parallel to prayer as monologue. But it may also be the disposition accompanying prayer as dialogue,[2] in bowing before the word of the Wholly Other encroaching upon life; here power is found in a voluntary powerlessness, which is however neither weakness nor hostility towards life, but simple acknowledgment of the validity of the word that has been heard. In this sense Jesus is said to have "learned obedience by the things which he suffered",[3] and in this way too He is the realization of that ideal of service which prevailed in Israelite prophecy:

> "He was despised and shunned by men,
>   a man of pain, who knew what sickness was; . . .
> He was ill-treated, yet he bore it humbly,
>   he never would complain,
> dumb as a sheep led to the slaughter,
>   dumb as a ewe before the shearers.
> Yes, many shall hold my servant blameless" (saith God)
>   "since 'twas their guilt he bore.
> Therefore shall he win victory,
>   he shall succeed triumphantly,
> since he has shed his life-blood,
>   and let himself be numbered among rebels,
> bearing the great world's sins,
>   and interposing for rebellious men."[4]

---

[1] Nietzsche, *Beyond Good and Evil*, 26 (Foulis Edition).   [2] Chap. 32.
[3] *Hebrews* v. 8.   [4] *Isaiah*, liii (Moffat); *cf.* Chap. 13.

CHAPTER 70

THE COVENANT WITH GOD

1. JUST as it is possible for men to enter into a covenant, and in association with one another to discover the sacred common element,[1] so too they can conclude a covenant with Power, with Deity. Certain rules are, as it were, laid down according to which the game between God and man is to be played;[2] man and Power both alike pledge themselves to some definite course of conduct. "Peace" must prevail between them; and in ancient Rome the entire life of the community was based upon a pact, *pax deorum*. This "peace" was a legally concluded covenant maintained by varied means, and when calamities fell on the people, when *portenta* occurred, *etc.*, it was a sign that the *pax* had been infringed; while the *pax* was preserved, the *status quo* assured, by sacrifice and prayer, the fulfilment of vows, purifications, conscientious investigation of the "situation" and attention to whatever was "unseasonable". In all this, however, there was no reference to trust in the gods; the Romans believed merely that correct words and acts securely determined the powers. Were this not the case, the reason was that some incorrect celebrations had been carried out; these were then corrected, or some new methods tried, for example a great repast of the gods: "For the purpose of imploring the favour of the gods there was a *lectisternium*, the third time since the building of the city."[3] The *pax* thus required a "conscientious observation" of the divine powers (*pietas*);[4] and with this the Germanic concept of "peace" may be compared.[5]

From the Old Testament, again, we can trace how the covenant with God arose from that between men, and was originally identical with this.[6] The human covenant was contracted on holy ground in the presence of the gods, and in this compact the deities of both parties were

---

[1] Chap. 33 *ff.*

[2] This comparison is in no degree depreciative, since there is scarcely anything in life more serious than play, especially child's play; *cf.* "the maturity of man—that means, to have recognized the seriousness that one had as a child at play". *Beyond Good and Evil*, 89 (Foulis Edition).   [3] Livy, VII, 2.

[4] Fowler, *Religious Experience*, 431; *cf.* 169 *ff.*, 261; also H. Wagenvoort, *Pietas*, 194.

[5] Grönbech, *op. cit.*, I, 20 *ff*   [6] On what follows *cf.* Pedersen, *Israel*, 201 *ff.*

included. The covenant rite was a communal meal (בְּרִית perhaps
means "food") of which gifts also formed part;[1] and the compact
inaugurated peace, *shalom*. Later there arose the idea of a covenant
between Jahveh and the people; and here the remarkable and typically
Israelite feature was that Jahveh himself concluded the covenant; a
covenant with Noah is referred to, with Abraham also, and later still
with the whole people, whose intermediary was Moses. The compact
demanded man's obedience to the divine commands (the Tables and
the Book of the Covenant), while on His part God pledged Himself to
conquest of the promised land and victory over their enemies. Here
too the rite was sacrifice, or the dismemberment of the sacrificial
animals,[2] while circumcision was regarded as the covenantal sign.

As has already been observed,[3] contract is never a merely rational nor
even advantageous affair; and the covenant, as it became apprehended
in Israel, was quite different from this. On the one hand trust in God's
word and on the other obedience to His commands became more
and more intensely, and at the same time more and more inwardly,
experienced: in this respect indeed the covenant approximates to the
relation of friendship, which will be discussed later;[4] it stood firmly
grounded in Jahveh's *truth* to eternity:

> He never forgets his compact,
>   the pledge given for a thousand generations,
> the compact made with Abraham,
>   the oath he swore to Isaac,
> confirming it as a decree to Jacob,
>   for Israel as a lasting compact,
> that he would give them Canaan's land,
>   to hold it as their own possession.[5]

The contrast with earlier ideas of the covenant was clearly perceived
and a "new" covenant distinguished from the "old": a new compact
having in the first place an eschatological significance: "I will remember
my compact with you in the days of your youth; I will ratify a lasting
compact with you";[6] while as the mediator of this renewed deliverance
Deutero-Isaiah presents the Servant of Jahveh, the obedient.[7] But

---

[1] Chap. 50.
[2] *Gen.* xv. For other examples of the idea of covenant, *inter alia* in Japan, *cf.* Jevons, *The Idea of God in Early Religions*, 1913, 92 *ff.*   [3] Chap. 50.
[4] Chap. 71.   [5] *Ps.* cv. 8 *ff.* (Moffat).
[6] *Ezekiel* xvi. 60 (Moffat); *cf. Isaiah*, lv, 3; lxi, 8; lxvi, 22.
[7] *Isaiah* xlii. 6; xlix. 8.

Jeremiah places beside its wide range into eternity its deep roots in experience: Jahveh declares that the new covenant consists in that

> I will put my law within them,
>   and write it on their hearts;
> and I will be a God to them,
>   and they to me a people.[1]

In this the significance of both the old and the new covenants is clearly exhibited, and the direction taken by the New Testament made possible; man recedes completely into the background: the covenant means solely the saving act of God in history, and His faithfulness means only His grace.

[1] *Jer.* xxxi. 33 (Moffat); *cf.* xxxii. 39 *f.*

CHAPTER 71

FRIENDSHIP WITH GOD

1. THOSE associated in any covenant are friends;[1] and thus the god who is accepted in the compact, or even concludes this, is a friend too. This friendship with the god, further, may awaken the sense of some likeness between god and man, and so we can well understand that in the sphere of religion man has been very chary of employing the title of friend. Peterson has discussed the genesis of the idea of friendship with the god in the Greek-Semitic world,[2] and has found it predominantly in Hellenistic circles or in those influenced by Hellenism. Previously employed by Plato, the concept of friendship with God was occasionally objected to,[3] but in later philosophy it became highly esteemed as one title of the sage. The designation of the patriarch Abraham also, as the friend of God,[4] probably originated from Hellenistically influenced quarters, while besides Abraham, Moses also appears as God's friend. For friendship with God, again, there were two conditions, the first being the possession of divine knowledge; and in this sense too St. John's *Gospel* speaks of the friends of Jesus: "Henceforth I call you not servants; for the servant knoweth not what his Lord doeth: but I have called you friends; for all things that I have heard of my Father I have made known unto you."[5] Thus friendship with God takes the place of service of God. In the second place, fulfilment of the commandments pertains to this: "Ye are my friends, if ye do whatsoever I command you";[6] obedience, which we have already discerned to be the presupposition of service, now becomes the condition of friendship also. Certainly St. John referred not to God but to Christ, as God revealed. The ultimate ground of this friendship, then, is divine love which expels fear: and this love is

---

[1] *cf.* Pedersen, *Israel*, 201 *ff.*

[2] On the original meaning of φίλος (θεοῦ) as "sanctified, dedicated" *cf.* Fr. Pfister in Pauly-Wissowa, *Realenzykl. d. klass. Alt.*, *Kultus*, § 5, 5. On φίλος as a title at the court of the Ptolemies *cf.* A. Deissmann, *Bibelstudien*, 1895, 159 *ff.* On the Israelites as friends of God: Strack-Billerbeck, *Kommentar zum N. T. aus Talmud und Midrasch*, II, 1924, 564 *f.*

[3] E. Peterson, *Der Gottesfreund* (*Zeitschr. für Kirchengeschichte*, 42, N. F. 5.), 166 *f.*

[4] *James* ii. 23.   [5] *John* xv. 15.   [6] *ibid.*, 14.

2. The mystical being and existing "*in Christo*", which finds undying expression in the parable of "The Vine and its Branches". All these features—the contrast with servitude and fear, the mystic community (with reference even to the sacrament!) and the knowledge of God, occur in the passage cited by Peterson from Origen:[1] "At first Christ the shepherd leads the sheep to pasture, but now the friend invites his friends to his table. 'For', he says, 'I no longer call you servants, but friends.' The fear of the Lord makes servants, but knowledge of the mysteries of God makes friends."

Friendship, to continue, includes a certain degree of intimacy; and this becomes stressed in mysticism; as al-Ghazali says: "When the mystic is overcome with joy at the nearness of God and the contemplation of what is imparted to him in revelation . . . a blissful mood arises in his heart; and this mood is called intimacy."[2] In *Sufi* mysticism, too, God is the friend, just as in fourteenth century German mysticism.[3] Conversely, man's turning towards God is friendship. "Thus man has turned to the best part, which is God . . . and then they are called the hidden friends of God";[4] the "cherubinic Wanderer" (Angelus Silesius) goes still farther: "Whoso would embrace him must be not merely his friend, but must even be his child and mother."[5]

In friendship love becomes visible, the blissful intimacy with God, while mysticism esteems it as the prologue to complete union: so in the words from *The Imitation of Christ*, with which Peterson also concludes: "That Thou alone wouldst speak to me and I to Thee, as a lover talking to his loved one, a friend at table with his friend. This is my prayer, my longing, to be made one with Thee. . . . Ah, my Lord God, when shall I be quite one with Thee, drawn in to Thee, myself utterly forgotten, Thou in me, I in Thee? Grant us to stay thus —one."[6]

---

[1] 191.   [2] A. J. Wensinck, *Semitische Mystiek* (*De Gids*, 83, 1919), 289 *f*.
[3] *cf.* E. Lehmann, *Mystik in Heidentum und Christentum*[2], 1923. Grete Lüers, *Die Sprache der deutschen Mystik des Mittelalters im Werke der Mechtild von Magdeburg*, 1926, 181.
[4] Lüers, *ibid.*, 182 (*Das Buch von geistlicher Armut*).
[5] Silesius, *Cherubinischer Wandersmann*, III, 17.   [6] IV, 13, 1.

CHAPTER 72

KNOWLEDGE OF GOD

1. POWER always requires knowledge; this has already been evident in our discussion of the close relationship between the ideas of Power and of capacity.[1] Whoever desires to exercise power must know something about both the sources of his potency and the object to be controlled; and although knowledge is not identical with ability, yet nevertheless capacity is always intimately linked with knowledge. Acquaintance with those formulas that induce power, therefore, becomes highly esteemed, and the knowledge of any tradition, preserved by elders or priests, determines the powerfulness of the community. At all times then, even under most primitive conditions, knowledge plays some part in religion.

If however there is to be any *knowledge of God*, not only must ability imply some degree of knowledge, but knowledge must *ipso facto* involve ability. Knowledge is power: to comprehend is to seize. But the validity of this dictum of liberal and optimistic learning, as we are familiar with it particularly in the nineteenth century, has in the present connection an altogether different character. For the knowledge implied here refers neither to the world in the technical sense, nor to the ego in the psychological sense, but solely to salvation: How am I to participate in Power? Whether I wish to assure myself of it, as being superior to it, or whether I kneel before it in fear and trembling, in any case I must know where it is to be found and how it is constituted. And I may also believe that this knowledge is the really essential matter, and that it of itself effects salvation. In that case, I am seeking the path of *the knowledge of God*, or theosophy. So pious Jews recognize the sacred duty of studying *Torah* and *Talmud*; in Warsaw, Jeremias found that among them every trade, bakers, coachmen, cobblers, *etc.*, had its "little room", in which the intervals between work were utilized to study the *Torah*.[2] The way to salvation, then, is study.[3]

To a far greater degree than this, however, we find the knowledge of God in India. For the brahmin, acquaintance with the sacred sacrificial formulas procures world-power.[4] He only, because of his know-

---

[1] Chap. 1.   [2] A. Jeremias, *Jüdische Frömmigkeit*, 1927, 26.
[3] Chap. 64.   [4] *cf.* Oldenberg, *Die Lehre der Upanishaden*, 6 *f.*

ledge, is competent to perform the sacrifice which sustains the world and upon which the gods depend, which indeed actually first of all produced both world and gods. "The dictum that knowledge is power has a completely different meaning from our own, since it implies not what we understand by it—that is the capacity for acting rightly—but rather that, in some mysterious way, it effects an immediate connection between the knower and his knowledge. . . . Here therefore it is not a matter of the intellectual ability to comprehend, but of some mystic equipment for accommodating knowledge and for protection against the hazardous powers dwelling therein."[1] The essential nature of the knowledge of God cannot be better expressed than in these words of Oldenberg; and he indicates a fine example in a *Brahmana Text*: "It (the sun) never actually sets." This, according to our views, is knowledge of a fact. But the *Text* continues: "Whoso knows this never sets, but attains to community with (the sun) and similarity thereto, and to life in its world."[2]

2. Magical knowledge, in the next place, becomes "transposed" *mystically*; and again we find this mystical transposition primarily in India. The realization that world and self are ultimately one[3] effects salvation; and the whole of Buddhism reposes on insight into the essence of the Universe and of man. Knowledge of the "four noble truths" brings with it the salvation of the cessation of births: "In me", says Buddha, "arose the knowledge and the conviction: the liberation of my spirit is assured; this is my last birth, and now for me there is no being reborn."[4] Certainly this insight is not "theoretical" in our sense; it is still magical-mystical, since it does not simply render man capable of attaining salvation, but actually imparts it; and the amalgamation of Hindu knowledge of God with the rationalist scientific consciousness of to-day was reserved for modern theosophy.

Knowledge of God, still further, is wholly mystical whenever it refers to the apprehension of the mystery of union with God. This also, of course, holds true of Hindu speculation, and in this respect Brahminic knowledge of God, as well as Buddhist, is absolutely mystical; and no less so was Hellenistic *gnosis*. "I proclaim the mystery of the sacred path: I call it knowledge", says the *Naassene Hymn*.[5] And it effects salvation through deification: "The high destiny of those who

---

[1] cf. Oldenberg, *Die Lehre der Upanishaden*, 6 f.   [2] *ibid.*, Note 1.
[3] Chap. 2.   [4] Bertholet, *Lesebuch*, 11, 40.
[5] Bertholet, *ibid.*, 5, 57.

have gained knowledge is to become divine".[1] This is very finely expressed in a gnostic thanksgiving prayer: "We thank Thee, Most High! for by Thy grace we received this light of knowledge, Thou unnameable, Whom we invoke as God and praise as Father, because Thou showest to each and all of us fatherly affection, benevolence and blessing power, favouring us with thought, reason and knowledge, that we may rejoice in knowing Thee. . . . We perceived Thee, the light apprehensible by thought alone: we have known Thee, life of human life: we apprehended Thee, the womb of all, imparting life in maternal generation; we knew Thee, the eternally enduring bestower of life. Worshipping Thee thus, we ask nothing of Thy goodness but that Thou mayest preserve us in Thy knowledge and that Thou mayest vouchsafe to let us never lose the life we have thus won."[2] Here too, then, knowledge bestows power, unites man with God and procures for him some portion of divinity. Again, it was no presumptive rationalism nor intellectualism to which the Christian church objected in Gnosticism, and which inspired the warning in *Timothy*: "avoid the profane jargon and arguments of what is falsely called gnosis".[3] Far more does this rejection, on the part of Christianity, apply to that essentially magical feature in all knowledge of God that *my* knowledge effects salvation and ultimately, indeed, creates God. In this sense therefore we understand the warning: "Knowledge puffs up, love builds up. Whoever imagines he has attained to some degree of knowledge, does not possess the true knowledge yet; but if anyone loves God, he is known by Him."[4] Thus love, and in fact the love of God, is placed at the very foundation of "true knowledge": nothing at all is permanent except what is erected on this basis.[5] And knowing itself reposes on a being-known.

3. Mysticism[6] attempted to remove the magical element from the knowledge of God by the fusion of subject and object: God then becomes apprehended by the God in man: or in Goethe's words, "were not the eye itself a sun, no sun for it could ever shine"; (this will be considered at a later stage).[7] To what has already been said there need be added only that the knowledge of God, although assigned its proper limits, is of course not absent from Christianity, and this indeed precisely as participation in God. St. John's *Gospel* is thoroughly imbued with the importance and the excellence of knowledge; but here

[1] Bertholet, *Lesebuch*, 74.   [2] *ibid.*, 5, 85.
[3] 1 *Tim.* vi. 20.   [4] 1 *Cor.* viii. 1 *f*. (Moffat).
[5] *cf.* 1 *Cor.* xiii. 8 *f*.   [6] Chap. 75.   [7] *cf.* p. 494.

"to know" is neither a matter of theory—in the modern sense—nor—in the primitive manner—an affair of the will to power. It is an imparted life. "And this is life eternal, that they might know thee the only true God, and Jesus Christ, whom thou hast sent."[1] But for St. Paul the apostle "knowing in part" is transformed into: "then shall I know even as also I am known"; and this will at some time render love possible.[2]

[1] *John* xvii. 3.   [2] 1 *Cor.* xiii. 12; *cf.* R. Bultmann, *RGG.* "Paulus".

CHAPTER 73

THE FOLLOWING OF GOD

1. IF Power possesses a form, and if it moves in some direction comprehensible by man, then he can *follow* it. This following, however, is not the non-obligatory and arbitrary attitude such as is often referred to (for example) in Protestant circles, when "merely following Jesus" is censured, as this is advocated by the modernist group. "To follow" always implies the union of the follower's life with that of him he follows: if I follow after someone I resolve to share his life, to make his fortunes, his victory and defeat, his gain and loss my own: to join my life to his and to allow my own powerfulness to be merged in his. Even when I decide to observe the instructions of the policeman, for instance, to "follow" the tram lines, I surrender to a specific powerfulness: that is to the direction, the ultimate goal, the turnings *etc.* of the route. But then I must be able to *see* how the line runs; it must have shown me an intelligible direction and this, again, in some fixed and permanent form. I cannot "follow" an airship because it immediately disappears from sight; I must have some support, some visible road.

There is therefore nothing remarkable in our encountering "following", or imitation, in connection with the mystery ideas about human life being concealed within the life of the saviour.[1] There was indeed in ancient Egypt a reference to the king "doing what Osiris does", and leading a life imitating or "following" the god; there too the basic idea of sacred drama was always "to repeat the life, death and resurrection of the god in dramatic form".[2] Not only was worship itself such a "repetition", but also the life of him who took part therein; we have already observed how the participant in the Osiris mysteries took the side of the god and fought for him,[3] and we know also that the essence of the Hellenistic mysteries consisted in the members "taking part" in the life and death of the saviour-god. The power of mystery consecration, in fact, lay in the initiate assimilating his own life wholly to

---

[1] Chap. 12. [2] Junker, *Stundenwachen*, 2.

[3] Chap. 66. Do the primeval *šmsw Ḥr*, the "followers of Horus", owe their names to this type of "Imitation"? The determination of the expression by the ship in the oldest period seems to indicate a connection with the (mock) water combats; *cf.* Flinders Petrie, *The Royal Tombs of the First Dynasty*, I, 16, 22; II, 8, 5; 12, 1. Sethe, *Beiträge*, 67 *f.*

that of the god, as may be seen from one of the best known exhortations, probably taken from Attis worship: "Be of good cheer, ye initiates, for the god has been saved; and you also shall be saved after toil":

$$\theta\alpha\rho\rho\epsilon\hat{\iota}\tau\epsilon \ \mu\acute{\upsilon}\sigma\tau\alpha\iota \ \tauο\hat{\upsilon} \ \theta\epsilon ο\hat{\upsilon} \ \sigma\epsilon\sigma\omega\sigma\mu\acute{\epsilon}\nu ου.$$
$$\overset{}{\epsilon}\sigma\tau\alpha\iota \ \gamma\grave{\alpha}\rho \ \acute{\eta}\mu\hat{\iota}\nu \ \grave{\epsilon}\kappa \ \pi\acute{ο}\nu\omega\nu \ \sigma\omega\tau\eta\rho\acute{\iota}\alpha.^1$$

In just the same way, St. Paul also preached following after Christ in the sense of practice of worship: "We believe that as we have died with Christ we shall also live with him."[2] And still more clearly in relation to baptism: "Our baptism into his death made us share his burial, so that, as Christ was raised from the dead by the glory of the Father, we too might live and move in the new sphere of Life. For if we have grown into him by a death like his, we shall grow into him by a resurrection like his, knowing as we do that our old self has been crucified with him in order to crush the sinful body and free us from any further slavery to sin."[3] Alike in the New Testament and in the Hellenistic mysteries of Isis and Mithra this following is occasionally conceived as military service, and as a sacred *militia*, fidelity to the god being compared to the soldier's loyalty;[4] in the service of Mithra, indeed, this idea found very fine expression in the refusal of the crown. The initiate who claims the rank of *miles* was presented with a crown as the symbol of victorious power; but he had to refuse it, saying that Mithra was his only crown. Later he had again to decline it, even when offered to him as a military honour, since it rightfully belonged only to his god, *invictus*.[5]

2. Following appears not only in worship, however, but in religious custom also, where the outstanding example is the Persian type. There the commandment of life is man's own participation in the great contest which Ahura Mazda has to sustain against the evil Power. This partaking, still further, is wholly practical: it is deed, virtue, and may be realized even in tilling the soil. For agriculture was regarded as a struggle against the malicious Power: cultivated land belonged to Ahura Mazda, desert country to the demons;[6] in the labour of civilization, therefore, man participates in the combat of the god, and thus

[1] Firmicus Maternus, *De errore prof. rel.* 22.   [2] *Rom.* vi. 8 (Moffat).
[3] *Rom.* vi. 4 ff. (Moffat).   [4] Reitzenstein, *Hell. Mysterienreligionen*[3], 192 ff.
[5] F. Cumont, *Die Mysterien des Mithra* (Gehrich)[3], 1923, 143 f.
[6] Chap. 57. Lommel, *Religion Zarathustras*, 250.

culture, morality and worship (*yaz*) find their unity in following the fighting god. "He who cultivates the grain crop cultivates the law, he promotes in the most advantageous way the religion of the Mazda worshippers . . . when there is grain the *devs* sweat (with dread)."[1] Among the Greeks, on the other hand, the idea of imitation in custom was quite rare; we find it however in Pythagoras, who demanded as the condition of deliverance a "Pythagorean life" which he described as a "following of the god".[2]

3. Mysticism, again, transfers imitation and following wholly into the realm of the inward, even when some external means are utilized such as the cross with the nails or meditation on the stations of the cross. The suffering and death of Christ must then be repeated within the soul of the faithful: like Christ, the mystic commences with mere humanity, in order by pain and death to rise to divinity. Mysticism of course found its starting-point in the New Testament itself: with Christ it desired to be crucified and raised again. In this, however, it not only proceeds to the complete effacement of all limits without exception, but it also regards following more as a salvation to be attained, to be won by asceticism, than as being imparted. Union with God, still further, is expressed even physically: we may recall the stigmata of St. Francis and of many other saints, while the self-sufficiency of following is manifested, according to the great schema of Dionysius the Areopagite, by the self-alienation of God (in the Incarnation) being regarded as a realization of man. The single foundational act is thus accomplished in two phases, "one of which ascends to the Trinity and the other descends to humanity";[3] and so God's act has a human, together with a divine, aspect. The existence of Christ thus becomes a paradigm of divine-human unity: in His ascension Christ has "shown all mysticism the path to the ultimate goal".[4]

4. For Christianity, however, imitation or following is practical in worship and custom; it is mystical also, and yet at the same moment something quite different, since it signifies that very self-renunciation which is the essential feature of the figure of Jesus; the path He indicates is precisely that of impotence, and at no time whatever that of the grasping of power: "Treat one another with the same spirit as you

---

[1] Bertholet, *op. cit.*, I, 37.
[2] G. van der Leeuw, *Goden en Menschen in Hellas*, 157.
[3] Thus *e.g.* Görres, *Christliche Mystik*, I, 168 *ff*.　　　[4] *ibid.*, 172.

experience in Christ Jesus. Though he was divine by nature, he did not snatch at equality with God but emptied himself by taking the nature of a servant; born in human guise and appearing in human form, he humbly stooped in his obedience even to die, and to die upon the cross."[1] Here then it is not divinity that is the stake, the goal, of following God, but obedience: not power but impotence: participation in God is not a triumph but a cross: "If anyone wishes to follow me, let him deny himself, take up his cross, and so follow me."[2] The single ground-colour then breaks out, in the history of the church, into an entire colour spectrum: the martyr is the follower of Christ in sacrificing his life—the monk by overcoming the world—the humble, because they have taken Christ's *humilitas*—the voluntarily poor, because they have accepted His poverty—the virtuous, because they have taken His obedience as an example. But in whatever way it is particularized, such imitation always remains a community of life which never elevates itself to God as its own example, but on the contrary humbles itself as did God Himself in Christ. So it is expressed in Zinzendorf's hymn, in which the way is indicated:

> Jesus, still lead on,
> Till our rest be won;
> And, although the way be cheerless,
> We will follow, calm and fearless;
> Guide us by Thy hand
> To our fatherland.

But this is to be found also in the New Testament, which shows the road not to him who would storm heaven, but to the little child: "Be ye therefore *followers* of God, as dear *children*; and walk in *love*, as Christ also hath loved us, and *hath given himself* for us an offering and a sacrifice to God for a sweet-smelling savour."[3]

[1] *Phil.* ii, 5 *ff.* (Moffat).   [2] *Mark* viii, 34 (Moffat).   [3] *Eph.* v, 1, 2.

CHAPTER 74

BEING FILLED WITH GOD

1. IN discussing Shamanism,[1] rapture was found to be one method of enhancing life's powerfulness. Somewhat crudely, it is true, this may be described as a radical evacuant, undertaken, however, with the intention of a no less thorough replenishing. In order to participate in higher and more potent life man attempts to suppress consciousness completely, whether by drugs of various kinds, by exercise and asceticism, or finally under the urge of his own psychical constitution or, again, some mental derangement.

Whether or not this inspiration is ascribed to demonic possession it is in any case an affair of decreasing one's own, and increasing a foreign, numinous and demonic life; the ancient Israelite judges, for example, led their people to victory because the spirit of Jahveh had come upon them.[2] This exaltation, this fullness of God, confers mighty power: we need think only of how Samson slew a thousand with the jawbone of an ass.[3] Similarly the old Germanic *berserkr*, who became beside themselves in battle, hacked their enemies to pieces in frantic exaltation and then, feeble and quite exhausted, once again became normal. The *Egils Saga* expresses this characteristically: "In their deeds they became so strong that nothing could resist them. But when their rage ceased they were weaker than usual."[4] It appears then that the emptying produces not mere power but a veritable power to attack: the man beside himself attacks others: he feels the urge to manifest his power destructively. This is true even when the struggle is carried on with spiritual weapons: Fox describes his appearance at the Court of King's Bench in London in a particularly impressive way:—"I was moved to look round, and turning to the people said 'Peace be among you'; and the power of the Lord sprang over the court."[5]

In ecstasy, therefore, there is an element of violence, equally in the

---

[1] Chap. 26.

[2] Schwally, *Semitische Kriegsaltertümer*, I, 100. *Judges* iii. 10; vi. 34; xi. 29. 1 *Sam.* xi. 6 *ff.* [3] Schwally, *ibid.*, 101.

[4] *Die Geschichte von Skalden Egil* (Niedner), 1914, 84; *cf.* also the psychosis of *amok* and *latah*, peculiar to the Malays; F. H. G. van Loon, *Revue Anthrop.* 37, 1927, 109 *ff.* [5] *Journal* (Parker), 313.

emptying and in being filled with God. To be beside oneself confers extraordinary powerfulness: even Nature becomes dominated by this frenzy: "Bacchic maidens draw milk and honey from the rivers when they are under the influence of Dionysus, but not when they are in their right mind."[1] It is as though, in rapture, closed doors are opened and all hindrances disappear, particularly those of the body: lightly and freely the ecstatics soar away. The transport due to chloroform, for instance, is described thus: "Simultaneously with the loss of taste and hearing, the body had completely lost its sense of orientation. It seemed as though it were nowhere at all, but were simply hovering in space."[2] The power thus acquired may involve either calm and serene happiness, destructive rage, mystic illumination, extraordinary energy, or productive capacity and intelligence. I should not, however, derive this wholly from loss of power on the side of the body, together with reinforcement on the side of the soul, as (among others) Leuba has suggested;[3] of course it may involve this also, and certainly ecstatic experience has played its own part in psychological theory. But here we are concerned with something more:—the enfeebling of life in general; all the senses are weakened, but at the same moment normal consciousness also. On the other hand, the newly acquired and foreign powerfulness affects both body and soul alike; the body is not lost merely in order to sustain the soul: both alike are lost, and a new body and a new soul gained.[4] We do not walk, but soar: nor do we think, but revelation comes to us; and as has already been observed, there is a harmonious, and a discordant, state of being beside oneself, pure happiness and also delirium; but the foundational experience is always the shrinking of one's own power and the becoming filled from without. Hence, too, the feeling of the expansion of life, of the collapse of all limitations, so that it seems as though the whole world were moving within oneself.[5]

As means of procuring ecstasy alcohol, opium, hasheesh, tobacco and other poisons have played a great part; while wine is the drink of the gods too, enhancing life. It addresses man:

---

[1] Plato, *Ion*, 534 (Jowett).

[2] J. H. Leuba, *Extase mystique et Révélation* (*Mercure de France*, 36, vol. 172, 1925), 673; for what follows, *cf.* Achelis, *Ekstase*.

[3] Chap. 42 *ff.*

[4] Were ecstasy dependent on the dualism between body and soul it would never occur among primitive peoples. Klages expresses the same opinion in *Vom Kosmogonischen Eros*[2], 1926, 63 *ff.*, although in other respects his assertions are very sweeping.

[5] Baudelaire, *Les paradis artificiels; cf.* Jaspers, *Allg. Psychopathologie*, 75.

En toi je tomberai, végétale ambroisie,
Grain précieux jeté par l'éternel Semeur,
Pour que de notre amour naisse la poésie
Qui jaillira vers Dieu comme une rare fleur![1]

The ancient Hindu *soma* was a drink of this kind which found its way into myth;[2] it conferred divine power: "Now we have drunk *soma*, we have become immortals, we have attained to the light, we have found the gods."[3] Here all the factors occur together: rapture elevates to divine existence, to immortality, but it also facilitates inner illumination. It is well known how, in mysticism, above all in its Mohammedan form, rapture became the stimulus, and the symbol also, of the fullness of God:

Knowest thou the cup-bearer who gives drink to spirits?
Knowest thou the beverage which the cup-bearer pours forth?
The cup-bearer is the beloved, who pours out for thee annihilation,
The drink is fire, wherein thou drinkest illumination.
Drink the draught of ecstasy, burn in the glow of love!
Gladly the droplet seeks extinction in its mighty flood.
The whole Universe is a wine lodge: every thing a goblet;
It is our friend who holds the chalice, and we are the drinkers.
Even wisdom is drunken and completely sunk in rapture.
Heaven and earth are drunken: every angel is drunken.[4]

And still more clearly: "In the drunken, my friends, you can see plainly that there is a link with God, where there is no being of one's own."[5]

In the case of the *sufis* it is usually not quite clear whether wine is still actually taken, or whether this has already become symbolical, but in any case the ecstasy is very real; it can also be attained by practice, asceticism, exercise, methodical meditation *etc*. In all this, too, dance and music exercise their functions equally with concentration and the greatest possible degree of immobility: there are ecstatic maenads as

---

[1] Within thee I shall plunge, ambrosial plant,
   Most precious grain cast by th' eternal Sower,
   So from our love shall poesy be born,
   As a rare flower that rises up to God.
                              Baudelaire, *L'âme du vin.*

[2] Chap. 52.   [3] Bertholet, *op. cit.*, 9, 57.

[4] Lehmann-Haas, *Textbuch*, 376; Mahmud's *Gulshan I Raz.*

[5] F. H. G. Tholuck, *Blütensammlung aus der morgenländischen Mystik*, 1825, 219; *cf.* also *Gulshan I Raz.*

well as ecstatic *yogis*. Mental derangement also, either individual or epidemic, may entail the emptying of the self. No precise diagnosis is possible here, and depersonalization, the collapse of the limits separating the individual from the external world, the rapturous state, *etc.*, occur in several forms of mental disorder.[1] We are concerned, however, not with the causes of the ecstatic condition, but with the fact that it affords us a very characteristic understanding of man in his relationship to Power.

2. Fullness of God, "the state of being filled with God", is not of course "enthusiasm" in the modern sense of the word, not even when this is so acutely elaborated as it has been, for example, by Jaspers.[2] The term must rather be understood in its original significance, derived from Dionysiac mysticism. This experience is distinguished from mere rapture and psychosis, since the ecstasy, the being beside oneself, is at the same moment connected with fulfilment; and the fulfilling element is Power, God. The enthusiast then, in the full sense of this word, knows that he is being swept away by some overruling power which lifts him completely out of himself and fills him with new insight, new strength, new life. We are familiar with the marvellous apologia for frenzy in Plato's *Phaedrus*:[3] "madness" is an excellent state, "the special gift of heaven", without which neither ecstatic mantic can be attained, nor dedication nor expiation, bringing release to the sick and the insane; nor is poetry possible in the absence of frenzy, since "he who, having no touch of the Muses' madness in his soul, comes to the door and thinks that he will get into the temple by the help of art— he, I say, and his poetry are not admitted"; "and his sane poetry is completely effaced by that of the mad poets". But more than any other, it is he who possesses the memory of the divine that he once saw who may speak about this frenzy; "as he forgets earthly interests and is rapt in the divine, the vulgar deem him mad, and rebuke him"; "for the many are not aware that he is full of God" (*enthousiazon*)[4]. This "madness" is the love of divine beauty, while for Plato it is the rapt

---

[1] It would be altogether too simple to connect ecstasy with manic-depressive derangement, or with the cyclic type of psychosis, although the conduct of the maenads, for example, at first abandoned and then apathetically silent, would accord with this. But hysteria, epilepsy, *etc.*, also exhibit ecstatic features, and identification with the environment is characteristic of the schizophrene or schizoid type; *cf.* Storch, *Archaisch-primitives Erleben*. Jaspers, *Psychologie der Weltanschauungen*, 1922, 137.

[2] *ibid.*, 117 *ff.*   [3] *Ion* 534 must also be considered.

[4] *Phaedrus*, 245, 249 (Jowett).

love of wisdom, *philosophia*.[1] But Platonic philosophy, as is well known, is no mere theory about life but rather life itself as, impelled by Eros, it rises to the gods. The idea therefore remains exactly the same as in Dionysiac mysticism: "The ekstasis, the temporary *alienatio mentis* of the Dionysiac cult was not thought of as a vain purposeless wandering in a region of pure delusion, but as a *hieromania*, a sacred madness in which the soul, leaving the body, winged its way to union with the god. It is now with and in the god, in the condition of *enthousiasmos*; those who are possessed by this are ἔνθεοι; they live and have their being in the god. . . . The ἔνθεος is completely in the power of the god; the god speaks and acts through him. The ἔνθεος has lost his consciousness of himself."[2] The person in the grip of ecstasy is himself a god, a βάκχος or a βάκχη. Hence there are but few of these: "For 'many', as they say in the mysteries, 'are the thyrsus-bearers, but few are the bacchoi'."[3]

3. Thus ecstasy is the condition of mysticism and being filled with God its goal.[4] Here too it may appear with a greater or less degree of turbulence; but the violent element is always retained, "for with a violence it is done, and as it were against nature", as Richard Rolle asserts.[5] Connected with this trait of violence, too, is the recoil that the ecstatic mystic experiences as soon as his transport ceases: a short time ago he was filled with God, and now it seems as though God has forsaken him again. It is like a bitter taste in his mouth, and he feels himself twice as impotent and abandoned as before.

> O dreadful is the check—intense the agony—
> When the ear begins to hear, and the eye begins to see;
> When the pulse begins to throb—the brain to think again—
> The soul to feel the flesh, and the flesh to feel the chain.[6]

In conclusion, I cite a Hindu and a modern example of emptying and filling. The Hindu poet Manikka Vachakar, in the first place, thus

---

[1] *Symposium*, 218; "madness and passion in your longing after wisdom" (Jowett).

[2] Rohde, *Psyche*, II, 19 f. with Note. E. T. 259, 275. He also cites Proclus: ἑαυτῶν ἐκστάντας ὅλους ἐνιδρῦσθαι τοῖς θεοῖς καὶ ἐνθεάζειν.

[3] *Phaedo*, 69.   [4] Chap. 75.

[5] In *Mysticism*, 440 (Underhill). The distinction drawn by Rolle between ecstasy (*raptus*, "ravishing"), as being "ravished out of fleshly feeling", and the "lifting of mind into God by contemplation", again shows that ecstasy essentially affects the whole man; *ibid*.

[6] Emily Brontë, *The Prisoner*. We may compare Tholuck's prosaic observation (*Blütenlese*, 115 f.), referring to a beautiful description of ecstasy by Jalaluddin Rumi: "intoxication remains intoxication, and after each debauch there follows a headache".

describes ecstasy: "I can neither comprehend it nor utter it. Miserable me, ah! how can I bear it. I do not understand what He has done to me. I do not know what Thou has given Thy slave; I taste it and am not satisfied: I drink it and do not retain it. As surging waves swell on the milk-white sea, so has He moved deep waters in my soul. Indescribable ambrosia penetrated my every pore: this is His gracious work! In each limb of my miserable body He filled me with honied sweetness. At His command ambrosial showers miraculously drenched my being. With loving soul He fashioned for me a form bestowing grace, as though He were making me like to Himself: and as an elephant seeks through a field of sugar cane, so sought He me and found me and brought me to life. He poured the pure honey of mercy into me, and in His grace gave me heavenly food—He whose nature not even Brahma knows."[1]

Similarly, Stefan George:

> White and soft as whey, the Earth is shaking—
> I mount above frightful chasms:
> I feel that I am swimming beyond the topmost clouds
> In a sea of crystal splendour—
> I am just a spark from the sacred Fire,
> I am but a murmur of the sacred Voice.[2]

---

[1] Lehmann-Haas, *Textbuch*, 148.   [2] *Der siebente Ring, Entrückung*.

CHAPTER 75

MYSTICISM

1. IN mysticism man, desiring to becoming dominant and to exercise power, breaks down the barriers alike of the self and of the external world. He ceases to experience anything whatever as objective, and likewise to be influenced or determined by anything as an object; both object and subject blend in formless and contentless fusion. Ecstasy, as we have just seen, induced the emptying of the self and the possibility of its being filled with some "Other". In mysticism, also, an evacuating has its place, but equally of object as of subject. Ecstasy, therefore, is certainly inherent in every mystical experience; but mysticism always goes still further than ecstasy, beyond all frontiers, beyond even the primeval relationship in which man himself subsists; to use the expression coined by Jaspers: in mysticism the schism between subject and object is in principle abolished. Man refuses not only to accept the given, but he also opposes care, strangeness and foreignness, and every possibility; he needs no rites whatever, no customs, no forms: he does not speak, he no longer bestows names and no longer wishes to be called by a name: he desires only "to be silent before the Nameless".[1]

Thus it is in "extreme" mysticism. Most mystics, however, either remain half-way, or return thence. Nevertheless in all mysticism, and essentially, the division between subject and object is suppressed, since its very essence lies in the yearning for this abrogation. And in this respect, too, the mystic differs from primitive man who also, like himself, restricts the whole world within the realm of the internal as in "magical" experience.[2] The mystic, however, not only transforms the entire external into the internal, but equally all that is internal into the external: only the completely void, the desert, remains:

> Where is my biding-place? Where there's nor I nor Thou.
> Where is my final goal towards which I needs must press?
> Where there is nothing. Whither shall I journey now?
> Still farther on than God—into a wilderness.[3]

---

[1] Mehlis, *Die Mystik in der Fülle ihrer Erscheinungsformen*, 13. Jaspers, *op. cit.*, 84 *ff.* Hofmann, *Rel. Erlebnis*, 45; *cf.* Jaspers, *Allg. Psychopath.* 262: "that primeval phenomenon—personality transcending itself".

[2] Chap. 82. On the distinction between magic and mysticism *cf.* Kraemer, *Javaansche Primbon*, 110 *ff.* Contrast Underhill, *Mysticism*, 85.

[3] Angelus Silesius, *The Cherubinic Wanderer*, I, 7.

2. Mysticism, again, is international and interconfessional; in this too it knows no limits. But in Neo-Platonic mysticism it has acquired a typical form that has shown itself most clearly, on the one hand in *Sufism*, and on the other in the Christian and partly ecclesiastical mysticism which began with Dionysius the Areopagite.[1] In these, too, it has developed a specific theory of knowledge which, derived originally from a sentence of Plato,[2] was given its classical expression by Plotinus and received from Goethe its most beautiful form:

> Were not the eye itself a sun,
> No sun for it could ever shine:
> By nothing godlike could the heart be won,
> Were not the heart itself divine.[3]

Sufism speaks exactly the same language: "He who discourses of eternity must have within him the lamp of eternity. . . . The light of intuitive certainty by which the heart sees God is a beam of God's own light cast therein by himself; else no vision of Him were possible", says Bayazid Bastami.[4] God is known by God. In the Thomist system, again, in which man knows by means of "likeness" (*similitudines*), the *lumen gratiae* must render the image of God visible; according to St. Thomas this is a created light, but for the genuine mystic Tauler it is uncreated. The conclusion, at which the scholastic halted, is then drawn that in man God loves and knows as both subject and object; but for St. Thomas, too, in the contemplation of God the divine essence was both that which is seen and that by which one sees (*et quod videtur et quo videtur*).[5]

The mysticism of the church is a restrained mysticism, that of Tauler unrestrained: St. Thomas desires to behold God through God, Tauler to enjoy Him, to make Him useful as it were (*visio essentiae Dei*, as contrasted with *fruitio Dei*).[6] St. Thomas halts at the divine barrier: Tauler breaks it down simultaneously with his own. Only the God Who is within knows the God Who remains without. Or better: where God becomes known, both without and within, here and there alike, are abolished. In the act of knowledge God and the self cannot be distinguished. "Cognition presupposes similarity between knower and known and produces equality."[7]

Here also, then, knowledge is powerfulness. Mysticism is nearer to

[1] On his reception by the Roman Catholic Church *cf.* A. Merx, *Idee und Grundlinien einer allgem. Geschichte der Mystik*, 1893, 24; *cf.* further H. Dörries, *Erigena und der Neuplatonismus*, 1925.   [2] *Republic*, VI, 508b.
[3] Dwight's translation.   [4] R. A. Nicholson, *The Mystics of Islam*, 51, 50.
[5] G. Siedel, *Die Mystik Taulers*, 1911, 22 f.   [6] *ibid.*, 20 f.
[7] Eckhart, in Lasson, *Meister Eckhart der Mystiker*, 96.

omnipotence than is magic, but of this truth it makes no use; its knowledge is a divine act, but in a "modeless mode", since the self which is to
harbour God must make room for Him. Here therefore "emptying"
assumes a specific and mystic form which, with ancient German
mysticism, we may call "deprivation of being" (*das Entwerden*).

3. Nothing is more characteristic of mysticism than the description
of the *path* which man must traverse in order to attain his goal. This
road is divided into *stages, stadia*; their designations are widely different,
but the fact remains unaltered.[1] There may be seven steps which, as in
Sufism, must be ascended: repentance, abstinence, renunciation,
poverty, patience, trust in God and satisfaction. There may be four,
like the Buddhist *jhanas*; or six, as with de la Badie: *touchement divin,
illumination, élévation, union divine, quiétude, sommeil*;[2] but it is always
the toilsome way from fullness of life to the sublime void of non-Being,
of dying in God. This mystic path might certainly be called asceticism,[3]
not however in the sense hitherto employed, but with its literal meaning
of "exercise"; and among its adepts mysticism counts Hindu *yogis*, who
have attained almost to immateriality, as well as emaciated Christian
saints, Persian epicureans and Dionysiac orgiasts. But all these *practise*,
and practise repeatedly, the loss of the self, either in self-indulgence or
in fasting; here there opens out the path of the deprivation of being,
the Neo-Platonic ἅπλωσις, *annihilatio*.[4] Fasting, rapture, control of

---

[1] *cf.* Field, *Mystics and Saints of Islam*, 124 *ff.*; Fr. Heiler, *Die buddhistische Versenkung*[2], 1922.

[2] H. Heppe, *Geschichte des Pietismus und der Mystik in der reformierten Kirche*,
1879, 294 *f.* Javanese mysticism distinguishes four stages, which it characteristically
designates by images borrowed from the indigenous drama: I. *scharé' at-Wajang*-play
(the creature puppets act only through the creator—*dalang*-puppet player); II. *tarékat-
Barongan*-play (unity between the actors and their leader, but concealed; for this
reason the players wear animal costumes); III. *hakékat-Topéng*-play (unity between
the actors and their leader, hidden merely by an animal mask); IV. *ma' ripat-Ronggèng*-
play, the dance girl (henceforth there is only *one* actor; the *ronggèng* appears unmasked;
complete unity between creator and created). Schuurman, *Myst. u. Glaube*, 22.

[3] Chap. 66.

[4] Heiler, *ibid.*, 10; *cf.* Mme Guyon:

> Ah! How happy is his fate
> Who has a self no more!
> How wretched is the soul
> When it lives ever within itself! . . .
>
> By ever dying to oneself
> No longer know we our own will:
> And then the Will of the Supreme
> In truth becomes our own.
>   (Segond, *Prière*, 107.)

breathing, contemplation, meditation, prayer—all these and yet more have only the one purpose, to induce unconsciousness, to reduce the self to nothingness. In the language of scholastic mysticism this is expressed by saying that the "images", which are the media of ordinary knowledge, must here yield ground: *Fili mi, tempus est, ut praeter-mittantur simulacra nostra*:—"My son, it is time to leave our images behind", says the youth in Dante's dream.[1] Here imagination fails and form disappears.

> Would ye know how I came forth from *images*?
> When I perceived the unity within me.
> That is true unity
> When nothing startles us, neither love nor sorrow:
> I *ceased to be*.

> Would ye know how I came forth from Spirit?
> When in myself I perceived nought whatever,
> Nought but *sheer unplumbed Deity*;
> Then no longer could I keep silence: I must proclaim it:
> I *ceased to be*.

> Since thus I have been lost in the *abyss*
> I would fain speak no more: I am dumb:
> Thus hath Deity
> Manifestly absorbed me in Itself . . .
> I have been *annihilated*.[2]

Or, again, in these lines from Strassburg:

> Whoso would love
> The Good that hath no ground,
> Must rise above the senses;
> Thus a splendid courage is gained.

> *Oh modeless mode!*
> Thou art so truly fine.
> Thou soarest o'er the senses,
> There is thy proper place.[3]

[1] *La Vita Nova.*
[2] In Merx, *Idee und Grundlinien*, 12 *f.* Here and in what follows the typically mystical expressions are in italics.
[3] In H. A. Grimm, *Von Gottes- und Liebfrauenminne*, 40.

Similarly in Konrad Immendorfer's *Hymn to the Trinity*:

> Around Him circles
> What Spirit hath never encompassed.
> There the *path* leads
> Into a strange *waste*,
> Immeasurable, endless,
> Where is *nor Time nor Place;*
> So unique is its Being.
>
> This *desert path*
> No foot hath trod.
> Created thought
> Came never there.
> *It is.—What?* No one knoweth.
> 'Tis here, 'tis there,
> 'Tis far, 'tis near,
> 'Tis deep, 'tis high!
> Yet have I lied:
> For 'tis *nor this nor that.*
>
> Become a child!
> Be deaf! Be blind!
> Let thy heart forget
> All that is!
> What is, what is not—let it be!
> Leave Place! Leave Time!
> Leave *image* far away!
> *Go with no road*
> Along the narrow path.
> So wilt thou find this desert track.[1]

Here both Deity and man alike become a waste, a qualitiless, unnameable Nothingness, the *ground*, of which German mysticism speaks so fluently. In other words, the abrogation of the division between subject and object, the fusion of God and man, are possible only when practice, deprivation of being, *annihilatio*, have reduced both man and God together to the same Nothingness: void meets void. And now, after it has dispensed with all images, mysticism speaks in images of such great beauty and impressiveness that they have never been forgotten.

---

[1] In Will Vesper's *Deutscher Psalter*, 43 *ff.*; *cf.* Siedel, *Tauler*, 99. On the images and the ground in Thomas and Eckhart *cf. ibid.*, 56: "The Deity hath nowhere wherein to secure a proper position except in the ground of annihilation" (Eckhart).

One is the simile of the *butterfly*, seeking the love-death in the flame. From al-Hallaj to Goethe it speaks the same language:[1]

> Tell it the wise alone, for when
> Will the crowd cease from mockery!
> Him would I laud of living men
> Who longs a fiery death to die.[2]

The *raindrop* also, happy in its dying as it strives toward the Ocean:

> The raindrop mourns: Far from the sea am I!
> But Ocean laughs: in vain is all thy grief!
> For we are all One: we all are God—
> Nought parts us but the tiny point of Time.[3]

Similarly:

> Drink the draught of ecstasy, burn in the glow of love!
> Gladly seeks the droplet extinction in its mighty flood.[4]

Again: "As the rivers flow to their rest in the ocean, released from form and name, so the knower, liberated from form and name, passes onward to the divine, supreme Spirit."[5] Or finally, Madame Guyon in her *Torrens spirituels*.

Love too is a metaphor of the mystic path, but always a love that leads to death: however sensuous its content, however richly coloured its portrayal, ultimately it is always a submersion in the beloved, a dissolution, a death:

> Upbraid me not for my love! Always do I offer myself to Death;
> For whenever love was true, Death was the loved one's fate.[6]

For the merging of God in man, of man in God, is possible only when the indescribable unites itself with the indescribable, and nothingness with nothingness. Mysticism therefore turns first of all inward, to seek therein the secret chamber, the *fundus animae*, the "ground of annihilation": for without, the lover has nought to search for. Thus when Madame Guyon complained to a Franciscan monk about her

---

[1] Massignon, *Al Hallaj*, 473. For Saadi *cf.* Tholuck, *Blütenlese*, 247 *ff.*; further, Field, *Mystics and Saints of Islam*, 128 *f.*
[2] *West-Eastern Divan*, 19; "Blessed Yearning" (Dowden).
[3] Omar Khayyám, in Lehmann, *Textbuch*[1], 296.
[4] Mahmud's *Gulshan I Raz*, in Tholuck, *Blütenlese*, 218; *cf.* Field, *op. cit.*, 180.
[5] Oldenberg, *Lehre der Upanishaden*, 147; *Mundaka Upanishad*.
[6] Saadi, in Tholuck, *op. cit.*, 248.

difficulties in prayer, he replied: "That, madame, is because you are
seeking outwardly what you possess within. Accustom yourself to search
for God in your heart, and you will find Him there"; words that wrought
a change in her life.[1] The modern mystic, also, directs us inwards:

> If you seek evil around you,
> If you strive to seize salvation without,
>> You are but pouring into leaky vessels,
> You only strive for what is valueless.
>
> You yourself are all and in all:
> The ecstatic note of prayer
>> Blends into one with all love,
> Calls it God, and Friend, and Bride.[2]

From the Inward the road leads to the Innermost, to the ground,
the *scintilla*, the "spark", the very soul of the soul. And this is no mere
abstraction, not some kind or other of "pure consciousness", but the
only real element in man, his nothingness which is his all. Brahminic
mysticism need coin no new concepts here: it employs the *ātman*, which
is really the ground of the soul rather than the soul itself: "It is the
ātman, which is called: No, No! It is impalpable, for it cannot be
seized: indestructible, since it cannot be destroyed: not clinging, since
it does not cling: unbound: it wavers not, and suffers no harm."[3] The
fundus animae, then, is precisely as inexpressible as is the essential
nature of God, with which it is one. "It is the place lying beyond this
contrast (between subject and object), where God and the soul are one
and the same."[4] The Buddhist mystic too knows that he "advances
completely beyond the place where neither consciousness nor unconsciousness subsists"[5]. Tersteegen's sensitive lines on the Ground may
be cited:

> Why is all so well with the soul
> When it finds its long sought Good
>> So *near its heart?*
> Now has it all, whate'er it will.
> Embraced, beloved, *it lies still*,
>> With its God, *in the ground*.[6]

[1] *Vie de Mme Guyon*, 1791, I, 78.   [2] Stefan George, *Der Siebente Ring*.
[3] Oldenberg, *Lehre*, 63; (*Brihad-Aranyaka Upanishad*).
[4] Fr. Delekat, *Rationalismus und Mystik*, ZTh K. N. F. 4, 1923, 280 *ff*.
[5] Heiler, *op. cit.*, 28; *cf*. Lasson, *op. cit.*, 101 *f*. Underhill, *Mysticism*, 120.
[6] *Geistliche Lieder*, 1897, 17.

In forcible and numinously primitive tones, again, Ruysbroek speaks of "eternal emptiness" and of "wild, *desolate and formless nakedness*":

> Call out, all ye with hearts open:—
> O! vast *abyss*!
> That hast *no orifice*,
> Lead us into thy *depths*,
> And proclaim to us thy love.[1]

And here too, even where it is a matter of the complete absence of image and form, we find an abundance of imagery: the colourless being described in glowing tints and the void as the greatest treasure. As has already been observed, the "ground" is the desert,[2] while the next image is silence. "Someone asked, 'Teach me Brahman, O exalted one!' But he (the wise Bāhva) remained silent. The other besought him a second and a third time. Then he spake: 'I teach it thee indeed, but thou perceivest it not. This *ātman* is silence.' "[3] Tersteegen again:

> By silence are they known
> Whose hearts are God's abode.[4]

Here the "paradox of expression" appears, as Jaspers calls it. For the very essence of mysticism is silence: in the ground mute silence rules. But this silence becomes apparent only in speech, and indeed in excessive and overhasty speech, one image being annulled by another which then, like its predecessor, is outstripped and suppressed. Behind the radiant splendour of the images stands the majestic bareness of the imageless: behind the diversified form of speech the fearful power of silence.[5] The mystic must be silent: but this he cannot be: he must

---

[1] In Huizinga, *Herfstty*, 375 *ff*.
[2] Tersteegen, *e.g. Geistliche Lieder*, 21.

> Into the waste I am enticed,
> Where God and I exist alone,
> And Spirit with spirit communes:
> O! Solitude, so far, so far
> From creature, space and time!
> The best loved stands without.

> *Man lockt mich in die Wüste ein,*
> *Da Gott und ich nur sind allein,.*
> *Da Geist mit Geist umgehet:*
> *O Einsamkeit, so weit, so weit*
> *Von Kreatur und Ort und Zeit!*
> *Das Liebste draussen stehet.*

[3] Oldenberg, *Lehre*, 133.   [4] *Geistliche Lieder*, 23.   [5] Chap. 63.

speak, "jubilate", break forth in "silent music".[1] "What the grace *jubilus* is, that ye shall observe. It is a grace exceedingly great: so great that no one can keep it secret, and yet no one can utter it completely," says the *Kirchberg Monastery Chronicle*.[2] Meister Eckhart, too, tells us that the "secret word" is born "in the Ground . . . there is profound silence, for thereto neither creature nor any kind of image has attained" . . . in this silence "are space and rest for that birth, that God the Father may speak His word there".[3]

Together with silence, sleep is the analogue of the mystical state; thus the *sufi* is like the seven sleepers of the legend,[4] while the quietist describes how her peaceful soul "often falls into mystic sleep, wherein all powers are silent".[5] Wholly devoid of will, man surrenders quite passively just like a tool, some instrument for writing or for music:

> Lutes are we, and Thou the player sounding through them;
> Art Thou not He who groaneth in our groaning?
> Flutes are we; but the breath, O Lord, is thine;
> We are the hills: the echo is still thine.[6]

Rapture, likewise, that renders possible deprivation of being.[7] "I mean by the chalice the wine of Eternity", asserts Hafiz; "and for me the meaning of this wine is the surrender of the self, the suppression of selfhood."[8]

4. But mysticism is most rapturous, and also most loquacious, when the long road ends, when perfect union is attained and the *unio mystica* completed. When the *sufi* mystic Rabi'a was asked how she

---

[1] St. John of the Cross.   [2] In N. von Arseniew, *AR*. 22, 1923–24, 271, 279.
[3] *ibid.*, 269.   [4] Tholuck, *op. cit.*, 62 f.   Field, *op. cit.*, 161.
[5] Mme Guyon, *Moyen court et très facile de faire oraison*, 12, 5.
[6] Jalaluddin Rumi in Tholuck, *op. cit.*, 66; *cf.* 62 f; Oldenberg, *Lehre*, 140 f.
[7] Chap. 74.
[8] In Merx, *Idee und Grundlinien*, 7; *cf.* Omar Khayyám (Lehmann, *Textbuch*[1], 296):

> I drink from no mere pleasure in carousing,
> Nor just to violate the Koran's teaching,
> But for the brief illusion of Non-Being—
> The ground of all the revels of the wise.

Similarly Jalaluddin Rumi: "Men incur the reproach of wine and drugs that they may escape for a while from self-consciousness, since all know this life to be a snare, volitional thought and memory to be a hell." Nicholson, *The Mystics of Islam*, 67.

achieved this union she answered: "By losing in Him all that I had found"; and again asked how she had gained her knowledge of God, she replied: "Oh Hassan, thou knowest in a certain way and manner, but I with no way nor manner."[1] This, once more, is the "modeless mode" of German mysticism, the overflowing of God into man characteristic of French mysticism: two mystics indeed, Madame Guyon and her friend Fénelon, did not *speak* of God at all, but between them "there went on an almost continual flowing of God".[2] "There are only these two truths: the All, and nothingness. Everything else is a lie. We can honour the divine All only by our own annihilation, and immediately we are annihilated God, Who can endure no void without filling it, fills us with Himself";[3] God is thus a sort of fluid which directs itself everywhere where room has been made for it. The *mirror* image is also employed here:

> Only one task the *sufis* have on earth—
> That their hearts may become clear mirrors of God.[4]

Here then negation preponderates, although it certainly remains a metaphorical negation, and must so remain: richness in poverty, a form obliterated again and again, a nullity that is nevertheless repeatedly endowed with form. Or can there be a crasser and more metaphorical description of the unity, which at the same moment more sharply stresses its inadequacy, than the Mohammedan *fana*, "evanescence", a depiction, however, immediately contradicted in the expression *fana al-fana*, the evanescence of even the consciousness of evanescence also?[5] The Buddhist, again, speaks of the "lonely island", of *Nirvana*: "In this state, rapture consists just in there no longer being any feeling in it."[6] Such too is the bliss of the concluding song in *Tristan and Isolda*:

---

[1] In Tholuck, *op. cit.*, 32.
[2] M. Masson, *Fénelon et Mme Guyon*, 1907, XXXVII.
[3] Guyon, *Moyen court*, 20, 4.
[4] Jalaluddin Rumi in Tholuck, *op. cit.*, 115; *cf.* Ghazali in Field, *op. cit.*, 16 f.
[5] The expression is probably of Indian origin, and was first employed in *Sufism* by Bayazid Bastami; *cf.* Nicholson, *op. cit.*, 17 ff., 60 f.; also Schuurman, *Myst. u. Glauben*, 17 f.
[6] Heiler, *Versenkung*, 36 ff.; *cf.* the beautiful lines:

> No standard can measure him who is at rest,
> There are no words wherewith to speak of him;
> All that thought could grasp has passed away,
> And every pathway's closed to human speech.

> Shall I sip them, dive within them,
> To my panting breathing win them,
>   In the breezes around,
>   In the harmony's sound,
> In the world's driving whirlwind be drowned?
>   And sinking,
>   Be drinking,
>   In a kiss
>   Highest bliss.[1]

And even when no other term is admissible except simple negation, and when "nothing" becomes the name for the best and dearest, then too the word has a resonance that promises inexpressible wealth, the "rich nothing" as it was called by the Christian mystic of the seventeenth century, Louvigny.[2]

In this respect, further, that man is God implies that God is man, and conversely. In so far as perfect union is possible only to man "deprived of his being" and emptied, mysticism's claim to divinity need be no presumption whatever. This had already been adduced in vindication of Mansur Hallaj, the fettered mystic, who had to pay for his bliss with the most fearful tortures. He said: *Ana' l-Haqq*, "I am the truth": that is, according to Muslim belief: "I am God". Hallaj himself, however, does not say this, but God by the mouth of the selfless Hallaj.[3] Certainly the prosaic al Junayd was not incorrect when he thus replied to him: "Nay: only through truth dost thou exist! What a gallows wilt thou stain with thy blood";[4] to the consciousness of the mystic himself, however, he is nothing more than "the hand that serves God as an instrument".[5] This effacing of limitations even proceeds so far that he can pray: "Oh my God, Thou knowest that I am powerless to offer Thee the prayer of thanksgiving Thou requirest. Come then, in me Thyself to thank. That is the true thanksgiving prayer! there is no other."[6] The mystics also outstrip and outbid each other just as mystic images do; so Bayazid Bastami asserts with mysterious profundity: "I went from God to God, until they cried out from me in me, 'Oh thou I'."[7]

Union then is submersion, that is to say dying. All the dreadfulness of delight in death lies in the celebrated lines in which al-Hallaj described his relations to God when, dancing in his chains, he was led

---

[1] Corder.   [2] Heppe, *Quietismus*, 90.
[3] Nicholson, *op. cit.*, 152.   [4] Massignon, *Al Hallaj*, 62.
[5] *ibid.*, 260.   [6] *ibid.*, 116.   [7] Nicholson, *op. cit.*, 18.

to the place of judgment;[1] when asked: "Oh master, how camest thou
into this condition?" he replied: "Through the caresses of His beauty
which attracts so intensely those who long for union." Then he recited:

> My host, in order not to seem to offend me,
> Has made me drink from the bowl from which he himself has drunk:
> like the host who honours his guest.
> Then, after the bowl has passed from hand to hand, the scourge
> and the sword are brought forth.
> Thus it befalls him who drinks wine with the dragon in Midsummer.

Here one primeval human experience is manifested in the sublimest
and tenderest mystical stirrings; a yearning for death is united with
the will to power, and forebodes the highest powerfulness in extinction.
The "thirty birds", similarly, whose pilgrimage is described by the
sufi Fariduddin Attar, at the goal find only themselves: *Simurgh* (a term
meaning "thirty birds"). God is a mirror in which everyone views
himself: "So they vanished in Him for ever, as the shadow disappears
in the sun."[2] Thus the ray that Deity emits is a "ray of darkness".[3]
Fear and the voluptuousness of death lie close beside each other: they
become one, indeed, in the fearful bliss of annihilation.

5. Since mysticism is essentially silent, for that very reason it speaks
all languages; it is fundamentally tolerant:

> Pagoda and ka'ba are the place of the pious,
> The music of the bells their melody;
> The Parsee's girdle, church, rosary and cross
> Are all, forsooth, the tokens of the pious.[4]

To mysticism therefore everything individual, distinctive and
historical in religion is ultimately quite indifferent. For the deprivation

---

[1] Massignon, *op. cit.*, 9, 301. The French Text as follows:

Celui qui me convie, pour ne pas paraître me léser,
M'a fait boire à la coupe dont il a bu; comme l'hôte qui traite un convive.
Puis, la coupe passée de mains en mains, Il a fait apporter le cuir du supplice et le
glaive.
Ainsi advient à qui boit le Vin, avec le Lion en plein Été.

cf. Tholuck, *op. cit.*, 322 *ff*. Field, *op. cit.*, 68 *ff*.
[2] Field, *op. cit.*, 131 *ff*. On union *cf.* further Tholuck, *op. cit.*, 64 *f.*, 87 *f.*, 105 (Jalaluddin Rumi). Oldenberg, *Lehre*, 126, 142, 181. Kraemer, *Primbon*, 72 (on the so-called
kawula-gusti of Javanese mysticism, "the truth of Lord and servant", *cf.* also Schuurman, *Mystik und Glauben*, 15).
[3] Dionysius Areopagita in Merx, *Idee und Grundlinien*, 20, 71.
[4] Omar Khayyám, in Merx, *op. cit.*, 26.

of being affects also all images, ideas and thoughts that religion regards
as important; and while mysticism speaks the languages of all religions,
no religion whatever is essential to it. The void remains void, the
nought nought, whether in Germany or India, in Islam or Christianity.
The mystic may be a faithful Muslim or a true son of the Christian
church: at bottom that counts for little. At best the particular symbols,
rites and ideas of the individual religions can assist him on his path
towards annihilation; but in the end they too must pass away like all
else. The true *Ka'ba*, says Jalaluddin Rumi, is a sorrowful and broken
heart;[1] and Bayazid Bastami, who wished to complete the sacred
journey around the *Ka'ba*, discovered a sage who said to him: "Give
me the two hundred pieces of gold thou needest for the journey, and
walk around me seven times"; Bastami did what he had been told to do,
for man is the true *Ka'ba*, the house of God.[2]

Christian mystics, indeed, often pay scant attention to scripture and
sacrament; the saints, and even the Virgin, must rest content with the
disappearance of their figures.[3] For the mystic even the very core
of Christianity, God assuming flesh, may be ultimately merely a symbol
of his own personal history: incarnation becomes *generatio aeterna* in
the hearts of men. And the remarkable feature is that, in this respect,
Mohammedan mystics hold quite similar views to Christians, and even
praise Jesus in passionate terms—of course as the Christ eternally born
in the heart.[4] The saviour can ·be only a messenger; and what does he,
who knows the sender, care for messengers?

> He who lies hidden in the sultan's bosom
> Demands no embassies nor documents.[5]

Celebration can no longer help, now that there is no support. Custom,
too, can no longer avail, when no conduct whatever can make any
difference in the indistinguishable. Thus mysticism has always been
hostile to every code of morality, not however from any immoral
tendency but simply because law and order attempt to bind where

---

[1] Field, *op. cit.*, 151.   [2] *cf.* Chap. 57. Field, *ibid.*, 54.
[3] Mme Guyon: "I could no longer perceive the saints and the Virgin apart from
God, but saw them all in Him, without being able to distinguish them from Him
except with difficulty." Heppe, *Quietismus*, 161. For Eckhart, Lasson, *op. cit.*, 323.
[4] St. Teresa, Molinos; *cf.* Heppe, *Quietismus*, 20. Eckhart, *cf.* Lasson, *op. cit.*, 129 *f.*,
120, 9, 12. Fénelon, Heppe, *ibid.*, 394 *ff.* For a modern parallel, Inge, *Personal Idealism
and Mysticism*. Jalaluddin Rumi, *cf.* Field, *op. cit.*, 159, 161, 211.
[5] Jalaluddin Rumi in Tholuck, *op. cit.*, 167. A remarkable parallel from heathendom:
late Hellenistic mysticism made the Attis myth the type of the history of the soul also,
as in Sallustius, in Murray, *Five Stages*, 246; *cf.* Gnosis generally.

there is no longer anything at all to be restrained. For he who has attained the *unio mystica* need give no further heed to any instructions. From Jalaluddin Rumi, who sets himself above the law:

> He to whom licence has been given
> May eat whate'er he will: he has permission,[1]

to the English mystic Blake, who permits heaven (good) and hell (evil) to marry,[2] and Browning, who infuses a naturalistic element into his mysticism:

> Type needs antitype:
> As night needs day, as shine needs shade, so good
> Needs evil: how were pity understood,
> Unless by pain?

the tone is ever the same. Not only what is hurtful, but also what is evil, loses its peculiar position; for there can be no special position whatever in the wholly undifferentiated divine.[3] Nothing therefore but complete repose, immersion, evanescence, can avail for the mystic: the ethics of mysticism is quietism: "Accustom thyself to absolute immobility, and lay not thy hand on the ark if thou seest it totter, as did Uzzah; for although this would be a good deed for another person, for thee, whom God desires to be completely passive, it is worthless."[4]

Thus mysticism is a hasty attempt at self-liberation through self-destruction, an endeavour to render the self powerful by death. "God is born as man, that I may be born as the same God . . . God's 'ground' is mine and my 'ground' is God's";[5] or in the language of the *sufi*:

> Yea, Jalaluddin, thou art the ocean, and the pearl art thou,
> Thou art thyself the secret of the Universe;
> Observe no other ceremonies.

Finally in the semi-naturalistic, semi-mystic Omar Khayyám:

---

[1] In Tholuck, *op. cit.*, 153.

[2] Spurgeon, *Mysticism in English Literature*, 141 *ff.*

[3] Julian of Norwich, for example, in *Revelations of Divine Love*, 26. Mme Guyon and the French quietists: E. Seillère, *Mme Guyon et Fénelon*, 1918, 32 *f.*, 217, 71. Masson, *op. cit.*, 55, 58, 227. Eckhart: Lasson, *op. cit.*, 8 *f.* The *sufis*: Field, *op. cit.*, 65. 188. Tholuck, *op. cit.*, 81, 96 *ff.*, 120 *f.*, 130, 159 *f.*, 212 *f.* Nicholson, *op. cit.*, 88, 99. Dionysius Areopagita: Merx, *op. cit.*, 19.

[4] Mme Guyon in Masson, *op. cit.*, 277; *cf.* Tersteegen, *Geistliche Lieder*, 19 *ff.* Siedel, *Tauler*, 118. A modern instance in Amiel's *Journal*, April 6, 1851.

[5] Lasson, *op. cit.*, 205.

> Heav'n but the Vision of fulfill'd desire,
> And Hell the Shadow from a Soul on Fire.[1]

Thus mysticism circles around the impenetrability of the ego itself:[2] at any moment it may become the most extravagant self-glorification but also, at any time, the most abysmal consciousness of nullity. In Meister Eckhart, for instance, self-deification turns into a "forceful doctrine of grace",[3] just as universally in mysticism, even in its Mohammedan type, predestination plays a prominent part. For both a "Cherubinic Wanderer" and a Rainer Maria Rilke, again, self-annihilation changes into the dependence, indeed into the nullity, of God:

> What wilt Thou do, O God, when I shall die?
> I am Thy tankard: (what if I should break?)
> I am Thy potion: (what if I should spoil?)
> I am Thy raiment and Thy calling,
> In losing me, Thou wouldst lose Thy significance.[4]

God is a fledgling that has fallen out of the nest! Human sonship, similarly, is converted into a fatherhood, or rather motherhood:

> I love thee as a dearly loved son
> Who once forsook me when he was a child,
> Because Destiny had called him to a throne,
> 'Fore which all lands are as valleys.[5]

Still more audaciously, and with the tone of concise finality, in Angelus Silesius:

> Deep calls to deep. My spirit's Deep doth cry amain
> To Deep of God: say, which is deeper of the twain?[6]

But we should not regard mysticism as one specific type of religion and raise the question, for example, whether Christianity and mysticism can be reconciled. Mysticism is a definite tendency in religion that may arise, and has indeed arisen, in every religion. It is a form of self-direction, of autism, of "living inside oneself"; not however the magical

---

[1] On Omar Khayyám and the various sources of his *Rubá'iyát cf.* A. Christensen, *Critical Studies in the Rubaiyat of Umar-i-Khayyám*, 1927.
[2] Hofmann, *Rel. Erl.* 47.
[3] *cf.* Otto, *Zeitschr. für Theol. und Kirche*, N. F. 6, 1925, 425.
[4] *Das Stundenbuch.*
[5] *ibid., cf.* A. Faust, *Der dichterische Ausdruck mystischer Religiosität bei Rainer Maria Rilke*, Logos, 11, 1923.   [6] *The Cherubinic Wanderer*, I, 68.

form[1] in which man transfers the world into himself, but a still more radical type in which man, by way of nothingness, constitutes himself the All. Mysticism, in other terms, is a forcible exaggeration of the consciousness of power, which finds its satisfaction in the omnipotence of death: no one can harm the dead, not even himself. Therefore, indeed, every religion can and must include mystical elements; but it can incorporate these within itself only in so far as they do not contradict its own essential character. Thus in primitive religion the boundary or frontier of mysticism is magic with its own practical aims; in Islam and Judaism, the overruling command of God; in Christianity, love.[2] With justice, then, has a "restrained mysticism" been discussed;[3] for except in such extreme cases as Angelus Silesius, Madame Guyon, Jalalludin Rumi, *etc.*, mysticism is almost always "restrained". Even "pure" mysticism is never wholly "pure". The mystic never suffers a complete loss of identity, just as little as does the schizophrene or the primitive, whose experience is similarly based on the abrogation of the division between subject and object, although it does not therefore attain the mystic's passionate level. Mysticism, then, is like Dante who, wholly absorbed in contemplation of Beatrice, immovably gazes at her. But life itself, its possibilities and faith also, resemble the three theological virtues which divert the poet's steady gaze with a *troppo fisso*—"too fixed a gaze"—and recall him to consciousness.[4] And it is no accident that it is precisely the theological virtues that pronounce this *troppo fisso*.

W. J. AALDERS, *Mystiek*, 1928.

K. BETH, *Frömmigkeit der Mystik und des Glaubens*, 1927.

F. HEILER, *Die Bedeutung der Mystik für die Weltreligionen*, 1919.

F. VON HÜGEL, *The Mystical Element of Religion* I, 1908, II[2], 1924.

K. JASPERS, *Die Psychologie der Weltanschauungen*[2], 1922.

A. LASSON, *Meister Eckhart der Mystiker*, 1868.

G. VAN DER LEEUW, *Mystiek*, 1925.

E. LEHMANN, *Mystik in Heidentum und Christentum*[3], 1923.

J. H. LEUBA, *The Psychology of Religious Mysticism*.

G. MEHLIS, *Die Mystik in der Fülle ihrer Erscheinungsformen*.

R. OTTO, *West-östliche Mystik*, 1926 (Eng. tr., *Mysticism East and West*, 1937, 1957).

C. F. E. SPURGEON, *Mysticism in English Literature*, 1913.

E. UNDERHILL, *Mysticism*.

[1] Chap. 82.   [2] Chap. 76.
[3] E. Brunner.   [4] *Purgatorio*, 31, 32.

CHAPTER 76

THE LOVE OF GOD

1. IN our discussion of fear we have already seen that religious experience is ambivalent: the relationship to Power is always simultaneously a being attracted *and* a being repelled whenever it attains any marked intensity: both *tremor* and fascination. Love in the religious sense, therefore, is by no means a purely harmonious attitude in life, since it never exists wholly free from its apparent opponent, fear, just as fear, on its part, is never present quite apart from love. Even hatred is closely connected with love: "everyone who hates is an unhappy lover without knowing it".[1] In this sense, then, the Power encountered in human life is always loved even when there is no implication of the love of God in any strict sense. This ambivalent experience of love may even be regarded as the basic experience in religion; for without the attraction there would be no fear, no celebration, indeed no religion whatever. Membership within some definite powerfulness, too—in the community or the covenant—is one form of love; being drawn to one's neighbour, to one's brothers or companions, the going forth from oneself, or rather the fusion of oneself with another, all repose on the common potency.[2]

2. Apart from this quite general sense, however, love appears as *surrender*. "In the purity of our hearts there surges the endeavour willingly to surrender, out of gratitude, to some higher, purer and unknown Being: thus unriddling the eternally unnamed One. This we call Piety!" Surrender thus implies the gift of oneself; while the gift which, as has been seen,[3] is itself always to a certain extent a surrender, is therefore the outward act pertaining to the inward experience. In the total experience, then, sacrifice and love are united; whence it follows that love always presupposes love in return, exactly as the gift presupposes a counter-gift. Or rather: as man's gift is always a counter-gift, so too his love is always a love in return.

It is thus that we find love in the Old Testament. There, originally, it pertains to the covenant in virtue of which Jahveh chose his people; in

---

[1] Künkel, *Einführung in die Characterkunde*, 16.
[2] Chap. 32 *ff. cf.* Marett, *Faith, Hope and Charity*, 178.   [3] Chap. 50.

Deuteronomy, indeed, love of God is an explicit commandment: "And thou shalt love the Lord thy God with all thine heart, and with all thy soul, and with all thy might";[1] this love of the people, and later of the individual also, is as it were the answer to Jahveh's love. His love is true and steadfast, even when that of the people (or of the individual) is deceitful. Hence the repeated parable of the faithless wife whose infidelity, however, never causes her husband's love to vacillate. Hosea, again, opposes love, as God's demand, to sacrificial ceremonial: "For I desired mercy, and not sacrifice; and the knowledge of God more than burnt offerings."[2] Jahveh loves his people, and among the members of the community especially the righteous, the obscure and the miserable,[3] while the people and its members requite his love by the praise of their reciprocal love. Here therefore there is no place for that antithesis found in Islam, where love to God plays a conspicuous and occasionally central rôle only among mystics and heretics, and where man's attitude towards God must therefore exhaust itself above all in the praise that he owes to God, because here too man rightly feels that all love is reciprocal even while, at the same moment, he cannot attribute to the exalted Creator any human and self-surrendering love.[4]

For religious sentiment in India, on the other hand, matters are altogether different; wherever Form and Will become manifested in Power, the otherwise preponderating celebration, even when it assumes the guise of asceticism, and also knowledge of God, yield place to surrender, *bhakti*. Here too, however, it is God's attitude, His deed of love, that first evokes man's love; and in *Mahayana* Buddhism surrender to the god Buddha replaced self-liberation in accordance with Buddha's own example—"I take my refuge in the Buddha". Buddha's vow not to desire to enter into *Nirvana* until all shall have been released is here regarded as the proof, the practical demonstration, of God's love which challenges surrender.[5] In Hinduism, then, the *Bhagavad-Gita* unites the two paths, of knowledge and of works, in the higher way of *bhakti*, of surrender; a personal lord, *Isvara*, who draws to himself man's love, is the focus of religion.[6] And the essence of this love and love in return is very beautifully expressed in the eighteenth song of the *Bhagavad-Gita*:

---

[1] *Deut.* vi. 5.
[2] *Hosea* vi. 6.
[3] *Ps.* cxlvi.
[4] *cf.* Massignon, *Al-Hallaj*, 161 *f.*
[5] This, and other aspects of the subject, are lucidly discussed in Tiele-Söderblom, *op. cit.*, 187 *ff.*
[6] "Love" and "surrender" appear to be more adequate renderings of *bhakti* than "faith"; *cf.* Chantepie, *op. cit.*, II, 148.

"The Lord abides in the heart of all things, O Arjuna, making all beings revolve mounted on a machine by his magic power.

Go even to him as refuge with thy whole being, O Bharata; through his favour thou shalt win the highest peace, an eternal abode.

Thus has knowledge more secret than the secret been declared to thee by me; examine it fully, and as thou wilt so do.

Listen again to my highest word, the most secret of all: dear art thou to me most surely; therefore I will speak what is for thy good.

Have thy mind on me, be devoted to me, sacrifice to me, do reverence to me. To me thou shalt come; what is true I promise; dear art thou to me."[1]

Here it can be very clearly observed how the knowledge of God, the most essential of all religious values in India, is gradually transformed into a love of God; and in this change the lord, from being a teacher, a supreme *guru*, becomes more and more an all-sufficing God: "Abandoning all (other) duties come to me, the one refuge; I will free thee from all sins; sorrow not."[2]

By the poets *bhakti*, although it hardly ever completely loses the subsidiary meaning of knowledge, is expressly opposed to rites and ascetic exercises:

> Why chant the *vedas*? why listen to the *sastras*?
> Why be taught moral principles every day?
> Why learn one *anga* (an auxiliary science) or all six?
> To bear the Lord in our hearts alone brings salvation.
> Why torment ourselves? Why observe fasts?
> Why chastise ourselves on high mountains?
> Why wander to and fro to sacred streams?
> To confess the Lord continually alone brings salvation.[3]

3. For the Greek, whom we must now consider, every experience bore a divine countenance. He spoke therefore not of love for God, and still less of God's love, since love itself is the god, indeed the oldest of gods:—Eros, the primal impulse of the Universe. And the entire life-movement, alike in its most sensuous as in its sublimest moments, whether directed to the beautiful, the good or the true, is for Plato an upward striving urge, Eros:[4] the Orphic primeval world-principle, the Sophoclean victor "resistless in fight", becomes love, highest and ultimate, the Idea. This Idea itself, however, cannot love. "God loves

---

[1] E. J. Thomas, *The Song of the Lord.*
[2] *Bhagavad-Gita*, 18, 66. (E. J. Thomas).
[3] Bertholet, *Lesebuch*, 14, 55.   [4] Chap. 95.

(Plato's Ideas do not love). Out of love to man God sent His Son to earth. Christ is the loving one: the man who loves God and God Who loves man. The dynamic of love no longer has one direction only, as in antiquity—from man to what is higher; but a dual course—also from what is higher to man; and Christ unites in Himself both tendencies."[1] "In Christianity, and wholly unplatonically, not only is loving central but also" (I prefer to say: essentially) "being loved . . . For antiquity Eros was a cult creation: for Christianity Eros is deliverance."[2] In this respect, then, a radical contrast exists between the Greek spirit and that of Christianity. Certainly Eros was surrender, but as instinct and subsequently as possession; as a sacred lunacy, but also always as the enhancing of power. The Christian *agape*, *caritas*, is however the surrender to Him who has surrendered Himself; neither instinct nor impulse therefore, but grace; neither possession nor increase of power, but pure gratitude.[3] In Christianity, then, the closest approach to Platonic love is shown in mysticism; for the similes of bridal love and of death from love are often nothing more than a transformation of childlike gratitude into a powerful impulse.

4. For Christian faith, then, love is not a god, but God is love.[4] And the Christian concept of love is not "spiritual," as the antithesis of "sensuous", love; rather does it subsist as "equally foreign to spiritual reality as to corporeal reality";[5] it implies a complete inversion of all the conditions of life without exception. Christians, in fact, sought their own specific term for love, *agape*, and rejected the various current expressions;[6] and the fundamental meaning of this word is "to receive, to welcome, to embrace". It already presupposes, therefore, the gift of a love; and in this it differs from φιλέω and ἐράω. In principle, therefore, *agape* is reciprocal love. It is neither instinct nor impulse, but readiness, preparedness, responding to God's act; and in this it is therefore not man's own conduct that is intrinsic, but the attitude of God. "I ask not for love in general and occasionally, but for that love with which I am loved";[7] and in this sense the striking assertion of the

---

[1] Marcuse, *Über die Struktur der Liebe, Jahrbuch der Charakterologie*, 5, 279.

[2] *ibid.*, 280.

[3] It is no accident that Islam, while rejecting love, was able to accept Platonic love; cf. Massignon, *Al-Hallaj*, 176.

[4] I *John* iv. 6, 18.   [5] Marcuse, *loc. cit.*, 283.

[6] Lohmeyer, *Rel. Gemeinschaft*, 59. Tromp de Ruiter, *Gebruik en beteekenis van* AGAPAN *in de grieksche literatuur, passim*.

[7] Bultmann, *Glaube und Verst.*, 242; cf. also 237.

so-called anti-Christian Nietzsche holds good, in which he distinguishes love from *pity*:[1] "all great love is above all its pity: for it seeketh— to create what is loved!"[2] God's love, then, is creative, while love for God is the creature's own gratitude. It is not even in the first place a giving, but rather a permitting oneself to receive.[3] "Love lies in this, not in our love for him but in his love for us—in the sending of his Son to be the propitiation for our sins. . . . We love, because he loved us first."[4] God descends to man: that is real love; and human love exists only as response. Christian love, therefore, is dynamic, for it is an activity of God and a reciprocal activity of man. Kierkegaard has referred to its "dialectic" and discussed this with ardent profundity: "the higher one stands above another whom he loves, the more, in human terms, will he feel inclined to raise him up to himself; but all the more, divinely speaking, will he feel impelled to descend to him. That is love's dialectic."[5] In Christianity, therefore, love can assume the central position because it coincides with God's act, with God becoming man. It is never merely a fine sentiment, a praiseworthy feeling, but an absolute deed; and as man's love for God it has its being only in God's powerfulness. "This impotent One then, who can save neither himself nor others, but brings misery to all who attach themselves to him, is the absolute. Who can believe that? man cannot. For he has an ineradicable idea of what Power is; and this impotence is not Power, and still less the Power of the Absolute."[6] We have become sufficiently familiar with this "ineradicable idea" in our previous discussions! In Christian love it is directly controverted: both the relationship between God and man, and that between man and man (community of love, the community grounded in the love of Christ) rest upon a Power which is neither a property nor an attribute of man, but a gift to him, a gift from the Father to the child. About this love, finally, the apostle Paul composed his great hymn, which is the very reverse of praise of any human excellence. For it is the song of the gift of God, of the absolutely indispensable, of the eternally existent:

> I may speak with the tongues of men and of angels,
>   but if I have no love,
>   I am a noisy gong or a clanging cymbal;
>   I may prophesy, fathom all mysteries and secret lore,

---

[1] Chap. 97.   [2] *Thus Spake Zarathustra*, 105 (Foulis Edition).
[3] Scholz, *Eros und Caritas*, 51 *ff.*   [4] 1 *John* iv. 10, 19 (Moffat).
[5] Geismar, *Kierkegaard*, 193; cf. 115, 194 *ff.*, 497 *f.*
[6] Kierkegaard, in Geismar, *op. cit.*, 412.

I may have such absolute faith that I can move hills from their place,
but if I have no love,
I count for nothing;
I may distribute all I possess in charity,
I may give up my body to be burnt,
but if I have no love,
I make nothing of it.

.   .   .   .   .   .

Thus "faith and hope and love last on, these three", but
the greatest of all is love.[1]

L. Marcuse, *Über die Struktur der Liebe* (*Jahrbuch der Charakterologie*, 5), 1928.

H. Scholz, *Eros und Caritas*, 1929.

S. Tromp de Ruiter, *Gebruik en beteekenis van* Agapan *in de grieksche literatuur*, 1930.[2]

[1] 1 *Cor.* xiii (Moffat)

CHAPTER 77

CHILDREN OF GOD

1. THE Orphic, appearing in the underworld before the gods, refers to his origin:

> Say: "I am a child of Earth and of Starry Heaven:
> But my race is of Heaven. This ye know yourselves."

Again:

> For I also avow me that I am of your blessed race, ye gods.[1]

The Homeric hero, too, boasts of his divine descent, and among numberless primitive peoples the link with Power is at the same time the relationship with divine, or at least extremely potent, ancestors. In all these examples, then, man advances this claim to common origin and common potency with the powers: among these, as it were, he includes himself. The Old Testament, still further, in addressing the people of Israel or the Messiah as the son of God, shows that an intense feeling of dependence may accompany this. For the son is intimately associated with the Father, obeys and trusts him; the Father's figure is perfectly familiar to him;[2] and in this sense the speech on the Areopagus can quote the words of the Greek poet: "For we are also his offspring."[3]

But in adopting this idea Christianity changes filiation to God, from being a matter of relationship, into one of *faith*.[4] For Christ alone and uniquely is "Son of God" in the sense of relationship. Man therefore is not the child of God, but he may become so. Or rather, because here least of all does any purely temporal relationship subsist, he is not the child of God in the tranquillity of immutable being, but in the agitation of faith. This sonship is a gift: "For the sons of God are those who are guided by the Spirit of God. You have received no slavish spirit that would make you relapse into fear; you have received the Spirit of sonship. And when we cry, 'Abba! Father!' it is this Spirit testifying

---

[1] (Cornford.) Gold tablets from Petelia and Thurioi, in Diels, *Vorsokratiker*, II, 175; Olivieri, *Lamellae orphicae*; *cf*. K. Kerenyi, *AR*. 27, 1928, 322 *f*. Kern, *Orph. Fragm.* 105 *f*.

[2] Chap. 20.   [3] *Acts* xvii. 28.   [4] *cf*. Piper, *Ethik*, I, 121.

along with our own Spirit that we are children of God";[1] similarly in
the Johannine trend of thought: "Think what a love the Father has
for us, in letting us be called 'children of God!' That is what we are."[2]
We are children of God, therefore, not in virtue of descent nor origin,
but of the selfless love of God that has chosen us.

[1] *Rom.* viii. 14 *ff.* (Moffat).   [2] 1 *John* iii. 1 (Moffat).

CHAPTER 78

ENMITY TO GOD

1. THE subject of this Chapter is enmity to God. We are no longer, therefore, discussing the infraction of Power which sets free a reaction, nor the observance of tabus. Nor again are we now concerned with celebration and conduct; or in other words, there is no reference whatever to custom.[1] But when we realize that, in the second half of this Section, *inward* action comes to the fore, this in no sense means that not custom, but an autonomous morality, is to be dealt with. Certainly morality too will appear in its diversity from religion, but only in a restricted aspect. For enmity against God has nothing whatever to do with moral failures; it refers to God alone. Nor can the various defences of morality that have been advanced in the course of centuries assist us at all. Thus it can by no means imply, for example, that experience which induced the Orphic, and subsequently the Christian also, to find his guilt in the captivity of the soul within the prison of the body: that would be misery, perhaps failure, but certainly not enmity.[2] Equally little can result from any utilitarian explanation of moral good in terms of the usefulness it serves. In accordance with the Old Testament and with many primitive peoples, we too assert "good" equally of a character, an action, of food and a nap;[3] but it never occurs to us that the lack of this type of goodness implies enmity. Neither does the grounding of inward action in Nature, nor in human caprice, assist us here. It is not at all a matter of man departing from Nature nor operating in opposition to his normal growth ($\phi\acute{v}\sigma\iota\varsigma$) nor, again, of his transgressing any universal principle ($\theta\acute{\epsilon}\sigma\iota\varsigma$). Rather does the issue concern his guilt. And "being guilty does not first of all result from some fault, but conversely: this itself is only possible on the ground of an original state of guilt".[4] This guilty condition, therefore, has nothing to do with either habit or custom, law, commandment or "Ought". It is not the absence of any kind of deed or disposition. As Heidegger finely

---

[1] Chap. 66.

[2] Brunner remarks that sin originates not in corporeality, but in the freedom of the spirit; *Gott und Mensch*, 84.

[3] Westermarck, *The Origin and Development of the Moral Ideas*, I, 132 *f.*

[4] Heidegger, *op. cit.*, 280 *ff.*

states this: man is not merely laden with guilt: he is guilty. The state of being " laden with guilt" originates in the circle of celebrations and cares; but guilt itself has no specific origin whatever: rather it pertains to the very being of man.

Sin and guilt, then, are related to the deepest element in man, to the ground of his being, just as he is, without any kind of possibility arising, or any sort of celebration producing any change.[1] As long as man clings to possibilities, as long as he celebrates his experience, he may continue to suppose that his power will never be entirely lost. But behind these possibilities there still lies nothingness; and in this nullity there subsists not only impotence but guilt. And as soon as conscience calls to man,[2] he becomes aware of this threatening nullity at the very ground of his being. How this comes about, however, it is difficult to say. For dread, which we have already encountered as dread of possibility, cannot explain guilt, although it "points towards it", as Kierkegaard has so impressively shown.[3] He who, standing on high, has become dizzy in his dread, falls and rises guilty. Between dread and guilt, however, there is a profound chasm, something not to be understood, something that is not apparent. Guilt therefore, with faith, falls quite outside the realm of Phenomenology.

Into experience, still further, this nullity enters as *enmity*. Regarded non-religiously, there is nothing whatever in his "being dust and ashes" with which man could be reproached. Religion, however, is never concerned with actions or dispositions that may deserve praise or blame, but with the very ground of being. And the nullity of this reveals itself as enmity against God. Conscience cries out to man that he hates God. The will that is hostile to God arises from man's deepest being. He will accept nothing as a gift, but will himself be God and bestow something on his God. But that is sin against God's very essence, against love. Even sacred actions are taken into his own service by self-sufficient man: in order to surmount his dread, celebration must help him to ignore the voice of conscience and to attain power in spite of everything. But then his conscience hurls him back into the nullity of impotence, which hates God. Awe, or primitive avoidance, may therefore be said to approach much more closely than does moral

---

[1] This is also the meaning of *original* sin; *cf.* G. Mensching, *Die Idee der Sünde* (1931), 50: "The distinctive peculiarity of the Christian idea of sin is to be perceived in the concept of general sin as original guilt"; *cf. ibid.*, 51 on the Vishnuite parallel to the parable of the Prodigal Son, and its characteristic distinction from this in its concept of sin.

[2] Chap. 68.   [3] *Begriff Angst (The Concept of Dread).*

failure to the consciousness of guilt, although it is by no means identical with it.

2. Sin, to continue, is enmity against God. But God cannot be measured by any human standards, however highly moral they may be. He is *holy*: that is, He is eternally superior, remote, incomprehensible: "For my thoughts are not your thoughts, neither are your ways my ways."[1] We do not even require to grasp the sublime idea of God in *Deutero-Isaiah* in order to realize the profound contrast between sin against God and every form of transgression, of lack of goodness or insight, *etc.* For this the moving prayer of a simple Egyptian workman, addressed to the "mountain peak", may quite well serve: "I am an ignorant man with no understanding, and cannot distinguish between good and evil. Once I transgressed against the mountain peak, and it has punished me: day and night I am in its hand. I sit on the tile like a pregnant woman; I call to the wind, but it does not come to me. I prayed to the mighty mountain summit, and to each god and goddess: 'Behold', I say to great and small among the workers: 'be humble before the summit of the mount, for there a lion dwells; it strikes just as does the fiercely glaring lion, and it pursues him who offends it'. I called to my mistress, and then I found that she came to me as a refreshing wind. She was gracious to me after she had let me see her hand (Providence). Graciously she turned to me and enabled me to ignore my suffering; she was like a breeze to me. Truly the mountain peak in the West is charitable, if we call upon it. Nofer-Abu says, and speaks: 'Truly, hear all ye with ears who live on earth: be humble before the Western mountain-top'."[2] It is probably but rarely that we discern the very essence of religion in such a simple garb as in this prayer of the worker thirsting in the desert. Deepest despair and the most blissful release lie close together, both being grounded in the essential nature of the god. That this is a grim mountain-top does not at all affect the issue; it is far nearer the essence of religion than the enlightened, rational and benevolent Lord God of so many Christian sermons! And this fully confirms Kierkegaard's dictum that the antithesis of sin is not *virtue*, but *faith*.[3] The Egyptian workman's prayer touches the same chords as do the profoundest terms of the Christian consciousness of sin. For "Lord, I am not worthy", "I am no more worthy to be

---

[1] *Isaiah* lv. 8.
[2] In G. Roeder, *Urkunden zur Religion des alten Ägypten*, 1915, 57.
[3] In Geismar, *op. cit.*, 328.

called thy son", refer to no sort of vice nor series of transgressions, but to the very nature of man as estimated by the absolute majesty of God: "Thou art worthy, O Lord."[1]

The essence of guilt also appears very clearly in the Babylonian hymns, the so-called penitential psalms; and here again primitive avoidance is very much nearer the religious consciousness of sin than is moral failure. For the Babylonian *Texts*, which are all spells, start from this avoidance. The lament is occasioned by illness or some other misfortune; and from the decline of his powers the sufferer infers the wrath of God, and his own unconscious guilt. Without being aware of it he has come into contact with Power and bears the consequences; and this is certainly never thought of as being at all a moral issue. But the poet's religion has, in this connection, a particularly suitable opportunity to appear.[2] The sick man allows himself to be exorcised and prays for the cure of his sickness; and both the spell and the cure are for him identical with divine liberation. But in this practical attitude he begins to realize the divine holiness and the depth of his own guilt; for although he is not immediately aware of his fault, still he is conscious of his guilt and unworthiness. His error may indeed have been a ritual one or—in our sense—moral. The god's anger, sickness, impurity, sin: it all amounts to the same thing: we offend God, even when we ourselves neither know nor desire this;[3] we are enemies of God, and indeed for no other reason than that He is our enemy. This appears most explicitly in the celebrated hymn that has been compared with the *Book of Job* (I have italicized the significant passages): "Just when I had almost *recovered* the (critical) moment passed. However I sought it was evil, very evil; my *agony* ever more increased; my right I found nowhere. If I called to my god, he vouchsafed me not his countenance; if I prayed to my goddess, she raised not her head to me. The *sacrificial diviner* could not decide the reason for things after an inspection, nor could the *dream interpreter* form a judgment about me by means of an incense offering. I approached the *soothsayer*, but he opened not my ear; the *exorcising priest* could not appease the *gods'*

---

[1] *Matt.* viii. 8; *Luke* xv. 19 ; *Rev.* iv. 11. Mark Connelly's modern Negro drama, *The Green Pastures*, is a very fine example of the genuinely religious consciousness of sin, especially Act I, Scene 4.

[2] *cf.* Morgenstern, *The Doctrine of Sin in the Babylonian Religion*, 1905. A. H. Edelkoort, *Het zondebesef in de babylonische boetepsalmen*, 1918. Ch. F. Jean, *Le péché chez les Babyloniens et les Assyriens*, 1925; *cf.* also A. van Selms, *De babylonische termini voor Zonde*, 1933.

[3] *cf.* Jastrow, *Religion Babyloniens und Assyriens*, I, 1, 68 *ff.* Paul Dhorme, *La religion assyro-babylonienne*, 1910.

wrath by his magical performance. Whence the changed actions everywhere? If I looked behind me, persecutions and afflictions! Like a man
who has not dedicated the gift to the god, and has not invoked the
name of the goddess over his food: who has shown no humility and
known no submission: in whose mouth supplication and prayer had
ceased and for whom the day of the god had ended: by whom feast
days were neglected: who laid his arms in his lap, disregarded the gods'
will, and has not taught his people the fear and adoration of the god:
has not called to his god, and has devoured the repast intended for
him: has abandoned his goddess, and has not offered the regular sacrifice: has neglected everything, forgotten his lord and has lightly sworn
by his holy god—so I appeared.

"And yet *I myself remembered supplication and prayer*; prayer was my
thought, sacrifice my rule; the day of the god's worship was the joy
of my heart, the day of the goddess's procession was gain and wealth
to me. My joy was to honour the king, and my pleasure to play on the
harp for him. I ordered my country to esteem the god's name, and
commanded my people to exalt the name of the goddess. The king's
worship I treated like that of a god, and taught the people to show
reverence before the palace.

"For I knew that such actions are acceptable to the god. *Yet what
appears beautiful to man is abominable to the god, and what is odious to
man's heart is most pleasing to the god.* Who has learnt (to understand)
the will of the gods in heaven, the gods' plan, full of wisdom? who can
comprehend it? *When have stupid mortals ever understood the ways of
the gods?* He who was alive yesterday, to-day is dead: suddenly he is
plunged into darkness and quickly dashed to pieces. One moment he
is singing and playing, and in a trice he is howling like a mourner.
Their wills are as different as light is from darkness." Again, of God:
"His *hand is too heavy*, I cannot bear it; his fearfulness is all too great
. . . His *word of wrath* is a storm flood—mighty is his stride. . . ."
Finally, the sick man is rescued by the god Marduk, who purifies him
by leading him through the twelve gates of E-sagila.[1] Here, therefore,
in this magical conception of sin, its true and essential character is
admirably manifested.[2]

An equally profound consciousness of guilt is to be found in the

---

[1] Lehmann-Haas, *op. cit.*, 312 *ff*. *cf.* Jastrow, *op. cit.*, I, 2, 124 *ff*.

[2] In the so-called *Shurpu-Texts* the type of offence is exhaustively investigated (a
complete list of vices is compiled) in order that it may be "set free"; Lehmann-Haas,
op. cit., 317 *ff*.

Hindu hymns to the god Varuna. This god pertains to those superior beings in the background of the Universe[1] who, as we have seen, are intimately linked with morality; but he is also the confessor of those who know that they must acknowledge actual sin: "I take counsel with myself about it: when shall I ever be in favour again with Varuna? Will he accept my sacrifice without anger? When shall I confidently see his grace? I examine myself closely about my sin, O Varuna. I go to the wise to enquire of them; and the sages tell me the same thing: Varuna is wroth with thee. What then was this most wicked sin, O Varuna, that thou wilt destroy him who praises thee, thy friend? Tell me that, thou infallible one, thou self-sufficient one! With obeisance and freed from guilt I would entreat thy pardon, anticipating this. Forgive the sins of our fathers: forgive us what we ourselves have done!".[2]

In the Old Testament again, as everyone knows, the same tone repeatedly resounds in the *Psalms* and elsewhere. And in the *Book of Job* the religious consciousness of guilt has certainly detached itself completely, not merely from its prior magical conditions, but also from the success of the prayer for deliverance. While Job is still plunged in abject misery, he places his hand over his mouth and is silent: from beginning to end God is here the first and the only One. But considered in its entirety, it is the *Book of Psalms* that exhibits the true. nature of sin and guilt more clearly than perhaps any other literature; and in this respect it certainly pictures a situation in most marked contrast with current moral preaching. Here again misery is the revelation of God's wrath: "Remove thy stroke away from me; I am consumed by the blow of thine hand. When thou with rebukes dost correct man for iniquity, thou makest his beauty to consume away like a moth."[3] "Lord, be merciful unto me: heal my soul for I have sinned against thee."[4] (But this is not the moral soul!). Misery, however, and above all sickness, are directly referred to Jahveh; they manifest his wrath, but to the contrite penitent, his mercy also:

> Oh the bliss of him whose guilt is pardoned,
> and his sin forgiven!
> Oh the bliss of him whom the Eternal has absolved,
> whose spirit has made full confession!

---

[1] Chap. 18.
[2] Bertholet, *op. cit.*, 9, 51; *cf.* Oldenberg, *Religion des Veda.*
[3] *Ps.* xxxix, 10, 11.
[4] *Ps.* xli. 4; *cf.* xxxviii, 19; cvii. 17.

So long as I refused to own my guilt,
　　I moaned unceasingly, life ebbed away;
　for thy hand crushed me night and day,
　　　my body dried up as in summer heat.
Then did I own my sin to thee,
　　uncovering my iniquity;
　and as I vowed I would confess,
　　thou didst remit my sinful guilt.
So let each loyal heart pray to thee in trouble:
　　the floods may roar,
　　　but they will never reach him.[1]

Here confession[2] and prayer have taken the place of the spell. Sin is a matter that man must fight out with his God. Our own consciousness of guilt still leaves avenues of escape open to us, but God's wrath only the sole remedy of His grace. For the ground of guilt is not transgression but the opposition between two wills, the divine and the human. So from the marvellously gracious word of God's compassion His anger, too, is not absent:

　　The Eternal is pitiful and gracious,
　　　slow to be angry, rich in love;
　　he will not always chafe,
　　　he will not hold to his anger for all time;
　　he treats us not according to our sins,
　　　he deals not with us as our guilt deserves;
　　but, high as heaven is over earth,
　　　so vast his love is to his worshippers.[3]

Sin therefore is hostile contact with God; but nevertheless it is an encounter with *God*; subsisting in the deepest essential being of man, it brings him close before God, where will opposes Will, and Power, power:

　　　It is against thee I have sinned,
　　　　I have done evil in thy sight.
　　　Yes, thou art just in thy charge,
　　　　and justified in thy sentence.
　　　Ah! 'twas in guilt that I was born,
　　　　'twas in sin that my mother conceived me.[4]

---

[1] *Ps.* xxxii (Moffat). 　　　　　[2] Chap. 62. 　　　　　[3] *Ps.* ciii. 8 *ff.* (Moffat).
[4] *Ps.* li. 4 *ff.* (Moffat). Kautsch observes with justice that it is not here a question of the adulterous origin of the community (as for Hosea) and still less of the sinfulness of sex relations, but solely of the fact that sin pertains to the essential nature of man.

Here too then, as in Babylon, sin is so deeply hidden that it is concealed even from the sinner, while God alone knows of it.[1] All this is apparently accompanied however, and this with no difficulty, by the consciousness of righteousness:

> Right me, O thou Eternal, for my life is right . . .
> blamelessly I wash my hands.[2]

For sin lies wholly elsewhere; and this is precisely its dreadful aspect:— that man is guilty without himself doing anything whatever towards it. Nor can he amend anything in his own conduct: just as Jahveh alone can avert his wrath, so Jahveh alone can pardon the guilt and "conceal it from view".

> If thou didst keep strict tally of sins,
>   O Lord, who could live on?
> But thou hast pardon
>   that thou mayest be worshipped.
> So I wait in hope for the Eternal,
>   my soul waits hoping for his promise;
>   my soul looks for the Lord
>   more eagerly than watchmen for the dawn,
>   than watchmen for the dawn.

> Put your hope in the Eternal, Israel,
>   for with the Eternal there is love,
>   there is a wealth of saving power;
>   'tis he who shall save Israel
>   from all their sins.[3]

For the marvellous mystery of guilt, of sin, of enmity against God, is that in it man discovers God:—certainly as an adversary, but nevertheless in the closest proximity. Thus the: "My God, my God, why hast Thou forsaken me?" of *Psalm* xxii is an expression not merely of estrangement, but equally of nearness. The God Who can "forsake" is a God Who has first been near. In the Confession of Faith of the Dutch and French reformed churches, being forsaken by God, the profoundest solitude, was made equivalent to the "dread of hell". But the grace of God then becomes heavenly joy. And precisely for this reason, both misery and bliss can transcend all else, reaching to the supreme height

---

[1] *Ps.* lxix. 6; xc, 7 *ff.*   [2] *Ps.* xxvi. 1, 6 (Moffat); *cf.* vii, 9; xi, 4 *ff.*
[3] *Ps.* cxxx (Moffat). On forgiveness as the act of God *cf. Theol. Wörterbuch z. N. T.*, "ἀφίημι" (Bultmann).

as to the profoundest depths, because it is not man who forsakes or finds the way back, but rather God Who forsakes or finds. Forcible and tender, regardlessly pressing on and almost inaudibly entreating, the prayer for the nearness of God resounds from the *Psalms*:

> Bestir thyself, Eternal One! Why sleep?
>   Awaken! ah, discard us not for ever!
> Why art thou hiding thy face,
>   forgetting our woe and distress?
> For our soul is bowed to the dust,
>   our body lies low on the ground.
> Come to the rescue!
>   For thy love's sake, oh save us.[1]

Here there is no longer any reference to piety or human weakness: everything is grounded in God: God alone remains important:

> The deer is panting for a stream,
>   and I am panting, O God, for thee.
> I am athirst for God, the living God.[2]

This is yearning. But fulfilment is proclaimed in the marvellous *Psalm* lxxiii, which advances from the enigma of the unrighteous course of the world to the praise of Jahveh; only his honour, his nearness, matters:

> Yet I am always beside thee;
>   thou holdest my right hand.
>
> .   .   .   .   .   .
>
> Whom have I in heaven but thee?
>   On earth I care for nothing else.
> Body and soul may fail,
>   but God my strength is mine for evermore.
> Those who leave thee are lost;
>   all who are faithless to thee, thou destroyest.
> But to be near God is my bliss,
>   to shelter with the Lord
>   that I may tell of all thy works.[3]

Here God's mercy is His essence, and His essential nature is to be near, while His being near is His own deed: *He* forsakes man, but *He* also finds him again. Always *He* alone, and again *He*.

---

[1] *Ps.* xliv. 23 *ff.* (Moffat); *cf. Ps.* lxxxviii. 15; lxxxix. 47; cxliii. 7.
[2] *Ps.* xlii. 1 *ff.* (Moffat).   [3] Moffat.

From here the path leads the believer into the dizzy fear of *quantus tremor est futurus*, to terrified adoration of *rex tremendae majestatis*, but also into trust: "Who savest whom thou savest free": *qui salvandos salvas gratis*. In this light therefore we can understand Peter's words: "Lord, leave me; I am a sinful man", together with the *miserere nobis* of the liturgy; but in the same spirit, "Who giveth joy to my youth": *qui laetificat juventutem meam*: of this liturgy, and the *felix culpa* of the church Father.

3. In view of this essential constitution of sin and of guilt, still further, a conflict between religion and morality is undeniably possible. This contest expresses itself now as a defence, on the part of religion, against an exaggerated morality, and again as an attempt at protection, by an "independent" morality, against the encroachments of the religious mentality. Thus Schleiermacher, in his second *Discourse upon Religion*, and later Rudolf Otto, have each in his own way detached morality in principle from religion. For according to Schleiermacher, religion is not at all concerned with man's practical activities; religious feeling should rather "accompany all human action like a sacred music, so that he should do everything together with religion, and nothing because of religion". Otto, indeed, distinguishes the holy, in the sense of moral perfection, from the holy as a purely religious quality, but afterwards unites the two once again in a composite category *a priori*. The group of problems raised by this relationship pertains however, with very few exceptions, to the Phenomenology of Morality, but on the other hand the remainder have already arisen in connection with my previous remarks about the essential nature of sin as being enmity against God. Here I need add only that the merging of religion within morality, as we are familiar with this in Confucianism, or our own eighteenth century, ultimately abolishes religion unless, as was the case with Kant, the moral law assumes on its own part a genuinely religious status and declares itself to be ultimate and unconditioned, and equally to be the Wholly Other.[1] Apart from this, "ethical culture"[2] remains mere "culture"; that is to say, it is religion only in so far as all culture is religion. Existence must be made a matter for "care", and this "caring for" can become a celebration equally in the sense of ritual

---

[1] On the essentially religious character of so much "mere" moralism *cf.* Otto, *Zeitschr. f. Rel.-Psych.*, 4, 1931, 9.
[2] Felix Adler founded his "Society for Ethical Culture" in 1875.

as of custom. But this does not reveal the deepest ground of the being of the "Other". So long as man still has something to care for, faith cannot for him acquire ultimate significance; so long as he still has something that he himself must do, he cannot completely become dust and ashes in his relation to God; and in this sense the saying which is often applied in altogether too edifying a way, "casting all your care upon him; for he careth for you",[1] becomes a terrifying, yet bliss bestowing, main commandment of religion.

The opposition between morality and religion, however, need by no means lead to any moral indifference. For in the obedience of faith, moral commands themselves find both their abrogation and their fulfilment. It is true that St. Paul, in the *Epistle to the Romans*, is striving for the correct understanding of sin, and his repeated: "Never!" when he alludes to the possibility of sinning in order that grace may "much more abound", discloses to us a forcible tension between the urge to care on the one hand, and on the other the tranquillity of justification by faith: "Sin increased, but grace surpassed it far. . . . Now what are we to infer from this? That we are to 'remain on in sin, so that there may be all the more grace'? Never! . . . Are we 'to sin, because we live under grace, not under law'? Never! Do you not know you are the servants of the master you obey, of the master to whom you yield yourselves obedient, whether it is Sin, whose service ends in death, or Obedience, whose service ends in righteousness?"[2] Here there opens out before the apostle the path of mysticism,[3] which eludes all care but also at the same moment knows nothing whatever of obedience. And St. Paul himself chooses the way of faith.

4. This commences with *repentance*. "It is the holy sorrow of the forgiven that places us in the most vital contact with the loving work of the Redeemer. It is the holy that appreciate the Holy One, and the conditions of His love. But I mean the holy of the swift and piercing conscience, the holy of the passionate and tragic soul, the holy who are forgiven much—it is they rather than those white flowers of the blameless life, the angelic purity, and the mystic mood; it is regenerate Launcelot more than noble Arthur."[4] These words of an English dogmatic theologian have precisely the same significance as the poet's lines:

---

[1] 1 *Peter* v. 7.   [2] *Rom.* v. 20; vi. 1, 15 *ff.* (Moffat).
[3] Chap. 75.   [4] P. T. Forsyth, *The Expositor*, X, 1915, 354 *f.*

528 RELIGION IN ESSENCE AND MANIFESTATION [78, 4

> God speaks to me and I to Him;
> With the same voice we speak.
> Yet what He means to say to me
> Is clearly manifested in His creation;
> And what I wish to say to His forbearance
> Lies deeply guarded in my guilt.[1]

Obviously it is here not a matter of repentance in the moral sense.[2] We are not concerned with grief over transgressions that have been committed; and repentance "first assumes its full significance when it is aroused no longer by evil alone, but by that evil in the eyes of God which is called sin";[3] and this repentance is "sustained by God's love", which first grants us the power to repent. "This impulse of love first appeared to us as our love; then we perceived that it was already reciprocal love."[4] Thus repentance leads immediately to conversion and to faith.

[1] Roel Houwink, *Strophen*, 1930, 12.   [2] *cf.* Piper, *Ethik*, I, 101.
[3] M. Scheler, *Vom Ewigen im Menschen*, I, 50 (1921).   [4] *ibid.*, 58.

CHAPTER 79

CONVERSION. REBIRTH

1. IN the previous discussion of human life[1] it was observed how its distinctive periods, indicated by rites, displayed on each of these occasions as it were a new life. Every transition, then, is a *rebirth*: the *rite de passage* designates a new beginning. Thus we found, for example, that in primitive initiation ceremonies the neophytes were greeted as just born and their adult life regarded as wholly new; in Greece, also, those adopted by the deity in the mysteries were looked upon as *deuteropotmoi*, "those to whom a second destiny was given".[2] As we then saw, too, life can be renewed either after death,[3] or previously in this existence; the initiate in the Mithraic mysteries called himself *renatus in aeternum*:—reborn in eternity. Christian baptism likewise effects a rebirth.[4] In all these cases, therefore, acquisition of power is a complete renovation.

We know nothing at all, however, about the psychical undercurrents of these outward events. But it is obvious that in every instance alike some inner experience corresponded to the outer process, so that when the Egyptian Pharaoh declared of himself that he *whm ankh*, that he was "repeating and renewing life", this certainly referred not merely to any definite rites subserving this renewal of life, but also presupposed an inner experience of which, however, we are quite ignorant. But this ignorance by no means releases us from the duty of depicting the inner structure of the external event as soon as this makes its appearance. And this happens in those occurrences which we call conversions, in which the main emphasis falls on the inner event, though not without this becoming outwardly observable also.

But an intermediate form between what we, with our inadequate means of expression, call "outward", and what we term "inner", is found in what Lévy-Bruhl has called "dispositions".[5] These are the "positive aspects" of affairs, about which man must know something before he can successfully apply himself to any kind of undertaking whatever. Are the beings with whom he has to deal beneficently, indifferently, or even perhaps inimically disposed? Here relations are

---

[1] Chap. 22.
[3] Chap. 47.   [4] Chap. 52.

[2] Rohde, *Psyche*, II, 421. E. T. 602.
[5] *Primitives and the Supernatural*, 65.

involved that are to our own minds completely incomprehensible and
imperceptible, such as the "disposition" of a weapon *etc*. But it is also
a matter of peculiarities that we too would call disposition or mood,
such as quarrelsomeness and the like; and the remarkable feature is
that these "dispositions" are conceived not as being subject to any
psychological influences, but precisely as being as objectively physical
as are magical attributes. Primitive man, in fact, drew no distinctions
at all in situations where we ourselves clearly differentiate. We can
understand how an attempt is made, by some concrete method, to
prevent a physical event happening, just as we can understand the
endeavour to influence a person's disposition by psychical means. But we
cannot at all comprehend anyone persuading a storm or a tree in a
friendly manner, and attempting to change someone's opinion by a rite.[1]
On the other hand, primitive man completely fails to understand our
stressing so heavily the differences between these two procedures.
We know, again, that men become baptized for their salvation, and we
can understand men being converted to the same end; but we scarcely
comprehend how baptism and conversion can both be the same. For
us the one is objective and pertains to ritual, the other subjective and
a matter of psychology. Essentially, however, they are both in the same
category: for inner and outer experience should not thus be separated
from each other. Here again our fatal predilection for the "spiritual"
(which is usually, nonetheless, merely something psychical!) has
destroyed our insight into the phenomena themselves. Conversion
is new birth, and new birth a conversion.[2]

2. But before considering conversion as this is familiar to us in the
great revivalist movements, it is worth while glancing at one example
of "inward-outward" conversion; and the story which Apuleius
narrates, in his celebrated romance about his hero Lucius, is in its
final chapters undoubtedly a genuine account of conversion. The way
in which the unfortunate hero, after so many excesses and afflictions,
dedicated himself to the service of the goddess, broken in spirit, repentant and contrite, indicates a unity between the outward and inward
occurrences which finds unequivocal expression in the exhortations of

[1] We may say, in brief, that we ask a maid for her love, but we "make use of" a
house in which to live with her; primitives, on the other hand, "make use of" a love
charm for the girl, while they implore the house for its blessing.
[2] The entire problem of the relationship between conversion and rebirth in systematic theology may be understood in the light of this false "modernization" of viewpoint.

the priest of Isis. For initiation, then, three conditions are laid down that supplement each other: the summons of the goddess in accordance with her "providence"; the neophyte's own readiness; and the rites that must be performed by and on the latter. These three together constitute rebirth, whose occurrence nevertheless depends not on any devout attitude of man, but solely upon the decision of the deity. "The day of each man's initiation", said the priest, "was fixed by the" *nod* "*of the goddess*, and the priest destined for her service was likewise chosen by *her providence*, and a like instruction appointed the sum required for the expenses of the ceremony. He bade me like others await all these ordinances with reverent patience, warning me that it was my duty to beware with all my soul of over-eagerness and petulance, to avoid both these faults, and neither to delay *when summoned* nor to hasten unbidden. 'There are none', he said, 'of all the order of priests of Isis so abandoned in spirit, or so given over to death, as to venture rashly and sacrilegiously to undertake the service of the goddess without *her express command* and thus to contract mortal guilt. For the gates of hell and the power of life are in the hands of the goddess, and the very act of dedication is regarded as a *voluntary death and*" *salvation by grace*, "inasmuch as the goddess is wont *to elect* those whose term of life is near its close and who stand on the threshold of the night, and are moreover men to whom the mighty mysteries of the goddess may safely be committed. These men the goddess by *her providence brings to new birth* and places once more at *the start of a new race of life*. Therefore thou too must await the command of heaven although long since appointed and ordained, by the clear and evident choice of the great deity, to be highly favoured in thy service at her shrine. And to that end thou like other servants of the goddess shouldst henceforth refrain from impious and unlawful foods, that so thou mayest more righteously win thy way to the secret mysteries of the purest of faiths.' "[1]

Only thus can we understand the far-reaching correspondence that exists, even in the expressions employed, between rites of initiation, and the experience of conversion. The initiates, whether primitive negroes or Hellenistic Greeks, are "new men" with new names, "newly born", *etc.*; and this holds good of converts too. In the first case however it is the outer, and in the second the inner aspect of the process that is presented to us. The fundamental experience, nonetheless, is the same: a new powerfulness enters into life which is experienced as "wholly other", so that life receives a new basis and is begun afresh. In other

---

[1] Apuleius, *Met.* XI, 21 (modified from Butler).

respects the rite is certainly absent from conversion, but by no means its external definiteness; on the contrary: conversion is fixed to a certain date, often indeed to some definite hour and minute. But instead of all the famous and the less well-known accounts of conversion, I shall cite here the marvellous document in which Blaise Pascal has recorded the experience of the night of his own conversion, the concise form of which brings us very close to that experience:

Mémorial de Pascal. † *L'an de grâce* 1654 *Lundi* 23 *Nov. le jour de St. Clément Pape et m.-veille de St. Chr. Depuis environ dix heures et demi du soir jusques environ minuit et demi.—Feu—Dieu d'Abraham, Dieu d'Isaac, Dieu de Jacob, non des philosophes et des savants. Joye certitude sentiment vue joye. Dieu de Jésus Christ. Deum meum et Deum vestrum. Jeh.* 20. 17. *Ton Dieu sera mon Dieu. Ruth. Oubly du monde et de tout hormis Dieu. Il ne se trouve que par les voyes enseignées dans l'Evangile. Grandeur de l'âme humaine. Père juste, le monde ne t'a point connu, mais je t'ay connu. Jeh.* 17. *Joye Joye Joye et pleurs de joye. Je m'en suis séparé. Dereliquerunt me fontem. Mon Dieu me quitterez-vous? que je n'en sois pas séparé éternellement.—Cette est la vie éternelle qu'ils te connaissent seul vrai Dieu et celuy que tu as envoyé . Jésus Christ. Jésus Christ. Je m'en suis séparé, je l'ay fui renoncé crucifié. Que je n'en sois jamais séparé, il ne se conserve que par les voyes enseignées dans l'Evangile. Rénonciation totale et douce. Soumission totale à Jésus-Christ et à mon directeur. Eternellement en joye pour un jour d'exercice sur la terre. Non obliviscar sermones tuos. Amen.* †.[1]

---

[1] "*Mémorial de Pascal.* † This year of Grace 1654, Monday, November 23rd, day of Saint Clement, pope and martyr; Eve of Saint Chrysogonus. From about half past ten at night, to about half after midnight. Fire. God of Abraham, God of Isaac, God of Jacob, not of the philosophers and the wise. Security, Feeling, Joy, Peace. God of Jesus Christ. *Deum meum et Deum vestrum. John* xx. 17. Thy God shall be my God. *Ruth.* Forgetfulness of the world and of all save God. He can be found only in the ways taught in the Gospel. Greatness of the human soul. O righteous Father, the world hath not known thee, but I have known thee. *John* xvii. Joy, joy, joy, tears of joy. I have separated myself from him. *Dereliquerunt me fontem.* My God, why hast thou forsaken me? That I be not separated from thee eternally. This is life eternal: That they might know thee the only true God, and him whom thou hast sent, Jesus Christ. Jesus Christ. I have separated myself from him; I have fled, renounced, cruci-fied him. May I never be separated from him. He maintains himself in me only in the ways taught in the Gospel. Renunciation total and sweet. Complete submission to Jesus Christ and to my confessor. In eternal joy for one day of affliction on earth. *Non obliviscar sermones tuos. Amen.* †." The French Text in *Pascal, Œuvres, Pensées* (C. Brunschvicg), I, 3 *ff.*, 1904: *cf.* the typical account of Stilling's conversion, Günther, *op. cit.*, 48., and of Sicco Tjaden, who called the year of his conversion the "miracle year 1716" (Heppe, *Pietismus*, 418). For Brakel, *ibid.*, 174 *f.* H. Martensen Larsen, *Zweifel und Glaube, Volksausgabe*, 1916, 114. The latter also gives on p. 271 a remark-able conversion document, a kind of gift of the self to the Lord. B. H. Streeter and A. J. Appasamy describe the Sadhu Sundar Singh's conversion in *The Sadhu*, 5 *ff.* Apart from Christianity *cf.* Lehmann-Haas, *Textbuch*, 147 *f.* (Manikkavasagar). Field, *Mystics and Saints*, 19 *ff.* (Hasan Basri), *etc.*

This experience of conversion is almost always the same in all religions: a second self stands over against the first: a completely new life begins: everything has become different. Thus Frick was able to place the conversion of St. Augustine and that of al-Ghazali in almost literal parallel.[1]

The cause of conversion is in itself not infrequently quite trivial: it may be some text often heard that suddenly appeals to the mind with extraordinary force, as in the celebrated instance of St. Augustine and of many Mohammedan mystics; it may be a vision or some other ecstatic state, as in the no less famous case of the apostle Paul. In his classical work on religious experience William James advanced a theory about conversion which, so far as it refers to the psychological process, probably deals with the essentials. He compared the process to the condition in which we find ourselves when searching our memory for some word or name or other; we exert ourselves in vain, but as soon as we discontinue the attempt and quietly settle down, then the word for which we sought suddenly occurs to us. It is exactly the same in the case of the solution of a scientific problem or musical composition *etc.* Conversion would then be an eruption of what has for long been accumulating beneath the threshold of consciousness, which finally and forcibly makes its way into the open. Hence the coerciveness and suddenness in the course of conversion; hence too the consciousness of something wholly new which overwhelms the convert; and thus we can also understand that conversion may occur in the reverse direction, from faith to unbelief. Of this also James quotes examples, while one that is extremely characteristic occurs in Romain Rolland's autobiographical romance *Jean Christophe.* Here the tones have the genuine ring: "Christopher woke up. He looked about him startled . . . He knew nothing. Around him and in him everything was changed. There was no God. . . . As with faith, so the loss of faith is often equally a flood of grace, a sudden light. Reason counts for nothing: the smallest thing is enough—a word, silence, the sound of bells. A man walks, dreams, expects nothing. Suddenly the world crumbles away. All about him is in ruins. He is alone. He no longer believes."[2] Thus conversion is a psychical eruption which, prepared for beneath the threshold of consciousness, is as it were incubated.

3. But although this theory of conversion is most pertinent psychologically, and phenomenologically also gives a satisfactory account

---

[1] H. Frick, *Ghazalis Selbstbiographie, ein Vergleich mit Augustins Konfessionen,* 1919.
[2] *John Christopher,* II, 27.

of the absolute reorientation in life, it is nevertheless insufficient as a description of what is here revealed. For in conversion it is a matter not merely of a thoroughgoing reorientation of Power, but also of a surrender of man's own power in favour of one that utterly overwhelms him and is experienced as sacred and as "wholly other". Of course we are not here discussing the possibility of any divine influence in the experience of conversion: that pertains to theology. But we cannot describe the structure of conversion in itself without taking this divine influence into account as one factor in our comprehension. Estimated by this criterion then it is, comparatively speaking, a matter of complete indifference whether or not conversion is connected with any definite rites, and indeed whether in general it becomes externally perceptible or not. For religion still continues to speak of conversion when it has completely relinquished equally rites and definite seasons, and even the character of suddenness. Thus it is not man who converts himself, but God Who converts him: God bestows new life; and with this, therefore, we revert once again to the basic conditions; primitive rites remain far closer to the essence of the situation than does modern psychology: *conversion, essentially, is rebirth*. God renews life, substitutes sanctity for wickedness, and makes possible a "repetition". Thus to begin life anew is wholly impossible for man: but what is impossible for him is possible to God; and in conversion it is a matter solely of this divine possibility. Exactly as in the case of celebration, we find ourselves confronted here also by the great possibility of "repetition"; "to renew life" was the ardent desire of the ancient Egyptian. Faith itself implies this very repetition. And the primeval yearning to return to the maternal womb becomes experienced here not as any natural process, but as an act of God, of the Father.[1]

[1] *cf*. Geismar, *Kierkegaard*, 185.

FAITH

1. FAITH is in the first place a conjecture. In saying: "I believe", we mean that we do not really know, but that we suppose something or other about the matter in question. Whoever believes in God, then, turns away from knowledge about Him; but he is conscious that he has an awareness (*Ahnung*) of God. The believer, however, has something more than a mere awareness. If someone tells me what at first sight appears incredible, I may eventually reply: "I believe you"; this by no means implies, however, that now I know about the fact told to me, but only that I accept its correctness from the narrator. Once again I know nothing (otherwise of course I need not believe it!), but I accept a truth from another person. To say: "I believe in God", therefore, is to admit the fact of God's existence; it has been declared to me, and has been believed. Thus in the structure of faith *obedience* to truth appears as a contrast to and in relation with, awareness (*Ahnung*). To speak of faith, then, is to speak of *truth*, in the sense not of correctness but of the authentic, valid, ultimate, conclusive and complete. And we observe immediately that we cannot speak about this truth, cannot say anything at all about it, until we have been seized by it, until we believe it: I have believed, and therefore I speak.

Finally, faith is *trust* also. Some affair, or task or person, demands our faith: that is to say, we must have confidence in them. I believe for example in the future of my own people: or I lack faith and can feel no confidence whatever in the matter: "I certainly hear the message, only I lack faith." But as trust, still further, faith presupposes will: we rely not upon a thing, but on a will. Whoever therefore believes in God has an assured sense of Him, obeys His truth and trusts in Him; and this again means that he does something of which no man, of himself, is ever capable. To know about God is easy: but in order to have this awareness of God, to obey Him, to be able to trust in Him, He must arouse some awareness of Himself, permit Himself to be apprehended, confide in man. The surrender involved in faith, therefore, presupposes surrender on the part of God: faith must be bestowed upon man; he can never give faith to himself. We say this even about quite ordinary affairs, and it is essentially correct. Faith is always a gift; even the faintest awareness of God can be the outcome of no human reflection alone. And here we forsake the domain of appearances and of inward experiences. Faith "appears" to us just as little as does guilt.[1]

2. With faith, therefore, an entirely new element enters into the religious life; although, taken quite literally, it does not "enter into" this life, since it would in that case be a phenomenon. Rather it bears upon life and indeed, in the first place, as a judgment passed on life, and then as its liberation. To the religious man who refuses simply to "accept" life and is troubled about it (in other words), three different ways are open: (*1*) *Domination*: man then finds his *locus standi* (*a*) magically, *locus standi in loco Dei*; or (*b*) theoretically: within the totality of his ideas he assigns a place to certain aspects of life, by means of which he presumes to dominate life; the Greeks adopted this course; (*c*) experience: so far as is possible, life becomes exhausted to its very foundations in feeling:—the path of Romanticism. (*2*) The second main course lies in *conduct*:—either in (*a*) rites, regulating life into an attained whole; or (*b*) custom; or again (*c*) prayer, which overcomes nothing whatever, but only expects, entreats, hopes:—and all this comprehends almost everything that precedes.

But now a further consideration arises :. for life does not belong to us at all. It belongs to God, Who has created it. We can therefore neither overcome it nor beg for it, since it always belongs to God alone, and any possibility it possesses lies in whatever we receive. Bustling about then, whether externally or internally, is quite futile; God's deed alone sets us free. God, Who created us, creates us anew, and makes us into a "new creation".[2]

Salvation, therefore, at which all religion without exception aims, is here no longer something to be won, but is simply a gift of grace; thus, indeed, it first becomes salvation in any actual sense. For life as such, even at its very highest power, is never genuine salvation.[3] Salvation is never something attained nor effected by man himself, not what has grown into his life or has become visible therein. It is the

---

[1] *cf.* Boulgakoff, *Orthodoxie*, 5.   [2] Chap. 45. καινὴ κτίσις.
[3] Scheler, *Rel. Erneuerung*, 335; Hofmann, *Erlebnis*, 12 *ff.*, 34 *f.*; *cf.* Piper, *Ethik*, I, 111.

hidden ground of life in God: it is the contrary, or rather the reverse side, of guilt. In truth, nothing becomes visible here: everything remains concealed.

Thus we can understand how it is that Christian *preaching* expounds the liberation that is trusted in as *forgiveness* of guilt, and as *atonement* for sin; and still more deeply does the idea of *election* penetrate, which arises in both Judaism and Islam and subsequently becomes the central idea in Christianity. Faith therefore is not a human sentiment, not a human deed, feeling nor volition, but man's state of being elected from the very beginning; out of His own free and incalculable grace God has chosen the believer, and imparted to him the *donum fidei*. And thus man's salvation lies wholly outside his own life (forensic justification, so-called), in God. The powerfulness of life in itself has utterly disappeared: only He has all Power; "with force of arms we nothing can". Involuntarily, we are here speaking the language of that religious movement, the Reformation, which constitutes faith the central point of all religion; and Luther's and Calvin's *sola fide* must be understood from this point of view. "For (faith) is the (Christian's) life, righteousness and bliss, which preserves the very self and makes it acceptable, and imparts to it all that Christ has, as has been previously observed, and as is confirmed by St. Paul in the *Epistle to the Galatians* ii, where he says: 'and the life which I now live in the flesh I live by the faith of the Son of God.' "[1]

[1] Luther, *Of the Liberty of a Christian.*

CHAPTER 81

ADORATION

1. FAITH itself and as such, therefore, does not "appear", nor become visible. But there is one phenomenon which, although it is certainly not the "appearance" of faith but its consequence, does reveal its presence. This is *Adoration*. Whoever believes, adores. He does not merely pray, since prayer originates from care.[1] Need teaches prayer but not *adoration*, as Scheler finely asserted.[2] Whoever adores has therefore forgotten his prayer and now knows only God's glory.

> God reveals His presence:
> Let us now adore Him,
> And with awe appear before Him.
> God is in His temple:
> All within keep silence,
> Prostrate lie with deepest reverence.[3]

Adoration, then, is the very culmination of worship, where inner and outer wholly coincide; and its almost muted tones resound not in Christianity alone, but also in Israel, in Islam and in India; Otto has compiled a wonderful selection of "numinous hymns" that give expression to adoration. Nevertheless the volume of sound is at its fullest where the worshipping community bows down before the presence of the Lord: "Lift up your hearts! We lift them up unto the Lord."

2. It is not only celebration, however, that culminates in adoration: custom also finds its ultimate fulfilment here; it too is transformed into praise and gratitude. Then the sole task of life is to extol God; and from this all moral conduct, as such, arises spontaneously. Thus the mystery of guilt sinks engulfed within the deeper mystery of God's love: only hope remains. And these notes too resound quite apart from Christianity (we recall the *Bhagavad-Gita*), although they were in fact most forcibly struck by the Reformers, and particularly by Calvin. All these elements united, then, reverberate in the church's hymn of adoration: *Te Deum Laudamus*:

---

[1] Chap. 62.   [2] *Rel. Erneuerung*, 300.   [3] Tersteegen.

We praise thee, O God: we acknowledge thee to be the Lord.
All the earth doth worship thee: the Father everlasting.
To thee all Angels cry aloud: the Heavens, and all the Powers therein.
To thee Cherubin, and Seraphin, continually do cry,
Holy, Holy, Holy: Lord God of Sabaoth;
Heaven and earth are full of the Majesty of thy Glory.
Vouchsafe, O Lord, to keep us this day without sin.
O Lord, have mercy upon us: have mercy upon us.
O Lord, let thy mercy lighten upon us, as our trust is in thee.
O Lord, in thee have I trusted: let me never be confounded.

PART FOUR

THE WORLD

CHAPTER 82

WAYS TO THE WORLD. CREATIVE DOMINATION

1. IN Chapter 8 I showed that for primitive man the modern concept of "world" does not really exist, and that far from regarding his environment as an object, he immediately constitutes it his own "conjoint world"; and in this principle the essential feature of the religious *Weltanschauung* has already been expressed. I may now repeat this, however, in the sense that a "religious *Weltanschauung*" is never merely a "point of view", but is always a *participation*, a *sharing*. For out of his own particular environment everyone constructs a world for himself which he believes himself able to dominate; there is therefore no *one* single world, but just as many *worlds* as there are human beings. Thus what holds good of the child is true universally: and "it should be the fundamental principle of every psychology, as contrasted with theories of knowledge, that for conscious experience reality is never a constant, but that it changes with the individual's psychical organization, and indeed with his stage of development; it must then be definitely stated, at the outset, that every child lives in a world quite different from ours".[1] In this sense the world is "objective mind";[2] the human spirit does not direct itself towards a world that is given to it, but allows what meets it to become part of itself, after it has sufficiently modified it. The "world" is therefore an essentially "celebrated", not merely an "accepted" but a dominated world.[3]

2. Herein lies the truth of the principle of participation, of sharing, advanced by Lévy-Bruhl. Things do not encounter each other "solidly in space", but have some share in one another and may mingle with, and appear in place of, each other. Accordingly, man does not conduct himself "objectively" towards the "world": he participates in it, just as it does in him. His path to the world, therefore, is neither that of contemplation, nor reflection, nor presenting himself as a subject and so forming a "substratum", but of existing as oriented *towards* the world. Man's domination of the world is thus a domination exerted always from within.

---

[1] Spranger, *Psychologie des Jugendalters*, 32.
[2] *cf.* Spranger, *Lebensformen*, 17 *f.*   [3] *cf.* Heidegger, *op. cit.*, 87.

This participation, still further, is an attitude deeply rooted in human nature; it is not a disposition that requires to be overcome, but is the perfectly natural mental outlook even of "modern" man, thoroughly accustomed as he is to theoretical and practical knowledge and to objective observation and experiment.[1] As Lévy-Bruhl himself profoundly observes on this subject: "Now the need of participation assuredly remains something more imperious and more intense, even among peoples like ourselves, than the thirst for knowledge and the desire for conformity with the claims of reason. It lies deeper within us and its source is more remote."[2] This mental attitude, therefore, which neither dissects nor abstracts, neither infers nor analyses, but deals with the whole, grasps it concretely, connects together its essentials and experiences "participation", is ours to-day just as much as it is that of primitive man. In the case of the latter, certainly, it has a wider range of control, although so-called "primitives" are obviously "modern" also, and are quite familiar with analytical and logical thought! But for us too it is the actual way to the world:[3] not indeed as "lazy thinking", as Thurnwald would regard it, but existing as oriented towards the world in contrast to merely observing it. The self, that is to say, is a partner with the world and the world with the self.[4]

This relationship (to continue) results in events in the world, equally with man's own activities, being dominated by "mystical" factors; I shall employ this expression, which was coined by Lévy-Bruhl, although I believe myself that it involves some misapprehension, and I would therefore prefer to restrict the terms "mysticism" and "mystical" to the phenomenon previously described in Chapter 75.[5] As regards the facts, however, Lévy-Bruhl is perfectly correct. When, for example, Gräbner attempts to invalidate his assertion by showing that "the Australian does not conceive the natural as supernatural, but conversely the supernatural as natural", and that the magic power he employs is

---

[1] cf. Marett, Faith, Hope and Charity, 86.

[2] How Natives Think, 385; cf. the remarkable discussion of Lévy-Bruhl's ideas in Bulletin 29, Société française de Philosophie, 1929, No. 4. Nothing is more significant of the low philosophic level of the historical and ethnological sciences than the misunderstanding of Lévy-Bruhl's views, exhibited by investigators in the most diverse fields. In this respect the urgent necessity becomes obvious of an understanding between Psychology and Phenomenology on the one hand, and on the other the so-called pure historic, anthropological and ethnological sciences, which to-day, almost without exception, set out, without being aware of so doing, from the most extraordinary epistemological, psychological and metaphysical principles.

[3] Thurnwald, Bequemes Denken.   [4] cf. Danzel, Grundlagen, 432.

[5] cf. Werner Entw. Psych. 270.

thought of as "grossly material",[1] this only indicates that the ethnologist has failed to perceive how our own antithesis between supernatural and natural, as this has gradually developed in Western European thought, does not exist at all in primitive and religious thought. That the primitive mind understands everything supernatural in some natural sense is indeed quite correct; but then his "naturalness" is far more "supernatural", more "mystical" or (still better) more numinous, than our "supernaturalness". And that Power is conceived as material is equally true; but we observed much earlier that the contrast between the material and the spiritual is far from being so fundamental as our current popular psychology would gladly believe it to be.[2]

I can influence the world therefore, just as the world can affect me, in a way that is justified by neither logic nor facts, but which constitutes a very real struggle at the closest possible range. I shall call this contest the *magical attitude*; and the armistice that follows the struggle, which is itself however also one kind of domination preluding a new combat, I shall call the *mythical form-conferring attitude*. The former is concerned with Powers, the latter with Will and Form, but both alike are conditioned by participation. For without participation there is no struggle: and similarly without proximity. This magical attitude, however, is not a structure of the spiritual life merely of the past, of which only meagre vestiges now persist for us; nor, again, is it a degeneration nor childish malady; it is neither "primitive science" nor elementary technique.[3] It is, on the contrary, a primal attitude very deeply grounded in human nature, as vital among ourselves as it ever was, in fact an eternal structure. This is evident, too, in the recurring predominance under certain conditions of the magical attitude. Children will be considered later, while Storch has discussed the reasoning of the mentally disordered and compiled remarkable examples of the magical attitude of mind, and has explicitly placed these parallel to "primitive" data. "As an underlying current of waking day-thinking there lies ready prepared, in every man, magical-archaic experience; but this comes into serious

---

[1] *Weltbild*, 16.

[2] K. Hidding has recently given an excellent description of so-called primitive mentality in his *Gebruiken en godsdienst der Soendaneezer, De Opwekker*, 1933, 3.

[3] Of a completely different opinion are Allier (Magic is degeneration), Lindworsky (primitives think rationally, but know nothing about the conditions of natural processes: magic is ignorance), Boas (feeling predominates among primitives), Bartlett (predominance of the play instinct); I have discussed these views elsewhere in my *Structure*. Closely akin to my own ideas is W. Mayer-Gross, *Zur Frage der psychologischen Eigenart der sog. Naturvölker*, VIII *Int. Congress of Psychology, Proc. and Papers*, 1927, 206 *ff.*

conflict with ordinary rational thinking only in specific schizoid types";[1] thus to victims of schizophrenic megalomania "the world, from being a differentiated objectivity, again becomes the immediate content of his own existence[2] . . . instead of being an object of objective consciousness, the world of things then becomes a mere modification of self-feeling."[3] One patient, for instance, "calls herself 'the goddess', relating how she has been placed in the domain of the sun and that the end of the world has been revealed to her, but that her joy in life could not be killed, as she wished to devour the time following the end of the world". We curtly describe this mental attitude as megalomania, but we must not forget that this mania subsists in the blood of us all without exception—this mania to dominate the world—and that anyone who had entirely relinquished this madness could no longer live. It is essentially human not to accept the given world, but to manipulate it until it has been adjusted to one's own life. "The world was not, till it I did create."[4] Thus a condition of struggle always prevails, whose victorious conclusion implies the decline of world power into that of the individual.[5]

3. He who thus assumes the magical attitude, according to Salomon Reinach's fine simile, resembles the conductor dominating his orchestra; and it may well be that he believes that he himself produces the uproar! The best parallel to the person who is magically disposed, however, is Chanticleer, who thinks that his crowing makes the sun rise, and who suffers the most tragic disillusioning when, one morning, the sun is there "of itself!" So man too assumes the offensive against the powers:[6] he overcomes them by the main force of his own will: he creates them as it were. The purely magical attitude, which of course nowhere actually exists, is therefore that of God, of the Creator:

> At my command, upon yon primal Night,
> The starry hosts unveiled their glorious light.[7]

In magic, then, the dictum *eritis sicut Deus*—"ye shall be as gods"—attains full reality; and in truth magical thinking is not literally thought "but willing".[8]

---

[1] Storch, *op. cit.*, 88 *f.*   [2] *ibid.*, 74.
[3] Storch.   [4] *Faust*, Part II, Act 2.
[5] Cassirer, *op. cit.*, II, 194: "Thus the ego exercises an almost limitless domination over reality in the magical world survey; it draws all reality back into itself."
[6] Reinach, *Orpheus*[2], 32 *f.* E.T. 23.   [7] *Faust*, Part II, Act 2 (Swanwick).
[8] Prinzhorn, *Bildnerei*, 311.

It is, therefore, never legitimate to set "religion" and "magic" in any definitely adverse relationship, as though religion were the successor of magic, the latter being non-religious and the former never magical. Magic itself is religion simply because it is concerned with powers; certainly it requires no "god", but a "godless" act may very well be religious. Magic differs, however, from all other forms of religion in that the desire to dominate the world belongs to its essential nature. Not every religion has this aim; nevertheless it is adopted by very many non-magical religions, only with other methods. Thus I can concede neither the antithesis between religion and magic as social-antisocial, nor as ethical-scientific, nor again that magic is anterior to religion:[1] wherever there is religion there is magic, even though the magical stream does not always follow the main channel of religion; similarly, wherever there is magic there is religion, although it can be only one specific type of religion. Saintyves, therefore, is quite correct: magic is an art, knowledge, a cult, only it deals with mystery.[2]

The magical attitude, then, is certainly religious: nevertheless it demands nothing "supernatural"; and the extent to which scholars of to-day take for granted the application of modern concepts to primitive religion, and in fact to religion in general, is astonishing. If I shoot an arrow at an enemy directly opposite me, this is to our modes of thought certainly a disagreeable, but perfectly logical, action. But if I aim my arrow at an opponent who is in another town a hundred miles away, then our logic ceases and we speak of an action grounded on the "supernatural", for whose results the supernatural may well be responsible. In primitive consciousness, however, these two acts are by no means so different: in any case we require a superior and numinous power for the success of both alike.[3] This is the truth in those theories of magic which emphasize the close relationship of ordinary *technique* to magical processes,[4] although the derivation of magical activity from primitive *technique*, attempted by Vierkandt,[5] has little force; and with his usual keen penetration Nietzsche has perceived the essential feature here: "when one rows, it is not the rowing that moves the boat, but rowing is only a magical ceremony by which one compels a *daemon* to

---

[1] *cf.* W. Otto's admirable observations on these problems: *AR.* 12, 1909, 544 *ff.*; *cf.* Clemen, *Wesen und Ursprung der Magie, Arch. f. Rel.-Psych.*, II-III; Beth, *Religion und Magie*; Bertholet, *op. cit.*, 23; Thurnwald, *Zauber*, 485, 498 *ff.* Vierkandt, *Die Anfänge der Religion und Zauberei, Globus*, 92, 64.

[2] *Force magique*, 9, 14.　　　　　　　　　　　[3] *cf.* Arbmann, *op. cit.*, 352.

[4] Söderblom, *Gottesglaube*, 68 *ff.* Vierkandt, *loc. cit.*, 21 *ff.*, 40 *f.*

[5] *cf.* Beth, *op. cit.*, 84.

move the boat" (I should myself substitute a "power"). "All maladies, even death itself, are the result of magical influences. Illness and death never happen naturally; *the whole conception of 'natural sequence' is lacking* . . . when a man shoots with a bow, there is still always present an irrational hand and strength . . . man is the *rule*, nature is irregularity."[1] To this I need add nothing.

But what really lends the magical attitude its intrinsic human interest is its character of protest: Preuss has observed how, in magical thinking, man opposed animal *instinct*, and so rose above himself; how too, in magic, lie the roots of all idealism and the possibility of the liberation of the human spirit.[2] Magical man, then, makes a "world", his own world, out of the "environment" of the animal; and thus magic was the earliest mode of uniting individual objects within one all-inclusive world-picture.[3]

This magical attitude, still further, appears even more clearly in the simplest examples than in complicated magic rituals. Lévy-Bruhl alludes, for instance, to the rite of reversing an action (*renverser un acte*): in certain tribes stepping over anyone is strictly prohibited and whoever inadvertently does so must nullify his action by once again stepping over the person concerned, only this time "in the reverse direction".[4] That is a magical action which many of us will recognize from our own youthful experience: a compulsive action consisting, for example, in not striking the right foot with the left without making this good immediately by touching the left foot with the right one. In this simple act, however, there lies a mastery of the world which permits whatever has happened to be modified, or even to be made retrogressive. Here then man raises his protest, utters his "Nevertheless", tenses his own will against what is simply given to him. It is thus not at all astonishing that a certain relationship exists between idealism and magic. We have already quoted the Bachelor in Goethe's *Faust*; we can also cite Amiel, who correctly discerned a magical tendency in Schleiermacher's *Monologues*: "The tameless liberty, the divine dignity of the individual spirit, expanding till it admits neither any limit nor anything foreign to itself, and conscious of a strength instinct with creative force."[5]

This domination of the world by will has, however, one essential condition:—before the world can be thus controlled it must be transferred inwards, and man must take it into himself: he can actually

---

[1] *Human, All Too Human*, I, 117, 118 (Foulis Edition).
[2] *Geistige Kultur*, 8.   [3] Kretschmer, *Medizinische Psychologie*, 34.
[4] *Primitives and the Supernatural*, 381.   [5] *Journal*, 1 Feb. 1852 (Ward).

dominate it only when it has in this way become an inner realm. For this reason all magic is autism, or "living within oneself".[1] "From the sensuous data of the environment the autistic-self-sufficient schizophrene makes for himself a totally different and more abundantly filled world, which he does not secure nor bring into accord with other people by means of any logical conventions, but which remains just raw material for his own fancies, caprices and needs. The actual environment, as such, is depreciated; it demands no recognition—it may be either utilized, or excluded, wholly at will."[2] And what is here asserted about mental disorder holds good almost precisely for magical man in general.[3] Man does not trouble himself at all about "reality": he dominates it creatively, since he immures himself against it; he erects a kingdom internally, a divine service in his own soul. Wherever any settled limits are given between man and the world, between object and subject, severe conflicts arise as in mental disease, or again in the contest between the artist and the world; and wherever these do not exist, as with primitive peoples, the magician receives his own official status, while everyone participates somehow or other in magical procedure. As Kretschmer correctly observes, myths and dogmas do not consider the world as it actually is, but deal with it wholly at will and make it into a world as it should be. In the fairy tale the idea that simultaneously expresses, and fulfils, a wish holds good even to-day, and the entire rite, the celebration, is quite incomprehensible apart from this autistic attitude: it is man himself who settles his own conditions. Thus primitive man firmly believes that unless certain words are recited and certain actions performed, it will not rain; and quite similarly, "only if you tidy up your chest of drawers now will you get your summer holiday", thinks the magically disposed child, who likewise lives in her own world. "When my dearest friend was very ill", said the same child, "I believed I could save her only by going up and down the street six times every day", and naturally with a most scrupulous avoidance of the gaps in the paving-stones![4] "Children stand nearer to the world of magic: the problem of the possibility of things does not

---

[1] In fuller detail *cf.* my *Structure.*

[2] Prinzhorn, *Bildnerei der Geisteskranken,* 55.

[3] In my *Structure* I have discussed the problem, which is scarcely pertinent here, of how it is that the same attitude arises in so widely diverse types of people as the mentally deranged, primitives, children, artists, *etc.* In any case we must be most cautious in making phylogenetic generalizations.

[4] Additional examples in Zeininger, *Magische Geisteshaltung im Kindesalter und ihrer Bedeutung für die religiöse Entwicklung.*

torment them, and although their thoughts are not debarred from the experience of reality, still they remain outside its domain; they are autistic, and live within themselves, not because they are turned away from the world but simply because they have not yet attained an adequate relationship to the real." In these terms H. C. Rümke[1] presents the essence of this mental attitude and, at the same time, reveals the reason why the norm that governs the life both of children and of primitives leads among modern adults to illness.[2]

When it is considered from the standpoint of its object, the world, the autistic "living within oneself" that characterizes the subject of experience appears as "catathymia"—a term employed by Kretschmer to describe that state of mind in which everything is perceived in accordance with one's own subjective mood, so that objective reality is to that degree distorted. Consequently the "world" becomes regarded entirely as one's own domain and experienced merely "in accord with human subjectivity", with its desires and demands. One catatonic patient, for example, crawled under his bed and tried to lift it with all his strength: that was the way in which he wanted "to lead the earth nearer to God",[3] while another person similarly afflicted would fall out of bed "in order to keep the world rotating, so that the wheel should go on turning".[4] For in all such cases the "world" lies within while, conversely, nothing whatever is perceived outside except the self: another patient felt fatigued and thought that her own strength was exhausted by the farmers working in the fields![5] I cannot agree with Kretschmer, however, in seeking the principle of this "catathymia" merely in feeling;[6] while this view is certainly not wholly incorrect, still in the wish for domination, in the emotional craving, the will is also manifested, and this has formed itself on the lines of the "wholly other". Once again then: magical man *protests*.

This "catathymic" attitude, again, extends to the entire Universe: the "underworld" becomes Hades, hell: heaven the abode of the blessed, the desert the resort of demons;[7] in all conditions, and in every event,

---

[1] *Geneeskundige Bladen*, 25. *Reeks*, X, 1927, 329; *cf.* also *Psych. und Neurol. Bl.*, 1928, 5–6, 29.

[2] Prinzhorn, *op. cit.*, 298 *f.* This by no means implies that primitive thought corresponds in every respect to that of children.   [3] Storch, *op. cit.*, 73.

[4] *ibid.*, 8; *cf.* 69, 80, and the characteristic case in Jaspers' *Psychopathologie*, 400.

[5] Storch, *ibid.*, 41.

[6] According to Kretschmer, causal thought connects things together in accordance with the principle of frequency, but magical thinking on the basis of the principle of community of feeling; *op. cit.*, 34.

[7] *cf.* Danzel, *Psych. Grundl.*, 436 *ff.* Werner, *Entwicklungspsychologie*, 62.

man perceives himself. He is Power: he is God. It may be, however, that in him Faust's yearning is manifested:

> Could I my pathway but from magic free,
> And quite unlearn the spells of sorcery,
> Stood I, Oh Nature, man alone 'fore thee,
> Then were it worth the trouble man to be![1]

This indeed the Greeks were able to do, since in the Homeric structure of their spirit they were the first to discover "Nature" in its modern sense.[2] Their religion (so far, of course, as it was Homeric and not mystical-Platonic) was that of the given, of quiescent Being, and as such it maintains a quite specific position among religions.[3]

A quite different victory over magic consists in the idea of *creation*. Magic is certainly by no means disavowed: but God, Who utters His creative word, is now the sole magician; and man's word, which is essentially an answer, can never possess magical power. But God speaks "So let it be!" and it is: He speaks again, and a second creation consummates the marvel of rebirth: He speaks "the word only, and my servant shall be healed".[4] Here, then, there is neither "acceptance" nor self-sufficient "celebration", but only receiving.

4. The second mode of creative domination, as has already been observed, may be understood as a quiescent pause following on the convulsive magical attainment of mastery. Man now retires from the world to a certain distance; and at first he seems to desire only to contemplate. Hence the static aspect of the mythical world: it wholly disregards time and, as it were, immobilizes it;[5] its forms are eternal, immutable. Every human passion, every desire, every thought, has there, in the realm of myth, its "eternal aspect".[6]

But this apparently contemplative domination is nonetheless control: man endows the world powers with form so that he can overcome them more effectively, even though in a manner wholly different from his magical attitude. Thus the form-imparting individual,[7] who invokes and evokes events as myths,[8] has adopted an attitude directly opposed to that of the magical individual. The latter absorbed the world within himself: but the other type of man ejects the world from himself. He projects experienced power into the external world; his own love assumes the form of the Cyprian goddess, his yearning becomes the

---

[1] *Faust*, Part II, Act 5.   Otto, *Götter Griechenlands*, 47.
[3] Chap. 95.   [4] *Matt.* viii. 8.   [5] Chap. 55, 60.
[6] Otto, *op. cit.*   [7] Chap. 17.   [8] Chap. 60.

Garden of Eden and his guilt the fall.[1] His death again, together with his hope of resurrection, he experiences "dually" (the dual experience of form!) in the myth of Light, and his dread in demonic figures.

Flight from the self, still further, corresponds to autism, to the passionate search for the self. "The poet draws the world within himself, in order to transfer it 'outwardly' afresh in the manifold forms of his work: the youth who has withdrawn from the world, into the depths of his own soul, attempts to bring its riches to light once more by writing poems."[2] Similarly, "primitive man has created a world for himself which, although it is for us only a product of imagination, implies for him a very concrete reality; but he thus elicits from his own soul all the possibilities that he has experienced. He peoples field and forest with the figures of his desires, his dread, his hope and his woe."[3] This is the animistic tendency of humanity, which here we encounter afresh, and in this sense spirits and gods are indeed "exponents of feeling".[4] "Under the pressure of a hostile world man, unsatisfied with a refuge in his inner being, creates a life apart from his own, a 'thou', in which he finds anew his own hate and his own love. Thus the two tendencies, of magical autism and of mythical endowment with form, correspond to and complete each other. They are both present simultaneously: now the one, and again the other, predominates. Only the attitude of the mentally disordered (the schizophrene) halts at the magical method, and hence it turns into a blind alley. But we too are just as much 'mythologists' as 'primitive man' ",[5] and are distinguished from him only by being conscious of the abyss separating our "primitive" from our logically grounded knowledge. It is true that Storch maintains that poetical images and metaphors hold their place in our own thought only as parallels or comparisons, or that these figures emerge only when our ideas relax.[6] But I believe that when Chesterton describes the Law of Gravitation as "that mad and quickening rush by which all earth's creatures fly back to her heart when released", he is expounding a genuinely vital "animistic" idea[7] which, despite its lack of scientific precision, exactly expresses the essence of the situation. For the time is past when poetry could be disposed of as merely playful comparison and religion as a similarly playful notion.

The form of myth, therefore, is that of experience; and whoever wishes to understand myth must first of all discover in it not any

---

[1] cf. Danzel, *Psych. Grundlagen.*   [2] cf. Spranger, *Psych. des Jugendalters*, 68.
[3] My *Structure*, 19 f.   [4] Wilamowitz.
[5] cf. Tillich, *Rel. Verwirkl.*, 96 ff   [6] *op. cit.*, 11.   [7] My *Structure*, 20 f.

"explanation" of certain natural phenomena, but an attaining of mastery over the world which, although certainly less forcible than the magical method, would still wrest from the "thou" what magic had extorted from the powers. In this connection, too, the newer mythological method is fully justified in its endeavour to understand the cult, in the first instance, in order to comprehend myths.[1] For what lives in myth subsists already in sacred action, in the "celebration" of the event, and conversely!

Like magic, still further, the mythical endowment with form comes to an end that is, however, never ultimate. Probably, therefore, we shall never be able to remove magic completely from our path, just as we are scarcely ever likely to discontinue spontaneous creation of form or ignore the traditionally given. Essentially, however, mythical endowment with form does reach its end where nothingness is the goal of all powerfulness. Mysticism, particularly the Hindu type, can instruct us on this point.[2] For where the void, or nullity, is to be attained in a "modeless mode", there every form without exception disappears. But the mythical form also comes to an end where an all-embracing form is given to faith,[3] which is not intended to subserve any acquisition of power but is itself that of a servitor. The belief in Incarnation, therefore, may essentially (that is, theologically and eschatologically) dispense with every form.

5. The two paths to the world, finally, with which we have thus become familiar, are actually only *one* road with two rails. Once again, however, this does not involve humanity following this road to its end until it notices that it raises a dilemma, and then striking another road such as that of science, of mysticism or of faith, as evolutionists and phylogenists are inclined to maintain. For we travel both roads now, just as previously and as always. But we are not restricted to them; and at this point the simile of the two roads ends: it must now be replaced by that of strata. The spiritual life of man then consists of different levels, one of which is at the same moment the most deeply situated and the most important:—that is the dual level of autism and myth, wherein "participation" is the fundamental law. Above this stratum others are deposited that are more or less based upon it.

To these other levels (to continue) the magical-mythical domination of the world is related in the same way as is dream life to waking consciousness. From recent psychology, then, we learn that dream experi-

[1] Chap. 60.   [2] Chap. 75.   [3] Chap. 80.

ence is in no degree less "real" than is daily life. The study of dreams is in fact a no less reliable path to the secret of life than is the investigation of waking consciousness; and Wilhelm Raabe observes that "we raise a corner of the curtain over the great mystery of the world when we reflect, and carefully consider the fact that stupid people and the poor in spirit may have the most marvellous and the most intelligent dreams; just as talented and strange as those of clever people, equally by day and by night".[1] Here again, therefore, we approach more closely to primitive feeling than to that of the nineteenth century when we regard dream facts as being valid of life, though not of waking life, just as Kamchadale tribesmen do who tell a young girl whom they desire that they have already won her favours in their dreams, whereupon the girl yields.[2] Similarly for primitive man his wife's infidelity, of which he has merely dreamt, is regarded as established;[3] while in Gaboon "a dream is more conclusive than a witness".[4] We must concede then that here a consciousness of reality is experienced, and this not only in the magical attitude. Thus the dream differs from waking consciousness in three respects: (*1*) "the supporting pillar of conscious experience, while we are awake, the tension between subject and object" disappears;[5] (*2*) the dream orders events in a way which compared with the experience of the day is asyntactic:—it has a loose or "diffuse structure",[6] its images being arranged in accord with the feelings, anxieties and desires of the dreamer, as in the previously defined "catathymia";[7] (*3*) the dream world is sharply separated from daily reality: it is mythical, having neither past nor future.[8]

The dream itself, of course, is not within the religious category; nevertheless it is life: life is a dream, the dream a life. And it displays life to us in rendering the domination of the world first of all possible in the magical-mythical manner; and also by the way in which it appears in its profoundest depths at the very frontier of the mechanized consciousness. In Prospero's words:

> We are such stuff
> As dreams are made on, and our little life
> Is rounded with a sleep.

---

[1] *Das Odfeld (Sämtl. Werke, 4, 90).*   [2] Lévy-Bruhl, *Primitive Mentality*, 115.
[3] R. Thurnwald, *Die Lüge in der primitiven Kultur: Die Lüge*, edited by O. Lippmann, 1927, 398.   [4] Lévy-Bruhl, *ibid.*, 101.
[5] Storch, *op. cit.*, 25; not however in the manner of mysticism, since the dream lacks the element of passion.
[6] Werner, *Entw. Psych.* 41.   [7] Kretschmer, *op. cit.*, 57 *f.*
[8] Kretschmer, *ibid.*, 64 *ff.* Binswanger, van der Leeuw, *Structure.*

R. ALLIER, *Le non-civilisé et nous*, 1927.

F. C. BARTLETT, *Psychology and Primitive Culture*, 1923.

A. BERTHOLET, *Das Wesen der Magie (Nachr. der Ges. d. Wiss. zu Göttingen, Gesch. Mitt.*, 1926–27).

L. BINSWANGER, *Wandlungen in der Auffassung und Deutung des Traumes von den Griechen bis zur Gegenwart*, 1928.

F. BOAS, *The Mind of Primitive Man*.

C. CLEMEN, *Wesen und Ursprung der Magie (Arch. f. Rel.-Psych.* II–III, 1921).

A. K. COOMARASWAMY, *De la Mentalité Primitive (Études Traditionnelles*, 44, 1939).

TH. W. DANZEL, *Kultur und Religion des primitiven Menschen*, 1924.
Die psychologischen Grundlagen der Mythologie (AR. 21, 1922).

F. GRAEBNER, *Das Weltbild der Primitiven*, 1924.

E. KRETSCHMER, *Medizinische Psychologie*[2], 1922.

J. LINDWORSKY, *Die Primitiven und das kausale Denken (Int. Woche für Religionsethnologie*, IV. *Tagung*, 1926).

H. PRINZHORN, *Bildnerei der Geisteskranken*[2], 1923.

A. STORCH, *Das archaisch-primitive Erleben und Denken der Schizophrenen*, 1922.

R. THURNWALD, *Zauber (in Lexikon der Vorgeschichte)*.
Bequemes Denken (Inst. intern. d'anthropologie, III Session, 1927).

A. VIERKANDT, *Die Anfänge der Religion und Zauberei (Globus*, 92, 1907).

K. ZEININGER, *Magische Geisteshaltung im Kindesalter und ihre Bedeutung für die religiöse Entwicklung*, 1929.

CHAPTER 83

WAYS TO THE WORLD. THEORETICAL
DOMINATION

1. SIDE by side with the domination of the world by means of magic and of the creation of form appears that achieved by *thought*. "Thought is one of the powers of Being, in which fate breaks loose from itself; it is an existential power."[1] But by the term "thought" alone the type of world domination referred to here is quite inadequately characterized. For the magical and the mythical form-creating attitudes also presuppose thinking.[2] We must therefore add that in specifically *theoretical thought* man frees himself so far as is at all possible from the environing world, and moves as far as he can from it, in order to *observe* it from a suitable distance as disinterestedly as possible. Both the magical and the mythical attitudes, again, always eliminate the contrast between subject and object: here, on the contrary, it becomes strictly observed: I *direct* my own thoughts towards the world, and therefore we speak of *directed thought*.

This has the same relation to the magic-mythical as waking experience has to the dream; but after what has been said in the preceding Chapter it need hardly be added that this by no means implies a relation like that between reality and appearance. For both waking thought and dream thought are ways to the world; there is a day-dream just as there is a night-thought, the distinction being that in waking thought man directs himself expressly towards an object and reflects upon this, so as to elaborate some *theory*, while in the dream there is no absolute object whatever, and equally little any stable subject. We discover a transitional stage, however, in those sciences and modes of knowledge which certainly elevate man expressly above the totality of the world, yet nevertheless contemplate him too as a sort of "world" that is, as it were, the reverse of the external world. We have previously discussed

---

[1] Tillich, *Philosophie und Schicksal*, 310.

[2] This type of thought is very finely characterized by Pedersen, *Israel*, 75: "For the Israelite, thought is not the solution of abstract problems. It is not connected link by link, and does not elaborate principal and subordinate sentences in order to draw conclusions therefrom. *For the Israelite, to think is to make a totality his own.* He directs his soul towards the principal factor, the decisive element in the totality, and takes this into his soul, which is thus set in motion and led in a definite direction."

astrology, which allots man the status of a microcosm over against the Whole as a macrocosm;[1] I may also allude further to Indian thought, which certainly gives prominence to the human mind as the *ātman*, but only in order immediately to identify it again with the spirit of the Universe. This type of theory I call, in Oldenberg's term, "prescientific science";[2] and within these relationships astrology falls in virtue of its casting life into fixed cosmic rhythm, and Hindu speculation because of its magical type of knowledge: "knowledge is power".[3]

Thought however, even directed thought, is of course no prerogative of culture. Primitives also think: "thinkers think, they who dwell here in their world. Behind their fires those present speak together: what are we to do with our thoughts? how are we to speak with our words?" say the Cora Indians.[4] But civilized thought also, on the other hand, is never without primitive-magical-mythical elements: man can never wholly succeed in abstracting his own mind from the world. Indeed he often feels, and quite justifiably, that in this intellectual activity he is abusing his actual life.

Science, in our modern sense of the term, was born in Greece; and it is very remarkable how the magical-mythical attitude only gradually receded before that of theoretic knowledge. Thus for Pherecydes cosmogony fashions itself, imperceptibly and *quasi*-spontaneously, into the myth of the marriage of Zeus and Chthonia; the entire Ionian monism reposes, in fact, upon the idea of participation: one thing participates in another, otherwise it could have no influence whatever on it; primeval power again, the *arche*, sought by the Ionian philosophy of Nature, is essentially related to the *mana*-power that primitive peoples believe in;[5] the philosophy of Nature (and, with this, science in general) is indeed "born from mysticism".[6] But later, with Socrates and the sophists, the great change appeared. Man discovered himself, that is to say, his own spirit; and then he began to objectivize the world: Protagoras' dictum πάντων χρημάτων μέτρον ἄνθρωπος:—Man is the measure of all things—becomes the criterion of all knowledge.

[1] Chap. 7, 54.
[2] *cf. Vorwissenschaftliche Wissenschaft. Die Weltanschauung der Brahmann-Texte*, 1919.
[3] Oldenberg, *Lehre der Upanishaden*, 6 f. In *Begriffsform*, 15 ff., Cassirer gives an excellent and comprehensive description of mythical thought and prescientific science.
[4] Preuss, *Nayarit-Expedition*, I, 88; *cf.* A. Titius, *Der Ursprung des Gottesglaubens*, 357 f.   [5] Chap. 2.
[6] Joel, *Der Ursprung der Naturphilosophie aus dem Geiste der Mystik, passim. cf.* K. Kuiper, *Mythologie en Wetenschap*, 1919, 16, 27 f. O. Gilbert, *Griechische Religions-philosophie*, 1911, 29 ff., 36.

Man learns to form concepts, and from these he soon fashions the eternal Ideas. In Plato's magnificent myth at the end of the *Republic* "the entire force of mythical endowment with form is once more manifested"; nevertheless "we no longer stand on the territory of the myth. For in opposition to the ideas of mythical guilt and mythical destiny there arises here that fundamental Socratic principle, the concept of moral self-responsibility: the significance and essence of human life, and that which constitutes man's actual destiny, are transferred to his inner self."[1] But in the Socratic love of wisdom this moral self-responsibility is primarily knowledge of virtue:—insight; and thus man has erected his own power of judgment as the supreme Power.

2. "The purely theoretical person is only a construction":[2] theoretic form is always the receptacle of non-theoretic content, and knowledge is always far more than merely theoretical knowledge.[3] Even in the mental process of geometrical knowledge all the others cooperate, the esthetic in perceiving spherical form and the religious in the appreciation of its perfection, *etc.*[4] "In every psychical process mind in its entirety participates."[5] The theoretical attitude towards the world is therefore not merely a construction but is also a compulsion, equally of the spirit which refuses all too impetuously to accept what is given to it, and of the world, which in this way is conquered too conveniently; and it has quite justly been pointed out that in all the basal concepts of natural science the pale and faded anthropomorphisms are still apparent: —in other terms, they are all mythical.[6] With equal correctness it has been shown that philosophy does not spring forth from the categories of reason alone, but expresses a total life experience[7]. At the basis of all knowledge, then, there lies a faith;[8] and the theoretical path to the world is a way around faith or belief which takes its start, however, from precisely the same crisis of Power that aroused faith. Thus instead of the celebrated Fichtean dictum: "Science supersedes all Faith, and changes it into Sight",[9] it should be said that the faith that evoked

---

[1] Cassirer, *op. cit.*, II, 166.   [2] Spranger, *Lebensformen*, 122.
[3] *ibid.*, 92 f.   [4] *ibid.*, 48.
[5] *ibid.*, 48.   [6] Joel, *op. cit.*, 57.
[7] Grünbaum, *Herrschen und Lieben als Grundmotive der philosophischen Weltanschauungen*, 2 f.
[8] *ibid.*, 62, 121; *cf.* Brunner, *Gott und Mensch*, 6: "All metaphysics, and all philosophical belief in God, is the descendant of some religion, and lives much more from its impulses than from its own grounds."
[9] Fichte's *Popular Works*, II, 375 (W. Smith): "The Way Towards the Blessed Life", Lecture V.

science also abrogates it once more. Science itself, therefore, exists only in virtue of faith.

The Greeks, who invented the theoretic conquest of the world, were nevertheless not ignorant of this dependence of science upon faith. Not only was calm submission commended:

> The world's Wise are not wise,
> Claiming more than mortal may;[1]

but the mystic ground of all science was disclosed also: "For it does not admit of exposition like other branches of knowledge: but after much converse about the matter itself and a life lived together, suddenly a light, as it were, is kindled in our soul by a flame that leaps to it from another, and thereafter sustains itself."[2]

A. A. GRÜNBAUM, *Hersschen und Lieben als Grundmotive der philosophischen Weltanschauungen*, 1925.

K. JOËL, *Der Ursprung der Naturphilosophie aus dem Geiste der Mystik*, 1906.

[1] Euripides, *Bacchae*, 395 f. (Murray): τὸ σοφὸν δ'οὐ σοφία, τὸ τε μὴ θνητὰ φρονεῖν.

[2] Plato, Letter 7. Harward, *The Platonic Epistles*, 135.

CHAPTER 84

WAYS TO THE WORLD OBEDIENCE

1. EITHER by mythical-magical methods therefore, or theoretically, man transforms the world into *his* world, and himself into its sovereign: this is the profound religious basis of all culture.[1] But faith[2] is essentially hostile to every form of domination of the world without exception, since it regards this as rivalry with God, as *pseudo*-creation whether magical, mythical or rational, and opposes itself also to culture, even to that which is recognized as essentially religious, seeking its own way to the world.[3] It questions, in principle, all human control: even its own pronouncements, so far as these necessarily participate in culture, are immediately disqualified again by faith.[4]

The path of faith, then, is *obedience*. This implies that to speak about the Universe is first and foremost to speak about God: or in other words, *theology*. For antiquity the term "theology" indicated systematic, though not theoretical, discourse about deity, as this was carried on by poets and teachers; in this sense Hesiod, in his *Theogony*, and Orpheus were theologians.[5] The *logia* was a logically connected utterance—neither doctrine nor theory, however, but myth; while later, as we shall observe, myth intellectualized itself into dogma, and form became theory. But by this the peculiar character of all theology was scarcely changed in its essentials; and in any case man's spirit must discuss the uncontrolled, and the never to be controlled, formatively and rationally, explanatorily and abstractly. Theology then is no theory of the non-theoretic, and just as little an imparting of form to the formless: it involves speaking about the unspeakable. This is its own essential

---

[1] *cf.* Fichte: "The acquisition of this skill—partly to subdue and eradicate the improper tendencies which have arisen within us prior to the awakening of Reason and the consciousness of our own independence—partly to modify external things, and alter them in accordance with our ideas—the acquisition of this skill, I say, is called Culture." *Popular Works* (W. Smith), I, 181: "The Vocation of the Scholar", Lecture 1.   [2] Chap. 80.

[3] On the relative justification of the hostility between faith and theory *cf.* E. Spranger, *Der Kampf gegen den Idealismus*, 20.

[4] *cf.* Tillich, *Rel. Verwirklichung*, 13 *ff.*

[5] *cf.* Plato, *Republic*, 379a: "what is said about the gods"; *cf.* F. Kattenbusch, *Die Entstehung einer christlichen Theologie* (*Zeitschr. f. Theol. und Kirche*, N. F. 11, 1930), 163 *ff.*

and specific tension, whose ground consists in having salvation as its goal instead of domination, and faith as its starting-point instead of its own potency.[1] Whatever theology produces is indeed either form-endowment or theory, both being essentially myths, as I have already observed: but an impalpable form, a "form of grace".[2] In other terms: theology never has its object at its disposal; all that it deals with is questionable, and whatever it controls vanishes away; what is given to it with and in its object is impalpable, yet discernible. Here also a "dual experience of form" is attained, now as a controlled object, myth or theory, and again as a "form of grace".

2. Theology, further, is one form of preaching. The earliest Christianity had no theologians at all, but contemporary antiquity was quite familiar with them, in fact as the official festival preachers; in the cult associations the sermon or address was called *theologia*.[3] And theology has always preserved this character of being proclamation; in the knowledge of sacred objects (knowledge of God),[4] of rites and formulas of worship, its task was already declared; then it became an attempt to regulate these affairs and effect their mutual adjustment. Actually, however, such theology is only theogony: it is the product of the poets and thinkers of polytheism. Thus we can—in somewhat loose terms—speak of a Heliopolitan theology in ancient Egypt, because attempts were repeatedly made by the ancient city of Heliopolis to subject the whole world of the gods to the sun-god, and to draw every myth into the realm of the light-myth; the distinctive feature of this theology being syncretism. Examples of this adjustment are provided principally by the exegesis of the ancient traditional formulas, or of sacred writings.[5] "The Egyptian king Akhnaton summarizes his sun-theology in the name he assigns to his god. The old god *Shu* is at first retained, but identified with the new god *Aton*. Later he is eliminated; and in his place we find the elaboration of the 'father of *Ra* who has returned as *Aton*'."[6] This is theological reinterpretation and adjustment; and in its seventeenth Chapter the ancient Egyptian *Book of the*

---

[1] *cf.* Boulgakoff, *Orthodoxie*, 197: "This astonishment when confronted with the divine mysteries, which manifest themselves in the church, is also the principle animating theological activity, whether theoretic or practical."

[2] Tillich, *Rel. Verwirkl.* 51, 53, *cf.* 50.　　　[3] Chap. 27. Kattenbusch, *op. cit.*, 201 *f.*

[4] Chap. 72.　　　　　　　　　　　　　　　　　　[5] Chap. 64.

[6] *cf.* H. Schäfer, *Amarna in Religion und Kunst*, 1931. G. van der Leeuw, *Achnaton*, 1927. Harnack has discussed the dangers of this theology of compromise: *History of Dogma*, IV, 341 *ff.*

Dead provides a very old commentary, which yields new meaning to
the still older *Text*. Similarly the Zarathustrian *Avesta* gives fresh
significance to the old god of the dead, Yima, "for whom it had no use",
as the fatherly protector of the oldest humanity.[1] So, too, in the New
Testament words from the Old were repeatedly introduced with new
constructions. This interpretative activity of theology is of long standing;
we discover it at a very early period operating in the practice of delivering
oracles, and Plutarch calls the interpreters of the utterances of the
Pythia οἱ Δελφῶν θεολόγοι—the theologians of Delphi.[2] More remote
from the genuine essence of theology is the scientific contemplation of
religion, which applies to it general philosophical ideas; and frequently
it seems as though theology is nothing more than the adaptation of
religious data to the prevailing philosophic world-view. Of this, in
antiquity, the Stoics provided the clearest example, and in modern
times the so-called liberal theology, which is almost completely oriented
to Kantian philosophy. The path to the world is then literally the same
as that of theoretical contemplation: religion is taken into account only
in so far as is compatible with attaining the goal of world domination;
and for this very reason faith, as the renunciation in principle of all
world control, can find no place here.

The precondition of genuine theology is the existence of the church:[3]
the church is the place for logically connected utterances about faith.
Whatever has been displayed, or is being exhibited, in religion, is then
investigated for its redemptive content. Myth, doctrine, law, rite, are
all examined as to their significance for human salvation. "From the
mass of myths there then stands forth the ἱερὸς λόγος, the sacred
story of salvation;[4] of the many rites, sacrament and sacrifice come forward into full light; and the community becomes regarded as the church
bringing salvation. From the sacred writings a canon is demarcated;
each individual factor that has been received is tested for its connection
with revelation. A theology, in this comprehensive sense, exists only
where there is a church, in Christianity, although tendencies towards
it appear in many places."[5]

3. The path to the world, therefore, is here a road by way of God;
and thus it must be an approach to the world in obedience, starting
from what God has done for the world. In Christianity therefore, as the

[1] Chantepie, *op. cit.*, II, 215.
[2] *On the Cessation of the Oracles*, 15; *cf.* Chap. 54, and *RGG. Theologie*, I.
[3] Chap. 36.   [4] Chap. 61.   [5] *RGG. Theologie*, I.

sole religion possessing a theology, this is in the first place creation, and secondly re-creation, liberation through the Incarnation of Christ. These two principles may certainly be distinguished, but not separated.

To seek the world in this manner, still further, is to discover history. If it be true that "the powers of history forbid an objective and commanding attitude to whoever sets out to know the world",[1] it is no less true that the attitude of obedience renders these historical potencies accessible. In its profoundest sense history is always the history of God. "There is such a thing as a human story; and there is such a thing as the divine story which is also a human story . . . every short story does truly begin with creation and end with a last judgment."[2] Historical contemplation of the world, then, begins only with the experience of the facts of salvation. Primitive peoples know merely a primal event in the background of the Universe;[3] the Hindu attitude to the world is completely unhistorical, and a timeless knowledge conditions salvation. For the peoples of antiquity, again, all events were accommodated within one settled and typical scheme: the king can do nothing but overthrow his enemies; on his gravestone an official's life is always described as exemplary in one and the same way; and whenever man reflects on the contemporary world, it is always a time of adversity in comparison with the past,[4] while the Greek spirit was by far the most thoroughly unhistorically attuned.[5] History commences with Abraham, for in his story God's saving Will manifests itself for the first time; subsequently, the festivals of the eternal periodicity of life are changed into celebrations of God's deeds. The Feast of the Passover celebrates the deliverance from Egypt, while in *Psalm* cxxvi the "salvation" produced by the harvest is transformed into the historical salvation of the return from exile.[6] Jahveh is the God of history, of his own history, which he experiences with his people.[7] Christianity is Israelite also in the sense that its God is a God in history (whose antithesis would be Power, such as is found in India, arising from a complete lack of the historical vein, and crushing life completely).[8] Windelband acutely remarks that the historical consciousness displays itself for the first time in the Christian representation of the world, which sets the facts of the fall and of liberation at the focal point of

---

[1] Tillich, *op. cit.*, 73.   [2] Chesterton, *The Everlasting Man*, 284 *f*.
[3] Chap. 18.
[4] *cf.* A. de Buck, *Het typische en het individueele by de Egyptenaren*, 1929.
[5] Cassirer, *op. cit.*, II, 151 *f*.
[6] Chap. 56.   [7] Söderblom, *Nat. Theologie*, 97 *ff*.   [8] Chap. 22.

world events;[1] and thus Christianity refuses to regard the significance of the world as detached from salvation.[2] What is disclosed in history therefore, and what proclaims itself to conscience as God's Will, are ultimately the same; this, it is true, is revealed only to faith; and its purpose is the "rendering the historic eternal, and making the eternal historical".[3] But this is a miracle, and indeed the miracle of the assumption of human form, of *Incarnation*.

4. Just as little as man is a dominating soul in a controlled body[4] is the Universe a ruling spirit in a world-realm that would be, as it were, its kingdom, its stuff. Like man, the Universe too is a *creation*, *creatura*. When man reflects upon himself, he certainly appears to himself as one advancing along a path to the world; but he knows full well that it is not he but God Who is traversing this road; God is the actual subject of all theology.[5] So when man himself desires to seek his way to the world nothing remains for him but following after God:[6] and for this he stands in need of *revelation*.

[1] *Präludien*, II[6], 1919, 156. The idea of a criticism of our own times (*Zeitkritik*), also, "has its root in the Christian concept of the whole of history as coordinated in accord with a plan of salvation". K. Jaspers, *Die geistige Situation der Zeit*[2], 1931, 7; *cf.* further Ad. Bauer, *Vom Judentum zum Christentum*, 1917.

[2] Frick; *cf. Rel. Gesch.* 25.   [3] Kierkegaard.   [4] Chap. 45.
[5] *cf.* Piper, *Ethik*, I, 252, Note 1.   [6] Chap. 73.

CHAPTER 85

GOALS OF THE WORLD. REVELATION.
MAN AS THE GOAL

1. BEFORE revelation Phenomenology comes to a halt. It may seem strange that what is "revealed" can never "appear"; and yet this is not so remarkable as we might anticipate. For the "appearance" of any phenomenon as such, that is in the sense of the familiar contrast between Appearance and Reality, must undoubtedly be essentially different from that Self-disclosure of God with which revelation is concerned. In part, experience is an affair of phenomena;[1] and this holds true equally of the experience of revelation. Yet this itself, and in principle, remains wholly withdrawn from our view: it is no making known, no manifestation nor exhibition. "Only what essentially is concealed, and accessible by no mode of knowledge whatsoever, is imparted by revelation. But in thus being revealed it does not cease to remain concealed, since its secrecy pertains to its very essence; and when therefore it is revealed it is so precisely as that which is hidden."[2] Tillich's extremely apposite words are sufficiently clear; and to adopt religious phraseology, in revelation something is disclosed to me that no eye has ever seen— not even mine! I hear something that no ear has ever heard—not even my ear! Something is prepared for me which has entered no human heart—not even my own heart! Only the phenomenon, as such, can appear to my reason;[3] but it is impossible, owing to the essential conditions of the situation, to understand revelation,[4] since a revelation comprehended would not be one. Any "insight" I may have, even if it comes to me suddenly and with coercive clearness, is therefore far from being a revelation, but is at best the "appearance" to me of some phenomenon; so that all reports about "illumination", or of connections disclosed to us "like a revelation", are mere metaphor, and a bad one at that. With the data of so-called occultism,[5] again, revelation is still less concerned; at most these could yield an expansion of our knowledge,

---

[1] Chap. 67.

[2] Tillich, *Die Idee der Offenbarung, Zeitschr. für Theol. und Kirche*, N.F. 8, 406.

[3] *cf.* further Chap. 107.

[4] "To understand" means here, of course, "rational or intellectual comprehension"; *in faith* the revelation is certainly understood, only not as any insight attained by man but as illumination bestowed by God.

[5] Or, as it appears to be termed to-day, Parapsychology.

but in no degree any deepening of our understanding, to say nothing
of imparting what surpasses our reason. Neither does the appeal to
some sort of religious *a priori*, nor to some religious fundamental
principle, avail: it may certainly account for man's own religious
predisposition, but not for the "Wholly Other" communicated in
revelation. Finally, the distinction between a "general" revelation to
everyone, and a "special" revelation bestowed upon the faithful alone
and in some particular way, is very mischievous. For in so far as it is
always originally given to myself, revelation is never "general" but
always "special". When therefore we refer to some universal revelation,
for example in Nature or history, this implies only that Nature and
history appear to the majority of mankind as media of revelation simply
because they have already become an actual revelation to so many.
But someone or other must have been the first, and for him revelation
was in no sense "general", as little as it is so for me if I do not regard
Nature or history as mere modes of revelation, but actually experience
them. As phenomenologists, therefore, we must regard as valid revelation whatever presents itself as such. We can attempt to differentiate
solely between genuine and spurious *experience* of revelation, and to
separate the derived or the counterfeit from the original and essential
type. *Revelation is the act of God.* Only he to whom something has been
done, or something has happened on the part of God, may speak of it:
"for he that is mighty hath done to me great things".[1] The phenomenologist can only discuss what is reported to him; he can listen for the
authentic sounds and describe the objects wherein, according to the
believer's own statements, revelation has for him been effected.

2. For revelation is consummated in an *object*: it has its proper
medium. This however does not become some kind of divine entity by
thus subserving revelation, just as little as the self-revealing loses its
essential secrecy by so revealing itself in an object, or committing itself
to some medium.[2] Here we meet once more almost all those objects
which, in variegated procession, have already passed before our eyes: a
thing or *place*, a *time* or *person*, is *sacred* precisely by virtue of its relation
to revelation. In all these objects some Power reveals Itself which,
however, does not display Itself, because essentially It always remains
concealed, "Wholly Other".

We have seen[3] how primitive man, in his characteristically empirical
fashion and without any theory whatsoever, experiences Power; *mana*,

---

[1] *Luke* i. 49.   [2] *cf.* Tillich, *loc. cit.*, 409 f.   [3] Chap. 1.

in objects. Some object, for example, becomes tabu in virtue of its character as a medium of revelation and, whenever this relationship to revelation is permanent, eventually a fetish. Here the experience of revelation occurs, as it were, from moment to moment and has no further consequences. The chief, for instance, has power, and some extra-ordinary fullness of the sacred "reveals" itself in him: but when age enfeebles him, then he has obviously lost his power and is therefore no longer a bearer of revelation.

Revelation through *oracles*, in the next place, is no longer entirely "primitive".[1] For primitive man all occurrences may be oracles and indicate a road to him; but to those no longer wholly primitive the way is shown only at definite places, and oracles are then consulted in some locality that has been proved to be sacred. This behaviour therefore involves some relaxation of the purely empirical consciousness of revelation: man no longer discovers the way by himself; neither powerful persons nor potent events (rites) suffice to discover the correct path. The oracle, then, is something special, set apart, which surprises him a little; the great mass of objects, actions, persons, *etc.*, is no medium of revelation, and indeed hardly can be such. Thus to the genuinely primitive individual any stone on which he steps is in certain circum-stances an oracle[2]; he who is no longer wholly primitive, on the other hand, must journey to some special stone, perhaps to the *ka'ba*, in order to find the essential revelation. Here, still further, there arises the idea of miracle as something markedly exceptional. For from the primitive mind the sense of the completely impossible is absent: "what we should call miraculous appears to primitives commonplace, and though it may cause them emotion it does not readily surprise them. . . . We might say that he lives in miracles, were it not that it is essential to the definition of a miracle that it shall be something exceptional. To him, miracles are of daily occurrence, and his medicine-man can make almost as many of them as he likes."[3] In the realms of semi-culture and of civilization, however, conditions are different, although in antiquity everything that happened "could be conceived as a miracle, even when it followed a wholly natural course". At that period therefore the boundary line between miracles and the non-miraculous was very unsettled, and the decision on the matter was left to man;[4] but still

---

[1] Chap. 54. For the Hebrew *Bath-Kol*, which comes from heaven like the ark, table and lamp, *cf.* A. Marmorstein, *AR.* 28, 1930, 286 *ff.*
[2] Chap. 3.   [3] Lévy-Bruhl, *Primitives and the Supernatural*, 5, 34.
[4] Weinreich, *Ant. Heilungswunder*, VII *f.*

it was arrived at in accordance with the criterion of revelation:—what does an event declare about the god or about divine activity? Thus the miracle is really a "sign": the element of astonishment (wonder, miracle, τέρας, Egyptian *bja-t*, Hebrew אלפ) accompanies the significance of powerfulness (δύναμις, ἀρετή) and token (σημεῖον, Hebrew אות). For the primitive mind, then, even the simple fact that it is raining may be a "marvel" of God;[1] it is merely a matter of the facts themselves declaring that they are media of revelation. The word goes forth to man:

> Listen to this, O Job, stand still,
> Think of the wonders of God.[2]

"At its deepest roots belief in miracles declares nothing other than: 'there is a living God' ":[3] certain objects, events and persons are, as it were, given prominence as against the world as a whole. Space for example, at some definite spot, becomes for man a "position" in the sense of Chapter 57; and from this viewpoint it may be said that certain experiences are thrown into relief within the experiential whole and called miracles, in the sense of being acts of God.

It is in itself, then, no prejudice whatever to the essence of miracle that it becomes conceived more and more as a rarity, and ultimately as a fact directly opposed to the course of the world and contrary to Nature. For this transposition is connected with the general transformation from the magical-mythical attitude to the theoretic, which has been previously discussed.[4] To primitive man, once again, everything can be a miracle, to the modern almost nothing; if however he does believe in miracles is his faith then all the more passionate. But a real injury to belief in miracles is done as soon as the rarity and the amazing element in miracle outweigh its character as a sign, for then miracle entirely loses its revelatory content, and therewith its very essence. The founders of great religions, therefore, warn against the mania for miracles, as in the case of Jesus and Buddha;[5] the marvel, in this its miraculous sense, may certainly still remain a medium of revelation, but it may also involve an obstacle to faith, equally in

---

[1] *Job* v. 9 *f.*   [2] *Job* xxxvii. 14 (Moffat).
[3] Joh. Wendland, *Der Wunderglaube im Christentum*, 1910, 1; *cf.* 60.
[4] Chap. 82, 85.
[5] *Mark* viii. 12. "When an *arhat* flew through the air, Buddha is represented as rebuking him: 'This will not conduce either to the conversion of the unconverted, or to the increase of the converted, but rather to those who have not been converted remaining unconverted, and to the turning back of those who have been converted'." J. A. MacCulloch, *ERE*. VIII, 676 *ff.*

theory as in practice; and of the second possibility Björnson's drama *Beyond Human Power* constitutes an impressive example:[1] Pastor Sang rests all his faith on the required miracle: but in this only human will, increased to colossal proportions, is manifested:—the will "beyond human power", the magic will. And when the miracle proves to be a failure, this betrays itself in the childlike words of the miracle priest: "But this was not the meaning of it—?"

As miracle becomes more and more strikingly exceptional, again, the objects in which Power reveals itself recede into the ever more remote and immaterial distance: solid fetishes become fleeting images of the dream, of illumination, of the vision. The dream has already been discussed;[2] and in Greek antiquity dream revelation was something very ordinary.[3] We have previously seen, too, how the young Red Indian, prepared by a prolonged fast, goes into solitude in order to become acquainted with his *nagual*, his individual totem, in a dream-like vision,[4] while the illuminations and visions of Buddha, Mohammed, St. Paul and of many other minor founders and reformers are universally known. As the type of vision in general that of Moses may serve:—the burning bush which becomes the medium of revelation.

In all these cases, then, the steadily expanding theorizing emphasizes the exceptional character of revelation. But just as happens in worship, man can attempt to regulate revelation too: in celebration, for instance, the god reveals himself to his people at specific times; he has his epiphany and his *epidemia*; "for an angel went down at a certain season into the pool, and troubled the water".[5] Thus in sacrament[6] or sermon,[7] at this or that definite place, man can be sure of the self-imparting of God; and almost all religious phenomena, in fact, subsist in relation to the experience of revelation. Among these, revelation in *words* occupies a very prominent place. And this is frequently flight from the burdensome concretely material into some rarer sphere which is apparently closer to the immaterial and is, still further, personal. But this is merely "apparently" since, even at its very highest, revelation in words cannot actually dispense with the object. Similarly in spiritual-evangelical Christianity, however passionately it may seek the spiritual-personal, some vestige is disclosed which is not merged in the word itself, and which leads to the doctrine of the sacrament. But neither is the word itself immaterial. For it presupposes a speaker[8] who personally exercises

[1] Act I.　　　　[2] Chap. 82.　　　　[3] Weinreich, *Heilungswunder.*
[4] Chap. 8.　　　　[5] *John* v. 4.　　　　[6] Chap. 52.
[7] Chap. 28, 61.　　　　　　　　　　　　[8] Chap. 27.

his function, and appeals therefore not to the visual but to the auditory, and subsequently to man's intellectual and moral capacities. Here, therefore, the more man relinquishes the primitive, the more does everything become inward: even the voice coming from heaven, as in St. Paul's vision, and the general hallucinatory condition of being directly spoken to, are still too "material". Thus the "inner voice", frequently associated with conscience,[1] and also the "inner light", are intended to be media of revelation that are wholly invisible and immaterial; and in this an inclination to mysticism manifests itself. The object must now be excluded: any medium is burdensome; revelation, as it were, must hover in the air. Of course there are various transitional forms here, in which inward perception of God's voice is associated with an outward one, and even with an objective vision: in the revelation of God upon Sinai, for instance, while the whole stress of the narrative falls on the intellectual and moral content of the revelation,[2] nevertheless Moses and Aaron "see" the Lord. But however this may be, flight from the material never succeeds completely and—what is more important—it never actually becomes flight from the objective. Human experience is—perhaps!—less "material" than the "life of sense". But it is no less objective—expressed in religious terms: no less on "this side", no less earthly and transient. Man cannot wholly elude the medium of revelation.

3. But he does his best! In Pietism and its related tendencies, for example, the miracle *par excellence* is the believer's own inner *experience*:

> Mercy has come to me,
> Mercy of which I was unworthy;
> And this I account *miraculous*.[3]

But the great, indeed the sole, miracle is *conversion*,[4] the experience of salvation; and Günther is quite correct in suggesting that this "transposition" of miracle was necessitated by pietism having passed through the period of the Enlightenment.[5] This was certainly one of the conditions: but the fundamental reason lies in the tendency towards spiritualizing, towards the exclusion of the object of revelation, a tendency wholly independent of historical conditions which has influenced theology too. One of its typical representatives is Wilhelm Herrmann. Seeberg had asserted that "to experience this miracle of

---

[1] Chap. 66.   [2] *Exodus* xxiv.   [3] Ph.ᵉFr. Hiller.
[4] Chap. 79.   [5] *Jung-Stilling*, 76.

rebirth and conversion is to enter into the sphere of the miraculous
by virtue of *one's own individual experience*";[1] and Herrmann adds:
"Our true aim is that the person to whom the redeeming love of God
in Christ appears *should find his own life becoming more and more a
miracle.*"[2] For this tendency towards the non-objective, then, special
"revelations" ultimately become quite indifferent:—the written word,
the locality which has become a "position", sacred time *etc.* But those
to whom such "experiences" occur readily forget that they too are
objective. Thus in pietistic and methodist circles the idea of guidance
is cherished; but this guidance can reach men only by means of certain
events which must then be regarded as the media of revelation. Self-
deception, which looks on whatever is gratifying as guidance while
all that is disagreeable is temptation, is certainly not excluded here,
and not infrequently leads to tragic conflicts. It cannot therefore be
sufficiently emphasized that revelation is concerned not with any
antithesis between external and internal,[3] but with that between man
and God, or what is essentially rational and comprehensible on the
one hand and what is essentially irrational and incomprehensible on
the other.

4. Here, however, a certain rationalization obtrudes itself; for we
must necessarily speak of the unutterable, and discuss the essentially
concealed, as though it had not been genuinely revealed but displayed
or demonstrated. Thus dogma, doctrine and law are frequently regarded
as imparting definite religious content, and so cause man to forget
that the content of genuine revelation can always be only God Himself.
So it was that the great revelation systems arose, whatever rites, myths
and customs already subsisted in a community being proclaimed anew
as "revelation". This certainly never happened without an actual
revelatory experience of some great founder—of a Moses, Mohammed,
Zarathustra—enriching whatever had been previously received and
invigorating this with fresh energy, and often indeed with a new spirit;
and in this connection the extremely important task of the *mediator of
revelation* is disclosed.[4] This mediator, still further, may ultimately
himself become the content of revelation, as in Christianity.[5] His
figure then constitutes the object of revelation, the miracle, the precondition of all other secondary "revelations".

[1] W. Herrmann, *Offenbarung und Wunder*, 1908, 53.
[2] *ibid.*, 63; *cf.* 49, 57 *f.*, 70; further, Bultmann, *Glaube und Verst.* 220 *ff.*
[3] Chap. 67.   [4] Chap. 101, 106.   [5] Chap. 106.

Conversely, again, the object of revelation may become extended over the whole of Reality. Monism and pantheism follow this direction, and then primitive conditions return to a certain extent. Certainly theory rules here without any restraint: not every object *can* be an object of revelation, but every object *is* so in virtue of the divinity residing within it. We have only to contemplate it from the correct angle, that is in its own divine aspect, and then miracle is "the religious name for whatever happens".[1] An extreme, but very characteristic, type of this experience of revelation is the great poet Whitman:

> I find letters from God dropt in the street.
> These with the rest, one and all, are to me miracles,
> The whole referring, yet each distinct and in its place.
> Why, who makes much of a miracle?
> As to me I know of nothing else but miracles.[2]

N. Söderblom, *Offenbarung* (*Int. Wochenschrift 10. Dezbr.* 1910).

P. Tillich, *Die Idee der Offenbarung* (*Zeitschr. für Theol. und Kirche*, N. F. 8, 1927).

O. Weinreich, *Antike Heilungswunder*, 1909.

[1] Schleiermacher.
[2] *Leaves of Grass*. "Song of Myself", 48; "Autumn Rivulets", "Miracles".

CHAPTER 86

GOALS OF THE WORLD. REVELATION.
THE WORLD AS THE GOAL

1. WE have previously observed how sacred life pursues a cycle and renews itself periodically.[1] The world too can revolve in one and the same orbit: it then includes its goal within itself and reveals to man its own powerfulness.

The fairy story, for example, reckons with periods of a century: the wight who has been all but released says sorrowfully to the fairy tale hero, who has just missed saving him: "now I must wander about for another hundred years"; and a century later the event is repeated. Between these critical points, however, fairy tale time is quite empty: nothing at all happens: nothing begins and nothing ends. It runs: "once upon a time", not: "there was at that time", and concludes: "they lived happily for a long time, and if they are not dead then they are still alive to-day", not: "and then at last they died". The self-revealing world, then, has neither beginning nor end: it is a circle.

So it was to the Greeks. The Greek mind dared to conceive the idea of eternal *repetition*, not merely of the individual life as in Orphism, but of the life of the Universe. So in Stoic doctrine the worlds, which are absolutely identical with one another, follow each other eternally, and the rhythm from the primeval fire to the world conflagration (ἀποκατάστασις) remains eternally the same.[2] As in Heraclitus: "This world (cosmos) the same for all, was not made by any god or man, but was always, and is, and shall be an everliving Fire, with measures of it kindling and measures being extinguished."[3] Here, therefore, the Universe cannot be the "object" of a revelation, it can "mean" nothing whatever: it is only itself.

Astrology, again, proceeded in just the same way. It derived all events without exception from the eternal movement of the Universe, destroying all that is specific and significant in favour of the eternal sameness subsisting at its base. To the ancient Babylonians, indeed, the writing of the heavens was a revelation; but it revealed merely itself. In India, finally, revelation is completely merged in insight

---

[1] Chap. 22. [2] cf. Windelband, *History of Philosophy*, 178 ff.
[3] *Frag.* 30, Diels (Cornford).

into the void, the unreality of the Universe. Here too the fairy story is completely divested of all its historical vestiges; Buddha narrates fairy tales: "When the master had imparted this instruction, he explained the truths and connected the Jataka (birth story); at that time Ananda was the Brahman (from the fairy tale), Sariputta was the divinity, the Buddha community was the assembly, but the wise Senaka was myself."[1] Here "then" and "there" have completely disappeared and all meaning become impossible. The Universe reveals itself, that is to say, its impotence; and Chesterton, who here as so often shows profound phenomenological insight, has observed somewhat inexactly, but on the whole appropriately: "To the Buddhist or the eastern fatalist existence is a science or a plan, which must end up in a certain way. But to a Christian existence is a *story*, which may end up in any way."[2] In other words: in the one case the Universe displays itself as a story, in the other as a process: on the one hand as the object of revelation, the sign of transcendent Power, on the other as revelation, as Power itself . . . or as impotence!

2. In revealing itself as a circle, further, the Universe is eternal. It can have no purpose of any kind: it can merely exist, and in it all Power is amassed. Man is then a part of the Universe: more he cannot become; he can only become aware that he pertains to the world, and can "celebrate" it in thought and imagery, though scarcely in worship. "What foolish person will appeal to some external and outer motive force? Who will assert that these limbs move of themselves? Who will be content with any prior or intermediate entity, subsisting between the soul and that which is moved? As for the soul itself, though it is an incorporeal substance, it is yet wholly contained within the whole and in every part thereof, just as the voice and the word are in each of the senses of those whom it reaches."[3] The tendency towards this revelation of the Universe as Power was already evident in the thought of the ancient Ionian philosophers; their *archai* or "origins" were regarded as the living, divine, primeval substance of the world, and its manifold activities derived from the eternally unchanging and immutable. [4]

[1] Lüders, *Buddh. Märchen*, 75 *et passim*. Chap. 22, 61.
[2] *Orthodoxy*, "The Romance of Orthodoxy", 250.
[3] Giordano Bruno, *De Immenso*, XV; *cf.* Goethe's lines, p. 185:
    What were a God, who outward force applying . . .
[4] *cf.* Rohde, *Psyche*, II, 142 *f.* E. T. 364 *f.* Joël, *Naturphilosophie*.

Here there certainly is revelation, because the actual divine essence of the Universe never unveils itself: it remains mysterious and essentially concealed. Euripides expresses this very finely in the marvellous prayer of which we have already spoken:[1]

> Thou deep Base of the World, and thou high Throne
> Above the World, whoe'er thou art, unknown
> And hard of surmise, Chain of Things that be,
> Or Reason of our Reason; God, to thee
> I lift my praise, seeing the silent road
> That bringeth justice ere the end be trod
> To all that breathes and dies.[2]

Thus the world is "the living garment of God"; this no longer has its own powerfulness, distinguished from the Universe, but is nothing more than just the Power of the world.[3] It no longer has a name of its own: a name is "sound and smoke" and by a colossal "transposition" the hymn phraseology, which adds name to name and as a precaution includes at the close the unknown god,[4] becomes the pantheistic apostrophe of Aeschylus: "Zeus, whate'er he be".[5] The impenetrable mystery of the Universe is certainly recognized; but he who sustains its "deep Base" is the same as he who has his "high Throne above the World"; he is the god, Zeus, and the world-reason. Again to return, in conclusion, to Bruno-Goethe:

> He from within lives through all Nature rather,
> Nature and Spirit fostering each other;
> So that what in Him lives, and moves, and is,
> Still feels His power, and owns itself still His.[6]

3. Against this fine faith, however, there repeatedly opposes itself that religion which seeks purpose wholly apart from the Universe, in God;[7] thus the religion of creation strives with the religion of birth:

---

[1] Chap. 2.
[2] *The Trojan Women*, 883 *ff*. (Murray); *cf.* Joel, *op. cit.*, 112 *f*. Diels, *Vorsokratiker*, I, 423 *f*. on the *arche*, here referred to, of Diogenes of Apollonia. Wilamowitz, *Gr. Trag.* III, 282 *f*. H. Diels, *Zeus, AR.* 22, 1923–24, 14. L. Parmentier and H. Grégoire, *Euripide* IV, 1925, 63, Note 3. Joel, *Geschichte der antiken Philosophie*, I, 637. Ferd. Dümmler, *Kl. Schriften*, I, 1901, 163, 174, 190, 209. G. van der Leeuw, *Een dramatische geloofsbelydenis, Hermeneus II*, 1929.
[3] *cf.* Marie Gothein, *AR.* 9, 1906, 337 *ff*.   [4] Chap. 17.
[5] *cf.* Kurt Latte, *AR.* 20, 1921–22, 275 and Note 2; further: Wilamowitz, *Gr. Trag.* III, 283.   [6] *Prooemium.* "God, Soul and World."   [7] Chap. 85.

the religion of the Father with that of the Mother.[1] "The main point of Christianity was this: that Nature is not our mother: Nature is our sister. We can be proud of her beauty, since we have the same father; but she has no authority over us; we have to admire, but not to imitate. . . . Nature was a solemn mother to the worshippers of Isis and Cybele. Nature was a solemn mother to Wordsworth or to Emerson. But . . . to St. Francis, Nature is a sister, and even a younger sister: a little, dancing sister, to be laughed at as well as loved."[2] But apart from the Jewish-Christian sphere, creation is not at all creation in the literal sense, but a birth. Life generates itself: the deity is a mother, eternally giving birth and eternally bringing back the living again into her womb.[3] Still more logical is the primeval Egyptian myth of the self-espousal of the god Atmu.[4] He is the god "who satisfied himself by his own hand", and even this extremely offensive idea involves a highly important value for a *Weltanschauung*: as Schäfer justly remarks, self-espousal is a crude conception of the maternal earth, a figure in other respects unknown in ancient Egypt.[5] The idea of self-espousal, indeed, is even more appropriate than that of the eternally bearing mother: for everything occurs in the mighty god-world-being itself; the one who conceives is also the impregnator.

The various myths which regard the Universe as emerging from the body of some primeval giant present yet another *Weltanschauung*, and an attempt to fix a "beginning" where essentially there can be no beginning.[6] In the *Edda* Ymir, in Babylon Tiamat, in China Pawn-ku and in India Purusha are the original beings whose limbs form parts of the world. In India, still further, this origin of the Universe is conceived as a mode of sacrifice, the giant being sacrificed and his limbs ritually dissected.[7] Prajapati, again, the world creator in the *Brahmanas*, brings forth the world from himself; first of all the waters emanate from him, and then he lays his seed therein which becomes the golden egg from which he himself is born.[8] Thus everything here happens wholly "of itself", from its own nature, as birth or at best as emanation, not as creation. "Separation or emanation emphasizes the relationship between the originator and man, and is therefore preferred by a

---

[1] Chap. 15, 25.   [2] Chesterton, *Orthodoxy*, "The Eternal Revolution", 205.
[3] Chap. 10.   [4] *Pyramidentexte* (Sethe), 1248.
[5] H. Schäfer, *Ägyptische und heutige Kunst und Weltgebäude der alten Ägypter*, 1928, 107. The expression *ḥtp–dt*, "satisfied by his own hand", was applied to the creator Ptah; *cf.* A. Wiedemann, *AR.* 21, 1922, 448.
[6] Alviella, *op. cit.*, 236 ff.   [7] Oldenberg, *Religion des Veda*, 270.
[8] J. S. Speyer, *De indische Theosophie en wy*, 37.

mysticism and pietism for which it is above all a matter of a fusion of humanity and divinity; while fabrication and creation stress the free act of will of the originator, and commend themselves to a belief in God which is profoundly agitated by the personal operation and Power of Deity."[1]

[1] Söderblom, *Gottesglaube*, 151. Chap. 21.

CHAPTER 87

GOALS OF THE WORLD. REVELATION.
GOD AS THE GOAL

1.   Among men I discovered this to be the highest knowledge—
That the Earth was not, nor the Heaven above,
Nor tree nor mountain,
Nor any star, nor shining sun,
Nor radiant moon, nor glorious ocean.
When there was nought of limit and boundary,
Then existed the one almighty God,
The gentlest of men, and with him
Many glorious spirits, and holy God.[1]

This so-called "Wessobrunn Prayer", an Old German poem from
a MS. of the ninth century, speaks in Christian language of the time
when there was "nought of limit and boundary", when the "Universe"
did not yet exist and God alone was there with His holy spirits. Here
therefore a *beginning* is assigned to the world in contrast to God; at
one time the world was not: not so with God. Consequently man rises
here to an *eschaton*, to an uttermost boundary of the Universe in its
entirety: he disregards both his own existence and that of the world,
seeking his goal neither in himself nor in the Universe. The "history"
in which he lives is certainly his own peculiar element, from which he
cannot disengage himself; but it began at some time or other. There
existed something "before" this commencement, and there will be
something "after" its end. And the description of the primeval condition,
in which whatever we know as existent was not yet present, frequently
occurs in the myths of all peoples. Usually too it includes a dim presage
of some better state of things, nearer to the divine. But the world that
preceded the world is also described without this longing for a better
Universe; in the myth of the Maya people, for example: "there were
neither men nor animals, no birds nor fish, no crabs, no trees and no
stones; there were neither caves nor gorges, neither plants nor forests.

---

[1] G. Ehrismann, *Geschichte der deutschen Literatur bis zum Ausgang des Mittelalters*,
I, 1918, 133; *cf.* K. Müllenhoff and W. Scherer, *Denkmäler deutscher Poesie und Prosa
aus dem VIII. bis XII. Jahrh.*³, 1892, II, 1. W. von Unwerth and Th. Siebs, *Geschichte
der deutschen Literatur bis zur Mitte des elften Jahrhunderts*, 1920, 149.

The heavens alone existed. The face of the earth was not yet visible, and the sea alone lay silent there under the wide expanse of heaven. There was not yet anything that coagulated or cohered, nothing which formed itself into strata nor formed a thread, nothing that had caused a rustling or a sound under the heavens. There was absolutely nothing there. . . . Everything was calm and motionless in darkness and night. One alone, Tepeu Gucumatz, existed: at once builder and generator, mother and father. . . ."[1]

Now the concept of the absolute non-being of what exists is altogether beyond human power; the Maya example is instructive also in this respect, since heaven and the sea are already present, and the earth too, although it is not yet visible. Creation therefore presents here the character of *arrangement* or *ordering*, of stratification of material which somehow or other is already present, a building up from stuff already provided; and thus the world creator is the demiurge,[2] the director, who overcomes chaos. Even the Old Testament, which places creation at the very beginning, does not escape the idea of chaos and describes the work of creation as a labour in several stages which, out of chaos, gradually forms the cosmos; while in other Old Testament allusions to creation (the struggle with the monster of chaos, *etc.*)[3] there survives the idea found elsewhere, according to which the demiurge subdues chaos. In this respect, still further, the light myth[4] has deeply influenced the creation myth: Marduk, who slays Tiamat, and Ra, who kills the Apap serpent, are light-gods who expel chaotic darkness. A different conception of the work of the demiurge is the Egyptian:— the potter making vessels, which occurs in the Old Testament also; here too there is some sort of foundation material that is utilized by the creator.

In these creation myths man struggles, as it were, with what is given apart from his own cooperation,[5] with the world just as he happens to find it, and tries to rise to belief in a deed which itself may be not "of this world". Certainly he cannot exclude himself and his world; but he does his utmost to follow the path of obedience to its end, to place the world's end and goal in God alone, and to experience revelation as a genuine act of God. In this connection, however, dogma can speak more clearly than myth; and in dogma *creatio ex nihilo* is asserted,

[1] W. Krickeberg, *Märchen der Azteken und Inkaperuaner, Maya und Muisca*, 1928, 121.
[2] Similarly in Plato's well-known account of creation, *Timaeus*, 30 ff.
[3] H. Gunkel, *Schöpfung und Chaos, in Urzeit und Endzeit*[2], 1921.   [4] Chap. 7.
[5] Chap. 21.

certainly in despite of all that is discernible.[1] For as soon as Will and Form receive their due recognition, the "Nought" gives way and the creator again becomes a demiurge. Thus the truly creative deed, as the self-surrender of God, is given to *faith*—neither to reason nor to utterance.

In all this, however, creation is never any explanation of the origin of the Universe. Or rather: the "origin" of the world is never a *causa* in religion, and least of all a *prima causa*. For a God-cause, as Brunner observes, would be itself part of the Universe;[2] but the idea of creation purports to assert something about what is not at all of this world. In this respect, then, the situation is exactly the same as with the so-called aetiological myth, which tells us why the raven is black and the heavens above the earth; all this is not some kind of primitive natural science, and from it every attempt at theoretical domination of the world is remote.[3] It is rather a grounding of the Universe in the numinous, in the mysterious and powerful primeval ground; and creation also is an aetiological myth, grounding the world in the primal ground of the divine Will.[4] Or in other terms: God is the sole magician: the magical attitude[5] pertains to Him alone; He has thoughts that are at the same moment deeds. The world is His *creatura*, and exists solely by virtue of His Will bringing it into existence.

2. If now the Universe has a beginning and an end, if it is both begun by God and by Him brought to its conclusion, then it must also have a *centre*.[6] If again its course is no eternally enduring process, but a drama, then the drama must have one focal point from which the whole reveals its significance; for when any phenomenon "appears" to man, he seeks for the point, the "centre", from which he can understand the whole and from which its meaning becomes perceptible. The Universe, however, is no "phenomenon"; and man cannot simply observe it, because he himself pertains to the Universe and can never think himself away. Nevertheless he can discuss its significance: but this he can do only in *faith*. For the Universe does not "appear" to him, but God reveals its meaning to him at its historic centre. In other words: that which, in the "phenomenon", is *significance* and is *comprehended*, is in the Universe *salvation* that is *bestowed*. *At the centre of history, therefore, God reveals the meaning of the world as salvation.*

---

[1] *cf.* Cassirer, *op. cit.*, II, 261.   [2] *Gott und Mensch*, 9.   [3] Chap. 83.
[4] *cf.* H. Frick, *Theol. Rundschau*, N. F. 2, 1930, 86. Piper, *Ethik*, I, 114 *ff.*
[5] Chap. 82.   [6] Tillich, *Rel. Verwirkl.* 116.

We can here, however, disregard the question (which falls within systematic theology) whether or not all history is the history of salvation.[1] The principle suffices that for the believer who seeks the goal and purpose of the Universe in God, the course of the world is in fact the *history of salvation*, from its beginning in God's creation to its end in His consummation. This is possible to him because on him, at the centre of this history, salvation was bestowed. In history, therefore, man seeks the history of God, that is to say, what is superior to himself, exactly as he did in the case of the soul. To him history first becomes living, and indeed becomes history proper, because of salvation; for just as history exists for us all solely in virtue of its meaning, which at first is only our own meaning but ultimately that of God, so it subsists for the believer only in virtue of salvation, which to begin with is his own powerfulness, but is in the last instance the saving power of God. History, then, is always dogmatized history: the Israelites fought the "wars of Jahveh", just as the Egyptians attacked the barbarians who were actually the mythical enemies of the sun-god. The king, again, stands as a god in the midst of a cosmic contest; his victory, still further, can never be in question, since he must conquer even if the enemy "in reality" has overcome him.[2] The history of the patriarchs in *Genesis* is indeed extremely "unnatural"; in other terms, it is a history of salvation. The birth and rescue of Isaac and Jacob's superiority over Esau, Joseph's status among his brothers, the favour shown to Ephraim and, conversely, the sinful self-assertion of Adam, Lamech and the Babylonian builders of the Tower—all this, as Lehmann has acutely described it in one of the last Articles he wrote,[3] is historical construction which we should not reject as childish nor as wanton forgery, but should rather apprehend as an attempt to depict the salvation which was given to man at the centre of history. In exactly the same way, the Synoptic *Gospels* provide no chronicle of Jesus' life but a recital of the historic salvation imparted in Him, while the fourth evangelist goes so far as almost to forget history altogether as compared with salvation.

In Christianity, to continue, this "centre" of history is the *Incarnation of Christ* and, as Tillich maintains, so far as the conception of history in general is Western European and Christian, all interpretation of

---

[1] Tillich, *Rel. Verwirkl.* 131.

[2] *cf.* R. Weill, *Les Hyksos et la Restauration nationale dans la tradition égyptienne* (*Journal asiat.* 16, 1910; 17, 1911). de Buck, *Het Typische en het Individueele*. G. van der Leeuw, *Historisch Christendom*, 1919.   [3] *La pensée du Jahviste, SM.* 3, 1927.

history leads in fact to Christology.[1] The Christian, then, has found in history the "concrete locality" where salvation is given to him. The beginnings of this religio-historical conception, however, are found in the people of Israel which not only, like all the peoples of antiquity, constructed its history in accordance with a scheme of salvation, but regarded the deeds of its God as direct leadership, as deliverance and guidance towards a goal which was nothing other than this God himself and his "service".

3. In this structure of the spiritual life, therefore, the world is the scene of a magnificent drama, whose redemptive history is disclosed to us in God's revelation:[2] a *divina commedia*. But with such a history we are already quite familiar: it is the "sacred story", *hieros logos*, which we have previously exhaustively discussed.[3] In the *hieros logos*, then, history becomes the *history of salvation*. The drama of the Cross is produced for us with the exhortation: *tua res agitur*—"thou art concerned". Now, however, the connection with Nature which we discerned in the "sacred story", of the mystery religions, for example, is absent. For the history of salvation is pure history, and salvation does not grow up for us "in the course of the world" from the eternal maternal womb, but is bestowed upon us by the divine Will. For this reason salvation, still further, can here mean *deliverance* also: the deed of salvation takes the world and man out of the "course" of the world and subjects them to a Will that transcends the world. Christology, therefore, is soteriology. Man no longer desires to make Nature bear the burden of his power, nor any longer to render her power serviceable to his own: he wishes neither to be himself a creator nor to live supported by the "given" potency. But he bows in obedience before the Creator, the Almighty, and receives deliverance from His hands alone.

4. But just because deliverance lies wholly in God's hands it must penetrate to the deepest element which, in man and in the world, opposes the tendency towards God; that is to *guilt*. Thus over against: "Look! At whom? At the bridegroom!" we find: "Look! Whither? At our guilt!" From the world, therefore, God produces something wholly different from what we ourselves find therein, even if we dig down to its profoundest ground. In other words: God changes the

---

[1] *ibid.*, 110 *f.*
[2] "To us":—that is to say "to our faith"; for to our understanding, as apart from faith, nothing "appears" here!   [3] Chap. 34, 61.

very essence of the world: deliverance is nothing less than *re-creation*. And God does not simply fit out a new world from the fragments of the old; here also He works with no material whatever; His creation is again *creatio ex nihilo*, from what is to the human intellect quite inconceivable—what exists, when nothing exists: or expressed in religious terms, from *grace*.[1]

In other words: deliverance and new creation are *atonement*: God sets the "bearing of guilt" in the very centre of history, and the Christian prays: *agnus Dei, qui tollis peccata mundi*.

5. The new creation, which has a beginning of the world as its condition, and a centre of history as its situation, must also fix an end to the world; and thus we enter the domain of *eschatology*. The renewal of the world, and its end, condition each other reciprocally. Of course we cannot contemplate exhibiting here all the pictures of the end of time as these have been painted at various periods in different religions, especially by Parsiism and Christianity, Judaism and Islam, and also among the Germanic peoples.[2] Instead of this, I shall attempt to sketch a few of the main features, together with some of the most important types, of eschatology.

It must be observed, first of all, that the *eschaton*, the uttermost limit, is not conceived merely in some remote future, but equally in a distant past: primeval time and the end of time, as we have already found, are associated. Man thus attempts to deal with his world as his nought and as God's All; but this he can do in mythical form, only at a time removed as far as possible from his own, in the earliest yesterday as in the farthest to-morrow. And this time is *God's time*. A golden age lies behind us: an eternal realm of salvation confronts us.[3] Some primitive peoples, indeed, can describe the primeval conditions when community between heaven and earth still subsisted, and they were united by a long liana— the Toradja of Celebes, for example.[4] The description in the *Rig-Veda*, again, has a typically acosmic tone: "The non-existent was not, the existent was not then; air was not, nor the firmament that is beyond. What stirred? (Was there any wind?) Where? Under whose shelter? Was (then) the deep abyss (of the sea) water? Death was not, immortality was not then; no distinction was there of night and day. That *One*

[1] The Orthodox church perceives in redemption-re-creation a *theosis*, a deification of humanity, but adopts therewith the mystical paradox of a "new creation, that is, an ultimate *creation* of man *as God*"; Boulgakoff, *Orthodoxie*, 153.

[2] A. Bertholet gives an excellent survey in *RGG. Eschatologie*, I.

[3] Lietzmann, *Weltheiland*, 44. [4] Adriani, *Animistisch Heidendom*, 5.

breathed, windless, self-dependent. Other than That there was none beyond."[1] This sounds, it is true, like a *Wessobrunn Prayer* with an Indian tinge, while the Greek myths of the golden age transpose the primeval world definitely nearer the divine.[2] Here too primeval time and ultimate time come into contact, while from these ideas the country of the soul[3] cannot be separated. Paradise lies at the beginning, as at the end; and in Egypt the same conception occurred: "the time of the eight primeval gods, which according to its actual nature is supposed to have been a period of nothingness devoid of all life, is nevertheless a happy past, a golden age, for this later Theban cosmogony", observes Sethe characteristically.[4] Similarly Yima's kingdom, according to Persian ideas, lasts without frost or heat, sickness or death, until it must retire into its stronghold before the advancing Winter of the world.[5]

The general scheme of this course of the world, from primeval time to its end, is at first the retarded and unified rhythm of periodicity.[6] In this train of thought, indeed, every new year was a fresh harvest, every sunrise a victory over darkness; the growth of vegetation a re-creation, the recommencement of life in Spring a repetition of the world's creation; the king too was the saviour of his own period.[7] To begin with, then, eschatology is only one "special case" of this periodic cosmology.[8] Later, however, all world history is comprehended within one single period, the many cyclic time series consolidated into one unique course: Jahveh, the god who overcomes darkness at the commencement of each year, then becomes the lord of the world who creates at the beginning and conquers at the end.[9] The many *peripeteiae* or recurring crises are now reduced to two only: initial creation and concluding, consummating victory; and in a quite similar way, the periodic change of Winter and Summer is in the North "transposed" into the idea of an extraordinarily long Winter, *Fimbulwinter*, which is nothing else than *Ragnarök*, the decline of the world.[10]

And thus the scheme of eschatology dogmatically intrudes into the everyday world: Egyptian wisdom-literature depicted a condition of

[1] Bertholet, *Lesebuch*, 9, 88. E. J. Thomas, *Vedic Hymns*, 127 (modified).
[2] L. Preller, *Griechische Mythologie*, 1, 1894, 87 *f*. Hesiod, *Works*, 109 *ff*.
[3] Chap. 46.
[4] K. Sethe, *Amun und die acht Urgötter von Hermopolis, Abh. der Wiss.*, 1929, *Phil. Kl.* 4, 63.   [5] Lehmann, *Zarathustra*, 1, 95 *f*.
[6] Chap. 22, 55.   [7] Chap. 13.
[8] Wensinck, *Semitic New Year*. Mowinckel, *Psalmenstudien*, II.
[9] cf. F. M. Th. Böhl, *Nieuwjaarsfeest en koningsdag in Babylon en Israel*, 1927.
[10] A. Olrik, *Ragnarök, die Sagen vom Weltuntergang*, 15 *ff*. (1922).

crisis in which everything was in a state of revolution; its features were certainly taken from some actual crisis, which need not however have been at all present for the poet himself, since it must occur in any case. The crisis is a genuine crisis, that is to say, not fact but judgment. The Jewish-Hellenistic apocalypse, for instance, is entirely filled with this scheme of crisis, following a period of happiness;[1] and ancient Greece also knew the "race of iron" and their era of misfortune.[2] Finally, the New Testament is familiar with a crisis that must inevitably come, and be proclaimed at a time when nothing whatever indicates it; and in this it conforms to the prophetic announcement of the "day of the Lord". But in the *Gospels* this schematism is not merely an apocalypse of the world (though it is this *also, St. Mark* xiii, *etc.*), but is in the first place the basis of belief, in accordance with which the life of the Messiah develops itself. For He must suffer, and His disciples with Him: a time of distress will arise: brother will deliver up brother, the father his child, and all natural relationships will be reversed.[3] Thus the course of the life of Jesus, as also the future which He described to His disciples, is intelligible only on the basis of this dogmatic-eschatological experience of history: afflictions must come so that glory may dawn.[4] The scheme of belief—this will be the world's fate—is applied by Jesus, as the mediator,[5] to Himself, and thus He makes the crisis the judgment upon Himself: "The Son of man came to give his life a ransom for many."[6]

This dramatization of history in the basis of faith desires, as it were, to "destroy" the world and time, so that the kingdom and era of God may dawn: it disowns to-day for the sake of "the day of the Lord". The *eschaton*, however, is not a nullity in the sense of the void, but in that of a violent reversal of all conditions with no exception. So man believes even with regard to Nature: "the sunshine will darken and evil winds blow in future Summers. Know ye still more? Mightily Garm barks at the mouth of the Gnipa-cave: the chains are broken, the wolf escapes. I know the tidings, I see far and wide: the mighty *Ragnarök* of the gods."[7] But the revolution concerns custom and culture also: "brothers will fight till both fall, cousins destroy their relatives; the world is dissolute, they commit adultery; there is no one who spares another."[8] Precisely the same too in the New Testament:

[1] Kampers, *Kaisermystik*, 102.
[2] Hesiod, *Works*, 174 ff. Murray, *The Rise of the Greek Epic*, 102.   [3] *Matt.* x.
[4] Probably the permanent significance of Schweitzer's *The Quest of the Historical Jesus* lies in this insight.   [5] Chap. 106.
[6] *Mark* x. 45.   [7] *Völuspá*; Lehmann-Haas, *Textbuch*, 245.   [8] *ibid.*

the sun will be darkened
and the moon will not yield her light,
the stars will drop from heaven,
and the orbs of the heavens will be shaken.[1]

But further: "Now the brother shall betray the brother to death, and the father the son; and children shall rise up against their parents, and shall cause them to be put to death."[2] But when everything has been thus reversed God's sovereignty begins: "Now learn a parable of the fig tree; When her branch is yet tender, and putteth forth leaves, ye know that summer is near: So ye in like manner, when ye shall see these things come to pass, know that it is nigh, even at the doors."[3]

According to its nature the end may be described as a dying, a decline, but also as a deed of God: the first type occurs in many places, being however most beautifully expressed in the Germanic myth of *Ragnarök*. There gods become heroes, while for the poet of the *Völuspá* the gods perish together with the world,[4] the essential traits of this description being probably taken from the typical decay of a tribe;[5] exactly like a clan, the gods and their world too are destroyed by impotence and unrighteousness. The world dies. And the gods also. Kahle has acutely perceived that this end of the world is directly contrary to the Christian conception. For in the former the gods are defeated: in the latter God triumphs; in the first the world passes on to its end: in the second God brings the world to an end.[6] Upon this Germanic picture of the world's collapse, however, there falls a gleam of magnificent tragedy: the tragedy of the sunset from which it arose. Man postulates the nullity of his whole world, and within the world he includes his gods.

Of the second type there is an abundance of examples: the many legends of a flood,[7] in which the god makes an end of the world because of guilt, already tend towards it; it is, however, seldom completed. In Persia, on the other hand, the "course of the world" was regarded as a path to a goal, and its periodicity as an ascent to the god's victory;[8] the will of the wise lord governs the whole. Subsequently, in Christianity, this Will, which in later Judaism was also the beginning and the end of the world, received the form of Him Who in His whole life posited an

---

[1] *Mark* xiii. 24 f. (Moffat).   [2] *Mark* xiii. 12.   [3] *Mark* xiii. 28, 29.
[4] Olrik, *op. cit.*, 51; *cf.* also his *Nordisches Geistesleben*[2], 1925, 101.
[5] Grönbech, *Folkeaet*, I, 176 f.
[6] *cf.* B. Kahle, *Der Ragnarök-Mythus*, AR. 8, 1905, 444 f.
[7] H. Usener, *Die Sintflutsagen untersucht*, 1899. G. Gerland, *Der Mythus von der Sintflut*, 1912. R. Andree, *Die Flutsagen*, 1891.
[8] *cf.* Lommel, *Zarathustra*, 130 ff.

end of the world. "For it is characteristic of Jesus that He looks forward, beyond the perfection and bliss of the individual, to a perfection and bliss of the world and of a chosen humanity. He is filled and determined by the will and hope for the kingdom of God'."[1] He proclaims the time of the end and brings this about. "The kingdom of God is at hand": and with the conclusion of His own history, in the final voluntary act, when He sends down His spirit on the disciples, the time of the end finally appears; for ever since then the world subsists only in an interim, and has lost its intrinsic value.

First of all, then, this end of the world is a *judgment*. Again Parsiism vigorously stresses this feature: the *frashokereti*, the world completion, is in the first place a purification, a judgment; and it is well known how closely the concepts of the end and of judgment are connected in Christianity too: the end is nothing but the nearness of God, judgment: no historical fact of the remote future therefore, but a revelation, a self-impartation of God. God's approach to the world is in itself the judgment and the end.

But again: the end of the world is also the commencement of God's sovereignty, of the *kingdom of God*:[2] the βασιλεία θεοῦ becomes actual. The world's completion begins: the goal of the world in God is realized. Dominion is linked with judgment; "judgment is the decisive characteristic of the event, perceived in the *eschaton*"; and conversely: "only from the point of view of the *eschaton* can the judicial nature of time be understood".[3] But dominion consists in the fact that the world exists solely in God:—that God is with the world, "*Emmanuel*." The kingdom of God, therefore, may also be called the kingdom of *the Spirit*: the third kingdom. But at no time whatever should it be severed from historic reality, as the sects have done repeatedly since the time of Joachim of Floris.[4] The world ever remains the world: and without the centre of history there can be neither beginning nor end. But the revelation of the world, as in its deepest ground belonging to God, comes to us from the *eschaton*, and with this the circle becomes completed of those "phenomena" which are not actually such, because they do not "appear" to us but are revealed only. Below the sphere of phenomenological transparency, therefore, is *life*; above it: *guilt, faith, the world* as God's sovereignty. Below and above, half understood, half believed in: the *church*.

---

[1] Schweitzer, *Leben-Jesu-Forschung*, 634; cf. 636 f.
[2] A parallel in Hindu Varuna-religion: R. Otto, *Das Gefühl des Überweltlichen* (*sensus numinis*), 1932, 168.   [3] Tillich, *Rel. Verwirkl.* 139, 136.
[4] Em. Gebhart, *L'Italie mystique*⁸, 1917, 75 f.

H. GUNKEL, *Schöpfung und Chaos*, in *Urzeit und Endzeit*, 1921.
A. OLRIK, *Ragnarök, Die Sagen vom Weltuntergang*, 1922.
R. OTTO, *Reich Gottes und Menschensohn*, 1934 (Eng. tr., *The Kingdom of God and The Son of Man*, 1938).

PART FIVE

FORMS

A. RELIGIONS

CHAPTER 88

RELIGIONS

1. "RELIGION actually exists only in religions", as Heinrich Frick very justly asserts with reference to Schleiermacher's fifth *Discourse upon Religion*.[1] This means that religion does not, as such, appear to us; what we can observe, therefore, is always only *one* concrete religion: in other terms, only its prevailing historical *form* appears to us.[2] From this it follows that "primeval religion" is here disregarded.[3] The primeval ground of religion, that is in the ontological or metaphysical sense, is in principle concealed. But the historic primeval ground of religion is merely a myth; it is obviously not prehistoric religion, about which, as it is, we know very little![4] but Adam's religion. Now either Adam is the first man, whose religion is plainly quite inaccessible to us: or he is "Everyman", and then the enquiry into his religion subdivides into two others: first, that concerning the awakening of the religious consciousness in everyone without exception, which would be the problem for psychology; and that into the revelation of God in every man: and to answer this question, again, would be the task of theology. The "primeval", then, altogether eludes our comprehension; and "primeval experience"[5] can neither be renewed nor observed. Certainly we may say that the origin of religion lies in God; but that is a theological assertion which (phenomenologically) scarcely assists us at all. For from the viewpoint of revelation every religion is primeval, because in order to be revealed[6] the content must be original and never previously perceived.

Research has attempted to arrive at primeval religion, however, in four different ways: (*A*) by advancing the idea of a "*natural religion*", which the essentially divine element in every human being discloses, either through creation (or Nature) or in conscience. On this general

---

[1] *Vergl. Rel. wiss.* 62.   [2] *cf.* Wach, *Rel. wiss.* 50 *f.*
[3] *cf.* H. Frick, *Theol. Rundschau*, N.F. 2, 1930, 72.
[4] C. Clemen, *Urgeschichtliche Religion*, I, 1932.
[5] Chap. 107.   [6] Chap. 85.

foundation the dome of historical religion may then be erected (in theological terms, as special revelation); and although this pallid abstraction has already been disposed of by Schleiermacher, nevertheless it repeatedly emerges. But with this Herder's fine maxim should be contrasted:—that every religion has "the focal point of its bliss in itself".[1] (B) Primeval religion, in the next place, was originally *one* and preceded all the current divisions. Specific religions are thus only specializations of the primeval, the various "idioms"[2] in which it addresses us. This romantic view still persists to-day in theosophy, which perceives in the actual religions the symbolic disguises of some primeval religion scrupulously guarded by initiates. (C) Primeval religion, again, is the germ of an unequivocal, unilinear *development*, being styled animism by some scholars and dynamism by others.[3] We find another modification of this in the French sociological school, for which primeval religion is supposed to imply a worship of humanity.[4] But in all these attempts at solution the common aim is to derive the plurality of actual religions from one simple origin in the sense of evolutionism. (D) Conversely, the so-called theory of degeneration tries to explain this plurality as being a descent from an original monotheism; while this monotheism, which is supposed to have comprised the essential features of belief in the creator and a morality sanctioned by God, closely approximates to (A), so-called natural religion.[5]

2. Now it is certainly not sufficient to reject primeval religion from the very outset; and the consistent advocacy of our own principle that religion exists only with and in *religions* unquestionably finds itself confronted with considerable difficulties. There is first of all the objection that the copiousness of religions cannot be surveyed adequately because, strictly speaking, each individual has his own religion. Thus my Christianity is often Poles apart from that of my nearest neighbour, and to a far higher degree is this true of a peasant's Christianity or that of a converted primitive, *etc*. It is of course undeniable that religion assumes some specific form in each person's own mind, so that just as my attitude in prayer diverges, however slightly, from my neighbour's, even when our general deportment during prayer corresponds, similarly my entire religious behaviour differs from his even when we belong to the same church and conform to the same type of piety. But this objection also concerns those cultures dealing with subject matter other

---

[1] *cf*. Wach, *Rel. wiss.* 84.   [2] Creuzer.
[3] Chap. 9, 1.   [4] Chap. 32.   [5] Chap. 18.

than religion:—esthetics, jurisprudence and ethics. Each artist, for example, has certainly a style of his own, and each individual his own mode of artistic appreciation. Nevertheless we all agree that there is no art purely in itself, and that in his creations every artist, and in his esthetic appreciation every individual, must submit to an objective ideal from which he began, within which he lives, and in whose construction or improvement he assists. There subsists a style, a consciousness proper to the period, an *objective spirit*:[1] it is quite impossible to begin the history of spirit entirely anew. I certainly have "my" religion, then, but I must nonetheless admit that it is "mine" only very conditionally; for in my own experience religion receives a special form which is, however, merely one specific form of the vast historic formation wherein I myself exist. In my own narrow sphere I assist in preserving the life of this historical religion; if I happen to be a "great man" then it is perhaps permitted to me to cooperate in its transformation, and ultimately in its dissolution and replacement by a new form. But even so this "new" religion could never be entirely "mine", but would always be simultaneously the perpetuation of what has been already given. All great founders, therefore, are essentially reformers.[2]

3. But objective spirit, still further, is so infinitely differentiated that the necessity of a *typology* is absolutely imperative; we must, then, attempt to attain an understanding of the historic forms of religion by appealing to certain ideal types. This typology may, however, follow two different courses. In the first place, and so far as is possible, it may disregard the historic and try to apprehend the specifically historical, to the highest attainable degree, under quite general points of view. Now not only is this typological method thoroughly justified: it is, still further, precisely that which has been pursued in my own investigation. Under these conditions, therefore, nothing more need be done except to draw the general conclusion from our specific considerations, in which case no new aspects whatever would come into view. But at the same time, in order to understand religions actually as forms, we must adopt a different course; and the ideal type that we discover must then be the result of the closest cooperation between phenomenological comprehension and the investigation of all that has been historically given. It follows that we are not concerned, for example, with any religion of compassion, but with Buddhism as the historically living form of this religion.

[1] Spranger, *Lebensformen;* Dilthey, *Werke, passim.*   [2] Chap. 94, 102.

Thus a general typology could be elaborated from the most varied points of view: I cite merely a few instances.

(*A*) A *collective* type becomes distinguished from an *individual* and personal type; and the whole of primitive religion then falls within the collective type. Well developed state religions rank as particularly characteristic instances of this; for example, the Roman, in which the entire social organization stood in a definite legal relationship to the powers, involving reciprocal obligations. To this the antithesis would be, for instance, the devoutness of pietism:

> If I only have Him
> Gladly will I leave all else behind
> And follow, leaning on my pilgrim's staff,
> In true devotion, my Lord alone;
> Content to let others
> Travel the wide, bright, crowded roads.[1]

(*B*) A *higher* religion is distinguished from a *lower*. Primitive religions then occupy the lowest level of all, and the advance proceeds by way of the religions of semi-culture, subsequently culminating in Christianity, or again in Judaism. But the unfortunate aspect of this typology, which is still very frequently advocated, is (first) that it estimates the historical religions exclusively from the standpoint of to-day; as the norm it presents Christianity, and in fact usually a modernized Christianity, to which all else must then be adapted. Secondly, again, this involves the error that the relatively lower and higher grades of religious development are evaluated exclusively in the light of the prevailing culture. The more closely, therefore, the scientific, moral and philosophic concepts of any given religion approach our own, so much the "higher" that religion is taken to be; a typical example of this is Tiele's classification of religions into "The Lowest Nature Religions, The Highest Nature Religions, and The Ethical Religions".[2] Quite differently, however, must this sort of typology be judged when the inadequate terms "high" and "low", which either convey nothing at all or are adopted from a shallow evolutionism, are replaced by the expressions "*primitive*" and "*modern*", provided always that these are not taken to involve stages or periods in the history of religion but eternal structures, and that they also serve to classify the historic religions according to the degree in which they participate in one or the other of these structures.

---

[1] Novalis, *Geistliche Lieder*.   [2] *Elements of the Science of Religion*.

(*C*) Still more hazardous than *B* is racial typology. We have already observed[1] that it is comparatively easy to contrast, for instance, a "Semitic" concept of God with an "Indo-Germanic". But the mere facts that "race" is an extremely dubious category, and that the religion with which we ourselves are most familiar has essential affiliations with the religions of at least two "races", should be a warning to us and induce us rather to describe the intrinsic features, which appear to us as typically "Semitic" or even "Aryan", in accord with their actual nature, and to represent them for example in the light of their relations either to Will or to impersonal Power.

(*D*) A very serviceable typology has been advanced by Frick,[2] distinguishing between the religions of *works* and those of *grace*, and exhibiting this contrast not merely within Catholicism and Protestantism alone, but in Hindu tendencies also. Whether any religious "original phenomenon" becomes perceptible here we may very well leave undecided; in any case this typology is inapplicable to the whole of religion, and primitive religion in general never draws this very momentous distinction.

(*E*) Typology in terms of form characteristics, however, is extremely important; the *religion of the father*, for example, contrasts sharply with that of *the mother*; but this has already been exhaustively discussed.[3]

(*F*) Söderblom's triple division of religion into *animism, dynamism* and the *religion of originators* (in my own terms: the religion of will and of form: that of formless Power: the religion of half-formed Power in the background) has the outstanding merit that it comprises the entire history of religion; and Söderblom himself has brilliantly demonstrated this by exhibiting the characteristic features of his own three types in all the great cultural religions alike: Judaism, Christianity and Islam— Indian religions—Chinese religions and Deism.[4]

(*G*) Reliable typologies may also be based on the character of the religious sentiment of each religion: I may refer here to Heiler's classification into mystical and prophetic piousness, with which many investigators have concurred. The two classical typologies of this type, however, are Hegel's and Goethe's. Hegel distinguished an objective stage, wherein God is the power of Nature, from a subjective, for which God appears as spiritual individuality; the third grade is Christianity, wherein God reveals Himself as Absolute Spirit.[5] It is true that the question may arise whether philosophic construction has not dis-

[1] Chap. 20. [2] *Vergl. Rel. gesch.* [3] Chap. 10, 20.
[4] *Gottesglaube.* [5] Hegel, *The Philosophy of Religion*, III, 107 *ff*

placed phenomenological observation. Far less is this the case with Goethe, who advanced *reverence* as the original phenomenon. In the first instance, this is felt towards whatever is superior to us; and this forms the religion of heathendom as a primary release from fear. In the second place, reverence is experienced with regard to what is equal to ourselves: that is philosophical religion. The Christian religion, on the other hand, involves reverence for what is inferior to us, for the weak and lowly, even the repulsive; it is the religion of suffering and of death. This is the ultimate and highest form which, it is true, then becomes once more apprehended as one of three special forms of higher religion, which consists in man's respect for himself.[1]

4. But all these typologies[2] bring us hardly any nearer to religions *as historical forms*. They are, undeniably, generalizations in definite guise of the data provided by the phenomenology of religion; nevertheless they do not constitute the phenomenology of *religions*. I can, for example, write the phenomenology of hero or saint, but I can also write that of Gustavus Adolphus or of St. Francis; and at present the latter must be our task—of course in its most abbreviated form. Hegel's much derided classification (not the general one already referred to, but that according to historic types) should be esteemed as a most necessary effort that well deserves consideration. Historical typology is a quite indispensable and essential subdivision of the phenomenology of religion. This typology excludes the non-historical and predominantly unhistorical (that is, the primitive) religions; and I need not repeat the contention that every religion is more or less primitive. Nevertheless there are religions which possess a sharply outlined historic form distinguishing them from all others. But this category does not include the religions of so-called primitive peoples, while extensive sections of so-called higher religions are omitted too: those, namely, which are also found in other religions, and thus possess no specific form of their own.

[1] *Wilhelm Meister's Apprenticeship*, II, 1.   [2] *cf.* Frick, *Vergl. Rel. gesch.* 10 *ff.*

CHAPTER 89

RELIGIONS OF REMOTENESS AND OF FLIGHT

1. HISTORICAL form, then, is presented first of all by the *religion of remoteness*, the essential nature of which has already been dealt with in Chapter 18, where it has also been pointed out that it received its historic form first of all in China and predominantly, in fact, in Confucianism. This form however, as indeed must be the case in any religion of remoteness, is extremely indefinite. It is not at all remarkable, therefore, that the advocates of so-called natural religion have sought their historical justification principally in that country.[1]

In China the mystical connection between objects, which is a form of the "participation" previously discussed,[2] becomes intersected by a marked disposition to consider Power only from a distance. But the immediate proximity of countless potencies in all the affairs of ordinary life, in every situation and at every moment, presents a remarkable contrast to this remoteness from Power in general, while the scrupulous observances by no means exclude an indifference approximating to flight. Observance then becomes morality and custom, the latter being omnipotent. "The master said: he who governs by virtue is like the Pole star: he stands immovably in his place and is therefore honoured by the mass of the revolving stars."[3] The leading virtue, however, is filial love (*hsiao*) in the sense of piety. "The master said: if the father is living, consider his will; if he is dead, then think of his conduct. Whoever follows his father's ways for three years may well be called *hsiao*, full of filial love."[4] This filial love is, in the first place, the guarantee of the potency of life taking its course in accord with custom; but it also expands into a universal love of mankind which shows powerful humanistic tendencies. This great-hearted philanthropic morality is restricted only by sagacity and by *li*, that is by propriety which, however, for Confucian sentiment coincides with the rites.[5] These are intended to make it possible for man to devote himself to an aristocratically tinged love of humanity, tranquilly remote from all that is exciting: "the master was not accustomed to speak about extraordinary things

---

[1] Söderblom, *Natürliche Theologie*, 30.
[2] Chap. 82. De Groot, *Universismus*.
[3] Bertholet, *Lesebuch*, 6, 68.
[4] *ibid.*, 6, 69.
[5] *ibid.*, 6, 71.

(miracles), about deeds of strength, rebellions or demons".[1] Custom is invariably observed; thus gods and spirits receive their rightful due, so that we may peacefully devote ourselves to mankind: "To be earnestly occupied in rendering full justice to man, to show reverence for demons and gods, but to keep oneself at a *distance from them*, may well be called wisdom."[2] Power is influential, then, only in its regulated, celebrated, human form; everything else causes alarm, so that both violent deeds and all that is specially sacred should alike be avoided: "To see a saint was not permitted to me. To be allowed to see a noble person would be sufficient for me."[3] "The master said: Is it not true, Shen, that all my teaching is expressed in a single principle? Yes: was the answer. When the master had gone out his disciples asked: what does that mean? and Master Dseng replied: our master's teaching is fidelity towards oneself and kindness to others: in this everything is included."[4] Here, therefore, nothing whatever is obligatory except custom and the virtue which springs from this; the encounter with a powerful will is in principle avoided. This will is certainly recognized, together with the wills of the many demons: nevertheless man remains at a proper distance, as God does also. Here, then, God is Power and Will in the background.[5] His proximity would involve violence, excitement, inhumanity. He is therefore circumvented; for He is just the God of heaven, and heaven is very far away.

2. A second historical form of the religion of remoteness is eighteenth century deism which, indeed, appealed to China; and exactly the same tendency existed in antiquity: "the gods attend to great matters; they neglect small ones".[6] In Western European eighteenth century culture, however, this attitude implies flight from God. Being so remote and so sublime, He is certainly praised; but it is believed to be just as well that He cannot observe us too closely, because we can manage very well without Him! Man says: "God is very far off", however, simply because he has withdrawn himself. In its most pious form, in the *Profession de foi du Vicaire savoyard*, where a sincere and warm feeling for divine reality unquestionably predominates, it nevertheless runs: "The first return to self has given birth to a feeling of gratitude and thankfulness to the author of my species, and this feeling calls forth my first homage to the beneficent Godhead. I worship his Almighty power and my heart acknowledges his mercies. I need no instruction in this religion,

---

[1] Lehmann-Haas, *Textbuch*, 19.   [2] *ibid.*, 19.   [3] *ibid.*, 21.
[4] *ibid.*   [5] Chap. 18.   [6] Cicero, *De Deorum Natura*, II, 167.

which *Nature herself* dictates to me. Is it not *a natural consequence of our self-love* to honour our protector and to love our benefactor?"[1] Great love as well as great defects come from man himself: let us then return to Nature; and even if Lisbon is devastated, that is not the fault of God for sending an earthquake, but of man for building Lisbon! And in a totally different spiritual climate the religion of the remote God becomes perceptible as the religion of remoteness from God:

> Pride! And nought but pride!
> The pot of iron wants to have been lifted
> With silver tongs from out the fire, that so
> 'A may think himself a pot of silver.—Pah!
> And what it harms, thou askest, what it harms?—
> What helps it? might I ask thee in reply:—
> For, for thy "nearer consciousness of God",
> 'Tis either nonsense or flat blasphemy.
> But harm it does:—yes, harm it does most surely![2]

Miracle, however, that is to say the direct and immediate presence of God, is the crucial issue upon which this religion of remoteness begins its struggle against other religions. The nearness of God in miracle and sacrament, in sacred word and church, fades away; God becomes the God of the unforgotten, but not very vivid, background:[3] He is recognized simply because man cannot dispense with Him entirely:

> This sublime mystery is indispensable to man.
> It is the sacred bond of society,
> The primal basis of sacred equity,
> The curb of the villain, the hope of the just.
> Should the heavens, despoiled of His august imprint,
> Ever cease to reveal Him—
> If God did not exist—then man must invent Him.[4]

The essential distinction between this religion of remoteness and the religion of love is most clearly discerned when we fully realize that the most essential characteristic in the parable of the Prodigal Son—the father hastening to meet him—must be completely excluded if the parable is to illustrate the first of these two religions.

---

[1] *Emile*, Book IV (p. 240, "Everyman's Library" Edition); my italics.
[2] Lessing, *Nathan the Wise*, Act I, Scene 2.
[3] Chap. 18; van der Leeuw, *Höchstes Wesen.*
[4] Voltaire, *Epître à l'auteur du Livre des trois Imposteurs*, XCVII, *Œuvres complètes*, XIII, 1785, 226. In this connection Balzac's dictum is not too severe: "*Le déiste est un athée sous bénéfice d'inventaire*" (Ursule Mirouet).

3. The religion of flight, to continue, is *atheism*. But it has never, under any conditions whatever, acquired historical form. Certainly there are again and again individuals who run away from God; nevertheless it is impossible for them to elaborate a religion from their flight. For no sooner have they escaped from one Power than they run into the jaws of the next; they can certainly desert from God to the devil; but then the devil too is (phenomenologically speaking) a sort of "god". Or they may return from God to man or to humanity; but again, in so doing, their flight only leads them back to one of the most primitive of all potencies. Obviously too there are religions opposed to any definite experience of God and any definite idea of God: (original) Buddhism, for example, recognized no gods at all as such.[1] There are indeed modern scholars who would refuse, for this reason, to call it a religion, presumably on the ground that it does not spring from the experience of a personal God. But this is merely to assert that Buddhism is neither Judaism nor Christianity, which we knew quite well already! Earlier investigators similarly denied the presence of religion among primitive peoples, because they served no "gods"; but this contention, fortunately, has now been abandoned; there are no peoples without religion: even at the very dawn of history there is no historic form of atheism. Religion exists always and universally. Even the explicitly atheistic systems of India are nevertheless religions; *Samkhya* is the religion of the soul and its liberation, while Jainism attains a *Nirvana* without the help of gods; and to a still greater degree is the religious character of so-called atheism apparent in some modern systems, such as the presumptive atheism of deism, naturalism and idealism.[2] For in all these cases alike some different god appears instead of the gods hitherto served:—morality, humanity, Nature, the Idea. And in each case its essence is powerfulness, always in the religious sense of this term. In modern communistic atheism, again, it is precisely the same: here the dream of a kingdom of God and the religion of humanity have been united in a new religious ideal, which is atheistic only when compared with the old religion, but which in itself is a search for God rather than a flight from Him.

Actually, however, we might well have omitted atheism altogether from our discussion of the historic forms of religion. For there is no religion of atheism: there is only the individual fleeing from God— long ago described by the believer as "the fool (who) hath said in his

---

[1] *cf.* Chap. 19.
[2] He also who "speaks of God in general truths" is essentially an atheist—that is to say, he flees from God. Bultmann, *Glauben und Verst.*, 27.

heart, There is no God".[1] And the reason why atheism is nevertheless adduced here is that there is no historical religion quite devoid of atheism. No religion, in other words, is the religion of atheism: nevertheless every religion without exception is atheism. For every religion recognizes the element of flight from God; and atheism, that is to say, the deepest doubt, induces in religion a radical tension and thus preserves it from stagnation.[2] As long as a religion is living, therefore, it will include among its adherents fools who say in their hearts, "There is no God". And these fools will not be the worst among the pious! For the existential doubt, concerned with reality, allied to guilt[3] and manifesting itself in flight, is at the same moment an acknowledging of God, even though it is repressed.

[1] *Ps.* xiv. 1; liii. 2.   [2] Tillich, *Rel. Verwirkl.* 102.   [3] Chap. 78.

CHAPTER 90

THE RELIGION OF STRUGGLE

1. PREVIOUSLY, in Chapters 19 and 21, we dealt in detail with the plurality and the unity of Powers; and unity implies either the victory of absolute Power (Monism), or that of Form (Theism). Powers, however, may be reduced in number to two which struggle with one another:—*Dualism*. Religion then becomes the contest between these Powers, and man's own participation therein.

Dualism subsists in many places, and we have already observed how, in the ancient Egyptian cult, persons assumed the part of the god against his enemies.[1] The Egyptians, indeed, possessed a perfect passion for dualism and divided everything—heaven, earth, the kingdom, the provinces and temples, *etc.* They regarded the whole world as, in principle, divided, the representative gods of the two hemispheres being usually Horus and Set.

But the historic form of dualism appears in the Persian religion of Zarathustra, in which the vision of a great founder and reformer has constituted a dualism of action out of that of Nature: the entire life of the Universe, as of man, being a ceaseless struggle.

Zarathustrian dualism, however, was concerned not with the antithesis of spirit and body, as was its Greek counterpart—although it certainly recognized this distinction—but with the still more penetrating dualism of good and evil. To the "wise mind" is opposed an "evil mind", and "bad" thought to "good": to "truth" the "lie," *etc.*,[2] while the antithesis to Zarathustra and to devout mankind is the inhuman, to domestic animals the wolf, to water drought, and to plants blight, *etc.*[3] Thus the whole world is apprehended, from the standpoint of the religious experience of conflict, in terms of contrasted pairs: "In this house obedience shall triumph over disobedience, peace over discord, generosity over parsimony, submission (resignation) over revolt (pride), the truthful word over the false, truth over the lie."[4]

---

[1] Chap. 53.

[2] H. Lommel, *Die Religion Zarathustras nach dem Awesta dargestellt*, 1930, 111. In this and the succeeding chapters no Bibliography of specific religions has been given; only the most valuable as regards Typology are cited; *cf.* also H. S. Nyberg, *Die Religionen des alten Iran*, 1938, 263, 372 *ff.*

[3] Lommel, *ibid.*, 120.

[4] *Yasna*, 60, 5; Lommel, *ibid.*, 86.

2. For the Persians, then, as for Northern peoples, "life is a struggle. But the Persian has the luminous faith of the worker that the effort will be useful; the Northerner dreams that everything will be destroyed."[1] The Persian himself was conscious of the positive struggle called work, and in this connection Zarathustra is typical: "He is to be elected as lord, even as master in the part of the law (*asha*), who prepares works of the good disposition (of *Vohu manah*) for Mazda in (this) life and the (future) kingdom for Ahura."[2] The sacred labour of agriculture is the practical form in which the struggle is sustained: "He who cultivates grain cultivates the law, and advances the religion of Mazda worshippers in the best possible way; he strengthens this religion by a hundred pillars, by a thousand supports, by ten thousand prayers. If there is grain the *devs* perspire (in dread); if there are ears of grain the *devs* are wetted; if there is flour they howl, and if there is dough they act extremely rudely."[3] Persian religion, again, did not distinguish "spiritual" work from this "corporeal" labour; on the contrary: all work based on agriculture is in the lord's service; virtue, also, is work, conflict.

This conflict, in fact, arises even before birth. For duality lies in the first cause of things, and the *daena* (spiritual primeval beings) of men choose between good and evil, exactly as the two great spirits themselves decide the world's destiny in one primeval choice. The kingdom of God too is called "what man should choose", *varya*, and the term for faith means not conviction nor its analogues, but "taking the part of, voluntary decision".[4] Religion is conflict.

This struggle finds its extreme limit, still further, not in the fact that Ahura Mazda is the lord, the creator, whose power is essentially and ultimately victorious. For theism, even the monotheism of Parsiism, does not exclude conflict, and the spirit of the lord is precisely the good spirit, the fighter opposing the evil spirit. But the contest finds its extreme limit in the monism of so-called *Zarvanism*, in the doctrine of infinite time, a factor of dissolution in the religion of Zarathustra, since the belief that Ahura Mazda and Ahriman both alike arose from *Zarvan Akarana*, from infinite time, takes the sting from the struggle and completely stultifies its moral aspect.[5]

3. Manichaeism, finally, which emerged from Zarathustrianism, can scarcely be regarded as a historic form of the religion of conflict. For

---

[1] Olrik, *Geistesleben*, 25. [2] Bertholet, *Lesebuch*, 1, 7.
[3] *ibid.*, 1, 37. [4] Lommel, *op. cit.*, 156 *ff.* [5] *ibid.*, 24 *f.* Nyberg, *op. cit.*, p. 388.

in this the world is abandoned as lost, in principle, only the individual soul being the goal of effort, this again being reinterpreted as asceticism; and the dualism concerns the antithesis between spirit and matter. But this also appears to abrogate conflict as being the basic essence of religion; and thus the religion of struggle subsides into that general dualism which we discern primarily in Greek Orphism and the gnostic religions: God is no longer the God of the world, and conflict has lost its standing.

H. Lommel, *Die Religion Zarathustras nach dem Awesta dargestellt*, 1930.
H. S. Nyberg, *Die Religionen des alten Iran*, 1938.

CHAPTER 91

THE RELIGION OF REPOSE

1. THE religion of repose has already been repeatedly discussed. It has, however, no historic form; nonetheless it must be referred to here because, like atheism and the religion of unrest, which will shortly be dealt with, it is an important element in all historical religions. It is, indeed, no other than mysticism.[1]

Whoever has experienced the *fascinans* of Power too intensely to withdraw from it or flee before it, but on the other hand shrinks from conflict, or at least cannot regard struggle as the characteristic element in his life, longs for calm, for repose, that shall rule both in the divine essence and within himself, between God and humanity as among men; and if he conceives this repose either as being essentially achievable, or as fully attained, then he possesses a religion of repose. But associated with it he always has a different religion also, the religion of repose being then at best one leading component. For not only do the religions of conflict and of will counteract repose, but the religions of infinity likewise do not leave it altogether unaffected. In the first place, a perfect religion of calm would abolish itself completely as a historical form, since without some activity there is no religion whatever; while (secondly) calm itself cannot be attained without struggle, and indeed severe struggle. Repose, therefore, is the goal of longing; nevertheless it may dominate a religion completely, and then monistic and pantheistic systems arise. But it may also be incorporated within the active tendencies of a religion, either as the ultimate human goal or eschatologically as the ultimate activity, the ultimate deed of God. An example of this second type would be St. Paul's declaration: "And when all things shall be subdued unto him, then shall the Son also himself be subject unto him that put all things under him, that God may be all in all."[2] This is certainly repose, but neither pantheism nor monism: it is the yearning for the unity in God called love, which is bestowed ultimately by God Himself. Hölderlin's fine pronouncement, again, would be an instance of the first kind: "The discords of the world are like lovers' quarrels. Reconciliation is to be found in the midst of strife,

---

[1] Chap. 75. [2] 1 *Cor.* xv. 28.

and there all that has been separated is again united. In the heart the arteries part and meet once more, and all becomes one single, eternal, glowing life."[1] In these words, though unquestionably as longing, as prospective, is depicted the union which *must* follow alienation.

[1] *Hyperion.*

CHAPTER 92

THE RELIGION OF UNREST

1. HERE also the religion of unrest, theism, must be assigned its specific position because it too is one element of every historic religion, although it never receives a proper form of its own. It is, then, neither conflict nor calm: it is ruled neither by the ethos of strife nor by the longing for peace. It is in fact the religion of a God Who rests not, Who "shall neither slumber nor sleep",[1] nor ever leave His people in repose. This, however, excludes neither conflict nor calm; for struggle is one form of unrest, while repose is its Pole and its aspiration. Still, disquietude ever remains the essential element in humanity. The conditions of conflict, too, are unambiguous. It may be that his God summons man to the contest; but it may also be a different unrest into which He plunges him, since he may be so good a fighter that he finds his peace in the very conflict itself; and this he must not do. For peaceful calm beckons as the final aim: we recall the familiar words, "our hearts are restless until they rest in Thee"; while every anticipation of this goal appears as sin.

Thus God is never-resting *Will*, which governs all human life. This is to be discerned at its best in the Old Testament, where God troubles and consoles, forsakes and seeks, punishes and shows compassion, is angry and loves:— but never for one single moment rests.

> Thou hast discarded us, crushed us in anger, O God;
>   restore us to power:
> thou hast shaken and shattered the land;
>   repair its tottering breaches.
> Hard times thou hast given to thy people:
>   and a cup to drink that has dazed them.
> Hast thou given thy worshippers a flag,
>   only that they might fly from the archers?
> To the rescue of thy dear folk!
>   Save by thy right hand, answer our entreaty,
> O thou Eternal who hast discarded us, shamed us,
>   who would'st not march out with our army.

[1] *Ps.* cxxi. 4.

> Help us against the foe,
>   for man's help is in vain.
> With God we shall do bravely;
>   he will trample down our foes.[1]

The religion of unrest, however, is not restricted to the historic form of Israel. It appears indeed not only in the closely allied religions of Islam and Christianity, but in all religions for which, however intense the element of calm may be, God is nevertheless a disquieting factor also. For Power, in the first place, is always the force that prevents man accepting life and indulging himself;[2] and this too finds its most pointed expression in the *Psalm*:

> Where could I go from thy Spirit,
>   where could I flee from thy face?
> I climb to heaven?—but thou art there;
>   I nestle in the nether-world?—and there thou art!
> If I darted swift to the dawn,
>   to the verge of the ocean afar,
> thy hand even there would fall on me,
>   thy right hand would reach me.
> If I say "The dark will screen me,
>   the night will hide me in its curtains",
> yet darkness is not dark to thee,
>   the night is clear as daylight.[3]

This we find to be repeated more or less in all religions with no exception, from the most primitive, in which the fear of God predominates, to the most mystical wherein the love of God consumes the devout. It is true that in these religions that foundation is absent which, in the religion of Israel, sustains the stirring drama of God and man:

> For thou didst form my being,
>   didst weave me in my mother's womb,[4]

and which constitutes the essence of Judaism as a historic religion. For there, and in Christianity also, God's creative Will is itself the cause of the unrest. The God Who descends to destroy the Tower of Babel descends a second time to deliver mankind; whether in anger, or in compassion, He never leaves humanity in peace. Wherever man goes, God's creative love pursues him.

---

[1] *Ps.* lx. 1–12 (Moffat).   [2] *cf.* Jaspers, *Psych. der Weltanschauungen*, 339.
[3] *Ps.* cxxxix. 7–12 (Moffat).   [4] *Ps.* cxxxix. 13 (Moffat).

CHAPTER 93

THE DYNAMIC OF RELIGIONS. SYNCRETISM. MISSION

1. IN Chapter 19 we discerned syncretism to be the process leading from polydemonism to polytheism. But we must now apprehend its essential nature somewhat more thoroughly:—in fact, as one form of the *dynamic of religions*. In other terms, if we wish to discover the essence of the so-called "great religions", which must now be discussed, it is imperative for us not merely to contemplate their static character, but also to consider their dynamic. A historic religion, then, is a form, an organized system. Nonetheless its characteristics are not fixed and rigid; rather they are in perpetual flux: not manufactured but growing, and in a state of incessant expansion. "Every religion, therefore, has its own previous history and is to a certain extent a 'syncretism'. Then comes the time when, from being a summation, it becomes a whole and obeys its own laws".[1]

Thus Egyptian, and similarly Greek, religion arose from a large number of local religions. In ancient Egypt this process of amalgamation had set in at a very early period, and proceeded very deliberately.[2] The priesthood of one of the capitals zealously pursued the unification of the prevailing local cults and the elucidation of the reciprocal relations between the gods. In Greece, on the other hand, this theogony was effected by the poets. Nonetheless at the culmination of Egyptian, and again of Greek, culture, there was still, for example, an Osiris religion and a Ra or Ptah religion, a religion of Apollo, and of Zeus or of Dionysus, which maintained their independence as against one another and whose incorporation into the great whole remained theoretical or poetic.[3] But as the "world" gradually became smaller, several religions came into contact, the most impressive example of this being the syncretism of the Hellenistic age, which attracted to itself the religions of the whole inhabited world and interwove and united

---

[1] Wach, *Rel. wiss.* 86.

[2] *cf.* H. Kees, *Zeitschr. für. ägypt. Sprache und Altertumskunde*, 64, 1929, 99 *f.*

[3] Chantepie, *op. cit.*, I, 75. To a certain degree, a "pantheon" is always theory or poetry; *cf.* Chap. 19 and G. Furlani, *Actes du V. Congrès*, 154. The Babylonian gods were regarded as the limbs of Nimurta.

them either into magical modes of activity, or mysteries, or philosophic speculation. It may indeed be asserted that at the close of the
imperial era there were countless religions in existence, since each
person had his private system of devotions, and many even had
several simultaneously; but it may also be said that there was only
one sole religion, since all the components, of the most varied origin,
had become unified within one single astrological-pantheistically
tinged piety, for which the name of Zeus signified a rallying-point
rather than any distinctive feature.

Every historic religion, therefore, is not one, but several; not of
course as being the sum of different forms, but in the sense that diverse
forms had approximated to its own form and had amalgamated with
this. This is true of even the great, and so-called world, religions, to a
quite specific degree. Restricting ourselves to Christianity and Islam,
for example, these are from the dynamic viewpoint syncretisms; and
thus in Christianity we find, together with the inheritance of Israel,
that of Greece and even a small bequest from Persia; and the scars on
the amalgam, especially that of the Greek and Israelite spirit, have not
yet completely healed! In Islam, similarly, Christianity, Judaism and
primitive religion met and fused together into a unique new form.[1]

In recent times, also, there exists a close parallel to the boundless
syncretism of the Roman imperial era, in the various semi-, or completely, occult tendencies which appear under the names of theosophy,
anthroposophy, Christian science or (new) *sufism*. These forms all pay
homage to syncretism, to some extent in principle, because of their
conviction that all religions, at bottom, are only one in different guise;
nevertheless they are all mixtures taken from religions and spiritual
tendencies occurring everywhere:—Oriental, Christian, modern idea-
listic, natural scientific, *etc.* Naturally these medleys often produce a
very peculiar and confused impression, which however does not at all
disturb their own adherents!

2. But at this point a more precise definition of a concept already
repeatedly encountered may be given:—the concept of *transposition*.
"Transposition", then, is the variation of the significance of any phenomenon, occurring in the dynamic of religions, while its form remains

---

[1] Shinto, the Japanese national religion, is a religion free from syncretism, and
therefore one that lacks a mission! In this instance religion has been wholly absorbed
within nationalism (*cf.* Chap. 37). R. Pettazoni, *Die Nationalreligion Japans und die
Religionspolitik des japanischen Staates, Orient und Occident,* 1932, 5.

quite unaltered. Thus the sacred word, the myth of Bethel, of the "house of God",[1] becomes "transposed" from a fetishist experience to that of a theophany, subsequently to an announcement of the nearness of God, and finally edifying consolation. Quite similarly, the killing of the ox, which was regarded in pre-Zarathustrian Parsiism as a praise-worthy release of life (for Mithra slays the animal not at all maliciously, but simply in order to render life as it were fluid), becomes "transposed" in Zarathustrianism and diabolized into Ahriman's first destructive deed.[2] In Christian worship, again, prayers of incense offering (by transposition) become an *epiclesis* of the eucharistic Lord.[3]

"Transpositions", to continue, appear at all times, but chiefly during reformations[4] and missions; and as a rule, the old possessions of religion were superseded to only a slight extent and retained in essentials with, however, an altered significance. Thus almost all Protestant religious communities retained the sacrament of communion but "transposed", with a changed meaning, and this too after the Roman Church itself had already accepted it from the ancient church and had transposed it. Israelitish prophecy, again, took over the Bedouin law of the *Decalogue* and interpreted it in a religio-ethical sense, since when we ourselves have not ceased repeatedly to transpose the Ten Commandments anew, from the Gospel down to Luther. Frequently, also, the actual character of a phenomenon is utterly lost in transposition, as in the previous example of incense prayers. But just as often we receive the impression that the essence of the phenomenon, at bottom, is retained even when its interpretation has been modified, as in the case of the Law.

3. The dynamic of religions, further, is displayed as mission. This may in the first place be completely unconscious, and merely a reciprocal influence of religions which is the outcome of local proximity, cultural interchange, *etc.* It is called mission, however, because it is a result of speaking forth, of utterance and of testimony,[5] and is accompanied by all sorts of transpositions in the life of both the influencing and the influenced religion. Frick has given an illuminating description of this effect of religions on one another.[6] Thus there occurs assimilation of religions by each other, and also substitution of a religious value with more or less changed meaning (transposition); but there likewise arises

---

[1] *Gen.* xxviii.   [2] Lommel, *op. cit.,* 183.
[3] Lietzmann, *Messe und Herrenmahl*; for liturgical transpositions *cf.* Will, *op. cit.,* II, 112 *ff.*   [4] Chap. 94.
[5] Chap. 58.   [6] *Vgl. Rel. wiss.* 53 *ff.*

the isolation of those elements which are, as it were, to be rendered harmless. Catholicism assimilated mysticism, for example, and substituted popular religion, while at the same time it isolated asceticism within monasticism.[1] This type of mission pertains to every living religion.

But as soon as missionary expansion is understood to be the essential activity of the community, it receives a quite different character. Its influence then becomes a fully conscious propaganda of doctrine and worship, and generally of the specific characteristics of a religion. It is in this sense that Judaism has made its proselytes, but has been frustrated because it has unified the "given" community with that of salvation;[2] for in general, deliberate missionary movements presuppose the collapse of this equivalence. The great mission religions, accordingly, are the "world religions" of Buddhism, Islam and Christianity. Of these three, again, Islam is at present the typical missionary religion, because it takes the dynamic power of its faith to be wholly a matter of course: conquest, then, lies in the very essence of Islam. Consequently, it sends out no specially trained missionaries at all, every follower of the prophet being, as such, a missionary who, by his example, advocates an extremely simple worship and an equally elementary creed.[3] But also in the essence of the Christian church, *una sancta catholica*, missionary activity is inherently incorporated, although Christians themselves are realizing this afresh only very gradually. Religion, however, lives only by being active; and in Christianity this ceaseless agitation is the life movement of the Holy Spirit, on Whom no limits whatever are imposed.

H. KRAEMER, *The Christian Message in a Non-Christian World*, 1938.
R. PETTAZONI, *Sencretismo e Conversione nella Storia delle Religione* (*Bull. du Com. Int. des Sciences Hist.*, 1933).

[1] *Vgl. Rel. wiss.* 55.   [2] Chap. 32 *ff.*
[3] Chap. 62; *cf.* W. H. T. Gairdner and W. A. Eddy, "Christianity and Islam", *The Christian Life and Message in relation to non-Christian Systems, Report of the Jerusalem Meeting of the Int. Miss. Council*, I, 1928, 252 *ff.*

CHAPTER 94

THE DYNAMIC OF RELIGIONS. REVIVALS. REFORMATIONS

1. EVERY religion is perpetually *reformanda*—to be reformed—although it is always already reformed—*reformata*—also. The dynamic of life compels religion continually to change its form; while it is living it is being reformed; and it is impossible to connect the occurrence of reformations merely with certain definite conflicts, even in the case of the most important, such as (for example) those involved in the different concepts of sin.[1] Reformation, in fact, can be associated with any given condition, any controversy whatever. That of Luther undoubtedly found its life and its justification in a profounder consciousness of sin; perhaps, also, that of Mohammed; but Buddha's case was quite different, and Zarathustra's reformation too had its roots elsewhere. Provisionally, however, we may say that the reformation of any religion begins in the reformer's own experience of God, and his being a special type of religious founder.[2] Luther's penitential struggle, Buddha's experience of suffering, Moses' theophany and Mohammed's visions—all alike imply, for the religious community to which each pertains, new life which then gradually flows out into channels of new doctrine, commandments, insight, *etc.*

The essence of "being reformed", however, is particularly distinct in the historic religions; thus Buddhism is the reformation of Brahminism, but this in its turn of the ancient Vedic polydemonism; similarly, Islam the reformation of Arabian animism, Zoroastrianism of the Persian "Nature religion"; Greek religion now as the "Homeric", and again as the "Platonic", reformation of local cults;[3] Christianity, finally, is the reformation of Judaism, which itself arose from the Jahvistic reformation of Canaanite animism. And in fact every religion without exception, as it appears in its concrete form, is the reformation of a reformation: Northern Buddhism of the original, which on its part, *etc.*; protestant Christianity of the medieval, and this again of the primitive Christian form, which in its turn, *etc.* No religion, therefore, is ever completed: every religion, even the "most primitive", was

---

[1] Mensching, *Sünde*, 68.   [2] Chap. 101 f.   [3] Chap. 95.

once different and will at some time be different again. Of course these reformations are not all on quite the same level, nor do they all attain an equal profundity. The reformations which produced the "great vehicle"—that is of salvation—from Buddhism, and the medieval church out of primitive Christianity, are rather processes of change[1] whose individual stages may indeed, to some degree, be based on religious experiences, but not on such as are markedly distinguished by any original power and specific character; in part, then, they also originate by accommodation and relapse into some ante-reform phase. It must certainly not be forgotten that (for example) St. Francis' experience of God was one factor in the construction of the medieval church—and subsequently an element, too, in its dissolution. The sole certainty, then, is that living religion is in perpetual activity, and reformation is therefore not some sort of arbitrary act, but *one form of the very life of a religion.*

Still further, a reformation that fails either because it lacks the requisite energy, or because it abandons the community it is seeking to reform as utterly lost, may lead to a sect or a schism: instances are the *Shiah* in Islam, and the great schism between West and East in Christianity.[2] From such controversies it frequently results that the sect, or the schismatic church, considers itself to be genuine and true, while its opponent concedes it only the status of a sect or indeed a heresy. Protestantism, for instance, regards itself as reformed Christianity, but to Roman Catholicism it is only a heresy.[3]

In general terms, then, three types of reformation should be distinguished: (*1*) that which has arisen from various historical developments, which in their turn are derived from unnumbered minor or major religious experiences. Such a reformation would be, for example, the gradual evolution of the medieval from the ancient church; this however need not be discussed further, because it is clear and simple in itself and hardly deserves the name of reformation, although it played an equally important rôle in the same dynamic as did the Reformation proper; but it may also be regarded simply from the viewpoint of transpositions and syncretisms.[4] (*2*) A reformation springing from mass experience:— from the revitalized collective experience of God: I

---

[1] Wach (*Rel. wiss.* 162) refers to "transpositions of strain", or corrections of the structure of a religion; in this broad sense the development of Homeric religion, *e.g.*, and Augustus' reform of the cult, were "reformations" of diverse type.

[2] *cf.* O. Piper, *Sekte und Konfessionskirche, Zeitschr. für Theol. und Kirche, N. F.* 11, 1930, 258.

[3] Chap. 35 *f.*   [4] Chap. 93.

describe such a reformation as revival. (*3*) One that is born from some individual person's experience of God: this is reformation in the full sense.

2. By the term revival I mean that a wave of religious feeling and desire flows over a community, and draws everything along with it in the broad stream of sentiment and resolution. It may be linked with ecstatic experiences,[1] but at all events it consists of some relaxation of life's potencies, all of which are then precipitated on the religious purpose without hindrance and freed from all compulsion of regulated celebration. It may be sustained by some single personality, but it may also operate *en masse* in every respect, though it certainly always requires leaders; and while it may reform a religious society, it may also establish itself as a sect quite apart from the existing community. Such a revival was the great Dionysiac wave which, in the early history of Greece, penetrated Hellas from the North with elemental power and carried everything along with it. Like all revivals this too was contagious, as may be clearly perceived from legendary narratives of the immigration of Dionysus; some few isolated individuals offer resistance,[2] but the majority are swept away in the whirlpool of divine insanity. Thus in Orchomenos the daughters of Minyas withstood the frenzy until vine-runners suddenly twined themselves around their looms, while milk and honey dropped from the ceiling; then they too seized one of their sons, tore him in pieces and sought their salvation in the mountains with the maenads.[3] Marvellously clear in this legend is the foil of the historical event itself: the epidemic seizes all the more fiercely those who at first resisted it, and the Dionysiac revival became a popular under-current of Greek religion that maintained itself not only in various sects such as Orphism and Pythagoreanism, but had also very lasting influence on the thought and aspiration of the entire Greek people; it may therefore be asserted that though it was not a reformation in the strict sense, still it thoroughly reformed Greek religion; and without this revival neither tragedy nor Platonism would ever have arisen.

The flagellant movement of the thirteenth and fourteenth centuries was a similar revival, directed in part against the clergy and carrying all before it in the stream of penitence, while analogous to this was the

---

[1] Chap. 74.   [2] Euripides, *Bacchae.*
[3] G. van der Leeuw, *Goden en Menschen,* 117 *f.* Nilsson, *A History of Greek Religion,* 207.

Anabaptist revival, whose raptures turned towards the new Jerusalem, the kingdom of God:

> I hear the trumpet's sounding,
> Its call is heard afar,
> In Jerusalem, in Edom, in Bashan,
> The messengers call everywhere.[1]

More recent revivals also, from pietism and methodism onwards, pertain to this category, even though they usually show no pronouncedly enthusiastic character. Nevertheless there always exists that passionate torrential surrender to the One which is necessary: in this case, to inwardness of belief, sanctification of life and the operations of the Spirit. These movements, still further, may once again become enthusiastic, as the pentecostal movement that arose from Evan Roberts's Welsh revival clearly proves to-day; while with a magnificent organization the Salvation Army hurls itself on the masses with the sole purpose of conversion.

3. As I have just observed, actual reformation arises from some one individual person's own experience of salvation. From this, new powerfulness springs into life which in part makes an end of old custom, doctrine and morals, and in general of the existing relationship between life and Power, and in part revivifies the torpid elements. Usually the second feature is stressed: the reformer comes "not to destroy, but to fulfil";[2] he wants to make the truly religious element, the very life of religion, resound once more in the vast desert calm of stagnation. This holds good of the Old Testament prophets—the Law—but that written in the heart: the sacrifice—but of a broken heart: just as it does of Jesus, of Buddha—the ideal of "true brahmins"—and of Mohammed —the appeal to Abraham.[3]

A typical reformation was that of the Egyptian "heretic king" Akhnaton.[4] Resuming primeval tendencies and endeavours, he placed in the centre the worship of the sun as that of the visible god. But in this he inevitably gave offence, on the one hand to the ancient traditional animal worship together with the anthropomorphic and theriomorphic representation of the gods in general, while on the other hand he

---

[1] Revivalist Song of the martyr Anneke Jans, in Lindeboom, *Stiefkinderen*, 211.
[2] *Matt.* v, 17.   [3] Frick, *Vgl. Rel. wiss.* 47.
[4] H. Schäfer, *Amarna in Religion und Kunst*, 1931. G. van der Leeuw, *Achnaton*, 1927.

believed that he was according the true essence of the sun-god its first proper estimation, as he had expressed this in the interpretation of his god's name. He also retained the ancient dogma of kingship,[1] filling it however with new and mystic content. It is no less typical of his reformation that, quite apart from the opposition to the old, and its fulfilment, he neglected one entire sphere of tradition:—the worship of the dead. And the same essential traits occur, more or less prominently, in all reformations. Zarathustra and Mohammed, Buddha and Jesus, Luther and Calvin: they all repeal, preserve and fulfil, or else they adopt a wholly indifferent attitude with reference to the religion they have reformed. In Jesus' own words: "Ye have heard that it was said by them of old time . . . But I say unto you . . . I am not come to destroy, but to fulfil";[2] the old is either annulled, fulfilled or set aside as quite immaterial. Luther may be similarly depicted: catholic penitential practice was abolished, while the church was affirmed in its essential nature, and worship left as it was with marked indifference.

[1] Chap. 13.   [2] *Matt.* v. 17 *f.*

CHAPTER 95

THE RELIGION OF STRAIN AND OF FORM

1. IN approaching the "great" forms among religions, and prepared by the consideration of their dynamic, we become increasingly aware that they can scarcely be characterized by any single term. In order to outline any adequately detailed description of these religions, therefore, nothing less than a vast number of intersecting lines would be adequate for the clear delineation of their contours. But even now, when we are concerned only with typology, we can satisfy ourselves with no single characteristic, as Hegel did. For it is undeniable that in dealing with such complicated historical structures as are the great religions, we should never analytically dissociate (at least not in phenomenology) what history itself has combined, since this has all grown up in the closest association, not merely been placed in juxtaposition. Yet at the same time we shall hardly be able to find any firm historic ground whatever without taking a cross-section which, while traversing the line that indicates the essential nature of a religion, still itself pertains to that very nature. Hence we must set to work as did the Romans when they laid out a camp, and decide on *cardo* and *decumanus*, the main road from North to South and its intersection East to West.

The *cardo* would be in the first instance strain, the *decumanus* form; and the religion of strain and of form is that of Greece. We have, in fact, long since been compelled altogether to abandon the classicist view of the Greek spirit:[1] the Greeks were not merely the people of "tranquil greatness and noble simplicity". Thus Rohde has emphasized the mystical aspect of the Greek sentiment for life, while although Nietzsche, with a brilliant anticipation of to-day's scientific achievements, has certainly modernized the discord in the Greek temperament, he nevertheless clearly perceived it. The Greeks, then, were the people of *hubris* and *sophrosyne*, of Dionysus and of Apollo, of the night of death and of bright day, of the dark stress of Eros and of clear, sharply outlined form. As Kern points out, the Dionysus of the Orphics was a god of liberation;[2] in the orgiastic cult, in the myth of the origin of sin, in mystic yearning for death, in transcendental speculation as in tragic art, Dionysus was the symbol of life ever striving beyond itself in

---

[1] G. van der Leeuw, *Goden en Menschen.*   [2] *Die griechischen Mysterien*, 48.

indomitable longing and seeking for deliverance, indeed for dissolution. To Dionysus they prayed: "Men shall send hecatombs at all seasons of the year, and shall celebrate orgies to bring about liberation from lawless ancestors, and shall celebrate them madly. And you, deriving strength from these, shall free whom you will from heavy toil and endless trouble."[1] The Bacchic mystic did not sing, like the worshipper of Apollo; once he had scaled the high peaks of ecstasy he remained silent.[2] But the philosopher, too, knows the moment when concepts fail him, so that he can do justice to his thought only in mystic guise. Thus the Greeks were keenly conscious of life's farthest frontiers, and of that beyond where actual life first begins: "who knows if this life be not death, and death be not accounted life in the world below?" as Euripides says.[3] In the dithyramb life becomes revealed as "deaths and vanishings, passages out of life and new births",[4] while out of the ecstatic experience of orgiastic worship sprang the belief in immortality.[5]

It is strain, therefore, that creates life and is the most ancient of gods, but which also overpowers life until it ceases to breathe and finds rest only in dissolution:

> Love resistless in fight, all yield at a glance of thine eye,
> Love who pillowed all night on a maiden's cheek dost lie,
> Over the upland fells thou roam'st, and the trackless sea,
> Love the gods captive holds. Shall mortals not yield to thee?
> Mad are thy subjects all.[6]

Eros, however, has already been discussed.[7] As a historical form he was adopted by Plato from the yearning dreams of Dionysiac Orphism, and fashioned into an eternal symbol. Divine strain, *Eros*, son of poverty and wealth: this is at once the eternally striving and the eternally vanishing, the love of the good and the beautiful, that which man has not, the generation of an eternal life, sexual desire and the most spiritual creation, instinct and loftiest volition. Generation,

---

[1] Kern, *Orphicorum Fragmenta*, No. 232.

> ἄνθρωποι δὲ τελήεσσας ἑκατόμβας
> πέμψουσι πάσῃσι ἐν ὥραις ἀμφιέτῃσιν
> ὄργια τ'ἐκτελέσουσι λύσιν προγόνων ἀθεμίστων
> μαιόμενοι· σὺ δὲ τοῖσιν ἔχων κράτος, οὕς κ' ἐθέλῃσθα,
> λύσεις ἐκ τε πόνων χαλεπῶν καὶ ἀπείρονος οἴστρου.

[2] Rohde, *Psyche*, II, 9; English Translation, 288.
[3] *Fr.* 639; Cornford, *Greek Religious Thought*, 155.
[4] Plutarch, *On the E at Delphi*, ix; Cornford, *ibid.*, 56.   [5] Chap. 44.
[6] Sophocles, *Antigone*, 781 ff. (Storr).   [7] Chap. 76.

indeed, is the very essence of the highest human capacity: "All men are bringing to the birth in their bodies and in their souls . . . procreation which must be in beauty . . . this procreation . . . is a divine thing; for conception and generation are an immortal principle in the mortal creature."[1] In the *Phaedrus Eros* leads to the turning away from body and form, the transition being here foreshadowed from the Greek spirit to Greek Christianity. But the polarity of the Greek spirit appears first of all in its proper guise in the *Symposium*: eternal strain, perpetually generating, nevertheless finds its supreme fulfilment in blissful contemplation of form.

2. For this is the other aspect of Greek religion: at one moment sober, at another rapt, but always tranquil *contemplation of form*: this is the truth of classicism and also of the famous Hegelian dictum at the transition from Egyptian to Greek religion: "The enigma is solved; the Egyptian Sphinx, according to a deeply significant and admirable myth, was slain by a Greek, and thus the enigma has been solved. This means that the content is man, free, self-knowing spirit."[2] For though Egyptian religion can scarcely be described as enigmatic, and though Oedipus' Sphinx is hardly an Egyptian, and if, still further, the "free, self-knowing spirit" could fashion itself only on free, self-conscious form, nevertheless a pedantic science should perceive that one aspect of Greek religion is quite clearly expressed here:—that is the purely human. No religion, in fact, has ever been so much a *religion of humanity* as the Greek; not even the entire oppressive weight of mysticism, pessimism and yearning for the "beyond" can stifle this pure humanity. Homer depicted the gods in beautiful human forms: but he did not deify man;[3] Homer's religion, as contrasted with Plato's— the religion of Apollo in antithesis to that of Dionysus—is perception of pure forms, contem₁ lation of form: not dominance over the divine, and scarcely indeed the longing for this.[4] "The Greeks enjoyed an astonishingly high degree of health—their secret was to revere even disease as a god, if it only possessed *power*", as Nietzsche observed;[5]

---

[1] *Symposium*, 206; *cf.* further 186*b*.; "how great and wonderful and universal is the deity of love, whose empire extends over all things, divine as well as human" (Jowett).

[2] Hegel, *The Philosophy of Religion*, II, 122.

[3] Murray, *The Rise of the Greek Epic*, 158 *ff.* On this aspect of Greek religion, *cf.* W. F. Otto, *Der Geist der Antike und die christliche Welt*, 1923; *id. Der europäische Geist und die Weisheit des Ostens*, 1931.

[4] This formulation shows to what extent I agree with W. F. Otto's fine and weighty, but one-sided, volume; *cf.* p. 621, n. 3.   [5] *Human, All Too Human*, I, 192.

and it is just this that is specially important for us. For it appears
almost as though the Homeric Greeks were deficient in that elementary
necessity of every religion:—not simply to accept life, but to undertake
something with it, to demand something from it, to resolve to make
some use of it. The Homeric Greek was neither magician nor believer
in the sense previously discussed:[1] he gazed upon the given world and
adored it as divine form; thus far, again, Hegel was correct (and many
after him), since if the other aspect of the Greek spirit is disregarded
Greek religion was certainly a religion of the beautiful, with an essentially esthetic character. Nevertheless this religion was indeed a genuine
religion, and was least of all estheticism. Reformed by poets and philosophers, it still lived among the people together with the mournful or
yearning cults of the grave and the mysteries.[2] In fact, precisely this
contemplation of form was "celebration" in this religion: the Greek
accepted the given world just as little as any others; and he celebrated
it as form. Certainly this form, for him, was neither a will which
dominated him nor which he dared hope to control, neither a power
that he constrained nor one that stifled himself. Otto suggests that the
fear of, and the longing for, the Wholly Other were equally lacking in
the Homeric Greek. In that case, however, one certainly could not
understand why his *Weltanschauung* should be called a religion at all.
But the Wholly Other subsists precisely in that *form* which is not
fortuitous and empirical but divine, perfect and eternal, radiantly rising
from the given life. And no. one has perceived and maintained this
better than Otto himself.

Let us follow him, then, awhile: the Greek domain of belief is "an
emanation from the wealth and profundity of existence, not from its
cares and longings".[3] For the Greek spirit, therefore, it was not events
and capacity that were significant, but "being. The divinities become
forms of reality, wherein the manifold being of Nature finds its perfect
eternal expression".[4] In form "there reposes the meaning of all being
and happening. It is the true reality, the divine. Present everywhere,
it is one with all the appearances of the life circle that it controls. But

---

[1] *cf.* further Chap. 82.   [2] *cf.* S. Wide, *Griechische Religion.*
[3] *Die Götter Griechenlands*, 1929[1], 371. This work, already cited, is particularly
significant with regard to the psychology and phenomenology of Form; *cf.* G. van der
Leeuw, *Gli dei di Omero, SM.* 7, 1931. On Greek religion, together with Rohde's
Psyche and Harrison's *Prolegomena, cf.* especially: Wilamowitz-Möllendorf, *Die Glaube
der Hellenen*, 1931–1932. O. Kern, *Die Religion der Griechen,* I, 1926. Nilsson, *History
of Greek Religion.* Farnell, *Outline History of Greek Religion.* Murray, *Five Stages of
Greek Religion.*   [4] *op. cit.,* 49.

as the highest essentiality and as persistent being it stands alone, high
above the earthly in etherial splendour".[1] This religious sentiment,
further, concerns itself little about the dead or death: the dead possess
form only as life that is ended; the "form of the person who has existed
is (indeed) not extinguished", but the deceased is not present as a
demon.[2] Nor again does it strive for any justification whatever, neither
of the world, nor of God nor man. Man should demand justice neither
from the course of the world, nor from the gods superior to it; as long
as "the consciousness of the divine presence" is vivid he asks absolutely
nothing.[3] Obscene myths may well have a quite comprehensible origin
in the syncretism of local cults,[4] but the Homeric gods do not require
any such justification; their sins never offended the Olympic Greeks,
simply because a god's sin is just the eternal form of an existing being,
and one does not censure being for existing.[5] Human guilt, too, is
indeed a fault; but it does not lead to contrition, and still less to any
metaphysics of sin as, for example, in Orphism. For the gods also
bring about evil deeds in man, and the passion to which these are due
"has its marvellous eternal countenance among the gods, to which
man may look up even out of his contrition".[6] What therefore deeply
distressed the Greeks of the first, Dionysiac type—that eternal gods
should allow themselves to be guilty of evil—is precisely the very
ground of Homeric religious sentiment; the Euripidean Hecuba, who
reproached Helen for being led astray not by the goddess but by her
own concupiscence, would here be wrong, since the goddess is precisely
this passion itself elevated to an eternal form.[7]

This religion of form is best displayed then—and here again we
may follow Otto—in Apollo's essential and true character. His form
certainly developed from various others on syncretistic lines; but in
Homer's religion it became a mighty and surpassing apparition, the
type of Homeric construction of form in general: embodying the ideal
of proper distance, it "repulses whatever is too near, the state of being
immersed in things, the trance-like glance, and equally the fusion of
souls, mystic rapture and its ecstatic dream".[8] Here then there appears a
sharp contrast between this religion and not merely—as Otto supposes—
Judaism and Christianity as the religions of Will and Love, but also
Greek mysticism and Dionysus, the god who plays almost no part at
all in Homer. For Apollo is an aristocratic figure who always maintains
his distance: "Are they, the perfect ones, to allow their bliss to be dis-

___

[1] 210.   [2] 182 ff.   [3] 331 f.   [4] Chap. 19.   [5] 311 ff.   [6] 225.
[7] cf. Chap. 19. Otto, op. cit., 242.   [8] 99.

turbed by any too serious a participation in man and his complaints?"[1]
Men are only men: eternal gods need not trouble too much about them;
when Poseidon challenges Apollo in battle before Ilium, the god replies:
"Shaker of Earth, as nowise sound of mind wouldest thou count me,
if I should war with thee for the sake of mortals, pitiful creatures, that
like unto leaves are now full of flaming life, eating the fruit of the field,
and now again pine away and perish."[2] And when his sister, Artemis,
chides the god for cowardice, he remains silent in his majestic self-
consciousness and self-esteem.

The religion of form, therefore, seeks no other world, but simply one
that has been given form and shape and which (in this I differ from
Otto!) precisely in thus acquiring form is then a kind of "new" world.
We stand here, in fact, at the uttermost frontier of religion: the "divine"
of the Homeric Greeks "is neither a justifying explanation, nor an
interruption and abolition of the natural course of the world; it is the
natural course of the world itself".[3] And here lies the limit already
indicated in Chapter 19: for as soon as Power thus becomes completely
identical with the world itself, no religion can live any longer; with the
"Other" it can never dispense. The salvation of Greek religion, then,
was the immortalizing and perfecting of the given form into timeless
sublimity: its weakness (deplored however by all its own "Dionysiac"
poets and philosophers!) was that it merely presupposed this sublimity
rather than strove for it. It may therefore be conceded to Otto that
Homeric religion not merely possesses esthetic value, but confronts the
Israelitish religion as an equal[4]—it may indeed even be maintained
that hardly any purer "antithesis" to Israelitish religion can anywhere
be found than just in this Greek religion. But on the other hand, we
cannot exclude the view that this polarity arises precisely from Homeric
religion having reduced the religious element to its utmost minimum.
And if it is true that it is not the striving, desiring, demanding, limitless,
uncanny and labyrinthic that is ever suggested in Homeric religion,
but form—if "the forms of being of the human appeared (to the Homeric
Greek) with such a degree of reality that he had to revere them as
gods"[5]—then, it is true, the Wholly Other may be saved in the perfection and eternity of these forms; it always hovers, nevertheless, in
danger of being entirely merged in the world itself and in humanity.
Thus this religion is sharply delimited from its own environment and
from the world of religion in general; no awful and imperious Will

---

[1] 165.   [2] *Iliad*, XXI, 461 (Murray).   [3] 218.
[4] 173.   [5] 299 f.

asserts itself against man: no unity entices, which might dissolve all that
has been separated: high and sublime stands Form, pure Form, and
man may contemplate it. "In the heavenly sphere the forms stand pure
and great before each other. There immaculate Artemis may gaze upon
the tenderness of Aphrodite with cool wonder."[1] That is beautiful, and
because it is perfect it is also sacred. But when Otto asserts that "immediate bodily presence and at the same time an eternal validity—that
is the marvel of Greek creation of form",[2] then the danger is at least not
at all illusory that the "immediate presence" stifles the "eternal validity".
It is indeed this peril that has made the tragedians suffer, while the
"Dionysiac" mystics and philosophers sought refuge from it in their
hatred of the body and the world.

3. It is one of the greatest of all marvels in the history of religion that
the religion of Form and that of Eros held their place in the soul of *a
single* people; and this, again, not side by side but in the unity of
tension and reconciliation. Eros is a beautiful *ephebos*, while Form
awakens Eros by its beauty;[3] and this is a miracle, witnessing to both
the affluence and the plasticity of Greek religion. For it could beget a
Pheidias but also a Euripides, a Homer, but a Plato too. Ultimately,
Homer's gods are no merely empirical Nature forms, but esthetically
"modelled forms"; Plato's ideas too are not without form and beauty,
being "in these akin to the marble statues of Pheidias".[4] And thus we
can understand how *Iliad* and *Phaedrus* sprang from the genius of one
and the same people.[5] To this unity of the religion of Form *and* of Eros,
in conclusion, Diotima's beautiful utterance may testify, revealing as it
does the ultimate vision of the Eros mystery: "He who" (in practice
and knowledge) "has been instructed thus far in the things of love, and
who has learned to see the beautiful in due order and succession, when
he comes toward the end will suddenly perceive a nature of wondrous
beauty (and this, Socrates, is the final cause of all our former toils)—
a nature which in the first place is everlasting, not growing and decaying,
or waxing and waning . . . And the true order of going or being led
by another to the things of love, is to use the beauties of earth as steps
along which he mounts upwards for the sake of that other beauty, going
from one to two, and from two to all fair forms, and from fair forms to

---

[1] 309.   [2] 321.
[3] For the comprehension of the Greek spirit, *cf.* J. Geffcken, *Kantstudien* 35, 1930,
427 *ff.* G. Mehlis, *Logos* 8, 1919–1920; van der Leeuw, *Goden en Menschen, Einleitung.*
[4] Mehlis, *op. cit.,* 45.   [5] G. van der Leeuw, *Gli dei di Omero,* 19.

fair practices, and from fair practices to fair notions, until from fair
notions he arrives at the notion of absolute beauty, and at last knows
what the essence of beauty is . . . a beauty not after the measure of
gold, and garments, and fair boys and youths . . . But what if man had
eyes to see the true beauty—the divine beauty, I mean, pure and clear
and unalloyed, not clogged with the pollutions of mortality, and all
the colours and vanities of human life—thither looking, and holding
converse with the true beauty divine and simple? Do you not see that in
that communion only, beholding beauty with the eye of the mind, he
will be enabled to bring forth, not images of beauty, but realities (for he
has hold not of an image but of a reality), and bringing forth and
nourishing true virtue to become the friend of God and be immortal,
if mortal man may. Would that be an ignoble life?"[1] Here equilibrium
between Form and Eros has been discovered, and the tension eschatologically relieved.

[1] *Symposium*, 210–212 (Jowett).

W. F. Otto, *Die Götter Griechenlands*, 1929.
M. P. Nilsson, *Geschichte der griecheschen Religion*, I, 1941; II, 1950.
M. P. Nilsson, *Greek Piety*, 1948.

CHAPTER 96

THE RELIGION OF INFINITY AND OF ASCETICISM

1. THE religions of India signify the victory of longing over form. And had the Greeks not been Greeks, they too would probably have carried the desire "to escape from the cycle" onward to the unconsciousness of a *Nirvana*, and intensified care for salvation to the point of asceticism. In the light of actual historical development, however, we find that with all their contempt for the world the Greeks never recognized formlessness as the norm, while in the classical Greek world the idea of asceticism and virginity was indulged only once—by Euripides:[1] a proof both of the greatness of the keen-sighted poet and of the essential distinction between the Greek and the Hindu spirit.

If for the moment we leave Buddhism, which occupies a place of its own, out of consideration, then the religions of India appear to us as the *religion of the infinite and of asceticism*. We know quite well, of course, that the "religions of India" comprise an almost endless variety; and like Greek religion, the Indian too are erected on a primitive religion of which they have preserved very much to this day. Still further, they find their limits in *bhakti* religion, which will be discussed later. The main stream of Hindu religious sentiment, however, which has also beaten against the coasts of Europe and still powerfully influences the modern world, directs itself towards the infinite, and attempts to attain it by asceticism.

The entire world-event, then, is the "universal sacrifice" of *Purusha*, the primeval man[2] from whom everything emanated; there are certainly gods who sacrifice *Purusha*, but they are not essential; there also exists, further, an old myth of the dismembered giant, but this likewise is inessential. What is really essential is the reduction of all that happens to one single event, of all that is to one sole being: "*Purusha* is the whole Universe, what was and what shall be . . . by sacrifice the gods sacrificed the sacrifice", says a celebrated hymn in the *Rig-Veda*.[3] Fear of solitude and of possibility, concern or "care" for the world, are infinitely intensified, and possibility becomes so potent that man ceases to breathe—literally, in fact, in *Yoga* discipline; "care" extends

[1] In *Hippolytus*.　　　　　　　　　　　　　　　[2] Chap. 86.
[3] Lehmann-Haas, *Textbuch*, 92 f.; *cf.* Otto, *India's Religion of Grace*, 68.

to the very ground of the Universe, dethrones the gods themselves and
bases the world in the self, the self in the world. "In the beginning this
world was only the *ātman* in human form (*purusha*). He gazed around
and saw nothing but himself (the *ātman*). Then first he spoke the word:
'It is I'. Thence arose the word 'I'. He was afraid. Therefore does he
fear who is absolutely alone. And he mused: If there exists nothing but
myself, of whom am I actually afraid? then his fear departed", says
Yajhavalkya.[1] Thus the great equilibrium prepared a way for itself,
which carries away all care that involves celebration, and all distance
implying fear and gods, in one intense passion: the Universe is the self
and the self is the Universe, *Brahman-Ātman.* Oldenberg has acutely
depicted the development of this equilibrium,[2] which received its finest
expression in Sandilya's words: "*Brahman* is the truth: therefore it
should be revered. Man consists of will alone. Whatever is his will in
passing from this world, such shall be his will on attaining the other
world. Thus let him revere the self (*ātman*): thought is its nature,
breath its body, light its form, the ether its self—it is formed like desire,
as swift as thought: it is true in thought, true in performance: rich
in all perfumes, rich in all essences, interpenetrating all regions of the
Universe, permeating the Whole, silent and heedless. Small as a grain
of rice or barley, or millet or a millet seed, this spirit dwells within
the self, golden as smokeless flame, greater than the heavens, greater
than the ether, greater than this earth, greater than all beings. This is
the self of the breath, this is my self. To this self I shall attain by
separation from this world. Whosoever truly possesses this knowledge
has no doubts. Thus spake Sandilya. Thus it is."[3] Just as the great
edifices of Hindu worship of the gods perpetuate the same *motif* in
interminable repetition—as the great epics of Hindu literature endlessly
accumulate epithet upon epithet—so Hindu religion expands what
exists, the Universe and the self, in eternal repetition into the infinite,
wherein the two are but one.

Then all celebration ceases; but to this culmination *asceticism*[4] should
lead. Usually we distinguish between the path of action and that of
insight and knowledge; but asceticism is equally acting and insight,
insight, as it were, that has become action. The ancient brahmin ideal,
indeed, places at the close of life the existence of the *yatin*, the self-
conqueror; the *yatin* no longer sacrifices, but in rigorous asceticism
dedicates himself to contemplation: life, so to say, is prolonged into the

[1] Bertholet, *Lesebuch,* 9, 102.   [2] *Die Lehre der Upanishaden,* 55 *ff.*
[3] Oldenberg, *Lehre,* 57 *f.*   [4] Chap. 66.

infinite. Commencing as a disciple of the brahmins, the adult performs his duties of sacrifice and procreation of children; then withdrawing into the forest, he "leaves his home";[1] from the variegated, fulfilled life there has arisen the void of the infinite. Man does not simply practice asceticism: life *is* asceticism as soon as it directs itself towards its actual powerfulness. "The 'great *Text*' indicates this powerfulness in the famous *tat tvam asi*, 'that art thou', 'thou, thy true essential being, thy spirit, art one with the unity in the All: thou art the Universe.' "[2] The religio-speculative passion of the *Vedanta* is separated from the infinite, which is the real and true world, only by the deceptive veil of *Maya*: "Man should know that Nature is merely illusion and the great god the deceiver. The whole Universe is filled with elements that are only fragments of him."[3] Both world and man, therefore, must be purified, the veil removed from them by either asceticism, insight or resignation: and Hindu religion is the way of infinity. Illusion (*Maya*), *avidya* (ignorance) must cease to deprive the relationship between the "I" and the "thou" of its essential unity. The world that "appears" was brought forth by *Brahman* with *Maya*: creation is therefore an illusory act; the personal god has a merely provisional task, and is only the object of unintelligent reverence. He who penetrates to essential being knows *advaita* (non-duality): that there are not two, but one only. This "one", however, actually exists; in this respect Sankara, the greatest of the commentators on the *Vedanta*, and perhaps the greatest of all prophets of the religion of infinity, differs from Buddhism, the religion of the nought. *Brahman* is timeless, eternal being with which the self merges after it has released itself, through insight, from the nullity of the world and the *tat tvam asi*.[4] It is therefore not sufficient to characterize the religion of India as the religion of unity: for into unity is entwined the All which is infinite, whereof the human self constitutes an indistinguishable part. *Brahman* has no predicates whatever: it merely exists; to it, or from it, there is no other path at all than that of being. Man can neither seek it, nor influence it, nor even love it; he can only be it. As religion, that is as one human attitude, Brahminism is therefore a religion of infinity: its goal, its task, are alike infinite. Already the nought advances its claim, but it is rejected.

2. The religion of infinity finds its logical consequence, and also its limit, in the nought of Buddhism: another limit, however, confronts it

---

[1] Chap. 34.   [2] Tiele-Söderblom, *Kompendium der Religionsgeschichte*, 157.
[3] Bertholet, *op. cit.*, 9, 140.   [4] *cf.* Otto, *op. cit.*, 30 *f.*

in *bhakti* religion:—submission to the lord *Isvara*; and Otto points out, with perfect justice, that in India there was not only a Sankara, but also a Ramanuja: "In India itself there has been waged the hottest battle against this 'monistic' mysticism of an impersonal Absolute."[1] One of Sankara's followers said to Otto: "You Christians are the same as our *bhaktas*. Your relation to God is that of a child to his father (*pitri-putri-bhava*). We also approve that. Still, the true and final completion of the *ekata-bhava*, the relation of complete unity and oneness with God, lies far above and beyond it."[2] In the theistic *bhakti* religion, then, God really is "a God to inspire personal trust, love, reverence, and loyal self-surrender",[3] no mere introduction and makeshift for popular piety. His lack of duality is primarily his uniqueness; *advaita* (non-duality), nevertheless, must be assigned its full validity, since God and the world become united as soul and body.[4] It is true that this constitutes one limit of the religion of infinity; but it is by no means a bridge to the religions of Will and Form. Formlessness is certainly limited, and the passionate flight into the infinite checked; in contemplating *bhakti* religion, therefore, we are repeatedly impressed by a far-reaching agreement with Islam, but above all with Christianity:—for here is a "religion of grace", and in a certain sense a religion of love too;[5] here also contrasts can arise such as that between release by works and deliverance by *bhakti* alone: *sola fide!* The *Bhagavad-Gita*, in fact, can be read with edification by the adept of a religion of Will and faith.[6] And what ultimately and definitely makes *bhakti* religion a religion of the infinite—in spite of all these features pointing in a different direction—is in the first place its conception of life, and secondly—but not detached from this—that of the Universe.

Otto points out, still further, that the term "rebirth", which in Christianity implies a completely new creation through the Spirit, can in *bhakti* mean nothing but *samsara*, the unbroken chain of births; what in one religion is supreme grace is regarded by the other as the dark foil for this grace; while what one calls liberation is, for the other, precisely that from which man must be freed. For the one, life is something to be created wholly anew; for the other, life is lost and must finally vanish in infinity.[7] As to the Universe, again, the religion of Will and of Love regards it as a creation, as the deed of God; for the religion of infinity however, even for that which in *bhakti* is mitigated and rendered much more a religion of the heart, it is merely the sport (*lila*)

---

[1] *cf.* Otto, *op. cit.*, 17.   [2] *ibid.*, 21, 22.   [3] *ibid.*, 29.   [4] *cf. ibid.*, 32 *f.*
[5] Chap. 76.   [6] *cf.* Otto, *op. cit.*, 50.   [7] *ibid.*, 87.

of the All-one. "When I consider the chaste women of honourable families, I see in them the divine mother garbed in the raiment of the chaste lady; and when I behold the prostitutes of the town, as they sit in their open verandahs wearing the clothing of immorality and shamelessness, in them too I see the divine mother as she plays the game in a quite different way", says Ramakrishna, the last great Hindu teacher.[1] All that "appears", therefore, is only the revelation of the One, here possessing a provisional form (that of the Hindu mother-goddess) which, however, makes everything else inessential; if the Universe moves the motion can be only a game of the sole Power with itself. And thus neither God nor man finds any assigned "place" in either space or time: infinite motion draws away with it even what is most immovable and once more dissolves the most rigid forms.

H. OLDENBERG, *Die Lehre der Upanishaden und die Anfänge des Buddhismus*, 1915.
R. OTTO, *India's Religion of Grace and Christianity Compared and Contrasted*.

[1] Bertholet, *op. cit.*, 14, 83 *f*.

CHAPTER 97

THE RELIGION OF NOTHINGNESS AND
OF COMPASSION

1. IN Buddhism the way of the infinite leads to *nothingness*. For the older Buddhism, most faithfully preserved in the "little vehicle" (of salvation), *Hinayana*, is hostile to all sensuous representation: Buddhist art lived in *Mahayana*[1]; nor is this to be wondered at, since in the former every presentation of the divine is proscribed: Form disappears, and Will must be annihilated. Buddhism, then, is in the first instance the insight that this vanishing and annihilation are real; it is therefore the religion of the negative.

In this connection Frick offers an illuminating comparison between the "sacred nights" of the three great religions. In Islam the night of power, *lailat al kadr*, is the occasion on which the *Koran* was sent down. In Christianity, again, the sacred night is that of the Saviour's coming. But in Buddhism, on the holy night, Buddha received illumination on the banks of the river Neranjara—that is to say, insight into the four noble truths and the path of liberation: "Here I have cut off the briars of passion from the tree of world-being with the axe of reflection, and burnt them in the fire of knowledge; the stream of sensual desires has been dried up by the sun of knowledge; here the eye of knowledge, in its purity, was opened for me and the fabric of madness rent; all the fetters of the existence of the world have been loosed for me."[2] Failure to know and to comprehend the noble truths of suffering and its origin, of its suppression, and the way leading to this, is the cause of the "erring and wandering on this long road".[3] The extirpation of the roots of suffering, then, effects the cessation of rebirth; and since the Hindu temperament cannot conceive existence except as a cycle, it leads to nothingness. The last word of the *Tathâgata* to the monks, in fact, refers to the nullity of this cycle: "Hearken, ye monks, I say unto you: doomed to vanish are the appearances of existence (*samkara*); strive on without ceasing."[4] Then the master enters *Nirvana*, which he attains

---

[1] Mensching, *Buddh. Symbolik*, 5.
[2] *Vergl. Rel. wiss.* 68 ff. cf. A. Bertholet, *Buddhismus im Abendland der Gegenwart*, 1928, 29.
[3] Bertholet, 11, 17.   [4] *ibid.*, 11, 24.

by stages: the four degrees of submersion (*jhana*) bring him to the realm of "infinite space", then he attains to that of "infinite consciousness", and finally to the sphere of "non-being". But this also is too positive: imagination and perception must cease completely. At this point, according to Ananda, the master has attained perfect rest; but Anuruddha understands the matter more adequately: the road returns once more to the first stage of submersion, and then follows precisely the same course again; but now, from the fourth *jhana* Buddha reaches "complete *Nirvana*" immediately (*Parinibbana*). And the king of the gods, Sakka, provides the commentary: "Alas! appearances of existence (*samkara*) are transitory, fated to arise and to pass away. After they have come into existence they are annihilated; *their cessation is bliss.*"[1] Buddha is no god, no *gandharva* nor *yaksa*, but neither is he man: he would indeed be all these were not the "basic evils" within him extirpated. "That whereby I might again come into being as a god, as a *gandharva* living in the air, or might become a *yaksa* or a man, the basic evils namely, are annihilated within me, destroyed, eradicated. And as the beauteous lotus does not become defiled in the water, so I remain unpolluted by the world. Therefore, Oh brahmin, am I a buddha."[2]

This nothingness, certainly, has a positive significance.[3] In the *Mahayana* the nought once more appears as "immeasurableness",[4] and even as form. Always, however, everything is again denied: the "great vehicle" (of salvation) "sets out with nothing. It will halt nowhere or, again, for omniscience it will stand still in the sense of not stopping."[5] "Standing still in the sense of not stopping": the secret of mysticism cannot be more eloquently expressed: Buddhism is mysticism *par excellence*. Salvation, *Nirvana*, is neither being nor non-being; "from still profounder depths than *Brahman*, than *Purusha*, the presage of *Nirvana* meets the gaze of the pious man, who strove not to solve its riddle but to lose himself within it. The way in which thought silently turned away from this enigma may seem feeble and fainthearted to the Faustian yearning to know 'the force that binds creation's inmost energies'.[6] But how completely had Buddhism rejected such a longing! An intrinsic greatness, and indeed a unique poetry, subsist within, as man stands here before the veiled image of the Beyond, free from the desire to unveil the glory unseen by any eye, while in the depths of his

---

[1] Bertholet, 11, 25 *f.*   [2] *op. cit.*, 11, 31 *f.*
[3] *cf.* the previous discussion of mysticism, Chap. 75.
[4] Bertholet, *op. cit.*, 15, 65.   [5] *ibid.*   [6] *Faust*, Part 1, "Night."

own being, silently and blissfully, he experiences this glory itself."[1] To these beautiful words of the sensitive specialist upon India it can only be added that the Christian longing for deliverance is also foreign to Buddhistic calm. For the *rex gloriae* does not rest, but is always "He that cometh in the name of the Lord". His image does not at all resemble the wonderful images of Buddha : in these desire is extirpated, and therewith life also; every potency, and this indeed in principle, is held at a distance. Nor is asceticism of any assistance, except that *exercitio spiritualis* which gradually denudes the individual in the sequences of submersion and leads to nothingness.[2]

2. If it possesses insight, however, what is born together and also suffers together must suffer *reciprocally*; and thus the essential meaning of Buddhism is *compassion*.[3] Involved in the same misery, carried wholly away into the same bliss—"be they visible or invisible, far or near, already born or still striving for birth—may all beings whatsoever be blessed in heart! As a mother protects her own child, her only son, even at the cost of her own life: so man should cherish a boundless benevolence for all beings! He should cultivate a limitless spirit of love for the whole world: above, below, on all sides, unhindered, without hate and without enmity."[4] A *bodhisattva* need only surrender himself completely to a single virtue, and all Buddha's virtues exist spontaneously within him; that is compassion: "Oh Lord, just as, when the organ of life is present all the other organs act, so, Oh Lord, when the great compassion exists all those other virtues which yield illumination become manifest."[5] The ground of this compassion, still further, is the essential unity of all beings involved in the cycle of births: "How could a *bodhisattva mahasattva*, who desires to approach all beings with his own essential being in order to help them, and who loves Buddha's teachings, eat the flesh of any creature or living thing, the flesh of a close relative, who has completed his existence in one birth and has been born again in the womb of a wild animal, a cow or bird?"[6] This is carried so far, indeed, that one brahmin disciple, who had observed his vow of chastity for 42,000 years, broke it out of compassion for a woman who would otherwise have died;[7] and it extends to such a degree that the *bodhisattva*, in the guise of a hare, roasts himself at the fire for the

---

[1] Oldenberg, *Lehre der Upanishaden*, 333.
[2] Bertholet, *op. cit.*, 11, 17; *cf.* Friedr. Heiler, *Die buddhistische Versenkung*², 1922.
[3] *cf.* Willy Lütge, *Christentum und Buddhismus*, 1916, 30 *ff.*
[4] Bertholet, *op. cit.*, 11, 84.   [5] *ibid.*, 15, 35.
[6] *ibid.*, 15, 50.   [7] *ibid.*, 15, 40.

benefit of a hungry brahmin—but not until he has conscientiously shaken from his fur all the vermin so that it should not be injured!¹

Compassion, however, is not love, "even though it is a manifestation of loving understanding. Compassion is oneself to suffer in the pain of another, no matter what kind of pain this may be. Pity has no relation whatever to the Absolute, but is merely a disavowal of suffering, and is in no degree directed to the individual as an individual, but generalized. It is therefore degrading for whomever it concerns . . . and arouses . . . in the compassionate a sense of superiority, because . . . in helping he feels his own power . . . We retain the attitude for which the value-contrast between pain and pleasure is absolute. We do not love when and because we are pitiful"; and Jaspers' observations,² founded on Nietzsche's merciless unmasking of virtue, can be applied quite freely to Buddhism. For, as has repeatedly been observed,³ love is always reciprocal love, and always directly related to the Absolute and to God's act, while compassion is insight into the universality of suffering. Pity is the magnanimous activity of one who knows that he can free himself: love is his act who knows that he himself is loved. Benevolence towards all living things invents neither hell nor heaven: but even in hell

Love is living when Pity is dead.⁴

3. The religion of nothingness finds its limits on the one hand in those of the infinite, and on the other in those of form and surrender. For strict Buddhism, therefore, Buddha's death is no essential loss, since the main factors, doctrine and insight, still remain. Nevertheless there have apparently been many whose sun was darkened when for them the light of salvation no longer shone from Buddha's features:— "When the Lord had finally departed to rest, many of the monks, who were not yet free from passion, wrung their hands and lamented; (others) suddenly fell to the ground and rolled to and fro (while they mourned): 'All too soon has the Lord finally gone to his rest, all too soon has the blessed one fallen completely to rest, all too soon the eye (that is, the light) of the Universe has disappeared.' But those monks who had overcome passion endured it with serious mind and keen insight (while they thought): 'all appearances of the existent are transient; how could it possibly (be otherwise) in this instance?' "⁵ The

¹ Lüders, *Buddhistische Märchen*, No. 53.
² *Psychologie d. Weltanschauungen*, 128.   ³ Chap. 76.
⁴ *Inferno*, Canto XX, 29.   ⁵ Bertholet, *op. cit.*, 11, 27.

trust of his disciples is directed, indeed, even towards the will of the departed, when Buddha Amitabha's "primeval vow" not to enter into perfect bliss until all who long for salvation have been released, transforms the "insight" and the "doctrine" into a very real act of will; for man should trust in this vow: it is a kind of deed of salvation that demands faith.[1] Here then a piety prevails which has been compared by missionaries, not without justice, with that of the Reformation, as in the case of Luther. Surrender, faith, make blessed. And Buddha's own resolve is itself a sort of sacrifice: "Out of the great abyss I must raise (all these beings), I must free them from all calamity, I must lead them out of the flood of *samsara*. I myself must take the entire mass of suffering of all beings upon myself . . . I am resolved to live countless millions of world-eras in each individual wretched form of existence. . . . Verily it is better that I alone should suffer, than that all beings should fall into situations of miserable forms of existence".[2] Nevertheless the salvation thus effected by Buddha is always blissful nothingness: "Looking for the maker of this tabernacle, I shall have to run through a course of many births, so long as I do not find him; and painful is birth again and again. But now, maker of the tabernacle, thou hast been seen; thou shalt not make up this tabernacle again. All thy rafters are broken, thy ridge-pole is sundered; the mind, approaching the Eternal, has attained to the extinction of all desires."[3]

H. Von Glasenapp, *Der Buddhismus*, 1936.
H. Oldenberg, *Buddha: His Life, His Doctrine, His Order*.

[1] *cf.* Frick, *Vergl. Rel. wiss.* 93 *f.*   [2] Bertholet, *ibid.*, 15, 34 *f.*
[3] *The Sacred Books of the East* (*The Dhammapada*), X, 153, 154 (Müller).

CHAPTER 98

THE RELIGION OF WILL AND OF OBEDIENCE

1. HISTORY offers in religion, as elsewhere, only a restricted number of possibilities: the religion of Form, or of formlessness: that of Will, or of nothingness: the religion of asceticism, or of strain: of compassion or of obedience—with these the entire wealth of history appears to be practically exhausted. Just as, in the course of history, mankind turns again and again to some few symbols, so there are also but few traits wherewith the essence of Power can be depicted, and only a few attitudes that can be adopted towards it.

In the first place, then, the religion of Will and of obedience arose in Israel from dynamistic-animistic foundations; any intermediate stage of polytheism, like that of India and Greece, was absent, or almost completely so. The powerfulness therefore, which the primitive Israelite perceived in his life, always had the pronounced character of a demonic will; and as Söderblom has justly observed, the religion of Israel, at least that of Jahvistic tendency, is of the animistic type, as is also that of Islam. Jahveh was thought of as the "destroyer, sinister, dangerous and unaccountably angered, as one who rejoices in destruction, ruins unexpectedly and craftily, who punishes without mercy, demands cruelty and creates evil."[1] A mighty warrior, he annihilates his people's enemies: but he attacks his own servant, Moses, too, in order to kill him,[2] and from his friend Abraham he exacts the sacrifice of his only son. His utterance is potent: "On the third day, in the morning, there was thunder and lightning, a dense cloud on the mountain, and a loud trumpet-blast, till all the people in the camp trembled . . . and the mountain of Sinai was all wrapped in smoke, as the Eternal descended in fire upon it; the smoke rose like steam from a kiln, till the people all trembled terribly. As the trumpet-blast grew louder and louder, Moses spoke and God answered him."[3] This is the description of a volcanic eruption, but at the same time of a numinous experience, of the experience of a demonic will falling upon a people. But when his oracles fail, God's silence is even more fearful and more sinister than his speech.[4] It is terrible when he comes forth "from his place" (prob-

---

[1] P. Volz, *Das Dämonische in Jahve*, 9 (1924). [2] *Exodus* iv. 24.
[3] *ibid.*, xix, 16, 18 *f.* (Moffat); Bertholet, 17, 39.
[4] 1 *Sam.* xiv. 37; xxviii. 6; *cf.* Volz, *op. cit.*, 13.

ably Sinai originally): "the Eternal descends, he strides on the heights of the earth! Mountains melt away before him, valleys split asunder, like wax before a fire, like water pouring over a fall".[1] For His will is in the first place wrath: He is like a hot breath sweeping the desert; and thus Israel experiences the sacredness of Power as an awful will. It is no different in the Prophets: "the Lord of hosts; 'tis he whom you should fear, 'tis he whom you should dread!".[2] Amos too hears Jahveh's voice as the roaring of a lion from Zion: "the Eternal thunders loudly from Jerusalem, then the pasture-lands are woe-begone, the ridge of Karmel withers".[3] Jahveh is "jealous" also; he enters man's life and ravages it in order to make it his own property: "a jealous god entered their lives, who had assisted them with fearful power, and who now desired their whole being and existence".[4] And with this something colossal has been accomplished for religion.

For now the fearful desert-will becomes the God of history, the God of *his own* people. He places the slothful people in the midst of the world's confusion, he drives it on and desires it to execute his demonic will, to know nothing whatever except him and his will. And actually, however frequently the people relapsed into idolatry, however thanklessly and unfaithfully it acted towards its stern but loving lord, it knew, as being unique among peoples, that its God was its sole salvation. Volz has given a penetrating and comprehensive description of how the experience of the powers, which Israel itself shared with all peoples, here led to neither polytheism nor dualism, but became incorporated within the overpowering experience of Jahveh, so that in Israel "the one Jahveh enfolded all".[5] "Jahveh became demonic; while conversely, since Jahveh absorbed everything demonic and was himself the mightiest demon of all, the Israelites no longer required any demons."[6] This, then, was the great and bold enterprise undertaken by the people of Israel: it was bound to its own God by such potent community, the might of the superior will which it felt to be laid upon itself was so vast, that it was quite impossible for it to believe in any other powers whatever except Jahveh, even if this forcible simplification of events should involve evil power being that of God. This adventure in faith in God, still further, was carried out by the people of Israel in all its gradations, by the editor of the tradition who ascribed what was most sublime and most atrocious simultaneously to Jahveh Elohim, as well as by the Mosaic popular consciousness which appears in the *Decalogue:* "Thou

---

[1] *Micah* i. 3, 4 (Moffat); Bertholet, 17, 40.   [2] *Isaiah* viii. 13 (Moffat).
[3] *Amos* i. 2 (Moffat).   [4] Volz, *op. cit.,* 27   [5] *ibid.,* 31.   [6] *ibid.*

shalt have no other gods before me"; and again in *The Book of Job*, for which "everything is united in the one God—and therewith its God himself becomes demonic and indeed almost Satanic."[1]

Something colossal then, to repeat, has been accomplished in this little people: *faith* is born. Power now becomes believed in as Will; and this, too, even when it leads to enigmatic and dubious historic confusion, even when it appears as more demonic than the very worst demon, even, in fact, when it "forsakes" the people.

In the light of this situation, further, a characteristic parallel can be drawn with the Greeks. For neither the Old Testament Jew nor the Homeric Greek ever recognized magic. Of course magic actually appeared in the first instance just as in the other: but, in principle, it was overcome. And the reason for this was that, in Greece, man desired *nothing* from God, and God nothing from man : while in Israel *everything* was demanded from God, and by God everything from man. "In the presence of such a monstrous and frightful God, who united all the might of God and demons, magic completely disappeared: before such a God, who was not only a demon but also God, no charm could avail."[2] Thus Israel *lives* with its God, in strife and discord, in anger and contrition, in repentance and self-will, in love and faith.

A further parallel, though now certainly in the negative sense, arises with the Greeks:—among them we found the religion of Form. Here however, in the religion of Will, *Form is absent*.[3] The relationship to deity, which the vision of the Greeks perceived in the remoteness of some radiant realm of the gods, is here all too close: God is far too much a reality ever to permit His features being portrayed. On Sinai certainly, according to *Deuteronomy*, a voice "spake out of the midst of the fire:"[4] Moses heard the sound of the voice, but he "saw no similitude".[5] And so the primeval awe before the nearness of Power in the image receives, in Israel, a quite special meaning: the Will, which forces itself upon man, is so close that he sees nothing whatever, but also so "Wholly Other" that it is good to perceive nothing. For whoever sees God must die: "Thou canst not see my face; for there shall no man see me, and live", says Jahveh to Moses.[6] But the voice resounding from the awful darkness of the mount of God rings too in man's innermost heart: it is therefore all the more dreadful simply because it is so much nearer.

---

[1] Volz, *op. cit.*, 30.   [2] *ibid.*, 31.
[3] And so, almost completely, is *myth*.
[4] *Deut.* v. 20; *cf.* Bultmann, *Zeitschr. f. d. Neut. Wiss.* 29, 1930, 169 ff.
[5] *ibid.*, iv. 12; *cf.* Chap 65.   [6] *Exodus* xxxiii. 20; Bertholet, *op. cit.*, 17, 45.

Thus the voice speaks of wrath: but of mercy also. Certainly this is always thought of in the guise of the cessation of the wrath: "the Lord is merciful . . . neither will he keep his anger for ever";[1] but it is precisely this conditioning of Jahveh's love and grace, of his gentleness and compassion, by his wrath, that gives them their intense reality which is simultaneously "Other" and beyond, and endows them with the character of "election." The same prophet who accuses Jahveh of deluding him, and who can no longer endure God's might,[2] finds for Jahveh's love the beautiful words: "I have loved thee with an everlasting love: therefore with lovingkindness have I drawn thee."[3]

2. The voice, resounding out of the darkness, delivers the *commandment*: man's *obedience* responds to God's Will. On this subject, however, little need be added to what has already been said in Chapter 69. In the commandment likewise God is close to the people: "For this commandment which I command thee this day, it is not hidden from thee, neither is it far off. It is not in heaven, that thou shouldest say, Who shall go up for us to heaven, and bring it unto us, that we may hear it, and do it? Neither is it beyond the sea, that thou shouldest say, Who shall go over the sea for us, and bring it unto us, that we may hear it, and do it? But the word is very nigh unto thee, in thy mouth, and in thy heart, that thou mayest do it."[4]

The great watchword of Israel, therefore, is the *Shema Israel*: "Hear, O Israel: The Lord our God is one Lord: and thou shalt love the Lord thy God with all thine heart, and with all thy soul, and with all thy might. And these words, which I command thee this day, shall be in thine heart."[5] Here the voice resounds within, dominating the entire life, the culmination of this faith being *The Book of Job*.

In the commandment,[6] certainly, the religion of Will and of obedience finds its limit. For as soon as God has become law he has lost his demonic character, and with this his essential nature; and the God of many prohibitions, against which the passionate preaching of Jesus is directed, can indeed be embarrassing, but scarcely dreadful! The marvellous love of the law, obedience to the voice sounding within the heart, has become a religion of book and legalism, in which the scorching breath of the desert has sunk for ever to rest.

[1] *Ps.* ciii. 8, 9.   [2] *Jer.* xx. 7 ff.; Bertholet, *op. cit.*, 17, 78.
[3] *Jer.* xxxi. 3; Bertholet, *ibid.*, 17, 93.
[4] *Deut.* xxx. 11 ff.; Bertholet, *ibid.*, 17, 112.
[5] *Deut.* vi. 4 ff.; Bertholet, *ibid.*, 17, 112.   [6] Chap. 62.

A quite different limit to this religion, again, occurs in the modern interpretation of the convenant[1] as a correlation between man and God. For now not only man, but God also, can speak of abandonment. "Thou hast cast me forth", says Adam: and God replies:

> My son, we are so closely united
> That with thine own words thou strikest at thyself.
>
> *Adam.*   Have mercy on me!
> *God.*   Have mercy on me![2]

But a God whom man must himself support, and to whom he must show pity, is such a thoroughgoing development of the all-consuming Will of the Old Testament that its very essence has been developed quite out of existence.

M. Buber, *Königtum Gottes* (*Das Kommende*, I, 1932).

J. Pedersen, *Israel*, I–II, 1920.

P. Volz, *Das Dämonische in Jahve*, 1924.

[1] Chap. 70.

[2] Franz Werfel, *Zwiegespräch an der Mauer des Paradieses*, in *Het wezen der joodsche religie*; K. H. Miskotte, 1932.

CHAPTER 99

THE RELIGION OF MAJESTY AND OF HUMILITY

1. "IN the Name of God, the Compassionate, the Merciful, say: He is God alone: God the Eternal! He begetteth not, and He is not begotten; and there is none like unto Him."[1] Here speaks the religion of majesty and of humility. Developed under powerful Jewish and Christian influences, and closely related to these two religions not merely in origin but also in its essence, Islam confronts us with the task of understanding how, nevertheless, it could become not only a "great" religion, but could acquire in this greatness a genuinely specific character. For Islam is not merely a spiritual world-power, but is also a spiritual form.

A friend who has laboured among Moslems for many years and who speaks the language (I mean of course their scientific and religious language), and can conduct a theological discussion on passages from the *Koran*, thus writes to me: "Islam is in the first, second and third place a religio-social complex, in which equal emphasis is due to each factor of this combination. . . . Its motive power is the longing to be a kingdom of God: its weakness that, quite unsuspectingly, it wishes to realize this goal from a spirit that is not reborn and remains at bottom worldly. . . . Itself historically dependent, an offshoot of Semitic prophetism, Islam is comparatively poor in thought and feeling. Nevertheless it develops a colossal power which is rooted in its faith in God, or in other words, it takes God's sovereignty in absolute seriousness."[2] For our own purposes, however, and in the light of what has already been said about the sacred community,[3] we can disregard the constitution of the kingdom of God in Islam (its peak, in the Khalifate, has in the meantime been snapped off),[4] and restrict ourselves to faith in God.

I shall begin with Nietzsche's impressive dictum: "Every religion has for its highest images an analogon in the spiritual condition of those who profess it. The God of Mohammed: the solitariness of the desert,

---

[1] *Koran, Sura* 112 ("Everyman" Edition); Lehmann-Haas, *Textbuch,* 350.

[2] Dr. H. Kraemer, Solo, Java; *cf.* further, W. H. T. Gairdner and W. A. Eddy, *Christianity and Islam (The Christian Life and Message in Relation to non-Christian Systems, Report of the Jerusalem Meeting of the Int. Miss. Council* I, 1928), 250.

[3] Chap. 32 *ff.*   [4] *cf.* R. Tschudi, *Das Chalifat,* 1926.

the distant roar of the lion, the vision of a formidable warrior. The God of the Christians: everything that men and women think of when they hear the word 'love'. The God of the Greeks: a beautiful apparition in a dream."[1] Jahveh too is a lion roaring in the desert, and a terrible warrior; and this he was long before Mohammed experienced his visions and heard Allah's voice. Nor is Islam distinguished from Judaism by the fact that Allah is a personal will, having a very definite relationship to the world,[2] and "demanding" something therefrom; for as has just been observed, we find this in the Old Testament certainly to no less a degree and with yet greater originality. And were there no more than this, Islam would indeed be nothing but an "offshoot of Semitic prophetism", a sect or, if we prefer, a reform of Judaism. But the unique feature in Islam is that (to repeat) "God's sovereignty is taken in absolute seriousness", or in Gairdner's words, that God possesses "unmitigated omnipotence", and that "man is every way surrounded by, nay, himself exists through the immediate working of Allah's will and power".[3] Islam is the "worship of unconditioned Might". "The uniqueness and living supremacy of Allah have sounded forth from every minaret through the centuries and halfway round the world."[4] In Islam, then, the concept of Power reaches its loftiest peak; just as in the Old Testament form completely disappears into the too intimate proximity of invisibility; but the burning, ardent will vivifies powerfulness and makes it the sole reality, universal Power.

We might well ask whether all this, too, was not already foreshadowed in the Old Testament; to a certain degree, indeed, it is so. For both religions, Islam and Judaism alike, are apotheoses of animism.[5] Gairdner's description of Mohammed's prophetic experience: "The Arabian prophet came to possess a fervid faith in Allah—the One God. Not only did he come to possess it; it came to possess him. He felt that he had *experienced* Allah, a living, absolutely all-powerful and irresistible being":[6] might equally well apply to that of Elijah or Jeremiah. But in Islam the distinctive and decisive factor is that enough can never be said about this omnipotence of God, while with it everything is said;[7] and this is probably what my friend meant by his "unsuspectingly". Neither of Greece nor of Brahminism, neither of Buddhism nor of Judaism, can it be maintained that they "unsuspectingly" worshipped

---

[1] *The Case of Wagner, We Philologists*, 165 (Foulis Edition).
[2] Gairdner, *op. cit.*, 239.   [3] *ibid.*   [4] *op. cit.*, 238.
[5] Chap. 9; *cf.* Frick, *Vergl. Rel. wiss.* 83.   [6] *op. cit.*, 237.
[7] On the "caprice" of this omnipotence *cf.* Mensching, *Sünde*, 90.

or assigned form to, abolished or obeyed, the Power or potencies they experienced. In all these religions, therefore, both in the founders and in the living communities, there occurred a struggle that is wholly absent from Islam. Thus the Greeks strove to assign form to Power: Islam, however, abhors all form in principle. The doctrine of *advaita* (non-duality), again, regarded the plurality of appearances as a deception, while Islam has never concerned itself with them at all; and while Buddhism ventured upon a passionate war of annihilation against life itself, Islam knows nothing whatever of this.   Finally, Judaism quarrelled with its God: but Islam never produced a Job! God's mighty power is indeed "unsuspectingly" believed in by the prophet's followers and, as it were, released into life "without further ado"; which certainly implies an intense faith, but at the same time a very feeble humanity. Paradoxically, then, we might say that Islam is the *actual religion of God*. Hence the marvellous "concentration" of the Mohammedan: "wherever he may be, the Muslim has learned, during his prayers, to be alone with himself; some of the Muslims to be alone with God."[1] But hence also the complete inessentiality of revelation, in spite of prophet and "book"; "Revelation is only a formal and mechanical link between incompatibles";[2] and the whole of Islamite theology is a contest for the unity of God, always of God alone. Nothing is so keenly dreaded as is *shirk*:—the association of any other independent being whatever with God.[3]

2. Islam, to continue, is the religion of *Judgment*: "When the day that must come shall have come suddenly, none shall treat that sudden coming as a lie: Day that shall abase! Day that shall exalt!"[4] God's absolute powerfulness, His majesty, restricted by nothing whatever, as this repeatedly appears even in the profane stories of *The Arabian Nights*, implies the judgment of man. Man's own attitude, therefore, can be only that of deepest *humility*: "Praise be to God, Lord of the worlds! The compassionate, the merciful! King on the day of reckoning! Thee only do we worship, and to Thee do we cry for help. Guide Thou us on the straight path, the path of those to whom Thou hast been gracious;—with whom Thou art not angry, and who go not astray."[5] "Abu Huraira relates that the Prophet—God grant him blessing and

---

[1] Gairdner, *op. cit.*, 246.   [2] *ibid.*, 267.
[3] *cf.* I. Goldziher, *Vorlesungen über den Islam*, 1910, 111.
[4] *Koran, Sura* 56 ("Everyman" Edition); Lehmann-Haas, *op. cit.*, 348.
[5] *Sura* 1 ("Everyman" Edition); Lehmann-Haas, *ibid.*, 350.

peace!—said: a man was wasting his life; when his end approached he
told his children: 'When I am dead you must burn me, grind my ashes
and scatter them before the wind; for if God seized me, He would
punish me as no man ever has been.' And when he was dead, so it
happened. But God commanded the earth: 'Assemble together what
there is in thee of him.' This was done, and accordingly he came forth.
'What made thee act thus?' God asked him. 'Fear of Thee, O Lord',
he replied. Then God forgave him."[1]

The lion roars in the desert: a prophet, *the* prophet, who "represents
all the prophets put together",[2] experiences his omnipotence; the book
descends from eternity, and the prophet's example (*sunnah*) interprets
the book. Now man knows what he has to do, and that he cannot
sufficiently humble himself. Of God he knows only that He *is*, and that
His Being is overpowering. This, undeniably, is very much: but on the
other hand, when measured against the more sophisticated religions, it
is very little.

[1] Lehmann-Haas, *ibid.*, 361.   [2] Gairdner, *op. cit.*, 249.

CHAPTER 100

THE RELIGION OF LOVE

1. IT has for long been the fashion in treating historical problems, especially in the sphere of religion, to set one's own religion as scrupulously as possible in the background and to create the impression that, with reference to religions, one was wholly free from prejudice. This attitude, however, was associated with the grave error of supposing that, in the spiritual realm, one may adopt any desired position or abandon it at will, as if it were possible to choose any *Weltanschauung* whatever, or to abstain provisionally from all partisanship. But gradually it is being perceived that man *exists* in the world in some quite definite way and that—with all due respect to his own *Weltanschauung*—any "unprejudiced" treatment is not merely impossible but positively fatal. For it prevents the investigator's complete personality becoming engaged in his scientific task. And even if the enquirer is not consciously a disciple of some religion or other, but is an eclectic or agnostic, or in other terms, if he is not aware of his religion (which he really has!) then too the attempt has a disastrous effect, since in his endeavour to gain a thorough understanding of religious subjects, the investigator renders his own living religious impulses inoperative; still further, this elimination is after all merely a pretence, since no one can ever release himself from his more or less definite rôle in the world. The sole possible result is an "unprejudiced"—but that is only to say unintelligent—treatment governed throughout by a religious attitude which has not been scientifically clarified, and which is therefore exempt from all criticism and discussion. For "unprejudiced" investigators are usually accustomed to beginning, without further ado, with an interpretation of religion borrowed either from some liberal Western European Christianity, or from the deism of the Enlightenment, or from the so-called monism of the natural sciences.

If then in this Chapter, as indeed in all its predecessors, I follow another course and deliberately begin our survey of religious phenomena from the Christian viewpoint, I certainly by no means advocate any dogmatic treatment which, in all religions except Christianity itself, can perceive only spurious religion and degeneration. Rather do I retain the typical phenomenological intellectual suspense (*epoche*), while at the same time I bear in mind that this is possible only in the light of one's own experience,[1] and that this can never be freed from its own religious determinateness. It would therefore be quite possible, in itself, for a buddhist to set out the phenomenology of religion, with his own as the starting point; and then he would naturally discover the culmination of religion in Buddhism. Whether he would be "right" in so doing is, however, not a matter for phenomenology itself to decide, but for theology or metaphysics. But he would be unable to proceed in any other way.

I myself regard Christianity, then, as the central form of historical religions;[2] and in general, the "comparison" of religions among themselves is possible only by thus beginning from one's own attitude to life. For religions are not wares that one can spread out on a table.[3] Surveying the realm of historic religions, therefore, from the point of view of Christianity, I consider that we perceive that the Gospel appears as the fulfilment of religion in general. But whether this "appearance" has its roots in any ultimate "reality" is again an issue which theology must decide.

The typology of Christianity needs only *one* word: *Love*.[4] This is because, in Christianity, God's activity and the reciprocal activity of man are essentially the same: the movement of Power towards the world is love, while that of the world towards God is reciprocal love; no other word is available. Mankind's love of God is the reflection of the divine love for man, or rather: "the form Christ has taken in man".[5]

2. The religion of love, still further, is *fulfilment* in the sense that it places Will at the focal point, but that it does so without disregarding

[1] Chap. 107, 109. The term *epoche* is a technical expression employed in current Phenomenology by Husserl and other philosophers. It implies that no judgment is expressed concerning the objective world, which is thus placed "between brackets", as it were. All phenomena, therefore, are considered solely as they are presented to the mind, without any further aspects such as their real existence, or their value, being taken into account; in this way the observer restricts himself to pure description systematically pursued, himself adopting the attitude of complete intellectual suspense, or of abstention from all judgment, regarding these controversial topics.

[2] *cf.* van der Leeuw, *Strukturpsychologie*.

[3] In this sense Comparative Religion is a fairly recent field of research; from its limited literature I select: Hegel, *The Philosophy of Religion*. Frick, *Vergl. Rel. wiss.* H. Frick, *Ghazalis Selbstbiographie*, 1919. van Gennep, *Religions Moeurs et Légendes* I, 67 *ff*. H. Groos, *Der deutsche Idealismus und das Christentum*, 1927. Lüttge, *Christentum und Buddhismus*. Mensching, *Sünde*. P. Masson Oursel, *Foi bouddhique et foi chrétienne* (*RHR*. 95, 1927). Otto, *West-östl. Mystik*. *ID.*, *India's Religion of Grace*. M. Schlunk, *Die Weltreligionen und das Christentum*, 1923.

[4] Chap. 76.
[5] *Gal.* iv. 19.

Form, and that it is also fully aware of the limits of Will and Form in their relation to infinite Power. God: Father, Son and Holy Spirit—thus are consummated, equally, the religion of Will (Israel), of Form (Greece), and also of Infinity (India). The Father's Will is glorified as God's creative deed, whose essence is love of the world. The impetuous energy of Jahveh (and also of Allah) is experienced as an impetuous deed of love: "God so loved the world" that He gave Himself to the world in the Form of the Son.

This Form of the Son, however, is not an endowment with form like that of the Homeric Greek. Equally visible in human appearance as Apollo or Athene, His "fulfilled" form is explicitly distinguished from the Greek by becoming experienced as "given" and, in fact, given in history. With regard to "endowment with form", indeed, Christianity remains to a great extent Jewish, or again Islamite. Power, that is to say, is not perceived as a form, but the Incarnation of God in human form is believed in; essentially, then, God is Will: the world, creation: and man belongs to the world.[1] But into this world God descends and brings salvation: that is, Himself. And as opposed to nineteenth century views, we cannot emphasize too strongly the fact that in Christianity no new *Weltanschauung* of any kind, no new idea of God, has arisen.[2] The Christian *Weltanschauung*, and the Christian idea of God, are in fact purely Jewish in origin, and subsequently modified by the general concepts of Hellenistic antiquity. What is really new and unique in Christianity is, however, that the love of God has "appeared". "And it came to pass *in those days*"; so begins the Christmas Gospel. This means that God fulfils time: in time itself He sets a bound to time. The "religion of Jesus" is therefore a prophetic-Jewish religion; faith in Jesus Christ is the belief that God's Will, as Form, has become visible and actual in this world:[3] "For unto you is born *this day* a Saviour."

But the doctrine of the Holy Spirit ensures, still further, that no limitation of any kind is involved in the Will of God and in the Form of Christ, in the sense that religion itself becomes transformed into either history or esthetics. Here both creative Will and consummated form are infinitely and limitlessly powerful:

[1] *cf.* J. de Zwaan, *Paulinische Weltanschauung, Zeitschr. für syst. Theol.* 8, 578. Connelly's drama, *Green Pastures*, shows here too the primitive form of the most sublime Christian faith, especially the end of Act II.

[2] *cf.* R. Bultmann's admirable article: *Urchristentum und Rel. gesch., Theol. Rundschau, N. F.* 4, 1932.

[3] *cf.* Bultmann, *Gl. u. Verst.* 144.

> Come, Holy Spirit!
> Fill the hearts of Thy faithful people,
> Enkindle within them the fire of Thy love.
> Thou Who hast gathered together,
> Within the one Faith,
> The peoples of all Earth's tongues.
> Alleluia! Alleluia!

3. Thus all that Christianity can ever declare about God is contained in this active love: it is the very essence of God, given to man as grace. To the exile from Paradise it was said:[1]

> Only add
> Deeds to thy knowledge answerable; add faith·
> Add virtue, patience, temperance; add love,
> By name to come called Charity, the soul
> Of all the rest: then wilt thou not be loth
> To leave this Paradise, but shalt possess
> A Paradise within thee, happier far.

All that man can either do or be, therefore, in his own attitude to Power, is contained in love: obedience, humility, holiness, hope.

The so-called "attributes" of God, too, are all comprehended within love. For these attributes are neither descriptions of God's uniqueness, nor edifying fantasies, nor even philosophic deductions, but experiences of the one love that is interpreted differently in each case. In love, again, the two demands, which we must address to religion,[2] concur in being realized. That God is ultimate is expressed by the "attributes" of omnipresence, omnisufficiency, omniscience and omnipotence; but in each of these instances alike this is only a proclamation of the love that is experienced as ultimate. But that God is "Wholly Other", that He is holy, perfectly good and perfectly just, this also is merely a proclamation of the same experience of the love that is "Wholly Other", exactly as it is ultimate; and thus in love the line ascending from man to God, and that descending from God to man, meet. The symbol of love is the Cross.

4. Reciprocal love, further, itself possesses a form: the church,[3] which displays its inseparable unity with love by being "the Body of Christ". The church's essential task, then, is to offer the sacrifice of thanksgiving,[4] which is a sacrifice of life and grants expression to reciprocal love.

---

[1] *Paradise Lost*, XII, 581 *ff.*   [2] Chap. 108.
[3] Chap. 36.   [4] Chap. 50.

But the church has always quite clearly realized that the Body of Christ is constantly being threatened:

> Far from us drive our hellish foe,
> True peace unto us bring,
> And through all perils bring us safe
> Beneath Thy sacred wing.[1]

However familiar this may be, it has nevertheless been frequently ignored in the church's history. It is forgotten that the spirit "bloweth, and thou canst not tell whence it cometh, and whither it goeth"; we forget, too, the dynamic character of love. "The Catholic type succeeds in transforming act into duration. It changes occurrence into being, and event into form. It believes that by spatializing the act it makes it eternal."[2] Against this the Protestant type of Christianity recalls to our recollection the "unconditioned menace"[3] that ever threatens man's being, and is fully aware that, within the church, the Christian occupies a frontier or "boundary situation", and that what he has he possesses merely in virtue of his status. It is true that Protestantism also ceases to be conscious of this "situation" as soon as it binds God's powerfulness to the words of the Bible, or to any immutable doctrine whatever: from being a living body the church then becomes merely a dead shell. On the other hand, if it is not to lose its essence in wholly objectless feeling, Protestant Christianity repeatedly needs the reminder addressed to it by the Roman and Orthodox Catholic churches: that God's Power in the life of the world possesses not only a ringing sound but a Form also, and that the church is not merely the period of proclamation, but is also the locus of the Incarnation, although only God's creative love can determine both the time and the place. "Surely the Lord is in this place; and I knew it not", is equally a Christian experience as is "this gate of the Lord, into which the righteous shall enter".

---

[1] *Hostem repellas longius,*
Pacemque dones protinus,
Ductore sic te praevio
Vitemus omne noxium.

[2] Frick, *Vergl. Rel. wiss.* 103 *f.*

[3] Tillich, *Rel. Verwirkl.*

B. FOUNDERS

CHAPTER 101

THE FOUNDER

1. IN Chapters 25 *ff.* the representation of Power by and in man was dealt with:—how men can become "sacred" by participating in Power and make their appearance sustaining some kind of holiness, their effectiveness being then described as that pertaining to status or "office".

Now we encounter these "sacred men" once again, but in a completely different connection: it is no longer a matter of the sacred man as a phenomenon, but of the historic bestowing of form upon religion within the respective religions, and of the question as to what part in this historical creation of form is taken by human personalities. Thus together with the historic "forms" of the various religions themselves there are the historical forms of those *founders* who, in different ways, have appeared at some turning-point of time and "established" some specific experience of Power. There are very many such "founders", quite as many as, and indeed more than, the religions themselves; I cannot deal with even all the historically known founders. But by means of a few examples I shall attempt to elucidate how religious experience assumes historic form, by considering the founder's own personality.

Of course a "founder" is not the "establisher" of a religion as he is depicted in works of reference, along with the founders of the "Gustavus Adolphus Union" and the like, or with the originators of socialism, *etc.* or, finally, any great inventors. Religions, in truth, are neither originated nor established; still, they appear as "founded". And this means that every experience of God is indubitably original, in so far as God is Himself its originator and executes nothing at second-hand. But every experience of God is also the outcome of some stimulus, and is extracted (as it were) from some predecessor; and whenever this initiating experience possesses special intensity, so that it arouses many subsequent experiences and continues to operate historically, then we speak of a "foundation of religion". This founding is, of course, not restricted merely to the "great" religions, and not even to religions in general:

every religious movement, every specific change in the course of
religious life, must have some founder. Such was St. Francis, just as
was Moses, and Mani equally with Zarathustra; and so, too, the "minor"
figures. In the literal sense, therefore, every genuine religious experience
is a *foundation*, from which some new experiences arise; but we are
concerned with founding only when its historical effects are visible on
a large scale. The mother, for example, may be the "founder" of her
children's religion, but we begin to discuss her only when her own
experience sets up historic waves. Founding, that is to say, is an
eminently historical affair.

2. A founder, in the first place, is primarily a *witness*[1] to revelation:
he has seen, or has heard, something; "to the numen there pertains a
seer". "Without him a rainbow remains a rainbow, and heaven a blue
roof of stone."[2] Then he speaks of his experience, and appears as
prophet.[3] Founders, again, usually base a (partially) new doctrine on
their own experience, some new law: in that case they are also *teachers*.[4]
They must then adapt themselves to what has already been given in
tradition, and can thus become *theologians*; but in any event they are
always to a certain degree *reformers*.[5] Their doctrine, however, possesses
power only in so far as their whole life enters into the "founding": then
they are *examples*,[6] archetypes of the genuinely pious life replete with
power. When, finally, they devote their entire existence to foundation,
they are called *mediators*. Certainly they are all without exception
mediators of revelation; nevertheless the term "mediator"[7] involves
something that is more than experience and utterance, doctrine and
example taken all together.

As has just been observed, then, there are infinitely many founders;
and it is characteristic of any given religion that either this plurality is
recognized, or else it is attempted to abolish it. In this respect, the
Greeks discerned nothing whatever that prevented ceaseless creation of
form; while in the case of the Jews the history of God's dealings with
His people extended over the individual prophets, so that their number
could be regarded as historically necessary.[8] But for Mohammedans, on
the other hand, all prophetic forms ultimately resolved themselves into
that of Mohammed; while for Christians all prophecies were "fulfilled"
in the form of the mediator.

---

[1] Chap. 29.   [2] Otto. *Gefühl des Überweltlichen*, 79; *cf*. 86 *f*.   [3] Chap. 27.
[4] Chap. 28.   [5] Chap. 94, 102.   [6] Chap. 105.   [7] Chap. 106.
[8] Leo Baeck, in Miskotte, *Wezen der joodsche religie*, 95; *cf. Hebrews* i. 1 *f*.

3. Frick[1] has drawn the parallel between the three nights which are accounted sacred by the three great religions: the night of illumination of Buddha, the *lailat al-kadr* (night of power) in Islam and, in Christianity, Christmas night.[2] Strictly regarded, however, the last is not a "foundation", and I prefer, therefore, to place in parallel the actual originative experiences in these three religions and in that of Israel— or at least those which have been elevated by tradition to the level of the principal experiences.

Apart then from pre-Mosaic tradition, the foundation of the Israelitish religion is related in the story of the burning bush. I do not wish to seek too profound a meaning in the bush burning without being consumed (although theophany as a flame of fire in the desert is certainly very characteristic); but here, as later in the historically less important circumstances connected with Samuel, the essential features are God speaking and the founder listening: "God called unto him out of the midst of the bush, and said, Moses, Moses. And he said, Here am I." This is summons and obedience; and what follows is equally characteristic: "And he said, Draw not nigh hither": and Moses put off his sandals and "hid his face." "Moreover he said, I am the God of thy father, the God of Abraham, the God of Isaac, and the God of Jacob ... I am come down to deliver (Israel) out of the hand of the Egyptians."[3] Thus it is the God, who manifests His own will in history, who here declares Himself to the founder, while the foundation is the fulfilling by Moses of his God's historical commission. His own experience is then perpetuated as obedience, and as the experience of the people it must express itself as loyalty.

The *lailat al-kadr* is the night of power; that is the night on which Mohammed received his first revelation and accordingly became a founder. Here the Power is the divine authority. "Verily, we have caused It to descend on the night of Power. And who shall teach thee what the night of power is? The night of power excelleth a thousand months. Therein descend the angels and the spirit by permission of the Lord for every matter; and all is peace till the breaking of the morn."[4] It is the book that was sent down; exactly as in Judaism, the originative experience here is the divine communication, and the absolute powerfulness, which I have earlier designated as all-sufficient majesty, gives

---

[1] *Vergl. Rel. wiss.* 68 *ff. cf.* Chap. 97.

[2] Chap. 97. His comparison between the founders' parting words is also valuable; 70 *ff.*   [3] *Exodus* iii. 4 *ff.* Bertholet, *op. cit.,* 17, 34.

[4] *Sura* 97 ("Everyman" Edition); Frick, *Vergl. Rel. wiss.* 69 *f.* Lehmann-Haas, *Textbuch,* 345.

this experience its distinctive colour. The rest is instruction which becomes the written word; and everything lies in the shadow of judgment.

"One night, the old traditions narrate, the decisive turning-point came, the moment wherein was vouchsafed to the seeker (Buddha) the certainty of discovery. Sitting under the tree, since then named the Tree of Knowledge, he went through successively purer and purer stages of abstraction of consciousness, until the sense of omniscient illumination came over him."[1] Insight into the primal cause of suffering was attained in the fourfold *jhana*. "When I apprehended this, and when I beheld this, my soul was released from the evil of desire, released from the evil of earthly existence, released from the evil of error, released from the evil of ignorance. In the released awoke the knowledge of release: extinct is re-birth, finished the sacred course, duty done, no more shall I return to this world; this I knew."[2] "This moment", Oldenberg continues, "the Buddhists regard as the great turning-point in his life and in the life of the worlds of gods and men: the ascetic Gotama had become the Buddha, the awakened, the enlightened. That night which Buddha passed under the tree of knowledge, on the banks of the river Neranjara, is the sacred night of the Buddhist world."[3] The originative experience here is clearly perceptible: illuminating insight into the world's nullity. The feeling of freedom and release certainly refers to concrete knowledge; but this, in its own turn, to nullity.

Finally, the originative experience of Jesus Christ cannot be unambiguously determined, although in the tradition the baptism in Jordan, the temptation, the transfiguration and the hour of Gethsamene can all be taken into consideration. Just as in Israel there is a history concerned with God, whose founders, together with Moses, are the many prophets, so there is in the Gospel a history dealing with God which is repeatedly "founded" anew. If then we select the four experiences just cited as historically symbolic, it can be affirmed that the originative experience of Jesus, as this became effective in history, exhibits the following four leading features: the consciousness of divine sonship or, more generally, of messiahship; the certainty of a task that was assigned to Him and must be accomplished in spite of everything; the assurance of the immediate presence of God; and readiness for the sacrifice which, at its culmination in the complete deprivation of being forsaken by God, called anew in question the three preceding factors.

---

[1] *Buddha: His Life, His Doctrine, His Order*, 107.
[2] ibid.; *cf.* Frick, *Vergl. Rel. wiss.* 69.
[3] *ibid.*, 107, 108.

We have discovered, therefore, as the typical originative experiences when expressed in their relation to Power:—Power speaks, and is obeyed: it speaks, and gives commands: Power reveals itself to insight as nothingness: the Power pertaining to the founder demands from Him, in absolute impotence, the complete surrender of Himself.

CHAPTER 102

THE REFORMER

1. IF every religion, in accord with its essential nature, is both reformed and to be reformed,[1] then every foundation must, to a certain extent, be at the same time a reformation; and this actually is the case. No "man of God" ever erects his experience on quite new ground, but all build afresh on the ruins of previous settlements. A reformer is thus a kind of founder, and we employ the narrower designation whenever the historic emphasis falls on the transformation of what has already been given. Thus Mohammed was a reformer, as were Buddha, Zarathustra and Jesus; but I prefer to call them founders. Luther was certainly a founder; but I call him preferably a reformer. The reformer's act is indeed "rediscovery",[2] but this discovery itself is an experiencing anew; just as the founder desires not to abrogate but to fulfil, so the reformer wishes the new system, which he sets up, proved to be the genuine ancient one, and the old, which he is combatting, to be shown as being falsely understood. Adam alone therefore, the "first man", could achieve a foundation with none of the significance of a reformation; and conversely, no reformer could ever fulfil his task without "foundation".

2. From these considerations it follows that most important founders were also more or less influential reformers; Zarathustra, Buddha, Mohammed, Jesus—but also Ramanuja, St. Paul, St. Francis, Ignatius Loyola, Wesley and Pusey—were founders whose labours had reforming value.

I have here selected two examples in order to make it quite clear how this type of founder arises historically. In the first place the Egyptian king Akhnaton, who has already been dealt with,[3] was a reformer of the purest stamp. No one who has read his *Hymn to the Sun* can deny the originality of his own experience of God;[4] and its reforming quality too is plainly shown: the king reverted to an old tradition, the fifth dynasty worship of the sun, kept alive through the centuries by the Heliopolitan

---

[1] Chap. 94; *reformata* and *reformanda*.   [2] Frick, *ibid.*, 48.   [3] Chap. 94.
[4] *cf.* H. Schaefer, *Amarna in Religion und Kunst* (1931); van der Leeuw, *Achnaton* (1927); further: *Altorientalische Texte zum A. T.* (edited by H. Gressmann)[2], 1926, 15 *ff.*; Lehmann-Haas, *op. cit.*, 259 *f.*; Roeder, *Urk. zur Rel. des alten Ägypten*, 62 *ff.*; Erman, *Literatur der Ägypter*, 358 *ff.*

priesthood, and opposed the beliefs of the Theban priesthood, which he regarded as false. The manner in which, in the development of the ceremonial name of his own god, he explained the ancient divine name Ra as the designation of a god who "has returned as Aton", testifies alike to the reformatory intention of converting the new experience of the god, connected with the name Aton, into a foundation, and to the endeavour to exhibit the truth of all that was sound in the tradition.[1] He emphasized the contrast with Amon, the "hidden god" of Thebes, as intensely as possible; his own god is the visible luminary that radiates its rays of love in all directions, and he developed the service of this god with such passion, indeed, that no room was left for the other gods; they either silently perished or were drastically expunged. Despite his theological experiments with the god's name, however, the king (perhaps, to some degree, just because he was a king) evidently failed to adapt himself to the religion in which he lived and from which he had set out; he underrated the old religion, above all the religious significance of belief in the beyond, and also of Osiris worship; and he had to suffer the penalty; despite the vehemence and purity of his own originative experience, revealed as this is in almost every word that has come down to us and in almost every form created by his art, his reform scarcely outlasted his own life.[2] Akhnaton may therefore be regarded as an extreme reformer, whose figure was decisively conditioned by this attempt at reformation.

If on the other hand we turn our attention to Luther, there appears a similar subjection to an original experience of God in penitential conflicts, but also a thorough intimacy with the religion from which he began; for Luther "would not have been the reformer had he not previously been a monk".[3] We might say, in fact, that almost nothing of importance in the old religion left Luther indifferent; the intense conviction that he stood in the true church of Christ and the confident assertion of the common treasure of Christian faith, unite with the struggle against abuse and unbelief which began with the experience of foundation. The sole living feature of the old religion which, so far as I myself can see, Luther contemplated neither with hatred against its

---

[1] Chap. 84.

[2] Schaefer; van der Leeuw; *op. cit. cf.* further: Ed. Meyer, *Gottesstaat, Militär-herrschaft und Ständewesen in Ägypten (Sitz. ber. der preuss. Ak. der Wiss., phil.-hist. Kl., 1928, 28).* K. Sethe, *Amon und die acht Urgötter von Hermopolis (Abh. der preuss. Akad. der Wiss., 1929, phil.-hist. Kl. 4).*

[3] Karl Holl, *Reformation und Urchristentum (Reden und Vorträge bei der 28. General-versammlung des Evang. Bundes, 1924).*

corruption nor with fidelity to the common Christian faith, was worship, apart (that is) from the sacrificial doctrine of the mass, which he condemned as idolatry. And here Luther, with wise discretion, treated the old practices with great consideration and granted them much liberty.

In their historical importance, then, the reformations of Akhnaton and Luther are scarcely comparable. But with regard to the manner of their emergence in history, on the other hand, they are not merely characteristic instances, but are direct antitheses. For the reformatory initial experience of the one lies almost completely outside the communal, while that of the other lies almost wholly within the common experience.

CHAPTER 103

THE TEACHER

1. THE teacher has previously been discussed in Chapter 28. His historical form also is that of a founder, its peculiarity consisting in the fact that his "foundation" becomes detached, as doctrine, from the experience lying at its base. He may be priest, apostle, missionary: in any case his own experience forces him to proclamation; and this then assumes the form of an interconnected whole. The doctrine itself, again, is independent of the teacher; it goes its own way even long after he has departed and his personal activities have been forgotten. A teacher such as Buddha was, indeed, himself desired this.[1]

2. Teachers, in the strictest sense, are found in India: Buddhism is doctrine, nothing other than doctrine. And wherever insight in itself leads to salvation, the doctrine that effects this insight can continue to operate independently. Buddha, therefore, is the teacher *par excellence*; his experience solidified into a doctrine which, despite all the humanizing and deifying of the founder himself, has always remained doctrine; and Buddha's historic form is that of an instructor: the ground of suffering is desire. To him this became clear in illumination; but it can be repeated quite apart from this illumination and, indeed, from the teacher himself. Such doctrine is certainly proclamation of salvation, not however of what has occurred or happened but only of what must be achieved, of what must be attained precisely through the doctrine; and so it is, to a certain degree, with every doctrine and every teacher in India, rich in *gurus* as it is.

A wholly different type of doctrine and teacher is the Jewish-Christian: the Jew, learned in scripture, was regarded by the people as "our teacher". This doctrine also is independent of the founder who places it within history; it becomes traditional. But it refers to something that actually happened, to the living relationship of God to the people, to the covenant; it is therefore the proclamation of an event rather than instruction proper, although it is this too. In this respect, then, the teacher has a more important historical status:

> he let Moses see his purpose,
> and Israel his methods.[2]

[1] Chap. 28.　　　　　　　　　　　　　　　[2] *Ps.* ciii. 7.

Doctrine thus becomes a living connection between God and man; it is indeed instruction, but above all proclamation. Similarly with the Christian teachers, of whom St. Paul may serve as the great example. He realized that he was only a late born disciple, that he himself was nothing and the word of the Cross everything; but he was equally conscious of standing in a great historical connection. Upon the *kerygma* of the original community he bestowed its historic form, and God's historical deed is the A and the Ω of his own proclamation. In other words: he himself was unimportant, but his teaching was equally so; the sole momentous factor was the redemptive history of Jesus. The teacher's own historic figure, therefore, just because it is negligible as compared with the occurrence of revelation, need not withdraw into the background so scrupulously as does that of Buddha in *Hinayana*. And in the living church it survives, like that of the Jewish teacher in the people.

CHAPTER 104

THE PHILOSOPHER AND THE THEOLOGIAN

1. IT appears quite undeniable to my own mind that the great systematists, who have influenced the religious thought of humanity, must be included among "founders". In the history of the spirit, it is true, Kierkegaard's simile of the man who builds a vast palace, and then sits down outside it, is repeatedly justified; the palace being the "system", the man the systematizer. And when we observe how the spirit's citadel again and again becomes its coffin, we can well understand Jaspers' preference for the great anti-systematizers Kierkegaard and Nietzsche. But this should not prevent us appreciating the originating influence of all system construction, since at bottom a great system springs from some primal experience, and exhibits the attempt to dominate the world from the viewpoint of this experience and to make it as it were capable of cultivation;[1] and it is not the artistic nor technical completion of systematic construction that is effective, but the power of this experience. St. Augustine, Thomas Aquinas, Luther, Calvin, obviously influenced the educated world by their logical arguments; nevertheless their actual spiritual effect sprang from the high emotional tension of their experience, and their boldness in applying it to the whole world. It is exactly the same with the great philosophers Socrates and Plato, Kant and Hegel; they all perceived something, contemplated the world from a certain definite standpoint, and had the courage to make this vision the starting point of a conquering invasion of spiritual territory.

In so doing, however, the philosophers follow the path from their own experience to the theoretical domination of the world,[2] while the theologians, on the contrary, choose the way of obedience.[3] The former look upwards from the plane of the world to that of Power; the latter down to the world level from the place of Power (the church). But of course there have frequently been philosophers who practised theological obedience and theologians who achieved philosophic dominance.

2. That philosophers pertain to the history of religion can scarcely be doubtful to anyone who regards theoretical investigation as in-

---

[1] Chap. 83.   [2] Grünbaum, *Herrschen und Lieben*, Chap. 83.   [3] Chap. 84.

separable from some commanding experience of Power. Here, however, it is not a matter of a phenomenology of philosophy, but merely of the way in which, as founder, the philosopher introduces his personal experience of Power into the historical world. Of this I have selected three examples: Hegel, to begin with, is the most philosophical of all philosophers; he lived his thought as no one else has done either before or after him. The movement of Spirit revealed itself in its majestic course; and in principle it is complete in itself. In it everything, from highest to lowest, has a place; but in it, and there alone, is the place of everything; the advance is dialectical, a monologue of Spirit; and the relationship with mysticism is obvious.[1] In this eternal movement the thinker himself participates. Here then everything is appointed, marked down and in a certain sense justified also.

Kant, again, represents the opposite type. Here too the movement of thought is contemplated; but its motion is open and unfinished. The system is thus a critique of its own authority, marked emphasis being laid on practical reason and action, and the spirit's path to absolute power leads only through this action. Not thought as such is worshipped, but something that is still purely formal: the moral law within. The human spirit is least of all the thought of God; nevertheless it is not forsaken by God. Philosophy is predominantly human and worldly, and yet a path is left open leading to the superhuman and supermundane.

Midway between these two modern philosophers stands the ancient thinker Plato. Setting forth from the interest in man and the self-criticism of Socrates, he rose to the contemplation of divine beauty. But the movement towards this vision was neither a way that had been left open, nor a dialectical necessity; it was a combat, a struggle; thus the proper place for Plato's philosophy is between heaven and earth, and its most characteristic language neither dialectic nor Socratic critical enquiry, but myth.

3. In accordance with the conception of their task, theologians follow the path of obedience; and they begin not with the world, but with revelation. They labour to serve the community: when they are Christians, the church. Between them and their own experience, therefore, there exists an intermediate factor: the proclamation of the prophets and the apostles; in this respect they are far less "founders" than are the philosophers. Nevertheless their labour, too, is an activated experience: they have heard the call of the church, to which they now

[1] Chap. 75.

give its historic form. They may share something with prophet or apostle, and they also have much of the teacher—but their true historic task consists in systematic utterance of God's deeds; they are therefore closely linked with those teachers of the second type dealt with in the preceding chapter.

Here again I would differentiate three types: There are theologians, in the first place, whose historical task lies in elucidating the collective experience of their own community in its relation to earlier tradition, to divergent experiences, to heresy, innovation and contemporary philosophy; they thus effect the connection with what is given in tradition and with the thought of their own day. In this respect, however, it may so happen that they concede too much to what is traditionally given, and endeavour to establish it anew merely because it is given; or, again, they submit their doctrine all too readily to current thought. Their true task, nonetheless, is to avoid these two extremes and is therefore mainly that of an intermediary. Every theologian has this task; both St. Paul and St. John attempted to execute it. Certain theologians, however, represent this type more or less purely, as for example in the era of the Greek apologists of the second century who tried to bring Christianity into agreement with the prevailing popular moral philosophy; and in modern times Herder and Schleiermacher, who sought to interpret the essentials of Christianity in accordance with the spirit of the age. But the foundation laid by the second century apologists, as well as that of the theologians at the beginning of last century, still exerts its influence to-day.

The second type is represented by those theologians who seek to embrace the revelation granted to the church within one vast and finally completed system of thought. They are the Hegels of theology, but with the difference that they themselves must follow the way of obedience and are bound to revelation. Still, the system indicates its fixed place for all that is contained in revelation and also for what arises subsequently, from this as its basis, in the church's life; and since the church is the sphere wherein the indications of grace are manifested, ecclesiastical theology is the totality of the indications thus given. The precise frontier between dogma and theology is indeed difficult to determine; nevertheless the significance of the *doctor ecclesiae* for the development of dogma is willingly recognized, the great representative of this type being Thomas Aquinas.

The third type, finally, is represented by those theologians who certainly attempt to combine the construction of a system with the first kind of task, but a system that is as it were open and unfinished and in which the original experience has, and should have, a markedly disquieting influence. This type is characterized by intense emotionalism and a personal note of address: St. Paul, St. Augustine and Luther fall within this category. At the frontier of this form of theology stands the anti-systematizer Kierkegaard, who showed himself to be a genuine member of this group by setting out from the revelation preserved in dogma, and also by the fabric he himself produced from this and intentionally left unfinished in both directions:—upwards to the aspect of the eternally active and divine revealing Will, and downwards to that of living, existential thought that deals with reality; nevertheless the fabric itself must never be finally completed.

CHAPTER 105

THE EXAMPLE

1. IN our previous discussions of following after God[1] the example of
the divine man came within our field of vision; and I shall now consider
the way in which a foundation appears historically as an example.
The personality of every founder, of course, is to a certain extent an
example to his own followers. His experience in itself is the standard;
but this very characteristic may become the preponderating factor in
the foundation. Thus Islamite *sufis* distinguish the "saint" from the
"prophet". The prophet warns, proclaiming the law in decisive terms:
he is the "messenger", *rasul*;[2] and the only personal quality that need be
demanded of him is faithfulness in delivering his message: he is not
necessarily a saint. He "has authority over the gifts of grace and distributes these, but they have no authority over him"; the saint, on the
other hand, is seized by grace and his very nature transformed, while
on his own part he cannot control grace; for this reason Jesus was
superior to Abu Bakr, for instance, the relationship of the former to
God being twofold, that of the latter merely single: he repeated only
what he had heard.[3] In this case, however, and exactly after the fashion
of Islam, an important insight is exaggerated. The prophet certainly
could not complete his own mission unless grace controlled him;
conversely, the saint transmits the grace that has seized upon him; and
Islam's striking dread of any dual relationship of any kind whatever
between God and man appears in its self-expulsion by the appeal to the
saint. *This*, nevertheless, has been quite accurately perceived: there are
founders whose instruction is not at all the principal factor, and whose
foundation can therefore be comprised in what has been manifested in
them through divine grace.

2. Here then it is the life and deed of the founders themselves that
are effective: they "found" a community, a communal life, a piety.
When Albert Schweitzer recently gave an organ recital in a Netherlands
town, many ordinary people came after the performance to the exit from
the organ gallery to see him—not however to hail the artist, and still
less to honour the scholar but, as someone expressed it, "to see the man

[1] Chap. 73.   [2] *cf.* Chap. 27.   [3] Massignon, *Al-Hallaj*, 738 *ff.*

who had done something while the others were only talking". This is precisely the power of example; we can point to some human life and say: something is happening there: in this life Power appears. St. Francis, again, was a purer type of this kind of foundation than Buddha who, though he was certainly an example to his disciples, laid chief stress on doctrine; the former's example, on the other hand, created the "Franciscan life" of poverty. Jesus also is the example for those who believe in Him, in a deeper sense, however, than as the example of one who is a founder. He too has done great deeds, but the following of this example is a mystical union with the Saviour; and St. Paul expressed this most clearly when he desired that "Christ be formed in you",[1] as did St. John in his parable of "The Vine and its Branches".[2]

[1] *Gal.* iv. 19; *cf.* Chap. 73.   [2] *John* xv.

CHAPTER 106

THE MEDIATOR

1. SINCE all "holy men" are mediators, their "representation" ensuring the relationship between Power and man, founders also are mediators. But in the truest sense he is a mediator whose whole being is mediation, and who surrenders his own life as the "means" for Power. In such cases foundation is not only an experience leading to some kind of instruction, doctrine or exemplary activity; it is identical with the founder himself: foundation and founder are one. This is most clearly perceived when we compare, for example, the salvation by the Buddha Amitabha with that by Christ. For the entrance into Buddha's Paradise is only a preparatory goal of salvation, a gateway to *Nirvana*; but Christ is Himself salvation.[1] And not merely His deed, the surrender of His life on the Cross, is effective in bringing salvation; His whole existence is the "means":—"Who for us men, and for our salvation, came down from heaven". Setting out from Judaistic Messiahism, born into the Greek-Oriental world, Jesus of Nazareth is worshipped by His followers as the mediator;[2] and what this means is most obvious in comparison with other saviours, for example with Apollonius of Tyana, who lived in the first century A.D. The life histories of both resemble each other in many respects; their busts were placed with those of Abraham and Orpheus, Alexander the Great and several emperors, all "divine" men, in the *lararium* or shrine of the emperor Alexander Severus.[3] But Apollonius is not a mediator in the truest sense, any more than was the Jewish messiah—for example, Zerubbabel. Jesus, however, is mediator because His whole essential being is a "means", a movement of man towards God and of God towards man.

2. Here, finally, we have reached the borderland of phenomenology, the region that proved to be inaccessible throughout our previous discussions of the world and the church, of guilt and faith. For Christian faith the figure of the mediator is no "phenomenon"; the phenomen-

---

[1] *cf.* Otto, *India's Religion of Grace*, Chap. I.

[2] *Hebrews* viii, 6; ix, 15; xii, 24: the mediator of the new covenant, as Moses is called the mediator of the old (*Gal.* iii, 19 *f.*).

[3] *cf.* Th. Hopfner, *Apollonius von Tyana und Philostratus* (*Seminarium Kondakovianum, Rec. d'Et.*, IV), Prag, 1931. *cf.* further Wendland, *Hell.-röm. Kultur*, 161.

ologist cannot perceive where and how it enters history. He observes prophet, reformer, teacher, example; but he cannot see the mediator in His historical effectiveness. It becomes apparent to him how the experience of Jesus of Nazareth has founded in history a mighty stream of faith experiences, but not how in history God gives Himself to man as mediator. He can perceive that Jesus sacrificed Himself: but he can only believe that Jesus was none other than God giving Himself. At best he can observe that the uniqueness of the mediator essentially pertains to this faith: the mediator of revelation has become revelation itself; the Word became flesh; and henceforth every revelation of God conforms to the sole revelation in Christ. "He is the head of the Body, that is, of the church, in virtue of his primacy as the first to be born from the dead—that gives him pre-eminence over all. For it was in him that the divine Fullness willed to settle without limit, and by him it willed to reconcile in his own person all on earth and in heaven alike." "It is in Christ that the entire Fullness of deity has settled bodily."[1] We can assert, further, that His mediation must concern what is deepest of all: guilt; the Saviour is the reconciler. And thus we can understand that every title of "saviour", and every representative function, belong to Him by right, from the dignity of the mediator of creation, in *The Epistle to the Colossians*, to that of the Hellenistic σωτὴρ τοῦ κόσμου, or *salvator mundi*, derived from the saviour-god and emperor;[2] from the Jewish messianic hero to the medieval champion of the joust;[3] from prophet to teacher, from reformer to example, from the merciful good shepherd to the Judge of the world at the last day. Since Christ's appearance a new comprehension of the world, of history and of man is possible:[4] "For 'there is one God' and 'one intermediary between God and men, the man Christ Jesus who gave himself as a ransom for all':—in due time this was attested."[5]

Here there lives a faith for which God, in human form, lovingly stoops over what is deepest in the world and in man, over guilt, and for which God's almighty Power assumes life in man's fragile frame. But at this point the contemplative and comprehending servant of research reverently withdraws; his own utterance yields place to that of proclamation, his service to that in the sanctuary.

---

[1] *Col.* i, 18 *ff.* ii, 9 (Moffat).   [2] *cf.* O. Weinreich, *Aegyptus*, 11, 1931, 17.
[3] Burdach, *Vorspiel*, I, 1, 245.
[4] *cf.* R. Bultmann, *Theol. Blätter* 8, 1929, 146 *f.*   [5] 1 *Tim.* ii. 5 (Moffat).

EPILEGOMENA

CHAPTER 107

PHENOMENON AND PHENOMENOLOGY[1]

1. PHENOMENOLOGY seeks the *phenomenon*, as such; the phenomenon, again, is *what "appears"*. This principle has a threefold implication: (*1*) Something exists. (*2*) This something "appears". (*3*) Precisely because it "appears" it is a "phenomenon". But "appearance" refers equally to what appears and to the person to whom it appears; the phenomenon, therefore, is neither pure object, nor *the* object, that is to say, the actual reality, whose essential being is merely concealed by the "appearing" of the appearances; with this a specific metaphysics deals. The term "phenomenon", still further, does not imply something purely subjective, not a "life" of the subject;[2] so far as is at all possible, a definite branch of psychology is concerned with this. The "phenomenon" as such, therefore, is an object related to a subject, and a subject related to an object; although this does not imply that the subject deals with or modifies the object in any way whatever, nor (conversely) that the object is somehow or other affected by the subject. The phenomenon, still further, is not produced by the subject, and still less substantiated or demonstrated by it; its entire essence is given in its "appearance", and its appearance to "someone". If (finally) this "someone" begins to discuss what "appears", then phenomenology arises.

In its relation to the "someone" to whom the phenomenon appears, accordingly, it has three levels of phenomenality: (*1*) its (relative) *concealment*; (*2*) its *gradually becoming revealed*; (*3*) its (relative) *transparency*. These levels, again, are not equivalent to, but are correlated with, the three levels of life: (*1*) *Experience*: (*2*) *Understanding*: (*3*) *Testimony*; and the last two attitudes, when systematically or scientifically employed, constitute the procedure of phenomenology.

By "experience" is implied an actually subsisting life which, with respect to its meaning, constitutes a unity.[3] Experience, therefore, is not pure "life", since in the first place it is objectively conditioned and, secondly, it is inseparably connected with its interpretation as experience. "Life" itself is incomprehensible: "What the disciple of Saïs unveils is form, not life."[4] For the "primal experience", upon which our experiences are grounded, has always passed irrevocably away by the time our attention is directed to it. My own life, for example, which I experienced while writing the few lines of the

---

[1] [In what follows a few passages of somewhat technical character are in small type.]

[2] The term "experience" (*Erlebnis*) is itself objectively oriented (we always experience something) and designates a "structure"; *cf.* Note, p. 461.

[3] Dilthey, *Gesammelte Schriften*, VII, 194.   [4] *ibid.*, 195.

preceding sentence, is just as remote from me as is the "life" associated with the lines I wrote thirty years ago in a school essay. I cannot call it back again : it is completely past. In fact, the experience of the lines of a moment ago is no nearer to me than is the experience of the Egyptian scribe who wrote his note on papyrus four thousand years ago. That he was "another" than myself makes no difference whatever, since the boy who prepared the school work thirty years ago is also, to my own contemplation, "another", and I must objectify myself in my experience of those bygone days. The immediate, therefore, is never and nowhere "given"; it must always be reconstructed;[1] and to "ourselves", that is to our most intimate life, we have no access. For our "life" is not the house wherein we reside, nor again the body, with which we can at least do something: on the contrary, confronted with this "life" we stand helpless. What appears to us as the greatest difference and the most extreme contrast possible—the difference, namely, between ourselves and the "other", our r eighbour, whether close by or in distant China, of yesterday or of four thousand years ago—all that is a mere triviality when measured against the colossal *aporia*, the insoluble dilemma, in which we find ourselves as soon as we wish to approach life itself. Even when we reduce life to its appearance in history, we remain perplexed: the gate remains closed, that to yesterday just as that to olden times; and every historian knows that he may commence anywhere at all, but in any case he ends with himself; in other words, he *reconstructs*.[2] What, then, does this reconstruction imply?

It may be described, to begin with, as the sketching of an outline within the chaotic maze of so-called "reality", this outline being called *structure*. Structure is a connection which is neither merely experienced directly, nor abstracted either logically or causally, but which is *understood*. It is an organic whole which cannot be analyzed into its own constituents, but which can from these be comprehended; or in other terms, a fabric of particulars, not to be compounded by the addition of these, nor the deduction of one from the others, but again only *understood* as a whole.[3] In other words: structure is certainly experienced, but not immediately; it is indeed constructed, but not logically, causally and abstractly. Structure is reality significantly organized. But the significance, in its own turn, belongs in part to reality itself, and in part to the "someone" who attempts to understand it. It is always, therefore, both understanding and intelligibility: and this, indeed, in an unanalyzable, experienced connection. For it can never be asserted with any certainty what is my own understanding, and what is the intelligibility of that which is understood; and this is the purport of the statement that the understanding

---

[1] cf. E. Spranger, *Die Einheit der Psychologie, Sitzber. d. Preuss, Akad. d. Wiss.* 24, 1926, 188, 191. F. Krüger, *Ber. über den VIII. Kongress für experim. Psych.*, 33.

[2] cf. on a different field of research, P. Bekker, *Musikgeschichte*, 1926, 2.

[3] The so-called hermeneutic circle, to which G. Wobbermin particularly drew attention; cf. Wach, *Religionswissenschaft*, 49.

of a connection, or of a person or event, *dawns upon us*.[1] Thus the sphere of meaning is a third realm, subsisting above mere subjectivity and mere objectivity.[2] The entrance gate to the reality of primal experience, itself wholly inaccessible, is *meaning*: *my* meaning and *its* meaning, which have become irrevocably one is the act of understanding.

Still further, the interconnection of meaning—structure—is experienced by understanding, first of all at some given moment; the meaning dawns upon me. But this is not the whole truth, since comprehension is never restricted to the momentary experience. It extends over several experiential unities simultaneously, as indeed it also originates from the understanding of these unities of experience. But these other experiences, which are at the same time understood in combination, and which cooperate in understanding, of course present a similarity to what has been instantaneously understood which, precisely in and through understanding itself, manifests itself as community of essential nature. The understood experience thus becomes coordinated, in and by understanding, within experience of some yet wider objective connection. *Every individual experience, therefore, is already connection*; and every connection remains always experience; this is what we mean by speaking of *types*, together with structures.[3]

The appearance, to continue, subsists as an image. It possesses backgrounds and associated planes; it is "related" to other entities that appear, either by similarity, by contrast, or by a hundred *nuances* that can arise here: conditions, peripheral or central position, competition, distance, *etc*. These relationships, however, are always *perceptible* relationships, "*structural connections*":[4] they are never factual relationships nor causal connections. They do not, of course, exclude the latter, but neither do they enunciate anything about them; they are valid only within the structural relations. Such a relation, finally, whether it concerns a person, a historical situation or a religion, is called a *type*, or an *ideal type*.[5]

"Type" in itself, however, has no reality; nor is it a photograph of reality. Like structure, it is timeless and need not actually occur in history.[6] But it possesses life, its own significance, its own law. The "soul", again, as such, never and nowhere "appears"; there is always and only some definite kind of soul which is believed in, and is in this its definiteness unique. It may even

---

[1] *cf*. A. A. Grünbaum, *Herrschen und Lieben*, 1925, 17. Spranger, *Lebensformen*, 6 *ff*. [2] Spranger, *ibid.*, 436.
[3] Spranger, *Einheit der Psychologie*, 177; *cf*. Wach's observation that the close connection between the theory of types and that of hermeneutics has not yet been adequately emphasized; *Religionswissenschaft*, 149.
[4] This term was introduced by Karl Jaspers: *verständliche Beziehungen*.
[5] On the history of the idea *cf*. B. Pfister, *Die Entwicklung zum Idealtypus*, 1928.
[6] Spranger, *Lebensformen*, 115; Binswanger, *Einführung in die Probleme der allgemeinen Psychologie*, 296; van der Leeuw, *Über einige neuere Ergebnisse der psychologischen Forschung und ihre Anwendung auf die Geschichte, insonderheit die Religionsgeschichte*, *SM*. II, 1926, *passim*; *cf*. further P. Hofmann, *Das religiöse Erlebnis*, 1925, 8.

be said that the ideas of the soul formed by any two persons, it may be in the same cultural and religious circle, are never wholly the same. Still there is a *type* of soul, a structural relation of distinctive soul-structures. The type itself (to repeat) is timeless: nor is it real. Nevertheless it is alive and appears to us; what then are we to do in order actually to observe it?

2. We resort to phenomenology: that is to say, we must discuss whatever has "appeared" to us—in this sense the term itself is quite clear.[1] This discussion, still further, involves the following stages, which I enumerate in succession although, in practice, they arise never successively but always simultaneously, and in their mutual relations far more frequently than in series:—

A. What has become manifest, in the first place, receives a *name*. All speech consists first of all in *assigning names*: "the simple use of names constitutes a form of thinking intermediate between perceiving and imagining".[2] In giving names we separate phenomena and also associate them; in other words, we classify. We include or reject: this we call a "sacrifice" and that a "purification"; since Adam named the animals, speakers have always done this. In this assignment of names, however, we expose ourselves to the peril of becoming intoxicated, or at least satisfied, with the name—the danger which Goethe represented as "transforming observations into mere concepts, and concepts into words", and then treating these words "as if they were objects".[3] We attempt to avoid this danger by

B. The interpolation of the phenomenon into our own lives.[4] This introduction, however, is no capricious act; we can do no otherwise. "Reality" is always *my* reality, history *my* history, "the retrogressive prolongation of man now living".[5] We must, however, realize what we are doing when we commence to speak about what has appeared to us and which we are naming. Further, we must recall that everything that appears to us does not submit itself to us directly and immediately, but only as a symbol of some meaning to be interpreted by us, as something which offers itself to us for interpretation. And this interpretation is impossible unless we experience the appearance, and this, indeed, not involuntarily and semi-consciously, but intentionally and methodically. Here I cite the impressive statement of Usener who, although he knew nothing of phenomenology, was fully aware of

---

[1] What I myself understand by the phenomenology of religion is called by Hackmann "The General Science of Religion"; other terms for this type of research that have appeared (once more to disappear, however) are "Transcendental Psychology", "Eidology" and *Formenlehre der religiösen Vorstellungen* (Usener).

[2] McDougall, *An Outline of Psychology*, 284.

[3] *Farbenlehre* in Binswanger, *op. cit.*, 31.

[4] The expression usually employed, "Empathy" (*Einfühlung*) overstresses the feeling aspect of the process, although not without some justification.

[5] Spranger, *op. cit.* 430.

what it implies: "Only by surrendering oneself, and by submersion in these
spiritual traces of vanished time[1] . . . can we train ourselves to recall their
feeling; then chords within ourselves, gradually becoming sympathetic, can
harmoniously vibrate and resound, and we discover in our own consciousness
the strands linking together old and new."[2] This too is what Dilthey describes
as the "experience of a structural connection", such experience, it is true,
being more an art than a science.[3] It is in fact the primal and primitively
human art of the actor which is indispensable to all arts, but to the sciences
of mind also:—to sympathize keenly and closely with experience other than
one's own, but also with one's own experience of yesterday, already become
strange! To this sympathetic experience, of course, there are limits; but these
are also set to our understanding of ourselves, it may be to an even greater
degree; *homo sum, humani nil a me alienum puto*: this is no key to the deepest
comprehension of the remotest experience, but is nevertheless the triumphant
assertion that the essentially human always remains essentially human, and
is, as such, comprehensible:—unless indeed he who comprehends has acquired too much of the professor and retained too little of the man! "When
the professor is told by the barbarian that once there was nothing except a
great feathered serpent, unless the learned man feels a thrill and a half
temptation to wish it were true, he is no judge of such things at all."[4] Only
the persistent and strenuous application of this intense sympathy, only the
uninterrupted learning of his rôle, qualifies the phenomenologist to interpret
appearances. In Jaspers' pertinent words: "Thus every psychologist experiences the increasing clarity of his mental life for himself; he becomes aware of
what has hitherto remained unnoticed, although he never reaches the ultimate
limit."[5]

  C. Not only is the "ultimate limit" never attainable in the sense referred
to by Jaspers: it implies, still further, the unattainability of existence. Phenomenology, therefore, is neither metaphysics, nor the comprehension of
empirical reality. It observes *restraint* (the *epoche*), and its understanding of
events depends on its employing "brackets".[6] Phenomenology is concerned
only with "phenomena", that is with "appearance"; for it, there is nothing
whatever "behind" the phenomenon. This restraint, still further, implies no
mere methodological device, no cautious procedure, but the distinctive
characteristic of man's whole attitude to reality. Scheler has very well expressed this situation: "to be human means to hurl a forcible 'No!' at this
sort of reality. Buddha realized this when he said how magnificent it is to
contemplate everything, and how terrible it is to *be*: Plato, too, in connecting
the contemplation of ideas to a diverting of the soul from the sensuous con-

---

[1] This applies equally to the so-called "present".   [2] *Götternamen,* 1896, VII.
[3] Binswanger, *op. cit.,* 246; van der Leeuw, *op. cit.,* 14 *f.*
[4] Chesterton, *The Everlasting Man,* 111; *cf.* Hofmann, *Religiöses Erlebnis,* 4 *f.*
[5] K. Jaspers, *Allgemeine Psychopathologie*[3], 1923, 204.   [6] *cf.* Note, p. 646.

tent of objects, and to the diving at the soul into its own depths, in order to find the 'origins' of things. Husserl, also, implies nothing different than this when he links the knowledge of ideas with 'phenomenological reduction'— that is a 'crossing through' or 'bracketing' of (the accidental) coefficients of the existence of objects in the world in order to obtain their *'essentia'*."[1] This of course involves no preference of some "idealism" or other to some kind of "realism". On the contrary: it is simply maintained that man can be positive only in turning away from things, as they are given to him chaotically and formlessly, and by first assigning them form and meaning. Phenomenology, therefore, is not a method that has been reflectively elaborated, but is man's true vital activity, consisting in losing himself neither in things nor in the *ego*, neither in hovering above objects like a god nor dealing with them like an animal, but in doing what is given to neither animal nor god: standing aside and understanding what appears into view.

D. The observance of what appears implies a *clarification* of what has been observed: all that belongs to the same order must be united, while what is different in type must be separated. These distinctions, however, should certainly not be decided by appealing to causal connections in the sense that *A* arises from *B*, while *C* has its own origin uniting it to *D*—but solely and simply by employing structural relations somewhat as the landscape painter combines his groups of objects, or separates them from one another. The juxtaposition, in other words, must not become externalization, but structural association;[2] and this means that we seek the ideal typical interrelation, and then attempt to arrange this within some yet wider whole of significance, *etc.*[3]

E. All these activities, undertaken together and simultaneously, constitute genuine *understanding*: the chaotic and obstinate "reality" thus becomes a manifestation, a revelation. The empirical, ontal or metaphysical *fact* becomes a *datum*; the object, living speech; rigidity, expression.[4] "The sciences of mind are based on the relations between experience, expression and understanding":[5] I understand this to mean that the intangible experience in itself cannot be apprehended nor mastered, but that it manifests something to us, an appearance: says something, an utterance. The aim of science, therefore, is to understand this *logos*; essentially, science is hermeneutics.[6]

Now when we are concerned, as in our own case, with the domain of historical research, this would appear to be the stage at which historical scepticism threateningly intrudes into our investigations, and renders all comprehension of remote times and regions impossible to us. We might then reply that we are quite ready to acknowledge that we can *know* nothing, and that we admit, further, that perhaps we understand very little; but that, on the

---

[1] Max Scheler, *Die Stellung des Menschen im Kosmos*, 1928, 63; *cf.* Heidegger, *Sein und Zeit*, 38.   [2] Binswanger, *op. cit.*, 302; *cf.* Jaspers, *Psychopathologie*, 18, 35.
[3] Spranger, *Lebensformen*, 11.
[4] Heidegger, *op. cit.*, 37; Dilthey, *op. cit.*, VII, 71, 86.
[5] Dilthey, *ibid.*, 131.   [6] *cf.* further Binswanger, *op. cit.*, 244, 288.

other hand, to understand the Egyptian of the first dynasty is, in itself, no
more difficult than to understand my nearest neighbour. Certainly the
monuments of the first dynasty are intelligible only with great difficulty, but
as an expression, as a human statement, they are no harder than my colleague's letters. In this respect, indeed, the historian can learn from the
psychiatrist: "If we are astonished by an ancient myth or an Egyptian head,
and confront it with the conviction that there is something that is intelligible
in accord with our own experience, although it is infinitely remote from us
and unattainable, just as we are amazed by a psycho-pathological process or
an abnormal character, we have at least the possibility of a more deeply comprehending glance, and perhaps of achieving a living representation. . . ."[1]

F. But if phenomenology is to complete its own task, it imperatively
requires perpetual correction by the most conscientious philological and
archaeological research. It must therefore always be prepared for confronta-
tion with material facts, although the actual manipulation of these facts
themselves cannot proceed without interpretation—that is without phenomenology; and every exegesis, every translation, indeed every reading, is
already hermeneutics. But this purely philological hermeneutics has a more
restricted purpose than the purely phenomenological. For it is concerned in
the first place with the Text, and then with the fact in the sense of what is
concretely implied: of what can be translated in other words. This of course
necessitates meaning, only it is a shallower and broader meaning than phenomenological understanding.[2] But as soon as the latter withdraws itself from
control by philological and archaeological interpretation, it becomes pure art
or empty fantasy.[3]

G. This entire and apparently complicated procedure, in conclusion, has
ultimately no other goal than pure objectivity. Phenomenology aims not at
things, still less at their mutual relations, and least of all at the "thing in
itself". It desires to gain access to the facts themselves;[4] and for this it requires a meaning, because it cannot experience the facts just as it pleases.
This meaning, however, is purely objective: all violence, either empirical,
logical or metaphysical, is excluded. Phenomenology regards every event in
the same way that Ranke looked on each epoch as "in an immediate and
direct relation to God", so that "its value depends in no degree on whatever
results from it, but on its existence as such, on its own self".[5] It holds itself
quite apart from modern thought, which would teach us "to contemplate the
world as unformed material, which we must first of all form, and conduct
ourselves as the lords of the world".[6] It has, in fact, one sole desire: *to testify*

---

[1] Jaspers, *Psychopathologie*, 404; *cf.* Usener. *Götternamen.* 62.
[2] Spranger gives an excellent example in his comparison of the ever more deeply
penetrating meanings of a biblical text; *Einheit der Psychologie*, 180 *ff.*
[3] Wach, *Religionswissenschaft*, 117; van der Leeuw, *op. cit., passim.*
[4] Heidegger, *op. cit.*, 34.   [5] L. von Ranke, *Weltgeschichte*, VIII[4], 1921, 177.
[6] E. Brunner, *Gott und Mensch*, 1930, 40.

to what has been manifested to it.[1] This it can do only by indirect methods, by a second experience of the event, by a thorough reconstruction; and from this road it must remove many obstacles. To see face to face is denied us. But much can be observed even in a mirror; and it is possible to speak about things seen.

E. Bernheim, *Lehrbuch der historischen Methode*[5–6], 1914.

L. Binswanger, *Einführung in die Probleme der allgemeinen Psychologie*, 1922. *Verstehen und Erklären in der Psychologie* (*Zeitschr. f. d. g. Neurologie und Psychiatrie* 107, 1927).

W. Dilthey, *Gesammelte Schriften*[2], 1923 ff.

H. Hackmann, *Allgemeine Religionsgeschichte* (*Nieuw Theol. Tydschrift*, 1919).

M. Heidegger, *Sein und Zeit, Erste Hälfte*[2], 1929.

Eva Hirschmann, *Phänomenologie der Religion*, 1940.

P. Hofmann, *Allgemeinwissenschaft und Geisteswissenschaft*, 1925.

G. van der Leeuw, *Über einige neuere Ergebnisse der psychologischen Forschung und ihre Anwendung auf die Geschichte, insonderheit die Religionsgeschichte* (*SM.* II, 1926).

E. Neumann, *Ursprungsgeschichte des Bewustseins*, 1949.

B. Pfister, *Die Entwicklung zum Idealtypus*, 1928.

F. Sierksma, *Phaenomenologie der Religie en Complexe Psychologie, Een Methodologische Studie*, 1950.

E. Spranger, *Lebensformen*[5], 1925.

Anna Tumarkin, *Die Methoden der psychologischen Forschung*, 1929.

J. Wach, *Das Verstehen*, I, 1926. II, 1929. III, 1933. *Religionswissenschaft*, 1924.

[1] *cf.* W. J. Aalders, *Wetenschap als Getuigenis*, 1930.

CHAPTER 108

RELIGION

1. WE can try to understand religion from a flat plain, from ourselves as the centre; and we can also understand how the essence of religion is to be grasped only from above, beginning with God. In other words: we can—in the manner already indicated—observe religion as intelligible experience; or we can concede to it the status of incomprehensible revelation. For in its "reconstruction", experience is a phenomenon. Revelation is not; but man's reply to revelation, his assertion about what has been revealed, is also a phenomenon from which, indirectly, conclusions concerning the revelation itself can be derived (*per viam negationis*).

Considered in the light of both of these methods, religion implies that man does not simply accept the life that is given to him. In life he seeks *power*; and if he does not find this, or not to an extent that satisfies him, then he attempts to draw the power, in which he believes, into his own life. He tries to elevate life, to enhance its value, to gain for it some deeper and wider meaning. In this way, however, we find ourselves on the horizontal line: religion is the extension of life to its uttermost limit. The religious man desires richer, deeper, wider life: he desires power for himself.[1] In other terms: in and about his own life man seeks something that is superior, whether he wishes merely to make use of this or to worship it.

He who does not merely accept life, then, but demands something from it—that is, power—endeavours to find some meaning in life. He arranges life into a significant whole: and thus culture arises. Over the variety of the given he throws his systematically fashioned net, on which various designs appear: a work of art, a custom, an economy. From the stone he makes himself an image, from the instinct a commandment, from the wilderness a tilled field; and thus he develops power. But he never halts; he seeks ever further for constantly deeper and wider *meaning*. When he realizes that a flower is beautiful and bears fruit, he enquires for its ampler, ultimate significance; when he knows that his wife is beautiful, that she can work and bear children, when he perceives

---

[1] Herein consists the essential unity between religion and culture. Ultimately, all culture is religious; and, on the horizontal line, all religion is culture.

that he must respect another man's wife, just as he would have his own respected, he seeks still further and asks for her final meaning. Thus he finds the secret of the flower and of woman; and so he discovers their religious significance.

The religious significance of things, therefore, is that on which no wider nor deeper meaning whatever can follow. It is the meaning of the whole: it is the last word. But this meaning is never understood, this last word is never spoken; always they remain superior, the ultimate meaning being a secret which reveals itself repeatedly, only nevertheless to remain eternally concealed. It implies an advance to the farthest boundary, where only one sole fact is understood:—that all comprehension is "beyond"; and thus the ultimate meaning is at the same moment the limit of meaning.[1]

Homo religiosus thus betakes himself to the road to omnipotence, to complete understanding, to ultimate meaning. He would fain comprehend life, in order to dominate it. As he understands soil so as to make it fruitful, as he learns how to follow animals' ways, so as to subject them to himself—so too he resolves to understand the world, in order to subjugate it to himself. Therefore he perpetually seeks new superiorities: until at last he stands at the very frontier and perceives that the ultimate superiority he will never attain, but that it reaches him in an incomprehensible and mysterious way. Thus the horizontal line of religion resembles the way of St. Christopher, who seeks his master and at last finds him too.

2. But there is also a vertical way: from below upwards, and from above downwards. This way however is not, like the former, an experience that is passed through before a frontier. It is a revelation, coming from beyond that frontier. The horizontal path, again, is an experience which certainly has an inkling or presage[2] of revelation, but which cannot attain to it. The vertical way, on the other hand, is a revelation, which never becomes completely experienced, though it participates in experience.[3] The first road is certainly not a tangible, but is all the more an intelligible, phenomenon. The second is not a phenomenon at all, and is neither attainable nor understandable; what we obtain from it phenomenologically, therefore, is merely its reflection in experience. We can never understand God's utterance by means of any purely intellectual capacity: what we can understand is only our

---

[1] Spranger, *op. cit., passim.*   [2] *Ahnung:* cf. p. 48, note 1.
[3] Chap. 67.

own answer; and in this sense, too, it is true that we have the treasure only in an earthen vessel.

Man, seeking power in life, does not reach the frontier; but he realizes that he has been removed to some foreign region. Thus he not only reaches the place from which a prospect of infinite distance is disclosed to him, but he knows too that, while he is still on the way, he is at every moment surrounded by marvellous and far-off things. He has not only a firm awareness (*Ahnung*) of the superior, but is also directly seized by it. He has not merely descried the throne of the Lord *from afar*, and fain would have sent on his heart in advance, but he realizes too that *this* place itself is dreadful, because it is a "house of God" and a "gate of heaven". Perhaps angels descend to his resting-place: perhaps demons press upon his path. But he knows quite definitely that *something meets him on the road*. It may be the angel who goes before him and will lead him safely: it may be the angel with the flashing sword who forbids him the road. But it is quite certain that something foreign has traversed the way of his own powerfulness.

And just because it is not to be found in the prolongation of man's own path, this strange element has no name whatever. Otto has suggested "the numinous", probably because this expression says nothing at all! This foreign element, again, can be approached only *per viam negationis*; and here again it is Otto who has found the correct term in his designation "the Wholly Other". For this, however, religions themselves have coined the word "holy".[1] The German term is derived from *Heil*, "powerfulness"; the Semitic and Latin, קדשׁ, *sanctus*, and the primitive expression, *tabu*, have the fundamental meaning of "separated", "set aside by itself". Taken all together, they provide the description of what occurs in all religious experience: *a strange, "Wholly Other", Power obtrudes into life*. Man's attitude to it is first of all *astonishment*,[2] and ultimately *faith*.

3. The limit of human powerfulness, in conclusion, and the commencement of the divine, together constitute the goal which has been sought and found in the religion of all time:—*salvation*. It may be the enhancing of life, improvement, beautifying, widening, deepening; but by "salvation" there may also be meant completely new life, a devaluation of all that has preceded, a new creation of the life that has been received "from elsewhere". But in any case, religion is always directed

---

[1] Chap. 4; *cf.* also Chap. 11, Section 1, and Otto, *The Idea of the Holy, passim.*
[2] Otto.

towards salvation, never towards life itself as it is given; and in this respect all religion, with no exception, is the religion of deliverance.[1]

P. HOFMANN, *Das religiöse Erlebnis*, 1925.
R. OTTO, *The Idea of the Holy*.

[1] Hofmann, *Das religiöse Erlebnis*, 12 *ff.*

CHAPTER 109

THE PHENOMENOLOGY OF RELIGION

1. PHENOMENOLOGY is the systematic discussion of what appears. Religion, however, is an ultimate experience that evades our observation, a revelation which in its very essence is, and remains, concealed. But how shall I deal with what is thus ever elusive and hidden? How can I pursue phenomenology when there is no phenomenon? How can I refer to "phenomenology of religion" at all?

Here there clearly exists an antinomy that is certainly essential to all religions, but also to all understanding; it is indeed precisely because it holds good for *both*, for religion and understanding alike, that our own science becomes possible. It is unquestionably quite correct to say that faith and intellectual suspense (the *epoche*)[1] do not exclude each other. It may further be urged that the Catholic Church, too, recognizes a *duplex ordo* of contemplation, on the one hand purely rational, and on the other wholly in accord with faith; while such a Catholic as Przywara also wishes to exclude every apologetic subsidiary aim from philosophy, and strenuously maintains the *epoche*.[2] But at the same time one cannot but recognize that all these reflections are the result of embarrassment. For it is at bottom utterly impossible contemplatively to confront an event which, on the one hand, is an ultimate experience, and on the other manifests itself in profound emotional agitation, in the attitude of such pure intellectual restraint. Apart from the existential attitude that is concerned with reality, we could never know anything of either religion or faith. It may certainly be advisable and useful methodically to presuppose this intellectual suspense; it is also expedient, since crude prejudice can so readily force its way into situations where only such an existential attitude would be justifiable. But, once again, how shall we comprehend the life of religion merely by contemplative observation from a distance? How indeed can we understand what, in principle, wholly eludes our understanding?

Now we have already found that not the understanding of religion alone, but *all* understanding without exception, ultimately reaches the limit where it loses its own proper name and can only be called "becoming understood". In other words: the more deeply comprehension

---

[1] *cf.* Note, p. 646. *Die Problematik der Neuscholastik, Kantstudien* 33, 1928.

penetrates any event, and the better it "understands" it, the clearer it becomes to the understanding mind that the ultimate ground of understanding lies not within itself, but in some "other" by which it is comprehended from beyond the frontier. Without this absolutely valid and decisive understanding, indeed, there would be no understanding whatever. For all understanding that extends "to the ground" ceases to be understanding before it reaches the ground, and recognizes itself as a "becoming understood". In other terms: all understanding, irrespective of whatever object it refers to, is ultimately religious: all significance sooner or later leads to ultimate significance. As Spranger states this: "in so far as it always refers to the whole man, and actually finds its final completion in the totality of world conditions, all understanding has a religious factor . . . we understand each other in God."[1]

What has previously been said with reference to the horizontal line in religion can also be translated into the language of the vertical line. And that ultimately all understanding is "becoming understood" then means that, ultimately, all love is "becoming loved"; that all human love is only the response to the love that was bestowed upon us. "Herein is love, not that we loved God, but that he loved us . . . we love him, because he first loved us."[2]

Understanding, in fact, itself presupposes intellectual restraint. But this is never the attitude of the cold-blooded spectator: it is, on the contrary, the loving gaze of the lover on the beloved object. For all understanding rests upon self-surrendering love. Were that not the case, then not only all discussion of what appears in religion, but all discussion of appearance in general, would be quite impossible; since to him who does not love, nothing whatever is manifested; this is the Platonic, as well as the Christian, experience.

I shall therefore not anticipate fruitlessly, and convert phenomenology into theology. Nor do I wish to assert that the faith upon which all comprehension is grounded, and religion as itself faith, are without further ado identical. But "it is plainly insufficient to permit theology to follow on philosophy (for my purpose, read "phenomenology") purely in virtue of its content, since the fundamental problem is one of method, and concerns the claim of philosophy (again, here, phenomenology) to justification in view of the obvious data, and also the impossibility of referring back faith, as the methodical basis of theology, to these data. In other terms: the problem becomes that of what is obviously

---

[1] *Lebensformen*, 418.   [2] I *John* iv. 10, 19.

evidence".[1] And I am prepared, with Przywara, to seek the intimate relationship that nevertheless exists between faith and the obvious data, in the fact that the evidence they provide is essentially a "preparedness for revelation".[2]

2. The use of the expressions: history of religion, science of religion, comparative history of religion, psychology of religion, philosophy of religion: and others similar to these, is still very loose and inexact; and this is not merely a formal defect, but is practical also.[3] It is true that the different subdivisions of the sciences concerned with religion (the expression is here employed in its widest possible sense), cannot subsist independently of each other; they require, indeed, incessant mutual assistance. But much that is essential is forfeited as soon as the limits of the investigation are lost to sight. The history of religion, the philosophy and psychology of religion, and alas! theology also, are each and all harsh mistresses, who would fain compel their servants to pass beneath the yoke which they hold ready for them; and the phenomenology of religion desires not only to distinguish itself from them, but also, if possible, to teach them to restrain themselves! I shall therefore first of all indicate what the phenomenology of religion is not, and what fails to correspond to its own essential character in the character or usage of the other disciplines.

The phenomenology of religion, then, is not the poetry of religion; and to say this is not at all superfluous, since I have myself expressly referred to the poetic character of the structural experience of ideal types. In this sense, too, we may understand Aristotle's assertion that the historian relates what has happened, while the poet recounts what might have occurred under any given circumstances; and that poetry is therefore a philosophical affair and of more serious import than history;[4] as against all bare historicism and all mere chronicle, this should always be remembered. Nor should it be forgotten that "art is just as much investigation as is science, while science is just as much the creation of form as is art".[5] But in any case there is a clear distinction between poetry and science, which forces itself into notice in the procedure of both from beginning to end: in his own work, then, the phenomenologist is bound up with the object; he cannot proceed without repeatedly confronting the chaos of the given, and without submitting again and again to correction by the facts; while although the artist certainly sets

[1] Przywara, *ibid.*, 92.   [2] *ibid.*, 95.   [3] Wach, *Religionswissenschaft*, 12.
[4] *Poetics*, Chap. 9.   [5] E. Utitz, *Ästhetik*, 1923, 18.

out from the object, he is not inseparably linked with this. In other words: the poet need know no particular language, nor study the history of the times; even the poet of the so-called historical novel need not do this. In order to interpret a myth he may completely remodel it, as for example Wagner treated the German and Celtic heroic sagas. Here the phenomenologist experiences his own limit, since his path lies always between the unformed chaos of the historical world and its structural endowment with form. All his life he oscillates hither and thither. But the poet advances.

Secondly, the phenomenology of religion is not the history of religion. History, certainly, cannot utter one word without adopting some phenomenological viewpoint; even a translation, or the editing of a Text, cannot be completed without hermeneutics. On the other hand, the phenomenologist can work only with historical material, since he must know what documents are available and what their character is, before he can undertake their interpretation. The historian and the phenomenologist, therefore, work in the closest possible association; they are indeed in the majority of cases combined in the person of a *single* investigator. Nevertheless the historian's task is essentially different from the phenomenologist's, and pursues other aims.[1] For the historian, everything is directed first of all to establishing what has actually happened; and in this he can never succeed unless he understands. But also, when he fails to understand, he must describe what he has found, even if he remains at the stage of mere cataloguing. But when the phenomenologist ceases to comprehend, he can have no more to say. He strides here and there; the historian of course does the same, but more frequently he stands still, and often he does not stir at all. If he is a poor historian, this will be due only to idleness or incapacity; but if he is a sound historian, then his halts imply a very necessary and admirable resignation.

Thirdly, the phenomenology of religion is not a psychology of religion. Modern psychology, certainly, appears in so many forms that it becomes difficult to define its limits with respect to other subjects.[2] But that phenomenology is not identical with experimental psychology should be sufficiently obvious, though it is harder to separate it from the psychology of form and structure. Nevertheless it is probably the common feature of all psychologies that they are concerned only with the psychical. The psychology of religion, accordingly, attempts to comprehend the psychical aspects of religion. In so far therefore as the

[1] Wach, *ibid.*, 56.   [2] *cf.* Spranger, *Einheit der Psychologie.*

psychical is expressed and involved in all that is religious, phenomenology and psychology have a common task. But in religion far more appears than the merely psychical: the whole man participates in it, is active within it and is affected by it. In this sphere, then, psychology would enjoy competence only if it rose to the level of the science of Spirit—of course in its philosophic sense—in general which, it must be said, is not seldom the case. But if we are to restrict psychology to its own proper object, it may be said that the phenomenologist of religion strides backwards and forwards over the whole field of religious life, but the psychologist of religion over only a part of this.[1]

Fourthly, the phenomenology of religion is not a philosophy of religion, although it may be regarded as a preparation therefor. For it is systematic, and constitutes the bridge between the special sciences concerned with the history of religion and philosophical contemplation.[2] Of course phenomenology leads to problems of a philosophic and metaphysical character, "which it is itself not empowered to submit";[3] and the philosophy of religion can never dispense with its phenomenology. Too often already has that philosophy of religion been elaborated which naïvely set out from "Christianity"—that is, from the Western European standpoint of the nineteenth century, or even from the humanistic deism of the close of the eighteenth century. But whoever wishes to philosophize about religion must know what it is concerned with; he should not presuppose this as self-evident. Nevertheless the aim of the philosopher of religion is quite different; and while he must certainly know what the religious issues are, still he has something other in view; he wishes to move what he has discovered by means of the dialectical motion of Spirit. His progress, too, is hither and thither: only not in the sense of phenomenology; rather is it immanent in the Spirit. Every philosopher, indeed, has somewhat of God within him: it is quite seemly that he should stir the world in his inner life. But the phenomenologist should not become merely frightened by the idea of any similarity to God: he must shun it as the sin against the very spirit of his science.

Finally, phenomenology of religion is not theology. For theology shares with philosophy the claim to search for truth, while phenomenology, in this respect, exercises the intellectual suspense of the *epoche*.[4]

[1] That psychology is concerned purely with actual, and not with historical, experiences, and that consequently a limit subsists here also, obviously cannot be admitted for one moment; without psychology we should be unable to deal with history; *cf.* Spranger, *Einheit der Psychologie*, 184.
[2] Wach, *Verstehen* I, 12.   [3] Wach, *Rel. wiss.* 131.   [4] *cf.* Note, p. 646.

But the contrast lies deeper even than this. Theology discusses not merely a horizontal line leading, it may be, to God, nor only a vertical, descending from God and ascending to Him. Theology speaks about God Himself. For phenomenology, however, God is neither subject nor object; to be either of these He would have to be a phenomenon— that is, He would have to appear. But He does not appear: at least not so that we can comprehend and speak about Him. If He does appear He does so in a totally different manner, which results not in intelligible utterance, but in proclamation; and it is with this that theology has to deal. It too has a path "hither and thither"; but the "hither" and the "thither" are not the given and its interpretation, but concealment and revelation, heaven and earth, perhaps heaven, earth and hell. Of heaven and hell, however, phenomenology knows nothing at all; it is at home on earth, although it is at the same time sustained by love of the beyond.

3. In accordance with what has been remarked in Chapter 107, the phenomenology of religion must in the first place assign names:— sacrifice, prayer, saviour, myth, *etc.* In this way it appeals to appearances. Secondly, it must interpolate these appearances within its own life and experience them systematically. And in the third place, it must withdraw to one side, and endeavour to observe what appears while adopting the attitude of intellectual suspense. Fourthly, it attempts to clarify what it has seen, and again (combining all its previous activities) try to comprehend what has appeared. Finally, it must confront chaotic "reality", and its still uninterpreted signs, and ultimately testify to what it has understood. Nevertheless all sorts of problems that may be highly interesting in themselves must thereby be excluded. Thus phenomenology knows nothing of any historical "development" of religion,[1] still less of an "origin" of religion.[2] Its perpetual task is to free itself from every non-phenomenological standpoint and to retain its own liberty, while it conserves the inestimable value of this position always anew.[3]

Kierkegaard's impressive description of the psychological observer, therefore, may serve not as a rule, and not even as an ideal, but as a permanent reproach: "just as the psychological investigator must possess a greater suppleness than a tight-rope walker, so that he can install himself within men's minds and imitate their dispositions: just as his

---

[1] Wach, *Rel. wiss.* 82.
[2] Th. de Laguna, "The Sociological Method of Durkheim", *Phil. Rev.* 29, 1920, 224. E. Troeltsch, *Gesammelte Schriften*, II, 1913, 490.
[3] Jaspers, *Allgemeine Psychopathologie*, 36.

taciturnity during periods of intimacy must be to some degree seductive and passionate, so that reserve can enjoy stealing forth, in this artificially achieved atmosphere of being quietly unnoticed, in order to feel relief, as it were in monologue: so he must have a poetic originality within his soul, so as to be able to construct totality and orderliness from what is presented by the *individuum* only in a condition of dismemberment and irregularity".[1]

G. VAN DER LEEUW, *Strukturpsychologie und Theologie* (*Zeitschrift für Theologie und Kirche*, N. F. 9, 1928).

N. SÖDERBLOM, *Natürliche Theologie und allgemeine Religionsgeschichte*, 1913.

E. SPRANGER, *Der Sinn der Voraussetzungslosigkeit in den Geisteswissenschaften* (*Sitzber. der preuss. Ak. der Wiss., phil.-hist. Kl.*, 1929, 1).

[1] *Begrebet Angest* (*The Concept of Dread*), Saml. *Vaerker*, IV², 1923, 360; *cf.* the entire fine passage.

CHAPTER 110

THE HISTORY OF PHENOMENOLOGICAL RESEARCH

1. THE history of the phenomenology of religion is brief. The history of religion is a young field of research, and its phenomenology is still in its mere childhood, having been systematically pursued only from the date of Chantepie's researches. But in the first place, no satisfactory history can ever be produced unless phenomenology is appealed to, whatever it may be called: secondly, at the most varied stages in the course of the history of religion there have arisen methodological approaches to a phenomenological mode of consideration; and these two circumstances enable us to trace the development of phenomenology to a comparatively early period. This is most readily carried out by discussing the outstanding eras in the history of religion. These are:

A. The history of religion during the age of enlightenment. The encyclopedic interest of the eighteenth century was, together with other subjects, directed to religions, which were—frequently in antithesis to the religion of revelation—interpreted as being expressions of natural religion and as forms of the innate ideas of God, immortality and virtue. There was therefore much enthusiasm for China, where all this was supposed to exist! The result was of course that the idea of toleration vaunted itself, priestly deception and thirst for power, bigotry and hypocrisy being decried, not without hinting at Christianity. In this connection the work of Meiners, the Göttingen investigator of religion, is for our purpose of outstanding importance.[1] As far as I am aware, he is the first systematic phenomenologist. Not only does he attempt a classification, an extensive allocation of names in which fetishism, worship of the dead, of stars and images, sacrifice, purifications, fasts, prayer, festivals, mourning customs, *etc.*, are discussed in an orderly manner, but his entire attitude, too, is in principle phenomenological. He wishes to discover what is essential in religion, and in doing this he does not halt at the frontier formed by the antithesis between heathen and Christian: "all religions may possess as many unique features as they please; it is nevertheless certain that each religion resembles others in many more respects than those wherein it differs from them".[2] A

[1] But *cf.* on a French predecessor, René Maurier, *Benjamin Constant, historien des Sociétés et des Religions, RHR.* 102, 1930.

[2] Meiners, *Allgemeine kritische Geschichte der Religionen*, I, 1.

general history of religion appears to him to be formless, and he therefore sets forth to seek the "elements": "since a series of the histories of all religions is either impracticable or is at least inadvisable, there remains for the historian of religion no other course than to resolve the known religions, especially the polytheistic, into their elements as it were, and then observe how each essential factor of the popular religions of ancient and modern times was, or still is, constituted".[1] He compares religions themselves with respect to their affinities, or their contrastedness;[2] and, primarily, he seeks a certain "harmony" that I should call structural order, and in virtue of which definite concepts bring definite modes of worship, *etc.*, to maturity; an "analogy or harmony . . . in virtue of which different aspects are mutually adapted, or accord with each other. Those peoples who recognized a certain type of god must worship them in a certain way, and conversely. Peoples who had certain ideas about superior beings, and about their worship, must accept a certain kind of priest and magician", *etc.*[3] Nor are finer distinctions lacking: that a people is poly- or monotheistic, of itself, proves nothing: if one God is worshipped in the polytheistic way, the monotheism is not true and genuine.[4]

B. The history of religion in the period of Romanticism is marked by many more suggestions with respect to its phenomenological aspects. Philosophic romanticism endeavoured to comprehend the significance of the history of religion by regarding specific religious manifestations as symbols of a primordial revelation. Thus Creuzer interpreted myths and legends as "idioms of one original and general mother tongue". For this purpose he employed a specific "mythological apperception", which is important in that it involved a religious immersion within the data of the history of religion.[5] In a completely different way, Hegel sought to permit the individual religions themselves to speak the language of reason, and thus to absorb historical diversity within the eternal dialectic of the Spirit. Phenomenology is thus "the phenomenology of Spirit", describing the development of knowledge as it first appears in the form of immediate spirit, which is mere sensuous consciousness devoid of spirit, and then steadily advances toward

---

[1] Meiners, *Allgemeine kritische Geschichte der Religionen*, I, 2.   [2] *ibid.*, I, 129.
[3] II, IV.
[4] II, VI; *cf.* H. Wenzel, *Christoph Meiners als Religionshistoriker*, 1917.
[5] O. Gruppe, *Geschichte der klassischen Mythologie und Religionsgeschichte*, 1921, 126 *ff.* It is most desirable that research should be undertaken on the other departments of the history of religion in the same way as Gruppe has dealt so admirably with classical antiquity.

Absolute Spirit.[1] Here the important feature is that what appears is not only a human mode of presentation, as for Kant, but a manifestation of Absolute Spirit, to exhibit which as Subject is the enduring task of Hegelian philosophy. The phenomenon would thus be an appearance of the eternal dialectical movement of Spirit in some definite situation; and religion then occupies the final position before that of absolute knowledge. It is the relationship of finite spirit to Absolute Spirit in the form of idea. Hegel is the first philosopher who treats history, including the history of religion, in its full seriousness: Absolute Spirit has its life in history as it is comprehended. Exceedingly fruitful for all history, and typical for all philosophy, the conclusion of the *Phenomenology* still remains: The "conservation (of spiritual forms), looked at from the side of their free existence appearing in the form of contingency, is *History*; looked at from the side of their intellectually comprehended organization, it is the *Science* of the ways in which knowledge appears (*"Phenomenology"*). Both together, or History (intellectually) comprehended, form at once the recollection and the Golgotha of Absolute Spirit, the reality, the truth, the certainty of its throne, without which it were lifeless, solitary, and alone. Only

> The chalice of this realm of spirits
> Foams forth to God His own Infinitude."[2]

The result of this merging of spirits with Spirit is that Hegel's phenomenology provides not merely a theory of knowledge and a philosophy of history, but a psychology of comprehension also.[3]

In romanticism, further, the two other extremely important names in connection with this branch of research are those of Herder and Schleiermacher. Herder was the first to understand the "voices of the peoples", and also the first for whom history became an experience and the writing of history the "art of empathy".[4] He was also the first to interpret the language of religion as poetry, and therefore as the actual mother tongue of mankind.[5] Schleiermacher, however, wished to comprehend religion solely and simply as religion, and rejected all derivation from metaphysical or moral interests; and in this way he destroyed the power of the age of enlightenment, which he also subjugated by banishing the bloodless "natural religion" into the lumber-room.

[1] Hegel, *The Phenomenology of Mind*, 85 f., 88 f.   [2] *ibid.*, 808.
[3] Fr. Brunstäd, *RGG*. "Hegel".   [4] *cf.* p. 674, note 4.
[5] *cf.* van der Leeuw, *Gli dei di Omero, SM.* 7, 1931, 2 ff.

C. The history of religion in the period of romantic philology represents, in the first place, a reaction from romanticism, since it substituted precise study of the sources for unfettered speculation. But it still continued to be romantic in its desire to comprehend religion as the expression of a universal mode of human thinking; and the conflict previously latent in Herder and Schleiermacher, between primal revelation and human predisposition, was here decided in favour of the latter. Philology and comparative philology were to be utilized to bring to light the thought of mankind when regarded in its unity. Thus comparative religion appeared on the scene, and this is still, in Anglo-Saxon countries, the name for the history of religion as such. This philological history of religion, which is connected with the names of Max Müller and Ad. Kuhn, is also romantic-symbolic in that it wishes to perceive the life of Nature symbolized in religious concepts. In the history of religion, however, this period was infinitely fruitful, owing to the discovery and exploration of yet more extensive territories; but for the phenomenological comprehension of religion, this was of less importance, since the comparative factor, which can never be more than one feature among others, was given undue prominence,[1] and thus obstructed the path to a profounder understanding.

D. The history of religion in the age of romantic positivism, although it subsists almost completely under the spell of the principle of development, remains romantic in so far as, here too, religion is taken to be the voice of humanity: in religion mankind has said something, and it has, unfortunately, spoken falsely. The primal revelation there became either an "elementary idea" (Bastian) or even the idea of humanity itself (Durkheim). During this period, undeniably, the results of research into the history of religion are incalculable: it is the culminating era in the history of religion. By this, however, phenomenology benefited comparatively little; and in the light of the conscious, or unconscious, evolutionism of that time, this is not at all strange. Yet out of its great wealth this very period produced men who sought and discovered other paths, and who to some extent prepared the way for phenomenology and, in part, actually initiated it: I refer to Hermann Usener and Albrecht Dieterich. Usener's "doctrine of religious forms", which regarded the creation of forms as the crucial feature, is phenomenologically of the utmost importance;[2] and Hackmann's *allgemeinen Religionsgeschichte* has already been mentioned. P. D. Chantepie de la Saussaye acquired the highest merit in connection with our subject in

---

[1] Wach, *Rel. wiss.* 181.   [2] *Vorträge und Aufsätze*[2], 1914, 57 *ff.*

his *Lehrbuch* of 1887, in which he first gave not merely an "Outline of the Phenomenology of Religion", but also sought to comprehend the objective apearances of religion in the light of subjective processes, and accordingly assigned a wide scope to psychology.[1] E. Lehmann followed him with an *Outline* in *RGG*[1]., which was subsequently rewritten.[2]

E. I can now be very concise. The position of phenomenology to-day is the natural outcome of previous investigations.[3] The history of religion, as influenced by psychology, produced the extremely important works of W. Wundt in Germany and of L. Lévy-Bruhl in France, which to a great extent touch upon our own subject. Attention, too, has been increasingly directed inwardly. F. Heiler has endeavoured not only to determine the direction of psychological research on the scientific aspects of religion,[4] but has given us, together with Rudolf Otto, some of its finest and most important fruits.

F. The history of religions as developed by the methodology of "Understanding", and in this regard, dealt with by W. Dilthey's school of thought, has recently enjoyed an ever freer course. Certainly this by no means implies that we to-day understand religious phenomena for the very first time, since the achievements of the nineteenth century, in this respect also, can scarcely be estimated sufficiently highly, but that we now, consciously and systematically, look upon such an understanding of the phenomena, just as they appear to us, as our goal. Among other investigators, J. Wach and myself have undertaken methodological research,[5] while a wealth, that may indeed be described as a profusion, of *Introductions to the History of Religion*, of a more or less phenomenological type, as well as of monographs, clearly shows the possibilities of fruitful labour. Nonetheless is it true that the phenomenological treatment of the greater part of the history of religion lies still in the future; but rather than cite many, I select here the great name of Nathan Söderblom. For without his acute insight and his deeply penetrating love of what "appears", we could not advance another step in our territory; and the change of direction in the history of religion, plainly set forth in the current phenomenological viewpoint, finds its symbol in this thinker's name.

---

[1] Chantepie, *op. cit.*[1] I, 48 *f.*   [2] Chantepie, *op. cit.*[4]

[3] On the history of the history of religion, and in relation to phenomenology, *cf.* my article in *RGG. Religionsgeschichte.*

[4] *Prayer*, xxiv *f.*

[5] *cf.* further, Max Scheler's "concrete phenomenology", *Vom Ewigen im Menschen*, I, 1921, 373.

2. But far more than all other spheres of knowledge, the phenomenology of religion is dynamic: as soon as it ceases to move it ceases to operate. Its infinite need of correction pertains to its innermost being; and so we may say of this volume, dedicated to phenomenology, what the fairy tale tells us for its own consolation and for ours: "and so everything has its end, and this book too. But everything that has an end also commences anew elsewhere".

E. HARDY, *Was ist Religionswissenschaft?* (*AR.* 1, 1898).
  Zur Geschichte der Religionsforschung (*AR.* 4, 1901).
G. W. F. HEGEL, *The Phenomenology of Mind.*
E. LEHMANN, *Zur Geschichte der Religionsgeschichte* (CHANT.⁴ I).
  Der Lebenslauf der Religionsgeschichte (*Actes du V⁸ Congrès Int. d'Hist.des Rel. à Lund*, 1929, 44 ff.).
C. MEINERS, *Allgemeine kritische Geschichte der Religionen*, 1806–07.
G. MENSCHING, *Geschichte der Religionswissenschaft*, 1948.
R. F. MERKEL, "Zur Geschichte der Religionsphänomenologie" (in *Deo Omnia Urum, Festschr*, FR. HEILIER, 1942).
R. PETTAZONI, *Svolgimento e carattere della storia delle religioni*, 1924.
H. PINARD DE LA BOULLAYE, *L'Etude comparée des religions*, 1922.
W. SCHMIDT, *Handbuch der vergleichenden Religionsgeschichte*, 1930.

APPENDIX

(NOTE: This appendix represents in condensed form the new material found in the revised German edition)

PART I

THE OBJECT OF RELIGION

CHAPTER 1—Power

Section 3: *Mana* is also a substance which lets itself become defined in various ways; *mana* is honour, authority, wealth: a rich man has *mana*; he has *auctoritas*! For further references see, M. Mauss, "Essai sur le Don, Forme Archaique de l'échange" (*Année Sociolog., nouv. série*, I, 1925, 97). *Mana* may also signify the prestige and success of the warrior as well as his weapon. (*cf.* R. Thurnwald, *AR.* 27, 1929, 101 *ff.*) The *dema* of the Marind-Anin (New Guinea) is even more comprehensive. Everything can become *dema* as soon as it stands as extraordinary or, if the thing is seen from a purely external viewpoint, thus taking on a distinctive form because of its individuality. Furthermore, ancestors are also *dema*; they have, that is to say, become concrete *dema*. (For further description of this see L. Lévy-Bruhl, *La Mythologie Primitive*, 1935, 56 *ff.*)

Section 4: The concept of power can also be translated into truth, in a way, however, which has more of a practical, rather than ethical meaning. Thus in this context *mana* among the primitive peoples often means the power of truth, effective truth, over against which the lie corresponds to bad luck. Whoever predicts a good catch of fish has *mana* if the prediction becomes true. If it does not the man has lied. (*cf.* R. Thurnwald, "Die Lüge in der primitiven Kultur", in O. Lippman and P. Plaut, *Die Lüge*, 1927, 402.)

Section 5: For a specific reference indicating a religion where power is not explicitly assigned a name see M. P. Nilsson, *Geschichte der griechischen Religion*, I, 1941, 60.

Section 6: The concept of power is also a "vox media" between a sacred substance and God. This is the meaning of the Hebraic *el* which is power as well as God. It is said that, "*el* is suspended from off my hand", that is to say, from the power of my hand (on the other hand, *elim* are personal deities). *cf.* O. Eisfeldt, "Der Gott Bethel", in *AR.* 28, 1930, 26.

CHAPTER 2—Theorizing About Power

Section 1: For further indications of what has already been cited under the first footnote see H. Oldenberg, *Die Religion des Veda*, 1917, 478 *ff.*; E. Cassirer, *Philosophy of Symbolic Forms*, Vol. II, 1955.

Section 4: Further examples of power as inherent in man, yet superior, or distinguished from him as impersonal power, can be seen in H. Oldenberg, *Religion des Veda*, 478 *ff.* The idea is also expressed in K. Zeininger, *Die magische Geisteshaltung im Kindesalter*, 1929, 60. In this later work we have reference to a sister warning her younger brother that certain death follows when anyone touches the mouth with certain picked flowers. Her little brother then asks her, "Is death in them?"

CHAPTER 3—Things and Power

Section 2: On the use of the word "fetishism", as coined by de Brosses, see his famous monograph, *Du Culte des Dieux Fétiches*, 1760. He was not the first, however, to use this word, since it appears in a study by Godofridus Carolinus, in 1661. (*cf.* R. F. Merkel, in *Forschung und Fortschritte*, II, 1935, 36, 451). It is certain that de Brosses used the word for the first time as a scientific and phenomenological expression. He used fetishism as a general term for the religion of the Negroes. He was also the first to write on the psychological origin of fetishism.

For an example of the development of fetishism into a higher form, *cf.* M. P. Nilsson, *The Minoan-Mycenean Religion and Its Survival in Greek Religion*, 1950, 407.

Section 3: For the significance of tools as potent, see E. Cassirer, Vol. II; L. Noire, *Das Werkzeug und seine Bedeutung für die Entwicklungsgeschichte der Menscheit*, 1880, also, E. Kapp, *Grundlinien einer Philosophie der Technik*, 1887.

Section 4: Potency as the hoard of a community is also found among the Zuni Indians in the form of a "medicine bundle" which is sacred. Only certain people (priests, *etc.*) can enter the room where it is located. For a description see Ruth Benedict, *Patterns of Culture* (Mentor Books, 1949) 60.

Power as manifested in family *pusaka* is also known in Goa (Southern Island of Celebes). Here it takes the form of a chain which is worn by the individual. The chain is weighed every year, if it weighs less at the end of twelve months it signifies bad luck. Again, only priests and kings have the right to view these *pusaka*. In times of crises they are known to be carried about in a procession. (*cf.* J. Ph. Duyvendak, *Inleiding tot de Ethnologie van de Indische Archipel*, 1935, 132 *ff.*, also L. Lévy-Bruhl, *Le Surnaturel et la Nature dans la Mentalité Primitive*, 1931, 5.

CHAPTER 5—Sacred Stones and Trees

Section 2: The presence of power in stones can be seen in villages where one finds a rock pile on the side of the street and upon which stones are thrown by those passing by. This ritual is still observed by the Amanebele in South Africa. (*cf.* Fourie, *Amanebele*, 99). These power-filled stones are able to guarantee the welfare of the community. Similarly, in Indonesia, the "village stones" give health and power. In many cases there is a differentiation made between male (phallic) and female (concave) stones. The accession of the king is also celebrated on these stones and in some cases they are believed to have fallen from heaven. See: A. C. Kruyt, "De West-Toradja's op Midden-Celebes" (in *Verh. K. Ned. Akad. V. Wetensch. Afd. Litt., N. R.* 40) I, 355 *ff.*, 401, 427 *ff.*, and 443, also J. C. van Eerde, "Investituursteenen in Zuid-Celebes (in *Tijdschr. K. Ned. Aardr. Gen.* 2, R., 47, 1930), 820.

There are also specific instances of power in metals; metals are born, not made, and they are also capable of marriage. Minerals are embryos which have prematurely glanced at the light of the world. Metallurgists and alchemists have the duty to ripen them until in the end they become gold. For further references, *cf.* Mircea Eliade, "Metallurgy" (*Cahiers de Zalmoxis*, I), 1938.

CHAPTER 6—Sacred Water and Fire

Section 1: Water in its essence corresponds to womanhood and the mother. It is the bounty of life and renews the life of all being. The water of chaos, out of which the world springs forth, and the water which surrounds the embryo in the mother are parallels. We can understand therefore the great difference between water and fire; the latter is in the sphere of anthropology, the former is essentially theological. In a communication from W. F. van Lier (1938), the following conversation took place with a Negro from Surinam: "A man cannot live without water." When the native was asked, "But what about fire?", he answered "Oh no, Sir, we cannot compare fire with water. Man can make fire, but water, only God alone can do this. Water is everything that lives, it is essential for man, animals and plants. It is only man who cannot live without fire."

CHAPTER 7—The Sacred World Above

Section 5: Rain is also related to the Sacred World Above; it is the heavenly powers that divide and impart the rain. Rain is a power which makes the earth fruitful. Thus in ancient Greece we find the origin of Zeus in pre-Homeric times as a magician and rainmaker. Dew is nothing but his own sperm with which he fertilizes the earth. For further references see A. B. Cook, *Zeus*, III, 31, 180; also, Nilsson, *Greek Popular Religions*; also R. Dussaud, *Les Découvertes de Ras Shamra et L'Ancien Testament*, 1937. Notice also that in the Old Testament it is claimed that Jaweh is as good as, if not better than, Baal in bringing rain.

CHAPTER 8—The Sacred "Conjoined World" Animals

Section 2: For another illustration of Nagualism in the Osage tribe of the Southern Plains see R. Benedict, *Patterns of Culture*, 36 *ff*. In this example of the "Mussel", individual totemism proceeds toward a social totemism. But the essential unity between the animal (here a mussel) and he who "finds" it is a very clear one.

On the meaning and role of dreams in totemism see L. Lévy-Bruhl, *Expérience Mystique et les Symboles chez les Primitifs*, 1938, 107, 122, *etc.*; also R. Thurnwals, under "Totem", in *Lexikon der Vorgeschichte*, for an Australian comparison.

CHAPTER 10—The Form of the Mother

Section 2: The form of the mother as gruesome and terrible is best seen in the goddess Kali of India. For a description of her ritual and sacrifice see H. Zimmer's article in *Eranos Jahrbuch*, 1938, 180 *ff.*, also S. Cave, *Hinduism or Christianity*, 1939, 152 *ff*.

CHAPTER 13—Power and Will in Man. The King

Section 2: That cosmic events are subject to kingly power can be documented from the Natchez tribe where the chief is called the Great Sun. He has the power of setting the sun on its course, he has the power over the growth of grain, the rain, *etc. cf.* R. R. Marett, *Sacraments of Simple Folk*, 1933, 129. Among the tribesmen of the Ba-Ronga in Africa, the king is called the "prince of the earth". He is the cock who is master of the yard, he is the bull without whom the cows cannot calve. Without him the earth is like a woman who has left her mate in the lurch. *cf.* R. Thurnwal's article under "Mana", in *Lexikon der Vorgeschichte*.

CHAPTER 14—The Mighty Dead

Section 5: All Souls Day is celebrated almost everywhere. For an example of its celebration among the Trobriands see B. Malinowski, *Myth in Primitive Psychology*, 1926, 97. In this example the dead live with the living, they visit once a year.

G. Meiners, in his work *Allgemeine Krit. Geschichte der Religionen*, 1806–1807, Vol. I, 290 *ff.*, had noticed quite accurately that the cult of the dead is a repetition of the funeral rituals. It is a "memoria" for the early Christians, *cf.* H. Lietzmann, *Geschichte der Alten Kirche*, Vol. II, 1936, 133, also J. Quasten, *Musik und Gesang in den Kulten der heidnischen Antike und christlichen Frühzeit*, 1930, 230 *ff.*

CHAPTER 17—Power and Will Given Form in the Name

Section 1: From the study of the names of God, it would be possible, as well as desirable, to write the typology of religions on the answer to the question: "Does God have a name?" The variations are vast; either God does not have a name or one names him with a generic name in plural form, or his name becomes specific because of characteristic actions, or, finally, he has a specific name in an essential way.

The Israelites did not find rest until they had given their God a truly particular name. This means that one could now know this God and that this God could now also reveal himself. On the other hand, the God of Goethe, who is without a name, cannot reveal himself. This had to be the case, since the name is not just a reference or a technique; the name is "the soul" of an essence. We do not need a name to differentiate one essence from another; we need it, however, to give form to the being which is expressed. This is the reason why name giving is man's privilege. Man finds specific names for specific things and thus creates his own world in a familiar way.

Section 3: For an example of special gods, *cf.* L. R. Farnell, "The Place of the Sondergötter in Greek Polytheism," in *Anthrop. Essays Presented to E. B. Tylor*, 1907, 81 *ff.*

CHAPTER 18—The Sacred World in the Background

Section 1: The extensive reading and enormous work of P. Wilhelm Schmidt finds its culmination in the Synthesis where he formulates his inferences (provisionally?) from the material; *cf.* "Endsynthese der Religionen der Urvolker Amerikas, Asiens, Australiens, Afrikas", in his *Der Ursprung der Gottesidee*, Vol. VI, 1935. The above mentioned section, though it is very diffuse, has the merit of presenting to us Schmidt's opinions. These opinions are typical of rationalism and are, unfortunately, far too Roman Catholic. The entire synthesis is concerned with the idea of God (which is, in any case, not theological) and not about God, faith or revelation. What we find is a system which attempts to pull together all religious innovations; thus we find God and his revelation, as well as other effective powers, inserted into history and thereby degraded in that very moment; God is only a very great man and revelation only a spiritual current. This approach, rich in material, can only become the occasion for discontentment for both historical and theological studies.

The thesis throughout his work is quite simple and finds its culmination in the phrase, "God is the origin of the oldest religion" (*cf.* 491). But one cannot, as Schmidt does, have history beginning before creation. By virtue of the above thesis, that "God is the origin of the oldest religion", he knows the complete chronology of our first relatives and can therefore quite naturally assert that it is only much later that "Naturism", "Mana-ism", in fact all "isms" come to have any share in primitive religions. In any case Naturism is only a "personification of nature" (379). Magic is also placed in a secondary position because, "anyone who was on guard against much of the jumble and disorder of magical thinking, through the light of a higher religion, as well as through the human spirit, illuminated positively, was able to think rationally and causally in a higher degree" (386).

The naïveté of this way of thinking, which is neither theological nor historical, could lead us to the loss of self-composure. P. Schmidt, however, is a scholar, who in the usual manner is thoroughly convinced about the infallibility and reasonableness of his system. Thus he can speak bluntly, for example, about "the oldest common religion", about an "isochronous whole, which as such stands before us from archaic times until now" (447, 469 *ff.*). A few years ago we could have countered this opinion with a description of primitive culture as composed of numerous cultures from various times and places. "This distinction no longer remains, for the investigations of the present volumes on 'The Origin of the Idea of God' have amply removed it" (471). This is indeed a conclusion which is amazing in its certainty, approximating a fifth gospel!

Sections 2 & 3: For further examples as given in these sections see also the following: N. Soederblom, *Werden des Gottesglaubens*, 176; Tor Andrae, *Mohammed, The Man and His Faith*, Chapter I; R. Otto, *Das Gefühl des Überweltlichen*, 200 *ff.*; and K. Th. Preuz, in *Zeitschr. f. Missionsk. und rel. Wissensch.*, 47, 1932, 236 *ff.*

CHAPTER 19—Powers

Section 1: The development of polydemonism and polytheism is certainly not a compulsory one. The *elohim* of Judaic religion are a typical polydemonistic phenomenon. *El*, however, is only a manifestation of power; opposed to this, Baal and Melek are men. Baal is the lord of the earth, Melek is the lord who leads through the wilderness, and *El* is power alone. Out of these specific powers arose a monotheism, not a polytheism; the plural *elohim*, an original polytheistic name, became quite simply a name for Jaweh. *cf.* M. Buber, *Königtum Gottes*, 63, and also A. J. Wensinck, *Semietische Studien*, 1941, 31.

Section 4: Christianity alone can advocate an anthropomorphism which is an essential and theological motif; God has become man. The central point of the incarnation gives us the right to represent God in human form. Thus anthropomorphism is not a last resort in the Christian religion, it is natural and is absolutely essential. For further literature on this see: H. Kraemer, *The Christian Message in a Non-Christian World*, 131; G. van der Leeuw, "L'Anthropomorphisme Comme Forme d'Anthropologie", in *Le Monde Non-Chretien*, N.S., 2, 1947, 170. For the opposite of the above in religious phenomenon *cf.* Fr. Altheim, *Rom. Rel. Gesch.*, II, 187, and M. P. Nilsson, "Mycenaean and Homeric Rel", in *AR*. 33, 1936, 87. *cf.* also Pearl S. Buck, *House of Earth, The Good Earth*, 67, 127 *ff.*, for a Chinese example of the divine and human conflict of power in polytheism.

PART II

THE SUBJECT OF RELIGION

CHAPTER 27—The Speaker
Section 2: There is a relationship which we shall call "displacement" between prophetism in the strict sense and shamanism. That is to say, the forms remain practically the same, while the content changes. There is, for example, a conformity between the prophet Jeremiah on the one hand, and the dancing, unruly prophets on the other. There is also, however, an essential difference. The shaman and prophet have a common trait; they are only a mouthpiece. *cf.* A. C. Kruyt, *De West-Toradja's op Midden-Celebes*, II, 506 *ff.*; H. S. Nyberg, *Rel. Iran*, 176, 187, 202, 215 and 224, where we see that Zarathustra was in the first place a prophet not a reformer. *cf.* also F. M. Th. de Laigre Bohl, "Priester und Prophet" (*N. Theol. Stud.* 22, 1940); S. Mowinckel, "Ecstatic Experience and Rational Elaboration in Old Testament Prophecy" (*Acta Orient.*, 13, 1935); H. Th. Obbink, "The Forms of Prophetism" (*Hebrew Union College Annual*, Cincinnati, 14, 1939, 23 *ff.*).

CHAPTER 29—The Consecrated
Section 2: There is a polarity between ritualistic licentiousness and temperance. In the first instance power is mobilized and, so to speak, squandered. In the second instance power is unified and, as it were, hoarded. From this arises the amazing fact that in religion the sacred prostitutes have almost the same function as the sacred virgins. *cf.* G. van der Leeuw, "Virginibus Puerisque, A Study on the Service of Children in Worship", in *Deus et Homo*, 1953.

CHAPTER 30—Saints
Section 1: The classical religion of relics is Buddhism. The cult of Buddha is to a great extent a relic cult. One carries a tooth of the Buddha in a procession; worships the impression of his feet, *etc.* The Pagoda is nothing else but a relic shrine. *cf.* H. Von Glasenapp, *Der Buddhismus*, 47, 132, 139.

CHAPTER 31—Demonic Human Beings
Section 2: For a more archaic example of the relationship of women

to demons see B. Malinowski, *Argonauts of the Western Pacific*, 239 *ff.* *cf.* also H. Th. Fischer, *Inleidung tot de Volkenkunde von Ned. Indie*, 1940, 194 *ff.*, for a description where women only can become united with demons. For an example of Shamans who change their sex, *cf.* Nyberg, *Rel. des alten Iran*, 255, where men possessed by a demon become, *ipso facto*, women,

CHAPTER 37—Nation and Humanity
    Section 2: Both nationality and authority construct the selfsame object: the state, which thus takes on a religious character of its own. It does not just possess its own gods, it becomes god itself. Carl Schmidt has shown in a convincing way that the ideology of states is nothing but secularized theology. (See his *Politische Theologie*, 1934, 51.)
    Christianity has caused the great break between the Kingdom of God and the state. The early Christians broke up the world and so vindicated the words of their Lord, "My Kingdom is not of this world." The archaic communities do not know of this kind of dualism; religion is collective-social and the political power has a religious and divine character. For examples of the identification and conflict between Church and State, see St. Augustine, *City of God*, 14.4; Jose Ortega y Gasset, *Über das Romische Imperium*, 1943; R. Pettazoni, *Religione e Politica Religiosa nel Giappone Moderno*, 1934; W. Gundert, *Japanische Religionsgeschichte*, 1935, 13 *ff.* and 127 *ff.*; H. Kraemer, *The Christian Message in a Non-Christian World*, 1938, esp 259 *ff.*, 395 *ff.*, 243-45; and C. Eschweiler, in *Religiöse Besinnung*, 4, 1931, 32, 72 *ff.*

CHAPTER 40—Souls In the Plural
    Section 1: Pater Trilles, in an article in the *XVI Congrès Intern. d'Anthropologie et d'Archéologie Préhistorique*, 1935, 803 *ff.*, gives the following account of the plurality of souls in an African tribe. "The soul is very complicated and comprehensive: 1. 'Eba' is the creative principle, situated in the head . . . it disappears at death. 2. 'Nlem', the knowing heart which administrates daily activity and also disappears at death. 3. 'Edzii', the individual name, which after death continues a certain mode of individuality. 4. 'Ki' and 'Ndem', power and sign (or mark) of the individual; they remain eternally connected to the 'stuff of the soul'. 5. 'Ngel' or 'Ngwel', the working principle of the individual soul as long as it lives in the human body. 6. 'Nsissim', the shadow, it is also the same as the essential soul. 7. 'Khun', the ghost, the spirit or that which is the 'soul-stuff'."

CHAPTER 45—The Creature

Section 1: N. Berdyaev was certainly correct when he wrote, "One could say that knowledge is founded on the rupture of man from himself because the knowing subject finds itself outside of being and likewise being as external to man." (*cf.* his *The Destiny of Man*, 1955, 1960.) The human being becomes human by the fact of consciousness, that is to say, by the fact that man is capable of standing at a distance from himself; that he knows himself and grasps his own point of selfhood from outside himself. The phenomenon "Man" can only be understood with the help of a dimension which is external to man, be it biological or theological. On this point what has been presented by modern anthropology harmonizes with archaic man. For an illustration of the above point see the conversation between Leenhardt and a New Caledonian native in M. Leenhardt's book, *Gens de la Grande Terre*, 1937, 194 *ff.*

In the awakening consciousness, which makes man human, man finally uncovers the inner life which is neither bodily, or, a life of the soul, nor spiritual life. We must never forget that religion begins of itself with this removal of man from himself. For the archaic cultures this religious externalization has its oldest form of manifestation in clothing and ornamentation. Man attempts to become distant from himself, thus he paints, mutilates and clothes himself.

This externalizing can lead of itself to a dualism of body and soul. It can also, however, lead to the comprehension of the "man-creature", the soul which comes from the hand of God. (*cf.* W. Sombart, *Vom Menschen*, 1938, 27, 61, *etc.*).

PART III

OBJECT AND SUBJECT IN THEIR RECIPROCAL OPERATION

CHAPTER 53—Service

Section 2: Movement and counter movement as constituting the "dramatic character" of service can also be seen in the Egyptian Mysteries; in the drama and conflict between the old and new gods in the Ras Shamra. (*cf.* Sethe, *Dramatische Texte*, and A. de Buck, "Egyptische Dramatischen Texten" in *Ex Oriente Lux, Meded, en Verh.*, I, 1934, 55 *ff.* See also René Dussaud, *Les Découvertes du Ras Shamra*, 1937; Joh. Friedrich, *Ras Shamra*, 1933; Th. Gaster, "An Ancient Semitic Mystery Play", in *S.M.S.R.* 10, 1934, 156 *ff.*)

As a summary we could say that service has the task of providing equilibrium between the power of man and the other powers. As soon as it is known that this equilibrium is or will be disturbed (*e.g.*, a catastrophe), we resort to extraordinary sacrifice, prayers, or the introduction of new cults, *etc.*

CHAPTER 55—Sacred Time

Section 2: Reversal in time is impossible. Yet, in most cases sacred time turns back upon itself as a time-cycle. The Pre-Asiatic peoples broke through this cycle and introduced a historical time. This history begins in Egypt and Persia, and is foremost in Israel where the acts of God are identified with the great events of national history. See H. Lommel, *Die alten Arier*, 1935, 34; J. H. Breasted in *Ancient Records of Egypt*, I, 1906, 51 *ff.*; M. P. Nilsson, "Again the Sothiac Period", in *Acta Orient.*, 19, 1941, 1 *ff.*, and O. Neugebauer, "Nochmals der Ursprung des ägyptischen Jahres" in *Acta Orient.*, 19, 1942, 138 *ff.*

CHAPTER 66—Endowment With Form in Custom

Section 2: Asceticism can replace any sacred action. In India asceticism is a mystical intensification of the Vedic sacrifice, its goal is immortality which is attained through a "continuous emptiness". For a description of this point see Mircea Eliade, *Les Techniques du Yoga*, 1948, 9, 102, 117, 98, *etc.*; and P. H. Pott, *Yoga en Yantra*, 1946.

CHAPTER 72—Knowledge of God

Section 3: Next to knowledge of God stands "Wisdom". We encounter this form of knowledge above all in countries around the Eastern Mediterranean and they carry much of international significance. *cf.* W. Zimmerle, *Die Weisheit des Predigers Salamo*, 1935, 111 *ff.*, and Paul Humbert, *Recherches sur les Sources Egyptiennes de la Litterature Sapientiale*, 1929.

From a phenomenological point of view we can speak of three kinds of Wisdom: 1. Epigrammatic saying (Proverbs). The typical virtues of this kind of wisdom are inspiration, prudence, retention and contentment. *cf.* Alex Scharff, "Die Lehre für Kagemni", in *Zeitschr. f. ägypt. Spr. u. Alt.*, 77, 1941, 15 *ff.*) 2. Wisdom which is anxious about life (the first is not anxious about anything). This wisdom is pessimistic just because it views life as powerless and as nothing. The typical utterances concern the despondency of the soul with life. 3. The wisdom which has the unrest of God as its subject. The uncomparable and greatest example of this is the Book of Job.

There is an interesting tendency in all of the above for the History of Religions, namely, they tend to emphasize the moral over the cultic. In fact, there is an anti-sacramental tendency in knowledge as wisdom and this is clearly seen in F. M. Th. de Liagre Bohl's article in *Jaarbericht Ex Oriente Lux*, 8, 1942, 673 *ff.* See also P. A. Munch, "Die jüdischen Weisheitspsalmen und ihr Platz im Leben", in *Acta Orient.*, 15, 1936.

CHAPTER 79—Conversion. Rebirth

Section 4: "The Inner Life". (The following summary is taken from the revised German edition where it is under a separate chapter heading. We have placed it here as Section 4 since it follows this chapter.)

What modern man finds in the history of religions does not correspond with what he expects to find. Yet he believes that in what he finds he will hear the religious feeling speaking to him, that feeling which Benjamin Constant has put before us as the essence of religion. We shall find rituals, *etc.*, but they are only the "forms" which, through the centuries, religious feeling has taken upon itself. (*cf.* B. Constant, *De la Religion*, I, 1824, 142, also, 27, 3, 13.) The opinion of Constant is in agreement with Schleiermacher's expression of it in Germany, and it has filtered through to our own contemporary way of thinking. It is the opinion, namely, that "until now we have only considered the externals of religion; the history of religious feeling remains wholly outside our present scope. Dogmas, creeds of faith, religious exercises, *etc.*, are all forms which the inner religious feeling elects but immediately breaks." What we find, however, is something completely different. We find the cultus, magic, and all that which belongs to the equilibrium of religion. Behind this a "religious feeling" may well be hidden, but we very seldom receive even a weak sign of its existence.

We can suppose, naturally, that rituals have always accompanied feeling. The totality of the history of religions, however, speaks against the supposition that feeling is everything and the external action is only a form which contains no meaning for the essence of the phenomenon. We have already shown, in Chapter 67, that outward and inward phenomena have the same essential unity. That which is "inner" unlocks itself only through time. The phenomena which one can use as the signs which reveal the inner religious life are very rare in those religions which strive to preserve equilibrium (or balance). In any case we cannot speak about personal faith or unbelief, at least in the sense which we have given these words, in the context of these religions. In relation to the religions of equilibrium the word "faith" is an anachronism and a failure in structure.

The inner religious life begins when this equilibrium is broken. The religions which speak of this rupture, Zarathustrian, Hebraic, Islamic, and Christian, have lost the meaning of what is natural and self-understood, as well as the tolerance which distinguishes them from the primitive and near primitive religions. The above-mentioned religions are exclusive since God has stepped into human life and has consummated the essential rupture. . . . A broken world reflects a broken humanity, and when the revelation is complete it corresponds to a broken God on a cross.

For an example of what is given here see St. Augustine's *Confessions*, I, 20; XI, 3; I, 6; X, 2, 3, and VIII, 2, 4; here we read that his soul has been given to him by God, and truth has been revealed without signs or words. Augustine knows himself through knowledge of God. See also H. Frick, *Ghazalis Selbstbiographie, ein Vergleich mit Augustine Konfessionen*, 1919; also, G. van der Leeuw, "Religionsgeschichte und Personliches Religioses Leben", in *Festschrift. f. Fr. Heiler*, 1942, also in van der Leeuw, *Deus et Homo*, 1953.

PART V

FORMS

CHAPTER 100—The Religion of Love

Section 5: "The Christian Confession". (The following summary is taken from the revised German edition where it was a separate chapter.)

Here we have open for us the way to a phenomenology of Church History. Since this remains undone and though it is impossible to develop it fully in this work, we do want to indicate its main outline.

The Christian Church has two aspects; the first is authoritative in the West, the second in the East. The fundamental differentiation is not to be found, as Frick sees it, between the conflict of Catholicism and Protestantism, but in the difference between the Western and the Eastern Churches.

The spirit of the Greek Church leans toward the mysterious. It is the religion of the "implicit" Word of God, which is revealed in spiritual pictures, art and song. The advent of the mystery of God has brought about a "heaven on earth". This is the gospel of John; the transformation of the world is accomplished through the mysterious, through the reality of the advent and resurrection of the Son of God. The art of the Eastern Church is reconstructed from this gospel.

In contrast to this aspect of the Church, the spirit of the Western Church translates the mysterious, which it holds in common, into the words and practices of daily life. The Word of God is "explicit" for this religion, it reveals itself in dogmas and instruction, becoming ever more explicit in discussion and commentating, and is proclaimed in preaching. Heaven is not on earth but the earth is proclaimed and renewed as the Kingdom of God. This new order, however, is not an obvious one, faith alone permits us to see the difference between a condemned and renewed world. One must work, therefore, to spread this faith everywhere. This takes place through proclamation and strict organization, which have as their goal the restoration of the Kingdom of God. This is the Gospel of the Synoptics, above all, the gospel of Paul.

Greek Catholicism is a religion of Sacrament. Latin Catholicism is a religion of proclamation. The latter in its Roman form has reduced the Sacrament to a resource and remarkable guarantee of the Hierarchy, while in the Protestant form it has become a resource for the power of proclamation. The endless conflict over the Sacrament in the Middle Ages and in the time of the Reformation is proof that the Western Church did not understand the East. The Church of the East seldom speaks about the Sacrament, it lives it; *cf.* my *Sacramentstheologie*, 1949.

Non-Roman Catholicism is certainly alive in the West only in the Anglican Church. The Church of England is essentially Catholic and only secondarily Protestant. (See Bishop of Gloucester, *Anglican Communion*, 5.)

Protestantism can be divided into two great confessions; Lutheran and Calvinist. Both are united in their sensitivity to any final definition of faith; every form is provisional. Thus Protestantism has restrained itself from any fixation of form, be it Sacrament or discipline, church or absolution. This reservation, however, does not always allow itself to be strictly followed and it is just those Protestant confessions that stress it as most important which become the exception to it. In this way scripture, doctrine and method become the great exception to the restraining principle within Protestantism.

For further references consult Karl Adam, *Das Wesen des Katholizmus*, 1934; H. Frick, "Der katholisch-protestantische Zwiespalt als Religioses Urphanomen", (*Kairos*, 1926); F. Heiler, *Die katholische Kirche des Ostens und Westens*; H. W. Rüssel, *Gestalt eines christlichen Humanismus*, 1940; P. Tillich, "Kairos und Logos" (*Kairos*, 1926).

EPILEGOMENA

CHAPTER 110—The History of Phenomenological Research

Section 1: Benjamin Constant was certainly one of the great names in the History of Religions; he belongs to the Romantic period as well as to the Enlightenment. His great work, *De la Religion*, 1924–31, was never very popular but his two theses as found in that work have influenced generations ever since, even though they have never known the author's name. The first thesis states that "religion is a feeling" (I, 13). His second thesis, even more important, is that religious feeling is not identical with life but is the very foundation of the nature of man. To ask a man why he is religious is to ask a question concerning the very ground of his bodily structure and being (I, 3).

For a more detailed description of his work and influence see M.

Saltet, *Benjamin Constant, Historien de la Religion*, 1905; Elizabeth W. Schermerhorn, *Benjamin Constant, His Private Life and His Contribution to the Cause of Liberal Government in France, 1767–1830*, 1924; also, René Maurier, "Benjamin Constant, Historien des Sociétés et des Religions", in *RHR.*, 102, 1930.

Section 2: The many important names in the development of the phenomenological point of view should not force us into silence. Among many we can name the following: Fr. Altheim, W. Baetke, C. J. Bleeker, Martin Buber, Odo Casel, H. Frick, V. Gronbeck, Romano Guardini, K. Kerényi, H. Lommel, R. R. Marett, Rudolph Otto, Walter Otto, Maurice Leenhardt, J. Pedersen, Geo. Widengren, Mircea Eliade, and R. Callois.

The history of the development of phenomenology in the History of Religions can be indicated by the universities which provided "chairs" in the faculties for these positions. The first was authorized at Basel in 1833, and was held by Joh. G. Muller. The second was authorized in 1873 at Geneva, followed by Lausanne, Zurich, and Bern. In the Netherlands four chairs were inaugurated in 1876; among others, they were filled by P. D. Chantepie de la Saussaye, and C. P. Tiele. France came next; in 1879, the College of France, in Paris, opened a position which was given to Albert Reville. In 1884 the free University of Brussels joined the list. In 1885 the Sorbonne called into existence a department for "The Science of Religion" in the "École des Hautes Études". Finally, in 1910, a chair was authorized in Germany at the University of Berlin (O. Pfleiderer and Ed. Lehmann), this was followed by Leipzig (N. Soderblom and then Hans Haas) and Bonn (by Carl Clemen, then G. Mensching). *cf.*, H. Pinard de la Boullaye, *L'Étude Comparée des Religions*, 1922, 331 *ff.*

INDEX

The figures in italics indicate the Chapters; those in ordinary type the Sections.

Lallation, Lalling, *63*, 2
Language, cult, *63*, 3
Language, tabu, *4*, 1
Law, *26*, 3; *54*, 2; *59*, 3; *64*, 2, 5; *66*, 2; *98*, 2: cf. Command
Law, domain of; *2*, 2; *5*, 3; *7*, 1, 2; *21*, 1
Law, matriarchal, *10*, 2
Legend, *60*, 4
Legend, cult, *61*, 1; *65*, 3
Letter, heavenly, *64*, 1
Levirate marriage, *33*, 2
Liberation, *66*, 2; *80*, 2; *84*, 3; *87*, 3
Lies, *58*, 1
Life, *22*; *23*, 3; *39*, 2; *79*, 1; *80*, 2; *82*, 5; *107*, 1
Life, rod of, *22*, 5; *49*, 2
Life, tree of, *5*, 3: cf. World-tree
Light myth, *7*, 2
Limits, *57*, 4; *100*, 4
Litany, *59*, 1
Liturgy, *53*, 3; *63*, 3; *64*, 2
Liver, *39*, 2
Locality, cf. Place
Localizability, *57*; *64*, 2, 3; *85*, 2
Logos, hieros, *61*, 1, 2; *84*, 2; *87*, 3: cf. Word of God
Love, *4*, 3; *7*, 4; *47*, 8; *68*, 2, 4; *71*; *72*, 2; *75*, 3; *76*; *78*, 4; *81*, 2; *92*; *96*, 2; *97*, 2; *98*, 1; *100*; *109*, 1: cf. agape, *76*, 3, 4; bhakti, *76*, 2; Eros, *76*, 3
Lucus, *57*, 2: cf. Shrine
Lycanthropy, *8*, 3; *31*, 2; *42*, 4

Magic; Magical attitude, *1*, 3; *17*, 3; *68*, 4; *72*, 2; *75*, 2, 5; *78*, 2; *82*, 2, 3, 5; *87*, 1; *98*, 1
Magical antecedent, *18*, 3; *62*, 2
Magical formula, cf. Formula
Majesty of God, *99*; *101*, 3
Man of words, *27*, 3
Mana, *1*, 3, 4; *5*, 3; *13*, 1; *39*, 1; *83*, 1
Manituism, *8*, 2; *42*, 4; *85*, 2
Mantic, *27*, 2; *54*
Marriage, *10*, 4; *20*, 2; *22*, 2, 6; *33*, 1, 2; *52*, 1; *62*, 1: cf. Nuptials of the dead

Marriage of gods, *17*, 2
Marriage, levirate, *33*, 2
Martyr, *29*, 4; *52*, 1; *73*, 4: cf. Witness
Masculine and feminine, *20*, 2; *23*, 1; *29*, 2: cf. Sex
Masks, *8*, 3; *26*, 1; *53*, 1
Mass, *50*, 4; *52*, 1; *60*, 1; *62*, 3; *64*, 3
Matriarchal law, *10*, 2
Matriarchate, *23*, 1: cf. Mother
Matter, *39*, 1
May king, May queen, *11*, 2; *12*, 6
Meal, sacramental, *22*, 6; *50*; *51*, 2; *52*, 2
Meal, sacrificial, *50*, 1, 3, 4; *51*, 2; *52*, 1, 2
Meaning, *87*, 2; *107*, 1; *108*, 1
Measa, *4*, 1
Medicine, *26*, 2
Medicine-man, *26*
Mediator, *85*, 4; *87*, 5; *101*, 2; *106*
Meditation, *74*, 1
Medium of revelation, *85*
Men's houses, *34*, 3; *57*, 3
Messenger of God, *16*, 2
Metals, *5*, 2
Metaphor, *58*, 1; *60*, 1; *82*, 4
Militia sacra, *73*, 1: cf. Service
Miracle, *30*, 3; *85*, 2, 3, 4; *89*, 2
Mission, *36*, 3; *37*, 3; *93*, 2, 3
Mock battles, *8*, 3; *53*, 2; *66*, 3: cf. Plays
Modesty, *10*, 3; *29*, 1, 2, 3
Momentary gods, *17*, 2, 3
Monastic community, *34*, 7
Money, *50*, 1
Monks, *29*, 3; *73*, 4
Moon, *7*, 2; *55*, 2
Monism, *2*, 1, 5; *21*, 4; *85*, 4; *90*, 2; *91*; *96*, 1
Monogamy, *33*, 1
Monotheism, *18*, 2, 3; *20*, 3; *61*, 3
Morality, *18*, 1, 2, 3; *47*, 4; *66*, 1, 2; *75*, 5; *78*; *89*, 1
Mother; Mother earth, *12*; *13*, 2; *20*, 2; *36*, 2; *46*, 2; *47*, 6; *86*, 3: cf. Matriarchate
Mountains, sacred, *5*, 2